Parker, Franklin, 1921-
 Women's education, a world view /
compiled and edited by Franklin
Parker and Betty June Parker. --
Westport, Conn. : Greenwood Press,
1979-
        v. <1   > ; 25 cm.
   Includes index.   Library has: v.1
   Contents: [v. 1] Annotated bibliography of
doctoral dissertations.
   ISBN 0-313-20891-3
   1. Women--Education--Bibliography--Collected
works. 2. Dissertations, Academic--United
States--Bibliography--Collected works. 3.
Dissertations, Academic--Canada--
Bibliography--Collected works. I. Parker,

                                    (continued)

WOMEN'S EDUCATION—
A WORLD VIEW

WOMEN'S EDUCATION—
A WORLD VIEW
Annotated Bibliography
of Doctoral Dissertations

Compiled and Edited by
Franklin Parker and Betty June Parker

GREENWOOD PRESS

WESTPORT, CONNECTICUT • LONDON, ENGLAND

Library of Congress Cataloging in Publication Data
Main entry under title:

Women's education, a world view.

   Includes index.
   1. Education of women—Bibliography.
2. Dissertations, Academic—United States—
Bibliography. 3. Dissertations, Academic
—Canada—Bibliography. I. Parker, Franklin.
1921-   II. Parker, Betty June.
Z7963.E2W65   [LC1481]   016.376   78-73791
ISBN 0-313-20891-3

Library of Congress Catalog Card Number: 78-73791
ISBN: 0-313-20891-3

First published in 1979

Greenwood Press, Inc.
51 Riverside Avenue, Westport, Connecticut 06880

Printed in the United States of America

10 9 8 7 6 5 4 3 2 1

To Jane Meadows Parker

CONTENTS

PREFACE

The editors have attempted to cite all locatable U.S. and Canadian doctoral dissertations in English that concern the education of girls and women at all ages and school levels in public and private institutions worldwide. Included with studies of women in liberal or traditional academic education are those in nursing education, home economics education (family life, domestic science), physical education, and other vocational or career training. Readers with specific interests will want first to consult the subject index as a key to the wide coverage attempted.

Entry is alphabetical by author. Where there are two authors for one dissertation, the listing is under the first author, and the second author is noted in the subject index. Citations include the degree (Ph.D., Ed.D., or other), degree-granting institution, and year, plus an abbreviation indicating the source of information. (See "Abbreviations of Sources.") Full bibliographical data is included except where Canadian university entries and the earlier University of Southern California and University of Chicago abstracts omitted pagination and where Xerox University Microfilm, Inc., omitted order numbers. Summaries following each citation attempt to describe the problem, research technique, subjects used in the study, and especially the findings and implications.

Thanks are due to university reference and interlibrary loan librarians and particularly to the dissertation writers and their families who provided bibliographical data, abstracts, summaries, articles based on dissertations, and tables of content from dissertations. Appreciation goes to Marilyn Brownstein of Greenwood Press, who suggested this project, encouraged its progress, and was patient during delays; and to Dr. Ray Koppelman, vice president for energy studies, graduate programs and research at West Virginia University, for financial aid in manuscript preparation.

The editors hope that this volume, together with a second volume in progress, which will compile and annotate *Books and Reports* in similar subject categories, will advance women's studies.

FRANKLIN PARKER
BETTY JUNE PARKER

West Virginia University, Morgantown
October 1978

ABBREVIATIONS OF SOURCES

CDI
Xerox University Microfilms, COMPREHENSIVE DISSERTATION INDEX (1861-1972). Ann Arbor, MI 48106: Xerox University Microfilms, 1973. A 37-volume subject and author index to over 417,000 doctoral dissertations accepted by U.S. colleges and universities and some foreign institutions. Subsequent CDI volumes since 1973.

Cordasco
& Covello
Francesco Cordasco and Leonard Covello, EDUCATIONAL SOCIOLOGY: A SUBJECT INDEX OF DOCTORAL DISSERTATIONS COMPLETED AT AMERICAN UNIVERSITIES, 1941-1963. New York: The Scarecrow Press, 1965.

Cruger
Doris M. Cruger (compilor), A LIST OF AMERICAN DOCTORAL DISSERTATIONS ON AFRICA (COVERING 1961/62 THROUGH 1964/65), FRANCE (COVERING 1933/34 THROUGH 1964/65), ITALY (COVERING 1933/34 THROUGH 1964/65). Ann Arbor: Xerox University Microfilm Library Service, 1967.

DAI
DISSERTATION ABSTRACTS INTERNATIONAL. Microfilm and/or xeroxed copy may be purchased by University Microfilm Order Number (use XUM Order No.) from Xerox University Microfilms, Inc., Ann Arbor, MI 48106, or phone free "Dissertation Hot Line Service": 1-800-521-3042. Chronology: MICROFILM ABSTRACTS, Volumes I-XI (1938-51); continued as DISSERTATION ABSTRACTS, Volumes XII-XXVI (1952-June, 1966); continued as DISSERTATION ABSTRACTS A: The Humanities and Social Sciences, and B: The Sciences and Engineering. Volumes XXVII-XXIX (July, 1966-June, 1969); continued as DISSERTATION ABSTRACTS INTERNATIONAL, Volume XXX- (July, 1969-), A and B as above.

Dossick
Jesse J. Dossick, DOCTORAL RESEARCH ON RUSSIA AND THE SOVIET UNION. New York: New York University Press, 1960.

Eells   Walter Crosby Eells, AMERICAN DISSERTATIONS ON FOREIGN
                   EDUCATION. Washington, DC: National Education
                   Association, 1959.

GPCFT   George Peabody College for Teachers, CONTRIBUTIONS TO
CONTRIBUTIONS   EDUCATION. New York: Reprinted by AMS Press, Inc.,
                   1972.

Gordon   Leonard H. D. Gordon and Frank J. Shulman (compilors and
& Shulman   editors), DOCTORAL DISSERTATIONS ON CHINA; A BIBLI-
                   OGRAPHY OF STUDIES IN WESTERN LANGUAGES, 1945-1970.
                   Seattle: University of Washington Press for the
                   Association for Asian Studies, 1972.

Kuehl   Warren F. Kuehl, DISSERTATIONS IN HISTORY. Lexington:
                   University of Kentucky Press, Vol. I, 1965; II, 1972.

Parker   Franklin Parker, LATIN AMERICAN EDUCATION RESEARCH:
                   AN ANNOTATED BIBLIOGRAPHY OF 269 UNITED STATES DOC-
                   TORAL DISSERTATIONS. Austin: University of Texas
                   Institute of Latin American Studies, 1964.

Selim   George Dimitri Selim, AMERICAN DOCTORAL DISSERTATIONS
                   ON THE ARAB WORLD. Washington, DC: Library of
                   Congress, 1970.

Shulman   Frank J. Shulman (compilor and editor), DOCTORAL DIS-
-ASIA   SERTATIONS ON SOUTH ASIA 1966-1970; AN ANNOTATED
                   BIBLIOGRAPHY COVERING NORTH AMERICA, EUROPE, AND
                   AUSTRALIA. Ann Arbor: Center for South and South-
                   east Asian Studies, University of Michigan, 1971.

Shulman   Frank J. Shulman (compilor and editor), DOCTORAL DIS-
-CHINA   SERTATIONS ON CHINA, 1971-1975; A BIBLIOGRAPHY OF
                   STUDIES IN WESTERN LANGUAGES. Seattle: University
                   of Washington Press, 1978.

Stucki   Curtis W. Stucki, AMERICAN DOCTORAL DISSERTATIONS ON
                   ASIA, 1933-1962, INCLUDING APPENDIX OF MASTER'S
                   THESES AT CORNELL UNIVERSITY. Ithaca, NY: Cornell
                   University Department of Asian Studies, 1963.

TCCU   Teachers College, Columbia University, CONTRIBUTIONS TO
CONTRIBUTIONS   EDUCATION. New York: Reprinted by AMS Press, Inc.,
                   1972.

TCCU DIGESTS   Teachers College, Columbia University, DIGESTS OF
                   DISSERTATIONS. New York: Teachers College Library
                   Reference Room.

UC, Berkeley   University of California, Berkeley, Library.

WOMEN'S EDUCATION—
A WORLD VIEW

DOCTORAL DISSERTATIONS

Abdel-Al, Hend (Ph. D.). "RELATING EDUCATION TO PRACTICE WITHIN A NURSING CONTEXT." University of Edinburgh (Great Britain), 1975. 693 pp. Source: DAI, XXXVII, 2A (August, 1976), 934-A-935-A. XUM Order No. 76-10,575.

The study presents the thesis that nursing, education, and practice stand in mutual interactive relatedness. Nursing is the abstract level which is conceptual and contextual in nature. Both education and practice are the concrete level which is of an applied and ex-perimental nature.

Abicht, Monika Maria (Ed. D.). "WOMEN'S LEADERSHIP ROLES IN TWO SELECTED LABOR UNIONS IN THE UNITED STATES AND BELGIUM: A COMPARATIVE, DESCRIPTIVE STUDY." University of Cincinnati, 1976. 191 pp. Source: DAI, XXXVII, 9A (March, 1977), 6098-A-6099-A. XUM Order No. 77-6044.

Belgian-U. S. cross cultural survey of women's leadership role in two blue-collar labor unions. Among many findings: women were strongly underrepresented in leadership roles; more men than women received and wanted leadership training; American men saw women leaders as less controlled than men in crisis situations; Belgians saw women leaders as more aggressive than men. The author believes that chan-ges in education and the whole society will be needed before more union women participate in leadership roles.

Ables, Jerry Leon (Ph. D.). "AN EVALUATION OF FOUR ASSOCIATE DEGREE NURSING PROGRAMS IN TEXAS BASED UPON CERTAIN SELECTED CRITERIA." East Texas State University, 1969. 181 pp. Source: DAI, XXX, 6B (December, 1969), 2770-B-2771-B. XUM Order No. 69-21,162.

Despite data indicating the need for fuller on-the-job experience during training, the associate nursing degree graduate appears to compare quite favorably with graduates of the diploma and baccalaure-ate programs in terms of work experience and performance as well as in annual income.

Abruzzese, Roberta Straessle (Ed. D.). "CONTINUING EDUCATION NEEDS OF DIRECTORS OF HOSPITAL NURSING INSERVICE EDUCATION IN NEW YORK STATE." Columbia University, 1975. 146 pp. Source: DAI, XXXVI, 3B (September, 1975), 1142-B-1143-B. XUM Order No. 75-20,182.

In ranking categories of learning needs, inservice directors gave priority to 4 major functional areas: (1) teaching and curriculum, (2) nursing practice, (3) counseling and guidance, and (4) adminis-tration and supervision.

Acheson, Eunice Mae (Ph. D.). "THE PERSONAL AND PROFESSIONAL CHAR-
ACTERISTICS OF A SELECTED GROUP OF DEANS OF WOMEN." Columbia University
Teachers College, 1932. 212 pp. Source: TCCU DIGESTS, VII (1932), pp.
1-3.

Questionnaires assessed characteristics of deans of women in widely
scattered, diverse colleges and universities. The 44 "successful
deans" were well balanced, intelligent, fairminded, and socially in-
clined.

Achord, Clifford David (Ph. D.). "IMPACT OF ATTRITION ON SELF-CON-
CEPT AND ANXIETY LEVEL OF FRESHMAN NURSING STUDENTS AT THE UNIVERSITY OF
NORTHERN COLORADO." University of Northern Colorado, 1972. 112 pp.
Source: DAI, XXXIII, 11A (May, 1973), 6166-A-6167-A. XUM Order No. 73-
10,974.

Tests concluded before entering the nursing program and after completing the freshman year showed that students who continued in the
program scored significantly higher on post-tests in total positive
self-concept and self-satisfaction self-concept than students who
withdrew at the end of the freshman year. No appreciable difference
was noted in anxiety levels of the 2 groups.

Adams, Kathleen Ann (Ph. D.). "ASSERTIVENESS TRAINING, ANDROGYNY,
AND PROFESSIONAL WOMEN." University of Texas at Austin, 1976. 392 pp.
Source: DAI, XXXVII, 12B, Part 1 (June, 1977), 6311-B. XUM Order No.
77-11,470.

For this study, 60 professional women recruited for a course entitled
"Problems Professional Women Face" were randomly assigned to 2 groups
in assertive training, discussion control, or waiting list control.
A rating system of unassertive, assertive, indirect aggressive, or
direct aggressive was used to determine reactions to managerial problem situations and stress job interview simulations. The results indicate that those in the assertive training group significantly increased overall assertiveness and significantly decreased unassertive
and direct aggressive responses. A masculinity-femininity questionnaire revealed that femininity scores remained constant despite significant increases in assertiveness.

Adams, Wesley James (Ph. D.). "SEX COMPOSITION IN GROUP DISCUSSION
AS RELATED TO ACQUISITION OF KNOWLEDGE AND ATTITUDINAL CHANGE AMONG WOM-
EN IN A FAMILY LIFE COURSE." Oregon State University, 1969. 215 pp.
Source: DAI, XXX, 7A (January, 1970), 3093-A. XUM Order No. 69-19,457.

Two assumptions held by many family life educators relative to learning processes in their courses were tested. The study's findings
provided no support for the assumption that mixed sex groups are optimal for learning arrangements and also discounted the assumption
that family and life knowledge gained from such courses is unrelated
to students' attitudinal changes.

Adams, Willie Gray (Ed. D.). "INFLUENCE OF CAREER EDUCATION ON MO-
TIVATION AND ASPIRATION OF MIDDLE SCHOOL AGE EDUCATIONALLY DISADVANTAGED
YOUTH." Pennsylvania State University, 1974. 124 pp. Source: DAI,
XXXV, 12A, Part 1 (June, 1975), 7641-A. XUM Order No. 75-12,715.

Findings supported the study's major hypothesis that career-oriented programs for educationally disadvantaged middle-school age learners, male and female, do not make a significant difference in the level of motivation, career maturity, aspiration, and expectation of these learners.

Addison, Carolyn Frances (Ed. D.). "EFFECTS OF VARIATIONS OF TARGET SIZE, DISTANCE, AND SHOOTING TECHNIQUE ON ARCHERY PERFORMANCE BY COLLEGE WOMEN BEGINNERS." Temple University, 1972. 121 pp. Source: DAI, XXXIII, 4A (October, 1972), 1481-A. XUM Order No. 72-27,172.

Among other findings, this study revealed that freshman college women without previous archery experience attained performance scores that are higher after 12 60-minute instruction periods.

Adix, Shauna McLatchy (Ph. D.). "DIFFERENTIAL TREATMENT OF WOMEN AT THE UNIVERSITY OF UTAH FROM 1850 TO 1915." University of Utah, 1976. 192 pp. Source: DAI, XXXVII, 11A (May, 1977), 6968-A. XUM Order No. 77-10,433.

This study on differential treatment for women at the University of Utah was based on the Records Center and the University Archives for the years 1850-1915 and on the archives and library of the Historical Department of the Church of Jesus Christ of Latter-day Saints, Salt Lake City. Results indicated that although women were part of the student body earlier than elsewhere, they did not have equal access to resources. Women received differential treatment in curricular offerings, leadership opportunities, and educational expectations and organizations.

Aguilera, Donna Conant (Ph. D.). "THE RELATIONSHIP OF PERFORMANCE IN SELECTED PROBLEM-SOLVING TASKS TO PARTICIPATION IN A CRISIS INTERVENTION COURSE FOR A SAMPLE OF NURSES IN A UNIVERSITY BACCALAUREATE PROGRAM." University of Southern California, 1975. 85 pp. Source: DAI, XXXVI, 1B (July, 1975), 160-B-161-B. XUM Order No. 75-15,513.

Findings supported the research hypothesis that an experimental group of student nurses participating in a university course in crisis intervention would show higher levels of fluency, flexibility, originality, and clinical nursing judgment than would students in a traditional course in patient care in a public health setting.

Aguren, Carolyn Tull (Ed. D.). "AN EXPLORATION OF SELF-ACTUALIZATION, SELF-CONCEPT, LOCUS OF CONTROL, AND OTHER CHARACTERISTICS AS EXHIBITED IN SELECTED MATURE COMMUNITY COLLEGE WOMEN." North Texas State University, 1974. 288 pp. Source: DAI, XXXV, 12A, Part 1 (June, 1975), 7641-A-7642-A. XUM Order No. 75-13,657.

Women 30 years of age or older enrolled at a metropolitan community college, most of them freshmen working toward a bachelor's degree, scored above the norm on self-concept tests and personality inventories.

Ahad, Mohammed Abdul (Ed. D.). "INNOVATIONS IN INDIAN NURSING: A STUDY OF FOREIGN RETURNED INDIAN NURSES AS INNOVATORS." Columbia University, 1973. 197 pp. Source: DAI, XXXIV, 9A (March, 1974), 5505-A. XUM Order No. 74-6387.

This study compared nurses from India trained in North America with those trained in British-oriented countries and found that all foreign training resulted in some useful changes in Indian nursing and practice. The majority of foreign-returned Indian nurses helped to introduce innovations in their fields of specialization.

Ahl, Sister Angelica (Ed. D.). "AN ANALYTIC STUDY OF DELIMITED IN-PUTS, STRUCTURES, AND OUTPUTS OF AN EDUCATIONAL ORGANIZATION DURING IN-TRA-SYSTEMIC RENEWAL." Boston University School of Education, 1975. 578 pp. Source: DAI, XXXV, 12B (June, 1975), 5964-B. XUM Order No. 75-12,223.

A case study of a significant change process in a well-established school of nursing. It relates to a recommendation of the nationwide study on nursing education in the U. S. (commonly referred to as the Lysaught Report) that strong diploma schools of nursing should become degree-granting institutions. The study reveals the complexity of this type of change for a diploma school. For nursing education administrators interested in initiating such a change, the case study provides a rich source of information regarding the problems and issues which occurred, and the processes, procedures, and methods used by the school during the 3 stages of its transition.

Ahl, Mary Ellen (Ph. D.). "PERCEPTIONS OF NURSE AND PHYSICIAN EDU-CATIONAL ADMINISTRATORS IN NEW YORK STATE CONCERNING THE COMPATIBILITY OF SELECTED NURSE ACTIVITIES WITH THE 1972 LEGAL DEFINITION OF NURSING." St. John's University, 1975. 217 pp. Source: DAI, XXXVI, 8B (February, 1976), 3868-B. XUM Order No. 76-2966.

As a group, administrators of New York State nursing schools tend to be more liberal in their interpretation of the 1972 legal definition of nursing than administrators of medical schools and internships. While the responses of nurse administrators indicated group consensus and decisiveness, physicians surveyed exhibited both less group consensus and less decisiveness.

Ahlers, April Ethel (Ph. D.). "THE WHOLE DUTY OF AN ENGLISHWOMAN, 1700-1792." Tulane University, 1974. 228 pp. Source: DAI, XXXV, 12A, Part 1 (June, 1975), 7827-A. XUM Order No. 75-11,890.

This examination of the feminist movement and feminist-oriented writings prior to Mary Wollstonecraft's 1792 publication, Vindication of the Rights of Women (long considered the beginning of the feminist movement) revealed that many earlier letters and diaries complained of inequality of the sexes. In 1758 a pamphlet appeared called Female Rights Vindicated.

Aiken, Wreathy Price (Ph. D.). "A SURVEY OF THE SOCIAL AND PHILO-SOPHICAL FACTORS WHICH HAVE AFFECTED THE HIGHER EDUCATION OF WHITE WOMEN IN TEXAS, 1825 TO 1945." University of Texas, 1946. 584 pp. Source: Dissertation, pp. 548-551.

This survey assessed the philosophies of women's education implicit in humanism, idealism, realism, and pragmatism and found that no complete philosophy of education for women existed.

Ainsworth, Dorothy Sears (Ph. D.). "THE HISTORY OF PHYSICAL EDUCA-
TION IN COLLEGES FOR WOMEN: AS ILLUSTRATED BY BARNARD, BRYN MAWR, EL-
MIRA, GOUCHER, MILLS, MOUNT HOLYOKE, RADCLIFFE, ROCKFORD, SMITH, VASSAR,
WELLESLEY AND WELLS." Columbia University Teachers College, 1930. 116
pp. Source: TCCU DIGESTS, IV, A-G (September, 1929-December, 1931), pp.
1-3.

This study traced the development of physical education in 12 colleges for women, finding that physical education has adapted itself
to the type of exercise which in each period seemed most beneficial
and appropriate for women.

Aitken, Margaret Helen (Ed. D.). "A STUDY OF PHYSICAL EDUCATION FA-
CILITIES FOR COLLEGE WOMEN WITH IMPLICATIONS FOR WESTERN WASHINGTON COL-
LEGE OF EDUCATION." Columbia University Teachers College, 1957. Source:
TCCU DIGESTS(1957), pp. 2-3.

Outcomes of this study included a handbook and suggested procedures
and institutional organization for long and short-range planning. A
definition of an accepted philosophy of physical education for college women was formulated.

Albanese, Naomi Gertrude (Ph. D.). "THE BEARING OF THE STUDENT
TEACHING EXPERIENCE IN HOME ECONOMICS UPON ATTITUDES TOWARD TEACHING AS
A CAREER AND TOWARD STUDENTS." Ohio State University, 1955. 294 pp.
Source: DAI, XVI, 1 (1956), 112-113. XUM Order No. 14,447.

Findings tend to support the study's major hypotheses that (1) student teaching experience elicits change in attitude toward teaching
as a career and toward students they will teach, and (2) background
factors prior to student teaching (such as academic competence), as
well as cooperative guidance and assistance from the supervising
teacher, may be identified with change in attitude.

Albino, Judith Elaine Newsom (Ph. D.). "THE MOTIVE TO AVOID SUCCESS
AND PROBLEMS REPORTED BY MALE AND FEMALE STUDENTS WITHDRAWING FROM THE
UNIVERSITY OF TEXAS AT AUSTIN." University of Texas at Austin, 1973.
197 pp. Source: DAI, XXXIV, 5A (November, 1973), 2375-A-2376-A. XUM
Order No. 73-25,968.

Reasons of 1,368 students (886 males and 482 females) for withdrawal
from college were sought. The study failed to establish that women's
wish to avoid success was a major cause for their dropping out of
college.

Alcoe, Shirley Yvonne (Ed. D.). "RESOURCES FOR THE PREPARATION OF
NURSE-TEACHERS--EXAMINATION OF A SITUATION." Columbia University, 1973.
251 pp. Source: DAI, XXXIV, 4A (October, 1973), 1743-A-1744-A. XUM
Order No. 73-22,703.

A study of the Canadian province of New Brunswick revealed that only
the New Brunswick Association of Registered Nurses (NBARN) held any
position regarding qualifications for nurse-teachers. No group had
any plans to prepare teachers, although government, universities,
and professional organizations agreed that they were jointly responsible for providing such preparation and should work together to en-
sure its availability.

Aldrich, Anita (Ed. D.). "A COMPARISON OF SECTARIAN COLLEGE WOMEN AND UNIVERSITY WOMEN IN MOTOR ABILITY, PERSONALITY ADJUSTMENT, SCHOLASTIC APTITUDE, AND BACKGROUND." Pennsylvania State University, 1957. 109 pp. Source: DAI, XVIII, 1 (January, 1958), 141. XUM Order No. 25,069.

Women attending a sectarian college, tending to come from smaller communities and smaller schools, scored significantly lower than university women in motor ability and academic aptitude. There were no significant differences in personality test scores.

Alexander, Florence Mary Anne (Ph. D.). "JOB PREFERENCES, MANIFEST NEEDS, AND OCCUPATIONAL VALUES OF FRESHMAN STUDENT NURSES." Syracuse University, 1962. 165 pp. Source: DAI, XXIII, 3 (September, 1962), 996-997. XUM Order No. 62-04012.

Two conclusions were: (1) that the groups' manifest needs, as measured, proved to have an overall similarity; (2) that occupational values, as ranked, constituted an identifiable difference among the groups, although there was a general similarity in such values.

Alexander, Margaret M. (Ph. D.). "EVALUATING THE HOME ECONOMICS CURRICULUM IN THE AREA OF CLOTHING." University of Chicago, 1952. 167 pp. Source: Dissertation, pp. 1-10.

This study shows that the present program in the area of clothing is contributing to the acquisition of information, the ability to select solutions to problems and reasons to support the choice, and to the development of suitable work habits and skills.

Alexander, Wanda Ruth Hammack (Ed. D.). "A STUDY OF BODY TYPES, SELF-IMAGE AND ENVIRONMENTAL ADJUSTMENT IN FRESHMAN COLLEGE FEMALES." Indiana University, 1967. 136 pp. Source: DAI, XXVIII, 8A (February, 1968), 3048-A-3049-A. XUM Order No. 67-16,386.

Women with heavily built bodies were found to be significantly less acceptant of their self-image than the other body types. Self-image acceptance was, however, related more to environmental perception than to body types.

Alibaruho, Gloria Lindsey (Ph. D.). "A STUDY OF SELF-CONCEPT OF BLACK COLLEGE STUDENTS." Wright Institute, 1976. 118 pp. Source: DAI, XXXVII, 4B (October, 1976), 1887-B. XUM Order No. 76-23,288.

This dissertation looked at the self-concept of black college students over a 5-year period. The data showed a difference in self concept between males and females, with females making more "self-enhancing and consensual statements about themselves."

Allan, Thomas Kenneth (Ph. D.). "THE RELATIONSHIP BETWEEN SUPERVISORY RATINGS AND THE PERSONALITY OF FEMALE STUDENT TEACHERS." University of Maryland, 1966. 126 pp. Source: DAI, XXVII, 9A (March, 1967), 2907-A. XUM Order No. 67-2357.

Results of this investigation of women students tended to support the hypothesis that certain aspects of the American system of training teachers might be reinforcing dogmatic tendencies of student teachers.

Allemang, Margaret May (Ph. D.). "NURSING EDUCATION IN THE UNITED STATES AND CANADA 1873-1950: LEADING FIGURES, FORCES, VIEWS ON EDUCATION." University of Washington, 1974. 316 pp. Source: DAI, XXXVI, 6A (December, 1975), 3467-A. XUM Order No. 75-28,308.

This inquiry traced developments in the thinking of U. S. and Canadian leaders in nursing education, 1873-1950. Findings confirmed that nursing education lacked system, order, and coherence. Despite this lack, nursing educators made great contributions because they worked toward humane goals.

Allen, Arthur Dequest (Ph. D.). "A STUDY OF EXISTING GRADUATE PUBLIC AFFAIRS AND ADMINISTRATION PROGRAMS IN AMERICAN UNIVERSITIES AND THEIR STATUS IN THE TRAINING OF BLACK AND MINORITY-GROUP STUDENTS." University of Pittsburgh, 1975. 240 pp. Source: DAI, XXXVI, 4A (October, 1975), 2412-A-2413-A. XUM Order No. 75-21,743.

Minority groups and women were clearly underrepresented in faculty, top-level administrative, and clerical positions in member schools of the National Association for Public Affairs and Administration, although slightly more than half of the respondents sponsored recruitment programs for these groups.

Allen, Dotaline E. (Ed. D.). "A STUDY OF SOME OPINIONS AND PLANS OF A SELECTED GROUP OF GRADUATE NURSES WITH REGARD TO GRADUATE NURSE EDUCATION." Indiana University, 1955. 146 pp. Source: DAI, XV, 11 (1955), 2109-2110. XUM Order No. 14,565.

The majority of graduate nurses believed graduate nursing education makes one a more capable nurse. Most wanted graduate nursing education to enhance personal development and their ability to provide better service rather than to prepare them for administrative or teaching posts.

Allen, Lawrence Stewart (Ed. D.). "AN EXAMINATION OF ACADEMIC AND BEHAVIORAL CHARACTERISTICS OF BOYS AND GIRLS WHO HAVE BEEN IDENTIFIED AS LEARNING DISABLED." University of Northern Colorado, 1975. 123 pp. Source: DAI, XXXVI, 11A (May, 1976), 7281-A-7282-A. XUM Order No. 76-10,822.

Learning disabled girls displayed higher achievement anxiety than normal girls and a greater need for closeness to their teacher than either learning disabled boys or normal girls.

Allen, Madeline May (Ph. D.). "AN HISTORICAL STUDY OF MORAVIAN EDUCATION IN NORTH CAROLINA: THE EVOLUTION AND PRACTICE OF THE MORAVIAN CONCEPT OF EDUCATION AS IT APPLIED TO WOMEN." Florida State University, 1971. 223 pp. Source: DAI, XXXII, 9A (March, 1972), 4998-A. XUM Order No. 72-10,014.

The educational concepts of the Moravians and their implementation as related to the education of women in North Carolina, while modified to fit the needs of the times, have changed little since the church was founded in 1457. Moravians have stressed that women as well as men must receive training for literacy and for a useful life.

Allen, Patricia (Ed. D.). "AN INVESTIGATION OF ADMINISTRATIVE LEA-
DERSHIP AND GROUP INTERACTION IN DEPARTMENTS OF PHYSICAL EDUCATION FOR
WOMEN OF SELECTED COLLEGES AND UNIVERSITIES." University of Oregon,
1972. Source: Author.

Identification and measurement of group and leadership behavior,
style, group acceptance, and position authority of selected women
physical education administrators yielded several conclusions: administrators as a group do not clearly favor one style of leadership
over another and believe that their leadership style is related to
the amount of authority their position has been given; administrators
and faculty members differ significantly as to their perceptions of
administrators' behaviors.

Allen, Roscoe Jackson (Ed. D.). "AN ANALYSIS OF THE RELATIONSHIP
BETWEEN SELECTED PROGNOSTIC MEASURES AND ACHIEVEMENT IN THE FRESHMAN
PROGRAM FOR SECRETARIAL MAJORS AT THE WOMAN'S COLLEGE OF THE UNIVERSITY
OF NORTH CAROLINA." Pennsylvania State University, 1961. 133 pp.
Source: DAI, XXIII, 1 (July, 1962), 122. XUM Order No. 62-2627.

A major conclusion was that achievement in the freshman program for
secretarial majors can be predicted by combining grade-point average,
SAT total, and the computational and clerical sections of the Kuder
Preference-Vocational Test.

Allerman, Geraldine Anne Golden (Ed. D.) and Britten, Mary Xenia
Wasson (Ed. D.). "NURSING STUDENTS' PERCEPTIONS OF THE RELEVANCE AND
USE OF THE CLINICAL LABORATORY IN LEARNING THE PRACTICE OF NURSING: A
TWIN STUDY." Columbia University, 1975. 332 pp. Source: DAI, XXXVI,
1B (July, 1975), 161-B. XUM Order No. 75-13,880.

Showing similar perceptions of their clinical laboratory activities,
both the baccalaureate and associate degree nursing students viewed
these clinical laboratories as providing the opportunity to learn
and practice skills associated with nursing.

Allos, Zeinab (Ed. D.). "AN ANALYSIS OF THE HOME ECONOMICS CURRICU-
LUM AT TAHRIR COLLEGE OF THE UNIVERSITY OF BAGHDAD, WITH SPECIAL ATTEN-
TION TO THE PROFESSIONAL PREPARATION OF PROSPECTIVE HOME ECONOMICS
TEACHERS." University of Tennessee, 1962. 184 pp. Source: DAI, XXIII,
9 (March, 1963), 3343-3344. XUM Order No. 63-2161.

Uneven allocation of semester credit hours, inadequate credit hours
required for graduation, and alumnae indication of inadequate preparation in college were among the findings of this analysis of a
home economics curriculum.

Almquist, Elizabeth M. (Ph. D.). "OCCUPATIONAL CHOICE AND CAREER
SALIENCE AMONG COLLEGE WOMEN." University of Kansas, 1969. 219 pp.
Source: DAI, XXX, 6A (December, 1969), 2634-A. XUM Order No. 69-21,484.

Those women who want to enter jobs in which over 70% of the workers
are now male were found to have had broad learning experience that
produced in them less stereotyped versions of the female role, of
which work in a high-level career is a significant part. The mothers
of such women had a more consistent history of working outside the
home.

Althof, Stanley Edward (Ph. D.). "A STUDY OF THE PERSONALITY VARI-
ABLES RELATED TO FEAR OF SUCCESS IN COLLEGE WOMEN." Oklahoma State Uni-
versity, 1975. 69 pp. Source: DAI, XXXVI, 10B (April, 1976), 5242-B.
XUM Order No. 76-9617.

In addition to several tentative findings, the exploratory hypothesis
that the high fear-of-success group would manifest significantly more
feminine interests and attitudes than the low fear-of-success group
was confirmed.

Altman, L. Doris (Ph. D.). "CHANGES IN GIRLS' SCHOOL PERFORMANCE
AND ATTITUDES TOWARD ACHIEVEMENT DURING THE YEARS SPANNING ADOLESCENCE."
City University of New York, 1974. 108 pp. Source: DAI, XXXIV, 12B,
Part I (June, 1974), 6188-B. XUM Order No. 74-13,437.

Data gathered in the research on girls and boys in grades 6, 9, and
12 supported the major hypothesis that higher needs for achievement
and approval, which are compatible in the academic setting during
the prepubertal years, come into conflict for girls during adoles-
cense, the greatest conflict and fear of success occurring in 9th
grade girls.

Alwine, Nevin Samuel (Ed. D.). "AN ANALYSIS OF STUDENT TEACHER SAT-
ISFACTION WITH THE MALE OR FEMALE SUPERVISING TEACHER AT THE UNIVERSITY
OF NORTHERN COLORADO." University of Northern Colorado, 1972. 90 pp.
Source: DAI, XXXIII, 3A (September, 1972), 1052-A. XUM Order No. 72-
23,793.

In comparing student teacher satisfaction, no significant differences were found between student teachers with like sex and opposite
sex supervising teachers, using the Student Teacher Satisfaction
Scale.

Amatea, Ellen Sherlock (Ph. D.). "A STUDY OF THE EFFECTS OF A
CAREER PLANNING PROGRAM FOR COLLEGE WOMEN." Florida State University,
1972. 208 pp. Source: DAI, XXXIII, 10A (April, 1973), 5485-A. XUM
Order No. 73-10,320.

Participants' initial attitudes and expectations about the program
and their initial level of career choice seemed to determine the
benefits they reportedly received from the program.

Amsterdam, Anne R. (Ph. D.). "A COMPARISON OF THE EFFECTIVENESS OF
THREE SELECTED GROUPS OF MARRIED WOMEN ELEMENTARY TEACHERS." New York
University, 1967. 177 pp. Source: DAI, XXVIII, 3A (September, 1967),
889-A. XUM Order No. 67-11,094.

Principals' evaluations of the teachers studied provided more accurate support of the research hypothesis than did interviews with the
teacher respondents. There are no statistical differences among 3
types of married elementary teachers (in terms of effectiveness)--
continuous career teachers, interrupted career teachers, and delayed
entrant teachers.

Anastasia, Antoinette Marie (Ed. D.). "THE IMPACT OF ANATOMY AND PHYSIOLOGY ON THE WORK OF THE NURSE." Columbia University, 1971. 110 pp. Source: DAI, XXXII, 7A (January, 1972), 3812-A-3813-A. XUM Order No. 72-4160.

The study concluded that the nature of anatomy and physiology used by graduate nurses in their work can be identified and that relative use and importance of the content of such courses can be measured effectively. The study found a correlation between work the nurse is engaged in and the significance attached to each area covered in the course work. In addition, the amount of time spent in nursing practice after graduation influenced the type of responses given.

Anderson, Edna Page (Ph. D.). "PROFESSIONAL IDENTITY OF HOME ECONO-MISTS: A SOCIALIZATION PROCESS." Pennsylvania State University, 1976. 246 pp. Source: DAI, XXXVII, 11A (May, 1977), 6993-A-6994-A. XUM Order No. 77-9645.

This study is concerned with the sources and nature of salient influences on home economists as they are socialized into the profession. Descriptions of socialization influences were obtained from the Professional Socialization Influence (PSI) using five successive versions, with Form A, the initial version, consisting of statements from selected literature, personal interviews, and discussions with home economists. It was found that home economics faculty (secondary and college/university) exert a strong influence on professional socialization of home economists.

Anderson, Janet Carol (Ed. D.). "THE EFFECTS OF COLLEGE EDUCATIONAL EXPERIENCES UPON PROFESSIONAL ROLE PERCEPTIONS OF STUDENTS OF NURSING." University of Wyoming, 1967. 127 pp. Source: Dissertation, pp. 93-98.

This research justified the following conclusions: (1) congruence between faculty and student role perceptions increased as students approached graduation, with the greatest difference in student perception occurring in their freshman and sophomore years; and (2) as a result of college educational experiences, nursing students changed their perceptions and descriptions of the nature of the ideal nurse.

Anderson, Lois Dorothy (Ph. D.). "STUDENT-FACULTY PERCEPTIONS OF EDUCATIONAL ENVIRONMENTS IN MINNESOTA SCHOOLS OF NURSING." University of Minnesota, 1961. 184 pp. Source: DAI, XXII, 11 (May, 1962), 3987-3988. XUM Order No. 62-1764.

The findings tend to support the assumption that the educational environment of basic collegiate and diploma nursing programs differ, apparently because collegiate programs are associated with institutions of higher education, and diploma programs are associated with service agencies.

Anderson, Margaret Harrington (Ed. D.). "FORCES AFFECTING THE EDU-CATION OF CHILD PSYCHIATRIC NURSES, 1954-1975." Boston University School of Education, 1976. 113 pp. Source: DAI, XXXVI, 9A (March, 1976), 5759-A. XUM Order No. 76-6631.

The study found that nursing still lacks a political base for influencing legislation; that nursing has been dependent on other groups to define its education and practice; and that federal funding has affected curriculum more than have faculty ideas.

Anderson, Mary Raleigh (Ph. D.). "PROTESTANT MISSION SCHOOLS FOR GIRLS IN SOUTH CHINA (1827 TO THE JAPANESE INVASION)." Columbia University, 1943. 365 pp. Source: Eells, p. 71; and Published, Mobile, AL: Heiber-Starke Printing Co., 1943, pp. 341-353.

Development of Protestant mission schools for girls in South China was traced, revealing various transitions and adaptations. Special emphasis was placed on these schools as having contributed to a modern intellectual or "scholar" class in China and to having influenced development of Chinese democracy and the Nationalist Movement.

Anderson, Mary Roberdeau (Ph. D.). "A DESCRIPTIVE STUDY OF VALUES AND INTERESTS OF FOUR GROUPS OF GRADUATE WOMEN AT THE UNIVERSITY OF MINNESOTA." University of Minnesota, 1952. 159 pp. Source: DAI, XII, 6 (1952), 851-852. XUM Order No. 4122.

Because 1 group can be differentiated from another by both values and interests, and because, in some instances, values differentiate between groups where interests do not, the conclusion was drawn that values as well as interests influenced the vocational decisions of the women studied.

Anderson, Robert Lee (Ph. D.). "AN EXPERIMENTAL INVESTIGATION OF GROUP COUNSELING WITH FRESHMEN IN A WOMAN'S COLLEGE." New York University, 1956. 93 pp. Source: DAI, XVI, 6 (1956), 1100-1101. XUM Order No. 16,581.

Conflicting conclusions emerged from this study: the areas in which freshman women showed greatest need for counseling were in adjustment to college life, social-recreational activities, and social and personal psychological relations. Group counseling in 8 sessions helped students deal with these problems, but no evidence proved that group counseling with college freshmen helped to minimize academic casualties and maximize academic achievement.

Anderson, Ruth Elizabeth (Ph. D.). "A STUDY TO FORMULATE PRINCIPLES OF NURSING PERTAINING TO THE MAINTENANCE AND PROMOTION OF HEALTH WHICH UNDERLIE PROFESSIONAL NURSING PRACTICE." New York University, 1963. 155 pp. Source: DAI, XXIV, 3 (September, 1963), 1144-1145. XUM Order No. 63-6656.

Functions and principles for the maintenance and promotion of health by the professional nurse were established in order to identify and further develop the theoretical body of knowledge unique to nursing.

Anthony, Teresa Ann (Ed. D.). "FACTORS RELATED TO A MEASURE OF PROFESSIONAL COMMITMENT AMONG HOME ECONOMICS TEACHERS IN UPSTATE NEW YORK." Columbia University, 1971. 197 pp. Source: DAI, XXXII, 3A (September, 1971), 1372-A. XUM Order No. 71-24,133.

Degree of professional commitment among home economics teachers was found to depend on a number of specific personal, professional, and educational characteristics. Level of job satisfaction varied and depended upon characteristics essentially similar to those relating to professional commitment.

Appleton, Christina Perry (Ph. D.). "DISTRIBUTION OF TEACHER ATTEN-TION IN THE PRE-SCHOOL CLASSROOM: THE EFFECTS OF CHILD SEX AND CHILD BEHAVIOR." University of Massachusetts, 1975. 195 pp. Source: DAI, XXXVI, 9B (March, 1976), 4659-B. XUM Order No. 76-5270.

Findings supported the hypothesis that teachers respond differently to children according to the type of behavior displayed by the child and according to whether the child is a male or female. Teachers appeared to be influenced by both the necessity to maintain order in the classroom and by sex-role stereotypes.

Aranha-Shenoy, Sister Marie Antoinette (Ph. D.). "HIGHER EDUCATION OF WOMEN IN INDIA--1963." Catholic University of America, 1964. 356 pp. Source: DAI, XXV, 6 (1964), 3336.

Among the findings: separate colleges for women have increased since 1947 with emphasis in the northern colleges on the humanities and in the southern colleges on the sciences.

Arias, Sister Maria Cecilia (Ed. D.). "A CASE STUDY OF THE PROGRAM OF THE OVERSEAS EDUCATION FUND INSTITUTE IN LEADERSHIP DEVELOPMENT FOR LATIN AMERICAN WOMEN IN THE UNITED STATES FROM 1963 TO 1970." Boston University School of Education, 1972. 470 pp. Source: DAI, XXXIII, 4A (September, 1972), 1399-A. XUM Order No. 72-25,410.

Assumptions about the need and purpose of the leadership program tended to remain stable. Other assumptions were relatively change-able, although tending to lag behind changes occurring in Latin American society.

Arnold, Fred Sidney (Ph. D.). "A MODEL RELATING EDUCATION TO FER-TILITY IN TAIWAN." University of Michigan, 1972. 369 pp. Source: DAI, XXXIII, 9A (March, 1973), 4618-A. XUM Order No. 73-6776.

Results suggested that because the educational level of couples of child-bearing age influenced fertility, the extension of compulsory education through the junior high school level in Taiwan will even-tually lead to a substantial reduction in fertility in that country.

Arnold, Vanessa Dean (Ed. D.). "ATTITUDES OF HIGH SCHOOL BUSINESS TEACHERS, BUSINESS STUDENTS, AND PARENTS OF FEMALE BUSINESS STUDENTS TOWARD THE SOCIAL, EDUCATIONAL, AND ECONOMIC ROLES OF WOMEN." Univer-sity of Florida, 1974. 143 pp. Source: DAI, XXXVI, 2A (August, 1975), 669-A. XUM Order No. 75-16,348.

Attitudes of the respondents were significantly related to their sex and to the position they held: i.e., female respondents were found to be significantly more favorable toward women's role in society than were male respondents, and teachers had higher mean scores than either students or parents.

Arnsdorff, Dorothy (Ed. D.). "PERCEPTIONS OF CRITICAL BEHAVIORS FOR WOMEN PHYSICAL EDUCATION TEACHERS AT THE SECONDARY SCHOOL LEVEL." Stanford University, 1959. 103 pp. Source: DAI, XX, 8 (February, 1960), 3180-3181. XUM Order No. 59-6866.

Differences in the way teachers and students perceive effective teaching behavior were found in such areas as planning and organization, presentation of materials, and guidance of learning experiences. No significant differences existed in their perceptions of teacher qualities, measurement, and evaluation.

Aroskar, Mila Ann (Ed. D.). "ATTAINING AUTONOMY THROUGH CURRICULUM PLANNING IN NURSING." State University of New York at Buffalo, 1976. 199 pp. Source: DAI, XXXVII, 1A (July, 1976), 106-A. XUM Order No. 76-13,311.

The data showed that students, faculty, and administrators agreed that development of autonomy in nursing students is very important. They all emphasized different elements in teaching-learning environments as critical. A conclusion was that the curriculum should contain planned opportunities for each student to develop autonomy.

Arteberry, Joan Kay (Ph. D.). "THE COMMUNICATOR AS ADVOCATE: AN EMBRYONIC ROLE FOR NURSES." University of Illinois at Urbana- Champaign, 1975. 218 pp. Source: DAI, XXXVI, 1A (July, 1975), 11-A. XUM Order No. 75-14,076.

On the basis of this study, it is premature to attempt to predict whether or not advocacy roles (serving the humanistic needs of a population by performing certain transactional services) will become an expected feature of professional nursing.

Arter, Margaret Helen (Ph. D.). "THE ROLE OF WOMEN IN ADMINISTRATION IN STATE UNIVERSITIES AND LAND-GRANT COLLEGES." Arizona State University, 1972. 221 pp. Source: DAI, XXXII, 10A (April, 1972), 5559-A. XUM Order No. 72-13,006.

This study concluded that very few women are in top-level administrative posts in state universities and land-grant colleges; that sex is indeed a factor in the selection of top-level administrators; and that the position, academic rank, and salary of women administrators are related to their educational and professional background.

Ashkenas, Thais Levberg (Ed. D.). "AIDS AND DETERRENTS TO THE PERFORMANCE OF ASSOCIATE DEGREE GRADUATES IN NURSING." Columbia University, 1972. 291 pp. Source: Dissertation, pp. 132-151.

Concluded that although the majority of the graduates of associate degree nursing programs pass the State Board Licensing Examination, they are not prepared to assume leadership roles upon graduation.

Ashley, Jo Ann (Ed. D.). "HOSPITAL SPONSORSHIP OF NURSING SCHOOLS: INFLUENCE OF APPRENTICESHIP AND PATERNALISM ON NURSING EDUCATION IN AMERICA, 1893-1948." Columbia University Teachers College, 1972. 337 pp. Source: DAI, XXXVII, 9A (March, 1977), 5622-A. XUM Order No. 77-4181.

This study determined that apprenticeship and paternalism had negative effects on nursing practices and nursing education. Apprenticeship and paternalism constituted a self-perpetuating system of structured inequality.

Aspy, Virginia Haynes (Ed. D.). "A SURVEY OF THE NEED FOR BACCALAUR-
EATE EDUCATION FOR REGISTERED NURSES IN NORTHEAST TEXAS AND THE DESIGN
OF A MODEL PROGRAM." East Texas State University, 1976. 125 pp. Source:
DAI, XXXVII, 11A (May, 1977), 6968-A-6969-A. XUM Order No. 77-9620.

This study centered on forming a model nursing education program in
30 counties in northeast Texas. A descriptive survey was made to
determine the current practices in baccalaureate nursing, contextual
variables of the nursing profession, the profile of nurses in the 30
counties, and a model baccalaureate program for registered nurses in
the study area. The Texas State Board of Nurses was the source of
the most current data available on the nurses. Directors of 15
schools with programs specifically for registered nurses leading to
a Baccalaureate Degree in Nursing were asked to submit information
on curriculum, philosophy, objectives, and conceptual framework of
programs. Only 1 of the 12 that responded was accredited by the
National League for Nursing. The findings of the study indicate a
shortage of professionally educated nurses with the "typical" nurse
being female, married, aged 30-39, and holding a diploma from a 3-
year program.

Atienza, Marie Fe Gonzales (Ph. D.). "A STUDY OF PRACTICES IN HOME
ECONOMICS TEACHER EDUCATION IN SELECTED COLLEGES AND UNIVERSITIES IN THE
UNITED STATES WITH IMPLICATIONS FOR THE HOME ECONOMICS TEACHER EDUCATION
PROGRAM IN THE PHILIPPINE WOMEN'S UNIVERSITY, MANILA." Michigan State
University, 1959. 320 pp. Source: DAI, XX, 5 (November, 1959), 1683-
1684. XUM Order No. 59-2630.

Practices and approaches used in preparing prospective teachers of
home economics in the U. S. were evaluated in terms of their applicability to the situation of the Philippine Women's University. Implications were suggested for the university's home economics teacher
education program.

Augustine, Grace M. (Ph. D.). "MANAGEMENT OF COLLEGE RESIDENCE HALLS
FOR WOMEN." Columbia University Teachers College, 1935. Source: TCCU
DIGESTS (1935), pp. 8-11.

Procedures of management in college residence halls for women were
studied and recommendations made for these procedures, with particular attention to staff members and their conditions of employment,
labor hours, and labor cost, as well as menu planning and budget
control.

Austin, Eilee Kay (Ed. D.). "CONTINUING EDUCATION NEEDS ASSESSMENT
OF TEACHERS IN ASSOCIATE DEGREE NURSING PROGRAMS IN FLORIDA." University of Florida, 1976. 85 pp. Source: DAI, XXXVIII, 2B (August, 1977),
588-B. XUM Order No. 77-16,995.

Teachers were willing to pay their own expenses and to attend courses taught by fellow faculty. The continuing education courses

which received the highest course need rating were Student Learning
Problems, Technical Nursing Practice, Curriculum Planning, Testing
and Measurement, and Clinical Supervision.

Bacon, Lucille Sleggs (Ed. D.). "A PROFESSIONAL EDUCATION PROGRAM
IN PHYSICAL EDUCATION FOR CATHOLIC TEACHER EDUCATION INSTITUTIONS FOR
WOMEN." New York University, 1950. 224 pp. Source: DAI, X, 3 (1950),
182-183.

Author suggested modifications to meet standards in professional physical education programs in 13 Catholic women teacher education institutions. She believed that some of the other 42 institutions surveyed should be able to promote the model program she presented.

Bahr, Sister Rose Therese (Ph. D.). "PROCEDURAL MODEL FOR ESTABLISH-
MENT OF NURSING PROGRAM IN LIBERAL ARTS COLLEGE ACCORDING TO CRITERIA:
PROFESSIONAL AND EDUCATIONAL." St. Louis University, 1967. 372 pp.
Source: DAI, XXVIII, 8B (February, 1968), 3350-B-3351-B. XUM Order No.
68-1209.

This pilot study's value to nursing educators is in assessing clinical and academic facilities that are needed for establishing collegiate nursing programs.

Bailey, Jane Lovenia (Ed. D.). "FACTORS AFFECTING CONTINUITY OF
LEARNING EXPERIENCES IDENTIFIED BY STUDENTS IN SELECTED BACCALAUREATE
PROGRAMS IN NURSING." University of Alabama, 1969. 169 pp. Source:
DAI, XXX, 11A (May, 1970), 4869-A. XUM Order No. 70-9324.

Seven major factors were found to affect continuity of student learning experiences. Of first importance was teacher behavior; second,
administration of nursing care; and third, quality of the curriculum.

Bailey, Janet Perry (Ed. D.). "CONSCIOUSNESS RAISING GROUPS FOR
WOMEN: IMPLICATIONS OF PAULO FREIRE'S THEORY OF CRITICAL CONSCIOUSNESS
FOR PSYCHOTHERAPY AND EDUCATION." University of Massachusetts, 1977.
155 pp. Source: DAI, XXXVIII, 1A (July, 1977), 164-A-165-A. XUM Order
No. 77-13,773.

Applies Brazilian adult educator Paulo Freire's theories to consciousness raising in the women's movement. Freire's theory: South
American oppressed people achieved liberation via these 3 stages:
(1) magical stage, when reality is thought to be controlled by fate
or luck; (2) naive stage, when people try to reform individuals in
order to improve conditions; and (3) critical stage, when people see
that the oppressive system needs to be transformed.

Bailey, Larry Joe (Ed. D.). "AN INVESTIGATION OF THE VOCATIONAL BE-
HAVIOR OF SELECTED WOMEN VOCATIONAL EDUCATION STUDENTS." University of
Illinois at Urbana-Champaign, 1968. 142 pp. Source: DAI, XXIX, 12A
(June, 1969), 4364-A. XUM Order No. 69-10,633.

The women studied experienced initial "floundering" in their occupation. Most of the women regarded their employment as temporary.
Substantial difference between women and men's vocational behavior
was indicated.

Bailey, Minnie L. (Ed. D.). "ATTITUDES TOWARD DEATH AND DYING IN NURSING STUDENTS." University of Houston, 1976. 135 pp. Source: DAI, XXXVIII, 1B (July, 1977), 139-B. XUM Order No. 77-13,961.

Instruction in death and dying did make a positive difference in the attitudes of 150 Texas senior baccalaureate nursing students.

Bain, Reba Joyce (Ed. D.). "A STUDY OF THE EFFECT OF SELECTED FAC- TORS ON THE PERFORMANCE OF NURSES ON THE STATE BOARD EXAMINATION." New Mexico State University, 1974. 109 pp. Source: DAI, XXXV, 6A (Decem- ber, 1974), 3320-A. XUM Order No. 74-27,515.

This study concluded that the length of the nursing program made a significant difference on student performance on the State Board Examination. Baccalaureate degree graduates were more likely to score higher; then came diploma graduates, followed by associate degree graduates.

Baird, Louise Claire (Ph. D.). "AN EXPERIMENTAL STUDY OF THE FRESH- MAN PROGRAM IN HOME ECONOMICS." Purdue University, 1947. 147 pp. Source: Dissertation.

A curriculum built around students' needs, interests, and abilities proved effective in speeding up mastery of subject matter and in im- proving personal adjustment.

Baker, Alma Jeanne Watkins (Ph. D.). "NURSING STUDENTS' CULTURAL KNOWLEDGE OF AND ATTITUDES TOWARD BLACK AMERICAN PATIENTS." University of Michigan, 1976. 139 pp. Source: DAI, XXXVII, 6B (December, 1976), 2768-B. XUM Order No. 76-27,440.

The study found that since white nursing students are poorly informed about the culture of their black patients, nursing education courses need to instruct all students in the cultural heritage of black Amer- icans.

Baker, Barbara Anne (Ed. D.). "ANALYSIS OF THE GIRL STUDENT ATTI- TUDES TOWARD THE PHYSICAL EDUCATION PROGRAM OF ARLINGTON, VIRGINIA." George Peabody College for Teachers, 1968. 191 pp. Source: DAI, XXX, 3A (September, 1969), 997-A-998-A. XUM Order No. 69-13,812.

The general response of the students surveyed was that their physi- cal education programs were effective. However, they felt that pro- gram adjustments were necessary and 22 recommendations for improve- ment were made.

Baker, Cecile Culp (Ph. D.). "SEX DIFFERENCES IN ACHIEVEMENT-RELA- TED BEHAVIORS IN UPPER ELEMENTARY SCHOOL CHILDREN." Florida State Uni- versity, 1973. 105 pp. Source: DAI, XXXIV, 4B (October, 1973), 1618- B-1619-B. XUM Order No. 73-25,112.

The girls studied were more likely to evaluate their efforts in terms of their own standards, rather than standards set by others. Girls also reported more anxiety about tests and more anxiety in general.

Bakke, Larry H. (Ph. D.). "A STUDY OF THE RELATIONSHIP OF AESTHETIC JUDGMENT TO SELF-ESTEEM AND SECURITY IN UNIVERSITY WOMEN." Syracuse University, 1971. 76 pp. Source: DAI, XXXII, 8A (February, 1972), 4410-A. XUM Order No. 72-6549.

Conclusions from this study reveal a higher sense of self-esteem of women in art as compared to non-art majors. The characteristics of "pushiness" and total commitment in the artistic personality need further exploration to determine if women need these attributes for artistic success.

Baldwin, Patricia Jane (D. N. Sc.). "CONGRUENCE BETWEEN THE EXPEC-TATIONS OF THE CLINICAL NURSE SPECIALIST AS PERCEIVED BY THE NURSE SPECIALIST, THE NURSE EDUCATOR, AND THE NURSE ADMINISTRATOR WITH IMPLI-CATIONS FOR CURRICULUM DEVELOPMENT IN GRADUATE NURSING PROGRAMS." Cath-olic University of America, 1975. 149 pp. Source: DAI, XXXVI, 3B (September, 1975), 1143-B. XUM Order No. 75-19,508.

Graduate programs for training clinical nurse specialists need to include courses in research theory, according to this study's find-ings.

Balentine, Margaret Ann B. (Ed. D.). "AN ANALYSIS OF TASKS OF OCCU-PATIONAL HOME ECONOMICS TEACHERS IN SECONDARY SCHOOLS OF ALABAMA WITH IMPLICATIONS FOR A COMPETENCY-BASED TEACHER EDUCATION PROGRAM IN HOME ECONOMICS." University of Alabama, 1976. 282 pp. Source: DAI, XXXVII, 12A, Part 1 (June, 1977), 7579-A-7580-A. XUM Order No. 77-12,169.

A random sample of occupational home economic teachers in Alabama was asked to keep a diary of all duties performed for a 6-day period distributed over 2 months. A questionnaire consisting of 5 cate-gories and containing 134 tasks was used to gather data. Teachers were asked to rate frequencies of task performance, degree of diffi-culty, and how competency was acquired. The findings showed that task analysis is a feasible approach to identifying competency. A preparatory program in home economics is needed; competency is gained through a combination of university training and job experience.

Balik, Muriel Jeanne (Ph. D.). "EFFECTS OF COGNITIVE STYLE ON ARITH-METIC ACHIEVEMENT IN SECOND, FOURTH, AND SIXTH GRADE BOYS AND GIRLS." Fordham University, 1976. 96 pp. Source: DAI, XXXVII, 2A (August, 1976), 872-A-873-A. XUM Order No. 76-17,951.

This research found that no significant sex differences in arithme-tic ability existed and that the effect of cognitive style operated independently of sex.

Ball, Patricia Gail (Ed. D.). "THE EFFECT OF GROUP ASSERTIVENESS TRAINING ON SELECTED MEASURES OF SELF-CONCEPT FOR COLLEGE WOMEN." Uni-versity of Tennessee, 1976. 120 pp. Source: DAI, XXXVII, 5A (November, 1976), 2731-A. XUM Order No. 76-24,820.

Assertiveness training sessions with an experimental group of women produced slight increases in assertiveness and self-concept, but these increases were not statistically significant.

Ballou, Mercedes Perrier (Ph. D.). "ORAL RESPONSES OF FIFTH GRADE GIRLS TO SELECTED STORYBOOKS." Ohio State University, 1975. 259 pp. Source: DAI, XXXVI, 11A (May, 1976), 7179-A. XUM Order No. 76-9931.

The range of the girls' oral reponses was related more to their reading achievement than to literary background.

Bancke, Linda Lee (Ph. D.). "BACKGROUND ANTECEDENTS OF AGGRESSIVE-NESS AND ASSERTIVENESS FOUND IN ACADEMICALLY ACHIEVING WOMEN." University of Cincinnati, 1972. 152 pp. Source: DAI, XXXIII, 6B (December, 1972), 2800-B-2801-B. XUM Order No. 72-31,741.

Women graduate students in 3 academic fields (education, psychology, science) differed in their ways of coping with their own aggressiveness. Science students relied most on intellectualization, psychology students most often turned against others, education students intellectualized but also turned against themselves more often than did the other women.

Bancroft, Judith Ann (Ph. D.). "PEDAGOGICAL MOVES AND SUBSTANTIVE MEANINGS COMMUNICATED IN THE VERBAL DISCOURSE OF BACCALAUREATE NURSING CLASSES." University of Wisconsin-Madison, 1974. 341 pp. Source: DAI, XXXVI, 1A (July, 1975), 99-A. XUM Order No. 75-9965.

The research methodologies developed, in part, in this study can be used by individual teachers of nursing to gather information about their own teaching behavior.

Banfield, Emiko Elaine Cunningham (Ph. D.). "WOMEN IN MIDDLE MANAGE-MENT POSITIONS: CHARACTERISTICS, TRAINING, LEADERSHIP STYLE, LIMITATIONS, REWARDS, AND PROBLEMS." U. S. International University, 1976. 158 pp. Source: DAI, XXXVII, 4B (October, 1976), 1952-B-1953-B. XUM Order No. 76-22,378.

No prescribed educational pattern was found among women in management. A majority valued their on-the-job training highly. They were women with well-integrated personalities who believed advancement most likely if one remained in one organization and gained acceptance.

Banker, Perin Kaikhushroo (Ed. D.). "A PLAN FOR THE REVISION OF TEACHER EDUCATION FOR THE RURAL GIRLS' SCHOOLS OF THE CHHATTISGARH AREA, CENTRAL PROVINCES, INDIA." Columbia University Teacher College, 1948. 158 pp. Source: Dissertation.

This plan for teacher education aims at utilizing educational facilities to prepare women teachers in order that they can improve living conditions in rural communities.

Banks, Anna Katherine (Ed. D.). "AN EVALUATION OF STUDENTS' ATTI-TUDES DEVELOPED THROUGH HOMEMAKING INSTRUCTION IN THE SECONDARY SCHOOLS OF OKLAHOMA." University of Oklahoma, 1939. 121 pp. Source: Dissertation, pp. 57-60.

Home economics instruction proved effective in building desirable attitudes toward home and family life.

Banks, Waldo Rice (Ph. D.). "SEXUAL AUTHORITY: AN EDUCATIONAL, HISTORICAL, PHILOSOPHICAL, AND SOCIOLOGICAL STUDY IN SUPPORT OF WOMEN'S EQUALITY." Claremont Graduate School, 1975. 179 pp. Source: DAI, XXXV, 12A, Part 1 (June, 1975), 8021-A-8022-A. XUM Order No. 75-12,738.

The conclusion was that women's equality with men is substantiated by educational, historical, philosophical, and sociological evidence. Men should support women's rights, specifically the Equal Rights Amendment, or they will inevitably face the challenge of women through more aggressive means.

Bannon, Carol (Ed. D.). "SEX STEREOTYPING IN HIGH SCHOOL CONSUMER EDUCATION TEXTBOOKS." Northern Illinois University, 1975. 140 pp. Source: DAI, XXXVI, 10A (April, 1976), 6585-A-6586-A. XUM Order No. 76-8905.

Content analysis revealed that the number and types of female role occupations were inadequately represented in consumer education text-books. In general the books reflected a stereotyped role system and not a changing society.

Barbee, Margaret S. (Ph. D.). "SKILL ASSESSMENT AND TRAINING FOR WOMEN MANAGERS." Colorado State University, 1976. 245 pp. Source: DAI, XXXVII, 12B, Part 1 (June, 1977), 6386-B. XUM Order No. 77-12,023.

The participants in this study were 37 women managers from 15 firms. An intervention program was used, including guest speakers, films, supervisory skills training, small group exercises, and discussions. A before-and-after evaluation model was used with randomly assigned experimental and no-treatment control groups. The hypothesis that the experimental group would be higher on measures of several dependent variables after the training program was not supported. Significant changes did occur in assertiveness, self-confidence, and motivation.

Barcus, Billie Jean (D. N. Sc.). "THE RELATIONSHIP OF NURSING STUDENTS' INFERENCE OF SUFFERING AND PERCEPTUAL REACTANCE." Catholic University of America, 1972. 67 pp. Source: DAI, XXXII, 12B (June, 1972), 7129-B-7130-B. XUM Order No. 72-18,348.

The findings of this study demonstrate a significant quadratic relationship between the nursing students' inference of suffering and the nursing students' perceptual reactance.

Barker, Virginia Adams (Ed. D.). "CHARACTERISTICS OF NURSING PROGRAMS LEADING TO AN ASSOCIATE DEGREE OFFERED BY INSTITUTIONS OF HIGHER EDUCATION." Indiana University, 1969. 86 pp. Source: DAI, XXX, 11A (May, 1970), 4669-A-4670-A. XUM Order No. 70-7968.

No standard curriculum was found for an associate degree in nursing. The requirements varied widely and many programs had an excessive number of total credit hours.

Barkley, Margaret Knotts (Ed. D.). "THE CONCEPT OF THE HOME ECONOMICS TEACHER HELD BY HIGH SCHOOL STUDENTS." University of Illinois, 1956. 165 pp. Source: DAI, XVII, 2 (1957), 307-308. XUM Order No. 19,795.

High school students were found to have a stereotyped concept of
home economics teachers. Most students believed the teacher would
rather be a housewife than a teacher. Students from small schools
had slightly clearer concepts about home economics teachers than did
students from large schools.

Barnartt, Sharon Naomi (Ph. D.). "SEX DIFFERENCES IN CORRELATES OF
ATTACHMENT TO THE PROFESSIONAL ROLE AMONG MEDICAL STUDENTS." University
of Chicago, 1976. Source: DAI, XXXVII, 9B (March, 1977), 4749-B-4750-B.

Competence in clinical tasks is more strongly related to professional
attachment than to enjoyment of those tasks for the women. For men
enjoyment is more strongly related. Spouse's encouragement is positively correlated for men but negatively correlated for women. The
women are more likely to interact with female faculty or students
while for the men, interaction with male classmates is more strongly
correlated than are other aspects of socialization.

Barnett, Rosalind Chait (Ph. D.). "VOCATIONAL PLANNING OF COLLEGE
WOMEN: A PSYCHO-SOCIAL STUDY." Harvard University, 1964. Source:
PROCEEDINGS, 75th ANNUAL CONVENTION, AMERICAN PSYCHOLOGICAL ASSOCIATION
(1967), pp. 345-346.

Behavior of college senior women concerning vocational planning was
classified with the help of behavioral indices. Drawing from developmental psychology, the research was able to predict stability or
change in the women's vocational plans.

Barnett, William Kester (Ph. D.). "AN ETHNOGRAPHIC DESCRIPTION OF
SANLEI TS'UN, TAIWAN, WITH EMPHASIS ON WOMEN'S ROLES OVERCOMING RESEARCH
PROBLEMS CAUSED BY THE PRESENCE OF A GREAT TRADITION." Michigan State
University, 1970. 585 pp. Source: DAI, XXXI, 7B (January, 1971),
3812-B-3813-B. XUM Order No. 71-2026.

Evidence from anthropological field study suggested that the structural position of Chinese women was not so inferior to that of men
as previously reported or as in Chinese literature. Many Chinese
women in this study were educated and economically important.

Barnes, Julia Herring (Ed. D.). "A STUDY OF THE COMPARATIVE PRE-
DICTIVE FUNCTION OF SELECTED PERSONALITY VARIABLES AS RELATED TO LOW AND
HIGH TEST PERFORMANCE GROUPS OF EXTENSION HOME ECONOMISTS." Mississippi
State University, 1976. 71 pp. Source: DAI, XXXVII, 12A, Part 1 (June,
1977), 7419-A. XUM Order No. 77-11,748.

The high performance group were more creative and more tolerant of
traditional ideas. When variables of age, length of service, and
level of education were statistically controlled, the high performance group was found to be more creative and imaginative. Age influenced factors of bright vs. dull, sensitive vs. tough minded,
and tense vs. relaxed. Length of service and level of education influenced the factor of enthusiastic vs. glum.

Baron, Eleanor B. (Ph. D.). "THE STATUS OF WOMEN SENIOR HIGH SCHOOL
PRINCIPALS IN THE UNITED STATES." University of Pittsburgh, 1976. 127
pp. Source: DAI, XXXVII, 7A (January, 1977), 4259-A-4260-A. XUM
Order No. 77-681.

Findings on returned questionnaires from a sample of 110 women senior high school principals in 1976 were compared with a similar study in 1955. Today's women principals are fewer in number, in charge of larger school enrollments, are associated more with community organizations, are more often married or were married, have more graduate education credits, and have had more administrative experience prior to their principalship; 74.3% do not teach and so devote more time to administration. Also assessed were statements they agreed with and disagreed with concerning reasons for the decline in the number of women as principals.

Baron, Gerald Thomas (Ed. D.). "A STUDY OF WOMEN IN INDUSTRIAL ARTS EDUCATION." Arizona State University, 1974. 117 pp. Source: DAI, XXXV, 3A (September, 1974), 1475-A. XUM Order No. 74-20,120.

Some findings in this study of women teaching industrial arts at the secondary level and women students majoring in secondary industrial education were: (1) most women teaching in the field did not major in it while in college; (2) industrial arts departments of teacher training institutions need to encourage women to overcome the social barriers to majoring in industrial arts; and (3) much resistance to women's entering the profession lies in the field of industrial arts itself.

Barritt, Evelyn Ruth Berryman (Ph. D.). "FLORENCE NIGHTINGALE'S VALUES REGARDING NURSING EDUCATION." Ohio State University, 1971. 124 pp. Source: DAI, XXXII, 7B (January, 1972), 4029-B. XUM Order No. 72-4418.

All of Florence Nightingale's values regarding nursing education were found to be viable in modern programs except the in loco paren- tis concept. The author's recommendations included further histori- cal research in nursing, analysis of Miss Nightingale's concepts, and the establishment of an International Nursing Hall of Fame.

Barron, Sister Marion (Ph. D.). "POSSIBLE CONSEQUENCES FOR DIPLOMA NURSING EDUCATION IN ONTARIO AS A SUBSYSTEM OF THE SYSTEM OF COLLEGES OF APPLIED ARTS AND TECHNOLOGY." Catholic University of America, 1972. 116 pp. Source: DAI, XXXIII, 2A (August, 1972), 512-A. XUM Order No. 72-22,147.

Although there would be positive consequences in making diploma nur- sing education a part of the Colleges of Applied Arts and Technol- ogy--including a broader program with more electives--the negative aspects present some unresolved questions. Differences in objec- tives, funding sources, and clinical nursing involvement need to be resolved.

Barter, Alice Knar Shamlian (Ph. D.). "A STUDY OF ELEMENTARY SCHOOL TEACHERS' ATTITUDES TOWARD THE WOMAN PRINCIPAL AND TOWARD THE ELEMENTARY PRINCIPALSHIP AS A CAREER." University of Michigan, 1957. 241 pp. Source: DAI, XVIII, 4 (April, 1958), 1313. XUM Order No. Mic. 58-878.

Teacher attitudes and school policies are not a problem in hiring more female principals. However, lack of interest in the job and lack of academic training prevents an increase in the number of women in administrative positions.

Bartok, Margaret Anne Riva (Ph. D.). "AN INVESTIGATION OF SELECTED
ATTITUDES AND PERSONALITY CHARACTERISTICS AS THEY RELATE TO CAREER COM-
MITMENT IN COLLEGE EDUCATED WOMEN." University of Pittsburgh, 1975.
204 pp. Source: DAI, XXXVI, 9A (March, 1976), 5816-A-5817-A. XUM Order No. 76-5413.

The attitude and personality factors measured did not affect career
commitment. Variables that did show significance were level of education, marital status, number of children, employment status, and
whether a job was male or female dominated.

Baruch, Grace K. (Ph. D.). "MATERNAL INFLUENCES UPON COLLEGE WOMEN'S
ATTITUDES TOWARD WOMEN AND WORK." Bryn Mawr College, 1970. Source:
Dissertation.

This study showed that women whose mothers have not worked devalue
feminine competence. Maternal employment did not, however, influence the subjects' attitudes toward combining a career with mother-
hood.

Basnyat, Prabha S. (Ph. D.). "BASIC GUIDELINES AND SUGGESTIONS FOR
IMPROVEMENT OF FUTURE HOME SCIENCE TRAINING, EXTENSION, AND RESEARCH
PROGRAMS IN NEPAL." Southern Illinois University, 1972. 268 pp.
Source: DAI, XXXIII, 3B (September, 1972), 1175-B-1176-B. XUM Order
No. 72-24,350.

A questionnaire about their learning needs was administered to a
random sample of 100 women in 4 villages. The researcher used the
findings, along with other materials, to devise guidelines for such
activities as basic education and vocational training in villages.

Bassett, Marion Blumer (Ed. D.). "THE CREATIVE THINKING ABILITY AND
PROBLEM-SOLVING SKILL OF ASSOCIATE AND BACCALAUREATE DEGREE NURSING STU-
DENTS." University of Alabama, 1976. 116 pp. Source: DAI, XXXVII,
12A, Part 1 (June, 1977), 6052-B. XUM Order No. 77-12,171.

Some difference between baccalaureate and associate degree students
was noted, but no significant differences in creative thinking or
problem-solving skills were found and no positive correlations between student perceptions of faculty and creative thinking were
noted.

Bates, Zelpha Mae (Ed. D.). "A STUDY OF THE NEEDS OF FRESHMAN HOME
ECONOMICS STUDENTS AND STUDENT PERSONNEL SERVICES IN THE SCHOOL OF EDU-
CATION OF NEW YORK UNIVERSITY." New York University, 1946. 261 pp.
Source: DAI, VII, 1 (1946), 27-29. XUM Order No. 823.

According to the data, personnel services in the School of Education
were not meeting freshman student needs. A coordinated program of
student personnel services was recommended with increased counseling
services, development of student activities, provisions for adequate
food and housing, and a year-long freshman orientation program.

Batz, Edna Todt (Ph. D.). "HOME ENVIRONMENT AND HOME-UNIVERSITY
RELATIONSHIPS OF A HOME-RESIDENT GROUP OF SENIOR WOMEN IN THE UNIVERSITY
OF PITTSBURGH." University of Pittsburgh, 1941. 180 pp. Source: Dis-
sertation, pp. 145-150.

Most senior women who commuted to an urban university had supportive families and favorable, though modest, home conditions. Despite the time and energy needed to commute, many enjoyed maintaining former friendships while cultivating new ones.

Baum, Paul B. (Ph. D.). "INVESTIGATION OF SOCIAL CONFLICTS OF JUNIOR COLLEGE WOMEN FOR COUNSELING." University of Wisconsin, 1945. 181 pp. Source: Dissertation, pp. 124-129.

The research revealed that parents and daughters considered certain aspects of personality development (such as poise) more important than academic achievement and that scholastic achievement provided no criterion for social adjustment.

Baur, Bonny Marsh (Ed. D.). "ADMISSION AND EMPLOYMENT PATTERNS OF WOMEN MATRICULATING IN EDUCATIONAL ADMINISTRATION AT SELECTED MIDWESTERN UNIVERSITIES." Ball State University, 1975. 97 pp. Source: DAI, XXXVII, 1A (July, 1976), 52-A. XUM Order No. 76-16,458.

Conclusions were: (1) the number of females completing specialist and doctorate degree programs in educational administration at selected midwestern universities is increasing annually; (2) these women are more likely to get elementary principalships than any other position; (3) women are not proportionately represented as faculty in educational administration departments; and (4) women are underrepresented in higher levels of educational administration positions.

Baylor, Ruth Markendorpff (Ed. D.). "THE CONTRIBUTION OF ELIZABETH PALMER PEABODY TO KINDERGARTEN EDUCATION IN THE UNITED STATES." New York University, 1960. 253 pp. Source: DAI, XXI, 10 (1960), 2976.

In 1870 Elizabeth P. Peabody established in Boston the first American public school kindergarten. This study reviews her humanistic educational philosophy and her efforts, through travel, lectures, and writing, to promote the kindergarten movement.

Beam, Walter Willis, Jr. (Ed. D.). "FACTORS ASSOCIATED WITH RESEARCH PRODUCTIVITY OF GRADUATE FACULTY MEMBERS IN HOME ECONOMICS UNITS." Oklahoma State University, 1976. 229 pp. Source: DAI, XXXVII, 9A (March, 1977), 5648-A-5649-A. XUM Order No. 77-5036.

For the nondoctoral group, research productivity was positively correlated with the direction of master's students, professional development activities, and expectations to conduct, disseminate, or become involved in research. Productivity was inversely correlated with undergraduate instruction and higher education experience. For the doctoral group, research productivity was correlated with work load and inversely correlated with publication credit ethics. Different factors were associated with research productivity for nondoctoral and doctoral members with respect to unit size.

Bean, Nancy McClain (Ph. D.). "A STATUS OF HOME MANAGEMENT IN HOME ECONOMICS PROGRAMS IN SECONDARY SCHOOLS OF MISSOURI." University of Missouri, Columbia, 1976. 181 pp. Source: DAI, XXXVII, 9A (March, 1977), 5649-A. XUM Order No. 77-4886.

The study concluded that home management subject matter is presented in secondary school home economics programs in Missouri. The "extent of inclusion" and the determination of which home management concepts are included in a program vary according to teachers' interpretation of the concept and the adequacy of their pre-service preparation.

Bearss, Kathryn Mildred (Ed. D.). "GENERAL EDUCATION IN THE PREPAR-ATION OF TEACHERS OF NURSING." Columbia University Teachers College, 1961. Source: TCCU DIGESTS (1961), pp. 31-32.

The data indicated a need to include general education at the under-graduate and graduate levels in schools of nursing.

Beck, Bonnie Ann (Ed. D.). "LIFESTYLES OF NEVER MARRIED WOMEN PHYSI-CAL EDUCATORS IN INSTITUTIONS OF HIGHER EDUCATION IN THE UNITED STATES." University of North Carolina at Greensboro, 1976. 375 pp. Source: DAI, XXXVII, 5A (November, 1976), 2715-A-2716-A. XUM Order No. 76-24,936.

Questionnaire data gathered from 153 single women faculty members showed a diversity and richness of lifestyles. Personal lifestyle was materialistic and outgoing; professionally the women were higher paid and very active. It was pointed out that personal life patterns could not be separated from professional accomplishments.

Beck, Burrel Henry (Ed. D.). "A COMPARISON OF THE ACHIEVEMENT LEVEL OF COLLEGE MEN AND WOMEN ENROLLED IN ENGINEERING DRAWING." University of Missouri, Columbia, 1967. 181 pp. Source: DAI, XXVIII, 12A, Part I (June, 1968), 4943-A. XUM Order No. 68-3594.

Although both men and women were able to achieve at a satisfactory group level, the men showed a higher level of achievement in tech-nical knowledge and manual dexterity. Scholastic aptitude of the men in the study was significantly higher than that of the women. Women's performance would likely improve if they were exposed earlier to the same type of training.

Beck, Esther Lily (Ed. D.). "AN ANALYSIS OF SELECTED FACTORS RELE-VANT TO THE EMPLOYMENT STATUS IN BUSINESS OFFICES OF MARRIED WOMEN COL-LEGE GRADUATES." Indiana University, 1963. Source: DAI, XXIV, 12, Part 1 (June, 1963), 5232-5233.

Interviews with 62 working women and with representatives of 27 firms having at least 100 employees each provided data. Major findings were that to reach managerial level, a woman must gener-ally have training beyond the bachelor's degree, remain with one firm for a long time, and be of high socioeconomic level. The smal-ler the firm, the better the chances for advancement.

Becker, Steven Joel (Ph. D.). "A COMPARISON OF BODY ATTITUDES IN WOMEN WITH MASCULINE VOCATIONAL INTERESTS AND THOSE WITH FEMININE VOCA-TIONAL INTERESTS." University of Maryland, 1971. 89 pp. Source: DAI, XXXII, 9B (March, 1972), 5421-B. XUM Order No. 72-10,061.

Findings did not support the hypothesis that women with masculine vocational interests would view their bodies as men do.

Becker, Susan Deubel (Ph. D.). "AN INTELLECTUAL HISTORY OF THE NA-
TIONAL WOMAN'S PARTY, 1920-1941." Case Western Reserve University, 1975.
499 pp. Source: DAI, XXXVII, 4A (October, 1976), 2345-A. XUM Order No.
76-16,032.

The National Woman's Party, the only "hard core" feminist organization during the 1920's and 1930's, was a closely knit elite group of
well-educated upper middle class women. Although its influence declined by 1940, it gained some support for the Equal Rights Amendment, which it first sponsored in 1923.

Bedwany, Therese Labib (Ph. D.). "THE STATUS OF WOMEN AND POPULA-
TION CONTROL: THE RELATIONSHIP OF GROSS REPRODUCTION RATE AND SELECTED
INDICATORS OF THE STATUS OF WOMEN IN DEVELOPED AND DEVELOPING COUNTRIES."
Michigan State University, 1974. 190 pp. Source: DAI, XXXV, 11A (May,
1975), 7417-A. XUM Order No. 75-7113.

Literacy was one of the indicators used to assess women's position
in various countries. This study found a direct relationship between
the status of women and fertility rate.

Beeker, Barbara Ann (Ed. D.). "SELECTED PERSONALITY TRAITS OF STU-
DENTS PREFERRING EPISODIC OR DISTRIBUTIVE NURSING." Columbia University
Teachers College, 1977. 137 pp. Source: DAI, XXXVII, 12B, Part 1
(June, 1977), 6052-B-6053-B. XUM Order No. 77-13,013.

Baccalaureate nursing students (139) were given the Omnibus Personality Inventory to test the hypothesis that those in distributive
nursing would score higher in altruism, complexity, and thinking introversion and lower in practical outlook than those in episodic
nursing. The curriculum included an area of concentration in either
episodic or distributive nursing in the January and spring terms of
the senior year. Analysis of the data indicated no significant differences in personality traits but differences were found in autonomy and estheticism.

Behling, Mary Alice (Ph. D.). "THE DEVELOPMENT OF A SCREENING PRO-
GRAM FOR THE SELECTION AND RETENTION OF WOMEN PHYSICAL EDUCATION MAJOR
STUDENTS." Florida State University, 1969. 106 pp. Source: DAI, XXX,
10A (April, 1970), 4258-A-4259-A. XUM Order No. 70-6287.

Success as a woman physical education teacher can be predicted by
measures of scholarship, personality, and motor ability.

Behymer, Alice F. (Ed. D.). "IMPLICATIONS FOR TEACHING PSYCHIATRIC
NURSING IN PRE-SERVICE NURSING EDUCATION PROGRAMS FROM A STUDY OF SATIS-
FYING AND STRESSFUL SITUATIONS REPORTED BY STUDENTS." Columbia Univer-
sity Teachers College, 1960. Source: Dissertation, pp. 47-49.

Data gathered from 29 schools of nursing indicated the need for improved orientation to psychiatric nursing, with improved clinical
experience and additional assistance in developing greater competencies in dealing with complex interpersonal relationships and in
other stressful situations.

Beighley, Kenneth Eldred (Ph. D.). "A STUDY OF FEMALE COLLEGE GRAD-
UATES CERTIFYING FOR ELEMENTARY SCHOOL TEACHING." Michigan State Univer-
sity, 1963. 237 pp. Source: DAI, XXIV, 11 (May, 1964), 4563-4564.
XUM Order No. 64-6864.

Female college graduates entering elementary teaching were found to
be committed and altruistic and primarily interested in intellectual
and individual development as teachers.

Belding, Robert E. (Ph. D.). "GUIDANCE PROGRAMS IN SMALLER COLLEGES
FOR WOMEN." Case Western Reserve University, 1953. 323 pp. Source:
Author.

This study identified significant guidance trends in small colleges
for women and made recommendations for improving guidance at one
such college.

Beldner, Judith (Ph. D.). "FEAR OF SUCCESS IN COLLEGE WOMEN AND ITS
RELATION TO PERFORMANCE IN ACHIEVEMENT SITUATIONS." New York University,
1976. 251 pp. Source: DAI, XXXVII, 2B (August, 1976), 946-B-947-B.
XUM Order No. 76-19,011.

The theories of 2 earlier researchers (Horner and Pappo) on fear of
success were tested with 102 female undergraduates. Using Horner's
measure, fear of success was significantly related to grade point
average, traditionality of occupational goal, and race. On Pappo's
test, such fear was significantly related to traditionality and level
of occupational goal.

Bell, Carmine Jane (Ph. D.). "THE ROLE OF MONASTIC WOMEN IN THE LIFE
AND LETTERS OF EARLY MEDIEVAL ENGLAND AND IRELAND." University of Vir-
ginia, 1975. 239 pp. Source: DAI, XXXVI, 5A (November, 1975), 2835-A.
XUM Order No. 75-26,015.

Monastic women's prominence in early medieval England (example,
Aethelthryth) and Ireland (St. Brigit) depended upon: (1) historical significance in the development of national monasticism; and (2)
literary and religious significance as the popular national counter-
part of the Virgin Mary.

Belson, Beverly Ann (Ph. D.). "JOURNAL OF THE NATIONAL ASSOCIATION
FOR WOMEN DEANS, ADMINISTRATORS, AND COUNSELORS: AN HISTORICAL ANALY-
SIS, 1938-1974." Michigan State University, 1974. 218 pp. Source:
DAI, XXXVI, 1A (July, 1975), 55-A-56-A. XUM Order No. 75-14,698.

Since analysis showed that only 20.28% of articles in the Journal
dealt primarily with concerns of female students and/or professional
personnel workers, the Journal proved to be useful to both sexes.

Benitez, Rosalyn P. Kartun (D. S. W.). "THIRTY RETIRED CAREER WOMEN:
AN EXPLORATORY STUDY OF PERCEIVED NEEDS." University of Southern Cali-
fornia, 1974. 250 pp. Source: DAI, XXXV, 5A (November, 1974), 3116-A.
XUM Order No. 74-23,569.

This study found 5 concomitant needs among retired women teachers.
Their personalities affected these needs.

Bennett, Donald Allison (Ed. D.). "A COMPARISON OF THE ACHIEVEMENT OF FIFTH GRADE PUPILS HAVING MALE TEACHERS WITH THOSE HAVING FEMALE TEACHERS." University of Denver, 1966. 249 pp. Source: DAI, XXVII, 12A (June, 1967), 4032-A-4033-A. XUM Order No. 67-3940.

Students having female teachers had higher levels of achievement than those with male teachers. Also female pupils showed more academic growth in the 5th grade than did male pupils.

Bennett, Donald Dean (Ed. D.). "SELECTED ATTRIBUTES WHICH INFLUENCE COMMITMENT TO TEACHING OF FEMALE ELEMENTARY TEACHERS WITH DIFFERENT PREP- ARATIONAL BACKGROUNDS." Indiana University, 1967. 171 pp. Source: DAI, XXVIII, 10A (April, 1968), 4019-A-4020-A. XUM Order No. 68-4705.

The data indicated that teaching commitment depended upon the under- graduate degree obtained, academic major, and plans for continued employment in education.

Bennett, F. Edward (Ph. D.). "A STUDY OF THE RELATIONSHIP OF PER- FORMANCE RATINGS TO THE LICENSING EXAMINATION SCORES AND OTHER SELECTED VARIABLES OF GRADUATE PRACTICAL NURSES." Southern Illinois University, 1974. 135 pp. Source: DAI, XXXV, 12B, Part 1 (June, 1975), 5965-B. XUM Order No. 75-13,262.

The study of 98 LPNs concluded that there was no significant predic- tive value between on-the-job performance and these selected vari- ables: licensing examination score, age, marital status, educational attainment, college GPA, and scores on 3 units of Content and Nursing Including Aspects of Pharmacology Achievement Tests.

Bennett, Leland R. (Ed. D.). "AIR FORCE NURSES' PARTICIPATION IN PROGRAMS OF CONTINUING EDUCATION AS RELATED TO SELECTED CRITERIA." Bos- ton University School of Education, 1968. 216 pp. Source: DAI, XXX, 6A (December, 1969), 2316-A-2318-A. XUM Order No. 69-7843.

Nurses appeared to be motivated to participate in continuing educa- tion programs by the learning opportunity presented and by a wish for greater personal achievement.

Bennett, Linda Lee Booker (Ed. D.). "THE RELATIONSHIPS BETWEEN SELF CONCEPT, PERCEPTUAL CHARACTERISTICS, AND TEACHING EFFECTIVENESS IN SE- LECTED GROUPS OF PROSPECTIVE SECONDARY TEACHERS." East Texas State Uni- versity, 1976. 135 pp. Source: DAI, XXXVII, 11A (May, 1977), 6969-A. XUM Order No. 77-9622.

Fifty prospective secondary teachers at East Texas University were given the Tennessee Self Concept Scale in February, 1976, and the Student Teacher Evaluation Form was completed by supervisors in pub- lic schools in order to determine the relationships between percep- tual characteristics (measured by the Perceptual Score Sheet), ef- fectiveness in teaching, and self concept. The results were that males and females with adequate self concepts had positive percep- tions of others, self, and teaching, with self concepts not being related to teaching effectiveness. No differences were found for males or females in relationships between self concept, perceptual characteristics, and teaching effectiveness.

Benningfield, Milo Francis (Ph. D.). "THE EFFECT OF GROUP DISCUS-
SION UPON SELECTED PERSONALITY VARIABLES OF STUDENT NURSES." North Texas
State University, 1974. 147 pp. Source: DAI, XXXV, 7A (January, 1975),
4177-A. XUM Order No. 75-869.

This study showed no change in sociometric status for participants
in group discussions. However, the significant change in self-actualization was found to warrant use of group discussion in nurses'
training.

Benoit, Sallye Starks (Ph. D.). "JOB SATISFACTION AMONG FACULTY WO-
MEN IN HIGHER EDUCATION IN THE STATE UNIVERSITIES OF LOUISIANA." Louisiana State University, 1976. 110 pp. Source: DAI, XXXVII, 11A (May,
1977), 6969-A-6970-A. XUM Order No. 77-10,356.

A stratified random sample of 220 women faculty selected from the
total population of the 1975-76 faculty women employed in state universities in Louisiana returned 2 questionnaires to determine what
aspects of their jobs gave them the most satisfaction. Factors contributing most to feelings of satisfaction were moral value, social
service and activity, with the least satisfying being university
policies and practices, advancement, and compensation. Compared to
the general satisfaction level of women in other occupations, women
faculty were the most dissatisfied with their positions.

Bentsvi-Mayer, Shoshanna (Ph. D.). "THE ATTITUDES OF ISRAELI TEACH-
ERS AND STUDENTS TOWARD THE TWO SEXES AND THEIR SEXUALLY STEREOTYPED BE-
HAVIORS." University of Connecticut, 1976. 250 pp. Source: DAI,
XXXVIII, 1A (July, 1977), 165-A-166-A. XUM Order No. 77-14,448.

Teachers preferred feminine behaviors when rating written essays.
Teachers and students considered masculine behavior in both sexes
indicative of leadership potential. Only women teachers showed same-
sex identification, exhibiting greater generosity when rating all
essays. The study also analyzed the development of the Israeli educational system and differential education received by females.

Berens, Anne Elizabeth (Ph. D.). "THE SOCIALIZATION OF ACHIEVEMENT
MOTIVES IN BOYS AND GIRLS." York University (Canada), 1973. Source:
DAI, XXXVII, 1A (July, 1976), 517-B.

For girls, independence training was found to be closely associated
with high achievement. As girls grew older, independent behavior
came into conflict with the feminine sex role.

Berg, Helen Margaret (Ed. D.). "FACTORS DIFFERENTIATING PARTICIPANT
AND NON-PARTICIPANT NURSES IN CONTINUING EDUCATION." Columbia Univer-
sity, 1973. 143 pp. Source: DAI, XXXIV, 4A (October, 1973), 1567-A.
XUM Order No. 73-22,706.

The data showed that participants in continuing education programs
were usually single, had been referred by friends and relatives to
join the classes, worked in mixed medical-surgical areas, and were
more likely to be members of other organizations than non-participants.

Berg, John Christian (Ph. D.). "GEOGRAPHIC MOBILITY OF GRADUATES FROM ASSOCIATE DEGREE AND BACCALAUREATE DEGREE NURSING EDUCATION PROGRAMS IN OKLAHOMA: 1972-1974." University of Oklahoma, 1975. 141 pp. Source: DAI, XXXVI, 8B (February, 1976), 3868-B-3869-B. XUM Order No. 76-3082.

Both baccalaureate and associate degree graduates from urban programs practiced in urban settings. While rural associate program graduates generally practiced in rural areas, over 50% of rural baccalaureate graduates practiced in urban areas.

Bergamini, Sister Marie Carmen (Ph. D.). "AN ASSESSMENT OF INTER-NATIONAL NURSING STUDENTS IN THE UNITED STATES: A CASE STUDY OF PHILIP-PINE EXPERIENCE." University of California, Berkeley, 1964. 360 pp. Source: DAI, XXV, 6 (December, 1964), 3517-3518. XUM Order No. 64-12,540.

The study revealed a need for in-service and continuing education programs for nurses in the Philippines.

Bergey, Stafanie Friday Antonakos (Ph. D.). "TEACHERS' RESPONSE TO SELF-DISCLOSURE OF CHILDREN." University of Pennsylvania, 1976. 85 pp. Source: DAI, XXXVII, 7A (January, 1977), 4220-A. XUM Order No. 77-812.

Male and female 4th, 5th, and 6th grade teachers were similar in rating student self-disclosure and in the referral of students for counseling, with more females being referred than males. Differences were found between the male and female teachers' opinions of student adjustment and their sex-role identification.

Bergman, Linda Susan (Ph. D.). "INTERPERSONAL ATTRACTION AS A SITU-ATIONAL DETERMINANT FOR THE AROUSAL OF MOTIVE TO AVOID SUCCESS IN THE COLLEGE FEMALE." Hofstra University, 1975. 131 pp. Source: DAI, XXXVI, 10B (April, 1976), 5337-B. XUM Order No. 76-5047.

Female college students (120) in competition with males to whom they felt attracted found that the level of fear of success, the sex of competitor, or the level of interpersonal attraction had no signifi-cant effects on achievement.

Bergman, Rebecca (Ed. D.). "TEAM NURSING IN PUBLIC HEALTH IN ISRAEL." Columbia University, 1963. 259 pp. Source: DAI, XXV, 1 (July, 1964), 412-413. XUM Order No. 64-5676.

Main recommendation: to teach team leadership to selected public health nurses and use teams of public health and practical nurses to expand health services in Israel.

Bergstrom, Joan Margosian (Ed. D.). "STUDY OF SWEDEN'S CHILD CEN-TERS--DAY NURSERIES: ITS APPLICABILITY IN DEVELOPING A CONCEPTUAL MODEL FOR AN EARLY CHILD CARE-DAY CARE PROGRAM IN THE UNITED STATES." Univer-sity of Massachusetts, 1972. 301 pp. Source: DAI, XXXIII, 9A (March, 1973), 4659-A. XUM Order No. 73-5528.

Administration, operation, and future goals of the Swedish day nur-sery system provided a model for a similar system for educating and improving the life of U. S. children, aged 6 months to 3 years.

Bernstein, Ruth Krugman (Ed. D.). "A PILOT STUDY OF THE EDUCATIONAL NEEDS OF NON-URBAN WOMEN (MISSOURI) AND A PROPOSAL FOR AN EXTENSION DIVISION PROGRAM TO MEET THESE NEEDS." Wayne State University, 1971. 237 pp. Source: DAI, XXXII, 5A (November, 1971), 2397-A. XUM Order No. 71-29,721.

Recommendation was that a conveniently located women's education center be established and that lay groups be involved in planning programs which reflect people's real needs.

Berry, Jane Batchelder (Ed. D.). "LIFE PLANS OF FRESHMAN AND SOPHO-MORE COLLEGE WOMEN." Columbia University Teachers College, 1954. Source: TCCU DIGESTS (1954), pp. 69-71.

About a quarter of the women planned to take graduate study. Most hoped to marry be age 23 and have 3 or 4 children. The conclusion was that the curriculum should provide preparation for home and family life.

Berwald, Helen D. (Ph. D.). "ATTITUDES TOWARD WOMEN COLLEGE TEACHERS IN INSTITUTIONS OF HIGHER EDUCATION ACCREDITED BY THE NORTH CENTRAL ASSOCIATION." University of Minnesota, 1962. 521 pp. Source: DAI, XXIII, 11 (May, 1963), 4161-4162. XUM Order No. 63-1854.

Only a few college administrators, faculty, and students were ready to accept women as faculty members on an equal basis with men. Only a quarter of women students had seriously considered becoming college teachers.

Bessent, Hattie (Ed. D.). "A CURRICULUM DESIGN FOR DISADVANTAGED STUDENTS IN A BACCALAUREATE NURSING PROGRAM." University of Florida, 1970. 89 pp. Source: DAI, XXXII, 3A (September, 1971), 1328-A. XUM Order No. 71-24,409.

In proposing curriculum changes, the study emphasized disadvantaged students' social, economic, and environmental experiences as they relate to educational achievement.

Best, William P. (Ph. D.). "THE PREDICTION OF SUCCESS IN NURSING EDUCATION." Purdue University, 1968. 143 pp. Source: DAI, XXIX, 8A (February, 1969), 2558-A. XUM Order No. 69-2888.

Statistical study designed to determine how accurately student nurses' success or failure in the first year of a 2-year associate degree program could be predicted.

Bevis, Mary Eileen (Ph. D.). "ROLE CONCEPTION AND THE CONTINUING LEARNING ACTIVITIES OF NEOPHYTE COLLEGIATE NURSES." University of Chicago, 1971. Source: Author.

Nursing education programs should continue efforts to professionalize the field, to intensify its service orientation, and to de-emphasize bureaucracy.

Bhaduri, Aparna (Ed. D.). "PARTICIPATION OF FACULTY MEMBERS IN CUR-
RICULUM DEVELOPMENT OF GENERIC BACCALAUREATE NURSING PROGRAMS IN INDIA."
Columbia University, 1974. 218 pp. Source: DAI, XXXV, 6B (December,
1974), 2846-B-2847-B. XUM Order No. 74-26,582.

Faculty members preferred more involvement for themselves and less
involvement of administrators and senior members. Faculty and administrators did not agree on the factors which enhanced or hindered
faculty participation in curriculum development. Faculty members
did not agree on how they actually participated in curriculum work.
Heavy faculty workload, high faculty turnover, and inadequate preparation for curriculum planning and evaluation inhibit faculty from
participating in curriculum development.

Bidelman, Patrick Kay (Ph. D.). "THE FEMINIST MOVEMENT IN FRANCE:
THE FORMATIVE YEARS, 1858-1889." Michigan State University, 1975. 420
pp. Source: DAI, XXXVI, 9A (March, 1976), 6254-A. XUM Order No. 76-
5521.

Neither the women's rights congresses (1878, 1889) nor the efforts
to reform divorce laws and education gave French women control over
their lives. The feminist movement's split weakened its impact and
left no foundation on which later feminists could build.

Biester, Charlotte Elizabeth (Ed. D.). "CATHARINE BEECHER AND HER
CONTRIBUTIONS TO HOME ECONOMICS." University of Northern Colorado, 1950.
198 pp. Source: Dissertation, pp. i-xii.

Beecher, founder of the home economics movement, prepared the necessary laboratory manual and textbook in the 1840's to establish home
economics as a subject-matter field. She saw education, not suffrage,
as women's greatest need. The 33 books she published referred in
some way to home economics.

Biklen, Sari Knopp (Ed. D.). "LESSONS OF CONSEQUENCE: WOMEN'S PER-
CEPTIONS OF THEIR ELEMENTARY SCHOOL EXPERIENCES, A RETROSPECTIVE STUDY."
University of Massachusetts, 1973. 523 pp. Source: DAI, XXXIV, 10A
(April, 1974), 6247-A-6248-A. XUM Order No. 74-8466.

The major finding was that women recalled their elementary years as
a time when they had few options because so much behavior was considered "improper" for girls.

Biles, Fay Reifsnyder (Ph. D.). "SELF CONCEPT CHANGES IN COLLEGE
FRESHMAN WOMEN IN A BASIC PHYSICAL EDUCATION COURSE USING TWO METHODS OF
INSTRUCTION." Ohio State University, 1968. 118 pp. Source: DAI, XXIX,
9A (March, 1969), 2979-A-2980-A. XUM Order No. 69-4847.

Comparing women students in 2 experimental basic physical education
classes with students in 3 sports classes, this study found the basic
physical education classes to be more effective in improving women
students' perceived self-concept.

Bird, Dorothy Jean (Ed. D.). "AN ANALYSIS OF PSYCHOLOGICAL NEEDS OF
GROUPS OF COLLEGE FRESHMAN WOMEN BY SVIB-W PATTERNS." University of Kansas, 1958. 141 pp. Source: Dissertation.

On 2 measures, all 399 freshman women preferred a future combining marriage with a career.

Bittman, Stanley Allen (Ph. D.). "PREDICTION OF PATIENT-TECHNIQUE ORIENTATION OF STUDENT NURSES AFTER ONE YEAR OF NURSING SCHOOL." Texas Tech University, 1973. 127 pp. Source: DAI, XXXIV, 9B (March, 1974), 4622-B-4623-B. XUM Order No. 74-5795.

Neither personality nor motivation was a reliable predictor of a student nurse's orientation regarding patients as opposed to techniques after 1 year of training.

Black, John Davies (Ph. D.). "THE INTERPRETATION OF MMPI PROFILES OF COLLEGE WOMEN." University of Minnesota, 1953. 174 pp. Source: DAI, XIII, 5 (1953), 870-871. XUM Order No. 5520.

This study, whose purpose was to investigate the validity of the Minnesota Multiphasic Personality Inventory (MMPI), concluded that counselors should use MMPI to locate girls who may have difficulty adjusting to college life.

Blackmore, Dorothy Smith (Ph. D.). "A COMPARISON OF SELECTED PERSONOLOGICAL ATTRIBUTES OF WOMEN ELEMENTARY TEACHERS PERCEIVED DURING PRESERVICE PREPARATION AND FIRST-YEAR TEACHING." University of California, Berkeley, 1963. 236 pp. Source: DAI, XXIV, 4 (October, 1963), 1476-1477. XUM Order No. 63-5481.

This study involving 60 women elementary teachers indicates that peer appraisals and members of academic departments are excellent predictors of success and college supervisors and public school teachers are satisfactory predictors when success is measured by principals' ratings.

Blackwell, Sara E. (Ph. D.). "DEVELOPMENT OF INSTRUMENTS FOR EVALUATING CERTAIN ASPECTS OF HIGH SCHOOL HOMEMAKING PROGRAMS." University of Minnesota, 1951. 297 pp. Source: Dissertation, pp. 157-162.

Outcomes of homemaking education in high schools were closely related to adequacy of space and equipment, reference and illustrative materials provided, the curriculum, and services contributed to the school and community. Home economic educators agreed about the relative desirability of certain characteristics of high school homemaking programs. Valid, reliable instruments can be developed for evaluating homemaking programs.

Blair, Karen J. (Ph. D.). "THE CLUBWOMAN AS FEMINIST: THE WOMAN'S CULTURE CLUB MOVEMENT IN THE UNITED STATES, 1868-1914." State University of New York at Buffalo, 1976. 327 pp. Source: DAI, XXXVII, 8A (February, 1977), 5296-A. XUM Order No. 77-3512.

Women, 1800-1850, became more involved in education and charity work through public, academic, and religious involvement. Increased leisure time enabled them to progress academically and culturally while acquiring self confidence and speaking skills. Through literary clubs the Women's Educational and Industrial Unions were formed. The clubs were highly committed to integrate women into public life.

Blaney, Doris Ruth (Ed. D.). "COMPARISON OF VALUE SYSTEMS OF THE GRADUATES OF TWO TYPES OF PROGRAMS IN NURSING." Indiana University, 1973. 187 pp. Source: DAI, XXXIV, 8B (February, 1974), 3877-B. XUM Order No. 74-2582.

Differences in values held by students from associate degree programs and baccalaureate programs were not great. Recommends that nursing educators examine these values and ascertain whether they should differ for different programs.

Blaylock, Enid Veronica (Ph. D.). "RELATIONSHIP BETWEEN SELECTED FACTORS IN CALIFORNIA ASSOCIATE DEGREE NURSING PROGRAMS AND PERFORMANCE BY THEIR GRADUATES." University of Southern California, 1966. 209 pp. Source: DAI, XXVII, 9B (March, 1967), 3157-B-3158-B. XUM Order No. 67-2103.

Among 14 factors tested in this study, only the academic training of full-time nursing instructors was important in student performance. An objective evaluation method was recommended for assessing the competence of professional nurses.

Bloch, Doris (Dr. P. H.). "ATTITUDES AND PRACTICES OF MOTHERS IN THE SEX EDUCATION OF THEIR DAUGHTERS." University of California, Berkeley, 1970. 446 pp. Source: DAI, XXXII, 1B (July, 1971), 406-B. XUM Order No. 71-15,701.

On the sex education test used, mothers were named as the most frequent source of sex information by a group of 7th grade girls, but the facts given were limited. The study suggested plans for sex education programs for both parents and children.

Blumenstein, Linda Ricker (Ph. D.). "THE EFFECTS OF SINGER'S JOB SURVIVAL SKILLS PROGRAM ON THE SELF CONCEPT AND WORK ATTITUDES OF DISADVANTAGED FEMALES." Georgia State University, 1976. 236 pp. Source: DAI, XXXVII, 2A (August, 1976), 773-A. XUM Order No. 76-16,958.

Singer's Job Survival Skills Program improved the girls' self concept but had only partial effect on work attitudes, perhaps because the experiment was conducted in too short a time span.

Bob, Sharon Helene (Ph. D.). "PARENTS' FINANCIAL SUPPORT OF THEIR MALE AND FEMALE CHILDREN'S POST-SECONDARY EDUCATION." University of Maryland, 1976. 253 pp. Source: DAI, XXXVII, 6A (December, 1976), 3403-A-3404-A. XUM Order No. 76-27,367.

This study investigated the college attendance patterns and family financial support within families where a male and a female were both attending college. It revealed that parents contributed more toward the cost of educating their daughters than their sons.

Bobbe, Carol Norwalk (Ph. D.). "SEX-ROLE PREFERENCE AND ACADEMIC ACHIEVEMENT." Yeshiva University, 1971. 156 pp. Source: DAI, XXXII, 3B (September, 1971), 1818-B-1819-B. XUM Order No. 71-23,923.

Both boys and girls sex-typed their school subjects, a process that increased with age. Although boys preferred "masculine" courses

and girls preferred "feminine" courses, this preference did not affect their achievement in these courses.

Bock, Dorothy Joleen (Ed. D.). "WOMEN IN INSTRUCTIONAL MIDDLE MAN-
AGEMENT IN CALIFORNIA COMMUNITY COLLEGES: A STUDY OF MOBILITY." University of Southern California, 1976. Source: DAI, XXXVII, 9A (March,
1977), 5624-A.

Women in middle management had greater opportunities in large, urban
colleges. Even though they possessed both teaching and supervisory
management experience, few women plan to move into the top 3 administrative levels in California community colleges; therefore few women seek doctoral degrees because of lack of career goals. Recommended a follow-up study in 1980 to determine whether those with
higher career goals achieved them.

Boehmer, Florence Elise (Ph. D.). "VOCATIONAL CONTINUITY OF COLLEGE
WOMEN: A STUDY BASED ON DATA SECURED FROM 6,466 WOMEN WHO MATRICULATED
IN LAND-GRANT COLLEGES BETWEEN 1889 AND 1922." Columbia University,
1932. 100 pp. Source: Published as After College, What?, Greensboro,
NC: The North Carolina College for Women, 1932.

Of the women studied, 81.8% had held remunerative positions. Married women and women who did not complete degrees had less continuous vocational histories. Women who made vocational decisions in
high school or as undergraduates and majored in subjects that equipped them to follow their chosen careers had a longer vocational
history.

Bohan, Kathleen Mary (Ph. D.). "PERFORMANCE RELATIONSHIP: NURSING
STUDENT TO PROFESSIONAL NURSE." Catholic University of America, 1966.
156 pp. Source: DAI, XXVII, 9A (March, 1967), 2931-A-2932-A. XUM
Order No. 67-1243.

Found no relationship exists between nursing course grades and professional nurse's performance. However, supervisors were highly
pleased with pre-service baccalaureate degree nurses and their adaptability to the nursing needs of patients and their families.

Bolton, Ina Alexander (Ph. D.). "THE PROBLEMS OF NEGRO COLLEGE
WOMEN." University of Southern California, 1949. Source: Abstract
from USC Reference Librarian.

The purpose was to investigate the extent to which a group of Southwestern black coeducational colleges assisted black women college
graduates in solving problems. Because these colleges were failing
to meet women's needs, the recommendations called for more practical
courses, better guidance programs, and improved job placement services.

Bomar, Willie Melmoth (Ph. D.). "THE EDUCATION OF HOMEMAKERS FOR
COMMUNITY ACTIVITIES: A STUDY OF THE COMMUNITY INTERESTS AND ACTIVITIES
OF REPRESENTATIVE HOMEMAKERS TO DISCOVER CERTAIN NEEDS FOR HOME ECONOMICS
EDUCATION." Columbia University Teachers College, 1930. 135 pp.
Source: TCCU DIGESTS, IV, A-G (September, 1929-December, 1931), pp. 1-3.

Higher education levels and course in home management did not increase participation in community activities. The results indicate
a need for more emphasis on desirable community activities in home
management courses.

Bone, Margaretta M. (Ed. D.). "A PERSONAL GUIDE FOR WOMEN STUDENTS
IN ELEMENTARY EDUCATION." New York University, 1949. 230 pp. Source:
DAI, X, 1 (1950), 22-24. XUM Order No. 1567.

This study involved the writing of an easily readable, non-technical
book containing the educational requirements, experiences, and personal prerequisites for women who plan to become elementary teachers.

Borod, Joan Carol (Ph. D.). "THE IMPACT OF A WOMEN'S STUDIES COURSE
ON PERCEIVED SEX DIFFERENCES, REAL AND IDEAL SELF-PERCEPTIONS, AND ATTI-
TUDES TOWARDS WOMEN'S RIGHTS AND ROLES." Case Western Reserve University,
1975. 150 pp. Source: DAI, XXXVI, 8B (February, 1976), 4127-B. XUM
Order No. 75-27,888.

It was hypothesized that women enrolled in a women's studies course
would become less stereotyped in their real and ideal self-perceptions and more liberal about women's rights. However, the data did
not support these hypotheses, perhaps because the experimental group
was initially profeminist and liberal.

Bourgeois, Mary Audrey (Ph. D.). "A STUDY OF THE PREPARATION FOR
THE ROLE OF PARENT-AS-EDUCATOR IN SELECTED CATHOLIC WOMEN'S COLLEGES."
Catholic University of America, 1961. 155 pp. Source: Dissertation,
pp. 121-128.

Of the 29 Catholic women's colleges studied, 17 offered some formal
preparation for family life. Programs in only 7 of the colleges
covered all material the consultants considered important as preparation for parenthood.

Bowden, Shirley Smith (Ph. D.). "THE INFLUENCE OF WORK VALUES IN
THE LIFE PLANNING OF TENTH GRADE GIRLS." Oregon State University, 1975.
272 pp. Source: DAI, XXXV, 7B (January, 1975), 3428-B-3429-B. XUM
Order No. 75-1093.

About 2/3 of the girls hoped to obtain post high school education,
almost 50% desired professional-technical careers, and over 90%
wanted to marry.

Bowe, Marion Blanche (Ph. D.). "THE ROLE OF CONTINUING EDUCATION IN
THE LIFE OF THE MARRIED WOMAN." University of Wisconsin, 1970. 244 pp.
Source: DAI, XXXI, 3A (September, 1970), 1393-A. XUM Order No. 70-
12,715.

Career and community-oriented women were found to be likely to continue education beyond high school but were also more likely to experience family conflict. Continued education affected the family
power structure of only 26% of the women.

Bowler, Sister Mary Mariella (Ph. D.). "A HISTORY OF CATHOLIC COL-
LEGES FOR WOMEN IN THE UNITED STATES OF AMERICA." Catholic University
of America, 1933. 145 pp. Source: Published, Same Title, Washington,
DC: Catholic University of America, pp. 123-125.

After 1896, as the number of Catholic colleges for women grew rapidly,
their curricula gave less emphasis to traditional subjects and more
attention to the social sciences, vocational education, and specialization.

Bowman, Betsy Linn Eells (Ph. D.). "A DESCRIPTIVE ANALYSIS OF TEACH-
ING ROLES IN CLINICAL LABORATORY SETTINGS IN BACCALAUREATE AND HIGHER
DEGREE NURSING PROGRAMS." University of Texas at Austin, 1976. 142 pp.
Source: DAI, XXXVII, 12A, Part 1 (June, 1977), 7559-A. XUM Order No.
77-11,475.

This study developed an instrument to aid in the categorization of 5
teaching roles: advising, conferring, steering, socializing, and
overseeing. Faculty volunteers from 2 state-supported schools of
nursing participated in the study, 15 from each school. A comparison of the faculty of the 2 schools indicated that the most commonly
perceived teaching roles were the steering roles; the teacher model
most frequently influenced perceptions of teaching roles.

Boyer, Micheline Francoise (Ph. D.). "A SURVEY OF THE CONTENT TAUGHT
IN FAMILY PLANNING IN THE NURSING SCHOOLS OF FRANCE." University of
North Carolina, 1975. 302 pp. Source: DAI, XXXVII, 3A (September,
1976), 1419-A. XUM Order No. 76-20,000.

Findings in this survey of 272 French nursing schools included that:
(1) they focused on technical content; (2) family planning was not
taught because of a lack of qualified personnel and lack of time;
and (3) post-basic schools, which train nursing instructors, teach
very little family planning.

Branegan, Gladys Alee (Ph. D.). "HOME ECONOMICS TEACHER TRAINING
UNDER THE SMITH-HUGHES ACT 1917 TO 1927: A STUDY OF TRENDS IN THE WORK
OF THE 71 INSTITUTIONS APPROVED UNDER THE NATIONAL VOCATIONAL EDUCATION
ACT." Columbia University Teachers College, 1929. Source: TCCU DIGESTS,
I (September, 1925-August, 1929), pp. 76-77.

An historical, descriptive, and analytical study of home economics
teacher training conducted during the first decade of the Smith-
Hughes Act.

Breck, Alice Rose Wolfe (Ed. D.). "PROFESSIONAL CONCERNS OF WOMEN
IN POSITIONS OF ADMINISTRATION IN PUBLIC SCHOOLS." University of Denver,
1960. 253 pp. Source: Dissertation.

A majority of women administrators said women had less chance than
men to gain high-level school posts. Most of the women were not convinced of the necessity of a doctorate degree for advancement. Other
problems were the burden of coordinating home responsibilities with
career and the limited opportunities for informal contact with community leaders. Problems in connection with their work (such as
budget, buildings, etc.) were unrelated to sex.

Breen, George Jefferson (Ed. D.). "AN INTERVENTIONIST GROUP COUNSE-
LING APPROACH WITH FIRST-YEAR DIPLOMA SCHOOL OF NURSING STUDENTS." Clark
University, 1974. 325 pp. Source: DAI, XXXV, 6A (December, 1974),
3418-A. XUM Order No. 74-25,988.

This study investigated the effects of interventionist group counseling with 3 groups of first-year student nurses. Findings indicated
that such counseling does expose differences, especially in the behavioral and personal aspects of group counseling.

Bresina, Bertha Mary (Ph. D.). "CONTRIBUTIONS OF THE CURRICULA OF
THE COLLEGE OF HOME ECONOMICS TO GENERAL EDUCATION." Iowa State Univer-
sity, 1961. 191 pp. Source: DAI, XXII, 10 (April, 1962), 3635-3636.
XUM Order No. 62-1344.

This study investigated the contribution of home economics education
to the achievement of commonly accepted goals of general education.
Found that no difference existed in the extent to which core courses
and professional courses in home economics enriched students' general
education.

Bresnan, Margaret Theresa (Ph. D.). "THE EFFECTS OF ETHNICITY, SEX,
AND LOCUS OF CONTROL ON VOCATIONAL MATURITY OF DISADVANTAGED HIGH SCHOOL
STUDENTS." Fordham University, 1976. 121 pp. Source: DAI, XXXVII, 2A
(August, 1976), 800-A. XUM Order No. 76-17,893.

Some findings were: (1) vocational maturity scores were lower for
internally controlled males; and (2) vocational maturity scores were
higher for internally controlled females and lower for externally
controlled females. One implication was that schools need programs
to strengthen the vocational maturity of inner-city disadvantaged
youth.

Brew, Alice Perrin (Ph. D.). "EFFECTS OF A COUNSELING WORKSHOP ON
ADULT WOMEN." University of Maryland, 1975. 107 pp. Source: DAI,
XXXVI, 10A (April, 1976), 6467-A. XUM Order No. 76-8383.

This investigation suggested that changes occurred in adult women's
self concepts and in their activities within 6 months after participating in a counseling workshop.

Briscoe, Marjorie B. (Ph. D.). "THE RELATIONSHIP OF CONCEPT UTILI-
ZATION BY VOCATIONAL HOME ECONOMICS STUDENTS AND NORM SCORES." Florida
State University, 1976. 133 pp. Source: DAI, XXXVII, 12A (June, 1977),
7580-A. XUM Order No. 77-13,308.

This study investigated the ability of 200 7th grade students to con-
ceptualize relationships and/or equivalencies about real world objects before and after a course in comprehensive vocational home
economics. Findings: having a course in comprehensive vocational
home economics education increased students' utilization of concepts.
Their socioeconomic status had a major effect on the pretest scores
but had no such effect after the course.

Brockway, Jacqueline Stevenson Frakes (Ph. D.). "A DESIGN FOR COUN-
SELING ADULT WOMEN USING A PARADIGM OF RATIONAL DECISION-MAKING." University of Oregon, 1974. 127 pp. Source: DAI, XXXV, 12A, Part 1 (June,
1975), 7642-A-7643-A. XUM Order No. 75-12,525.

Confirmed that many troubled women are willing to seek counseling
help, but many were unwilling to change decision-making patterns or
to disengage from their current situations.

Brody, David S. (Ph. D.). "DEVELOPMENTAL FACTORS AFFECTING SOCIALI-
TY TRAITS AND WORK HABITS AMONG COLLEGE WOMEN." University of Minnesota,
1952. 411 pp. Source: DAI, XII, 5 (1952), 580. XUM Order No. 4121.

Popularity among their peers was a result of participation in outside
activities. Girls with good work habits, though not highly popular
with their peers, were regarded favorably.

Bromley, Ann (Ph. D.). "A STUDY OF WOMEN MATRICULANTS OF THE CHICAGO
UNDERGRADUATE DIVISION OF THE UNIVERSITY OF ILLINOIS." Northwestern Uni-
versity, 1954. 223 pp. Source: DAI, XIV, 10 (1954), 1617-1618. XUM
Order No. 9226.

Among the needs of women students identified were (1) more financial
aid; (2) more survey courses; and (3) more personnel and guidance
services.

Brooke, Marinez Layfield (Ph. D.). "AN INVESTIGATION OF DIFFERENCES
IN ATTITUDES AND VALUES BETWEEN FRESHMAN AND SOPHOMORE WOMEN AT THE UNI-
VERSITY OF ALABAMA." University of Alabama, 1970. 127 pp. Source:
DAI, XXXI, 10A (April, 1971), 5117-A-5118-A. XUM Order No. 71-9060.

No significant differences were found between the total group of
freshman and sophomore women. All other statistically significant
differences were between cultural subgroupings except the one between
black non-sorority freshmen and sophomores.

Brooke, Mary Joan (Ph. D.). "STATUS INCONGRUENCE AND SUPPORT FOR
CHANGE IN SEX-ROLE IDEOLOGY: A STUDY OF WOMEN IN VARIOUS PROFESSIONS."
Loyola University of Chicago, 1976. 126 pp. Source: DAI, XXXVI, 11B
(May, 1976), 5858-B-5859-B. XUM Order No. 76-11,709.

The majority of professional women studied regardless of field, support change in sex-role ideology and believe that sex discrimination
can be eliminated by social and political means.

Brookhart, Ruth Aileen (Ph. D.). "AN ANALYSIS OF THE CHANGING PROB-
LEMS OF A BUSINESS EDUCATION PROGRAM IN THE LIBERAL ARTS COLLEGE, WITH
SPECIAL EMPHASIS ON THE PROBLEMS OF THE PREPARATION OF WOMEN FOR TEACHING
AND BUSINESS EMPLOYMENT." University of Iowa, 1967. 417 pp. Source:
DAI, XXVIII, 1A (July, 1967), 29-A-30-A. XUM Order No. 67-9045.

Because small liberal arts colleges were de-emphasizing secretarial
courses, this study concluded that they are curtailing the preparation of high school business teachers and are necessitating on-the-
job training or specialized graduate work for those entering business
fields, especially women.

Brooks, Barbara Jean Roberts (Ph. D.). "A PROFILE OF BLACK FEMALES IN SELECTED ADMINISTRATIVE POSITIONS IN THE PUBLIC SCHOOL SYSTEMS OF FLORIDA." University of Michigan, 1975. 184 pp. Source: DAI, XXXVI, 10A (April, 1976), 6385-A. XUM Order No. 76-9353.

Institutionalized sexism and racism in hiring practices are the main reasons for the scarce number of black female administrators.

Brooks, Lois Phillips (Ed. D.). "THE SEX-ROLE STEREOTYPING OF OCCU-PATIONAL PERCEPTIONS BY SIXTH GRADE STUDENTS." Wayne State University, 1973. 175 pp. Source: DAI, XXXIV, 7A (January, 1974), 3862-A. XUM Order No. 73-31,698.

The students perceived that boys can enter more female-dominated occupations than girls can enter male-dominated professions. The middle socio-economic white students had the least stereotyped sex-role perceptions. Girls who had the least occupational sex-role stereotyped perceptions also had high self-esteem.

Brooks, Margaret Bilkey (Ph. D.). "THE EFFECT OF EMPLOYMENT ON INDI-VIDUAL MODERNITY AMONG WOMEN IN FOUR SOCIETIES." Case Western Reserve University, 1976. 198 pp. Source: DAI, XXXVII, 12A, Part 1 (July, 1977), 7998-A-7999-A. XUM Order No. 77-11,937.

A strong relationship existed between the score of married women and the educational level of their husbands in Nigeria, Puerto Rico, U. S., and Yugoslavia. Another finding suggested a threshold level of formal education above which women respond to the experience of employment with more modern attitudes and values. Below this level, employment has no effect or negative effect on individual modernity.

Brousseau, Mary Aline (Ed. D.). "COMPARISON OF DISCIPLINED AND NON-DISCIPLINED WOMEN RESIDENTS, MARQUETTE UNIVERSITY, 1967-68." Marquette University, 1969. 130 pp. Source: DAI, XXXI, 9A (March, 1971), 4451-A. XUM Order No. 71-5290.

The women who had been disciplined for breaking rules were younger, were financially supported by parents, came from better economic-educational backgrounds, and had lower grades in high school than did those women who had not been disciplined.

Brown, Anna Caroline Baker (Ph. D.). "A STUDY OF WOMEN INFLUENTIALS IN THREE MICHIGAN COMMUNITIES, THEIR ATTITUDES TOWARDS AND PERCEIVED ABILITY TO INFLUENCE ADULT EDUCATION PRACTICES." University of Michigan, 1963. 332 pp. Source: DAI, XXIV, 5 (November, 1963), 1913. XUM Order No. 63-8140.

Concluded that there is a woman's world and that women gain a reputation of leadership primarily through accepting responsibility and performing successfully in areas of primary interest. Top women leaders were well educated. Though most were not involved in adult education, they were favorably disposed toward adult education programs.

Brown, Billye Jean (Ed. D.). "THE HISTORICAL DEVELOPMENT OF THE UNI-VERSITY OF TEXAS SYSTEM SCHOOL OF NURSING, 1890-1973." Baylor University, 1975.   462 pp.   Source: DAI, XXXVI, 6B (December, 1975), 2724-B.   XUM Order No. 75-27,838.

Extensive use of documents and interviews traced the growth of the school from its initial 2-year program to the present one offering 3 higher degrees.

Brown, Geraldine Starke (Ph. D.). "THE RELATIONSHIP BETWEEN AUTHORI-TARIANISM, SOCIAL CLASS, AND SOCIAL PERCEPTION OF PATIENTS AMONG STUDENTS OF NURSING." New York University, 1970. 166 pp. Source: DAI, XXXI, 7B (January, 1971), 4154-B. XUM Order No. 70-26,413.

The degree of authoritarianism of 208 female nursing students of varying social classes was measured and related to their reactions to patients of different classes. Findings: (1) most students per-ceived patients of their own class positively; (2) high authoritarian students only perceived patients of the lowest class negatively; and (3) low authoritarian students showed no difference among the social classes except the lowest class, of whom they have a negative social perception.

Brown, Herbert R. (Ed. D.). "A STUDY TO DETERMINE THE RELATIONSHIP BETWEEN SELECTED CHARACTERISTICS AND THE DURATION OF CONTINUOUS SERVICE OF FEMALE, PUBLIC ELEMENTARY SCHOOL TEACHERS." American University, 1967. 161 pp. Source: DAI, XXIX, 11A (May, 1969), 3793-A-3794-A. XUM Order No. 69-6720.

This study of female teacher turnover found that those most likely to stay on a job were (1) between 40 and 44 years old; (2) married and had 2 or 3 dependents; and (3) previously employed for 7 or 8 years.

Brown, Lynn E. (Ph. D.). "HOUSING OF WOMEN STUDENTS AT THE NORMAL SCHOOLS AND TEACHERS COLLEGES IN NEW YORK STATE." New York University, 1933. Source: New York University, School of Education, ABSTRACTS OF THESES (1933), pp. 1-7.

This study, done when no New York state-owned teacher-training ins-titution had housing facilities found ample evidence of such need. Two recommendations were (1) that halls of residence for women be established; and (2) that these halls be an integral part of the teacher-training program.

Brown, Naomi B. (Ed. D.). "THE NATIONAL ASSOCIATION OF WOMEN DEANS AND COUNSELORS, 1951-1961." University of Denver, 1963. 520 pp. Source: DAI, XXIV, 12 (June, 1964), 5166-5167. XUM Order No. 64-4860.

The history of this Association during a 10-year period showed how it functioned in exchanging ideas, discovering ways of accomplishing goals, and strengthening the professional status of its members.

Brown, Theresa Kennedy (Ed. D.). "A STUDY OF HOME ECONOMICS GRADU-ATES AT MORGAN STATE COLLEGE, BALTIMORE, MARYLAND, FROM 1944 TO 1953: AN INVESTIGATION FOR CURRICULUM DEVELOPMENT." New York University, 1958.

264 pp. Source: DAI, XX, 2 (August, 1959), 656-657. XUM Order No. Mic. 59-1044.

The study's findings were the basis for proposals to improve present practices in: (1) curricular offerings; (2) guidance services; and (3) physical facilities.

Bruemmer, Rick (Ed. D.). "ACADEMIC DIFFERENCES AND CHANGES IN MAJOR BETWEEN FEMALE STUDENTS ENROLLED IN AN ORIENTATION CLASS AND THOSE NOT ENROLLED." Brigham Young University, 1974. 64 pp. Source: DAI, XXXIV, 7A (January, 1974), 3862-A. XUM Order No. 74-899.

Women enrolled in an orientation class had a lower dropout rate, as did those with a higher HSGPA, CCGPA and ACT composite score.

Brumbaugh, Sara Barbara (Ph. D.). "DEMOCRATIC EXPERIENCE AND EDUCA- TION IN THE NATIONAL LEAGUE OF WOMEN VOTERS." Columbia University Teach- ers College, 1946. Source: TCCU CONTRIBUTIONS No. 916, pp. 106-111.

Political education of women by the League involved both study and action. The need for such education is unending.

Bryan, William Edward (Ed. D.). "A COMPARISON OF THE CAREER ORIEN- TATION OF COLLEGE WOMEN IN CONTRASTING MAJORS." Wayne State University, 1968. 125 pp. Source: DAI, XXX, 3A (September, 1969), 980-A. XUM Order No. 69-14,658.

Compared the career orientation of elementary education and natural science majors at a Catholic women's college. Significant differences were found in intelligence, scholastic ability, interests, father's occupation, and self-concept of the 2 groups of women students.

Buckley, Lola Elizabeth (D. S. W.). "THE USE OF THE SMALL GROUP AT A TIME OF CRISIS: TRANSITION OF GIRLS FROM ELEMENTARY TO JUNIOR HIGH SCHOOL." University of Southern California, 1970. 214 pp. Source: DAI, XXXII, 2A (August, 1971), 1078-A. XUM Order No. 71-21,441.

Tested the effectiveness of short-term social work intervention with girls entering junior high school and found that the treatment group scored significantly higher in each of 4 adjustment areas.

Buckner, Kathleen Ellen (Ed. D.). "THE RELATIONSHIP BETWEEN PREFER- ENCE FOR INDEPENDENT STUDY OR PREFERENCE FOR TEACHER-DIRECTED INSTRUCTION AND PERSONALITY FACTORS OF ASSOCIATE DEGREE NURSING STUDENTS." Northern Illinois University, 1976. 203 pp. Source: DAI, XXXVII, 12A, Part 1 (June, 1977), 7500-A-7501-A. XUM Order No. 77-12,335.

Subjects were 194 nursing students from 5 Illinois community college associate degree nursing programs, 2 emphasizing independent study, 2 emphasizing teacher-directed instruction, and 1 combination pro- gram. The results indicated few significant differences in prefer- ence for either independent or teacher-directed study. It was con- cluded that little if any relationship exists between first-year associate degree nursing students' preferences and personality traits.

Buescher, Ruth Marie (Ph. D.). "THE RELATIONSHIP BETWEEN SELECTED NONCOGNITIVE VARIABLES AND ACADEMIC ACHIEVEMENT OF COLLEGE WOMEN IN VARIOUS FIELDS OF STUDY." Fordham University, 1969. 210 pp. Source: DAI, XXX, 5A (November, 1969), 1858-A-1859-A. XUM Order No. 69-16,227.

An examination of freshman women in the arts, natural science and mathematics, social science and humanities found that such noncognitive predictors as motivation for grades, liberalism, and family independence helped to predict academic achievement. Significant differences were found in the noncognitive predictors among the 4 curricular groups.

Buie, Grace Elizabeth (Ed. D.). "AN EVALUATION OF THE WOMEN'S NON-MAJOR PHYSICAL EDUCATION PROGRAM IN SELECTED AMERICAN COLLEGES AND UNIVERSITIES." University of Florida, 1956. 321 pp. Source: DAI, XVI, 11 (1956), 2086-2087. XUM Order No. 17,546.

This study explored the extent to which college physical education (non-major) programs are being adapted to fit women's changing role. It found that these programs differed in democratic procedures, emphases, and grading standards.

Burdett, Rita Anne (Ph. D.). "A COMPARATIVE STUDY OF WOMEN GRANTED DOCTORAL DEGREES FROM THE NEW YORK UNIVERSITY SCHOOL OF EDUCATION AND WOMEN IN GENERAL WITH PH.D. AND ED.D. DEGREES." New York University, 1958. 380 pp. Source: DAI, XX, 4 (October, 1959), 1124-1125. XUM Order No. Mic 58-1984.

Compared the status of women holding doctorates from New York University with a national sample in such characteristics as family background, motivation, marriage, age at time of degree, income, and employment status.

Burgemeister, Bessie B. (Ph. D.). "THE PERMANENCE OF INTERESTS OF WOMEN COLLEGE STUDENTS: A STUDY IN PERSONALITY DEVELOPMENT." Columbia University Teachers College, 1940. 60 pp. Source: ARCHIVES OF PSYCHOLOGY, No. 255, p. 56.

Major findings were that successful achievement of college women and a withdrawal attitude favored the permanence of interests.

Burggraf, Margaret Zeidler (Ph. D.). "HOLLAND'S VOCATIONAL PREFERENCE INVENTORY: ITS APPLICABILITY TO A GROUP OF TECHNICAL COLLEGE WOMEN AND THE RELATIONSHIP OF SOCIAL LEVEL, SELF CONCEPT AND SEX ROLE IDENTITY TO THE SOCIAL PERSONALITY TYPE." Ohio University, 1975. 136 pp. Source: DAI, XXXVI, 10A (April, 1976), 6467-A-6468-A. XUM Order No. 76-8876.

A study of women nursing students found that the Tennessee Self Concept Scale, the Bem Sex Role Inventory, and the Index of Social Position were not valid predictors of Holland's Vocational Preference Inventory social personality type. Showed the need for further study of normative data on non-university women and longitudinal studies of women's career choices.

Burke, Judith Lee (Ph. D.). "SCHOOL AND PARENTAL VIEWS OF GIRLS ADOPTED OR BORN TO FIRST VERSUS LATER ORDINAL POSITION." Bryn Mawr College, 1976. 191 pp. Source: DAI, XXXVIII, 1B (July, 1977), 348-B-349-B. XUM Order No. 77-13,823.

Contrary to prediction, adopted girls were rated by their teachers as poorly adjusted. However, these ratings were countered by normal commentaries in their cumulative files, referral rates for psycho-educational problems comparable to that for non-adopted children, and comparable social desirability scores. It was concluded that adoptees encounter some negative bias because of their known adoptive status.

Burlin, Frances-Dee (Ph. D.). "AN INVESTIGATION OF THE RELATIONSHIP OF IDEAL AND REAL OCCUPATIONAL ASPIRATION TO LOCUS OF CONTROL AND TO OTHER SOCIAL AND PSYCHOLOGICAL VARIABLES IN ADOLESCENT FEMALES." Syracuse University, 1974. 128 pp. Source: DAI, XXXVI, 1A (July, 1975), 181-A-182-A. XUM Order No. 75-13,963.

Using Rotter's Internal-External Control Scale, this researcher found women who were internally controlled more apt to aspire to innovative occupations (those in which fewer than 30% are women). More than half of the subjects attributed the discrepancy between their ideal and real occupational aspiration to sexism.

Burns, Dorothy M. (Ed. D.). "WOMEN IN EDUCATIONAL ADMINISTRATION: A STUDY OF LEADERSHIP IN CALIFORNIA PUBLIC SCHOOLS." University of Oregon, 1964. 215 pp. Source: DAI, XXV, 5 (November, 1964), 2821-2822. XUM Order No. 64-12,150.

This study found no correspondence between women's level of assignment and academic degree held and predicted that the number of women in leadership positions in California public schools would continue to decline.

Burns, Patia Jane Herbert (Ph. D.). "PROFILES OF ACHIEVEMENT-RELATED BEHAVIORS IN CAREER AND NON-CAREER WOMEN." Fordham University, 1976. 142 pp. Source: DAI, XXXVII, 5B (November, 1976), 2474-B-2475-B. XUM Order No. 76-25,715.

Married graduates of a women's college perceived vocational commitment as a social risk. Those with traditional career choices conformed more to stereotypes than women with unconventional vocations. Achievement-related behaviors were: fear of success and failure, risk-taking, gender role deviance, and self-sabotage.

Burns, Rosemary (Ph. D.). "PERCEPTUAL COGNITIVE DEVELOPMENT AND ITS RELATION TO ACTIVITY IN ADOLESCENT GIRLS." Catholic University of America, 1974. 58 pp. Source: DAI, XXXV, 3B (September, 1974), 1400-B. XUM Order No. 74-19,500.

Explored the relationships among behavioral activity level, impulsivity of motor response, and maturity of perceptual-cognitive development in girls, and found them not related.

Burson, Linda Sharon (Ed. D.). "CAREER MATURITY: A COMPARISON OF AFFECTIVE AND COGNITIVE PROGRAMS WITH COLLEGE FRESHMAN WOMEN." Mississippi State University, 1976. 130 pp. Source: DAI, XXXVII, 3A (September, 1976), 1397-A. XUM Order No. 76-21,201.

Compared an affective approach with a cognitive approach to enhancing career maturity in freshman women; found no significant differences between the 2 approaches.

Buseck, Sally Ann (Dr. P. H.). "CHARACTERISTICS AND ROLE EXPECTATIONS OF NURSES CARING FOR THE ELDERLY IN THE NURSING HOME AND IN ACUTE CARE." University of Pittsburgh, 1975. 101 pp. Source: DAI, XXXVI, 9B (March, 1976), 4382-B. XUM Order No. 76-5420.

Nurses were not prepared for the increase in elderly patients but were interested in continuing education concerning geriatric care. A need for basic and continuing education to train geriatric nurses properly was indicated.

Cabotaje, Arsenia Abellera (Ed. D.). "A COMPARATIVE STUDY OF THE QUALIFICATIONS FOR DEANS OF WOMEN IN INSTITUTIONS OF HIGHER EDUCATION IN THE UNITED STATES AND IN THE REPUBLIC OF THE PHILIPPINES." American University, 1962. 216 pp. Source: DAI, XXIII, 9 (March, 1963), 3185. XUM Order No. 62-4523.

Qualifications of deans of women at institutions of higher education in the Philippines were found to be significantly similar to qualifications of deans of women in the U. S.

Cacy, Lora Belle (Ed. D.). "IDENTIFICATION AND EVALUATION OF SELECTED INTEGRATIVE BEHAVIORS AS RELATED TO HOME ECONOMICS EDUCATION." Oklahoma State University, 1962. 193 pp. Source: DAI, XXIV, 1 (July, 1963), 274. XUM Order No. 63-4038.

Observation data on profile charts showed change in all 9 of the selected behaviors, although no consistent or outstanding patterns of progress were observed.

Calderwood, Deryck David (Ph. D.). "ADOLESCENT APPRAISALS AND OPINIONS CONCERNING THEIR SEX EDUCATION IN SELECTED INSTITUTIONS." Oregon State University, 1970. 271 pp. Source: DAI, XXXI, 8A (February, 1971), 4295-A-4296-A. XUM Order No. 71-2465.

Male and female 9th through 12th graders indicated different sources of information regarding sex, although in this order: home, school, youth organizations, church. Respondents indicated desire for sex information at ages earlier than they had received it.

Calhoun, Harriott Dixon (Ph. D.). "COMMUNITY COLLEGE WOMEN STUDENTS: CHARACTERISTICS, MOTIVATIONS, AND ASPIRATIONS." University of Alabama, 1975. 105 pp. Source: DAI, XXXVI, 9A (March, 1976), 5853-A. XUM Order No. 76-4797.

The typical female community college student studied was white, single, between ages 17-21 (many were older), and had anticipated college attendance for many years with the goal of career preparation.

Although generally satisfied with programs and services offered, a major complaint was the unavailability of financial aid.

Callin, Diane Tomcheff (Ph. D.). "A THREE HOUR CREDIT COURSE IN WO-MEN IN LITERATURE: TOWARD A PROTOTYPE." University of Illinois at Ur-bana-Champaign, 1976. 162 pp. Source: DAI, XXXVII, 10A (April, 1977), 6228-A. XUM Order No. 77-8949.

Culled from a collection of materials from 83 similar courses, a com-posite college course was composed on Women in Literature to be made available for colleges in Illinois and elsewhere.

Callis, Virginia Carolyn (Ph. D.). "INTERACTIVE EFFECTS OF ACHIEVE-MENT ANXIETY, ACADEMIC ACHIEVEMENT, AND INSTRUCTIONAL MODE ON PERFORMANCE AND COURSE ATTITUDES." Ohio State University, 1976. 175 pp. Source: DAI, XXXVII, 8A (February, 1977), 4915-A. XUM Order No. 77-2362.

With respect to non-academic outcomes, the findings suggest that posi-tive attitudes may be fostered by providing adequate instructional support for a wide range of ability types and providing opportunities for student decision-making so that they may select and devise those experiences which will be most meaningful to them.

Callsen, Margaret Signora (Ph. D.). "AN IDENTIFICATION OF PROFES-SIONAL COMPETENCIES NEEDED BY HOME ECONOMISTS WHO ARE PART-TIME ADULT EDUCATORS." Kansas State University, 1974. 148 pp. Source: DAI, XXXV, 6A (December, 1974), 3379-A. XUM Order No. 74-25,595.

Competencies in communications, motivation, selection of teaching techniques, time management, technical material, and self-confidence were very important to adult-educator home economists who devoted 50% or less of their time to adult education. They showed greatest in-terest in improving subject competence and teaching techniques.

Cameron, Anna Margaret (Ph. D.). "THE DEVELOPMENT OF AN INSTRUMENT TO EVALUATE THE ABILITY OF COLLEGE HOME ECONOMICS STUDENTS TO APPLY HOME MANAGEMENT GENERALIZATIONS AND FACTS IN THE SOLUTION OF HOMEMAKING PROB-LEMS." Ohio State University, 1954. 191 pp. Source: DAI, XX, 7 (Janu-ary, 1960), 2638-2639. XUM Order No. Mic 59-6626.

The hypothesis tested was that a valid, reliable instrument could be developed to evaluate the ability of college home economics students to apply home management generalizations and pertinent facts in sol-ving homemaking problems. The instrument proved effective in samp-ling students' ability to see logical relationships. The conclusion was that the instrument might be more effective if used with other kinds of evidence.

Campbell, Barbara Kuhn (Ph. D.). "PROMINENT WOMEN IN THE PROGRESSIVE ERA: A STUDY OF LIFE HISTORIES." University of Illinois at Chicago Cir-cle, 1976. 336 pp. Source: DAI, XXXVII, 7A (January, 1977), 4550-A-4551-A. XUM Order No. 77-270.

Education is one of many factors mentioned in this examination of personal and professional backgrounds of 9,000 women leaders listed in the Woman's Who's Who of America, 1914-1915.

Campbell, Margaret Amelia (Ed. D.). "THE SELECTION OF NURSING EDU-
CATION PROGRAMS BY NURSING STUDENTS IN BRITISH COLUMBIA." Columbia Uni-
versity, 1970. 280 pp. Source: DAI, XXXI, 7A (January, 1971), 3434-A.
XUM Order No. 71-1092.

Students' age, educational level, size of family, and parents' educational level appeared to have the strongest relationship to the type
of nursing program selected--either hospital diploma, 2-year diploma,
or baccalaureate degree--with length of program as another major determinant. The persons most influencing students' selection were
parents and graduates of nursing programs.

Campos, Adela B. (Ed. D.). "A STUDY OF ACCREDITED MASTER'S DEGREE
PROGRAMS IN NURSING IN STATE INSTITUTIONS OF HIGHER EDUCATION." Indiana
University, 1970. 129 pp. Source: DAI, XXXI, 6A (December, 1970), 2699-
A-2700-A. XUM Order No. 70-25,197.

Data from 22 nursing school deans and from school bulletins showed
that: (1) the philosophy and objectives of each of the master's
programs were in accord with the teaching, research, and public service aspects of the universities; and (2) because the majority of
universities offered master's degrees in medical-surgical and psychiatric-mental health nursing, the possibility existed that these institutions were neglecting or under-emphasizing other clinical areas.

Canaday, Martha Helen (Ed. D.). "THE SOCIAL ROLES OF MARRIED MIDDLE-
AGED WOMEN WITH IMPLICATIONS FOR ADULT EDUCATION." Pennsylvania State
University, 1966. 116 pp. Source: DAI, XXVII, 11A (May, 1967), 3687-
A-3688-A. XUM Order No. 67-5900.

A sample of middle-aged women, their husbands, and their teenaged
daughters assessed these women as wife, mother, homemaker, and individual person and evaluated feelings of satisfaction with their role
performances. All respondents had very similar scores on perception
of the roles and on feelings of satisfaction with the women's role
performances. Scores were, however, consistently low in the individual person role. Adult education programs can help women to develop
themselves in the individual person role area.

Cannell, Mary Elizabeth (Ed. D.). "COMPETENCIES REQUIRED FOR THE
DIRECTOR OF THE NURSING PROGRAM IN THE COMMUNITY JUNIOR COLLEGE." Colorado State College, 1968. 173 pp. Source: DAI, XXIX, 8B (February,
1969), 2950-B-2951-B. XUM Order No. 69-2830.

Competency in nursing was seen by respondents (nursing directors and
college presidents) as having the highest priority for the role of
nurse director. It was felt that other required skills and understandings, such as administrative duties and curriculum, could be
learned. A high degree of agreement on the importance of various
competencies for nurse directors was noted between nurse directors
and college presidents.

Cannon, Mary Agnes (Ph. D.). "THE EDUCATION OF WOMEN DURING THE
RENAISSANCE." Catholic University of America, 1916. Source: Published,
Same Title, Washington, DC: National Capital Press, 1916, p. 3.

Presented the education of women in Renaissance Italy, Spain, Portugal, England, France, and other northern European areas.

Cannon, Nona H. (Ed. D.). "PROPOSALS FOR DEVELOPING A MORE FUNCTIONAL PROGRAM OF HOME AND FAMILY LIFE EDUCATION AT HARDING COLLEGE." Columbia University Teachers College, 1953. 144 pp. Source: Dissertation, pp. 133-139.

Eleven characteristics of a functional program of home and family life education were described. Seven proposals suggested: (1) a coordinating committee be formed; (2) creation of a course in interpersonal, family, and community relations for freshman students; (3) creation of a course in problems of homemaking; (4) greater emphasis placed upon occupational orientation; (5) sociology course be made more functional; (6) develop a home economics core curriculum; and (7) provision be made for an interdisciplinary minor in home and family life education. Suggested a more thorough study before effecting changes.

Canter, Rachelle Joan (Ph. D.). "AN ANALYSIS OF ACHIEVEMENT-RELATED EXPECTATIONS AND ASPIRATIONS IN COLLEGE WOMEN." University of Colorado, 1975. 142 pp. Source: DAI, XXXVI, 11B (May, 1976), 5860-B. XUM Order No. 76-11,559.

Data on 200 undergraduate women supported the thesis that women's achievement is hindered by low occupational and educational expectations. The inhibiting effect of men's attitudes on women seemed to operate indirectly; i.e., women who perceive traditional expectations in close male friends expect more negative consequences of success and so they lower their aspirations.

Capps, Julia Anna (Ed. D.). "THE ROLES OF ASSISTANT SUPERINTENDENTS AND SUPERVISORS IN NORTH CAROLINA RELATIVE TO SEX DIFFERENCES." Duke University, 1976. 175 pp. Source: DAI, XXXVIII, 3A (September, 1977), 1140-A. XUM Order No. 77-18,765.

Data collected from 306 supervisors and 176 assistant superintendents indicated that males held higher degrees, had concentrated more in administration, had more experience as administrators, missed half as many days, and were more frequently assigned to administratively oriented jobs than women.

Carey, Joan (Ed. D.). "AN ANALYSIS OF CERTAIN TRAITS AS EXHIBITED BY A GROUP OF WOMEN SELECTED FOR ELEMENTARY EDUCATION AT SYRACUSE UNIVERSITY." Syracuse University, 1954. 353 pp. Source: DAI, XV, 8 (1955), 1356. XUM Order No. 11,864.

A comparison of sophomore women who had chosen elementary education as a career with sophomore women in other areas of study yielded several conclusions, among them the following: although the teacher group scored higher on a psychological exam, participated in more service-type organizations, and came from higher socio-economic status than the non-teacher group, the traits compared showed few differences between the 2 groups. The teacher group showed no greater leadership ability or more favorable attitude toward past school experience.

Carino, Oliva Palafox (Ph. D.). "THE RELATIONSHIP BETWEEN NEED PAT-
TERNS OF STUDENT NURSES AND SATISFACTION WITH NURSING EDUCATION." University of Nebraska, 1959. 122 pp. Source: DAI, XX, 1 (July, 1959), 201-
202. XUM Order No. Mic 59-1780.

Using the Edwards Personal Preference Schedule and the Nursing Education Satisfaction Scale, differences in need patterns between satisfied and dissatisfied student nurses were established. Six personality traits--Deference, Exhibition, Autonomy, Nurturance, Endurance,
and Heterosexuality--showed highly significant relationships with satisfaction with nursing education.

Carlson, Karen Louise (Ph. D.). "FACTORS IN VOCATIONAL CHOICES OF
LIBERAL ARTS WOMEN." Northwestern University, 1948. 467 pp. Source:
Dissertation, pp. 412-413.

Information gathered from 446 participants indicated the following as
influential: attitude toward higher education, national cultural factor, parental educational background, and economical background of
parents.

Carlson, Nancy L. (Ph. D.). "OCCUPATIONAL CHOICE AND ACHIEVEMENTS OF
WOMEN GRADUATE STUDENTS IN PSYCHOLOGY AS A FUNCTION OF EARLY PARENT-CHILD
INTERACTIONS AND ACHIEVEMENT AS RELATED TO BIRTH ORDER AND FAMILY SIZE."
University of Kansas, 1970. 170 pp. Source: DAI, XXXI, 6A (December,
1970), 2679-A. XUM Order No. 70-25,311.

Study showed no support for Anne Roe's hypothesis: that parental attitudes toward children influence the child's eventual orientation
toward the child's environment and the people in it; such parental
treatment determines the child's choice of person or nonperson-oriented
vocations. However, some evidence suggested that the vocational development of men and women is different.

Carpeno, Linda (Ed. D.). "EXPECTATIONS OF MALE/FEMALE LEADERSHIP
STYLES IN AN EDUCATIONAL SETTING." Boston University School of Education,
1976. 243 pp. Source: DAI, XXXVII, 3B (September, 1976), 1482-B. XUM
Order No. 76-21,223.

Expectations of leadership styles are basically unrelated to sex despite some sex-related differences in perceptions of leaders. Qualities associated more with women leaders were efficiency, organization,
and friendliness. The quality associated more with male leaders was
strength.

Carper, Barbara Anne (Ed. D.). "FUNDAMENTAL PATTERNS OF KNOWING IN
NURSING." Columbia University Teachers College, 1975. 185 pp. Source:
DAI, XXXVI, 10B (April, 1976), 4941-B. XUM Order No. 76-7772.

The 4 fundamental patterns of knowing--empirics (nursing science),
aesthetics (nursing art), ethics, and the component of personal knowledge in nursing--were described and interpreted in relation to their
relevance to nursing education and practice. In addition, the study
showed that each pattern is necessary for the development of mastery
in nursing and that each pattern of knowing has special significance.

Carr, Norma June (Ph. D.). "THE EFFECT OF OBJECTIVE AND SUBJECTIVE TELEVISION CAMERA TREATMENTS ON THE LEARNING OF SELECTED PSYCHOMOTOR AND COGNITIVE ASPECTS OF BADMINTON ACHIEVEMENT OF COLLEGE WOMEN." Ohio State University, 1971. 112 pp. Source: DAI, XXXII, 7A (January, 1972), 3754-A. XUM Order No. 72-4439.

Using 3 groups of college women--control, television subjective camera group, and television objective camera group--several conclusions seemed justifiable: (1) that a single television lesson, laboratory experience, and testing sequence can produce significant gains in selected psychomotor and cognitive aspects of badminton with the use of subjective or objective camera techniques; and (2) camera technique affects cognitive, but not psychomotor, badminton learning.

Carrell, Juanita (Ed. D.). "AN ANALYSIS OF LEADERSHIP ABILITIES OF SENIOR NURSING STUDENTS." Texas Tech University, 1976. 136 pp. Source: DAI, XXXVIII, 2B (August, 1977), 590-B. XUM Order No. 77-16,026.

The senior nursing students did not demonstrate high levels of leadership. Senior nursing students who have completed a patient care management course tend to demonstrate a significantly lower level of the structure factor of leadership than do students who have not completed a patient care management course. Recommended that nursing programs include effective leadership development.

Carrington, Dorothy Helen (Ed. D.). "AN ANALYSIS OF FACTORS AFFECTING THE DECISION OF COLLEGE WOMEN SENIORS OF THE SOUTHEAST TO ENTER GRADUATE SCHOOL." Florida State University, 1961. 132 pp. Source: DAI, XXII, 9 (March, 1962), 3036. XUM Order No. 61-5633.

Analysis of 3 groups from among 1,171 women college seniors in 28 Southeastern colleges: those with no plans for graduate school, those already enrolled in graduate school, and those planning to enter who had not applied or enrolled in a graduate program. Women planning to enter graduate school had better educated parents, were older at graduation, and a larger proportion of them had attended private colleges.

Carruth, Beatrice Fontella (Ed. D.). "PURPOSES AND CONTENT OF DOCTORAL PREPARATION FOR PSYCHIATRIC NURSES." Columbia University, 1967. 238 pp. Source: DAI, XXVIII, 5B (November, 1967), 2493-B-2494-B. XUM Order No. 67-16,749.

Responding faculty members of graduate programs in psychiatric-mental health nursing said that doctoral preparation is most necessary for those who will do research and/or teaching in psychiatric-mental health nursing. The majority of respondents favored a therapeutic rather than a resocialization role for the clinical specialist.

Carter, Frances Tunnell (Ed. D.). "A STUDY OF SELECTED ASPECTS OF HOME ECONOMICS PROGRAMS IN JUNIOR COLLEGES." University of Illinois, 1954. 231 pp. Source: DAI, XIV, 10 (1954), 1607-1608. XUM Order No. 9047.

In most cases, the home economics departments of responding junior colleges were staffed by suitably trained instructors, had adequate facilities and operating budgets, and placed more emphasis on practical training for terminal students than for university-preparatory students. There was little emphasis, however, on job preparation for terminal students.

Cartwright, Lillian Kaufman (Ph. D.). "WOMEN IN MEDICAL SCHOOL." University of California, Berkeley, 1970. 301 pp. Source: DAI, XXXI, 10B (April, 1971), 6237-B. XUM Order No. 71-9775.

Considerable diversity in personality and background characterized the 58 women medical students studied. Findings: (1) most came from small, stable families. The father's educational and occupational achievement was considerable; 93% of the mothers, though well educated, were in traditional female occupations. (2) These students' behavior as measured was effective both socially and intellectually. (3) Reasons for entering medicine, though diverse, showed that women were more likely than men to choose the field as a route to self-discovery via challenging work.

Carty, Helen Margaret Christine Stewart (Ph. D.). "SIX SELECTED FACTORS AND THEIR RELATIONSHIP TO THE EXPRESSED ATTITUDE OF THE HIGH SCHOOL GIRL TOWARD PHYSICAL EDUCATION." University of Michigan, 1968. 120 pp. Source: DAI, XXIX, 8A (February, 1969), 2547-A. XUM Order No. 69-2297.

Among 578 high school girls enrolled in physical education courses, attitude toward physical education was affected by amount and type of previous physical education, high or low intelligence scores, and variety of activity within the physical education programs.

Casey, Timothy John (Ph. D.). "THE DEVELOPMENT OF A LEADERSHIP ORIENTATION SCALE ON THE STRONG VOCATIONAL INTEREST BLANK FOR WOMEN." University of Notre Dame, 1974. 53 pp. Source: DAI, XXXIV, 7A (January, 1974), 3457-B. XUM Order No. 74-46.

Dividing the sample of freshman coeds into leaders, intermediates, and non-leaders, the study revealed that leaders responded "Like" to 90% more scale items than non-leaders; inversely, non-leaders answered "Dislike" to 90% more scale items than leaders. The scale was developed to aid counselors in helping women plan extracurricular activities.

Cassidy, Claudia Lenore (Ph. D.). "THE RELATIONSHIP OF SOME ATTITUDINAL VARIABLES TO CAREER DECISION-MAKING AMONG COLLEGE WOMEN." University of California, Berkeley, 1976. 128 pp. Source: DAI, XXXVII, 11A (May, 1977), 6948-A. XUM Order No. 77-4405.

Juniors and seniors (138) from Mills College were given a Background Questionnaire and the Wellesley Role Orientation Scale to determine their attitudes about sex-roles, with the level of self-esteem determined by the Coopersmith Self-Esteem Inventory. They were further categorized by career group with 56 being nontraditional and 82 being traditional. No significant difference was found between traditional and non-traditional subjects on self-esteem; responses fo the background questionnaire revealed no significant differences between the groups. Scores on the Wellesley scale were low, indicating a rejection of stereotyped role orientations.

Cassidy, George F. (Ph. D.). "THE RELATIONSHIP BETWEEN AN INVENTORY AND A PROJECTIVE TECHNIQUE APPROACH TO THE EVALUATION OF EMOTIONAL ADJUSTMENT IN A GROUP OF STUDENT NURSES." Fordham University, 1954. Source: Dissertation Summary Report, pp. 1-10.

There is a positive and statistically significant relationship between the MMPI (Minnesota Multiphasic Personality Inventory) and the projective tests as indicators of general adjustment, but little or no relationship was found between the psychopathological syndromes mutually indentified on both tests. The evaluations of general adjustment on both types of tests yielded generally positive but statistically insignificant correlations with the external indices. The findings relative to the meaning of low MMPI scores failed to show poor psychological adjustment.

Catapusan, Flora Encarnacion Diaz (Ed. D.). "AN APPRAISAL OF THE HOMEMAKERS AND MOTHERS COOPERATIVES, INC. (HOMOCO) IN RELATION TO UNESCO'S FUNDAMENTAL EDUCATION AND OTHER CRITERIA." University of Michigan, 1959. 347 pp. Source: DAI, XIX, 12 (June, 1959), 3203-3204.

Despite inadequate facilities and technically unqualified personnel, the study revealed that typical activities of the Philippines' Homemakers and Mothers Cooperative (HOMOCO) had creatively implemented, and in some cases gone beyond, the aims and principles of UNESCO's Fundamental Education. HOMOCO's primary objective was to help homemakers, the unschooled, and the low-income groups to learn how to solve their practical problems and to improve their living conditions.

Cathcart-Barker, Narviar Clemencia (Ph. D.). "THE EFFECTS OF RACE AND SEX ON THE EVALUATION OF COUNSELORS BY CLIENTS IN AN URBAN UNIVERSITY COUNSELING CENTER." Georgia State University School of Education, 1976. 118 pp. Source: DAI, XXXVII, 7A (January, 1977), 4127-A-4128-A. XUM Order No. 76-30,365.

Women counselors, particularly black women counselors, were rated higher than men counselors by black and white student clients in an urban university.

Cato, William Hall (Ph. D.). "THE DEVELOPMENT OF HIGHER EDUCATION FOR WOMEN IN VIRGINIA." University of Virginia, 1941. 436 pp. Source: Dissertation, pp. 30-32ff.

The first school founded specifically for women was Richmond Female Academy (1806). In 1893 Randolph Macon, a full-fledged liberal arts college, opened in Lynchburgh. This historical study showed the relationship of women's status to provisions for women's higher education.

Cawley, Sister Anne Mary (Ph. D.). "A STUDY OF THE VOCATIONAL INTEREST TRENDS OF SECONDARY SCHOOL AND COLLEGE WOMEN." Catholic University of America, 1951. Source: GENETIC PSYCHOLOGY MONOGRAPHS, XXXV (1947), pp. 241-244.

Intelligence as measured by group tests is a stronger factor in developing vocational interests among secondary school girls than among college girls.

Cawley, Helen L. (Ed. D.). "THE INFORMAL EVALUATION AS A TEACHING TECHNIQUE FOR SOME OF THE LESS TANGIBLE ASPECTS OF A HOMEMAKING PROGRAM AT THE SEVENTH AND EIGHTH GRADE LEVELS." Pennsylvania State University, 1958. 174 pp. Source: DAI, XIX, 1 (July, 1958), 129. XUM Order No. Mic 58-2278.

Informal evaluation devices developed in the areas of personal, family, and social relations were most effective.

Chadwick, Ida Frances (Ph. D.). "A COMPARISON OF THE PERSONALITY TRAITS AND KINESTHETIC AUGMENTATION AND REDUCTION OF COLLEGE FEMALE ATHLETES AND NON-ATHLETES." Florida State University, 1972. 192 pp. Source: DAI, XXXIII, 3A (September, 1972), 1005-A-1006-A. XUM Order No. 72-22,992.

After sorting the 30 women athletes and 30 women non-athletes into augmenters, moderates, or reducers on the basis of kinesthetic stimulation tests, results of personality inventories showed the athletes to be significantly more tough-minded, group-dependent, extraverted, subdued, and less intelligent than the non-athletes.

Chamberlain, Jeanette Goodwin Nehren (Ed. D.). "TURNOVER RATES OF NURSING AIDES AS COMPARED TO SELECTED FACTORS RELATED TO DIRECTORS OF NURSING IN LONG-TERM CARE FACILITIES IN THE STATE OF MARYLAND." George Washington University, 1977. 167 pp. Source: DAI, XXXVIII, 3B (September, 1977), 1139-B. XUM Order No. 77-20,076.

Turnover rate of nursing aides is not significantly affected by the academic achievement level of nursing directors, although fewer turnovers tend to occur where directors have the bachelor's or master's degree.

Chambers, Mildred Jean (Ph. D.). "DEVELOPMENT OF AN INSTRUMENT TO ASSESS ACHIEVEMENT OF MINIMUM ACADEMIC COMPETENCIES ESTABLISHED BY THE AMERICAN DIETETIC ASSOCIATION." Ohio State University, 1975. 313 pp. Source: DAI, XXXVI, 8B (February, 1976), 3893-B. XUM Order No. 76-3399.

An instrument was developed to assess student competence upon completion of a program designed to meet academic requirements for membership in the American Dietetic Association. The instrument was administered to 186 students completing undergraduate programs in dietetics and was then evaluated. It was concluded that the test instrument needed further refinement.

Champoux, Ellen Miles (Ed. D.). "INTERPERSONAL RELATIONSHIPS ASSOCIATED WITH TWO EDUCATION EXPERIENCES OF COLLEGE HOME ECONOMICS EDUCATION STUDENTS." Pennsylvania State University, 1962. 135 pp. Source: DAI, XXIII, 3 (September, 1962), 918-919. XUM Order No. 62-4089.

Findings did not support the hypothesis that skill in interpersonal relationships was (1) associated with educational experience planned to give knowledge and understanding of adolescent development; or (2) associated with college level maturity.

Chandra, Arvinda Ramesh (Ph. D.). "RESEARCH NORMS OF HOME ECONOMICS EDUCATION GRADUATE FACULTY." Iowa State University, 1969. 186 pp.

Source: DAI, XXX, 11B (May, 1970), 5119-B-5120-B. XUM Order No. 70-7682.

Data from 112 faculty members from 47 graduate departments of home economics identified norms of professional characteristics and research productivity. Although the data showed little research productivity among faculty, they did identify research as a desirable norm.

Chandy, Annamma Kollathottathil (Ed. D.). "FAMILY PLANNING OPINIONS OF FIRST AND THIRD YEAR STUDENTS OF DIPLOMA NURSING SCHOOLS IN UTTAR PRADESH, INDIA." Columbia University, 1974. 166 pp. Source: DAI, XXXV, 1B (July, 1974), 346-B. XUM Order No. 74-15,972.

Second and third-year students who received information about birth control through formal instruction showed more favorable opinions about their intentions to utilize birth control programs than the 1st-year students who had no formal instruction about birth control.

Channing, Rose Marie (Ed. D.). "INCREASED ENROLLMENT AND THE ASSOCIATE DEGREE NURSING ADMINISTRATOR." Columbia University, 1973. 177 pp. Source: DAI, XXXIV, 6A (December, 1973), 2948-A-2949-A. XUM Order No. 73-31,268.

This study identified how the functioning of nursing education administrators changed as enrollment increased beyond 250 students. Several changes occurred when the faculty numbered over 20, including some loss of administrative control from an increase in delegation of functioning. Of the 3 role relationships identified within which such administrators functioned, there was a noticeable shift in emphasis from the Educational Leadership Role to the Managerial Role.

Chapman, Muriel Elizabeth (Ed. D.). "NURSING EDUCATION AND THE MOVEMENT FOR HIGHER EDUCATION FOR WOMEN: A STUDY IN INTERRELATIONSHIPS, 1870-1900." Columbia University, 1969. 559 pp. Source: DAI, XXXI, 7B (January, 1971), 4154-B. XUM Order No. 70-26,769.

Between 1870 and 1900 nurses' schools and women's colleges faced similar problems; a definite relationship existed between them. By 1900 women's higher education had been accepted into the mainstream of American education. The quality of nursing education by contrast, did not improve because for many years it was rooted in hospitals.

Chase, Genevieve (Ph. D.). "FACTORS THAT INTERFERED WITH THE PROGRESS OF WOMEN STUDENTS AT THE STATE UNIVERSITY OF IOWA." University of Iowa, 1936. Source: Dissertation, pp. 75-82.

Because emotional factors caused many problems, the study recommended that mental health and guidance services by provided.

Chater, Shirley Sears (Ph. D.). "DIFFERENTIAL CHARACTERISTICS OF GRADUATE STUDENTS IN NURSING AND IMPLICATIONS FOR CURRICULUM DEVELOPMENT." University of California, Berkeley, 1964. 99 pp. Source: DAI, XXV, 7 (January, 1965), 3965-3966. XUM Order No. 64-12,975.

Personality characteristics were not significantly different between students who had graduated and those who withdrew or deferred graduation. The study showed differences in personality characteristics when students were compared by areas of specialization (i.e., students majoring in medical surgical nursing and in maternal child nursing were more dependent and conforming).

Checkley, Kenneth Lloyd (Ph. D.). "THE INFLUENCE OF A HUMAN RELATIONS LABORATORY ON THE EFFECTIVENESS OF THIRD YEAR PSYCHIATRIC NURSES." University of Alberta, 1971. Source: Dissertation.

Data obtained from the 12 participants revealed no significant changes in the personality of the students nor any changes in the behavioral adjustments of the patients involved; it did reveal differences in the way subjects interacted with their patients.

Cheska, Alyce Taylor (Ed. D.). "THE RELATIONSHIP OF AUTHORITARIANISM IN WOMEN STUDENTS TO THEIR PERCEPTION OF TEACHERS' INSTRUCTIONAL BEHAVIOR." University of California, Berkeley, 1961. 104 pp. Source: Dissertation, pp. 64-66.

This study used (1) verbal responses to statements in an opinion-attitude scale showing anti-democratic disposition; and (2) responses to an Adjective List, measuring authoritarian and equalitarian behavior of instruction in a classroom situation. The significant relationship occurred between the level of students' own authoritarianism and their description of their teacher's instructional behavior.

Chioni, Rose Marie (Ph. D.). "THE RELATIONSHIPS BETWEEN PREDICTED AND REPORTED SUCCESS IN ONE COLLEGIATE NURSING EDUCATION PROGRAM." Ohio State University, 1964. 175 pp. Source: DAI, XXV, 11 (May, 1965), 6543-6544. XUM Order No. 65-3835.

Although the typical nursing student could be described, no selective variables proved predictive of both student groups. Some of the selective variables were not predictors of any criterion of success. Recommendations concerned definition of success, evaluation of psychological testing, and need for further research.

Chipp, Sylvia A. (Ph. D.). "THE ROLE OF WOMEN ELITES IN A MODERNIZING COUNTRY: THE ALL PAKISTAN WOMEN'S ASSOCIATION." Syracuse University, 1970. 430 pp. Source: DAI, XXXII, 2A (August, 1971), 1030-A-1031-A. XUM Order No. 71-21,516.

Though highly educated and well traveled, the members of the All-Pakistan Women's Association saw themselves as "liberals" within their traditional roles in Islamic society rather than as activists seeking overt, radical change. They sought gradual national improvement within the framework of Islamic culture.

Chishti, Khawar Khan (Ph. D.). "AN EVALUATION OF THE EDUCATIONAL EXPERIENCE AT THE COLLEGE OF HOME ECONOMICS, LAHORE, PAKISTAN, BASED ON THE OPINIONS OF THE GRADUATES, THEIR PARENTS AND THE ADVISORY COUNCIL ON ISLAMIC IDEOLOGY FOR REVISIONS IN THE STRUCTURE AND CURRICULUM OF THE COLLEGE." Cornell University, 1974. 391 pp. Source: DAI, XXXV, 8A (February, 1975), 4855-A. XUM Order No. 75-4247.

Data confirmed the hypothesis that graduates of the College of Home Economics set up by Americans in Lahore, Pakistan, fall into 2 groups: modernists, who viewed their educational experience positively, and traditionalists, who viewed their experience negatively. Modernists agreed with traditionalists that the curriculum ignored Islamic ideals and values that relate to home and family life.

Christian, Johnie (Ph. D.). "A SUGGESTED PROGRAM FOR THE RECONSTRUC-TION OF HOME ECONOMICS IN SECONDARY EDUCATION." Ohio State University, 1941. 381 pp. Source: Dissertation, pp. 274-281.

Surveyed the history of home economics as background for the assertion that the home economics curriculum should advance the American demo-cratic ideal and not merely sustain class-oriented cultural traditions.

Christy, Teresa Elizabeth (Ed. D.). "A HISTORY OF THE DIVISION OF NURSING EDUCATION OF TEACHERS COLLEGE, COLUMBIA UNIVERSITY, 1899-1947." Columbia University, 1968. 229 pp. Source: DAI, XXXI, 1B (July, 1970), 265-B. XUM Order No. 70-12,511.

In nearly 50 years, over 25,000 nurses were enrolled, many of whom became leaders in nursing and nursing education around the world--in keeping with the program's goal of training leaders in the field.

Cibik, Rosemarie Scavariel (Ed. D.). "THE PERSONAL, SOCIAL AND PRO-FESSIONAL BACKGROUNDS AND THE DUTIES AND RESPONSIBILITIES OF WOMEN HIGH SCHOOL PRINCIPALS IN THE UNITED STATES." University of Pittsburgh, 1957. 229 pp. Source: DAI, XVII, 10 (1957), 2186. XUM Order No. 22,845.

The typical woman high school principal in 1954 was married, over 50 years of age, had graduate hours in education, and although she had 9.7 years of principalship, was found to be scantily prepared for ad-ministrative problems and responsibilities.

Clark, Carolyn Chambers (Ed. D.). "A COMPARISON OF LEARNING OUTCOMES FOR TEACHER AND STUDENT PLAYERS IN A PEER-MEDIATED, SIMULATION GAME FOR ASSOCIATE DEGREE NURSING STUDENTS." Columbia University Teachers College, 1976. 120 pp. Source: DAI, XXXVI, 12B, Part 1 (June, 1976), 6069-B-6070-B. XUM Order No. 76-13,790.

Students (100) in a psychiatric nursing program assumed roles as student-teacher pairs. Students but not teachers exhibited a warm-up effect in the games. All students increased their learning, but students who taught others learned more than those who did not teach. The teacher group scored higher than the student group.

Clark, Laura Veach (Ph. D.). "A STUDY OF THE RELATIONSHIP BETWEEN THE VOCATIONAL HOME ECONOMICS TEACHER-TRAINING CURRICULA OF A GROUP OF WOMEN'S COLLEGES AND THE EXPECTED RESPONSIBILITIES OF BEGINNING TEACHERS." Columbia University Teachers College, 1933. 82 pp. Source: TCCU CON-TRIBUTIONS No. 586, pp. 25-27, 37-39, 46, 69-70.

Certification requirements in 7 states lacked uniformity. Factors examined were: (1) the relationship between college emphasis and corresponding high school courses; and (2) background information on colleges and steps to execute the Federal Vocational Education Act.

Clark, Louise Rhodes (Ed. D.). "THE STUDENT TEACHING PROGRAM IN VO-
CATIONAL HOME ECONOMICS AT JACKSONVILLE STATE UNIVERSITY--STUDY IN EDUCA-
TION." University of Alabama, 1968. 152 pp. Source: DAI, XXIX, 10B
(April, 1969), 3812-B. XUM Order No. 69-6875.

Strengths of the program included the setting of definite objectives
as organized under a director who provided strong leadership, while
the primary weakness of the program appeared to be lack of communication among the administrators.

Clark, Marilyn L. (P. E. D.). "AN ASSESSMENT OF CHARACTERISTICS OF
SUCCESSFUL WOMEN INTERCOLLEGIATE ATHLETIC COACHES." Indiana University,
1972. 162 pp. Source: DAI, XXXV, 8A (February, 1975), 5089-A-5090-A.
XUM Order No. 75-1543.

Highest of 12 characteristics of successful women coaches were: (1)
knowledge of the sport; (2) ability to teach; (3) personal appear-
ance; and (4) fairness in dealing with each player.

Clark, Martha Kate (Ed. D.). "A STUDY OF SIMULATION TRAINING AND ITS
EFFECT ON THE SELF-CONCEPT, DOGMATISM, PERCEPTION, AND VERBAL BEHAVIOR OF
VOCATIONAL HOME ECONOMICS STUDENT TEACHERS." West Virginia University,
1976. 258 pp. Source: DAI, XXXVII, 8A (February, 1977), 5050-A-5051-A.
XUM Order No. 77-2546.

Simulation training was not as effective in changing behavior as was
actual classroom experience. However, the students who participated
in simulation felt that it helped them understand themselves and
others.

Clarke, Florence June (Ed. D.). "AN INVESTIGATION OF THE EXPRESSED
GOALS OF CERTAIN HOME ECONOMICS EDUCATORS AND THEIR STUDENTS WITH IMPLI-
CATIONS FOR HOME ECONOMICS EDUCATION." Cornell University, 1960. 238
pp. Source: DAI, XXI, 12 (June, 1961), 3677-3678. XUM Order No. Mic
61-1006.

Four hypotheses were tested: (1) that it is possible to identify and
investigate stated goals of certain teacher-educators and senior students in home economics colleges in the U. S.; (2) that the stated
goals of senior home economics students are related to those of their
teachers; (3) that statements of teacher and student goals have implications for pre-service and in-service training of home economics
teachers; and (4) that the home economics education beliefs of
teacher-educators consciously and unconsciously become part of the
underlying philosophy of their students. Results: the 4 hypotheses
could be accepted in part, hypotheses 2 and 3 being completely acceptable.

Clarke, Judith Alta (Ph. D.). "SURVEY OF THE GRADUATES OF PROFES-
SIONAL PROGRAMS IN PHYSICAL EDUCATION FOR WOMEN AT THE UNIVERSITY OF
IOWA." University of Iowa, 1971. 120 pp. Source: DAI, XXXII, 9A
(March, 1972), 5015-A. XUM Order No. 72-8227.

Found that most graduates were teaching at college or secondary school
levels, were affiliated with some professional group, and regularly
read professional journals. Most graduates rated their education at
Iowa as superior, citing "high quality of instruction."

Clay, John Thomas (Ph. D.). "PERSONALITY TRAITS OF FEMALE INTER-
COLLEGIATE ATHLETES AND FEMALE INTERCOLLEGIATE ATHLETIC COACHES." University of Utah, 1974. 129 pp. Source: DAI, XXXV, 8A (February, 1975),
5090-A. XUM Order No. 75-4964.

Hypothesis was that there would be no significant differences in personality traits between female intercollegiate athletes and female
intercollegiate athletic coaches. It was suggested that there would
be little difference in such traits between large and small school
coaches, and large and small school athletes. Results revealed that
certain personality traits significantly discriminated between female athletes and their coaches; coaches were more intelligent and
less suspicious than athletes. There were also significant differences in personality traits between large-school and small-school
female athletes.

Clayton, Bonnie Clare Wilmot (Ph. D.). "HISTORICAL PERSPECTIVES OF
PSYCHIATRIC NURSING IN HIGHER EDUCATION: 1946-1975." University of
Utah, 1976. 174 pp. Source: DAI, XXXVII, 5A (November, 1976), 2683-A.
XUM Order No. 76-25,845.

This study used documentary and other evidence about events which initiated and advanced psychiatric nursing in higher education. Recommended continued efforts to develop knowledge needed to support clinical practice.

Cleary, Frances Mae (Ph. D.). "AN APPLICATION OF A CLIENT-CENTERED
MODEL FOR STUDY OF SERVICE-ORIENTED ORGANIZATIONS: A BACCALAUREATE SCHOOL
OF NURSING." Case Western Reserve University, 1968. 309 pp. Source:
DAI, XXIX, 12A (June, 1969), 4561-A. XUM Order No. 69-9335.

In this application of the Lefton-Rosengren model for study of service organizations to a baccalaureate school of nursing, 3 objectives
were formulated. Findings on the lateral client concern supported
the general hypothesis that faculty perceptions of students were specific in nature. The longitudinality hypothesis that there would be
long-term responsible interest in the graduated student was only partially supported.

Cleek, Jo Beatrice (Ed. D.). "PERCEPTUAL MOTOR MATCH: IMPACT OF TWO
MOTOR TRAINING PROGRAMS." East Tennessee State University, 1976. 87 pp.
Source: DAI, XXXVII, 7A (January, 1977), 4093-A. XUM Order No. 76-
30,256.

In the experimental group all scores increased significantly. The
impact of motor training on verbal intelligence was more effective
in males than in females.

Cleino, Elizabeth White (Ph. D.). "DOCTORAL EDUCATION FOR THE PREP-
ARATION OF COLLEGE TEACHERS OF NURSING." University of Alabama, 1964.
348 pp. Source: DAI, XXV, 12 (June, 1965), 7209-7210. XUM Order No.
65-4060.

Data gathered from nurse-educator respondents recommended that doctoral programs include: (1) both research and professional-type
doctorates; (2) majors in clinical, teaching, and administrative

nursing; and (3) a dissertation that makes an original contribution to nursing knowledge.

Cline-Naffziger, Claudeen (Ph. D.). "A SURVEY OF COUNSELORS' AND OTHER SELECTED PROFESSIONALS' ATTITUDES TOWARDS WOMEN'S ROLES." University of Oregon, 1971. 160 pp. Source: DAI, XXXII, 6A (December, 1971), 3021-A. XUM Order No. 72-955.

Women counselors and teachers of all ages described their ideal woman as more extra-family oriented than the ideal women described by their male counterparts, thus disproving one hypothesis that age is a factor in varying attitudes of respondents in defining the ideal woman. Support was found for the hypothesis that differences in professional and educational experience and work setting have a significant effect on respondents' attitudes.

Clough, L. Bradley (Ph. D.). "A FACTOR ANALYSIS OF VARIABLES RELATED TO FEMALE COLLEGE ACHIEVEMENT." University of Connecticut, 1965. 130 pp. Source: DAI, XXVI, 9 (March, 1966), 5221-5222. XUM Order No. 66-831.

Correlations were found between each of the personality factor areas-- home anxiety, autonomy, ego, hostility, orientation, and school--and the female respondents' cumulative grade average. Differences in grade average corresponded with differences in personality characteristics and the way students perceived themselves and their environment.

Coates, Susan Winship (Ph. D.). "FIELD DEPENDENCE-INDEPENDENCE, SEX ROLE STEREOTYPING AND SEX-TYPED PREFERENCES IN CHILDREN." New York University, 1976. 104 pp. Source: DAI, XXXVIII, 2B (August, 1977), 890-B. XUM Order No. 77-16,474.

Both boys and girls showed that field independence was associated with less sex-role stereotyping. Field-independent girls had more feminine preferences than field-dependent girls.

Coble, Madge Albright (Ph. D.). "IMPLICATIONS OF WARTIME CHANGES IN HOME ECONOMICS TEACHER EDUCATION IN HIGHER INSTITUTIONS FOR POSTWAR IN-SERVICE TRAINING PROGRAMS." Ohio State University, 1945. 224 pp. Source: Dissertation, pp. 2-3.

Wartime adjustments and anticipated postwar socio-economic conditions were considered in developing an in-service program for home economics teachers and non-professional leaders of home and family life education. Socio-economic conditions resulting from the war intensified the need for the program. Nature, extent, and effectiveness of wartime adjustments were examined and related to the postwar situation.

Coe, Charlotte R. (Ed. D.). "IDENTIFICATION OF EDUCATIONAL OBJECTIVES IN NURSING." University of Wyoming, 1965. 84 pp. Source: Dissertation, pp. 59-69.

Three important objectives identified were: (1) being technically competent and skillful in giving nursing care; (2) making accurate evaluations of required nursing care; and (3) performing within a nurse's legal responsibility.

Coffey, Margaret Alyce (Ph. D.). "THE DEVELOPMENT OF PROFESSIONAL PREPARATION IN PHYSICAL EDUCATION FOR WOMEN IN THE COLLEGES AND UNIVERSITIES OF THE NORTHWEST." State University of Iowa, 1963. 242 pp. Source: DAI, XXIV, 2 (August, 1963), 606. XUM Order No. 63-4725.

Trends in the development of women's physical education were drawn from the programs; major requirements and professional training and degrees of the faculties of the colleges were studied.

Cohelan, Evelyn Ellis (Ed. D.). "NURSING ACTIVITIES DESCRIBED BY STUDENTS AS USEFUL FOR PROVIDING EMOTIONALLY SUPPORTIVE CARE TO PATIENTS." University of California, Berkeley, 1963. 154 pp. Source: DAI, XXIV, 9 (March, 1964), 3697. XUM Order No. 64-2163.

Many student nurses found that they lacked emotional support skills. Nursing literature has emphasized verbal skills in emotional support, but neglected the importance of physical care to aid a patient.

Cohn, Lucile M. (Ph. D.). "EFFECTS OF GROUP COUNSELING ON FRESHMAN NURSING STUDENTS." Marquette University, 1972. 156 pp. Source: DAI, XXXIII, 10A (April, 1973), 5489-A. XUM Order No. 73-8265.

Group counseling may be effective for beginning nursing students in decreasing dogmatism and authoritarianism, and in improving self-concepts and interpersonal relationships.

Cole, Dorothy (Ed. D.). "A TYPOLOGICAL STUDY OF THE WOMEN'S RIGHTS MOVEMENT: IMPLICATIONS FOR BLACK WOMEN AND EDUCATION." Rutgers University, 1976. 383 pp. Source: DAI, XXXVII, 6A (December, 1976), 3948-A. XUM Order No. 76-27,310.

Inequities exist between black and white females, currently reinforced by racism and sexism toward blacks. To improve their situation, black women must strive for educational growth and the betterment of their own race while subordinating feminist priorities.

Cole, Eleanor Mabel (Ed. D.). "INVESTIGATION OF THE FREQUENCY, VARIETY, AND INTENSITY OF PROBLEMS REPORTED BY SELECTED WOMEN PHYSICAL EDUCATION MAJORS." University of California, Los Angeles, 1956. Source: Author.

Principal problems found were: inadequate finances, poor study techniques, and lack of reading skill.

Cole, Katherine Witherspoon (Ed. D.). "THE PERCEPTIONS OF LEADER BEHAVIOR OF MALE AND FEMALE ADMINISTRATORS IN THE ARCHDIOCESE OF WASHINGTON, D.C., SECONDARY SCHOOLS." Catholic University of America, 1977. 88 pp. Source: DAI, XXXVIII, 4A (October, 1977), 1769-A. XUM Order No. 77-20,452.

Data from 15 administrators and 136 teachers indicated no significant differences between male and female administrators and that females are as competent in administration as males.

Coles, Anna Louise Bailey (Ph. D.). "DOCTORAL EDUCATION OF NURSES IN THE UNITED STATES." Catholic University of America, 1967. 150 pp. Source: DAI, XXVIII, 6B (December, 1967), 2494-B. XUM Order No. 67-15,427.

Guidelines developed included: (1) exposure to programs that provide rigorous training in disciplined, critical, and analytical thinking; and (2) extensive review of current literature relating to higher education and doctoral programs.

Collazo-Collazo, Jenaro (Ph. D.). "OCCUPATIONAL PLANS OF PUERTO RICAN YOUTH." Cornell University, 1967. 139 pp. Source: DAI, XXVIII, 4A (October, 1967), 1534-A-1535-A. XUM Order No. 67-12,336.

Boys are more likely to have higher occupational plans than girls. Younger male students more often planned for high professional occupations. Older female students tended to plan for low professional occupations.

Collins, Sister Mary Lucille (Ph. D.). "HISTORY OF THE DOMINICAN CONGREGATION OF OUR LADY OF THE ROSARY OF SPARKILL, NEW YORK, 1876-1951." St. Louis University, 1953. 401 pp. Source: DAI, XXXVIII, 1A (July, 1977), 418-A. XUM Order No. 77-13,942.

The Congregation was established by Alice Mary Thorpe as a shelter for needy women and children. After 1900, the emphasis shifted to elementary and secondary education of Catholic youth.

Connolly, Mary Kennedy (Ed. D.). "THE ANOMALY OF CATHOLIC HIGHER EDUCATION FOR WOMEN." Columbia University Teachers College, 1976. 269 pp. Source: DAI, XXXVII, 2A (August, 1976), 843-A. XUM Order No. 76-17,277.

To see if Catholic colleges for women are still valuable, author examined history of women's higher education and specifically 4 Catholic academies which became women's colleges. Author believes that the role of strong, dedicated women who valued religion has been and remains incalculable, although the new nuns and lay faculty now contribute within society and not apart from it.

Connor, Ruth (Ph. D.). "THE SCHOLASTIC BEHAVIOR OF A SELECTED GROUP OF UNDERGRADUATE HOME ECONOMICS STUDENTS." Columbia University Teachers College, 1931. Source: TCCU DIGESTS, IV, A-G (September, 1929-December, 1931), pp. 1-2.

Among the findings: when home economics majors in high school, college, and graduate school were compared on intelligence tests, the pattern of behavior was essentially the same.

Cook, Barbara Ivy Wood (Ph. D.). "ROLE ASPIRATION AS EVIDENCED IN SENIOR WOMEN." Purdue University, 1967. 364 pp. Source: DAI, XXVIII, 6A (December, 1967), 2067-A-2068-A. XUM Order No. 67-16,627.

Among the findings: academic majors influenced career and homemaking expectations of senior women.

Cook, Ruth Helen (Ph. D.). "THE PARTICIPATION OF GRADUATES OF THE NEW YORK STATE COLLEGE OF HOME ECONOMICS, CORNELL UNIVERSITY, 1911-49, IN COMMUNITY AND PROFESSIONAL ORGANIZATIONS." Cornell University, 1954. 182 pp. Source: DAI, XIV, 11 (1954), 1945. XUM Order No. 9792.

The findings indicated the need for the college program to prepare most of its students for good citizenship as well as for the role of homemaker and home economist.

Cordova, F. David (Ed. D.). "A STUDY OF THE ATTITUDES OF ASSOCIATE DEGREE NURSING INSTRUCTORS TOWARD PROGRAMMED INSTRUCTION." East Texas State University, 1974. 112 pp. Source: DAI, XXXV, 5B (November, 1974), 2278-B. XUM Order No. 74-25,628.

Instructors who receive preparation in the use of programmed instruction through formal college courses or workshops develop significantly more positive attitudes toward programmed instruction.

Cornelison, William Hedrick (Ph. D.). "A COMPARATIVE STUDY OF ACADEMIC ACHIEVEMENT AND SOCIAL ADJUSTMENT OF HIGH SCHOOL STUDENTS IN RELATION TO THEIR ATTENDANCE AT COEDUCATIONAL AND SINGLE-SEX HIGH SCHOOLS." United States International University, 1973. 178 pp. Source: DAI, XXXIV, 4A (October, 1973), 1475-A-1476-A. XUM Order No. 73-22,660.

The environment of a coeducational school is less academically demanding than the environment of a single sex school, especially a girls' school.

Costick, Rita Marie (Ph. D.). "AN EXPLORATORY STUDY OF THE DEVELOPMENTAL PROCESSES OF CONTINUING EDUCATION PROGRAMS AND SERVICES FOR WOMEN IN SELECTED MICHIGAN COMMUNITY COLLEGES." Michigan State University, 1975. 215 pp. Source: DAI, XXXVI, 9A (March, 1976), 5675-A. XUM Order No. 76-5537.

Among the findings: the majority of the colleges surveyed offered such courses as self-awareness and women's studies.

Counts, Mona Marie (Ph. D.). "AN ANALYSIS OF A SELECTED ASSOCIATE DEGREE AND BACCALAUREATE DEGREE NURSING CURRICULUM AS RELATED TO GRADUATES' PERFORMANCE OF FUNCTIONS IN THE MEDICAL-SURGICAL AREA." University of Texas at Austin, 1975. 260 pp. Source: DAI, XXXVI, 5B (November, 1975), 2152-B. XUM Order No. 75-24,855.

Graduates' performance of nursing functions in a medical-surgical area was not affected by the curriculum of the program from which they graduated.

Coyle, Jean Marie (Ph. D.). "JOB INVOLVEMENT, WORK SATISFACTION, AND ATTITUDES TOWARD RETIREMENT OF BUSINESS AND PROFESSIONAL WOMEN." Texas Woman's University, 1976. 257 pp. Source: DAI, XXXVII, 7A (January, 1977), 4630-A-4631-A. XUM Order No. 77-735.

The 2 factors of job involvement and work satisfaction were directly and significantly related. A significant inverse relationship between job involvement and a favorable attitude toward retirement was discovered.

Cozy, Helen Marie Brandt (Ph. D.). "POST HIGH SCHOOL ACADEMIC
ACHIEVEMENT IN THE CONTEXT OF SPECIFIED VALUE INDICANTS IN HIGH SCHOOL
CUMULATIVE RECORDS OF SCHOLASTICALLY SUPERIOR WOMEN." University of Wis-
consin, 1972. 340 pp. Source: DAI, XXXIII, 8A (February, 1973), 4084-
A-4085-A. XUM Order No. 72-31,523.

There appeared to be no predictive relationship between values expressed during high school and later academic achievement for scholastically superior women.

Crogan, Corinne Almyra (Ed. D.). "THE REPORTED PREFERENCES AND PRAC-
TICES OF TEACHERS OF GOLF FOR WOMEN AT THE COLLEGE LEVEL." University of
Michigan, 1953. 293 pp. Source: DAI, XIII, 3 (1953), 334-335. XUM Or-
der No. 3985.

There is agreement in the preferences and practices as to content
and teaching methods. Preferences and practices are not influenced
by experience but are influenced by the source of learning. Teachers
of golf learn more from each other and professional associates than
from references.

Crossland, Kathryn McAllister (Ed. D.). "INFLUENCE OF THE CHARACTER-
ISTICS OF MASTER'S PROGRAMS ON THE RECRUITMENT OF TEACHERS OF NURSING."
University of Florida, 1967. 80 pp. Source: DAI, XXIX, 1B (July, 1968),
255-B. XUM Order No. 68-9561.

Characteristics influencing decisions to enter or not to enter graduate education for teachers of nursing are location of school, curriculum, accreditation, and admission requirements.

Curran, Connie Lea (Ed. D.). "FACTORS AFFECTING PARTICIPATION IN
CONTINUING EDUCATION ACTIVITIES AND IDENTIFIED LEARNING NEEDS OF REGIS-
TERED NURSES." Northern Illinois University, 1974. 161 pp. Source:
DAI, XXXV, 12B, Part 1 (June, 1975), 5965-B-5966-B. XUM Order No. 75-
13,156.

Recommended that a greater number of continuing education programs
be offered to meet the many different learning needs expressed by
registered nurses.

Dahl, Paul Eugene (Ph. D.). "SOME FACTORS WHICH DIFFER BETWEEN MAR-
RIED AND NEVER-MARRIED L.D.S. MALES AND FEMALES WHO ATTENDED 1969 SUMMER
SCHOOL AT BRIGHAM YOUNG UNIVERSITY IN RELATIONSHIP TO THEIR FAMILIES OF
ORIENTATION." Brigham Young University, 1971. 143 pp. Source: DAI,
XXXII, 1A (July, 1971), 562-A. XUM Order No. 71-19,143.

Never married female summer session students reported the most positive feelings toward their mothers and had the highest college grade
averages.

Dake, Marcia Allene (Ed. D.). "STATE UNIVERSITY OF NEW YORK AND PRE-
SERVICE NURSE EDUCATION." Columbia University Teachers College, 1958.
Source: Dissertation, pp. 137-145.

Author found that NY state support of nursing education was below
the National League for Nursing standard for accreditation and recom-

mended that state tax money be used more effectively to coordinate nursing education in the state.

Daley, Sister Mary Anselm (Ph. D.). "HISTORICAL DEVELOPMENT OF THE MEDICAL-SURGICAL NURSING COURSE IN THE UNITED STATES FROM 1873 TO 1950." Saint Louis University, 1963. 321 pp. Source: DAI, XXV, 1 (July, 1964), 413. XUM Order No. 64-4238.

The historical developments of the medical-surgical nursing course were traced, the forces shaping its features examined, and recommendations made for a reorganization of the learning experience into a new curriculum.

Dalrymple, Julia Irene (Ph. D.). "THE RELATION OF EXPERIENTIAL BACKGROUND TO PROFICIENCY IN STUDENT TEACHING IN THE FIELD OF HOME ECONOMICS." Ohio State University, 1953. 228 pp. Source: DAI, XIX, 7 (January, 1959), 1648-1650. XUM Order No. Mic 58-7194.

Concluded that more contact and experience with homes and children is desirable for the professional preparation of home economics teachers.

Dalsimer, Katherine Damen K. (Ph. D.). "THE DEVELOPMENT, IN ADOLESCENT GIRLS, OF FEAR OF ACADEMIC SUCCESS." New York University, 1973. 129 pp. Source: DAI, XXXIV, 12B, Part 1 (June, 1974), 6207-B. XUM Order No. 74-13,319.

Found in this study of white middle-class students in 8th, 10th, and 12th grade honors classes, that fear of academic success, more prevalent among girls, increased as the girls advanced in the high school years.

Dalsimer, Marlyn Hartzell (Ph. D.). "WOMEN AND FAMILY IN THE ONEIDA COMMUNITY, 1837-1881." New York University, 1975. 332 pp. Source: DAI, XXXVI, 11A (May, 1976), 7587-A-7588-A. XUM Order No. 76-10,160.

Social history of a utopian community which discussed, among other factors, women's access to educational and cultural opportunities.

D'Amelio, Rosalie F. (Ed. D.). "NURSING EDUCATION IN THE REPUBLIC OF ITALY IN 1971." Columbia University, 1972. 277 pp. Source: DAI, XXXIV, 9A (March, 1974), 5472-A. XUM Order No. 74-6397.

Italian nursing education: (1) was hospital-based and dominated by vested interests; (2) had no baccalaureate programs; (3) its nationally approved curriculum was prescribed in a 1938 law; and (4) was conducted by private and public agencies with the approval of the Ministries of Public Instruction and Interior.

Daniel, Elnora Delores Belle (Ed. D.). "ESSENTIAL ELEMENTS OF INDIVIDUALIZED INSTRUCTION AS PERCEIVED BY FACULTY MEMBERS AND LEARNERS IN A BACCALAUREATE NURSING EDUCATION PROGRAM." Columbia University Teachers College, 1976. 445 pp. Source: DAI, XXXVII, 12B, Part 1 (June, 1977), 6053-B. XUM Order No. 77-13,016.

In a private black college having an accredited baccalaureate nursing program, students (203) consistently differed from faculty (26) in their perceptions of the program. Agreement was noted on how the program should be used in the future. Sophomore students and faculty tended to perceive more individualization of the program than did freshman, junior, and senior faculty and students.

Daniel, Julia Ellen (Ph. D.). "DEVELOPMENT OF AN INSTRUMENT TO EVAL-UATE CERTAIN AFFECTIVE COMPETENCIES OF VOCATIONAL HOME ECONOMICS TEACHERS." University of Georgia, 1976. 112 pp. Source: DAI, XXXVII, 8A (February, 1977), 4915-A-4916-A. XUM Order No. 77-4111.

Instrument was developed, tested, and found valid relating to vocational home economics teacher-student human relations.

Daniels, Daisy Holloway (Ed. D.). "THE DEVELOPMENT OF PROPOSED AF-FECTIVE OBJECTIVES FOR COLLEGE UNDERGRADUATE HOME MANAGEMENT PROGRAMS." Oklahoma State University, 1973. 145 pp. Source: DAI, XXXIV, 10B (April, 1974), 5053-B-5054-B. XUM Order No. 74-7992.

Information from college home economics teachers of home management was used to enhance teacher-student relations.

Daniels, Doris Groshen (Ph. D.). "LILLIAN D. WALD: THE PROGRESSIVE WOMAN AND FEMINISM." City University of New York, 1977. 345 pp. Source: DAI, XXXVII, 11A (May, 1977), 7268-A. XUM Order No. 77-11,171.

A biography of social welfare reformer Lillian Wald, who established the Henry Street Settlement House in New York City. Rarely mentioned as a feminist, she was for 40 years an active feminist, helping to organize the Women's Trade Union League, lobbying for labor legislation, and often serving as spokeswoman for the Woman's Peace Party whose goal was female participation in international affairs. She tried to convert the middle class to the cause of the working girl and supported passage of such legislation as the Sheppard-Towner and Cable Acts.

Dannison, Linda Louise Silverman (Ph. D.). "STUDENT ATTITUDES TOWARD SECONDARY HOME ECONOMICS CURRICULUM." Kansas State University, 1976. 13 pp. Source: DAI, XXXVII, 9A (March, 1977), 5649-A-5650-A. XUM Order No. 77-5495.

Kansas high school girls in the 8th and 12th grades showed positive attitudes toward home economics and the curriculum concept areas.

Darby, Merlin Duane (Ed. D.). "THE RELATION OF SENSITIVITY TRAINING TO MARITAL INTEGRATION OF GRADUATE STUDENT HUSBANDS AND THEIR WIVES." Oregon State University, 1968. 52 pp. Source: DAI, XXIX, 3A (September, 1968), 795-A. XUM Order No. 68-12,897.

Compared role tension and marital integration among wives of graduate students by dividing the wives into 3 groups who: (1) received sensitivity training; (2) were active outside the home; or (3) had no activities nor sensitivity training. Findings were inconclusive.

Darian, Jean Catherine (Ph. D.). "LABOR FORCE PARTICIPATION OF MAR-RIED WOMEN IN THE UNITED STATES: AN INVESTIGATION OF THE ROLE OF OCCUPA-TION." University of Pennsylvania, 1972. 246 pp. Source: DAI, XXXIII, 4A (October, 1972), 1860-A. XUM Order No. 72-25,561.

During 1940-70 more married women entered the work force, more women did white-collar jobs, and the work week was shortened. After 1960, less work was required of women in the home and the more positive general attitude about their working freed them for the work force.

Darnell, Richard E. (Ph. D.). "THE INFLUENCE OF PROFESSIONAL ROLE IDENTIFICATION UPON THE DEVELOPMENT OF INTEREST IN HORIZONTAL CAREER MOBILITY BY NURSING STUDENTS." Michigan State University, 1971. 190 pp. Source: DAI, XXXII, 6A (December, 1971), 3022-A. XUM Order No. 71-31,184.

Found that 3 types of career information about the new field, nurse physician associate, made no difference in interest level among junior and senior nursing students but aroused some sophomore in-terest. Concluded that treating the nurse physician associate as a distinctly different profession will make it more interesting than to identify it with nursing or medicine.

Da Silva, Sonia (Ph. D.). "FOOD PRACTICES OF FAMILIES IN A BRAZILIAN CITY." Iowa State University, 1970. 342 pp. Source: DAI, XXXI, 9B (March, 1971), 5458-B. XUM Order No. 71-7259.

Food and nutrition habits of Brazilian homemakers were correlated with their educational and socio-economic levels. Information was then used to improve the educational programs of the School of Home Economics, Federal University of Vicosa, Brazil.

Daugherty, Kathryn Mary (Ph. D.). "DEVELOPMENT AND UTILIZATION OF A CONCEPTUAL MODEL TO DESCRIBE THE RELATIONSHIP OF SELECTED RESEARCH VARI-ABLES TO FEMALE CHOICE OF OCCUPATIONAL, VOCATIONAL, OR TECHNICAL PRO-GRAMS." University of Pittsburgh, 1975. 138 pp. Source: DAI, XXXVI, 9A (March, 1976), 5980-A. XUM Order No. 76-5425.

The model developed was a useful and flexible research paradigm for identifying and examining factors related to the vocational choice of public school girls.

Dauria, Anne Mary (Ed. D.). "A DESCRIPTIVE ANALYSIS OF THE NURSE-FACULTY ROLE IN INSTITUTIONS OF HIGHER EDUCATION IN VIRGINIA." Univer-sity of Virginia, 1976. 181 pp. Source: DAI, XXXVII, 8B (February, 1977), 3869-B. XUM Order No. 76-22,862.

Found among Virginia college teachers of nursing that, as they rose in academic rank and degree level, such non-teaching activities as administration, counseling, and research also tended to increase.

Davenport, Irvin Warren (Ed. D.). "ANALYSIS OF THE PERCEIVED LEADER BEHAVIOR OF MALE AND FEMALE ELEMENTARY SCHOOL PRINCIPALS." University of Missouri, Columbia, 1976. 305 pp. Source: DAI, XXXVII, 9A (March, 1977), 5476-A. XUM Order No. 77-4899.

Concluded that: (1) the sex of elementary school principals was not
significant in their overall behavior; (2) the claim that men behave
differently as leaders than women do was not justified; and (3) male
superordinates tended to favor male elementary school principals.

Daves, Martha Marise (Ph. D.). "A STUDY OF PRACTICES USED BY WOMEN'S
ATHLETIC ASSOCIATIONS IN ILLINOIS COLLEGES TO CONDUCT EXTRAMURAL SPORTS
PROGRAMS." New York University, 1964. 270 pp. Source: DAI, XXV, 12
(June, 1965), 7062-7063. XUM Order No. 65-965.

The weakest areas of women's extramural sports programs in Illinois
were publicity, officiating, balance of team and individual activities, lack of emphasis on social activities, and standards for practice and participation time.

David, Deborah Sarah (Ph. D.). "CAREER PATTERNS AND VALUES: A
STUDY OF MEN AND WOMEN IN SCIENCE AND ENGINEERING." Columbia University,
1971. Source: Dissertation, pp. 219-225.

Author's suggestions for maximizing women entering science and engineering fields include: (1) eliminate barriers toward their entering
these fields; (2) maximize their educational opportunities; and (3)
for those with family obligations, facilitate their need for time
for the family and for part-time schooling.

Davidoff, Ida Fisher and Markewich, May Elish (Ed. D.). "THE POST-
PARENTAL PHASE IN THE LIFE-CYCLE OF FIFTY COLLEGE-EDUCATED WOMEN." Col-
lumbia University Teachers College, 1961. Source: TCCU DIGESTS (1961),
pp. 126-127.

Found that 75% of post-parental women studied had made a satisfactory
adaptation, were in excellent health, and had an improved marital relationship. Greater involvement with people was the primary role
change.

Davidson, E. Wayne (Ed. D.). "PROBLEMS AND PRACTICES OF MISSOURI
PUBLIC HIGH SCHOOLS RELATED TO GIRLS' INTERSCHOOL ATHLETICS." University
of Missouri, Columbia, 1976. 158 pp. Source: DAI, XXXVII, 9A (March,
1977), 5476-A-5477-A. XUM Order No. 77-4900.

Found in Missouri public secondary schools that girls' interschool
athletic programs lacked community interest and financial support.

Davidson, Jane Ansalee Stovall (Ph. D.). "THE RELATIONSHIP OF FUTURE
HOMEMAKERS OF AMERICA PROGRAM OF WORK AND CURRICULUM PLANNING FOR SECON-
DARY HOME ECONOMICS EDUCATION." Texas Woman's University, 1974. 207 pp.
Source: DAI, XXXVI, 9A (March, 1976), 5889-A. XUM Order No. 76-5055.

Concluded that the Future Homemakers of America's work program can
enrich learning experiences provided in home economics education
classes.

Davies, Michael Martin (Ph. D.). "A COMPARISON OF THE EFFECTS OF
SENSITIVITY TRAINING AND PROGRAMMED INSTRUCTION ON THE DEVELOPMENT OF
HUMAN RELATIONS SKILLS OF BEGINNING NURSING STUDENTS IN AN ASSOCIATE
DEGREE PROGRAM." Saint Louis University, 1970. 114 pp. Source: DAI,
XXXII, 2A (August, 1971), 734-A-735-A. XUM Order No. 71-21,377.

Davis, Ella Kathleen Clements (Ph. D.). "A COMPARATIVE STUDY OF DEMOGRAPHIC AND PERSONALITY CHARACTERISTICS OF OLDER AND YOUNGER WOMEN STUDENTS ENROLLED IN A TEACHER PREPARATION PROGRAM." University of Texas at Austin, 1973. 205 pp. Source: DAI, XXXIV, 5A (November, 1973), 2382-A-2383-A. XUM Order No. 73-25,995.

The older women students studied were more focused on work and education, less concerned with peers and parents, more successful in academic performance, and less anxious, hostile, and depressed than their younger students counterparts.

Davis, Frances (Ed. D.). "THE HEAD NURSE AND THE IN-SERVICE EDUCATION OF PROFESSIONAL NURSING STAFF." Columbia University, 1965. 163 pp. Source: DAI, XXVII, 1B (July, 1966), 215-B-216-B. XUM Order No. 66-2653.

Concluded that most head nurses supported in-service education programs but were not actively involved in them.

Davis, Gail Roberta Comer (Ed. D.). "DIFFERENTIATION OF NURSING EDUCATION PROGRAMS THROUGH IDENTIFICATION OF NURSING FUNCTIONS." Texas Tech University, 1972. 254 pp. Source: DAI, XXXIV, 1A (July, 1973), 132-A. XUM Order No. 73-16,267.

Findings on 3 groups of variously trained nurses included the following: diploma graduate nurses performed 76% more nursing functions than the other groups. Baccalaureate degree graduates functioned independently, provided leadership, and performed the greatest number of functions in desirable practice. The associate degree graduate has not been accepted as a vital nurse practitioner by diploma educators or nursing service administrators.

Davis, Linda Sue Covert (Ph. D.). "SEX DIFFERENCES IN ACHIEVEMENT AND COMPETITION IN RELATION TO CONSEQUENCES AND AFFILIATION." University of Texas at Austin, 1975. 135 pp. Source: DAI, XXXVI, 10B (April, 1976), 5226-B-5227-B. XUM Order No. 76-8016.

Found in a competitive motor skill achievement test that college women who wanted to win performed like men and improved on each trial. Study suggested that women who wanted social approval achieved more than women who wanted to win so long as there was no competition. In competition, women who wanted social approval inhibited their performance.

Davis, Lorraine Cohen (Ed. D.). "THE INFORMATION AND PERCEPTIONS OF TWELFTH GRADE STUDENTS ABOUT THE ECONOMIC AND POLITICAL ROLES OF WOMEN." Indiana University, 1974. 249 pp. Source: DAI, XXXV, 9A (March, 1975), 5984-A-5985-A. XUM Order No. 75-5610.

Concluded that girls more than boys among 235 Wisconsin high school seniors had insufficient and unrealistic information about women's economic and political roles.

Davis, Reba Jones (Ed. D.). "THE RELATION BETWEEN NUTRITION KNOWLEDGE AND THE DIETARY INTAKE OF SELECTED WOMEN: A BASIS FOR ADULT EDUCATION PROGRAM DEVELOPMENT." University of Illinois at Urbana-Champaign,

1971. 180 pp. Source: DAI, XXXII, 8A (February, 1972), 4320-A. XUM
Order No. 72-6908.

Compared nutrition knowledge and dietary intake of 3 groups of women.
Found that: (1) nutrition knowledge and dietary quality were positively related; (2) food preferences and dietary quality were positively related; and (3) all groups needed more nutrition knowledge.
Recommended to nutrition educators that their instructional programs
be based on food preferences in order to evoke greatest interest.

Davis, Sandra Lee Ottsen (Ph. D.). "FACTORS RELATED TO THE PERSIS-
TENCE OF WOMEN IN A FOUR-YEAR INSTITUTE OF TECHNOLOGY." University of
Minnesota, 1973. 556 pp. Source: DAI, XXXIV, 7A (January, 1974),
3460-B. XUM Order No. 74-693.

Contradicting common stereotypes of women in technical fields, this
study found that such women: (1) seek rather than avoid social relationships; (2) have broad rather than narrow interests; and (3)
have incorporated feminine role behaviors into their life plans.

Davis, Sidney Thomas (Ph. D.). "WOMAN'S WORK IN THE METHODIST
CHURCH." University of Pittsburgh, 1963. 457 pp. Source: DAI, XXV,
2 (August, 1964), 1018. XUM Order No. 63-7795.

Historical and analytical account showed that women provided more
than half the Methodist Sunday school teachers, were more numerous
than men as missionary teachers, and initiated more dynamic projects
in education.

Davis, Wesley Alexander (Ed. D.). "ACADEMIC ACHIEVEMENT AND SELF-
DISCLOSURE OF HIGH SCHOOL STUDENTS AND THEIR PARENTS." University of
Florida, 1969. 77 pp. Source: DAI, XXXI, 1A (July, 1970), 145-A. XUM
Order No. 70-11,738.

More female high school students than males were found to have volun-
tarily revealed more about themselves to their parents.

Davison, Kathryn Mary (Ph. D.). "SIMULATION VERSUS CASE STUDY STRAT-
EGY FOR DEVELOPING PRE-SERVICE TEACHER VERBAL COMMUNICATION COMPETENCY."
Ohio State University, 1976. 158 pp. Source: DAI, XXXVII, 11A (May,
1977), 6994-A. XUM Order No. 77-10,512.

Among home economics students, it was found that the simulation
strategy was feasible for developing teacher verbal communication
abilities and confidence, with significantly higher post-test scores
for those who participated in the experiment than for those in the
case-study experiment.

Davison, Marian Bigelow (Ed. D.). "EDUCATIONAL OUTCOMES AND IMPLI-
CATIONS OF ACADEMICALLY OR VOCATIONALLY FOCUSED SMALL GROUPS OF UNDER-
GRADUATE STUDENTS IN A WOMEN'S RESIDENCE HALL." Pennsylvania State Uni-
versity, 1964. 118 pp. Source: DAI, XXV, 9 (March, 1965), 5046-5047.
XUM Order No. 64-10,770.

Because participation in academically or vocationally focused groups
improved women's grades, author recommended that more such groups
should be organized.

deAlmeida, Eleanor Engram (Ph. D.). "A DESCRIPTIVE AND ANALYTICAL STUDY OF THE EARLY ADULT ROLES OF BLACK AND WHITE WOMEN." Duke University, 1977. 123 pp. Source: DAI, XXXVIII, 4A (October, 1977), 2351-A. XUM Order No. 77-21,869.

Nearly equal percentages of women students planned to work, marry, or do both. White women were more likely to have enacted a work role if planned and black women, a marital role. Mothers' education levels influenced daughters' nontraditionality more for whites than blacks.

Dean, Betty Marlene (Ed. D.). "DEVELOPMENT AND VALIDATION OF AN INSTRUMENT TO PREDICT PROBABLE SUCCESS IN ASSOCIATE DEGREE NURSING PROGRAMS." Brigham Young University, 1976. 232 pp. Source: DAI, XXXVII, 2B (August, 1976), 696-B. XUM Order No. 76-18,324.

Found that students' success in associate degree nursing programs could be predicted by the grade point average obtained in 1st year nursing courses and by such characteristics as integrity and judgment when caring for patients.

Dean, Diana Jean Hill (Ph. D.). "AN ANALYSIS OF THE EFFECTS OF USING DIRECT MEASURES IN A COMPETENCY BASED PROFESSIONAL EDUCATION PROGRAM: AN EXAMPLE IN NURSING." University of Oregon, 1973. 90 pp. Source: DAI, XXXIV, 9A (March, 1974), 5577-A-5578-A. XUM Order No. 74-6820.

Specific competencies taught to student nurses in an Oregon community college nursing program were found to have been achieved in practice.

Dean, Margaret (Ed. D.). "PERCEIVED ACTIVITIES OF NURSE-MIDWIVES FOR LABOR AND DELIVERY IN SELECTED HOSPITALS IN PUNJAB STATE, INDIA." Columbia University, 1975. 209 pp. Source: DAI, XXXVI, 3B (September, 1975), 1145-B-1146-B. XUM Order No. 75-20,193.

Found that given the opportunity and within a conducive environment, nurse-midwives could handle normal deliveries and recognize abnormalities.

Dear, Joseph Donald (Ed. D.). "STUDENTS' PERCEPTIONS OF VARIABLES THAT RELATE TO ACADEMIC SUCCESS IN COLLEGE AMONG BLACKS AND WHITES, MALES AND FEMALES, AND SOPHOMORES, JUNIORS AND SENIORS." Northern Illinois University, 1974. 149 pp. Source: DAI, XXXV, 12A, Part 1 (June, 1975), 7675-A-7676-A. XUM Order No. 75-13,157.

The characteristics most related to college success for all students were: attendance of predominantly white high schools; residence in small towns and suburban areas; and higher family income.

DeBarbrie, Margaret Anne Brown (Ph. D.). "FACTORS ASSOCIATED WITH THE PREDICTION OF SUCCESS IN AN EDUCATIONAL PROGRAM FOR LICENSED VOCATIONAL NURSES." University of Texas at Austin, 1972. 135 pp. Source: DAI, XXXIII, 7A (January, 1973), 3373-A. XUM Order No. 73-424.

There were significant differences on entrance exam scores for black, Mexican-American, and Anglo junior college student nurses but no difference in their performance after finishing the 1-year course.

DeBoer, George Edward (Ph. D.). "A COMPARISON OF TWO METHODS OF TEACHING CHEMISTRY TO FRESHMAN STUDENT NURSES: AN INDIVIDUALIZED APPROACH VERSUS LECTURE." Northwestern University, 1972. 170 pp. Source: DAI, XXXIII, 6A (December, 1972), 2610-A-2611-A. XUM Order No. 72-32,419.

Concluded that individualized instruction which used a learning guide and small group discussion was as effective as the lecture method in a chemistry course for student nurses.

DeCrespo, Patria Cintron (Ed. D.). "PUERTO RICAN WOMEN TEACHERS IN NEW YORK: SELF-PERCEPTION, AND WORK ADJUSTMENT AS PERCEIVED BY THEMSELVES AND BY OTHERS." Columbia University, 1965. 229 pp. Source: DAI, XXVI, 9 (March, 1966), 5225. XUM Order No. 65-14,963.

Women teachers' dissatisfactions included inability to do more for Puerto Rican school children, lack of cooperation from some school officials, prejudice, and lack of interest from Puerto Rican parents and children.

De Dona, Frank Ettere (Ed. D.). "EVALUATION OF AN INTERDISCIPLINARY PROGRAMMED SUBSTANCE ABUSE SERIES FOR INDUSTRIAL NURSES USING A FUNCTIONAL APPROACH." Wayne State University, 1975. 279 pp. Source: DAI, XXXVI, 11A (May, 1976), 7330-A-7331-A. XUM Order No. 76-10,937.

Findings from industrial nurses who participated in a drug use and abuse educational program were used to improve nursing and health programs in several schools at Wayne State University, MI.

Deegan, Dorothy Yost (Ph. D.). "THE STEREOTYPE OF THE SINGLE WOMAN IN AMERICAN NOVELS: A SOCIAL STUDY WITH IMPLICATIONS FOR THE EDUCATION OF WOMEN." Columbia University, 1951. 252 pp. Source: Published: Same Title; New York: King's Crown Press, 1951; pp. 193-197.

Recommended that through encouraging the reading of fiction and biography, and through drama and the other arts, schools bring to girls' education a realistic awareness of their life options and opportunities whether they marry or not.

DeFabaugh, Gretchen Lee (Ph. D.). "ATTITUDES OF POTENTIAL PROFESSIONAL WOMEN TOWARD WOMEN'S UNCONVENTIONAL OCCUPATIONS." University of Rochester, 1975. 143 pp. Source: DAI, XXXVI, 1B (July, 1975), 468-B. XUM Order No. 75-15,197.

How views of their life roles influenced 96 female graduate students preparing to enter male-dominated fields as physicians, Ph. D. educators, and nursing administrators.

Deguire, Kathryn S. (Ph. D.). "ACTIVITY CHOICE, PSYCHOLOGICAL FUNCTIONING, DEGREE OF SATISFACTION, AND PERSONALITY FACTORS IN EDUCATED, MIDDLE-AGED WOMEN." Fordham University, 1974. 147 pp. Source: DAI, XXXV, 5B (November, 1974), 2424-B. XUM Order No. 74-25,045.

Found: (1) that the nature of a woman's activity was not predictive of the quality of her psychological functioning; and (2) personality traits were not significant determinants of an educated, middle-aged, married mother's choice of activity.

Delange, Janice Mae (Ph. D.). "RELATIVE EFFECTIVENESS OF ASSERTIVE
SKILL TRAINING AND DESENSITIZATION FOR HIGH AND LOW ANXIETY WOMEN."
University of Wisconsin-Madison, 1976. 284 pp. Source: DAI, XXXVIII,
1B (July, 1977), 351-B-352-B. XUM Order No. 77-8087.

Assertive skill training was effective both in increasing assertive
performance and reducing anxiety for both low and high anxiety women. Desensitization was also effective in reducing anxiety about
situations used in treatment but did not reveal an increase in performance nor generalized effects to new situations.

Delano, Phyllis Janes (Ed. D.). "CASE STUDIES OF CONTINUITIES AND
DISCONTINUITIES IN THE EMPLOYMENT-EDUCATION-FAMILY PATTERNS OF WOMEN'S
LIVES." Columbia University Teachers College, 1961. Source: TCCU DI-
GESTS (1960), pp. 128-130.

Of the 55 women studied, most who continued their formal education
were part-time students. Their interrupted work or study was caused
by: mobility, family responsibilities, calamities, required upgra-
ding of skills, retirement, economic and social conditions, and age
or sex discrimination.

Del Bueno, Dorothy Joan (Ed. D.). "AN EMPIRICAL EVALUATION OF THE
RELATIONSHIP BETWEEN CONTINUING EDUCATION AND NURSING BEHAVIOR." Col-
umbia University Teachers College, 1976. 107 pp. Source: DAI,
XXXVII, 2A (August, 1976), 928-A. XUM Order No. 76-17,280.

Concluded that traditional continuing education programs for nurses
did not change on-the-job behavior and that the cost of such continuing education can be justified only if the program improved
nursing performance and patient care.

DeLisle, Frances Helen (Ph. D.). "A STUDY OF THE RELATIONSHIP OF
THE SELF-CONCEPT TO ADJUSTMENT IN A SELECTED GROUP OF COLLEGE WOMEN."
Michigan State College, 1953. 277 pp. Source: DAI, XIII, 5 (1953),
719. XUM Order No. 5916.

Found that women students with high academic achievement: (1) had
a more realistic self-concept; (2) were more realistic about problems; and (3) used available resources to strengthen skills and
overcome difficulties than did lower achieving women students.

Del Papa, Lillian (Ed. D.). "DECISION-MAKING IN AN INTEREST GROUP:
AN ANALYSIS OF THE PROCESSES USED BY THE NATIONAL LEAGUE FOR NURSING IN
THE DEVELOPMENT OF ITS POLICY STATEMENT ON THE OPEN CURRICULUM IN NUR-
SING EDUCATION." Columbia University Teachers College, 1975. 487 pp.
Source: DAI, XXXVII, 3B (September, 1976), 1177-B-1178-B. XUM Order
No. 76-20,868.

De Maldonado, Aida Quinones (Ph. D.). "PERCEIVED NEED DEFICIENCIES
OF AGRICULTURAL AND HOME ECONOMICS EXTENSION AGENTS IN PUERTO RICO."
Pennsylvania State University, 1972. 140 pp. Source: DAI, XXXIII,
10B (April, 1973), 4889-B-4890-B. XUM Order No. 73-7459.

Information from agricultural and home economics extension agents
in Puerto Rico revealed their need for personal growth and development and a need for more opportunities for women workers.

De Martino, Hugo A. (Ph. D.). "THE RELATIONS BETWEEN CERTAIN MOTI-
VATIONAL VARIABLES AND ATTITUDES ABOUT MENTAL ILLNESS IN STUDENT PSYCHI-
ATRIC NURSES." St. John's University, 1970. 103 pp. Source: DAI,
XXXI, 6A (December, 1970), 3036-A. XUM Order No. 70-22,265.

Found that those student nurses whose opinions about mental illness
were less authoritarian: (1) were more able to think critically;
(2) were judged "Best"; and (3) had less need for abasement. Concluded that attitudes about mental illness were complex and multifaceted.

Deno, Evelyn Dreier (Ph. D.). "CHANGES IN THE HOME ACTIVITIES OF
JUNIOR HIGH SCHOOL GIRLS OVER A TWENTY-SEVEN YEAR PERIOD." University
of Minnesota, 1958. 340 pp. Source: DAI, XIX, 4 (October, 1958), 904-
905. XUM Order No. Mic 58-3540.

Found that in 1956: (1) fewer girls had regular home jobs for which
they assumed full responsibility (more "helped"); and (2) more girls
were responsible for tasks involving their own well-being, such as
making their beds and pressing their dresses.

Dereli, Atila Hasan (Ph. D.). "AN EXPLORATORY STUDY OF ATTITUDES
TOWARD SEX AND ITS RELATIONSHIP TO CERTAIN PERSONALITY FACTORS AMONG
PRESENT AND FUTURE SEX EDUCATORS." University of Oregon, 1973. 89 pp.
Source: DAI, XXXIV, 3A (September, 1973), 1357-A-1358-A. XUM Order No.
73-20,198.

Results of study indicated that health educators who teach sex education need sensitivity training.

DeRose, Anne Louise (Ph. D.). "PERCEPTIONS OF FEMALE SENIORS EN-
ROLLED IN COOPERATIVE OFFICE EDUCATION IN MICHIGAN HIGH SCHOOLS." Mich-
igan State University, 1976. 171 pp. Source: DAI, XXXVII, 12A, Part 1
(June, 1977), 7487-A. XUM Order No. 77-11,633.

Surveyed 937 past and present students and a coordinator; studied
perceptions of the Cooperative Office of Education program in 54
Michigan schools. The results indicated an overwhelmingly positive
perception with only 11 of the 937 giving negative responses to the
questionnaire.

DeSagasti, Heli Ellen Ennis (Ph. D.). "SOCIAL IMPLICATIONS OF ADULT
LITERACY: A STUDY AMONG MIGRANT WOMEN IN PERU." University of Pennsyl-
vania, 1972. 306 pp. Source: DAI, XXXIII, 7A (January, 1973), 3789-A.
XUM Order No. 73-1374.

Increase in literacy level among Peruvian migrant women was found to
result in their increased hopes for a university education and professional status for their children.

Desjean, Georgette (Ph. D.). "THE PROBLEM OF LEADERSHIP IN FRENCH
CANADIAN NURSING." Wayne State University, 1975. 417 pp. Source:
DAI, XXXVI, 5B (November, 1975), 2152-B-2153-B. XUM Order No. 75-25,235.

Nurses sampled believed: (1) that the indistinct work roles of
nurses caused confusion; and (2) social lags in the health system
lessened nurses' influence compared to other professionals.

Desmond, Sarah Ellen (Ph. D.). "PERSONALITY ORIENTATION, WORK VALUES AND OTHER CHARACTERISTICS OF PIONEER AND TRADITIONAL ACADEMIC WOMEN." University of Pittsburgh, 1975. 229 pp. Source: DAI, XXXVI, 12A (June, 1976), 7891-A-7892-A. XUM Order No. 76-14,124.

Found that pioneer and traditional women differed significantly in personality orientation, educational background, and career development but differed little in work values and biographical background.

Despain, Loy Keate (Ph. D.). "EDUCATION ACCOUNTABILITY: THE RATE OF RETURN TO NURSING EDUCATION AT MESA COMMUNITY COLLEGE." University of Arizona, 1975. 167 pp. Source: DAI, XXXVI, 11A (May, 1976), 7550-A-7551-A. XUM Order No. 76-11,333.

Found that money spent for nursing education at Mesa Community College brought high returns to the individuals involved and to society.

Desrosiers, Muriel C. (Ed. D.). "A DEMONSTRATION OF THE PARTICIPATION OF PROFESSIONAL NURSES IN THE EVOLVEMENT OF A CRITERION FOR THE EVALUATION OF PROFESSIONAL NURSING CONSCIENTIOUS PERFORMANCE." Boston University School of Education, 1977. 189 pp. Source: DAI, XXXVII, 12A, Part 1 (June, 1977), 7414-A. XUM Order No. 77-11,358.

Data from 107 baccalaureate degree nurses employed in New England general hospitals supported the evolvement of a criterion and its use in a role model peer review process.

Deutsch, Francine (Ph. D.). "COGNITIVE AND SOCIAL DETERMINANTS OF FEMALE PRESCHOOLERS' EMPATHIC ABILITY, HELPING, AND SHARING BEHAVIOR." Pennsylvania State University, 1972. 206 pp. Source: DAI, XXXIII, 12A (June, 1973), 6585-A-6586-A. XUM Order No. 73-13,968.

Author used instrument scales to discover the empathy, helping, and sharing behaviors of 67 kindergarten girls.

Devi, Leela (Ph. D.). "A PROPOSED COLLEGE HOME SCIENCE CURRICULUM FOR NEPAL." Southern Illinois University, 1972. 182 pp. Source: DAI, XXXIII, 2B (August, 1972), 804-B. XUM Order No. 72-22,479.

After surveying Nepal's home economics needs and measuring these needs against actual practice, a model home economics curriculum guide was developed.

DeVincenzo, Doris Kremsdorf (Ph. D.). "SOCIO-CULTURAL RELOCATION AND CHANGES IN ANXIETY AND ATTITUDES TOWARD THE UNITED STATES AS HOST COUNTRY AMONG EXCHANGE VISITOR NURSES." New York University, 1970. 139 pp. Source: DAI, XXXI, 7B (January, 1971), 4155-B. XUM Order No. 70-26,415.

Explored the concept of culture shock among 73 foreign nurses in the U. S. Found a significant relationship between their anxiety and their attitudes toward the U. S.

Devitt, Grace A. (Ph. D.). "COMMONALITIES OF CURRICULAR OBJECTIVES IN THE PREPARATION OF NURSES, PHYSICAL THERAPISTS, OCCUPATIONAL THERAPISTS, AND THERAPEUTIC DIETITIANS AT THE BACCALAUREATE LEVEL." University of Pittsburgh, 1970. 154 pp. Source: DAI, XXXI, 12B (June, 1971), 7379-B-7380-B. XUM Order No. 71-16,183.

Suggests objectives and content of a core health field program to serve as the common professional preparation of nurses, physical therapists, occupational therapists, and therapeutic dietitians.

Devore, Alline Burks Cato (Ed. D.). "SELECTED CHARACTERISTICS OF SUCCESSFUL AND UNSUCCESSFUL FEMALE PARAPROFESSIONAL STUDENTS IN A BAC- CALAUREATE DEGREE PROGRAM." Fordham University, 1976. 76 pp. Source: DAI, XXXVII, 5A (November, 1976), 2577-A. XUM Order No. 76-25,767.

Characteristics of successful female paraprofessionals were higher high school grade point averages and previous college attendance. Factors unrelated to success were age, marital status, years of paraprofessional employment, and pattern of college attendance.

DeWever, Margaret Kenney (Ed. D.). "AN INVESTIGATION OF THE RELA- TIONSHIP OF BACCALAUREATE NURSING STUDENTS' PERSONALITY AND THEIR PER- CEIVED DISCOMFORT IN TOUCHING PATIENTS." University of Houston, 1972. 75 pp. Source: DAI, XXXIII, 8A (February, 1973), 4113-A. XUM Order No. 73-4317.

Baccalaureate nursing students need help in coping with any emotions involved in touching patients.

Dezelsky, Thomas Leroy (H. S. D.). "ROLE APPERCEPTIONS OF SCHOOL HEALTH NURSES AND PUBLIC HEALTH NURSES WORKING IN SELECTED SCHOOLS IN WISCONSIN." Indiana University, 1966. 136 pp. Source: DAI, XXVII, 8B (February, 1967), 2756-B-2757-B. XUM Order No. 66-15,272.

Study compared how: (1) Wisconsin public school nurses and (2) pub- lic health nurses working in public schools each saw their roles. The results had implications for nursing education programs.

Dhaliwal, Manmohan S. (Ph. D.). "PREFERENCES IN THE SIZE OF FAMILY AMONG SENIOR GIRLS IN BLACK SEGREGATED HIGH SCHOOLS IN SOUTH, CENTRAL, AND WESTERN PARTS OF MISSISSIPPI." Utah State University, 1970. 116 pp. Source: DAI, XXXII, 3A (September, 1971), 1638-A. XUM Order No. 71-19,119.

Found that: (1) girls whose parents had either the lowest or the highest levels of education preferred larger families; (2) girls who believed in birth control preferred smaller families; and (3) the higher the grade point average, the larger the preferred size of family.

Dhanagom, Davirashmi (Ph. D.). "THE ROLE OF HOME ECONOMICS IN DEMO- CRATIC FAMILY LIVING WITH REFERENCE TO CHILD WELL-BEING AND PROPOSALS FOR SUCH EDUCATION IN THAILAND." Ohio State University, 1954. 319 pp. Source: DAI, XX, 2 (August, 1959), 559-562. XUM Order No. Mic 59-2556.

Recommended better home economics teaching at all school levels as a way to improve Thai children's physical and mental well-being and to emphasize parental responsibility for child development.

Dible, Isabel Wallace (Ed. D.). "FACTORS RELATED TO SUCCESS OF WO-
MEN WHO SEEK ELEMENTARY TEACHING CREDENTIALS WHEN THEY ARE BETWEEN THE
AGES OF THIRTY AND FORTY-FIVE." University of California, Los Angeles,
1962. 244 pp. Source: Dissertation, pp. 203-206.

Reasons it was easier for the older women studied to become successful elementary teachers include the fact that their children were
grown, their families encouraged them to take responsibilities outside the home, their test scores and academic performances were superior, and their maturer experiences equipped them to more readily
assume teaching duties.

Dibner, Lillian Adler (Ed. D.). "DUMPING THE DEMONS: A STUDY OF
WOMEN OVER TWENTY-FIVE YEARS OF AGE WHO ARE STUDENTS AT DALEN COMMUNITY
COLLEGE; THEIR GOALS, PROBLEMS, AND REFERENCE GROUPS." Columbia University Teachers College, 1976. 234 pp. Source: DAI, XXXVII, 3A (September, 1976), 1399-A-1400-A. XUM Order No. 76-21,015.

The goals of older women students surveyed were either to become more
skilled in their present occupations or to prepare for new careers.
The most frequently mentioned difficulties were having to manage a
home and/or work while going to college.

Dickerson, Kitty Gardner (Ph. D.). "A STUDY OF FEMALE COLLEGE STU-
DENTS' ACADEMIC-VOCATIONAL ASPIRATIONS AND HOW THEY PERCEIVE THAT THE
FACULTY AND ADMINISTRATION OF THEIR INSTITUTION SEE THEIR ROLES AS FE-
MALES." Saint Louis University, 1972. 249 pp. Source: DAI, XXXIV,
9A (March, 1974), 5657-A. XUM Order No. 74-4499.

Testing the "Pygmalion effect" (that one's behavior is influenced by
another's expectations), author found among women college students
that many perceived that faculty and administration had low expectations of them.

Dickerson, Thelma Mathes (Ed. D.). "AN EXAMINATION OF COMPETENCY
RATINGS FOR BEGINNING NURSE PRACTITIONERS." University of Tennessee,
1975. 162 pp. Source: DAI, XXXVI, 8B (February, 1976), 3870-B. XUM
Order No. 76-1937.

Compared ratings made by 165 nursing education administrations and
127 nursing service administrators of the competencies of beginning
baccalaureate, associate, and diploma nurses.

Dickman, John Frederick (Ed. D.). "THE PERCEPTUAL ORGANIZATION OF
PERSON ORIENTED VERSUS TASK ORIENTED STUDENT NURSES." University of
Florida, 1967. 82 pp. Source: DAI, XXIX, 4A (October, 1968), 1101-A.
XUM Order No. 68-13,000.

Found no accurate way to predict person-oriented nurses on the basis
of their perceptual organization. Urged that nursing schools stress
both technical proficiency and perceptual development in their students.

Dietz, Margaret R. (Ed. D.). "A STUDY OF SELF-CONCEPT OF DIPLOMA
NURSING SCHOOL STUDENTS." University of Pittsburgh, 1973. 62 pp.
Source: DAI, XXXIV, 8B (February, 1974), 3878-B. XUM Order No. 74-
2083.

Conclusions were that the self-concept scores of the freshman and senior nursing students in the 5 diploma nursing schools were not significantly different from the self-concept scores of college students in general nor from other nursing students.

DiLeo, Jean Cohen (Ph. D.). "INFLUENCES ON WOMEN'S SEX-ROLE ATTITUDES, ASSERTIVENESS, MODES OF INTERACTION, SELF-CONCEPT, AND SELF-ESTEEM: EVALUATION OF A TRAINING PROGRAM." Tulane University, 1975. 138 pp. Source: DAI, XXXVI, 8B (February, 1976), 4225-B. XUM Order No. 76-3990.

Women who discussed women's changing role became significantly less traditional in their sex-role attitudes and: (1) often worked outside the home as career persons or volunteers; (2) had majored at college in non-traditional fields; and (3) had fewer traditionally feminine hobbies.

Di Mattia, Judith Anne (Ph. D.). "FACTORS RELATING TO EDUCATIONAL ASPIRATIONS OF PRINCETON WOMEN." University of Pittsburgh, 1975. 103 pp. Source: DAI, XXXVI, 12A (June, 1976), 7892-A. XUM Order No. 76-14,125.

Found among 249 Princeton senior women that: (1) 7% had low self-esteem; (2) 93% had high self-esteem; (3) 89% were high in personal competencies; (4) 95% had contemporary sex-role views; (5) 21% had limited educational aspirations; (6) 32% had medium educational aspirations; and (7) 47% had high educational aspirations.

Dirks, Marie Metta (Ph. D.). "FACTORS ASSOCIATED WITH THE SOCIAL ACCEPTANCE OF COLLEGE STUDENTS IN HOME ECONOMICS WITH IMPLICATIONS FOR GUIDANCE." Ohio State University, 1946. 251 pp. Source: Dissertation, pp. 198-201.

Implications for guidance for college students in home economics were drawn from findings that friendliness increased when students became acquainted in class; and that religion, nationality, and other background factors except race did not affect friendliness.

Ditty, Dona Doreen (Ph. D.). "SOCIAL-PSYCHOLOGICAL ASPECTS OF CLOTHING PREFERENCES OF COLLEGE WOMEN." Ohio State University, 1962. 200 pp. Source: DAI, XXIV, 1 (July, 1963), 274-275. XUM Order No. 63-4652.

Found that socially mature women used clothing for self-expression, while socially immature women used clothing as a way of conforming to a social role.

Djung, Lu-dzai (Ph. D.). "DEMOCRATIC TENDENCIES IN THE DEVELOPMENT OF MODERN EDUCATION IN CHINA." Stanford University, 1930. 277 pp. Sources: Eells, p. 72; and Published as A HISTORY OF DEMOCRATIC EDUCATION IN MODERN CHINA; Shanghai: Commercial Press, 1934; Stanford University, ABSTRACTS OF DISSERTATIONS (1930-31), pp. 182-188.

Nineteenth century Christian missionaries started China's first girls' schools. The government in 1908 issued its first regulations for girls' elementary and normal schools. Co-education was allowed

in primary schools after 1912 and after 1919 in colleges. The proportion of girls, though low, was higher in the 1920's in Christian
schools than in public schools.

Dobry, Alberta M. (Ph. D.). "SELECTED CHARACTERISTICS OF MICHIGAN
HOME ECONOMICS TEACHERS IN RELATION TO THE SCHOOL SITUATIONS OF THEIR
EMPLOYMENT." Michigan State University, 1973. 230 pp. Source: DAI,
XXXIV, 9A (March, 1974), 5579-A. XUM Order No. 74-6030.

Significant relations found were: (1) between teachers' ages and
the amount of their influence on curriculum decisions; and (2) between years of teaching and the helpfulness of various printed sources used for class content.

Dobson, Margaret June (Ed. D.). "AN EVALUATION OF THE PORTLAND STATE
COLLEGE WOMEN'S PHYSICAL EDUCATION CLASSIFICATION TEST." University of
Oregon, 1966. Source: Author.

The previously established test and testing procedure for identifying selected physical education objectives proved to be valid. This
research established valid test norms for use in interpreting individual women's test results.

Dodds, Jon Howard (Ph. D.). "AN ATTRIBUTION THEORY APPROACH TO THE
CORRELATIONS OF CHILDREN'S ANXIETY WITH IQ, SEX, SES, AND SCHOOL ACHIEVE-
MENT." Syracuse University, 1975. 123 pp. Source: DAI, XXXVII, 4A
(October, 1976), 1957-A-1958-A. XUM Order No. 76-18,507.

Anxiety measures of 150 7th grade boys and girls showed that girls
were more anxious than boys. IQ and achievement, though negatively
related to test anxiety, were unrelated to general anxiety.

Dodge, Norman Barnes (Ed. D.). "DEMOCRACY AND THE EDUCATION OF WO-
MEN: THE COLORADO WOMAN'S COLLEGE STORY." Columbia University Teachers
College, 1960. Source: TCCU DIGESTS (1960), pp. 138-139.

History of Colorado Woman's College and its trend toward shared
rather than centralized administration were examined in the larger
context of U. S. women's higher education.

Doherty, Elizabeth Catherine (Ph. D.). "EDUCATIONAL MOBILITY IN
DIETETICS." University of Pittsburgh, 1976. 125 pp. Source: DAI,
XXXVII, 3A (September, 1976), 1425-A. XUM Order No. 76-19,906.

Investigated competence of dietitians who had associate and baccalaureate level training which emphasized either general, clinical,
or community nutrition. Found common areas of competence among subjects. Little educational mobility existed in the field.

Doherty, Patricia McGinn (Ed. D.). "SELF ACCEPTANCE AS A FUNCTION
OF SAME-SEX PEER RELATIONSHIPS IN ADOLESCENT AND YOUNG ADULT WOMEN."
Boston University School of Education, 1976. 186 pp. Source: DAI,
XXXVII, 3A (September, 1976), 1400-A. XUM Order No. 76-21,228.

Used high school and college women to test the hypothesis, based on
Erikson's theory, that women who disclosed more to female friends

would have higher self-acceptance. Major finding: disclosures to
fathers and male friends were better predictors of self-acceptance
than disclosure to mother or female friend.

Dolan, Frances Anne (Ph. D.). "PERSONAL QUALITIES AND CHARACTERIS-
TICS IMPORTANT IN THE SELECTION OF UNDERGRADUATE STAFF MEMBERS FOR WO-
MEN'S RESIDENCE HALLS." Northwestern University, 1965. 125 pp. Source:
DAI, XXVI, 6 (December, 1965), 3124. XUM Order No. 65-12,071.

Effectiveness of undergraduate women's residence hall staff members
could be improved by: (1) identifying personal qualities and values
needed for the job; (2) informing applicants of precise job requirements; and (3) using well constructed instruments for evaluating
staff.

Dolecki, Lawrence Stanley (Ph. D.). "THE EFFECTS OF ALPHA FEEDBACK
TRAINING ON ANXIETY IN INTERNALLY AND EXTERNALLY CONTROLLED FEMALE STU-
DENTS." University of Georgia, 1975. 126 pp. Source: DAI, XXXVI, 9B
(March, 1976), 4724-B-4725-B. XUM Order No. 76-6396.

This study failed to prove that internally controlled students are
better able to increase their EEG alpha activity than externally controlled subjects.

Donahue, Thomas Joseph (Ph. D.). "DISCRIMINATION AGAINST YOUNG WO-
MEN IN CAREER SELECTION BY HIGH SCHOOL COUNSELORS." Michigan State Uni-
versity, 1976. 217 pp. Source: DAI, XXXVII, 2A (August, 1976), 802-A.
XUM Order No. 76-18,612.

Counselors studied tended to suggest to females lower paying, more
highly supervised jobs which required less education. Female counselors over 40 showed the greatest discrepancy between careers chosen for female and male students while male counselors over age 40
discriminated least against females. Counselors in city schools
discriminated less than did counselors in rural schools.

Donaldson, Mary Louise Moore (Ph. D.). "THE VIDEO TAPE RECORDER AS
A TOOL FOR EVALUATION OF TECHNICAL NURSING SKILLS IN A BACCALAUREATE
NURSING PROGRAM." George Peabody College for Teachers, 1974. 51 pp.
Source: DAI, XXXV, 7B (January, 1975), 3413-B. XUM Order No. 74-
29,160.

Evaluations of nursing students who studied a skill with or without
viewing a video replay of the skill failed to prove conclusively
that such video recordings have value in nursing education.

Donnalley, Mary Jane Metcalf (Ed. D.). "A STUDY OF THE FACTORS
WHICH INFLUENCE WOMEN COLLEGE STUDENTS TO WITHDRAW BEFORE COMPLETING
THEIR DEGREE REQUIREMENTS." University of Virginia, 1966. 75 pp.
Source: DAI, XXVII, 8A (February, 1967), 2388-A. XUM Order No. 66-
15,219.

The most prevalent reason for students' transferring from a woman's
college was to enter a co-educational state university with broader
course offerings. Marriage and low academic achievement caused
most dropouts.

Donnelly, Anne (Ed. D.). "A CURRICULAR FRAMEWORK FOR PROGRAM DEVEL-
OPMENT IN NURSING." Temple University, 1974. 84 pp. Source: DAI,
XXXV, 7A (January, 1975), 4312-A. XUM Order No. 74-28,167.

Explored theoretically the professionalism inherent in nursing as
distinct from the biological and other content aspects of the nursing curriculum.

Donovan, Molly Walsh (Ph. D.). "BELIEFS OF WOMEN IN ROLE INNOVATIVE
AND TRADITIONAL PROFESSIONS ABOUT THEMSELVES AND THEIR FEMALE COLLEAGUES."
George Washington University, 1976. 131 pp. Source: DAI, XXXVII, 11B
(May, 1977), 5809-B. XUM Order No. 77-10,126.

Subjects were 127 first year white female graduate and professional
school students in male-dominated professions (law, medicine, archi-
tecture/urban planning, and computer science) and female-dominated
professions (education, nursing, library science, and social work).
A comparison was made of beliefs on competence and possession of
"feminine" and "masculine" personality traits of those entering each
field. The subjects evaluated how much ability, effort, task ease,
and luck affected their success, using the Personal Attributes Questionnaire. The expected differences were not found. Both groups
attributed their success to ability and effort.

Dooley, Emilie Phoebe (Ed. D.). "AN EXPLORATORY STUDY OF THE EDUCA-
TIONAL VALUES INHERENT IN VARIOUS PATTERNS OF HOUSING FRESHMAN WOMEN IN
COLLEGE RESIDENCE HALLS." Columbia University Teachers College, 1957.
Source: TCCU DIGESTS (1957), pp. 153-155.

More freshman women living in residence halls with upper class women
reported that their study habits were improved than did students in
all-freshmen residences. Students in single-class residence developed stronger class loyalty.

Doran, Lindley Elizabeth (Ph. D.). "THE EFFECT OF ASSERTION TRAIN-
ING WITHIN A CAREER AWARENESS COURSE ON THE SEX-ROLE SELF-CONCEPTS AND
CAREER CHOICES OF HIGH SCHOOL WOMEN." University of Illinois at Urbana-
Champaign, 1976. 147 pp. Source: DAI, XXXVII, 10A (April, 1977),
6270-A-6271-A. XUM Order No. 77-8976.

The study's main hypothesis was supported; i.e., that the experimental group would become more androgynous and less conscious of sex-
role differences.

Dorgan, Jean Nostrand (Ed. D.). "EIGHTEENTH-CENTURY VOICES OF EDU-
CATIONAL CHANGE: MARY WOLLSTONECRAFT AND JUDITH SARGENT MURRAY." Rutgers University, 1976. 217 pp. Source: DAI, XXXVII, 2A (August, 1976),
843-A. XUM Order No. 76-17,312.

This documentary search proved that Wollstonecraft and Murray,
though themselves influenced by their contemporaries, were prophetic
educational theorists whose writings on education are still relevant.

Dorris, Jo Freida (Ed. D.). "THE EFFECTS UPON FRESHMAN WOMEN OF
RESIDENCY IN AN ALL-CLASS HALL." Arizona State University, 1969. 221
pp. Source: DAI, XXXI, 1A (July, 1970), 145-A-146-A. XUM Order No.
70-11,879.

Although residents of all-class halls scored higher on self control
and good impressions, the study found little difference between residents of freshman versus all-class halls in terms of basic college
survival (grades, attrition, and discipline problems).

Dorsch, Helen Elizabeth (Ph. D.). "FACTORS BEARING UPON SELECTION
OF NURSING EDUCATION AS A PROFESSION." Ohio State University, 1957.
179 pp. Source: DAI, XIX, 1 (July, 1958), 117. XUM Order No. Mic 58-
2061.

These factors influenced nurses to become teachers of nursing: marital status, interest in teaching and students, and satisfactions
from teaching.

Dorse, Jeanne Loree (Ed. D.). "CONSUMER AND HOMEMAKING EDUCATION:
A SUGGESTED CURRICULUM MODEL FOR COMMUNITY COLLEGES." University of
Southern California, 1974. 175 pp. Source: DAI, XXXV, 4A (October,
1974), 2003-A-2004-A. XUM Order No. 74-21,468.

After investigating programs in California community colleges, the
researcher recommended for curriculum development: (1) study the
community's composition; (2) verify what resources are available to
students; and (3) examine current literature.

Douglas, Priscilla Delahunt (Ph. D.). "AN ANALYSIS OF DEMOGRAPHIC
CHARACTERISTICS AND CAREER PATTERNS OF WOMEN ADMINISTRATORS IN HIGHER
EDUCATION." University of Connecticut, 1976. 195 pp. Source: DAI,
XXXVIII, 2A (August, 1977), 653-A-654-A. XUM Order No. 77-16,705.

The average administrator was 44 years old, first born, and from a
small family of average means. Her husband was professionally employed, well educated, and they had no children. Her father had a
grammar school education. Her mother had a high school education.
She attended a 4-year co-educational college with a degree in the
humanities. She was more likely to be a non-academic than an academic administrator. She had few periods of unemployment, usually
had been employed primarily at 1 college, and decided late in life
to be an administrator.

Douglin, Junette Jennilin (Ph. D.). "NURSE EDUCATORS' RECEPTIVITY
TO EDUCATIONAL CHANGE: AN EMPIRICAL STUDY." University of Toronto
(Canada), 1973. Source: DAI, XXXV, 1B (July, 1974), 346-B-347-B.

Analyzed the reactions of nurse educators from all Ontario nursing
schools to a basic reform in nursing education.

Dowd, Alice G. (Ed. D.). "A SYSTEMS ANALYSIS OF PERCEPTIONS BY BASIC
VERSUS REGISTERED NURSE BACCALAUREATE STUDENTS OF A COURSE IN NURSING
LEADERSHIP AND ITS EFFECT ON SELF-ESTEEM AND PRODUCTIVITY." Boston Uni-
versity School of Education, 1971. 203 pp. Source: DAI, XXXII, 4A
(October, 1971), 1828-A. XUM Order No. 71-26,696.

All participating students (72) saw a tendency toward synergy in the
nursing course. No significant relationship was found between this
synergistic perception and the students' self-esteem.

Dowe, Mary Catherine (Ed. D.). "A STUDY OF THE CHARACTERISTICS OF TWO SELECTED GROUPS OF STUDENT NURSES." University of Kentucky, 1973. 75 pp. Source: DAI, XXXV, 3B (September, 1974), 1310-B. XUM Order No. 74-19,612.

In intellectual, social, and personality comparisons, the 2 groups of nursing students (in associate degree and baccalaureate programs) were more alike than different.

Downing, Beverly May (Ed. D.). "THE ELECTION OF HOME ECONOMICS BY COLLEGEBOUND GIRLS." Columbia University, 1963. 155 pp. Source: DAI, XXV, 1 (July, 1964), 446-447. XUM Order No. 64-7194.

Some conclusions: A slight tendency existed for college-bound girls in lower socio-economic classes to elect home economics courses. More college-bound girls elected home economics courses if junior high school home economics courses had been satisfying and if senior high schools offered a good home economics program.

Doyle, Sister Margaret Marie (Ph. D.). "THE CURRICULUM OF THE CATH-OLIC WOMAN'S COLLEGE." University of Notre Dame, 1932. 144 pp. Source: Published; Same Title: Berrien Springs, MI: College Press, 1932; pp. 126-128.

Reviewed the history of women's education in the U. S. Recommended a Catholic woman's college curriculum that would, first, prepare women for home responsibilities but also make them an efficient part of society, able to maintain themselves economically.

Doyle, Mary Peter (Ph. D.). "A STUDY OF PLAY SELECTION IN WOMEN'S COLLEGES." Columbia University Teachers College, 1935. Source: TCCU CONTRIBUTIONS No. 648, pp. 55-66.

Analyzed content and likely influence of dramatic plays selected and performed in 51 women's liberal arts colleges.

Drachman, Virginia G. (Ph. D.). "WOMEN DOCTORS AND THE WOMEN'S MEDI-CAL MOVEMENT: FEMINISM AND MEDICINE 1850-1895." State University of New York at Buffalo, 1976. 250 pp. Source: DAI, XXXVII, 8A (February, 1977), 5299-A. XUM Order No. 77-3530.

This reinterpretation of the role of early women medical doctors as-serted that they were important not only for breaking into a male-dominated field. By providing accurate medical data about women, they contributed to the woman's rights movement.

Dreidame, Ruth Elaine (Ph. D.). "A SURVEY OF THE ORGANIZATION AND ADMINISTRATION OF WOMEN'S INTERCOLLEGIATE ATHLETIC PROGRAMS IN THE 1973-74 AIAW ACTIVE MEMBER SCHOOLS." Ohio State University, 1974. 166 pp. Source: DAI, XXXV, 8A (February, 1975), 5094-A. XUM Order No. 75-3049.

Among the findings were: fewer than 10% of institutions studied gave any type of athletic scholarship to women students in 1973-74. In general, women's intercollegiate athletic programs were severely underfinanced.

Dua, Prem Sakhi (Ph. D.). "IDENTIFICATION OF PERSONALITY CHARACTER-ISTICS DIFFERENTIATING ELECTED WOMEN LEADERS FROM NON-LEADERS IN A UNI-VERSITY SETTING." Pennsylvania State University, 1963. 136 pp. Source: DAI, XXIV, 8 (February, 1964), 3145. XUM Order No. 64-1388.

Characteristics identified showed that leaders tended to: (1) take action that would resolve problems; and (2) have a low tolerance for situations that involved dependence on others in taking action or that involved evading an issue.

Dubois, May (Ph. D.). "AN EVALUATION OF THE CURRICULA OF THE SCHOOL OF HOME ECONOMICS, OREGON STATE COLLEGE, BASED ON THE JUDGMENTS OF GRAD-UATES." Ohio State University, 1951. 436 pp. Source: Dissertation, pp. 395-407.

This study showed the extent to which courses fulfilled the criteria set for home economics. Recommendations are about ways home economics courses further democratic living, the teaching methods employed, and necessary guidance facilities.

Ducker, Dalia Golan (Ph. D.). "THE EFFECTS OF TWO SOURCES OF ROLE STRAIN ON WOMEN PHYSICIANS." City University of New York, 1974. 150 pp. Source: DAI, XXXV, 7B (January, 1975), 3552-B. XUM Order No. 74-29,248.

Whether or not a woman physician had ever been married or had children was an important influence on the level of her professional activity and on her feeling that her personal life had suffered.

Dudgeon, Ruth Arlene Fluck (Ph. D.). "WOMEN AND HIGHER EDUCATION IN RUSSIA, 1855-1905." George Washington University, 1975. 454 pp. Source: DAI, XXXVI, 6A (December, 1975), 3922-A-3923-A. XUM Order No. 75-26,000.

Despite women's unrest which began during the Crimean War, Russian authorities restricted women's search for education and jobs. Revo-lutionary groups, having other political concerns, demanded that feminist issues not interfere with revolutionary goals. By 1905, however, the state recognized women's right to higher education.

Duggan, Anne Schley (Ph. D.). "A COMPARATIVE STUDY OF UNDERGRADUATE WOMEN MAJORS AND NON-MAJORS IN PHYSICAL EDUCATION WITH RESPECT TO CERTAIN PERSONAL TRAITS." Columbia University Teachers College, 1936. 117 pp. Source: TCCU CONTRIBUTIONS No. 682, pp. 107-111.

Author developed an interest questionnaire to help counselors identi-fy potential physical education majors. Other important factors in choosing future professional women physical educators were: broad cultural background, high intelligence, motor ability, and satis-factory personality.

Dugger, June Armistead (Ph. D.). "A STUDY OF MEASURABLE PERSONAL FACTORS OF LEADERS AND NON-LEADERS AMONG UNIVERSITY FRESHMAN WOMEN." Florida State University, 1969. 114 pp. Source: DAI, XXX, 5A (Novem-ber, 1969), 1817-A. XUM Order No. 69-17,671.

The most significant discriminators found were grade point average, social extroversion, and autonomy.

Dugo, James M. (Ph. D.). "A TYPOLOGICAL ANALYSIS OF THE PERSONALITY OF THE STUDENT NURSE." Illinois Institute of Technology, 1973. 113 pp. Source: DAI, XXXIV, 5B (November, 1973), 2279-B-2280-B. XUM Order No. 73-27,047.

Student nurses' personalities were like those of college women in general.

Dunagan, Frances Acker (Ed. D.). "A STUDY OF THE RELATIONSHIP BE-TWEEN NURSING EDUCATION ADMINISTRATIVE CLIMATE AND NURSING TEACHER MORALE AS PERCEIVED BY TEACHERS OF NURSING." University of Southern Mississippi, 1976. 106 pp. Source: DAI, XXXVII, 9A (March, 1977), 5479-A-5480-A. XUM Order No. 77-5936.

Significant relationships were found between nursing education's ad-ministrative climate and nursing teacher morale as perceived by nur-sing teachers: (1) employed in baccalaureate schools of nursing; (2) employed for 2 years or more; and (3) employed for 2 years. Length of employment had no significant effect on perceptions of ad-ministrative climate and teacher morale.

Dunbar, Donald Stuart (Ph. D.). "SEX-ROLE IDENTIFICATION AND ACHIEVE-MENT MOTIVATION IN COLLEGE WOMEN." Ohio State University, 1959. 134 pp. Source: DAI, XX, 10 (April, 1960), 4161-4162.

The general hypothesis of a relationship between subjects' sex-role orientation and their achievement projections onto male and female pictures was firmly supported.

Dunbar, Sharon Mae Berliner (Ph. D.). "COLLEGE WOMEN'S SELF ESTEEM AND ATTITUDES TOWARD WOMEN'S ROLES." Michigan State University, 1975. 119 pp. Source: DAI, XXXVI, 9B (March, 1976), 4752-B-4753-B. XUM Or-der No. 76-5549.

This study attempted, first, to delineate 4 female "types" based on levels of self-esteem and degrees of liberality in their attitudes toward women. The only hypothesis tentatively supported was that high esteem groups rated their parents as more communal than low esteem groups.

Duncan, Wanda Louise (Ph. D.). "THE EDUCATIONAL IMPLICATIONS FOR INSTITUTIONS OF HIGHER-ADULT EDUCATION OF A STUDY OF TWENTY WOMEN CREA-TIVES IN THE FIELD OF LITERATURE." University of Oklahoma, 1976. 161 pp. Source: DAI, XXXVII, 5A (November, 1976), 2663-A. XUM Order No. 76-24,379.

All 20 of the creative women had others to care for their homes and businesses during their most productive periods. Half of them were married and only 3 had children.

Dunkerley, Mary Dorothea (Ph. D.). "A STATISTICAL STUDY OF LEADER-SHIP AMONG COLLEGE WOMEN." Catholic University of America, 1940. Source: Author's Article, same title, in STUDIES IN PSYCHOLOGY AND PSYCHIATRY FROM THE CATHOLIC UNIVERSITY OF AMERICA; Washington, DC: Catholic Uni-versity of America Press, 1940, pp. 55-60.

Leaders were found to take initiative in specific situations rather than to have general leadership ability. Intellectual leaders had high IQ scores, high scholastic averages, and extroverted and dominant personalities. Social leaders were more neurotic, more introverted, and more dominant. Religious leaders were less neurotic, more extroverted, and less dominant than non-leaders.

Dunlap, Marjorie Snyder (Ed. D.). "THE DEVELOPMENT OF A PROFESSIONAL GRADUATE PROGRAM IN NURSING." University of Southern California, 1959. 476 pp. Source: DAI, XX, 2 (August, 1959), 643. XUM Order No. Mic 59-2610.

This study recommended 5 areas as essential for preparing nursing teachers and administrators: research (although nursing teachers and administrators themselves rated research as relatively unimportant), statistics, interpersonal relationships, current professional issues, and group behavior.

Dunn, Charleta J. (Ed. D.). "THE DEAN OF WOMEN IN TEXAS STATE-SUPPORTED SENIOR COLLEGES AND UNIVERSITIES, 1965-1966." University of Houston, 1966. 190 pp. Source: DAI, XXVII, 9A (March, 1967), 2770-A. XUM Order No. 66-15,274.

Surveyed deans of women in Texas state colleges and universities in order to develop a common job description. Their duties in public relations, administration, and academic work varied. A doctor's degree was recommended as preparation by 71%; while 100% recommended college courses in counseling and guidance.

Dunnington, Leslie G. (Ph. D.). "THE PERCEIVED ROLE OF THE NURSE AS JUDGED BY NURSING STUDENTS AT VARIOUS STAGES IN THEIR EDUCATIONAL PROGRAMS." University of Wyoming, 1965. 71 pp. Source: Dissertation.

Students' perceptions of the nurse's role became more like faculty perceptions the longer they continued in nurses' training. Freshman students' grades in nursing courses seemed to be related to their perception of the nurse's role.

Duquin, Mary Elizabeth (Ph. D.). "INSTITUTIONAL SANCTION FOR GIRLS' SPORT PROGRAMS: EFFECTS OF FEMALE HIGH SCHOOL STUDENTS." Stanford University, 1975. 85 pp. Source: DAI, XXXV, 12A, Part 1 (June, 1975), 7705-A. XUM Order No. 75-13,517.

Evidence supported the view that, by strongly sanctioning physical education programs, high schools can influence young women to hold favorable attitudes toward sports.

Durazzo, Emma Cash (Ph. D.). "WELFARE WOMEN TRAINED AS TEACHER-AIDES." Pennsylvania State University, 1972. 96 pp. Source: DAI, XXXIII, 10A (April, 1973), 5432-A. XUM Order No. 73-7430.

Systematic interviews showed that their training improved the women's self-image and their ability to work with others toward constructive goals.

Durnall, Edward J., Jr. (Ph. D.). "A COMPARISON OF STUDENT PERSON-NEL PRACTICES IN JUNIOR COLLEGES FOR WOMEN." Oregon State University, 1953. 323 pp. Source: Author's Article (co-author Robert R. Reichart), Same Title, JUNIOR COLLEGE JOURNAL (September, 1954), pp. 41-45.

Junior colleges for women provided as many student personnel services as did public and private junior colleges. Some smaller colleges were unable to offer services with a high degree of professionaliza-tion.

Durongkadej, Somchai (Ed. D.). "A STUDY OF EDUCATION AND TRAINING FOR PUBLIC HEALTH NUTRITIONISTS IN THAILAND." Columbia University, 1974. 218 pp. Source: DAI, XXXV, 4B (October, 1974), 1769-B-1770-B. XUM Or-der No. 74-23,516.

Modifications of the existing curriculum were proposed, including plans for field training in rural areas.

Durrant, Laurice Kafrouni (Ed. D.). "EXPLORING THE EFFECTS OF CERTAIN LEARNING STRATEGIES IN AN AUDIOVISUAL-TUTORIAL INSERVICE NURSING PROGRAM." Stanford University, 1971. 115 pp. Source: DAI, XXXII, 10B (April, 1972), 5887-B-5888-B. XUM Order No. 72-11,695.

Student performance was positively related to time spent using ins-tructional materials. Performance also improved when tests were given after daily instruction.

Dustan, Laura Corbin (Ed. D.). "CHARACTERISTICS OF STUDENTS IN THREE TYPES OF NURSING EDUCATION PROGRAMS." University of California, Berkeley, 1963. 236 pp. Source: DAI, XXIV, 9 (March, 1964), 3697-3698. XUM Or-der No. 64-2164.

Students (379) in 4 nursing programs (1 baccalaureate, 1 associate, and 2 diploma programs) were examined for such characteristics as scholastic aptitude, values and interests, social and economic back-ground, and career expectations. Students in the baccalaureate and diploma programs were appropriately matched with the curricula cho-sen. But many associate degree students were not in the program best suited to their abilities and interests.

Dutton, Ronald Pearson (Ph. D.). "COMMITMENT BY WOMEN TO EDUCATIONAL CAREERS." Harvard University, 1965. Source: Dissertation, pp. 1-5.

Statements by 42 students in diaries kept during 1 academic year were used to devise hypotheses about differences in career develop-ment by sex and training program. Normally less committed to careers than men, women were much more committed who had role models in their field before entering graduate training. Because of a strong sense of service, women were more likely than men to choose teaching and counseling careers.

Dwyer, Sister Mary Bernard (Ph. D.). "HOMEMAKING EDUCATION IN THE CATHOLIC FOUR YEAR COLLEGE FOR WOMEN." University of Nebraska, 1940. 160 pp. Source: Dissertation, pp. 109-113.

Only 2/3 of the colleges studied offered home economics, and their programs were mainly designed to prepare for careers rather than for home making. No general pattern existed in course offerings. A recommended curricular plan was included in the conclusion.

Dye, Celeste Ann Lombardi (Ph. D.). "AN ANALYSIS OF THE EFFECTS OF HUMAN RELATIONS TRAINING UPON STUDENT NURSES' MEASURED ANXIETY, SELF CONCEPT, AND GROUP PARTICIPATION." Purdue University, 1972. 138 pp. Source: DAI, XXXIII, 2B (August, 1972), 795-B. XUM Order No. 72-21,181.

No significant differences in the student nurses were measured as a result of the training given.

Dyer, Annie Isabel Robertson (Ph. D.). "THE ADMINISTRATION OF HOME ECONOMICS IN CITY SCHOOL SYSTEMS." Columbia University Teachers College, 1928. 143 pp. Source: TCCU DIGESTS, I (September, 1925-August, 1929), pp. 152-153.

No marked differences in home economics practices were found. Marked differences existed between home economists and school superintendents, perhaps because superintendents regard home economics as having less value.

Eberhart, Ozella Mae Yowell (Ph. D.). "ELEMENTARY STUDENTS' UNDERSTANDING OF CERTAIN MASCULINE AND NEUTRAL GENERIC NOUNS." Kansas State University, 1976. 165 pp. Source: DAI, XXXVII, 7A (January, 1977), 4113-A-4114-A. XUM Order No. 76-29,993.

Studied the extent to which 121 students in grades 1, 3, and 6 understood that women were included in such generic nouns as "mankind."

Economou, Nick (Ed. D.). "RELATIONSHIPS BETWEEN IDENTITY CONFUSION, IDENTITY CRISIS RESOLUTION, SELF-ESTEEM AND CAREER CHOICE ATTITUDES IN FRESHMAN COLLEGE WOMEN." Rutgers University, 1974. 138 pp. Source: DAI, XXXVI, 2A (August, 1975), 703-A. XUM Order No. 75-17,344.

Freshman college women (140) who resolved their identity crisis had more mature career choice attitudes.

Eddleman, Edna Jacqueline (Ph. D.). "DEVELOPMENT, USE, AND EVALUATION OF AN INDIVIDUALIZED INSTRUCTION UNIT TO TEACH THE CONCEPT 'EVALUATION' AS IT RELATES TO HOME ECONOMICS EDUCATION." Southern Illinois University, 1970. 264 pp. Source: DAI, XXXI, 12B (June, 1971), 7403-B-7404-B. XUM Order No. 71-9987.

All participants judged the approach as at least as good as more traditional group approaches. The objectives of the course were achieved to a larger degree.

Edmondson, Marilyn Annette Ellison (Ed. D.). "THE RELATIONSHIP BETWEEN SELF-CONCEPT AND ACHIEVEMENT IN NURSING EDUCATION." University of Cincinnati, 1976. 118 pp. Source: DAI, XXXVII, 3B (September, 1976), 1178-B. XUM Order No. 76-21,455.

It was concluded that self-concept is not a significant predictor of clinical, theory, or achievement test performance in nursing.

Edwards, Joy White (Ph. D.). "THE RELATIONSHIP OF CREATIVE THINKING ABILITY TO SOCIOMETRIC STATUS AND SEX OF ELEMENTARY SCHOOL CHILDREN." Texas Woman's University, 1973. Source: Dissertation, pp. 61-70.

Found among 122 children aged 8-12 no significant difference between creative thinking ability of boys and girls.

Egan, Mari Jeanne (Ph. D.). "A STUDY OF THE EFFECT OF EDUCATIONAL LEVEL, AGE, AND SEX ON THE VALUES AND SELF CONCEPTS OF ADULT STUDENTS AND ALUMNI OF AN ADULT BACCALAUREATE DEGREE PROGRAM." Ohio State University, 1976. 97 pp. Source: DAI, XXXVII, 11A (May, 1977), 7034-A-7035-A. XUM Order No. 77-10,521.

Results indicated that college experience had little effect on values and self concepts of mature adult students. Several sex differences in values and self concepts were noted with the women's mean scores being significantly more positive in total self concepts.

Ehrhardt, Maryann (Ed. D.). "A SOCIOMETRIC STUDY OF THE FRIENDSHIP STATUS OF COLLEGE WOMEN." Indiana University, 1955. 122 pp. Source: DAI, XV, 9 (1955), 1663-1664. XUM Order No. 13,216.

Among the conclusions: higher friendship status students tended to have higher academic averages than lower friendship status students.

Eidens, Clyde Otis (Ed. D.). "THE WORK OF THE SCHOOL NURSE-TEACHER AS PERCEIVED BY SELECTED PUBLIC SCHOOL STAFF PERSONNEL." Columbia University, 1963. 236 pp. Source: DAI, XXIV, 8 (February, 1964), 3296. XUM Order No. 64-1471.

Perceptions of school nurse duties by principals, teachers, and school nurses indicated that pre-service educational experiences of school nurses should include classroom health instruction.

Eisenhauer, Laurel Antoinette (Ph. D.). "A STUDY OF VARIABLES ASSO-CIATED WITH PERCEIVED ROLE CONFLICT AND ROLE AMBIGUITY IN NURSING FACUL-TY." Boston College, 1977. 152 pp. Source: DAI, XXXVIII, 3A (September, 1977), 1248-A. XUM Order No. 77-18,625.

Suggested that faculty with the least amount of exposure and experience in academia had less role conflict and role ambiguity than those with a moderate amount of such exposure. The group with the highest degree of academic experience generally had less role conflict and role ambiguity than the other groups.

Ekstrom, Doris Evangeline (Ph. D.). "THE BEARING OF THE EXPERIMEN-TALIST'S APPROACH TO GENERAL EDUCATION UPON HOME ECONOMICS IN HIGHER EDUCATION." Ohio State University, 1948. Source: Ohio State University, ABSTRACTS OF DOCTORAL DISSERTATIONS, No. 55 (1949), pp. 83-89.

Advocated general education as an integral part of home economics study in higher education.

Ekstrum, James Michael (Ed. D.). "SEX ROLE PATTERNS AND READING SCORES OF FIRST GRADE CHILDREN." Indiana University, 1972. 52 pp. Source: DAI, XXXIII, 9A (March, 1973), 4934-A. XUM Order No. 73-6972.

Found among 210 first grade girls that those categorized as masculine had better reading vocabularies.

El Bindari, Aleya Mohamed Kamel (Ed. D.). "A CULTURAL APPROACH TO NURSING EDUCATION IN THE UNITED ARAB REPUBLIC." Boston University School of Education, 1965. 461 pp. Source: DAI, XXVI, 9 (March, 1966), 5378. XUM Order No. 66-346.

Results showed that the programs of the Higher Institute of Nursing were not meeting the needs of the Egyptian culture.

Eller, Vercie Massengill (Ed. D.). "ROLE ORIENTATION TOWARD PROFES-SIONAL NURSING OF STUDENTS COMPLETING ASSOCIATE DEGREE, DIPLOMA, AND BACCALAUREATE NURSING EDUCATION PROGRAMS." North Carolina State University at Raleigh, 1976. 137 pp. Source: DAI, XXXVII, 6B (December, 1976), 2770-B. XUM Order No. 76-28,474.

Found that baccalaureate nursing students were more professionally oriented than associate degree and diploma nursing students.

Elliott, Dorothy Virginia (Ed. D.). "A PROPOSED REDESIGN OF THE PATTERN OF THE EDUCATIONAL PROGRAM FOR U. S. ARMY NURSE CORPS OFFICERS." Columbia University Teachers College, 1955. Source: TCCU DIGESTS (1955), pp. 194-195.

Among the recommendations: the pattern of the education program should be redesigned to provide the needed educational opportunities.

Elliott, Eileen Davis (Ph. D.). "EFFECTS OF FEMALE ROLE MODELS ON OCCUPATIONAL ASPIRATION LEVELS OF COLLEGE FRESHMAN WOMEN." University of Missouri-Columbia, 1972. 116 pp. Source: DAI, XXXIV, 3A (September, 1973), 1075-A. XUM Order No. 73-21,412.

Increased information presented via videotaped interviews with female career role models had the effect of increasing the occupational aspiration levels of college freshman females.

Elliott, Eileen Elizabeth (Ed. D.). "AN ANALYSIS OF HOME MANAGEMENT EDUCATION IN COLLEGES AND UNIVERSITIES." University of Missouri, 1947. 213 pp. Source: Dissertation, pp. 139-142.

Author made a national survey of aims, skills needed, and status of home management teachers in colleges and universities.

Elliott, Vida Coe (Ph. D.). "THE EDUCATION OF HINDU WOMEN FROM ANCIENT DAYS WITH ITS BEARING ON THE PREPARATION OF THE HINDU WOMAN FOR HER PLACE IN SOCIETY." Hartford Seminary Foundation, 1947. 436 pp. Source: Dissertation.

Included the influence of western civilization on Indian women's education.

Ellis, Elizabeth Myrna (Ph. D.). "A COMPARATIVE STUDY OF FEMINIST VS. TRADITIONAL GROUP ASSERTIVENESS TRAINING WITH UNASSERTIVE WOMEN." Emory University, 1977. 100 pp. Source: DAI, XXXVIII, 3B (September, 1977), 1397-B. XUM Order No. 77-19,431.

Concluded that the success of feminist therapy may not be attributable to their consciousness-raising format but perhaps to the single-sex composition of such groups and to the type of client who seeks this form of treatment.

Elmore, Joyce Ann (Ph. D.). "THE IDENTIFICATION OF PROBLEMS AND ISSUES OF INTRODUCING COMPUTER APPLICATIONS INTO BACCALAUREATE NURSING PROGRAMS." Catholic University of America, 1974. 189 pp. Source: DAI, XXXV, 4B (October, 1974), 1765-B-1766-B. XUM Order No. 74-22,691.

Among the recommendations: nursing curricula should include content related to computer/electronic data processing with specific modules or courses at undergraduate and graduate levels.

Elmore, Marjorie Jane (Ed. D.). "PROPOSALS RELATING TO THE SELECTION AND ORGANIZATION OF LEARNING EXPERIENCES FOR NURSING STUDENTS IN THE CARE OF OLDER PATIENTS." Columbia University, 1964. 235 pp. Source: DAI, XXV, 9 (March, 1965), 5218. XUM Order No. 65-4727.

It was concluded that the geriatric nursing aspects of the curriculum received little attention in the total planning and evaluation activities in participating schools of nursing.

El-Sanabary, Nagat Morsi (Ph. D.). "A COMPARATIVE STUDY OF THE DISPARITIES OF EDUCATIONAL OPPORTUNITIES FOR GIRLS IN THE ARAB STATES." University of California, Berkeley, 1973. 546 pp. Source: DAI, XXXV, 11A (May, 1975), 6936-A. XUM Order No. 75-8496.

Economic constraints and cultural barriers account for limited progress in women's education in the Arab States.

El-Shamy, Susan Elaine (Ed. D.). "THE EFFECTS OF TIME-SPACING ON OUTCOMES IN ASSERTION TRAINING FOR WOMEN: THE EFFECTIVENESS OF A WORKSHOP MODEL." Indiana University, 1976. 93 pp. Source: DAI, XXXVII, 8A (February, 1977), 4861-A-4862-A. XUM Order No. 77-3333.

Found no differences in outcomes in assertion training of 50 women students, some of whom participated in a shorter workshop and others of whom participated in a longer course.

Elster, Shulamith Reich (Ed. D.). "AN EVALUATIVE STUDY OF A CAREER INFORMATION AND ADVISORY SERVICE FOR WOMEN." George Washington University, 1975. 151 pp. Source: DAI, XXXVI, 6A (December, 1975), 3402-A. XUM Order No. 75-28,855.

Suggested that vocational counseling for women had to be done by trained personnel because paraprofessionals, though helpful, could not effectively do it alone.

Emerson, Shirley Armstrong (Ph. D.). "GUILT FEELINGS IN RETURNING WOMEN STUDENTS." University of Michigan, 1977. 174 pp. Source: DAI, XXXVIII, 3A (September, 1977), 1224-A. XUM Order No. 77-17,989.

Older women (40) returning to college were studied to ascertain the degree of their guilt feelings at leaving husband and children at home.

Engel, Annette (Ph. D.). "THE EFFECTS OF CHILD STUDY ACTIVITIES ON ADOLESCENT GIRLS' ATTITUDES TOWARD CHILD REARING PRACTICES." Arizona State University, 1973. 94 pp. Source: DAI, XXXIV, 7A (January, 1974), 3866-A. XUM Order No. 73-21,887.

Found that girls in grades 7 and 8 learned more about child-rearing practices when the learning goals were clear, the learning methods familiar, and the learning sources authoritative.

Engel, Barbara Alpern (Ph. D.). "FROM FEMINISM TO POPULISM: A STUDY OF CHANGING ATTITUDES OF WOMEN OF THE RUSSIAN INTELLIGENTSIA: 1855-1881." Columbia University, 1974. 345 pp. Source: DAI, XXXVI, 9A (March, 1976), 6242-A. XUM Order No. 76-7356.

A history of the educational advances of Russian women.

Engelman, Herta (Ph. D.). "THE IDEAL ENGLISH GENTLEWOMAN IN THE NINETEENTH CENTURY: HER EDUCATION, CONDUCT, AND SPHERE." Northwestern University, 1956. 411 pp. Source: DAI, XVI, 12 (1956), 2445-2446. XUM Order No. 19,557.

This study covered the early Victorian era, when women's subjugation was stressed, to the late 19th century, when the women's movement had brought about changes.

Englander, Meryl Edwin (Ph. D.). "AN EXPLORATION OF CERTAIN PSYCHO-LOGICAL COMPONENTS RELATED TO THE SELECTION OR REJECTION OF ELEMENTARY TEACHING BY COLLEGE WOMEN." University of Michigan, 1958. 133 pp. Source: DAI, XIX, 3 (September, 1958), 482. XUM Order No. Mic 58-3659.

Concluded that self-concept (the individual's perceptions of personal characteristics and occupations) is important when choosing a vocation.

Enzle, Michael Evans (Ph. D.). "SOMETHING OLD, SOMETHING NEW, SOME-THING BORROWED: AN INTEGRATIVE APPROACH TO RECIPROCAL HELPING." University of Connecticut, 1975. 153 pp. Source: DAI, XXXV, 11B (May, 1975), 5614-B. XUM Order No. 75-10,618.

Women college students responded better when fellow students offered academic and other help out of an internal desire to be helpful.

Epstein, Cynthia Fuchs (Ph. D.). "WOMEN AND PROFESSIONAL CAREERS: THE CASE OF THE WOMAN LAWYER." Columbia University, 1968. 413 pp. Source: DAI, XXX, 2A (August, 1969), 824-A. XUM Order No. 69-9188.

Studied 54 women lawyers and other sources to document that being a woman was more important than were professional qualifications in determining a woman lawyer's success. Found that, despite sex bias, women lawyers who worked long hours and were active in professional organizations could have stable law careers.

Ericksen, Julia Ann (Ph. D.). "WORK ATTACHMENT AND HOME ROLE AMONG A COHORT OF AMERICAN WOMEN." University of Pennsylvania, 1976. 319 pp. Source: DAI, XXXVII, 11A (May, 1977), 7341-A. XUM Order No. 77-10,161.

Results indicated that there was a tradeoff for women between home and work. Age had little effect on women staying at home or working. As education increased, ability to find work increased. Black women were more likely to have a higher work attainment with a higher level of education.

Erickson, Vera Lois (Ph. D.). "PSYCHOLOGICAL GROWTH FOR WOMEN: A COGNITIVE-DEVELOPMENTAL CURRICULUM INTERVENTION." University of Minnesota, 1973. 173 pp. Source: DAI, XXXIV, 7A (January, 1974), 3829-A-3830-A. XUM Order No. 74-766.

A conclusion was that counselors can become psychological educators able to employ their skills to promote personal growth in regular high school classes.

Espin, Oliva Maria (Ph. D.). "CRITICAL INCIDENTS IN THE LIVES OF FEMALE COLLEGE STUDENTS: A COMPARISON BETWEEN WOMEN OF LATIN AMERICA AND THE UNITED STATES." University of Florida, 1974. 120 pp. Source: DAI, XXXVI, 2A (August, 1975), 703-A. XUM Order No. 75-16,379.

Study explored anti-sex and other discriminatory incidents experienced by college women in Latin America and the U. S.

Eustace, Sister Frances Regis (Ph. D.). "FRESHMAN ENGLISH IN SELECTED LIBERAL ARTS COLLEGES FOR WOMEN." Catholic University of America, 1963. 150 pp. Source: DAI, XXIV, 9 (March, 1964), 3639. XUM Order No. 63-7370.

Results showed that the course basically stressed writing, with subject matter varying from lecture courses to reading, rhetoric, and grammar courses.

Evans, Betty Louise (Ph. D.). "THE EDUCATIONAL PREPARATION OF NURSES FROM ABROAD TO FUNCTION IN THEIR HOMELANDS." University of Pittsburgh, 1968. 243 pp. Source: DAI, XXIX, 4B (October, 1968), 1415-B. XUM Order No. 68-13,972.

Recommended that the nurses from India should be enrolled in educational programs offering a combination of clinical and functional preparation.

Evans, Lura Elizabeth (Ph. D.). "THE INFLUENCE OF RELAXATION TECHNIQUES ON THE VARYING LEVEL OF TENSION IN COLLEGE WOMEN." State University of Iowa, 1954. 96 pp. Source: DAI, XIV, 12 (1954), 2284. XUM Order No. 10,209.

Author stated that the average woman college student can be taught physical activities to reduce everyday tensions.

Everett, Anna Elizabeth (Ed. D.). "THREE DIFFERENT APPROACHES TO TEACHING THE CONCEPTS OF OPERATING ROOM NURSING WITHIN THE COURSE OF MEDICAL-SURGICAL NURSING." University of Maryland, 1970. 180 pp. Source: DAI, XXXII, 1B (July, 1971), 393-B-394-B. XUM Order No. 71-17,214.

Among the conclusions: the surgical cycle clinical experience
proved to be more effective than either planned observation or surgical follow-through clinical experience in learning the concepts
of operating room nursing.

Fagerburg, Joan Emeline (Ph. D.). "A COMPARATIVE STUDY OF UNDER-
GRADUATE WOMEN IN RELATION TO SELECTED PERSONAL CHARACTERISTICS AND CER-
TAIN EFFECTS OF EDUCATIONAL INTERRUPTION." Purdue University, 1967.
139 pp. Source: DAI, XXVIII, 11A (May, 1968), 4445-A-4446-A. XUM Order No. 68-6299.

Among the conclusions: women who have had their education interrupted differ from those who have not. Young and single women have
the least academic success. Married women have more academic success than single men.

Faherty, William Barby (Ph. D.). "RECENT POPES ON WOMAN'S POSITION
IN SOCIETY." Saint Louis University, 1949. 318 pp. Source: Dissertation, pp. 50, 187-192, 217-223.

Analyzed papal statements on women's education, religious and secular, including home, school, reading, and other media influences.

Fahey, Sister Mary Ralph (Ph. D.). "THE IN-SERVICE TRAINING OF
RELIGIOUS SECONDARY SCHOOL TEACHERS IN CONGREGATIONS OF WOMEN IN THE
UNITED STATES." Fordham University, 1960. 143 pp. Source: Disserta-
tion, pp. 107-113.

Examined in-service education of Catholic women's order who teach
in Catholic high schools.

Fahy, Ellen Therese (Ed. D.). "PROPOSALS FOR FACILITATING INTER-
NATIONAL EXCHANGE OF RESOURCES OF PROFESSIONAL NURSING (WITH SPECIAL EM-
PHASIS ON FOUR SCANDINAVIAN COUNTRIES)." Columbia University, 1963.
212 pp. Source: DAI, XXV, 1 (July, 1964), 413-414. XUM Order No.
64-5681.

Concluded that the American nursing profession had the responsibility
for instituting programs of international education exchanges involving personnel and educational materials.

Fairhurst, Claire Perrault (Ph. D.). "THE ASSESSMENT OF COUNSELORS'
ATTITUDES TOWARD THE COMBINING OF A CAREER AND MARRIAGE BY WOMEN." Ohio
University, 1969. 145 pp. Source: DAI, XXX, 6A (December, 1969),
2329-A-2330-A. XUM Order No. 69-19,861.

Women public school counselors were more positive than men about
women combining career and marriage; men were not against it.

Fallon, Sister Marjorie (Ph. D.). "AN EXPLORATORY STUDY TO DETER-
MINE ATTITUDES OF YOUNG WOMEN AT ST. JOSEPH COLLEGE, WEST HARTFORD, CON-
NECTICUT, TOWARD THEIR FUTURE ROLE IN THE CHURCH." New York University,
1973. 228 pp. Source: DAI, XXXIII, 10A (April, 1973), 5573-A-5574-A.
XUM Order No. 73-8195.

Women in a Catholic college wanted more opportunities in church leadership.

Fand, Alexandra Botwinik (Ph. D.). "SEX ROLE AND SELF CONCEPT; A STUDY OF THE FEMININE SEX ROLE AS PERCEIVED BY EIGHTY-FIVE COLLEGE WOMEN FOR THEMSELVES, THEIR IDEAL WOMAN, THE AVERAGE WOMAN AND MEN'S IDEAL WOMAN." Cornell University, 1955. 144 pp. Source: DAI, XV, 6 (1955), 1135-1136. XUM Order No. 11,901.

Found among 85 freshman women in a college of home economics that their self-concept influenced their views of women's role.

Farley, Jennie Tiffany Towle (Ph. D.). "WOMEN ON THE MARCH AGAIN: THE REBIRTH OF FEMINISM IN AN ACADEMIC COMMUNITY." Cornell University, 1970. 289 pp. Source: DAI, XXXI, 12A (June, 1971), 6730-A. XUM Order No. 71-13,805.

Includes suggestions for changing the place of women in any academic community.

Farnoodymeher, Nehzat Salehian (Ph. D.). "PSYCHOSOCIAL SURVEY OF ATTITUDES TOWARD EQUAL RIGHTS FOR WOMEN (IRAN)." United Stated International University, 1975. 97 pp. Source: DAI, XXXVI, 3B (September, 1975), 1504-B. XUM Order No. 75-19,111.

Both male and female respondents chose higher education and working with men in organized groups as the preferred way for women to overcome discrimination.

Farrell, Richard J., Jr. (Ed. D.). "AN EXPLORATION OF THE REASONS FOR INITIAL ENROLLMENT IN COLLEGE COURSES BY MIDDLE-AGED WOMEN: TWELVE CASE STUDIES." State University of New York at Albany, 1975. 116 pp. Source: DAI, XXXV, 12A, Part 1 (June, 1975), 7594-A. XUM Order No. 75-13,862.

Personal factors were most important in the decision to enroll in college.

Farrelly, John Francis (Ph. D.). "THE EFFECTS OF COACTORS, SEX OF COACTORS, AND ABILITY LEVEL UPON PERFORMANCE OF A SIMPLE MOTOR TASK." Florida State University, 1976. 142 pp. Source: DAI, XXXVII, 12A, Part 1 (June, 1977), 7612-A. XUM Order No. 77-13,314.

Results indicated that female performance is affected when coaction between males and females occur whereas males performed better with coactors of high ability, regardless of sex. Low ability groups showed no significant differences.

Farthing, Frances Marian (Ed. D.). "BACKGROUNDS, CAREER DECISIONS, AND JOB SATISFACTIONS OF NURSING FACULTY IN ASSOCIATE AND BACCALAUREATE DEGREE PROGRAMS IN THE SOUTHERN REGION." Florida State University, 1968. 134 pp. Source: DAI, XXX, 2B (August, 1969), 721-B-722-B. XUM Order No. 69-11,295.

The trend in nursing education is changing from a hospital-related diploma school to a university-sponsored one.

Feagans, Janet (Ph. D.). "FEMALE POLITICAL ELITES: CASE STUDIES OF FEMALE LEGISLATORS." Howard University, 1972. 196 pp. Source: DAI, XXXV (December, 1974), 3826-A. XUM Order No. 74-15,957.

Found that 22 women in the U. S. Congress and 2 state legislatures were: married, half were mothers, 17 had been to graduate school, had advanced through long volunteer political party work, and generally were from small towns or rural areas.

Fecher, Agnes Anne Rohlof (Ed. D.). "CAREER PATTERNS OF WOMEN IN COLLEGE AND UNIVERSITY ADMINISTRATION." Indiana University, 1972. 148 pp. Source: DAI, XXXIII, 11A (May, 1973), 6115-A. XUM Order No. 73-10,765.

Found that women do not have similar educational backgrounds. Generally, they accept new positions within the same institution rather than look for positions elsewhere.

Feeney, Helen Marie (Ph. D.). "INTEREST VALUES AND SOCIAL CLASS AS RELATED TO ADULT WOMEN WHO ARE CONTINUING THEIR EDUCATION." New York University, 1972. 145 pp. Source: DAI, XXXIII, 10A (April, 1973), 5835-A. XUM Order No. 73-8163.

Author studied the intellectualism of 2 social classes among 126 married women college students.

Fein, Sophia Richman (Ph. D.). "CONCEPTUAL TEMPO AND ABSTRACT REASONING IN COLLEGE STUDENTS: A STUDY OF THE EFFECTS OF INDIVIDUAL DIFFERENCES IN SPEED AND CONFIDENCE OF JUDGMENT ON ABSTRACT REASONING PERFORMANCE OF COLLEGE FEMALES." New York University, 1970. 139 pp. Source: DAI, XXXI, 11A (May, 1971), 5840-A-5841-A. XUM Order No. 71-13,639.

Studied the abstract reasoning abilities of 12 college freshman women.

Feinburg, Sylvia Gruber (Ed. D.). "SEX DIFFERENCES AND SIMILARITIES IN CHILDREN'S PICTORIAL REPRESENTATIONS OF FIGHTING AND HELPING." Harvard University, 1976. 171 pp. Source: DAI, XXXVII, 6B (December, 1976), 3045-B-3046-B. XUM Order No. 76-26,746.

Second and 3rd grade children drew pictures in response to the words "fighting" and "helping" and then described their pictures. Girls personalized, boys depersonalized "fighting." Girls represented the person being "helped" as an integral part of the picture, boys as an event in isolation. Concluded that differences were caused by subject matter preference rather than by sex-bound predisposition.

Feinman, Clarice (Ph. D.). "IMPRISONED WOMEN: A HISTORY OF THE TREATMENT OF WOMEN INCARCERATED IN NEW YORK CITY, 1932-1975." New York University, 1976. 336 pp. Source: DAI, XXXVIII, 2A (August, 1977), 970-A. XUM Order No. 77-16,480.

Initially, women were imprisoned for short terms and received mainly custodial care. After 1954 they were taught to be cooks, waitresses, seamstresses, beauticians, typists, homemakers, and mothers. Currently, they are offered mental health services, coeducation, home-like environment, counseling, and contact visits with children.

Feldman, Gail Carr (Ph. D.). "THE ONLY CHILD AS A SEPARATE ENTITY: AT ATTEMPT TO DIFFERENTIATE ONLY FEMALES FROM FIRSTBORN FEMALES." University of New Mexico, 1976. 144 pp. Source: DAI, XXXVII, 5A (November, 1976), 2633-A-2634-A. XUM Order No. 76-25,661.

Found among 75 firstborn college women that: (1) those with brothers were responsible, confident, and thoughtful; (2) those with sisters were more conventional and dependent; and (3) those who were only children were confident, resourceful, and assertive.

Feldman, Saul Daniel (Ph. D.). "ESCAPE FROM THE DOLL'S HOUSE: WOMEN IN GRADUATE AND PROFESSIONAL SCHOOL EDUCATION." University of Washington, 1972. 268 pp. Source: DAI, XXXIII, 5A (November, 1972), 2509-A. XUM Order No. 72-28,596.

This study examined the status of sex-based inequality. It verified that barriers exist for women that are not present for men.

Felmly, Merritt Frederick (Ph. D.). "THE UTILITY OF BIOGRAPHICAL, PERSONALITY, AND ATTITUDINAL VARIABLES IN THE PREDICTION OF SUCCESS IN NURSES' TRAINING." Baylor University, 1974. 146 pp. Source: DAI, XXXV, 11B (May, 1975), 5615-B. XUM Order No. 75-10,775.

The results showed that biographical data were the most reliable source for predicting success in nurses' training.

Ferguson, Helen Louise (Ed. D.). "AN AUTO-TUTORIAL AUDIO-VISUAL AID RELATED TO TEACHING BASIC MATHEMATICAL SKILLS TO NURSING STUDENTS." Indiana University, 1976. 126 pp. Source: DAI, XXXVII, 8B (February, 1977), 3869-B-3870-B. XUM Order No. 77-3286.

Compared how associate degree nurse students and vocational nursing students learned basic math skills.

Ferguson, William Franklin (Ed. D.). "A COMPARISON BASED ON MEAN SCORES OF CERTAIN PRE-COLLEGE TESTS AND INVENTORIES OF SELECTED GROUPS OF FEMALE TEACHERS AND NON-TEACHER GRADUATES OF THE UNIVERSITY OF MISSISSIPPI." University of Mississippi, 1969. 116 pp. Source: DAI, XXXI, 1A (July, 1970), 262-A-263-A. XUM Order No. 70-11,483.

Compared pre-college tests of 152 women with tests taken at their graduation; some qualified as elementary school teachers, others as secondary school teachers, and the rest were non-teachers.

Fernandez, Louise S. (Ed. D.). "AN EXPLORATION OF WOMEN COLLEGE STUDENTS' INTERPRETATION OF MARITAL ROLES OF MEN AND WOMEN AS INDICATED BY THEIR RESPONSES TO FAMILY LIVING SITUATIONS IN SELECTED MOTION PICTURES WHERE ALL STUDENTS WERE IN THE HOME ECONOMICS DEPARTMENT." New York University, 1953. 277 pp. Source: DAI, XIII, 4 (1953), 515-516. XUM Order No. 5433.

The findings of this study have implications for content, methods, and techniques of family life courses.

Ferris, Patricia Ann (Ph. D.). "AN EXPERIMENT TO DETERMINE THE VALUE OF SYSTEMATIC FEEDBACK TO NEW TEACHERS OF NURSING IN CHANGING SELECTED CLASSROOM VERBAL BEHAVIORS." University of Washington, 1972. 72 pp. Source: DAI, XXXIII, 1A (July, 1972), 141-A. XUM Order No. 72-20,864.

Explored the value of student verbal feedback to instructors by 8 new teachers of college nursing.

Filella, James Ferrer (Ph. D.). "EDUCATIONAL AND SEX DIFFERENCES IN THE ORGANIZATION OF ABILITIES IN TECHNICAL AND ACADEMIC STUDENTS IN COLOMBIA, SOUTH AMERICA." Fordham University, 1957. 178 pp. Source: Dissertation, pp. 1-9.

In a comparison of boys and girls in a private academic school, found that: (1) the two sexes had striking similarities; but (2) boys' abilities were less highly differentiated than were those of girls.

Finger, Bernice (Ed. D.). "AN ADMINISTRATIVE GUIDE FOR THE PROGRAM OF PHYSICAL EDUCATION FOR COLLEGE WOMEN." Columbia University Teachers College, 1956. Source: TCCU DIGESTS (1956), pp. 216-218.

Survey of how 187 college women's physical education programs were organized and administered.

Finger, Marie M. (Ph. D.). "A STUDY OF FRESHMAN WOMEN IN A TEACHERS COLLEGE." Northwestern University, 1940. 302 pp. Source: Dissertation, pp. 225-227.

A conclusion is that the colleges which train teachers should attempt to set up a more adequate standard for admission and should maintain throughout the entire program progressive minimum standards of development.

Finlayson, Elizabeth Mason (Ed. D.). "A STUDY OF THE WIFE OF THE ARMY OFFICER: HER ACADEMIC AND CAREER PREPARATION, HER CURRENT EMPLOYMENT AND VOLUNTEER SERVICES." George Washington University, 1969. 183 pp. Source: DAI, XXXI, 4A (October, 1970), 1564-A-1565-A. XUM Order No. 70-19,727.

Found that the Army officer's wife is well educated, that over 80% have education past high school and 40% have bachelor's degrees.

Finley, Esther M. (Ed. D.). "FACTORS INFLUENCING EDUCATION FOR NURSING IN THE NEAR EAST." Columbia University Teachers College, 1955. Source: TCCU DIGESTS (1955), pp. 213-215.

Cultural factors and a code of ethics were seen as needs for the education of nurses in the Near East, along with education of village nurses and paraprofessional auxiliaries.

Fisher, Robert Lawrence (Ph. D.). "AN EMPIRICAL TYPOLOGY OF COLLEGE WOMEN'S PERSONAL ROLE CONCEPTIONS." University of California, Berkeley, 1973. 183 pp. Source: DAI, XXXIV, 9B (March, 1974), 4660-B. XUM Order No. 74-7508.

Found 8 role-preference types among college women, 4 of which were psychologically analyzed.

Fisher, Robert Thaddeus (Ed. D.). "A HISTORICAL STUDY OF THE EDUCA-
TIONAL THEORIES CONTAINED IN THE CLASSICAL UTOPIAS." Michigan State Uni-
versity, 1959. 293 pp. Source: DAI, XXI, 2 (August, 1960), 310-311.
XUM Order No. Mic 60-1711.

Equal educational opportunity for women characterized such utopian
works analyzed as Plato, The Republic; Thomas More, Utopia; Campanel-
la, City of the Sun; Andreae, Christianopolis; Francis Bacon, New
Atlantis; and Jean Jacques Rousseau, Social Contract and Emile.

Fitzgerald, Tom J. (Ed. D.). "AN ANALYTICAL AND EVALUATIVE STUDY OF
SELECTED ASPECTS OF CERTAIN SECONDARY SCHOOL GIRLS' PHYSICAL EDUCATION
PROGRAMS IN NEBRASKA." University of Nebraska, Lincoln, 1974. 140 pp.
Source: DAI, XXXV, 8A (February, 1975), 5094-A-5095-A. XUM Order No.
75-3404.

High school girls' physical education programs taught by women were
of better quality than programs taught by men. But measured against
national fitness levels, the girls' physical education programs were
rated poor.

Flaherty, Sister Mary Rosalie (Ph. D.). "PATTERNS OF ADMINISTRATION
IN CATHOLIC COLLEGES FOR WOMEN IN THE UNITED STATES." Catholic Univer-
sity of America, 1960. Source: Published; Same Title; Washington, DC:
Catholic University of America Press, 1960, pp. 88-90.

Studied 39 Catholic women's colleges in the eastern U. S. Concluded
that: (1) their administrators showed sound understanding and use
of principles of administration; and (2) patterns of administration
in Catholic colleges for women were similar to those of American
higher education generally.

Fleniken, Dennis Wayne (Ph. D.). "A LONGITUDINAL STUDY OF ACADEMIC
ACHIEVEMENT IN TERMS OF AGE OF ENTRY INTO FIRST GRADE." Louisiana State
University, 1974. 86 pp. Source: DAI, XXXVI, 1 (July, 1975), 238-A.
XUM Order No. 75-14,247.

Concluded that sex as a factor in achievement was shown to increase
in influence as the years of study progressed.

Flynn, Shirley Katherine (Ed. D.). "AN ANALYSIS OF THE RECREATIONAL
BEHAVIOR AND PERSONALITY CHARACTERISTICS OF A SELECT GROUP OF COLLEGE
WOMEN WHO EXHIBITED ATYPICAL SOCIAL BEHAVIOR." University of North Carolina at Greensboro, 1972. 87 pp. Source: DAI, XXXIII, 4A (October,
1972), 1535-A. XUM Order No. 72-24,941.

Found among 37 college women who were drug or alcohol violators that
drug violators were less interested and alcohol violators more interested in physical recreation and that the drug violators responded
randomly and in a less meaningful way.

Foley, Margaret Mary (Ph. D.). "THE HOSPITAL SCHOOL OF NURSING: AN
ANALYSIS AND AN EVALUATION." Saint Louis University, 1961. 175 pp.
Source: DAI, XXII, 9 (March, 1962), 3162. XUM Order No. 61-6466.

From a review of literature about Catholic nursing education, the author concluded that the redirection of nursing from task-technique to personal patient service fitted Catholic nurse educators' concept of "the spirit of nursing."

Follingstad, Diane Ruth (Ph. D.). "DECREASING CONFORMING BEHAVIOR IN WOMEN--AN INTERVENTION UTILIZING MALE SUPPORT FOR FEMALES' ABILITIES AND AN EXPLORATION OF PERSONALITY VARIABLES INFLUENCING LEVELS OF CON-FORMITY." University of Colorado, 1974. 116 pp. Source: DAI, XXXV, 12B, Part 1 (June, 1975), 6163-B-6164-B. XUM Order No. 75-13,475.

This highly structured study of conforming behavior failed to find a significant difference between men and women. As hypothesized, those women with less need for social approval conformed significantly less than did those with more need for social approval.

Ford, Betty Joan (Ph. D.). "A STUDY OF THE RELATIONSHIP BETWEEN CERTAIN PREDICTIVE MEASURES AND ON-THE-JOB PERFORMANCE IN A SELECTED GROUP OF NURSES." University of Wisconsin, 1967. 55 pp. Source: DAI, XXVIII, 8A (February, 1968), 2982-A-2983-A. XUM Order No. 67-12,423.

The major finding was that the most effective predictor of nursing success was the students' course grade.

Ford, Eddy Lucius (Ph. D.). "THE HISTORY OF THE EDUCATIONAL WORK IN THE METHODIST EPISCOPAL CHURCH IN CHINA: A STUDY OF ITS DEVELOPMENT AND PRESENT TRENDS." Northwestern University, 1936. 294 pp. Source: Eells, p. 73; and Northwestern University, SUMMARIES OF DOCTORAL DISSERTATIONS, IV (1936), pp. 82-86.

This mission had trouble getting girl students in its first (1859) boarding school for girls because of the low estimate the Chinese had for their daughters. Author described subsequent educational efforts, including those for women, up through higher education.

Ford, Roxana Ruth (Ph. D.). "DEVELOPMENT AND USE OF EVALUATIVE CRI-TERIA FOR ADULT EDUCATION IN HOMEMAKING IN THE PUBLIC SCHOOLS WITH SPE-CIAL REFERENCE TO IOWA." Iowa State University, 1949. 224 pp. Source: Dissertation, pp. 178-184.

Developed and found criteria useful for judging the value of adult education homemaking programs in Iowa public schools.

Forest, Betty Lucille (Ed. D.). "THE UTILIZATION OF ASSOCIATE DE-GREE NURSING GRADUATES IN GENERAL HOSPITALS." Columbia University, 1965. 149 pp. Source: DAI, XXVI, 8 (February, 1966), 4583-4584. XUM Order No. 65-14,967.

Associate degree nursing graduates performed functions for which they had been prepared and additional functions for which they had not been prepared.

Forest, Sister Cecile Agnes (Ph. D.). "THE RELIGIOUS ACADEMIC WOMAN: A STUDY OF ADJUSTMENT TO MULTIPLE ROLES." Fordham University, 1966. 336 pp. Source: DAI, XXVII, 6A (December, 1966), 1939-A. XUM Order No. 66-13,507.

In a study of Catholic teaching sisters in 28 Catholic women's colleges the author found that the sisters experienced strains in integrating their religious and academic responsibilities.

Forst, Florence Handy (Ph. D.). "DESIGN DECISIONS OF WOMEN AFTER
COLLEGE." University of Pittsburgh, 1962. 129 pp. Source: DAI, XXIII,
6 (December, 1962), 1968. XUM Order No. 62-5122.

The study provided a basis for planning art education for college
women. It was recommended that for art education to be effective
the interdependence of social and aesthetic values should be stressed.

Fort, Ada (Ed. D.). "PLANNING GRADUATE EDUCATION AT EMORY UNIVERSITY
TOWARD THE IMPROVEMENT OF NURSING PRACTICE." Columbia University Teachers College, 1961. Source: TCCU DIGESTS (1961), pp. 196-198.

Author recommended adding a moral and spiritual value unit to the
graduate nursing program at Emory University, GA.

Foss, Jean Lois (Ph. D.). "A HISTORY OF PROFESSIONAL PREPARATION IN
PHYSICAL EDUCATION FOR WOMEN IN THE TEACHERS COLLEGES OF WISCONSIN, ILLI-
NOIS, AND IOWA." University of Iowa, 1966. 229 pp. Source: DAI, XXVII,
9A (March, 1967), 2847-A-2848-A. XUM Order No. 67-2614.

An historical treatment of the undergraduate and graduate programs
in women's physical education in the teachers' colleges of the 3
states.

Foster, Grace R. (Ph. D.). "SOCIAL CHANGE IN RELATION TO CURRICULAR
DEVELOPMENT IN COLLEGIATE EDUCATION FOR WOMEN." Columbia University
Teachers College, 1933. Source: TCCU DIGESTS, VIII (1933), pp. 117-120.

Findings revealed 2 needs: (1) for the revision of college programs
along vocational lines; and (2) for educational and vocational guidance.

Foster, Rosebud Lightbourn (Ed. D.). "THE DEVELOPMENT OF CURRICULUM
GUIDELINES BASED UPON THE ROLE AND PERCEPTION OF PROFESSIONAL NURSES IN
HEALTH AND LICENSURE-RELATED LEGISLATION IN THE STATE OF FLORIDA." University of Miami, 1976. 277 pp. Source: DAI, XXXVIII, 2B (August,
1977), 580-B-581-B. XUM Order No. 77-12,920.

Significant differences were found between nurse groups on the issues
of familiarity with current laws related to health. Teaching skills
were significant and identified as a means to promote responsiveness
and to strengthen the nurses' political influence. Significant differences were found between the attitude of nurses related to age,
length of experience, and type of degree possessed.

Fought, Carol Ann (Ph. D.). "THE HISTORICAL DEVELOPMENT OF CONTINU-
ING EDUCATION FOR WOMEN IN THE UNITED STATES: ECONOMIC, SOCIAL, AND
PSYCHOLOGICAL IMPLICATIONS." Ohio State University, 1966. 413 pp.
Source: DAI, XXVII, 9A (March, 1967), 2838-A. XUM Order No. 67-2444.

The study emphasized the influence of women's needs for power and
the development of women's continuing education.

Fowler, Anne Clerke (Ph. D.). "THE CONTEMPORARY NEGRO SUBCULTURE: AN EXPLORATORY STUDY OF LOWER-CLASS NEGRO WOMEN OF NEW ORLEANS." Tulane University, 1970. 296 pp. Source: DAI, XXXI, 9A (March, 1971), 4922-A. XUM Order No. 71-8046.

Influence of education was one of the factors considered in this study of 120 lower-class southern urban black women.

Fowler, Marguerite Gilbert (Ph. D.). "PERSONALITY DYNAMICS AND BIO-GRAPHICAL FACTORS ASSOCIATED WITH OCCUPATIONAL ROLE-INNOVATION IN FE-MALES." University of Florida, 1976. 147 pp. Source: DAI, XXXVII, 10B (April, 1977), 5350-B. XUM Order No. 77-6868.

Among advanced university students, studied the relationship of the female sex role to female self-concept. Found that: (1) high femi-ninity was not significantly related to locus of control or to trad-itionality in sex role; (2) women in innovative roles were not more masculine; and (3) women with greater self-devaluation tendencies showed less psychological dominance.

Fowler, Stanley Earl (Ph. D.). "FAMILY RELATIONSHIPS AS VIEWED BY TEENAGERS." Florida State University, 1955. 107 pp. Source: DAI, XV, 5 (1955), 1136-1137. XUM Order No. 11,678.

Studied attitudes toward family relationships among 572 white male and female high school students. Found that: (1) boys and girls' attitudes did not differ significantly regarding 3 family life styles; but (2) their attitudes showed great variation and differed significantly with their parents' attitudes. Recommended that those teaching family life courses study parental attitudes and plan pro-grams to narrow the gap between adolescents and their parents.

Fox, Frances Jaunita (Ed. D.). "BLACK WOMEN ADMINISTRATORS IN THE DENVER PUBLIC SCHOOLS." University of Colorado, 1975. 167 pp. Source: DAI, XXXVI, 11A (May, 1976), 7089-A-7090-A. XUM Order No. 76-11,574.

Found in Denver, CO, public schools that there were disproportion-ately fewer black women administrators and that they had more ob-stacles to advancement than did other women and men administrators.

Fox, Loreda Lynn White (Ed. D.). "A COMPARATIVE ANALYSIS OF INTER-NAL-EXTERNAL LOCUS OF CONTROL AND SEX-ROLE CONCEPTS IN BLACK AND WHITE FRESHMAN WOMEN." East Texas State University, 1975. 79 pp. Source: DAI, XXXVI, 8A (February, 1976), 5143-A-5144-A. XUM Order No. 76-4631.

Found among 329 black and white college freshman women no differences in sex-role orientation or in locus of control.

Fox, Lynn Hussey (Ph. D.). "FACILITATING THE DEVELOPMENT OF MATHE-MATICAL TALENT IN YOUNG WOMEN." Johns Hopkins University, 1974. 218 pp. Source: DAI, XXXV, 7B (January, 1975), 3553-B. XUM Order No. 74-29,027.

The special summer program was designed to improve young girls' com-petence in math by appealing to their social interest. This program was more successful than were 3 co-educational accelerated math class-es.

Fox, Margaret Mary (Ed. D.). "A STUDY OF PROFESSIONAL ACTIVITIES OF REGISTERED NURSE GRADUATES OF A CAREER LADDER PROGRAM." University of Southern California, 1975. Source: DAI, XXXVI, 9A (March, 1976), 5848-A-5849-A.

Descriptive, longitudinal, and follow-up study of a San Diego City College, CA, nursing career progression program which enabled licensed vocational nurses to become state-licensed registered nurses.

Francis, Barbara Richardson (Ph. D.). "EFFECT OF MATERNAL EMPLOYMENT ON THE SOCIALIZATION OF SEX ROLE AND ACHIEVEMENT IN NEW ZEALAND." Cornell University, 1975. 349 pp. Source: DAI, XXXVI, 4A (October, 1975), 2452-A-2453-A. XUM Order No. 75-22,994.

New Zealand working mothers were more important than working fathers as role models for their daughters, setting higher expectations and standards which the daughters fulfilled.

Francis, Eileen Marian Casey (Ph. D.). "SELECTED CLOTHING USAGE AND BUYING PRACTICES OF A SPECIFIED GROUP OF COLLEGE WOMEN AND THEIR MOTHERS." Pennsylvania State University, 1971. 181 pp. Source: DAI, XXXIII, 1B (July, 1972), 304-B. XUM Order No. 72-19,303.

Studied differences in clothing selection and consumer behavior between 50 non-home economics college women and their mothers.

Francis, Margaret Rose (Ed. D.). "RELATIONSHIPS AMONG SCHOOL NURSES' VERBAL BEHAVIOR IN TEACHER-NURSE CONFERENCES, THEIR KNOWLEDGE OF PRINCIPLES OF HUMAN DEVELOPMENT AND ATTITUDES TOWARD CHILDREN'S BEHAVIOR." University of Maryland, 1968. 157 pp. Source: DAI, XXX, 2A (August, 1969), 581-A-582-A. XUM Order No. 69-12,938.

Found among 35 public health nurses who worked part-time in Washington, DC, public schools that their knowledge of human development was positively related to their attitude toward children's behavior.

Franken, Mary L. (Ed. D.). "SEX ROLE EXPECTATIONS IN CHILDREN'S VOCATIONAL ASPIRATIONS AND PERCEPTIONS OF OCCUPATIONS." Drake University, 1976. 140 pp. Source: DAI, XXXVII, 10A (April, 1977), 6271-A-6272-A. XUM Order No. 77-8346.

Interviewed 120 boys and girls from 3 grades and 2 socio-economic levels about their job goals; also showed slides about 30 occupations. Found that: (1) first choice for their future occupations was significantly related to their being boys or girls; (2) perceiving jobs as sex-related decreased as the students' grade levels increased; and (3) lower socio-economic children perceived jobs as sex-related more often than did middle-class children. Recommended that school programs try to broaden children's sex-role expectations.

Franklin, Doris Rosalie (Ed. D.). "THE RELATIONSHIP BETWEEN SELECTIVE AND NON-SELECTIVE ADMISSIONS CRITERIA IN JUNIOR COLLEGE NURSING PROGRAMS IN NEW YORK STATE AND ATTRITION, REASONS FOR ATTRITION, FINAL CUMULATIVE GRADE POINT AVERAGES, AND STATE BOARD EXAMINATION SCORES." Columbia University, 1970. 167 pp. Source: DAI, XXXII, 6A (December, 1971), 2945-A. XUM Order No. 72-1232.

Among the findings: selective admissions graduates showed a closer correlation between final grade point average and state board exam scores. More of them succeeded in passing state boards on the first attempt.

Franzblau, Rose Nadler (Ph. D.). "RACE DIFFERENCES IN MENTAL AND PHYSICAL TRAITS STUDIED IN DIFFERENT ENVIRONMENTS." Columbia University, 1935. 44 pp. Source: ARCHIVES OF PSYCHOLOGY, No. 177 (April, 1935), pp. 41-42.

Except for slightly earlier physical maturity, no intelligence or other important differences were found in Danish-American and Italian-American girls compared with their counterparts in Denmark and Italy.

Frazier, Frances (Ed. D.). "GUIDES FOR NURSING EDUCATION CONSULTANTS IN PLANNING AND ORGANIZING PROGRAMS OF STUDY FOR GRADUATE NURSES IN OTHER LANDS." Columbia University Teachers College, 1955. Source: TCCU CONTRIBUTIONS (1955), pp. 232-233.

Described the nursing, cultural, and psychological needs of nursing educators and administrators serving as consultants at the University of Sao Paulo School of Public Health, Brazil.

Frede, Martha Chambers (Ph. D.). "SEXUAL ATTITUDES OF BEHAVIOR OF COLLEGE STUDENTS AT A PUBLIC UNIVERSITY IN THE SOUTHWEST." University of Houston, 1970. 168 pp. Source: DAI, XXXI, 11B (May, 1971), 6898-B-6899-B. XUM Order No. 71-12,509.

Found that: (1) male college students were more sexually active than female students; and (2) female sexual attitudes were more orthodox.

Frederickson, Keville Conrad (Ed. D.) and Mayer, Gloria Helen Gilbert (Ed. D.). "PROBLEM-SOLVING BY NURSING STUDENTS: A TWIN STUDY." Columbia University, 1975. 154 pp. Source: DAI, XXXV, 12B, Part I (June, 1975), 5966-B. XUM Order No. 75-12,583.

There was no significant difference between the performance of associate degree and baccalaureate degree nursing students in solving simulated nursing problems.

Freedman, Estelle Brenda (Ph. D.). "THEIR SISTERS' KEEPERS: THE ORIGINS OF FEMALE CORRECTIONS IN AMERICA." Columbia University, 1976. 468 pp. Source: DAI, XXXVII, 2A (August, 1976), 1170-A. XUM Order No. 76-17,844.

Traced reforms and reformers in delinquent and criminal women's correctional institutions, 1840s-1920, including social, educational, vocational, and professional rehabilitation of both inmates and of wardens and administrators.

Freeman, Kenneth Howard (Ed. D.). "AN EXAMINATION OF THE GENERAL EDUCATION PROGRAM OF YOUNG WOMEN IN A PRIVATE JUNIOR COLLEGE." University of Missouri, 1947. 97 pp. Source: Dissertation, pp. 76-79.

Found that the general education at a private junior college for women was poorer when compared with that of the high school studied.

Freese, Frances (Ph. D.). "DIFFERENTIAL PERCEPTIONS OF INTERPERSONAL
RELATIONSHIPS AMONG DORMITORY WOMEN." University of Texas, 1955. 140
pp. Source: Dissertation, pp. 82-88.

Found among 106 freshman college women living in a dormitory that
they chose friends whom they perceived as similar to their ideal
selves.

Frels, Lois Marian Parnell (Ph. D.). "THE BACCALAUREATE NURSING EDU-
CATION PROGRAM: FACULTY AND STUDENT ASSESSMENT OF STUDENT CAPABILITIES
THROUGH THE USE OF A BEHAVIORAL OBJECTIVES INVENTORY." University of
Minnesota, 1977. 203 pp. Source: DAI, XXXVIII, 3B (September, 1977),
1126-B. XUM Order No. 77-18,987.

Baccalaureate nursing students (167) rated themselves and were also
rated by 15 nursing faculty members. The correlation was found to
be low when the student and faculty ratings were compared.

Frerichs, Sarah Cutts (Ph. D.). "ELIZABETH MISSING SEWELL: A MINOR
NOVELIST'S SEARCH FOR THE VIA MEDIA IN THE EDUCATION OF WOMEN IN THE
VICTORIAN ERA." Brown University, 1974. 339 pp. Source: DAI, XXXV,
11A (May, 1975), 7303-A. XUM Order No. 75-9150.

Life and influence of British educator and writer Sewell (1815-1906)
and an analysis of her factual books and novels on women's education.

Frey, Bernice Gertrude (Ph. D.). "A STUDY OF TEACHING PROCEDURES IN
SELECTED PHYSICAL EDUCATION ACTIVITIES FOR COLLEGE WOMEN OF LOW MOTOR
ABILITY." University of Iowa, 1947. 105 pp. Source: Dissertation,
pp. 55-57.

Found that college women of low motor ability: (1) had fewer physical education opportunities in elementary school and high school;
(2) enjoyed physical education less than those with high motor ability; and (3) did not respond consistently to different teaching
methods tried with an experimental group.

Friedberg, Marjorie Helene (Ed. D.). "A STUDY TO EXPLORE AND ASSESS
HOW NURSERY SCHOOL TEACHERS, DIRECTORS AND EARLY CHILDHOOD EDUCATION STU-
DENTS VIEW TEACHING IN THE NURSERY SCHOOL." New York University, 1964.
196 pp. Source: DAI, XXVI, 7 (January, 1966), 3697-3698. XUM Order
No. 65-6598.

As college students, nursery school teachers had been motivated to
enter that field by relaxed nursery school atmosphere. They liked
their work, thought early childhood education extremely important,
and favored incorporating nursery schools into public schools.

Friedman, Walter (Ph. D.). "THE DEVELOPMENT OF PROFESSIONAL ATTI-
TUDES IN THE DIPLOMA SCHOOL OF NURSING: A FAILURE IN PROFESSIONALIZA-
TION." University of Pennsylvania, 1970. 128 pp. Source: DAI, XXXII,
2A (August, 1971), 1085-A. XUM Order No. 71-19,224.

In testing professional attitudes against a "perfect model," author found among 264 diploma nurses that seniors were less "idealistic" about nursing than were freshmen.

Friery, Catherine M. (Ph. D.). "IDENTIFICATION OF CRITERIA FOR THE DEVELOPMENT OF ASSESSMENT MEASURES IN NURSING EDUCATION PROGRAMS." Fordham University, 1974. 157 pp. Source: DAI, XXXV, 5B (November, 1974), 2278-B-2279-B. XUM Order No. 74-25,096.

Studied nursing students in 790 nursing programs in the U. S. Found that: (1) practical nurses differed significantly from other types of nurses in selected behaviors; and (2) except for practical nursing, regional differences among nursing programs were negligible. Concluded that critical standards could be established and measured nationally for diploma, associate, and baccalaureate nursing programs.

Fritschner, Linda Marie (Ph. D.). "THE RISE AND FALL OF HOME ECONOMICS: A STUDY WITH IMPLICATIONS FOR WOMEN, EDUCATION, AND CHANGE." University of California, Davis, 1973. 403 pp. Source: DAI, XXXIV, 10A (April, 1974), 6770-A. XUM Order No. 74-8506.

History of home economics in higher education from a critical sociological and contemporary women's liberation viewpoint.

Fritts, Robert Mason (Ed. D.). "THE EFFECTS OF PUPIL-TEACHER SEX INTERACTION ON KINDERGARTEN CHILDREN'S PERCEPTIONS OF THEIR TEACHERS AND THEMSELVES." Mississippi State University, 1976. 83 pp. Source: DAI, XXXVII, 7A (January, 1977), 4114-A-4115-A. XUM Order No. 76-30,057.

Ten female and 10 male kindergarten teachers who were similar in experience, certification, race, and locality were studied. The data revealed no significant differences in the children's self-concept and their perception of their teachers when the children and teacher's sex and the interaction effects were considered.

Fritz, Edna Lillian (Ed. D.). "FACULTY SELECTION, APPOINTMENT, AND PROMOTION IN COLLEGIATE NURSING PROGRAMS." Columbia University, 1965. 206 pp. Source: DAI, XXVI, 3 (September, 1965), 1599-1600. XUM Order No. 65-8841.

Collected information from 46 baccalaureate nursing programs about their policies and problems in selecting, appointing, and promoting faculty.

Fritzsche, Bertha Maude (Ph. D.). "IMPLICATIONS FOR TEACHER EDUCATION SUGGESTED BY THE RESPONSIBILITIES AND LIMITATIONS OF HOMEMAKING TEACHERS IN THE TOTAL SCHOOL PROGRAM FOR EDUCATION FOR FAMILY LIVING IN FIFTY-SEVEN PUBLIC SCHOOLS IN MISSISSIPPI." Ohio State University, 1951. 134 pp. Source: Ohio State University, ABSTRACTS OF DOCTORAL DISSERTATIONS, No. 65 (1954), pp. 73-80.

Findings implied that those preparing to teach homemaking education need to see and promote a total school program infused with the improvement of family living.

Frost, Hazel (Ed. D.). "A MEASURE OF SKILLS AND INFORMATION DEVEL-
OPED THROUGH HOME ECONOMICS INSTRUCTION IN THE SECONDARY SCHOOLS OF
OKLAHOMA." University of Oklahoma, 1939. 116 pp. Source: Disserta-
tion, pp. 56-59.

Survey of Oklahoma high school home economics courses revealed that:
(1) students needed more instruction in house furnishing, art in the
home and in clothing; (2) food and nutrition were effectively taught;
and (3) home economics courses needed to be coordinated more with
other school subjects.

Frost, Kenneth Bradley (Ph. D.). "THE EFFECTS OF THREE LEVELS OF
FRUSTRATION AND SEX DIFFERENCES ON FIGURAL CREATIVE EXPRESSION OF HIGH
SCHOOL JUNIORS AND SENIORS." University of Georgia, 1976. 80 pp.
Source: DAI, XXXVII, 5A (November, 1976), 2738-A-2739-A. XUM Order No.
76-26,473.

Found on Torrance Test of Creative Thinking that high school girls
scored lower than boys in fluency, flexibility, and originality.

Fry, Patsy Stubbs (Ed. D.). "CURRICULAR CONCOMITANTS IN THE EDUCA-
TIONAL BACKGROUNDS OF SELECTED WOMEN LEADERS IN EDUCATION, FINE ARTS,
AND LITERARY FIELDS." University of Southern California, 1968. 278 pp.
Source: DAI, XXIX, 7A (January, 1969), 2147-A-2148-A. XUM Order No.
69-614.

Women subjects who were chosen at random from Who's Who in America
said that in high school and college foreign language, English, and
social science were their 3 most influential subject areas.

Fuller, Andrew Reid (Ph. D.). "A STUDY OF THE RELATIONSHIP BETWEEN
PERSONALITY VARIABLES, SEX, RETENTION INTERVAL, AROUSAL, AND OBSERVA-
TIONAL AND PAIRED-ASSOCIATE LEARNING." New School for Social Research,
1976. 125 pp. Source: DAI, XXXVII, 2B (August, 1976), 1033-B. XUM
Order No. 76-18,115.

Found no difference between men and women's observational learning
abilities, regardless of extraversion, introversion, or neuroticism.

Fullingim, Billie G. (Ph. D.). "A COMPARISON OF SEX DIFFERENCES IN
THE TEST PROFILES OF UNDER-ACHIEVERS IN READING." Texas Woman's University, 1972. Source: Author.

On reading tests and in relation to boys, elementary school girl
underachievers did less well on vocabulary.

Furlong, Virginia June (Ed. D.). "ANTI-SOCIAL BEHAVIOR IN YOUTHFUL
FEMALE OFFENDERS." University of Northern Colorado, 1971. 121 pp.
Source: DAI, XXXII, 2A (August, 1971), 1094-A. XUM Order No. 71-20,721.

Juvenile girl offenses and offenders increased, 1957-1967. Many more
girls' cases than boys' cases were dismissed because of victim re-
luctance to press charges and arresting officers' belief that a rep-
rimand was sufficient.

Garrett, Pauline Bertie Gillette (Ed. D.). "THE IDENTIFICATION OF CERTAIN COMPETENCIES IN TEACHING VOCATIONAL HOME ECONOMICS IN THE SECONDARY SCHOOLS OF MISSOURI." University of Missouri, 1958. 430 pp. Source: DAI, XIX, 10 (April, 1959), 2544-2545. XUM Order No. Mic. 58-5239.

No definite relationships were found between certain identified competencies and the ratings of teachers as inadequate, competent, or unusually competent.

Garrison, Viann Roggow (Ed. D.). "EQUAL ACCESSIBILITY TO AND PARTICIPATION IN CONSUMER AND HOMEMAKING EDUCATION PROGRAMS BY BOTH SEXES IN COLORADO PUBLIC SCHOOLS." University of Northern Colorado, 1975. 141 pp. Source: DAI, XXXVI, 11B (May, 1976), 5531-B. XUM Order No. 76-10,837.

Accessibility to and participation in consumer and homemaking education programs, on the basis of sex, were unequal in 65.5% of Colorado public schools. Equality was considered desirable by 84.5% of department heads.

Gavin, Sister Rosemarie Julie (Ph. D.). "TRAINING TEACHERS OF SECONDARY SCHOOL ENGLISH IN CATHOLIC COLLEGES FOR WOMEN." Stanford University, 1955. 266 pp. Source: DAI, XV, 10 (1955), 1792. XUM Order No. 13,264.

Criteria for an ideal program in training women English teachers were developed.

Gawne, Eleanor Jerner (Ed. D.). "THE GRADUATE PROGRAM FOR TEACHERS OF HOME ECONOMICS AT SIMMONS COLLEGE." Columbia University Teachers College, 1957. 243 pp. Source: Dissertation, pp. 31-33, 62-63, 100-102, 158-162, 190-193.

Alumnae surveyed recommended that the program provide more emphasis on teaching methods and more opportunities for observing new techniques. Among other recommendations were: (1) integrating the graduate program into the School of Home Economics; and (2) improving library resources.

Gaza, Caesar Thomas (Ph. D.). "THE PREDICTION OF SUCCESS IN NURSING TRAINING: THE USE OF THE INTERPERSONAL SYSTEM OF MULTILEVEL PERSONALITY DIAGNOSIS AS AN ADJUNCT TO THE SELECTION PROGRAM OF A HOSPITAL SCHOOL OF NURSING." New York University, 1963. 142 pp. Source: DAI, XXIV, 4 (October, 1963), 1684-A-1685-A. XUM Order No. 63-6662.

Personality tests used did not succeed in predicting students' grade point averages.

Geitgey, Doris Arlene (Ed. D.). "A STUDY OF SOME EFFECTS OF SENSITIVITY TRAINING ON THE PERFORMANCE OF STUDENTS IN ASSOCIATE DEGREE PROGRAMS OF NURSING EDUCATION." University of California, Los Angeles, 1966. 197 pp. Source: DAI, XXVII, 6B (December, 1966), 2000-B-2001-B. XUM Order No. 66-11,908.

Nursing students who received sensitivity training were rated by their patients, peers, and instructors. Good interpersonal relations with patients suggested that such training was effective.

Gelwick, Beverly Prosser (Ph. D.). "THE ADULT WOMAN STUDENT AND HER PERCEPTIONS AND EXPECTATIONS OF THE UNIVERSITY ENVIRONMENT." University of Missouri-Columbia, 1975. 124 pp. Source: DAI, XXXVIII, 1A (July, 1977), 171-A-172-A. XUM Order No. 76-7492.

Conclusions in this study of 318 women were: a match between the individual and the environment led to increased satisfaction; and behavior was functionally related to the person and the environment. Women students (27 years and older) were: (1) more likely to drop out of the university for nonacademic reasons; and (2) more satisfied with administrative rules than were younger students.

Gibson, Harold Elmer (Ed. D.). "PUBLIC RELATIONS PRACTICES IN INSTITUTIONS OF HIGHER EDUCATION FOR WOMEN." University of Missouri, 1946. Source: University of Missouri, ABSTRACTS OF DISSERTATIONS IN EDUCATION, 1946-1950, pp. 58-59.

Among conclusions: (1) the general movement for public relations departments in women's colleges began in senior colleges in 1929 and in junior colleges in 1937; and (2) the most helpful preparations for public relations directors were journalism courses, newspaper experience, and teaching.

Gibson, Irene Ann (Ph. D.). "THE DEAN OF WOMEN'S OFFICE AT WORK." University of Colorado, 1949. 335 pp. Source: Author.

Traced the history of the position, described trends, and considered its future possibilities.

Gilbert, Gratia (Ed. D.). "CAREER MATURITY OF VOCATIONALLY UNDECIDED MIDDLE-AGED WOMEN." University of South Dakota, 1976. 132 pp. Source: DAI, XXXVIII, 1A (July, 1977), 112-A-113-A. XUM Order No. 77-13,947.

Middle-aged women have acquired more occupational information and hence are vocationally more mature than freshman women.

Gilcoyne, Katharine (Ed. D.). "THE PROFESSIONAL PREPARATION OF WOMEN FOR PHYSICAL EDUCATION IN THE FIRST HALF OF THE TWENTIETH CENTURY." Columbia University Teachers College, 1958. Source: TCCU DIGESTS (1958), pp. 220-222.

Some historic highlights: (1) early 20th century psychology laid groundwork with its focus on purposeful activity; (2) between 1917 and 1929 emphasis shifted from physical development to social and recreative values and to individual needs and interests; and (3) the 1948 National Conference on Undergraduate Professional Preparation set new directions.

Gilliam, Jack Rhine (Ed. D.). "THE STATUS OF TEXAS HIGH SCHOOL COUNSELORS' ATTITUDES TOWARD THE ROLES OF WOMEN." East Texas State University, 1975. 128 pp. Source: DAI, XXXVI, 11A (May, 1976), 7207-A. XUM Order No. 76-11,947.

Male counselors were more sexist than were female counselors. The location and size of the employing school were significant in relation to attitudes toward women. Counselors who attended seminars

about attitudes toward women's roles were less sexist than those who
did not.

Girard, Kathryn Lee (Ed. D.). "HOW SCHOOLS FAIL WOMEN: A STUDY OF
FEMINISTS' PERCEPTIONS OF THEIR SCHOOLING EXPERIENCES AND WOMEN'S SCHOOL-
ING NEED." University of Massachusetts, 1974. 254 pp. Source: DAI,
XXXV, 5A (November, 1974), 2529-A-2530-A. XUM Order No. 74-25,834.

Some feminists' views on schooling were: (1) elementary and secondary schools used uninteresting curricular materials and enforced
sex-appropriate behaviors; (2) secondary schools and higher institutions failed to encourage women to enter traditionally male careers;
and (3) leadership roles in education were male-dominated.

Glancy, Sister Francesca (Ph. D.). "THE PRESENT STATUS AND ROLE OF
THE REGISTRAR IN A SELECTED NUMBER OF CATHOLIC FOUR-YEAR LIBERAL ARTS
COLLEGES FOR WOMEN." Catholic University of America, 1962. 209 pp.
Source: DAI, XXIII, 9 (March, 1963), 3200. XUM Order No. 63-301.

Conclusions: (1) the registrar envisioned her position as one of
service to administrators, faculty, students, and the public; and
(2) most colleges use the title "registrar."

Glass, Helen Preston (Ed. D.). "TEACHING BEHAVIOR IN THE NURSING
LABORATORY IN SELECTED BACCALAUREATE NURSING PROGRAMS IN CANADA." Columbia University, 1971. 347 pp. Source: DAI, XXXII, 6A (December, 1971),
3152-A. XUM Order No. 72-1235.

Characteristics of 53 teachers in 3 Canadian nursing school laboratories   showed that educational experience is often distorted
by teachers' "status" and "autonomy" problems.

Glass, Kenneth Denton (Ed. D.). "A STUDY OF RELIGIOUS BELIEF AND
PRACTICE AS RELATED TO ANXIETY AND DOGMATISM IN COLLEGE WOMEN." University of Tennessee, 1970. 78 pp. Source: DAI, XXXI, 7A (January, 1971),
3637-A. XUM Order No. 71-347.

Females with high scores in religious beliefs were more dogmatic on
social, political, and economic issues. Females who practiced their
religion regularly tended to be more secure.

Glogowski, Diane Rose (Ed. D.). "AN INVESTIGATION OF THE RELATION-
SHIPS AMONG AGE CATEGORY, CURRICULUM SELECTED, AND MEASURES OF WORK
VALUES HELD AND CERTAINTY OF CAREER CHOICE FOR WOMEN STUDENTS IN A COM-
MUNITY COLLEGE." Indiana University, 1976. 111 pp. Source: DAI,
XXXVII, 8A (February, 1977), 4864-A. XUM Order No. 77-3339.

Concluded that an understanding of work values may be a useful ele-
ment in the career counseling of women in a community college.

Glotzbach, Charles Jerome (Ph. D.). "INTELLECTUAL AND NONINTELLEC-
TUAL CHARACTERISTICS ASSOCIATED WITH PERSISTENCE OF WOMEN IN AN ELEMEN-
TARY AND NURSERY SCHOOL TEACHER-EDUCATION PROGRAM." University of Min-
nesota, 1957. 167 pp. Source: DAI, XVIII, I (January, 1958), 146-147.
XUM Order No. 23,933.

The best predictors of persistence in the program were high school
graduating class rank and students' test scores. Marriage plans accounted for dropouts among those who were predicted as persistent
students.

Goble, Eva Lenora (Ph. D.). "THE PARTICIPATION OF YOUNG HOMEMAKERS
IN GROUP LEARNING ACTIVITIES." University of Chicago, 1964. Source:
Dissertation, pp. 1-19.

The 161 young women non-members interviewed believed that a home
demonstration club was a closed social group which selected members.
They felt excluded and had less experience in relating to groups than
did the 108 young women club members.

Godlasky, Charles Andrew (Ed. D.). "THE DEVELOPMENT OF FITNESS IN
COLLEGE WOMEN." Pennsylvania State University, 1962. 117 pp. Source:
DAI, XXIII, 10 (April, 1963), 3760. XUM Order No. 63-3047.

The study proved that physical fitness levels of college women can
be greatly increased by a vigorous program of physical activities.

Goering, Orlando James (Ph. D.). "MARRIAGE AMONG HIGH SCHOOL GIRLS
IN IOWA." Iowa State University, 1959. 139 pp. Source: DAI, XX, 1
(July, 1959), 409-410. XUM Order No. Mic 59-2415.

Married high school girls had started dating early. Strong parent-
child relationships were more common among married high school girls.

Goldberg, Rochelle Lois (Ph. D.). "THE RUSSIAN WOMEN'S MOVEMENT:
1859-1917." University of Rochester, 1976. 405 pp. Source: XXXVII,
5A (November, 1976), 3106-A-3107-A. XUM Order No. 76-23,994.

The Trubnikova circle, a group of gentry women, accomplished some
philanthropic and educational projects. The intelligentki, mainly
women graduates of higher courses, enabled over 8,000 to join the
Women's Equal Rights Union. The women's movement declined until re-
vived by International Women's Day Celebration. The comprehensive
equal rights decree came in the revolution of October 1917.

Goldman, Myra Frances (Ph. D.). "THE LEARNING, RETENTION, AND BI-
LATERAL TRANSFER OF A MOTOR SKILL BY COLLEGE WOMEN AS A FUNCTION OF
MENTAL PRACTICE, PHYSICAL PRACTICE AND MIXED PRACTICE." New York Univer-
sity, 1972. 165 pp. Source: DAI, XXXIII, 5A (November, 1972), 2148-A.
XUM Order No. 72-26,595.

Mental practice proved to be as effective as physical practice in
women's learning a motor skill. This study supported previous
studies' conclusion that physical practice is the most effective way
to teach motor skills.

Goldsmith, Herbert Burton (Ph. D.). "THE CATEGORICAL DOMINANCE OF
SEX, RACE AND NATIONAL ORIGIN IN THE PREFERENCES OF WHITE, BLACK, HIS-
PANIC MALE AND FEMALE NEW YORK CITY ELEMENTARY SCHOOL TEACHERS FOR WHITE,
BLACK AND HISPANIC MALE AND FEMALE ELEMENTARY SCHOOL PRINCIPAL CANDIDATES
BY MEANS OF A SIMULATION ACTIVITY." New York University, 1976. 306 pp.
Source: DAI, XXXVIII, 3A (September, 1977), 1148-A-1149-A. XUM Order
No. 77-16,424.

Black, Hispanic male and female teachers preferred candidates similar in race and national origin. White male and female teachers more often preferred black, Hispanic candidates.

Goldstein, Mark Kane (Ph. D.). "BEHAVIOR RATE CHANGE IN MARRIAGES: TRAINING WIVES TO MODIFY HUSBANDS' BEHAVIOR." Cornell University, 1971. 156 pp. Source: DAI, XXXII, 1B (July, 1971), 559-B. XUM Order No. 71-17,094.

Wives (10) who wished to alter their husbands' behavior were taught to give positive social reinforcements when the desired response occurred. Husbands' behavior changed in 8 out of 10 cases.

Goliber, Sue Helder (Ph. D.). "THE LIFE AND TIMES OF MARGUERITE DURAND: A STUDY IN FRENCH FEMINISM." Kent State University, 1975. 198 pp. Source: DAI, XXXVI, 12A (June, 1976), 8232-A. XUM Order No. 76-14,358.

Editor Marguerite Durand formed her own newspaper, La Fronde, which was operated by an all-woman staff from December 9, 1897, until March, 1905. Until her death in 1936 she worked for equality and justice in education and other fields.

Goltra, Raylene Denise (Ph. D.). "WOMEN'S STUDIES: A NEW PROGRAM FOR THE COMMUNITY COLLEGE." Oregon State University, 1974. 83 pp. Source: DAI, XXXV, 2A (August, 1974), 751-A-752-A. XUM Order No. 74-18,269.

Preliminary sections gave data about women's disadvantages and about the failure of American institutions to improve women's status. A community college course for male and female students was then outlined. The course, designed to use existing facilities and often existing personnel, was intended to hasten equality throughout American society.

Goltz, Diane L. (Ph. D.). "THE RELATIONSHIP OF PERCEPTIONS OF SEX ROLES AND OCCUPATIONAL CHOICE AMONG WOMEN." University of Oklahoma, 1977. 127 pp. Source: DAI, XXXVIII, 4A (October, 1977), 1918-A-1919-A. XUM Order No. 77-21,374.

Of the women studied in law, medicine, education, and homemaking, those in homemaking seemed not to have utilized fully their intellectual abilities or potential.

Good, Shirley Ruth (Ed. D.). "PREPARATION OF UNIVERSITY TEACHERS OF NURSING IN CANADA: PROPOSALS FOR THE PROFESSIONAL EDUCATION COMPONENT OF A MASTER'S PROGRAM." Columbia University, 1967. 166 pp. Source: DAI, XXVIII, 7B (January, 1968), 2914-B. XUM Order No. 67-16,757.

Four major areas of study were proposed: (1) history and development of higher education; (2) educational psychology including guidance and counseling; (3) knowledge and skills of teaching; and (4) faculty-institution problems and policies.

Goodman, Lillian Rachel (Ed. D.). "A MODEL OF OBJECTIVES FOR A PRO-
GRAM OF CONTINUING EDUCATION FOR PSYCHIATRIC NURSES IN COMMUNITY MENTAL
HEALTH WORK IN MASSACHUSETTS." Boston University School of Education,
1969. 202 pp. Source: DAI, XXXI, 2B (August, 1970), 774-B. XUM Order
No. 70-12,174.

Supervisors and nurses believed that the most important function was
to provide general nursing care. The authorities believed that such
collateral functions as administration were important. The model
focused on 3 main areas of learning needs: (1) direct and collateral
nursing services; (2) concepts of community and culture; and (3)
planning for institutional change.

Goodwin, Gail Crow (Ed. D.). "THE WOMAN DOCTORAL RECIPIENT: A STUDY
OF THE DIFFICULTIES ENCOUNTERED IN PURSUING GRADUATE DEGREES." Oklahoma
State University, 1966. 231 pp. Source: DAI, XXVII, 12A (June, 1967),
4038-A. XUM Order No. 67-7224.

In contrast to single women students, married women and particularly
those with children came from families with a higher level of parental educational attainment. Women doctoral students who faced the
most difficulties (1) were those enrolled in private institutions;
or (2) were majoring in the social sciences or the humanities; or
(3) had children.

Gordon, Barbara Jane Arthur (Ed. D.). "THE DETERMINATION AND STUDY
OF ACADEMIC UNDERACHIEVEMENT IN THE NEW YORK STATE COLLEGE OF HOME ECO-
NOMICS AT CORNELL UNIVERSITY WITH IMPLICATIONS FOR COUNSELING AND AD-
MISSIONS." Cornell University, 1959. 350 pp. Source: DAI, XX, 5
(November, 1959), 1675-1676. XUM Order No. Mic 59-5289.

Overachievers' parents tended to have more education and to be employed mainly in managerial and professional fields. Underachievers
worked more hours, had more dates per week, and felt academically
insecure.

Gordon, Gale Lynn (Ed. D.). "DIVERGENT AND SPONTANEOUS ART STRATEGY
COMPARISON PROFILE FOR ART AND NON-ART FEMALE COLLEGE STUDENTS." Penn-
sylvania State University, 1966. 127 pp. Source: DAI, XXVII, 11A
(May, 1967), 3615-A-3616-A. XUM Order No. 67-5917.

Findings suggested that art experience may tend to alter women students' problem solving outlook and artistic growth.

Gordon, Ruby Daniels (Ph. D.). "A STUDY OF COMMUNITY COLLEGE NURSING
STUDENT VALUES." Arizona State University, 1975. 105 pp. Source: DAI,
XXXVI, 6A (December, 1975), 3331-A-3332-A. XUM Order No. 75-28,485.

Conclusions: (1) freshman and sophomore community college nursing
students held significantly different views on the value of variety;
and (2) nursing courses, non-nursing courses, faculty, and social
institutions apparently caused students' values to change as they
proceeded through the nursing program.

Gordon, Susan Ellen (Ed. D.). "BACCALAUREATE EDUCATION FOR REGIS-
TERED NURSES IN NEW YORK, NEW JERSEY, AND PENNSYLVANIA: 1971-1972."
Columbia University, 1972. 276 pp. Source: DAI, XXXIII, 8A (February,
1973), 3951-A-3952-A. XUM Order No. 73-2596.

Survey revealed that: (1) there were no accredited baccalaureate
programs solely for registered nurses (RN); (2) evaluation of basic
baccalaureate students and RNs differed at the time of admission;
and (3) only a few schools provided a way for RN students to shift
from technically oriented to professional training. The major
strenghs of both programs were flexibility and individualized instruction.

Gordon, Verona Christofferson (Ph. D.). "EVALUATION OF A SIMULATED
GROUP-THERAPY FILM TEST IN TEACHING PSYCHIATRIC NURSING." University of
Minnesota, 1976. 193 pp. Source: DAI, XXXVII, 6B (December, 1976),
2771-B. XUM Order No. 76-27,894.

Potential uses of the observation skills test were in: (1) measuring
student competency and growth in observation skills; (2) identifying
students needing help in observing patient behavior; (3) indicating
what emphasis should be given to communication skills; and (4) developing student skill in observing patient behavior.

Gore, William Eugene (Ph. D.). "THE EFFECTS OF AGE, SEX, INTELLI-
GENCE AND RACE UPON STATEMENT VOLUME AND ABSTRACTNESS IN WRITTEN IMPRES-
SIONS." University of South Carolina, 1974. 80 pp. Source: DAI,
XXXVI, 2B (August, 1975), 908-B. XUM Order No. 75-16,481.

Among findings: (1) the older the subject, the more lengthy the impression; (2) female descriptions were longer than those made by
males; and (3) the amount of abstraction increased with the age of
the subject.

Gorgone, Kathleen (Ph. D.). "A COMPARISON OF PERCEPTIONS HELD BY
SUPERINTENDENTS, SCHOOL BOARD MEMBERS, AND TEACHER REPRESENTATIVES RE-
GARDING THE ROLE OF WOMEN SCHOOL BOARD MEMBERS IN THE STATE OF INDIANA."
Southern Illinois University, 1976. 236 pp. Source: DAI, XXXVII, 9A
(March, 1977), 5485-A. XUM Order No. 77-6217.

Questionnaires revealed that: (1) both male and female board members
and male superintendents felt that there were enough women board
members; and (2) teacher representatives felt that there were too
few women board members. Women board members seemed to have a higher
interest than men in: (1) the regulations of superintendents; (2)
employment of certified and non-certified personnel; (3) student ex-
pulsion; (4) instructional programs; and (5) school and community
relations.

Gorman, Anna Marguriette (Ed. D.). "TEACHING AND NON-TEACHING GRADU-
ATES OF HOME ECONOMICS EDUCATION CURRICULA: A COMPARISON OF THEIR VALUES
AND OTHER CHARACTERISTICS." University of Illinois, 1959. 125 pp.
Source: DAI, XX, 1 (July, 1959), 212. XUM Order No. Mic 59-2022.

Findings: (1) need to emphasize the social service role home economics teachers play in society; and (2) programs need to enable

students to better understand their reasons for teaching, to more fully appreciate graduate study opportunities, and to read and use professional literature.

Gortner, Susan Reichert (Ph. D.). "NURSING MAJORS IN TWELVE WESTERN UNIVERSITIES: A COMPARISON OF REGISTERED-NURSE STUDENTS AND BASIC SENIOR STUDENTS." University of California, Berkeley, 1964. 305 pp. Source: DAI, XXV, 7 (January, 1965), 3971-3972. XUM Order No. 64-13,008.

Concluded that registered nurses were less socially and more theoretically oriented, had lower feminine interests than basic senior students, and were interested in professional advancement. Basic senior students were interested in general professional education and reported greater stress.

Gorvine, Elizabeth Sturtevant (Ed. D.). "A STUDY OF DECISION MAKING IN CERTAIN ADMINISTRATIVE FUNCTIONS OF SELECTED HOME ECONOMICS PROGRAMS OF UNIVERSITIES AND COLLEGES." New York University, 1954. 604 pp. Source: DAI, XIV, 12 (1954), 2332-2333. XUM Order No. 8022.

Conclusions were that: (1) decision making in home economics administration is not generally understood; (2) staff frequently interpret situations differently; (3) department head and staff desire wider participation in decision making; (4) when given the opportunity, more constructive ideas were given; and (5) formalized procedures for participation offered no assurance that the individuals felt they had participated.

Gould, Terri F. (Ph. D.). "THE EDUCATED WOMAN IN A DEVELOPING COUNTRY: PROFESSIONAL ZAIRIAN WOMEN IN LUBUMBASHI." Union Graduate School, 1976. 314 pp. Source: DAI, XXXVII, 9A (March, 1977), 6089-A. XUM Order No. 77-4332.

Women secondary school teachers, university instructors, and directors of clinics and homemaking schools were studied in relation to work, economic independence, urbanization, education, ethnic politics, class formation, and the sexual class system. They were struggling to resolve the conflict between traditional and modern values and regarded themselves as pioneers in breaking down sex-role stereotypes. Current economic, social, and political structures in Zaire made it impossible for women to become fully integrated into the socio-political structure.

Gover, Virginia Frances (Ph. D.). "THE DEVELOPMENT AND TESTING OF A NURSING PERFORMANCE SIMULATION INSTRUMENT." University of North Carolina at Chapel Hill, 1971. 230 pp. Source: DAI, XXXII, 10B (April, 1972), 5888-B. XUM Order No. 72-10,684.

The Nursing Performance Simulation Instrument (NPSI) was designed to measure the discrepancy between expected and observed nursing behaviors on 1 variable problem-solving proficiency. Reliability, validity, and discriminatory power of NPSI were estimated from data obtained by administering the NPSI to 179 nursing practitioners and 200 nursing educators.

Goza, John Thomas (Ph. D.). "AN INVESTIGATION OF THE ACADEMIC PO-
TENTIAL, ACADEMIC ACHIEVEMENT, AND PERSONALITY OF PARTICIPANTS IN AN
ASSOCIATE DEGREE NURSING PROGRAM." East Texas State University, 1970.
153 pp. Source: DAI, XXXI, 9B (March, 1971), 5442-B. XUM Order No.
71-8642.

Some conclusions: (1) all students had the same potential for success; (2) minimum academic success of dropouts was due to their ir-
responsible attitude; (3) academically superior students did better
on the State Board Test Pool Examination; (4) Gordon Personal Inventory and Profile could be used to identify potential dropouts and
potential State Board failures; (5) some graduates' poor on-the-job
performance resulted from personality differences; and (6) counseling
program could be improved by use of the involved tests.

Gradel, Dorothy V. (Ed. D.). "THE RELATIONSHIPS BETWEEN STUDENTS'
NEEDS-ENVIRONMENTAL PRESS AND ACHIEVEMENT IN NURSING EDUCATION OF STU-
DENTS IN SELECTED ASSOCIATE DEGREE NURSING EDUCATION PROGRAMS IN WASHING-
TON STATE." Washington State University, 1965. 76 pp. Source: DAI,
XXVI, 1 (July, 1965), 321. XUM Order No. 65-7701.

Findings: (1) student needs profiles were similar in all 3 colleges;
(2) significant relationships existed among the environmental press
patterns for the 3 colleges; (3) student responses agreed with faculty responses on environmental patterns; (4) no significant relationship between personality needs and grades was demonstrated; (5) requirements for admission were similar; (6)differences in students'
ages, past achievement, and ability scores existed in each college;
(7) students felt high needs for caring for those unable to help
themselves; and (8) all 3 colleges de-emphasized self-depreciation
and hostility toward others.

Grady, Roslyn Marie (Ph. D.). THE INTERRELATIONSHIPS OF: (1)
CIVILIAN OR MILITARY HOME BACKGROUND; (2) STABILITY OR MOBILITY; AND
(3) SEX CLASSIFICATION UPON ADJUSTMENT AND ACADEMIC POTENTIAL REALIZED
BY FIFTH-GRADE CHILDREN FROM THE MIDDLE SOCIO-ECONOMIC CLASS." University of Alabama, 1965. 185 pp. Source: DAI, XXVI, 10 (April, 1966),
5865-5866. XUM Order No. 66-2935.

Results indicated: (1) no differences in academic potential were
found in civilian or military homes and the stability or mobility
of educational experience; (2) difference between boys and girls
resulted from the interaction effect of sex, and from civilian or
military home life; (3) no significant differences existed in feelings of security; (4) no significant differences existed in self-
reports of adjustment problems; (5) stable students received significantly higher mean acceptance by peers and girls had higher mean
scores than boys; (6) no differences existed in teacher ratings of
pupil adjustment; and (7) there was a significant relationship between adjustment variable scores and academic achievement.

Graef, David William (Ph. D.). "EFFECT OF FEEDBACK VARIATION ON
ACHIEVEMENT AND COMPLETION TIME OF STUDENT NURSES STUDYING DOSAGES AND
SOLUTIONS IN A PROGRAMMED FORMAT." Arizona State University, 1971. 97
pp. Source: DAI, XXXII, 6A (December, 1971), 3089-A. XUM Order No.
71-24,391.

Conclusions: (1) variation in feedback had little or no consistent
effect on time or achievement; and (2) the program had a consistent,
significant effect on student achievement.

Gray, Carol Joyce (Ed. D.). "A STUDY OF HOW NURSES FINANCE DOCTORAL
EDUCATION." Columbia University, 1970. 253 pp. Source: DAI, XXXI, 8B
(February, 1971), 4797-B. XUM Order No. 71-5581.

Recommendations: (1) a change is needed in financial aid administration; (2) financing system is ineffective; (3) because planning
and cost control are inadequate, the educative process suffers; and
(4) the federal government gives the most support.

Gray, Lyle Asa (Ph. D.). "A SOCIOLOGICAL STUDY VIA PARTICIPANT OB-
SERVATION OF A TWO-YEAR PRIVATE LIBERAL ARTS COLLEGE FOR WOMEN." Syracuse University, 1970. 279 pp. Source: DAI, XXXI, 6A (December, 1970),
3054-A. XUM Order No. 70-24,082.

Survey of 80% of 500 women students found that: (1) the junior college was the students' second choice; and (2) they preferred social
experiences over academic emphasis.

Green, Helen Bagenstose (Ph. D.). "SOCIALIZATION VALUES IN THE NEGRO
AND EAST INDIAN SUB-CULTURES OF TRINIDAD." University of Connecticut,
1963. 119 pp. Source: DAI, XXIV, 11 (May, 1964), 4832-4833. XUM Order
No. 64-3535.

Findings: (1) Negro mothers had a wider extent of social reference
than East Indian women; (2) Negro mothers gave their children more
independence training; (3) Negro mothers emphasized less internalization; and (4) differing socialization values seemed to be associated with differing roles of Negro and East Indian mothers in maintaining subcultural differences.

Green, Lennis Harris (Ph. D.). "AN INVESTIGATION OF FACTORS WHICH
INFLUENCE THE VOCATIONAL CLASSIFICATION OF CAREER ORIENTED AND HOME
ORIENTED WOMEN." Ohio State University, 1971. 125 pp. Source: DAI,
XXXII, 4B (October, 1971), 2377-B-2378-B. XUM Order No. 71-27,475.

Findings were: (1) women scored higher than men on the vocational
preference inventory social scale; and (2) men scored higher on the
realistic scale.

Greendorfer, Susan Louise (Ph. D.). "THE NATURE OF FEMALE SOCIALI-
ZATION INTO SPORT: A STUDY OF SELECTED COLLEGE WOMEN'S SPORT PARTICIPA-
TION." University of Wisconsin, Madison, 1974. 336 pp. Source: DAI,
XXXV, 9A (March, 1975), 5902-A-5903-A. XUM Order No. 74-27,738.

Conclusions were: (1) peers and family were the significant agents
of socialization into sports during childhood, peers and schools
were significant during adolescence, and peers were the most significant agents in adulthood; (2) male models were a dominant influence
during childhood, but not in adolescence or adulthood; (3) a stronger
reference group was associated with younger ages; and (4) the sports
type chosen was a function of socio-economic status.

Greene, Margaret Duncan (Ed. D.). "THE GROWTH OF PHYSICAL EDUCATION FOR WOMEN IN THE UNITED STATES IN THE EARLY NINETEENTH CENTURY." University of California, Los Angeles, 1950. 269 pp. Source: Author.

Early efforts in women's physical education programs were studied with emphasis on the work of 5 educators: Emma Hart Willard, Almira Hart Lincoln Phelps, Mary Lyon, William Bentley Fowle, and Catharine Beecher.

Greenhill, Elizabeth Dianne (Ed. D.). "THE ROLE OF THE SCHOOL NURSE AS PERCEIVED BY PRINCIPALS, TEACHERS, COUNSELORS, AND SCHOOL NURSES IN MEMPHIS AND SHELBY COUNTY, TENNESSEE." Memphis State University, 1976. 99 pp. Source: DAI, XXXVII, 8B (February, 1977), 3870-B. XUM Order No. 77-3148.

Conclusions were: (1) there was strong support for a school nursing program; (2) educators perceived the school nurse functioning in newer areas of health education and health; (3) teachers had the most divergent perceptions of the school nurse's role; (4) professional training or experience was not related to perception of the school nurse's role; and (5) school nurses could not agree on some roles.

Greenspan, Laurie Judge (Ph. D.). "SEX ROLE ORIENTATION, ACHIEVEMENT MOTIVATION AND THE MOTIVE TO AVOID SUCCESS IN COLLEGE WOMEN." Case Western Reserve University, 1974. 83 pp. Source: DAI, XXXV, 9A (March, 1975), 5813-A-5814-A. XUM Order No. 75-5061.

The 2 groups of women, 30 with a traditional sex-role orientation and 30 with a nontraditional sex-role orientation, had equivalent levels of achievement motivation. The difference was that the direction of their achievement strivings corresponded to their sex-role orientation.

Grieder, Frieda Anne (Ed. D.). "AMERICAN WOMEN IN THE PROFESSIONS: A STUDY OF TRENDS, 1870 TO 1940, AND THEIR IMPLICATIONS FOR THE COUNSELING OF COLLEGE WOMEN." Stanford University, 1950. 325 pp. Source: Dissertation, pp. iii-vii.

Topics covered include: (1) the status of women in America from colonial days; (2) women in the professions; and (3) the significance of occupational trends in counseling college women.

Griffin, Aileen (Ph. D.). "A PORTRAIT OF THE WOMAN TEACHER IN TWENTIETH CENTURY POPULAR MAGAZINES." Columbia University Teachers College, 1960. Source: TCCU DIGESTS (1960), pp. 237-238.

Popular magazines' depictions of women teachers in 5,364 short stories and 61 references to women teachers in 10,572 articles indicated that she was not interesting, glamorous, or dramatic enough to draw readers. A hierarchy of characteristics rather than a single stereotype emerged from magazine fiction. Nonfiction was more positive about women teachers than fiction.

Griffin, Gerald Joseph (Ed. D.). "RECOMMENDATIONS FOR PROGRAM DEVELOPMENT BY THE BOARD OF REVIEW OF ASSOCIATE DEGREE NURSING PROGRAMS OF THE NATIONAL LEAGUE FOR NURSING AND HOW THEY ARE IMPLEMENTED." New York

University, 1971. 139 pp. Source: DAI, XXXII, 5B (November, 1971), 2819-B-2820-B. XUM Order No. 71-28,579.

The study found that recommendations made by the Board of Review in the accreditation process were not an effective means of program development.

Griffin, John Chaney, Sr. (Ed. D.). "A PREDICTION STUDY OF FIRST YEAR COLLEGE PERFORMANCE OF HIGH SCHOOL GRADUATES BY SEX AND ETHNIC BACK-GROUND." University of Wyoming, 1972. 128 pp. Source: DAI, XXXIII, 12A (June, 1973), 6664-A-6665-A. XUM Order No. 73-14,273.

This effort to predict first year college grade point average conclu-ded that: (1) women are more predictable; (2) high school grade point average was the best indicator; (3) males and females need separate predictor formulas; and (4) general formulas do not account for differences between ethnic and sex groups.

Griffin, Wilma Pitts (Ph. D.). "THE DEVELOPMENT OF A SELF-APPRAISAL INSTRUMENT FOR HOME ECONOMICS STUDENT TEACHERS." University of Texas at Austin, 1976. 108 pp. Source: DAI, XXXVII, 8A (February, 1977), 4916-A. XUM Order No. 77-3906.

A high degree of agreement was found between respondents that student teachers were effective; and student teachers tended to underrate their teaching effectiveness.

Griggs, Mildred Barnes (Ed. D.). "ATTITUDES OF HIGH SCHOOL SENIORS TOWARD MOTHERS AND WIVES WORKING OUTSIDE THE HOME." University of Illi-nois at Urbana-Champaign, 1971. 70 pp. Source: DAI, XXXII, 8A (Febru-ary, 1972), 4500-A. XUM Order No. 72-6940.

Conclusions were: (1) females had more favorable attitudes about working mothers; (2) males had more favorable attitudes toward working wives; and (3) social class did not cause different attitudes.

Gross, Alice Dzen (Ed. D.). "SEX DIFFERENCES IN AN ISRAELI KIBBUTZ SYSTEM: READING DISABILITIES, MATURATION AND SEX-ROLE STANDARDS." Bos-ton University School of Education, 1977. 213 pp. Source: DAI, XXXVIII, 4A (October, 1977), 1998-A. XUM Order No. 77-21,645.

Although boys saw reading as significantly more masculine, no other sex differences were found among the groups in reading levels, reading readiness levels, and reading disability cases.

Haag, Sister Barbara Ann (Ph. D.). "A STUDY OF LIFE GOALS AND OCCU-PATIONAL ORIENTATION OF COLLEGIATE NURSING STUDENTS AND REGISTERED NUR-SES." University of Maryland, 1976. 176 pp. Source: DAI, XXXVII, 11A (May, 1977), 6853-A. XUM Order No. 77-10,271.

Registered nurses with associate degrees (62) had significantly higher scores in fame, power, and task-orientation with no significant dif-ferences in other goals. Blacks scored significantly higher in es-teem, security, and self-expression. Whites scored higher in leader-ship. There were no significant differences between black and white nurses with baccalaureate degrees. Race did not seem to be a factor

in influencing the goals and occupational orientations of either
black or white associate or baccalaureate degree students.

Haas, Mary Helen (Ph. D.). "A STUDY OF CERTAIN FACTORS RELATED TO
THE VOCATIONAL ACTIVITY OF HOME ECONOMICS-EDUCATION GRADUATES." University of Minnesota, 1957. 259 pp. Source: DAI, XVIII, 4 (April, 1958),
1413. XUM Order No. Mic 58-1152.

Found that a favorable attitude toward alternative vocations is related to the job performed. Among homemakers but not teachers a
favorable attitude toward alternative jobs and perceived adequacy of
income was associated with persistence in a job. Commitments to and
satisfaction with current job were not associated with persistence
in that job.

Haase, Patricia Ann Thompson (Ph. D.). "A STUDY OF MASTERY AND IN-
TERNALITY TRAINING TO IMPROVE ACHIEVEMENT IN NURSING CURRICULA." Purdue
University, 1972. 121 pp. Source: DAI, XXXIII, 9A (March, 1973),
4797-A. XUM Order No. 73-6034.

This study investigated the effectiveness of 2 teaching strategies in
improving achievement in the beginning nursing course. Findings indicated that mastery training improved student achievement more on
theory tests than did traditional methods of instruction.

Habryl, Joy (Joan M.) (Ph. D.). "AN ANALYSIS OF THE LABOR FORCE PAR-
TICIPATION OF WOMEN WITH COLLEGE AND GRADUATE DEGREES IN VARIOUS OCCUPA-
TIONAL FIELDS RANGING FROM THE TRADITIONALLY MALE TO THE TRADITIONALLY
FEMALE PROFESSIONS." Northwestern University, 1971. 214 pp. Source:
DAI, XXXII, 6A (December, 1971), 3170-A-3171-A. XUM Order No. 71-30,816.

Women with graduate degrees in liberal arts working in non-male
fields (such as nursing, music, speech, education, and social work)
spend more time in the labor force before they reach age 40 than do
women with graduate degrees in traditionally male fields (such as
math, law, and science) and with college degrees in all fields.

Hagey, Sylvia Joan Joy (Ph. D.). "RISK TAKING, SELF COMPLEXITY, AND
ROLE CHOICE AT TWO STAGES IN THE LIVES OF COLLEGE WOMEN." University of
Oregon, 1970. 167 pp. Source: DAI, XXXI, 7A (January, 1971), 3638-A.
XUM Order No. 71-1316.

Found that risk-taking performance had no apparent effect on role
choice. Interruption of college was related to such things as marital status, marriage plans, and academic major.

Haglund, Alma Hebel (Ph. D.). "PREDICTING SUCCESS IN COLLEGIATE NUR-
SING PROGRAMS." University of Wisconsin, Madison, 1975. 263 pp. Source:
DAI, XXXVII, 1A (July, 1976), 64-A. XUM Order No. 76-8586.

The results suggest that admissions officials should look closely at
individual grades in the traditional academic subjects to predict
the expected nursing program grade point average.

Hakkio, Joan S. (Ph. D.). "A COMPARISON OF 1958 AND 1970 WOMEN STU-
DENT LEADERS AT NORTHWESTERN UNIVERSITY: THEIR CHARACTERISTICS, SELF-

CONCEPTS, AND ATTITUDES TOWARD THE UNIVERSITY." Northwestern University, 1972. 218 pp. Source: DAI, XXXIII, 6A (December, 1972), 2710-A-2711-A. XUM Order No. 72-32,449.

It was concluded that the 2 groups' self concepts and attitudes toward the university were similar. The women thought greater independence, increased self-awareness, and acceptance of responsibility were the most important self concepts and attitudes.

Halas, Celia Mary (Ph. D.). "SEX-ROLE STEREOTYPES: PERCEIVED CHILD-HOOD SOCIALIZATION EXPERIENCES AND THE ATTITUDES AND BEHAVIORS OF MATURE WOMEN." Arizona State University, 1974. 297 pp. Source: DAI, XXXV, 3A (September, 1974), 1499-A. XUM Order No. 74-20,133.

The purpose was to investigate the association of early socialization experiences with sex role stereotypes of mature women and to determine the impact of the Women's Liberation Movement upon these women. Sex role stereotypes were found in the attitudes and behaviors of the subjects.

Halbrook, Diane Christine Ronning (Ph. D.). "HOME ECONOMICS EDUCA-TION STUDENTS' ATTITUDES TOWARD THE FUTURE HOMEMAKERS OF AMERICA." Iowa State University, 1976. 294 pp. Source: DAI, XXXVII, 7A (January, 1977), 4177-A-4178-A. XUM Order No. 77-1030.

Concluded that training future home economics teachers for the role of advisors to FHA/HERO programs is essential.

Hale, Elwynn Stephens (Ed. D.). "IDENTIFICATION OF THE RANGE OF FUNCTIONS PERFORMED BY GRADUATES OF ASSOCIATE DEGREE NURSING PROGRAMS AND GRADUATES OF BACCALAUREATE DEGREE NURSING PROGRAMS." University of Alabama, 1975. 136 pp. Source: DAI, XXXVI, 9B (March, 1976), 4383-B. XUM Order No. 76-4816.

The educational preparation of the 2 groups made no statistically significant difference in identifying nursing problems. However, there were significant differences in stating objectives and specifying nursing actions.

Hall, Betty Arlene Woodring (Ph. D.). "THE EFFECT OF SEX OF THE LEADER ON THE DEVELOPMENT OF ASSERTIVENESS IN WOMEN UNDERGOING GROUP ASSERTIVE TRAINING." University of Missouri, Kansas City, 1975. 210 pp. Source: DAI, XXXVI, 11A (May, 1976), 7208-A. XUM Order No. 76-11,488.

The results indicated no significant difference between women led by females and women led by males. It was concluded that the sex of the leader is unimportant in planning educational activities for women unless the now traditional role modeling effect of female leadership is an objective.

Hall, Ruth Eleanor (Ph. D.). "THE PLACE OF TEXTILES AND CLOTHING IN THE REQUIRED CURRICULUM AND IN SELECTED SPECIALIZATIONS IN HOME ECO-NOMICS." University of Minnesota, 1964. 328 pp. Source: DAI, XXV, 5 (November, 1964), 2883-2884. XUM Order No. 64-10,824.

Among the findings: students tended to recommend more emphasis on most objectives than did the experts.

Hall, William Joseph (Ph. D.). "COLLEGE WOMEN'S IDENTIFICATIONS WITH THEIR FATHERS IN RELATION TO VOCATIONAL INTEREST PATTERNS." University of Texas, 1963. 171 pp. Source: DAI, XXIV, 12 (June, 1964), 5192-5193. XUM Order No. 64-6602.

Women with stronger father identification tended to imply femininity of interests and interests resembling those characterizing women engaged in traditionally male occupations.

Haller, Lola Marie (Ed. D.). "THE FUTURE ROLE OF THE HIGHEST RANKING WOMAN STUDENT PERSONNEL ADMINISTRATOR IN THE COLLEGE OR UNIVERSITY AND A SUGGESTED TRAINING PROGRAM." Michigan State University, 1967. 147 pp. Source: DAI, XXVIII, 10A (April, 1968), 3933-A. XUM Order No. 68-4146.

Concluded that the role of the highest ranking woman student personnel administrator is in transition. This administrator's role is becoming primarily administrative and educational as opposed to the traditional role, which was basically custodial.

Hands, Sandra Lee (Ph. D.). "AN EVALUATION OF A COURSE FOR WOMEN DIRECTED TOWARD THE DEVELOPMENT OF SELF-ACTUALIZING LIFE STYLES." University of Texas Health Science Center at Dallas, 1974. 209 pp. Source: DAI, XXXV, 8A (February, 1975), 5117-A-5118-A. XUM Order No. 75-1122.

The results indicated that the 8-week course was largely successful in achieving its objectives of developing self-actualizing life-styles.

Hansen, Norma Jones (Ph. D.). "A STUDY OF THE ASSOCIATE DEGREE NURSE PROGRAM AT WEBER STATE COLLEGE (1953-69)." University of Utah, 1970. 148 pp. Source: DAI, XXXI, 6B (December, 1960), 3508-B-3509-B. XUM Order No. 70-23,823.

One finding was that the associate degree program had fulfilled the purposes for which it was developed.

Hanson, Doris Elizabeth (Ed. D.). "HOME ECONOMISTS IN OVERSEAS WORK." Columbia University, 1964. 213 pp. Source: DAI, XXVI, 1 (July, 1965), 346. XUM Order No. 65-4731.

Found that overseas home economists were highly diverse in age, background, and experience, and held proportionately more advanced degrees than those in the profession as a whole.

Hardester, Laura Mae (Ph. D.). "AN ANALYSIS OF IMMEDIATE AND DELAYED VERBAL COGNITION INFORMATION PROCESSING, MENTAL OPERATION LEVELS AND COURSE PERFORMANCE OF COLLEGE FRESHMEN BY SEX." University of Pittsburgh, 1976. 164 pp. Source: DAI, XXXVIII, 2A (August, 1977), 657-A-658-A. XUM Order No. 77-15,192.

The results showed a difference between the sexes in ability to recall science terms. It was established that female subjects tended to forget more science passage terms than male subjects.

Male students earned higher biological science course grades compared to women. It was concluded that male and female subjects differed in the operational structure of memory.

Harms, Mary Terwilliger (Ed. D.). "PROFESSIONAL EDUCATION IN UNIVERSITY SCHOOLS OF NURSING." Stanford University, 1955. 418 pp. Source: DAI, XV, 3 (1955), 396. XUM Order No. 11,158.

This study traced the historical evolution of nursing education, described the establishment and expansion of university schools of nursing and their programs, and summarized their present status.

Harrington, JoAnn Condit (Ed. D.). "THE STATUS OF WOMEN WITH DOCTORAL DEGREES IN COLLEGIATE BUSINESS EDUCATION." Arizona State University, 1971. 274 pp. Source: DAI, XXXII, 1A (July, 1971), 198-A. XUM Order No. 71-18,952.

Findings showed that there were few complaints of discrimination and that individual abilities rather than sex were more important in attaining professional status.

Harris, Elizabeth Simpkins (Ed. D.). "CALIFORNIA WOMEN SCHOOL SUPERINTENDENTS: CHARACTERISTICS AND TRENDS." University of California, Los Angeles, 1976. 129 pp. Source: DAI, XXXVII, 11A (May, 1977), 6871-A. XUM Order No. 77-9344.

The results indicated that no women held the titles of associate or deputy superintendent during the 1974-1975 school year. Women were generally older than men when they received their first administrative appointment. Women superintendents tended to be in rural and suburban areas; women assistant superintendents tended to be in larger, urban districts.

Harris, Ianthe Clothilde (Ed. D.). "COMPETENCIES DEMONSTRATED BY NURSE PRACTITIONERS IN PROVIDING CARE FOR INFANTS IN SELECTED AMBULATORY HEALTH CARE SETTINGS." Columbia University Teachers College, 1976. 203 pp. Source: DAI, XXXVII, 6B (December, 1976), 2772-B. XUM Order No. 76-27,703.

This study concluded that the nursing education curriculum should place a greater emphasis on wellness care and that it should provide opportunities for students to learn about social and cultural behaviors of ethnic groups.

Harris, Martha Jean (Ph. D.). "SEX-TYPING OF IN-SCHOOL MOVEMENT BEHAVIORS: PERCEPTIONS AND RATIONALES OF SIXTH GRADE BOYS AND GIRLS." University of Oregon, 1974. 263 pp. Source: DAI, XXXV, 8A (February, 1975), 4983-A. XUM Order No. 75-3880.

This study found a high level of agreement between the sexes regarding which behaviors are expected of a given sex within the school environment.

Harris, Mary Elizabeth Barnes (Ed. D.). "DEVELOPMENT, IMPLEMENTATION, AND EVALUATION OF EARLY PROFESSIONAL OPPORTUNITIES IN HOME ECONOMICS EDUCATION." Oklahoma State University, 1975. 173 pp. Source: DAI, XXXVI, 11A (May, 1976), 7251-A. XUM Order No. 76-9680.

Among the findings: home economics educators should be encouraged
to offer more and varied types of activities that would involve more
students.

Harrison, Clyde Eugene (Ph. D.). "THE SEX-ROLE CLASSIFICATION OF
SCHOOL-RELATED OBJECTS BY SELECTED FOURTH-GRADE SUBJECTS FROM CONTRASTING
LEARNING ENVIRONMENTS INCLUDING A TREND ANALYSIS, K-4." Ohio State Uni-
versity, 1976. 139 pp. Source: DAI, XXXVII, 11A (May, 1977), 6942-A.
XUM Order No. 77-10,536.

It was found that the classroom learning environment was an insignificant factor because it did not seem to affect the sex-role classification of school-related objects.

Harrison, Ella Vardha (Ph. D.). "CLOTHING SELECTION PRACTICES, IN-
TEREST, KNOWLEDGE, AND PERCEPTION FOR A GROUP OF EDUCATED WOMEN CONSUMERS
IN INDIA." Pennsylvania State University, 1969. 243 pp. Source: DAI,
XXXI, 2B (August, 1970), 785-B. XUM Order No. 70-13,833.

This study found that clothing interest was related to clothing knowledge which in turn was related to clothing perception.

Harrison, Omeera Anne Jasper (Ed. D.). "AN EXPERIMENTAL STUDY OF
PSYCHOMOTOR SKILL LEARNING OF A NURSING PROCEDURE USING TWO METHODS OF
CRITIQUE IN INSTRUCTION." University of Colorado, 1972. 151 pp. Source:
DAI, XXXIII, 8A (February, 1973), 4059-A. XUM Order No. 73-1780.

Results showed that self critique by means of videotapes of performance and checklists resulted in the same learning level as did
teacher critique.

Hart, Margaret Elder (Ed. D.). "NEEDS AND RESOURCES FOR GRADUATE
EDUCATION IN NURSING IN CANADA." Columbia University, 1962. 303 pp.
Source: DAI, XXIII, 5 (November, 1962), 1665-1666. XUM Order No. 62-
4897.

The results of this study justified the conclusion that graduate education in nursing is needed in Canada, that potential candidates are
available, and that the universities have the resources for developing
graduate programs.

Hart, Wynelle Mims (Ed. D.). "THE EVALUATION OF THE PERFORMANCE OF
BACCALAUREATE STUDENTS IN CLINICAL NURSING." Indiana University, 1974.
125 pp. Source: DAI, XXXV, 9B (March, 1975), 4519-B. XUM Order No.
75-5560.

Concluded that the evaluation of performance in clinical nursing is
difficult but necessary and that the student's ability to meet the
needs of the patient are a top priority in preparing a professional
practitioner.

Hartley, Gordon Eugene (Ed. D.). "A COMPARISON OF BACCALAUREATE AND
ASSOCIATE DEGREE NURSING STUDENTS ON SELECTED PERSONALITY CHARACTERIS-
TICS." Washington State University, 1974. 96 pp. Source: DAI, XXXV,
10B (April, 1975), 4963-B-4964-B. XUM Order No. 75-7642.

Concluded that both graduating baccalaureate and associate degree nursing students may possess the same potential characteristics for the assumption of leadership responsibilities.

Harvey, Elaine Butler (Ed. D.). "PREDICTION OF STATE BOARD TEST POOL EXAMINATION SCORES UTILIZING GRADES ACHIEVED ON BASIC SCIENCE ASSESSMENT TESTS IN NURSING." Indiana University, 1976. 106 pp. Source: DAI, XXXVII, 8A (February, 1977), 5014-A-5015-A. XUM Order No. 77-3344.

Major findings were that science prerequisite courses like anatomy, microbiology and pharmacology should be retained as prerequisites to the upper division nursing courses.

Harvey, Lillian Holland (Ed. D.). "ELEMENTS IN THE ESTABLISHMENT OF PRESERVICE BACCALAUREATE PROGRAMS IN NURSING IN SENIOR COLLEGES AND UNIVERSITIES DURING 1949-1958." Columbia University, 1966. 180 pp. Source: DAI, XXVII, 12B (June, 1967), 4455-B-4456-B. XUM Order No. 67-6526.

Among the recommendations: colleges and universities whose preservice baccalaureate programs are sound should expand in order to graduate the maximum number. Selected publicly supported and private colleges should be encouraged to establish new programs.

Hastings, Dolores Buehler (Ed. D.). "THE RELATIONSHIP OF SELECTED VARIABLES TO THE POSTGRADUATE EDUCATIONAL PLANS OF MEMPHIS STATE UNIVERSITY SENIOR WOMEN." Memphis State University, 1971. 151 pp. Source: DAI, XXXII, 8A (February, 1972), 4349-A. XUM Order No. 72-7573.

It was concluded that high marks tend to characterize the students planning to attend graduate school.

Hauf, Barbara Judith (Ed. D.). "AN EVALUATIVE STUDY OF A NON-TRADITIONAL FIELD PLACEMENT FOR COMMUNITY HEALTH NURSING STUDENTS." University of Montana, 1975. 237 pp. Source: DAI, XXXVI, 6B (December, 1975), 2725-B. XUM Order No. 75-26,197.

The findings show that nursing students were able to accomplish the community health nursing course objectives through a non-traditional family and community entry point.

Hausdorff, Joyce (Ed. D.). "INDEPENDENT STUDY EXPERIENCE OF BACCALAUREATE NURSING STUDENTS AND PERCEIVED AUTONOMY." Columbia University, 1973. 83 pp. Source: DAI, XXXIV, 6A (December, 1973), 3023-A. XUM Order No. 73-31,275.

This study did not find that students who had independent study experiences felt more autonomous than students who had no such experience.

Hausmann, Sister M. Daniel (Ph. D.). "THE ROLE OF THE PRESIDENT IN AMERICAN FOUR-YEAR LIBERAL ARTS COLLEGES CONDUCTED BY THE BENEDICTINE SISTERS." Catholic University of America, 1963. 208 pp. Source: DAI, XXIV, 9 (March, 1964), 3602. XUM Order No. 63-6759.

Found that although the religious superior of the community operating the college had traditionally served as college president, the complexities and demands of modern administration required separate roles for the religious superior and the college president.

Haynes, John Sherman (Ph. D.). "A STUDY TO DETERMINE THE IMPACT OF A SEX-ROLES COURSE ON CHANGING ATTITUDES TOWARDS SELF AND WOMEN." West Virginia University, 1976. 125 pp. Source: DAI, XXXVII, 12B, Part 1 (June, 1977), 6405-B. XUM Order No. 77-12,312.

Women authors received better ratings on the pre and posttest articles written on male-related professions but scored significantly lower on nonsex-related articles. Changes in attitudes towards sex roles of men and women occurred mainly because of previously formed stereotyped attitudes and not because of the sex-roles course.

Healy, Frances Patricia (Ph. D.). "A HISTORY OF EVELYN COLLEGE FOR WOMEN, PRINCETON, NEW JERSEY, 1887 TO 1897." Ohio State University, 1967. 207 pp. Source: DAI, XXVIII, 9A (March, 1968), 3478-A. XUM Order No. 68-2999.

This women's college closed in 1897 because of poor financial support, the early death of its founder (the Rev. Joshua Hall McIlvaine), and the general backwardness of New Jersey education.

Hearn, Martha B. (Ed. D.). "ATTITUDES OF A SELECTED GROUP OF PHYSICIANS AND NURSES TO RECOMMENDED ROLES FOR THE NURSE PRACTITIONER." University of Alabama, 1974. 215 pp. Source: DAI, XXXV, 11B (May, 1975), 5505-B-5506-B. XUM Order No. 75-9904.

Identified the perceptions of practicing and prospective health professionals regarding the roles of nurses. Findings: (1) the expanded role of the nurse was perceived as providing one solution to the shortage of adequate health care; and (2) nursing education should include awareness of an expanding role for nurses.

Hedman, Edwin Randolph (Ph. D.). "EARLY FRENCH FEMINISM: FROM THE EIGHTEENTH CENTURY TO 1848." New York University, 1954. 206 pp. Source: DAI, XVII, 10 (1957), 2253-2254. XUM Order No. 22,950.

Poverty, factions, and lack of educational facilities were obstacles to the feminist movement among working class French women of the period.

Heins, Margaret Jones (Ed. D.). "A COMPARISON OF THE PERFORMANCE OF HIGH RISK STUDENT ADMISSION TO NURSING WITH THAT OF REGULARLY ADMITTED STUDENTS." University of Tennessee, 1975. 101 pp. Source: DAI, XXXVI, 7B (January, 1976), 3311-B. XUM Order No. 76-1943.

Ascertained whether students rejected from a school of nursing through traditional admission procedures could succeed at school and on the job with special assistance. Results showed that if they persisted and graduated, their performance closely matched that of regularly admitted students.

Henderson, Grace Mildred (Ph. D.). "PROPOSALS FOR THE ADMINISTRATION OF HOME ECONOMICS IN THE LIGHT OF CO-ORDINATED COMMUNITY EDUCATIONAL EFFORTS IN HOME AND FAMILY LIFE." Ohio State University, 1944. 578 pp. Source: Dissertation, pp. 556-561.

Among the author's 10 suggestions to accomplish a democratic, community-oriented home economics training program were: (1) interdependent student residence, research, and field work; (2) making home economics a university-wide responsibility; (3) administration and teaching staff sharing responsibility for all home and family life problems; and (4) administration and staff use of democratic values.

Henderson, Jean Carolyn Glidden (Ph. D.). "WOMEN AS COLLEGE TEACHERS." University of Michigan, 1967. 171 pp. Source: DAI, XXVIII, 6A (December, 1967), 2026-A-2027-A. XUM Order No. 67-15,635.

Compared the careers as college teachers of Woodrow Wilson Fellows of 1958 and 1959 to determine whether women had the same opportunities as men, and if not, whether the differences were due to the women's preferences or to discrimination against them. It was concluded that women college teachers with Ph. D. degrees were not given the same opportunities as men and were discriminated against.

Henderson, Linnea Elizabeth (Ed. D.). "A PROPOSAL FOR PRESERVICE NURSING PROGRAMS IN WEST VIRGINIA." Columbia University, 1962. 224 pp. Source: DAI, XXIII, 5 (November, 1962), 1666. XUM Order No. 62-4898.

Recommended that associate degree nursing programs be established in selected 4-year colleges and that pre-nursing programs be discontinued.

Hennessey, Sister Mary Agnes (Ph. D.). "A STUDY OF THE ATTITUDES OF COLLEGE WOMEN TOWARD SELECTED INTERGROUP PROBLEMS AND THEIR RELATION TO CERTAIN BACKGROUND FACTORS." St. Louis University, 1958. 234 pp. Source: DAI, XIX, 11 (May, 1959), 2807-2808. XUM Order No. Mic 59-898.

Explored the attitudes in Catholic colleges for women toward certain intergroup problems in American society. Conclusions: (1) interreligious problems--freshmen and seniors vary significantly with seniors holding more favorable attitudes; (2) interracial problems--a majority of students favor racial integration on social, economic, educational, and political levels (students whose parents are in higher income brackets have less favorable attitudes); and (3) socioeconomic problems--seniors show more favorable attitudes.

Henning, Sister Gabrielle (Ph. D.). "A HISTORY OF CHANGING PATTERNS OF OBJECTIVES IN CATHOLIC HIGHER EDUCATION FOR WOMEN IN MICHIGAN." Michigan State University, 1969. 213 pp. Source: DAI, XXX, 4A (October, 1969), 1413-A. XUM Order No. 69-16,143.

The 6 women's colleges studied historically held certain common objectives, including (1) a Catholic philosophy of education; and (2) intellectual, moral, service, and teacher training objectives. Another objective since the Second Vatican Council is community involvement.

Henry, Grant George (Ph. D.). "A COMPARISON OF THE EMPLOYMENT STATUS OF BLACK MEN AND WOMEN PHYSICAL EDUCATORS IN BLACK INSTITUTIONS OF HIGHER EDUCATION." University of Illinois at Urbana-Champaign, 1975. 143 pp. Source: DAI, XXXVI, 9A (March, 1976), 5920-A-5921-A. XUM Order No. 76-6789.

Concluded that the women physical educators were more dissatisfied than men because men received higher salaries, held more tenured positions, had higher academic rank, and taught lighter loads.

Henry, Iona Shulenberger (Ed. D.). "A STUDY OF THE EDUCATIONAL POLICY AND EFFORT OF THE WOMAN'S DIVISION OF CHRISTIAN SERVICE OF THE METHODIST CHURCH." New York University, 1960. 312 pp. Source: DAI, XXI, 10 (April, 1961), 2945-2946. XUM Order No. Mic 61-367.

No specific common policies were in operation. Cultural conditions within ethnic groups served by the schools were appreciably affected by the schools.

Henschel, Beverly Jean Smith (Ed. D.). "A COMPARISON OF THE PERSON-ALITY VARIABLES OF WOMEN ADMINISTRATORS AND WOMEN TEACHERS IN EDUCATION." University of Utah, 1964. 144 pp. Source: DAI, XXV, 11 (May, 1965), 6313. XUM Order No. 64-10,534.

The 136 women administrators, teachers, and supervisors exhibited more masculine responses than feminine responses, which indicated leadership qualities. They scored higher than women in general in ability to analyze and predict behaviors in others, were less likely to feel inferior, and were not as likely to help others in need.

Herald, Eunice Elizabeth (Ph. D.). "RELATIONSHIP BETWEEN VARIOUS FACTORS AND TYPES AND FREQUENCIES OF PROBLEMS BROUGHT TO VOCATIONAL HOME-MAKING TEACHERS IN SEVENTY-SEVEN MICHIGAN HIGH SCHOOLS." University of Michigan, 1952. 180 pp. Source: DAI, XII, 4 (1952), 512. XUM Order No. 3763.

There was a significant relationship between the types and frequen-cies of the problems and each of the following factors: the size and type of community; the size of school and the number of guidance personnel available; the teachers' guidance training; the students' grade placement, work experience, number of siblings, and status of the home as indicated by the fathers' occupations. There was no significant relationship between the types and frequencies of the problems and each of the following factors: teachers' experience; ages of students; and extracurricular activities.

Herberg, Dorothy Mary Chave (Ph. D.). "CAREER PATTERNS AND WORK PARTICIPATION OF GRADUATE FEMALE SOCIAL WORKERS." University of Michi-gan, 1970. 269 pp. Source: DAI, XXXII, 2A (August, 1971), 1079-A. XUM Order No. 71-15,177.

One important finding was the sequence of marriage and education as a consistently strong predictor of work participation.

Hereford, Julia J. (Ph. D.). "SELF CONCEPTS AND CHILDHOOD RECOLLEC-TIONS OF UNDERGRADUATE WOMEN PREPARING FOR NURSING OR TEACHING." Univer-sity of Chicago, 1971. Source: Dissertation, pp. 1-25.

Supported the hypothesis that mothers, fathers, and a teacher will be important in the memory of childhood relationships for all women stu-dents; however, a teacher will be more important for those students planning to teach. A nurse and doctor will be more important for

the nursing students. A father and a doctor will be most important
for the students preparing for masculine fields.

Herkenhoff, Louis Henry (Ed. D.). "A COMPARISON OF OLDER AND YOUNGER
WOMEN STUDENTS AT SAN JOSE CITY COLLEGE WITH IMPLICATIONS FOR CURRICULUM
AND STUDENT PERSONNEL SERVICES." University of California, Berkeley,
1966. 250 pp. Source: DAI, XXVII, 8A (February, 1967), 2443-A. XUM
Order No. 66-15,304.

Findings: women 30 years or older were more education-minded, had a
superior tested verbal aptitude and achievement, and were more active
readers.

Hernandez, Aurea Rosario (Ph. D.). "A COMPARATIVE STUDY OF FEAR OF
SUCCESS IN MEXICAN-AMERICAN AND ANGLO-AMERICAN COLLEGE WOMEN." California School of Professional Psychology, Los Angeles, 1976. 155 pp.
Source: DAI, XXXVIII, 2B (August, 1977), 900-B-901-B. XUM Order No.
77-17,176.

Fear of success was divided into 3 related parts: competition,
anxiety and self esteem. The women studied proved to be more competitive than males. The Mexican-American college women were a
highly competitive and acculturated group with significantly higher
levels of anxiety and lower self esteem than Anglo-American women.

Hesiak, Thomas Ervin, Sr. (Ed. D.). "A STUDY OF SEX DISCRIMINATION
IN EMPLOYMENT, ADMISSION OF STUDENTS, AND TREATMENT OF STUDENTS ENROLLED
AT THE SENIOR HIGH SCHOOL LEVEL OF THE MILWAUKEE PUBLIC SCHOOLS." 217
pp. Source: DAI, XXXVII, 7A (January, 1977), 4264-A. XUM Order No.
77-802.

Recommended that all school personnel should discuss in seminars or
meetings how best to implement Title IX (prohibition of sex discrimination).

Hewitt, Shirley Ann (Ed. D.). "THE STATUS OF WOMEN FACULTY IN DE-
PARTMENTS OF BUSINESS EDUCATION OF NABTE INSTITUTIONS." Utah State University, 1975. 218 pp. Source: DAI, XXXVI, 9A (March, 1976), 5862-A-
5863-A. XUM Order No. 76-6226.

Significant differences were found between male and female faculty
members in academic rank, salaries, academic degrees, and marital
status. Female faculty members held lower rank and received less
pay.

Hiatt, Helen Garner (Ed. D.). "AN ASSESSMENT OF SEX KNOWLEDGE AND
ATTITUDES TOWARD SEX OF STUDENTS AND FACULTY IN FIVE NURSING EDUCATION
PROGRAMS." Memphis State University, 1975. 118 pp. Source: DAI,
XXXVII, 1A (July, 1976), 112-A-113-A. XUM Order No. 76-10,868.

Definite differences were found in sex knowledge and attitudes in
the 5 programs. Sexual myths are less believed by nursing students
and faculty. Entering nursing students and nursing faculty did not
differ in their attitudes about or knowledge of human sexuality.
Baccalaureate nursing graduates were somewhat more liberal about
sexual attitudes.

Hickey, Betty Gene (Ed. D.). "WASTED WOMANPOWER: FACTORS AFFECTING THE PLANS OF GIFTED GIRLS TO GO OR NOT TO GO TO COLLEGE." Columbia University Teachers College, 1959. Source: TCCU DIGESTS (1959), pp. 281-282.

Described the attitudes of 50 gifted high school girls, 25 of whom planned to attend and 25 of whom did not plan to attend college. There were differences in the influences which affected college bound and non-college bound gifted girls. Motivation for higher education was especially low in rural areas.

Higgs, Zana Rae (Ed. D.). "EXPECTATIONS AND PERCEPTIONS OF THE CUR-RICULAR LEADERSHIP ROLE OF ADMINISTRATORS OF NURSING EDUCATION UNITS." Columbia University, 1975. 167 pp. Source: DAI, XXXV, 12A, Part 1 (June, 1975), 7558-A-7559-A. XUM Order No. 75-13,893.

Purpose was to compare opinions of chief administrative officers and select faculty members on their expectations and perceptions of the curricular leadership role of the chief administrative officers of baccalaureate nursing education programs.

Hill, Ann G. (Ed. D.). "PERCEPTIONS OF WOMEN DOCTORAL GRADUATES IN EDUCATION AT THE UNIVERSITY OF ALABAMA RELATIVE TO ADMISSION AND SELECTED ACADEMIC AND PROFESSIONAL EXPERIENCE." University of Alabama, 1970. 145 pp. Source: DAI, XXXI, 10A (April, 1971), 5034-A. XUM Order No. 71-9098.

Over 1/3 of the participants felt that the doctoral program should have provided more insight into the functions and roles of women in educational leadership positions.

Hill, Helen Thacker (Ed. D.). "CHARACTERISTICS OF HEAD RESIDENTS AND A PROPOSED COURSE OF STUDY FOR HEAD RESIDENTS OF WOMEN'S RESIDENCE HALLS." Oklahoma State University, 1970. 140 pp. Source: DAI, XXXI, 11A (May, 1971), 5765-A. XUM Order No. 71-11,167.

Concluded that the head resident should possess certain social and personality traits, be a college graduate, and be a stable, healthy individual.

Hiller, Jeannette Snyder (Ed. D.). "THE EDUCATION OF NURSES FOR SOCIAL RESPONSIBILITY IN THE OUTPATIENT CLINIC--THE SCHOOL OF NURSING, UNIVERSITY OF CALIFORNIA, THE MEDICAL CENTER, SAN FRANCISCO." Stanford University, 1952. 152 pp. Source: Dissertation, pp. 104-111.

Nursing students and nurse educators were handicapped by their in-ferior status in relation to other out-patient staff. Recommenda-tions for improving nurse education in the out-patient clinic inclu-ded developing relationships with social workers and volunteers, in-creasing nursing students' awareness of community resources, and allowing nurses to participate in the formulation of out-patient department policies.

Hillier, Elizabeth Charlotte (Ph. D.). "THE HOMEMAKING PROBLEMS, SATISFACTIONS, AND GOALS OF RECENT HOME ECONOMICS GRADUATES AND THEIR IMPLICATIONS FOR THE COLLEGE CURRICULUM." Ohio State University, 1952.

272 pp.   Source: DAI, XVIII, 4 (April, 1958), 1413-1416.   XUM Order No.
25,447.

A relationship existed between the values which some individuals saw
in their home economics training and their satisfactions. A similar
relationship was seen between problems of some homemakers and what
they reported as weaknesses in the curriculum.

Hilton, Margaret J. (Ed. D.).   "THE EMPLOYMENT STATUS OF MEN AND
WOMEN BACCALAUREATE GRADUATES FROM THE COLLEGE OF BUSINESS ADMINISTRATION
AT THE UNIVERSITY OF TENNESSEE FROM 1969 TO 1973." University of Tennes-
see, 1974.   234 pp.   Source: DAI, XXXV, 8A (February, 1975), 4787-A.
XUM Order No. 75-3603.

Males had significantly higher salaries and greater job satisfaction
than females.

Hilton, Martha Eunice (Ph. D.).   "THE DEAN OF WOMEN IN THE PUBLIC
CO-EDUCATIONAL JUNIOR COLLEGE." Syracuse University, 1934.   322 pp.
Source: Dissertation, pp. 146-166.

Among activities considered desirable for deans of women: teaching,
academic guidance, advising on student activities, conducting freshman orientation, sponsoring student government, and helping develop
social and academic policies.

Hincker, Etta Anne (Ed. D.).   "INDUCTION PROGRAMS FOR BEGINNING
TEACHERS IN BACCALAUREATE NURSING." Memphis State University, 1970.
126 pp.   Source: DAI, XXXI, 9B (March, 1971), 5442-B-5443-B.   XUM Order
No. 71-6532.

Beginning teachers of baccalaureate nurses desired a more extensive
and carefully planned orientation program than they had been receiving.

Hinders, Duane Curtis (Ed. D.).   "AN EXPLANATION OF SEX DIFFERENCES
IN STUDENT EFFORT IN MATHEMATICS: THE IMPACT OF DIFFERENCES IN SOCIAL
INFLUENCE, ARTICULATION TO FUTURE WORK, AND RELATING GRADES TO ABILITY."
Stanford University, 1977.   242 pp.   Source: DAI, XXXVII, 12A, Part 1
(June, 1977), 7591-A-7592-A.   XUM Order No. 77-12,720.

Findings: males tended to have more math-related jobs, attached
greater importance to mathematical knowledge, and put forth more
effort in the learning process. Females tended to attribute poor
grades to lack of ability. Those with mothers in "male" jobs showed
more of the "male" tendencies.

Hinkley, Nancy Emily Engstrom (Ed. D.).   "THE RELATIONSHIP BETWEEN
SEX AND INTRINSIC JOB SATISFACTION OF ADULT EDUCATORS." North Carolina
State University at Raleigh, 1975.   147 pp.   Source: DAI, XXXVII, 1A
(July, 1976), 97-A-98-A.   XUM Order No. 76-14,322.

Female adult educators found less intrinsic job satisfaction than
males. Both were seeking the gratification of higher level needs
in their work.

Hinsvark, Inez Genieve (Ed. D.). "A CASE REPORT OF THE APPLICATION OF PROGRAMMED INSTRUCTION TECHNIQUES FOR NURSING EDUCATION." University of California, Los Angeles, 1965. 321 pp. Source: DAI, XXVI, 1 (July, 1965), 322. XUM Order No. 65-7317.

Programmed instruction techniques in nursing education can be used successfully and can save teachers' time if the skills to be taught are identified.

Hipps, Opal Shepard (Ed. D.). "THE STATUS OF NURSING ELECTIVES IN GENERIC BACCALAUREATE NURSING EDUCATION PROGRAMS." University of South Carolina, 1976. 123 pp. Source: DAI, XXXVII, 10A (April, 1977), 6176-A-6177-A. XUM Order No. 77-6764.

Nursing electives are offered mainly at the junior and senior levels, make the curriculum more flexible, and seem to be a beneficial trend.

Hirose, Hamako (Ed. D.). "A GUIDE FOR CURRICULUM DEVELOPMENT FOR RELIGIOUS EDUCATION DEPARTMENT OF SEIWA WOMAN'S COLLEGE IN NISHINOMIYA, JAPAN." Columbia University Teachers College, 1950. Source: TCCU DIGESTS (1950), pp. 221-222.

Curriculum changes should meet the needs of school, society, and students; be a cooperative and continuous process; and be attempted with administrative tact and skill.

Hitchman, Gladys Symons (Ph. D.). "THE PROFESSIONAL SOCIALIZATION OF WOMEN AND MEN IN TWO CANADIAN GRADUATE SCHOOLS." York University (Canada), 1976. Source: DAI, XXXVII, 12A, Part 1 (June, 1977), 7979-A-7980-A.

The findings indicated that women encountered status contradictions, discriminatory treatment, and suffer more stress than men. Membership in professionally supportive groups increased professional identification for female graduate students.

Hixson, Florence A. (Ed. D.). "CURRICULUM OFFERINGS IN ADVANCED NURSING EDUCATION IN 1947-1948." Columbia University Teachers College, 1952. Source: TCCU DIGESTS (1952), Part I, pp. 369-371.

Surveyed curriculum offerings in 42 U. S. advanced nursing education programs. Among the findings: (1) many schools of nursing education were reviewing their courses; and (2) some schools were experimenting with integrated courses which cut across subject-matter boundaries, especially in the clinical fields and in foundations of nursing education.

Ho, Kuo Cheng (Ph. D.). "THE STATUS AND THE ROLE OF WOMEN IN THE CHINESE COMMUNIST MOVEMENT, 1946-1949." Indiana University, 1973. 288 pp. Source: DAI, XXXIII, 11A (May, 1973), 6481-A. XUM Order No. 73-12,331.

Wanting women to be mobilized for socio-political development and change, the Chinese Communist Party set about giving women complete equality and full membership in the revolution. A 3-tiered organizational structure and pragmatic leadership techniques helped elevate

women. Complex reforms weakened parental and male authority in the
family, awakened women's class consciousness, raised their cultural
and economic standard, militarized them, equalized their socio-political conditions, and made them productive members of society.

Hoban/Hopkins, Frances T. (Ed. D.). "A STUDY OF THE RELATIONSHIPS
BETWEEN FRESHMAN STUDENT NURSES' ACADEMIC PERFORMANCE, SAT SCORES AND
SPECIFIED PERSONALITY VARIABLES." University of Toledo, 1975. 179 pp.
Source: DAI, XXXVI, 10A (April, 1976), 6473-A-6474-A. XUM Order No.
76-8355.

Results indicated that administrators and counselors can use the
tests with caution to predict academic success, failure, and attrition among freshman student nurses.

Hobson, Abigail Kyzer (Ph. D.). "A STUDY OF VALUES OF RURAL AND
URBAN NEGRO FAMILIES IN ALABAMA WITH IMPLICATIONS FOR HOMEMAKING EDUCA-
TION." Michigan State University, 1962. 226 pp. Source: DAI, XXIV,
2 (August, 1963), 721-722. XUM Order No. 63-3719.

Findings included: (1) carryover from class to home was low for both
urban and rural girls; (2) both urban and rural girls were close to
mothers; and (3) within limits, love, religion, comfort, tradition,
security, play, and health were important values in the families
studied.

Hockin, Katharine Boehner (Ed. D.). "A METHOD AND PLAN OF WORK FOR
DEVELOPING A PROGRAM IN RELIGIOUS EDUCATION FOR CHRISTIAN SECONDARY
SCHOOLS FOR GIRLS IN SZECHUAN, CHINA." Columbia University Teachers Col-
lege, 1948. 338 pp. Source: Eells, p. 73; and RELIGIOUS EDUCATION,
XLV (May-June, 1950), pp. 176-177.

Analyzed Chinese society and culture in transition, with youths'
facing adjustment problems complicated by the civil war. Christian
education was needed to clarify national issues and to help determine the goals and standards of Christian youths in China.

Hoey, Sister Ann Francis (Ph. D.). "A COMPARATIVE STUDY OF THE PROB-
LEMS AND GUIDANCE RESOURCES OF CATHOLIC COLLEGE WOMEN." Catholic Univer-
sity of America, 1957. 220 pp. Source: Published; Washington, DC:
Catholic University of America Press, 1957; pp. 200-210.

Catholic college students (1,056) and 455 Newman Club members reported these problems: academic (38.7%), vocational (22.8%), personal adjustment (11.34%), opposite sex (10.8%), religious and moral
(6.07%), home and family (5.24%), financial (4.14%), and health
(.83%).

Hoffman, Barbara Rodamer (Ph. D.). "SEX-ROLE PERCEPTIONS, SEX-ROLE
SELF-CONCEPTS AND FUTURE PLANS OF TEENAGE GIRLS." Boston University
Graduate School, 1973. 175 pp. Source: DAI, XXXIV, 4B (October, 1973),
1749-B-1750-B. XUM Order No. 73-23,488.

Found that: (1) perception of sex-role differences varied with age;
(2) self-concept of competency attributes may be related to experience; (3) relatively few relationships existed between sex-role

perceptions and future plans; (4) ideal number of children was related to self-concept and perception of male-female differences on
the warmth-expressiveness attributes; (5) actual number of children
planned was related to societal norms; and (6) subjects' future
plans were largely concerned with interpersonal rather than career
goals.

Hoffman, M. Marian Kasabian (Ph. D.). "THE BEGINNINGS OF BASIC
BACCALAUREATE NURSING EDUCATION: 1916-1929." Ohio State University,
1968. 228 pp. Source: DAI, XXX, 4B (October, 1969), 1771-B-1772-B.
XUM Order No. 69-11,649.

Encouraging the development of a baccalaureate program were: (1)
changing roles of women; (2) advancement of science and technology;
(3) World War I impact on nursing; (4) number of college women attracted to nursing; (5) Rockefeller report on nursing; and (6) extensive communication among advocates of university nursing education.

Hofland, Sharon Leech (Ph. D.). "FACTORS ASSOCIATED WITH THE ACCEP-
TANCE BY NURSING STUDENTS OF ROLE FUNCTIONS AS CHARACTERISTICS OF AN
EXPANDED ROLE FOR NURSES." South Dakota State University, 1976. 109 pp.
Source: DAI, XXXVII, 10A (April, 1977), 6769-A. XUM Order No. 77-646.

Major conclusions were: (1) the specific role functions were accepted as characteristics of an expanded role for nurses; and (2)
acceptance of expanded role functions was associated with the type
of program students were in and their concerns about professionalism.

Hofstrand, Richard Kent (Ph. D.). "THE OCCUPATIONAL EXPECTATIONS OF
HIGH SCHOOL SENIORS BY SEX, SOCIAL CLASS, CURRICULUMS, AND OTHER SELECTED
VARIABLES." University of Illinois at Urbana-Champaign, 1973. 181 pp.
Source: DAI, XXXIV, 2A (August, 1973), 677-A. XUM Order No. 73-17,560.

Females indicated more intensive expectancies and value for expectations in relations with other persons outside and within the job
environment.

Hogan, Carilee Ann (Ph. D.). "REGISTERED NURSES' COMPLETION OF A
BACHELOR OF SCIENCE DEGREE IN NURSING--ITS EFFECT ON THEIR ATTITUDE
TOWARD THE NURSING PROFESSION." Saint Louis University, 1972. 65 pp.
Source: DAI, XXXIII, 3B (September, 1972), 1170-B. XUM Order No. 72-
23,953.

Professional attitudes may increase after completing a bachelor's
degree in nursing but tend to diminish during the first year on the
job. Professional attitudes may increase again if the nurse remains
employed more than 1 or 2 years.

Hogstel, Mildred Onelle (Ph. D.). "ANALYSIS OF NURSING FUNCTIONS
AND PREPARATION." North Texas State University, 1974. 188 pp. Source:
DAI, XXXV, 10B (April, 1975), 4964-B. XUM Order No. 75-7044.

Graduate nurses (109 associate degree and 236 baccalaureate) were
asked to report on their performance of 80 activities and their
preparation for each. Employers (100) were asked to rate the

readiness of graduate nurses to perform each activity. More associate degree nurses were in leadership roles. The only difference in
the 5 functions studied was that baccalaureate nurses performed more
community health care functions. Associate degree nurses perceived
themselves as better in physical care and technical skills while
baccalaureate nurses felt better prepared for community health care.
Employers said baccalaureate nurses were better prepared for 4 of
the 5 functions studied.

Hohlogh, Faith Jefferson (Ed. D.). "FUNCTIONS OF NURSES WITH
DOCTOR'S DEGREES IN ACCREDITED BACCALAUREATE AND HIGHER DEGREE PROGRAMS
IN NURSING." Indiana University, 1974. 94 pp. Source: DAI, XXXV,
9B (March, 1975), 4519-B-4520-B. XUM Order No. 75-5628.

Conclusions about nurses with doctoral degrees: (1) those who had
administrative positions spent all their time in administration;
(2) those on teaching faculties had both instructional and administrative responsibilities; (3) those in research positions participated in the educational programs; (4) none of them participated in
clinical practice; and (5) there was a relationship between type of
degree and their function.

Holbrook, Viola Rose Funfsinn (Ed. D.). "A STUDY OF ATTITUDE AND
PERFORMANCE IN GYMNASTICS OF COLLEGE WOMEN PHYSICAL EDUCATION MAJORS."
University of New Mexico, 1970. 97 pp. Source: DAI, XXXI, 10A (April,
1971), 5178-A-5179-A. XUM Order No. 71-9303.

Conclusions were: (1) women physical education majors expressed a
positive attitude toward gymnastics, which was related to their pre
and post performance in gymnastics; (2) difference existed within 3
attitude level groups in the relationship between attitudes and performance; and (3) rural women had a less positive attitude toward
gymnastics than did urban women. The differences in attitudes and
skill diminished with instruction and practice.

Holcomb, Josephine Chandler (Ph. D.). "WOMEN IN THE LABOR FORCE IN
THE UNITED STATES, 1940-1950." University of South Carolina, 1976. 300
pp. Source: DAI, XXXVII, 10A (April, 1977), 6702-A-6703-A. XUM Order
No. 77-6765.

Women's training for World War II industrial jobs was crisis-oriented
and realistic but the skills they learned were not convertible to
postwar work.

Holcombe, Lee (Ph. D.). "MIDDLE-CLASS WORKING WOMEN IN ENGLAND,
1850-1914." Columbia University, 1962. 543 pp. Source: DAI, XXIII,
3 (September, 1962), 1004-1005. XUM Order No. 62-3696.

During these years middle class women became more interested in being
educated for jobs in 5 major fields: teaching, nursing and mid-
wifery, distributive trades, clerical labor, and the civil service.
The first 2 rose in status while the latter 3 areas declined in
status and work conditions. Inequality with men was their major
problem in entering the labor force.

Holland, John Lee (Ed. D.). "DIFFERENCES IN SCHOLASTIC-ENVIRONMENTAL PERCEPTION AMONG 6TH GRADE STUDENTS OF THE PROVO SCHOOL DISTRICT GROUPED ACCORDING TO SEX AND READING ACHIEVEMENT." Brigham Young University, 1974. 117 pp. Source: DAI, XXXV, 7A (January, 1975), 4130-A. XUM Order No. 75-549.

Sex factors were significant on 7 of the 11 reading tests. Girls were superior on 5 tests.

Hollandsworth, Helen Lorena (Ed. D.). "FACTORS INFLUENCING MONTANA STATE COLLEGE HOME ECONOMICS GRADUATES FOR THE YEARS 1935 THROUGH 1955 TO ENTER, TO LEAVE, OR TO REMAIN IN THE TEACHING PROFESSION." Michigan State University, 1959. 178 pp. Source: DAI, XX, 9 (March, 1960), 3649. XUM Order No. Mic 60-549.

There was a significant difference in teaching satisfaction of the women graduates who (1) had taught but were full-time homemakers; (2) had taught but were employed in other work; and (3) were teaching. Those who were teaching scored highest in level of satisfaction.

Holley, Jeanne Lowry (Ph. D.). "AN ANALYSIS OF PERSONALITY NEEDS AND CERTAIN BACKGROUND FACTORS WHICH MAY INFLUENCE CAREER CHOICE OF WOMEN BUSINESS EDUCATION MAJORS." University of Mississippi, 1969. 132 pp. Source: DAI, XXXI, 1A (July, 1970), 223-A-224-A. XUM Order No. 70-11,486.

Concluded that background factors and personality needs figured prominently in the women's choice of business education as a profession.

Hollinger, Constance Louise (Ph. D.). "THE EFFECTS OF STUDENT DEPENDENCY, SEX, BIRTH ORDER, AND TEACHER CONTROL IDEOLOGY OF TEACHER-STUDENT INTERACTION." Case Western Reserve University, 1975. 135 pp. Source: DAI, XXXVII, 2A (August, 1976), 883-A. XUM Order No. 76-16,050.

Results indicated that the control ideology of a teacher influenced her perception of students and the way she interacted with them. Students' sex influenced the teacher's perception of dependency. Birth order of students was related to the amount of praise or criticism received by the student. No clear relationship was shown between dependency score and teacher-student interaction.

Holmes, Lulu H. (Ph. D.). "A HISTORY OF THE POSITION OF THE DEAN OF WOMEN IN A SELECTED GROUP OF COEDUCATIONAL COLLEGES AND UNIVERSITIES IN THE UNITED STATES." Columbia University Teachers College, 1938. Source: TCCU DIGESTS, XIII (1938), pp. 57-60.

An historical study of Boston University, Cornell, Swarthmore, Oberlin, Northwestern University, and Universities of Chicago, Wisconsin, Michigan, Kansas, California, and Oregon provided data about problems of women students in housing, social life, and health as they were related to the work of deans of women.

Holmstrom, Lynda Lytle (Ph. D.). "INTERTWINING CAREER PATTERNS OF HUSBANDS AND WIVES IN CERTAIN PROFESSIONS." Brandeis University, 1970. 384 pp. Source: DAI, XXXI, 6A (December, 1970), 3055-A-3056-A. XUM Order No. 70-24,637.

Conclusions were that most problems of 2-career couples were connected with rigidity of occupations and the isolation of the nuclear family.

Holsopple, Frances Quinter (Ph. D.). "SOCIAL NON-CONFORMITY: AN ANALYSIS OF FOUR HUNDRED AND TWENTY CASES OF DELINQUENT GIRLS AND WOMEN." University of Pennsylvania, 1919. 43 pp. Source: Dissertation, pp. 42-43.

The majority of girls picked up on the street by protective officers were from mill districts, self-supporting, and not foreign born. The only preventive treatment for delinquency is recognition, special care, stabilizing influences, health and housing care, education, and good recreational facilities.

Holt, Barbara Alice (Ph. D.). "PRAXIS AND COMMITMENT IN FAMILY PLAN-NING EDUCATION: EVALUATION OF AN IN-SERVICE PROGRAM WITH HOME ECONOMISTS IN PANAMA." Cornell University, 1975. 264 pp. Source: DAI, XXXV, 10B (April, 1975), 4979-B-4980-B. XUM Order No. 75-8596.

Concluded that in-service education effectiveness, defined by Paulo Freire's praxis, was predictable by a combination of the 8 independent variables used with 167 home economists.

Holtzclaw, Katharine (Ph. D.). "SOME FACTORS RELATED TO CURRICULUM DEVELOPMENT FOR A MINORITY SEGREGATED GROUP AS REVEALED BY A STUDY OF HOME-ECONOMICS EDUCATION IN NORTH CAROLINA." New York University, 1945. Source: New York University, School of Education, ABSTRACTS OF THESES (October, 1944-June, 1945), pp. 81-84.

Black social problems of economics, health, housing, child welfare and guidance, family, and general education were examined. Recom-mendations were made for ways home economics could assist black women in solving them.

Honeycutt, Karen (Ph. D.). "CLARA ZETKIN: A LEFT-WING SOCIALIST AND FEMINIST IN WILHELMIAN GERMANY." Columbia University, 1975. 483 pp. Source: DAI, XXXVI, 6A (December, 1975), 3925-A-3926-A. XUM Order No. 75-27,425.

Clara Zetkin was a principal theoretician on women's status among European socialists before World War I, was the leader of the social-ist women's movement in Germany in the early 1900's, and the head of the socialist women in the Second International after 1907. On the basis of her correspondence and writings, the study traced her per-sonal, political, and intellectual development from 1857 through 1914.

Hood, Grace Gordon (Ph. D.). "A STUDY OF THE CONTENT OF PREREQUISITE CHEMISTRY COURSES IN RELATION TO THE CONTENT OF UNDERGRADUATE COURSES IN HOME ECONOMICS." University of Minnesota, 1934; Source: Published; Same Title; Minneapolis, MN: Burgess Publishing Co., 1934; pp. 105-110.

Found that: (1) there was a marked lack of agreement about the amount and nature of the chemistry courses required for home economics cour-ses; (2) experts disagreed about what chemistry content had home eco-nomics applications; (3) students were required to study material ir-relevant to home economic; and (4) students' ability to apply chemis-try to home economics was influenced by several factors.

Hopwood, Kathryn Louise (Ph. D.). "EXPECTATIONS OF UNIVERSITY FRESH-
MAN WOMEN." Ohio State University, 1953. 139 pp. Source: DAI, XIX, 7
(January, 1959), 1652-1655. XUM Order No. Mic. 58-7179.

Most preferred to combine home making, personal development, and
marriage with a job.

Horn, Marcia A. (Ed. D.). "IDEAS OF THE FOUNDERS OF THE EARLY COL-
LEGES FOR WOMEN ON THE ROLE OF WOMEN'S EDUCATION IN AMERICAN SOCIETY."
Rutgers University, 1977. 157 pp. Source: DAI, XXXVII, 12A, Part 1
(June, 1977), 7577-A. XUM Order No. 77-13,465.

Focused on the educational and social views of such prominent college
founders as Emma Willard, Catharine Beecher, Mary Lyon, Sophia Smith,
Henry Durant, Matthew Vassar, and M. Carey Thomas. Troy Female Seminary, Hartford Seminary, Mount Holyoke, Elmira, Vassar, Wellesley,
Smith, and Bryn Mawr were the main colleges studied. These founders
of women's colleges were opposed to the woman suffrage movement.
They believed that women should use their advanced education in the
home and should work for altruistic and religious motives.

Hosford, Marian Hauck (Ed. D.). "THE CONTINUING EDUCATION OF SCHOOL
NURSE-TEACHERS IN NEW YORK STATE: A DESCRIPTIVE STUDY." Columbia University, 1962. 185 pp. Source: DAI, XXIII, 4 (October, 1962), 1233-
1234. XUM Order No. 62-4900.

Data showed an evolution of an extremely diversified educational pattern for school nurse teachers. Findings: former in-service education had become part of pre-service preparation; present pre-service
practice exceeded legal requirements; and certification requirements
caused wide diversity in pre-service preparation.

Hosinski, Sister Marion (Ph. D.). "SELF, IDEAL SELF, AND OCCUPATIONAL
ROLE: PERCEPTUAL CONGRUENCE IN VOCATIONALLY COMMITTED COLLEGE WOMEN. A
CROSS SECTIONAL STUDY OF SELF PERCEPTION, SELF ASPIRATION, AND OCCUPATION-
AL PERCEPTION AMONG UNIVERSITY NURSING STUDENTS." University of Notre
Dame, 1964. 248 pp. Source: DAI, XXVIII, 11A (May, 1968), 4481-A. XUM
Order No. 67-15,999.

Findings were: (1) nursing roles are broad enough to accommodate a
range of personalities and intellectual abilities; and (2) there are
trends toward high and increasing self-ideal-occupational percept
congruence among vocationally committed college women. These trends
are not adequately explained by experience, age, ego strength, or
intellectual awareness.

Howard, Michael Steven (Ph. D.). "THE EFFECTIVENESS OF AN ACTION
TRAINING MODEL (USING ROLE PLAYING, DOUBLING, AND ROLE REVERSAL) IN IM-
PROVING THE FACILITATIVE INTERPERSONAL FUNCTIONING (EMPATHY, RESPECT, AND
GENUINENESS) OF NURSING STUDENTS WITH DYING PATIENTS." University of
Maryland, 1975. 169 pp. Source: DAI, XXXVI, 6B (December, 1975), 3005-
B-3006-B. XUM Order No. 75-28,744.

Georgetown University nursing students were divided into discussion
training, action training, and control groups. Results indicate that
there were no significant differences among the 3 groups. The model

was not effective in improving levels of empathy, respect, and genuineness.

Howell, Samuel Ernest (Ed. D.). "THE FUNCTIONS OF THE HEAD RESIDENT
IN A WOMEN'S RESIDENCE HALL IN ACCREDITED COLLEGES AND UNIVERSITIES IN
MISSISSIPPI." University of Mississippi, 1971. 190 pp. Source: DAI,
XXXII, 1A (July, 1971), 91-A-92-A. XUM Order No. 71-18,629.

Profile of 97 head residents: most were widows between ages 56 and
65, had been a head resident 3 to 5 years, had some college education,
had a background in counseling, and earned $317 per month. Duties
included administration, student personnel service, and academic responsibilities. Major functions were counseling, maintaining a
friendly homelike atmosphere, and being available.

Hoyte, Stephney Keyser (D. S. W.). "THE WOMEN' JOB CORPS--PATTERNS
OF BEHAVIOR RELATING TO SUCCESS OR FAILURE." Catholic University of
America, 1969. 330 pp. Source: DAI, XXX, 6A (December, 1969), 2630-A-
2631-A. XUM Order No. 69-19,922.

Significant differences were noted on months in Job Corps, age, reading grade score, and highest grade completed before Job Corps. Findings indicated that: (1) the success group was more economically
deprived than the failure group; (2) there was a greater proportion
of medical defects in the success group; (3) no significant differences were found between the voluntary and referred groups; and (4)
comments during interviews indicated that the Job Corps was a rewarding, productive experience helping women develop a value preference for a productive life.

Hrebiniak, Lawrence George (Ph. D.). "A MULTIVARIATE ANALYSIS OF
PROFESSIONAL AND ORGANIZATIONAL COMMITMENT ORIENTATIONS AMONG TEACHERS
AND NURSES." State University of New York at Buffalo, 1971. 389 pp.
Source: DAI, XXXII, 6A (December, 1971), 3445-A. XUM Order No. 72-225.

Nurses (395) and 318 elementary and secondary teachers had common,
underlying similarities in professional commitment transcending occupational boundaries.

Hrubetz, Joan (Ph. D.). "MEASUREMENT OF CHANGES IN NURSING STUDENTS'
LEVELS OF EMPATHY, SELF-DISCLOSURE, AND CONFRONTATION AS OUTCOMES OF SYS-
TEMATIC HUMAN RELATIONS TRAINING." Saint Louis University, 1975. 108 pp.
Source: DAI, XXXVI, 6B (December, 1975), 2725-B. XUM Order No.75-26,267.

Lectures in the behavioral sciences on human relations were not effective in providing nursing students with skills of empathy, self-disclosure, and confrontation.

Hsu, Jennie (Ph. D.). "A STUDY OF CERTAIN PROBLEMS IN THE HIGHER
INSTITUTIONS FOR WOMEN IN CHINA." Columbia University Teachers College,
1931. 133 pp. Source: Eells, p. 73; and TCCU DIGESTS, VI (1929-1931),
n. p.

Health, academic, social, family, and financial problems were identified as influenced by changing conditions in China.

Huang, May Weifenne (Ph. D.). "PROFESSIONAL ATTITUDES, COMMITMENT, AND SELECTED DEMOGRAPHIC VARIABLES AS INDICATORS OF HOME ECONOMISTS' EMPLOYMENT SATISFACTION." Ohio State University, 1976. 153 pp. Source: DAI, XXXVII, 11A (May, 1977), 6996-A. XUM Order No. 77-10,542.

Results indicated that employment satisfaction was positively correlated with professional attitudes, administration, income, age, years as home economist, and degree earned. There was a negative correlation with commitment and teaching responsibility.

Huffman, Mabel (Ph. D.). "THE ADVANCEMENT OF AMERICAN WOMEN'S EDUCATION IN RELATION TO THE KONDRATIEFF THEORY OF BUSINESS CYCLES." Southern Illinois University, 1976. 248 pp. Source: DAI, XXXVII, 9A (March, 1977), 5630-A. XUM Order No. 77-6227.

In consonance with the Kondratieff Wave Theory, American women's advancement in education evolved through prosperous upswings of fervor and reform and downswings of economic contraction and self concern. More options in work and education occurred in low and peak wartime needs. Advancement of women's education was a part of the movement for equal rights. Four periods were studied as being closely related to the women's movement and their education: 1790-1844, 1844-1896, 1897-1950, and 1950-2004.

Hughes, Mary Angela (Ed. D.). "ATTITUDES OF WIVES OF U. S. ARMY OFFICERS IN THE CONTINENTAL U. S. TOWARD THEIR EDUCATIONAL AND EMPLOYMENT OPPORTUNITIES." Arizona State University, 1973. 208 pp. Source: DAI, XXXIV, 3A (September, 1973), 1026-A-1027-A. XUM Order No. 73-20,431.

Conclusions: (1) the length of marriage was directly related to satisfaction with the military establishment and available employment and educational opportunities; (2) frequent moves lessened problems in these 2 areas; (3) wife mobility had no adverse effects on education or employment; and (4) a direct relationship existed between educational attainment and satisfaction with education and job opportunities.

Hughes, Ruby Darlene Mentze (Ed. D.). "A COMPARISON OF THE RESPONSES OF 1974-75 SENIOR NURSING STUDENTS IN KANSAS COMMUNITY COLLEGES TO SELECTIVE QUESTIONNAIRE ITEMS." University of Kansas, 1976. 108 pp. Source: DAI, XXXVII, 8A (February, 1977), 4880-A. XUM Order No. 77-2235.

Findings: (1) the growth of community colleges in the last decade has been a large factor in meeting health care needs; (2) as a result of the impact of community colleges, more people can have a diploma in nursing than ever could before; and (3) each college should have ongoing evaluation to maintain quality and quantity.

Hulett, Sarah Anne (Ed. D.). "SELECTED VERTICAL MOBILITY DETERMINERS OF WOMEN EDUCATORS IN MISSOURI." University of Missouri-Columbia, 1976. 100 pp. Source: DAI, XXXVII, 9A (March, 1977), 5490-A. XUM Order No. 77-4916.

Some conclusions were: (1) vertically mobile women educators differed significantly on conformity; (2) significant determiners of upward mobility were achievement, goal orientation, recognition, benevolence, and leadership; (3) non-determiners were marital status, practical mindedness, variety, decisiveness, orderliness, support, and independence.

Hummer, Patricia Myles (Ph. D.). "THE DECADE OF ELUSIVE PROMISE: PROFESSIONAL WOMEN IN THE UNITED STATES, 1920-1930." Duke University, 1976. 261 pp. Source: DAI, XXXVII, 6A (December, 1976), 3852-A-3853-A. XUM Order No. 76-27,977.

Despite popular belief, American women made only modest gains in the labor force in the 1920's. Rising professional standards counterbalanced the expanding number of schools accepting women and the lessening of restrictions in the professions.

Hunkele, Catherine Eileen (Ph. D.). "FACULTY DEVELOPMENT PROGRAMS IN SELECTED SCHOOLS OF NURSING IN WESTERN PENNSYLVANIA." University of Pittsburgh, 1976. 173 pp. Source: DAI, XXXVII, 3A (September, 1976), 1428-A. XUM Order No. 76-19,914.

Most effective in improving teaching were: (1) support for participation in seminars; (2) support for faculty research; (3) tuition assistance; and (4) administrative system for reward or recognition.

Hunnicutt, John Manley (Ph. D.). "AN INVESTIGATION OF THE RELATION BETWEEN THE ELEMENTS OF THE SOCIAL SYSTEM AND WITHDRAWALS OF STUDENT NURSES." University of Nebraska, 1962. 280 pp. Source: DAI, XXIII, 10 (April, 1963), 4005-4006. XUM Order No. 63-2402.

Findings included: (1) schools with the greatest emphasis on professional objectives had the highest withdrawals; (2) schools with emphasis on marriage and the family had the lowest withdrawals; (3) there were no significant differences among students' goals, ends, and objectives; (4) different patterns of interaction existed; and (5) withdrawing students were not concerned about parents' opinions while graduating students saw family as the deciding factor in their finishing school.

Hunnicutt, Theo M. (Ed. D.). "DEFINING AND PROJECTING THE OFFICE OF THE DEAN OF WOMEN AT THE UNIVERSITY OF HOUSTON." University of Houston, 1956. 246 pp. Source: DAI, XVII, 3 (1957), 543-544. XUM Order No. 19,358.

Role and duties were compiled from old records, newspaper files, and other media. Students (193) were surveyed to determine the effectiveness of the Dean of Women office, and to evaluate services, attitude, philosophy, and shortcomings.

Hunt, Beverly English (Ed. D.). "CHARACTERISTICS, PERCEPTIONS AND EXPERIENCES OF MARRIED WOMEN STUDENTS AT LANSING COMMUNITY COLLEGE 1965." Michigan State University, 1966. 152 pp. Source: DAI, XXVIII, 1A (July, 1967), 104-A-105-A. XUM Order No. 67-7551.

Findings included: (1) marriage and finances were major reasons for not continuing education after high school; (2) most had started college education at Lansing; (3) women with children were not waiting until they were grown to resume education; (4) grades were significantly higher for married women; (5) pressure of time was the greatest problem; and (6) friends and family encouraged women to continue education.

Hunt, Delores Mae (D. A.). "A STUDY OF ADMINISTRATIVE DUTIES AND THEIR IMPORTANCE BY THOSE WHO ADMINISTER INTERCOLLEGIATE ATHLETIC PROGRAMS FOR WOMEN IN TENNESSEE." Middle Tennessee State University, 1976. 102 pp. Source: DAI, XXXVII, 3A (September, 1976), 1453-A. XUM Order No. 76-19,771.

Most directors of women's intercollegiate athletic programs in 66 Tennessee colleges performed administrative duties, did coaching, and taught classes.

Hurwitz, Robin Elaine (Ph. D.). "THE EFFECT OF SEX OF PARTICIPANTS ON DECISION MAKING IN SMALL TEACHER GROUPS." Columbia University, 1976. 115 pp. Source: DAI, XXXVII, 7B (January, 1977), 3677-B. XUM Order No. 76-29,395.

It was concluded that males and females initially responded equally in the decision-making process but that final decisions were more likely to be proposed by males.

Hutchinson, Sister Mary Kathleen (Ph. D.). "A COMPARATIVE STUDY OF THE INTELLIGENCE, ACHIEVEMENT, CULTURAL BACKGROUND, SOCIOECONOMIC STATUS, AND PERSONALITY OF TEACHER TRAINING AND NON-TEACHER TRAINING SOPHOMORES IN FIVE CATHOLIC LIBERAL ARTS COLLEGES FOR WOMEN." Fordham University, 1959. 216 pp. Source: Dissertation, pp. 192-198.

Conclusions about the 2 groups: (1) no significant differences existed in their intelligence, in freshman achievement, or in scores on the American Council on Education psychological examination; (2) no significant differences existed in socio-economic background or in fathers or mothers' employment; and (3) significant differences existed in the cultural background of science students not in teacher education.

Hyde, Frances C. (Ph. D.). "A STUDY OF THE TRAINING AND EXPERIENCE OF 150 BUSINESS WOMEN NOW OCCUPYING MANAGERIAL POSITIONS IN BUSINESS." University of Iowa, 1952. Source: Dissertation, pp. 130-140.

Questionnaire data from 150 successful business women revealed: education needed, work experience, participation in civic and community affairs, character traits, physical stamina required, factors which retard advancement, factors which foster advancement, and remarks about their success.

Iannotti, Mary Margaret (Ph. D.). "THE RELATIONSHIP BETWEEN CERTAIN NONCOGNITIVE FACTORS AND THE ACADEMIC ACHIEVEMENT OF JUNIOR COLLEGE WOMEN." Fordham University, 1970. 185 pp. Source: DAI, XXXI, 7A (January, 1971), 3271-A. XUM Order No. 71-30.

Differences in the perception of college climate were related more to grade placement (i.e., age) and to experience than to academic achievement.

Icaza, Susana Judith (Ed. D.). "PROGRAMED INSTRUCTION MATERIALS FOR TEACHING CHILD FEEDING PRACTICES TO NURSING STUDENTS IN EL SALVADOR." Columbia University, 1969. 223 pp. Source: DAI, XXX, 9B (March, 1970), 4224-B-4225-B. XUM Order No. 70-4511.

Nursing students had successful learning experiences with programmed instruction.

Infante, Mary Sue (Ed. D.). "THE LABORATORY CONCEPT IN BACCALAUREATE EDUCATION IN NURSING." Columbia University, 1971. 232 pp. Source: DAI, XXXIII, 8A (February, 1973), 4061-A. XUM Order No. 73-2604.

Found that students' clinical laboratory activities were chiefly oriented toward patient care.

Ingmire, Alice Elizabeth (Ed. D.). "ATTITUDES OF STUDENT NURSES AT THE UNIVERSITY OF CALIFORNIA." Stanford University, 1949. 253 pp. Source: Author.

Nursing students with good academic records had fewer negative attitudes toward their family and fewer personal problems than did academically poor students.

Ingram, Margaret Helen (Ed. D.). "DEVELOPMENT OF HIGHER EDUCATION FOR WHITE WOMEN IN NORTH CAROLINA PRIOR TO 1875." University of North Carolina, 1961. 285 pp. Source: DAI, XXIII, 1 (July, 1962), 144-145. XUM Order No. 62-3129.

Women's higher education began in 1800. Quaker and Moravian religious groups were important forces. Later on academies for young ladies were founded. In 1875 the state started direct support of higher education for women.

Inman, Lydia Lucille (Ph. D.). "EXPLORATORY STUDY OF HOUSEHOLD EQUIPMENT SUBJECT MATTER FOR SECONDARY SCHOOL HOME ECONOMICS CURRICULA." University of Minnesota, 1963. 199 pp. Source: DAI, XXIV, 2 (August, 1963), 574. XUM Order No. 63-6066.

Recommended that high school homemaking classes teach students about construction and operation requirements of such basic home equipment as ranges and refrigerators.

Insko, William Robert (Ed. D.). "A STUDY OF WOMEN DIRECTORS OF CHRISTIAN EDUCATION IN THE PARISHES OF THE EPISCOPAL CHURCH IN THE CONTINENTAL UNITED STATES." Duke University, 1960. 305 pp. Source: DAI, XXI, 3 (September, 1960), 551. XUM Order No. Mic 60-2962.

Questionnaire results showed that 59% held a bachelor's degree and 29% had no degree although most had an average of 2 years of college.

Ireson, Carol Jean (Ph. D.). "EFFECTS OF SEX ROLE SOCIALIZATION ON THE ACADEMIC ACHIEVEMENT, EDUCATIONAL EXPECTATIONS, AND INTERPERSONAL COMPETENCE OF ADOLESCENT GIRLS." Cornell University, 1975. 236 pp. Source: DAI, XXXVI, 10B (April, 1976), 5349-B. XUM Order No. 76-8173.

Found that traditional female sex role socialization had negative effects on female academic achievement and educational expectations, and mixed effects on girls' interpersonal competence.

Irland, Marquita L. (Ed. D.). "AN ANALYSIS OF THE HOME ECONOMICS TEACHER EDUCATION PROGRAM IN THREE MICHIGAN COLLEGES." Wayne University, 1956. 121 pp. Source: DAI, XVII, 1 (1957), 135-136. XUM Order No. 19,063.

The purpose was to determine why individuals entered, remained to graduate, or dropped out of the home economics education major. Findings showed that the majority did complete the requirements. This majority felt that too few electives were permitted.

Isenberger, Wilma E. (Ph. D.). "SELF-ATTITUDES OF WOMEN PHYSICAL EDUCATION MAJORS AS RELATED TO MEASURES OF INTEREST AND SUCCESS." State University of Iowa, 1957. 122 pp. Source: DAI, XVII, 12 (December, 1957), 2911-2912. XUM Order No. 23,752.

Results indicated that the self attitudes of teachers differed significantly from those of students enrolled in a liberal arts college and a university teachers college, but were similar to those of students in a teacher education institution.

Istiphan, Isis (Ph. D.). "ROLE EXPECTATIONS OF AMERICAN UNDERGRADU- ATE COLLEGE WOMEN IN A WESTERN COEDUCATIONAL INSTITUTION." University of Southern California, 1962. 211 pp. Source: DAI, XXIII, 7 (January, 1963), 2613-2614. XUM Order No. 62-6068.

Family, school, and church were not as strong influences as was the student culture on student ideas, behavior, and role expectations.

Jackson, Pamela Rochelle (Ph. D.). "SELF-CONCEPTIONS IN BLACK MALE AND FEMALE COLLEGE STUDENTS." Michigan State University, 1972. 114 pp. Source: DAI, XXXIII, 9B (March, 1973), 4509-B-4510-B. XUM Order No. 73-5406.

Two of three tests used found that the self concept of black men and women students did not differ significantly.

Jacobi, Eileen M. (Ed. D.). "ACADEMIC FREEDOM IN BACCALAUREATE PRO- GRAMS IN NURSING." Columbia University, 1968. 170 pp. Source: DAI, XXIX, 2B (August, 1968), 666-B. XUM Order No. 68-11,137.

This study indicated that: (1) faculty felt they had a degree of academic freedom, but (2) they felt inhibited by not having a doc- toral degree, which they regarded as necessary educational prepara- tion for academic leadership.

Jacobs, Mary G. (Ed. D.). "AN EVALUATION OF THE PHYSICAL EDUCATION SERVICE PROGRAM FOR WOMEN IN CERTAIN SELECTED COLLEGES." New York Uni- versity, 1957. 242 pp. Source: DAI, XVIII, 5 (May, 1958), 1715-1716. XUM Order No. 25,494.

Concluded that physical education service program for women in pub- licly controlled four-year colleges needed improvement.

Jacobson, Margaret Jane Davis (Ph. D.). "EFFECTIVE AND INEFFECTIVE BEHAVIOR OF TEACHERS OF NURSING AS DETERMINED BY THEIR STUDENTS." George Peabody College for Teachers, 1965. 125 pp. Source: DAI, XXVII, 5B (November, 1966), 1525-B. XUM Order No. 66-10,703.

Nursing students (961) regarded their teachers as significantly more effective than ineffective.

Jacobson, Phyllis Audrey (P. E. D.). "KNOWLEDGE AND PRACTICE OF WOMEN PHYSICAL EDUCATION TEACHERS IN INDIANA REGARDING NEGLIGENCE." Indiana University, 1974. 142 pp. Source: DAI, XXXV, 5A (November, 1974), 2751-A. XUM Order No. 74-24,519.

Many of the 190 women secondary physical education teachers had limited knowledge about liability in case of accidents. Development of undergraduate course material concerning the legal responsibilities of physical education teachers was recommended.

Jacobson, Rovena Furnivall (Ed. D.). "THE ORGANIZATION AND ADMINIS-TRATION OF SPECIAL COUNSELING PROGRAMS FOR ADULT WOMEN IN COLLEGES AND UNIVERSITIES." University of Southern California, 1969. 282 pp. Source: DAI, XXX, 5A (November, 1969), 1778-A. XUM Order No. 69-19,377.

This study evaluated special counseling programs for women in college and recommended ways to develop ideal programs. Two findings were that there is a trend toward establishing such counseling programs and that more financial aid and child-care facilities should be made available for these women.

Jacokes, Lee Edward (Ph. D.). "COEDUCATIONAL AND SINGLE SEX RESI-DENCE HALLS: AN EXPERIMENTAL COMPARISON." Michigan State University, 1975. 159 pp. Source: DAI, XXXVI, 9B (March, 1976), 4755-B-4756-B. XUM Order No. 76-5577.

Women significantly increased their non-conformity ratings within the first 2 months at the university. They dated more non-residents more often than did men. Both men and women experienced a signifi-cant decline in belief in church doctrines. Women were more in-volved in informal conversations with men and women; men were more involved in college organizations.

Jamann, JoAnn Shafer (Ed. D.). "JOB SATISFACTION AND DISSATISFACTION OF NURSE-FACULTY IN B.S.N. PROGRAMS." Lehigh University, 1974. 110 pp. Source: DAI, XXXV, 8A (February, 1975), 4914-A-4915-A. XUM Order No. 75-4729.

In both job satisfaction and dissatisfaction, achievement and use of best abilities were identified as most important factors. Inter-personal relationship was an important part of achievement for women employed as teachers in nursing baccalaureate programs.

James, Elizabeth Ann (Ed. D.). "THE ROLE OF WOMEN'S PRIVATE JUNIOR COLLEGES." Columbia University, 1962. 312 pp. Source: DAI, XXIV, 5 (November, 1963), 1938. XUM Order No. 63-5854.

Recommended that women's private junior colleges should remain small enough to provide guidance for individuals yet large enough to sustain themselves economically.

Jarrard, Mary Elizabeth W. (Ph. D.). "AN EMPIRICAL INVESTIGATION: TEACHING A COURSE IN ORAL COMMUNICATION TO SEXUALLY SEGREGATED CLASSES." University of North Carolina at Chapel Hill, 1976. 122 pp. Source: DAI, XXXVII, 8A (February, 1977), 4923-A. XUM Order No. 77-2055.

All-male and all-female classes had significantly more favorable attitudes toward the basic oral communication course than did the 2 mixed classes.

Jay, Winifred Tom (Ed. D.). "SEX STEREOTYPING IN SELECTED MATHEMATICS TEXTBOOKS FOR GRADES TWO, FOUR AND SIX." University of Oregon, 1973. 168 pp. Source: DAI, XXXIV, 6A (December, 1973), 3028-A. XUM Order No. 73-28,604.

Although 3 famous females were featured in 2 grade 6 textbooks, sex stereotyping clearly existed. Girls were generally observers and helpers.

Jenkins, Jeanette Marion Davis (Ed. D.). "THE RELATIONSHIP BETWEEN MATERNAL PARENTS' MUSICAL EXPERIENCE AND THE MUSICAL DEVELOPMENT OF TWO- AND THREE-YEAR-OLD GIRLS." North Texas State University, 1976. 150 pp. Source: DAI, XXXVII, 11A (May, 1977), 7015-A. XUM Order No. 77-11,111.

Data showed that the strongest and most positive relationship was between girls' musical development and musical environment; all other factors (ethnicity, social class, age, and others) were statistically insignificant.

Jenkins, Marlyn King (Ph. D.). "CONTRIBUTIONS OF TEXTILE AND CLOTHING COURSES TO THE GOALS OF GENERAL-LIBERAL AND PROFESSIONAL EDUCATION." Ohio State University, 1969. 227 pp. Source: DAI, XXXI, 2B (August, 1970), 786-B. XUM Order No. 70-14,045.

All students viewed courses supplemented by laboratory experience as contributing more than non-laboratory experience to liberal education goals. The teachers had different perceptions than the students; students thought that laboratory assignments were more beneficial than other materials.

Jenkins, William Job (Ed. D.). "A STUDY OF THE ATTITUDES OF ELEMEN- TARY SCHOOL TEACHERS IN SELECTED SCHOOLS IN MONTGOMERY COUNTY, PENNSYL- VANIA, TOWARD THE WOMAN ELEMENTARY SCHOOL PRINCIPAL." Temple University, 1966. 258 pp. Source: DAI, XXVII, 5A (November, 1966), 1223-A-1224-A. XUM Order No. 66-11,266.

A conclusion was that women teachers have a more favorable attitude than men toward women principals.

Jenkins, Wilsie Greene (Ph. D.). "THE EXTENT TO WHICH TRENDS THAT EMERGED DURING THE UNITED NATIONS FIRST DEVELOPMENT DECADE, 1960-1970, RELATIVE TO EDUCATIONAL OPPORTUNITIES FOR WOMEN ARE STILL PREVALENT DURING THE UNITED NATIONS SECOND DEVELOPMENT DECADE." Florida State

University, 1976. 151 pp. Source: DAI, XXXVII, 7A (January, 1977), 4162-A. XUM Order No. 76-29,451.

There were positive changes in trends in educational opportunities for women during the first half of the second development decade in all geographical areas. More changes occurred in developed nations, where women had better salaries, more leadership opportunities, and better vocational counseling. Because of low status, most women in developing nations could contribute little to economic and social development.

Jenks, Paul Everett (Ph. D.). "MALE AND FEMALE INTEREST FOR OPPOSITE SEX SCALES OF THE STRONG VOCATIONAL INTEREST BLANK." Brigham Young University, 1976. 117 pp. Source: DAI, XXXVIII, 1A (July, 1977), 177-A. XUM Order No. 77-13,805.

Although definite male-female differences in vocational interests existed, the findings substantiated that tests of vocational interest should offer both men and women a broader choice of occupations.

Jensen, Frances (Ph. D.). "HOME ECONOMICS IN GENERAL EDUCATION IN INSTITUTIONS OF HIGHER LEARNING: THE ROLE OF HOME ECONOMICS IN EDUCATION FOR HOME AND FAMILY LIVING AS A PART OF THE GENERAL EDUCATION OF STUDENTS IN SIX SELECTED LAND-GRANT COLLEGES." Cornell University, 1953. Source: Abstract in JOURNAL OF HOME ECONOMICS, XLV, No. 3 (March, 1953), pp. 202-203.

The study hypothesized that: (1) education leaders consider home economics education to be a vital part of the general education of land-grant college students; and (2) home economic departments have responsibility for providing a home and family living education.

Jensen, Judith Lee (Ph. D.). "THE DEVELOPMENT OF STANDARDS FOR WOMEN'S ATHLETICS AND THEIR INFLUENCE ON BASKETBALL COMPETITION IN THE STATE OF NEW YORK." Ohio State University, 1972. 461 pp. Source: DAI, XXXIII, 8A (February, 1973), 4155-A-4156-A. XUM Order No. 73-2029.

This historical study showed the evolution of women's basketball in New York from 1891 to 1972, when a national women's intercollegiate basketball championship was held.

Jensen, Mary Elizabeth (Ed. D.). "DEVELOPING INSTRUCTIONAL UNITS IN NURSING EDUCATION." University of California, Los Angeles, 1971. 287 pp. Source: DAI, XXXII, 11A (May, 1972), 6102-A. XUM Order No. 72-13,622.

This study assessed the effectiveness of utilizing single-concept films as the major medium in learning. Findings showed that single-concept films were suitable for teaching cognitive and psychomotor skills.

Jernigan, Marinell Hargrove (Ed. D.). "THE IMAGE OF THE UNIVERSITY OF ALABAMA SCHOOL OF NURSING HELD BY ITS ALUMNI, UNDERGRADUATE STUDENTS, AND POTENTIAL STUDENTS." University of Alabama, 1971. 416 pp. Source: DAI, XXXII, 9B (March, 1972), 5273-B. XUM Order No. 72-8442.

Major findings were that junior and senior students have a more negative image of the school than freshmen and sophomore students and
that the alumnae's image is less negative than the junior and seniors,
but more so than the freshmen and sophomores.

Jeu, Fongee (Dr. P. H.). "DESCRIPTIVE STUDY TO IDENTIFY VARIABLES
RELATED TO ATTRITION AND SUCCESS OF SPANISH SURNAMED VERSUS NON-SPANISH
SURNAMED STUDENTS IN TWO BACCALAUREATE PROGRAMS OF NURSING IN TEXAS."
University of Texas Health Science Center at Houston School of Public
Health, 1975. 115 pp. Source: DAI, XXXVII, 8B (February, 1977), 3870-
B-3871-B. XUM Order No. 77-2983.

Most frequent obstacles to success were financial, personal and family
problems.

Jimenez, Carmen Tombo (Ed. D.). "A PROPOSED STUDENT PERSONNEL PROGRAM
FOR THE PHILIPPINE WOMEN'S COLLEGE, ILOILO CITY, PHILIPPINES." Columbia
University Teachers College, 1951. 283 pp. Source: Eells, p. 122; and
TCCU DIGESTS (1951), pp. 295-296.

The study's purpose was to identify the needs of students at the
Philippine Women's College and to suggest ways these needs can be met
through an organized student personnel program. Plans and activities
were suggested and recommendations made for immediate and future
action in carrying out the proposals.

Joel, Lucille Ann Roncoroni (Ed. D.). "AN EXPLORATORY STUDY OF SOME
FACTORS WHICH MAY INFLUENCE CAREER CHOICE IN PSYCHIATRIC NURSING." Columbia University, 1970. 328 pp. Source: DAI, XXXII, 6B (December,
1971), 3458-B. XUM Order No. 72-1243.

The purpose was to identify factors which influence seniors graduating
from basic programs in nursing to choose or not to choose psychiatric
nursing. Major deciding factors were the course itself and the particular nurse instructor in psychiatric nursing.

Johanson, Alva Judith (Ph. D.). "FACTORS RELATED TO CAREER CHOICE BY
WOMEN PHYSICAL EDUCATION MAJORS AND IMPLICATIONS FOR EARLY RECRUITMENT."
University of Southern California, 1967. 582 pp. Source: DAI, XXVIII,
10A (April, 1968), 3986-A-3987-A. XUM Order No. 68-5866.

The hypothesis that the image of the physical education teacher was
influential in recruiting young college women into physical education
teaching was supported statistically in this study.

John, Alex, Jr. (Ed. D.). "AN ANALYSIS AND COMPARISON OF THE EFFECTS
OF STUDENT SEX, STUDENT RACE, TEACHER BEHAVIOR, AND TEACHER RACE UPON THE
ACHIEVEMENT OF TENTH GRADE ENGLISH STUDENTS." Northeast Louisiana Univer-
sity, 1972. 88 pp. Source: DAI, XXXIII, 7A (January, 1973), 3259-A.
XUM Order No. 72-34,031.

Some findings: (1) males had a greater gain in mean achievement than
did females; (2) female low achievers had a higher mean achievement
gain than did males; and (3) white males had a higher mean gain in
achievement than did white females.

Johnson, Allan Griswold (Ph. D.). "MODERNIZATION AND SOCIAL CHANGE: ATTITUDES TOWARD WOMEN'S ROLES IN MEXICO CITY." University of Michigan, 1972. 301 pp. Source: DAI, XXXIII, 11A (May, 1973), 6471-A. XUM Order No. 73-11,159.

The modernity of women's attitudes toward their roles was directly related to the level of their educational attainment.

Johnson, Bernadine (Ph. D.). "FAMILY RELATIONS AND SOCIAL ADJUSTMENT SCORES ON THE MINNESOTA PERSONALITY SCALE AS RELATED TO HOME AND SCHOOL BACKGROUNDS OF A SELECTED GROUP OF FRESHMAN WOMEN." Florida State University, 1956. 73 pp. Source: DAI, XVI, 8 (1956), 1438-1439. XUM Order No. 17,027.

Statistically significant differences were found between proportions of students with satisfactory and unsatisfactory scores in relation to size of high school, average high school grade, extra curricular activities, and time spent in college.

Johnson, Florence DeVida Howard (Ed. D.). "RELATIONSHIP BETWEEN RULE ADMINISTRATION, LEADERSHIP BEHAVIOR AND THE SEX OF ELEMENTARY SCHOOL PRINCIPALS." Pennsylvania State University, 1977. 146 pp. Source: DAI, XXXVIII, 2A (August, 1977), 571-A-572-A. XUM Order No. 77-17,698.

Female principals were perceived as more representative and punishment-centered in their application of rules. Female principals were seen to exercise a significantly greater degree of leadership than males in all other dimensions except tolerance of uncertainty, tolerance of freedom, and consideration.

Johnson, Genevieve Beulah (Ed. D.). "AN EXPLORATION OF THE USE OF TWO-WAY CAR RADIOS AND TELEPHONES BY STUDENTS AND INSTRUCTORS IN PUBLIC HEALTH NURSING LABORATORY IN BACCALAUREATE NURSING EDUCATION." Columbia University, 1969. 133 pp. Source: DAI, XXX, 5B (November, 1969), 2270-B. XUM Order No. 69-16,802.

Students and teachers in a rural public health nursing laboratory demonstrated a need to discuss specific subject matter with each other when separated regardless of the medium. Radio communication was found to be convenient, accessible, and reliable.

Johnson, Georgia Borg (Ph. D.). "ORGANIZATION OF THE REQUIRED COURSE IN PHYSICAL EDUCATION FOR WOMEN IN STATE UNIVERSITIES." Columbia University Teachers College, 1927. Source: TCCU DIGESTS, II (September, 1925-August, 1929), pp. 67-68.

Findings: (1) teachers' estimates are inadequate measures of students' innate physical efficiency and of their motor abilities; (2) men in physical education rank higher than do women; and (3) physical education teachers as a whole are of lower academic ranking than teachers in English, psychology, history, and chemistry.

Johnson, Hazel Muriel (Ph. D.). "PERCEPTIONS OF TEACHING RESPONSI-BILITIES IN BACCALAUREATE NURSING PROGRAMS." University of Minnesota, 1969. 229 pp. Source: DAI, XXX, 4B (October, 1969), 1772-B. XUM Order No. 69-16,419.

Purpose: to understand the expectations held by instructors and administrators regarding the teaching role in baccalaureate nursing programs. Findings included: (1) beginning instructors rated as most important those responsibilities related to improving their professional competence; and (2) instructors derived much satisfaction from their relationships with students, patients, and colleagues.

Johnson, Helen R. (Ed. D.). "A HISTORY OF PURDUE UNIVERSITY'S NURSING EDUCATION PROGRAMS." Indiana University, 1975. 195 pp. Source: DAI, XXXVI, 9B (March, 1976), 4383-B-4384-B. XUM Order No. 76-6277.

The author concluded that the associate and baccalaureate degree programs in nursing education should continue to operate and expand in enrollment by only a moderate degree.

Johnson, Josephine Louise (Ed. D.). "WOMEN LEADERS IN NATIONAL GUIDANCE AND COUNSELING ASSOCIATIONS: SOME IMPLICATIONS OF THEIR BACKGROUNDS AND LEADERSHIP ROLES." University of Wyoming, 1972. 267 pp. Source: DAI, XXXIII, 6A (December, 1972), 2713-A. XUM Order No. 72-32,789.

Most women leaders in national guidance and counseling associations had studied at private universities and as undergraduates had majored in the social sciences.

Johnson, Leon Johanson, Sr. (Ph. D.). "A COMPARATIVE STUDY OF THE WOMANHOOD EXPERIENCES OF BLACK YOUNG ADULT FEMALES AND WHITE YOUNG ADULT FEMALES." University of South Carolina, 1976. 97 pp. Source: DAI, XXXVIII, 1A (July, 1977), 177-A. XUM Order No. 77-13,890.

Black women more than white women had suffered much more mistreatment and had a greater number of humiliating experiences that reflected negatively on their womanhood.

Johnson, William Richard (Ed. D.). "THE MEASUREMENT AND EVALUATION OF STUDENT AND FACULTY PERCEPTIONS OF NURSING EDUCATION ENVIRONMENTS." University of Rochester, 1970. 174 pp. Source: DAI, XXXI, 7A (January, 1971), 3169-A-3170-A. XUM Order No. 71-1444.

Significant differences were found among baccalaureate degree, associate degree, and diploma nursing programs in 6 selected dimensions of perceived nursing school environments.

Johnston, Anita Faye (Ed. D.). "LITIGATION BEARING UPON WOMEN IN SECONDARY AND HIGHER EDUCATION." University of Oklahoma, 1977. 165 pp. Source: DAI, XXXVIII, 4A (October, 1977), 1787-A. XUM Order No. 77-21,379.

Job discrimination existed in cases involving litigation of women employed in secondary and higher education. Main concerns were equality of treatment and such problems as promotion and tenure, appointment, dismissal, and pregnancy.

Johnston, Hubert S. (Ph. D.). "MALE AUTHORITARIANISM: THE ATTITUDES OF MALE GRADUATE STUDENTS IN PROFESSIONAL SCHOOLS TOWARD WOMEN." Cornell University, 1974. 89 pp. Source: DAI, XXXV, 7A (January, 1975), 4159-A. XUM Order No. 75-1617.

Attitudes toward women's rights and equality were found to be favorable among male graduate students in the professional schools.

Jones, Agnes A. (Ph. D.). "A FOLLOW-UP STUDY OF BEGINNING HOME ECONOMICS TEACHERS GRADUATED FROM THE UNIVERSITY OF WISCONSIN TO ASCERTAIN EDUCATION NEEDS." University of Wisconsin, 1954. Source: Author.

New home economics teachers evaluated their own experience as student teachers as inadequate and recommended ways to improve student teaching.

Jones, Ann Fondren (Ph. D.). "MOTIVE TO AVOID SUCCESS, SEX ROLE, PARENTAL ROLE MODEL, ACADEMIC ABILITY, AND ACADEMIC CLASSIFICATION: PREDICTORS OF COED COLLEGE MAJOR." Mississippi State University, 1977. 81 pp. Source: DAI, XXXVIII, 4A (October, 1977), 2000-A. XUM Order No. 77-20,642.

Findings: undergraduate women felt anxious about possible negative consequences of choosing a major field that was traditionally male-dominated.

Jones, Carolyn W. (Ed. D.). "MODELS FOR PREDICTING ACADEMIC SUCCESS AND STATE BOARD SCORES FOR ASSOCIATE DEGREE NURSING STUDENTS." Illinois State University, 1977. 97 pp. Source: DAI, XXXVIII, 4A (October, 1977), 1890-A. XUM Order No. 77-20,941.

Found that pre-admission nursing students' success in grades and on the State Board examination could be accurately predicted by referring to their ages and their standardized test scores in English, mathematics, social studies, and natural sciences.

Jones, Erna Beatrice (Ph. D.). "ANALYSIS OF PRINCIPLES AND GENERALIZATIONS FOR CURRICULUM MAKING IN HIGHER EDUCATION WITH IMPLICATIONS FOR HOME ECONOMICS." Cornell University, 1959. 140 pp. Source: DAI, XX, 6 (December, 1959), 2268. XUM Order No. Mic 59-6128.

Recommended that principles derived from this study by applied toward (1) revising the philosophy of home economics; and (2) selecting some aspects of general education which might provide experiences for both majors and non-majors in home economics.

Jones, Irene Ann (Ph. D.). "A RECOMMENDED PROGRAM OF TRAINING FOR NORTHERN BAPTIST WOMEN LAY LEADERS." University of Pennsylvania, 1949. Source: Published; Same Title; Ann Arbor, MI: Edward Brothers, Inc., 1949; pp. 276-277.

The most successful and popular training for women lay leaders occurred in non-credit conferences and institutes.

Jones, Jacqueline (Ph. D.). "THE 'GREAT OPPORTUNITY': NORTHERN TEACHERS AND THE GEORGIA FREEDMEN, 1865-73." University of Wisconsin-Madison, 1976. 475 pp. Source: DAI, XXXVII, 6A (December, 1976), 3853-A. XUM Order No. 76-20,116.

The need for teachers in schools for former black slaves gave educated northern women a welcome opportunity to enter the male-dominated teaching profession. Despite their great numbers, women teachers remained on the lowest rung of the profession and received paternalistic treatment from their male administrators and colleagues.

Jones, Jane Gaudette (Ph. D.). "CAREER PATTERNS OF WOMEN PHYSICIANS." Brandeis University, Florence Heller Graduate School for Advanced Studies in Social Welfare, 1971. 197 pp. Source: DAI, XXXII, 7A (January, 1972), 4125-A-4126-A. XUM Order No. 72-1581.

This study examined the choices women made during medical training. The women, generally daughters of professional parents, defined their occupational interests early in life. Their schools were chosen for location and reputation. The study concluded that if more women are to be recruited for medicine, the system of medical education must be changed to insure women's steady progress.

Jones, Jane Louise (Ph. D.). "A PERSONNEL STUDY OF WOMEN DEANS OF COLLEGES AND UNIVERSITIES." Columbia University Teachers College, 1929. Source: TCCU DIGESTS, II (September, 1925-August, 1929), pp. 74-75.

The analysis of the duties of 107 women deans in institutions of highest rank indicated that work done by the 3 types of deans corresponded to the 3 general types of college organization: the college for women affiliated with a university, the independent college for women, and the co-educational institute. The affiliated college dean has more administrative duties, the independent college for women more academic duties, and the co-education institution more duties related to social life.

Jordan, Annie Wilhelmina (Ph. D.). "RELATIONSHIP BETWEEN SELECTED COLLEGIATE EXPERIENCES AND BEGINNING JOBS FOR WOMEN." Ohio State University, 1956. 143 pp. Source: DAI, XVII, 5 (1957), 1041. XUM Order No. 20,691.

Women's major field in college and their beginning salaries were positively related, but individual women's beginning salaries varied greatly.

Jordison, Nancy Sittig (Ph. D.). "A NURSING CURRICULUM AND ATTITUDE CHANGES." State University of Iowa, 1957. 138 pp. Source: DAI, XVII, 12 (December, 1957), 2983-2984. XUM Order No. 23,757.

Confirmed the hypothesis that students in the nursing curriculum developed a more accepting attitude than did students in other curricula.

Jorgenson, D. Elaine (Ed. D.). "ANALYSIS OF VERBAL BEHAVIOR OF BE-GINNING HOME ECONOMICS TEACHERS AS A BASIS FOR RECOMMENDATIONS FOR IN-SERVICE EDUCATION." Oklahoma State University, 1968. 109 pp. Source: DAI, XXX, 3B (September, 1969), 1228-B. XUM Order No. 69-14,271.

Using the interaction analysis technique, the study showed that second-year teachers spent more time lecturing than did first-year teachers.

Jutten, Jessie Bernadine (P.E.D.). "A JOB ANALYSIS OF WOMEN PHYSICAL EDUCATION TEACHERS IN SELECTED SENIOR HIGH SCHOOLS IN MISSOURI WITH IM- PLICATIONS FOR TEACHER EDUCATION." Indiana University, 1961. 216 pp. Source: DAI, XXII, 6 (December, 1961), 1915. XUM Order No. 61-6502.

Some recommendations were: (1) increased efforts should be made to recruit able teachers; and (2) the local community, school adminis- trators and teachers, boards of education, and state department offi- cials should work together to improve physical education programs.

Kagan, Lillian (Ph. D.). "THE RELATIONSHIP OF ACHIEVEMENT SUCCESS, HETEROSEXUAL RELATIONSHIP SATISFACTION, SEX-ROLE ORIENTATION, AND SELF- ESTEEM IN MALE AND FEMALE LAW SCHOOL STUDENTS." New York University, 1976. 157 pp. Source: DAI, XXXVII, 9B (March, 1977), 4651-B-4652-A. XUM Order No. 77-5311.

Males' self-esteem was statistically higher than that of females. Satisfaction with heterosexual relationships was more highly corre- lated with females' self-concept than with males.

Kahng, Hewon (Ph. D.). "CLOTHING INTERESTS AND CLOTHING ASPIRATIONS ASSOCIATED WITH SELECTED SOCIAL-PSYCHOLOGICAL FACTORS FOR A GROUP OF COLLEGE WOMEN IN KOREA." Pennsylvania State University, 1971. 139 pp. Source: DAI, XXXII, 9B (March, 1972), 5286-B-5287-B. XUM Order No. 72-9485.

Among home economics students (109) in Yonsei University, Seoul, Korea, those with low aspirations in professional goals, education, and community interests were found to be clothing conformists, mar- riage-oriented, extraverted, feminine, and holders of traditional attitudes toward women's roles.

Kaiser, Joan E. (Ed. D.). "A COMPARISON OF STUDENTS IN TWO TYPES OF NURSING PROGRAMS." Columbia University, 1974. 149 pp. Source: DAI, XXXV, 9A (March, 1975), 5861-A-5862-A. XUM Order No. 75-6469.

Concluded that: (1) students in associate degree nursing and practi- cal nursing were more similar than dissimilar in background; (2) nursing educators should clarify differences among various nursing programs; and (3) they should recruit students into the specific nur- sing program which matches their abilities and career goals.

Kajander, Cheryl Ann (Ph. D.). "THE EFFECTS OF INSTRUCTOR AND STU- DENT SEX ON VERBAL BEHAVIORS IN COLLEGE CLASSROOMS." University of Texas at Austin, 1976. 157 pp. Source: DAI, XXXVII, 5A (November, 1976), 2743-A-2744-A. XUM Order No. 76-26,645.

Few significant sex differences were found in teacher behavior. But students responded more frequently to female teachers, who in turn gave students more feedback than did male teachers. Conclusions: (1) female teachers were more sensitive than male teachers to the needs and feelings of their students; and (2) male students were more adept than female students at handling course material indepen- dently.

Kalisch, Beatrice Jean (Ed. D.). "AN EXPERIMENT IN THE DEVELOPMENT OF INTERACTIVE AND PREDICTIVE EMPATHY IN NURSING STUDENTS." University of Maryland, 1970. 353 pp. Source: DAI, XXXI, 11B (May, 1971), 6715-B. XUM Order No. 71-13,202.

Of 49 first-year students, those who underwent didactic training, experiential training, role playing, and a role model of empathy improved significantly. Experimental subjects maintained gains made on interactive empathy at the 6-week follow-up, while the controls showed no significant improvement.

Kalish, Barbara Jane (Ph. D.). "ADULT PRESENCE AND REINFORCEMENT WITH GIRLS IN GRADES K, 3, AND 6." Hofstra University, 1976. 126 pp. Source: DAI, XXXVII, 10B (April, 1977), 5399-B. XUM Order No. 77-7649.

Having an adult present helped assure the success of kindergarten and 3rd grade girls but was not necessary for 6th grade girls. The adult's role as reinforcer was proved important.

Kalka, Beatrice Sybol (Ed. D.). "A COMPARATIVE STUDY OF FEMININE ROLE CONCEPTS OF A SELECTED GROUP OF COLLEGE WOMEN." Oklahoma State University, 1967. 139 pp. Source: DAI, XXVIII, 12A (June, 1968), 4822-A. XUM Order No. 68-8435.

Comparisons of freshman and senior women in the Colleges of Arts and Sciences and of Home Economics indicated no significant differences in Own Self, Average Woman, and Men's Ideal Woman concepts.

Kanger, Kay Elizabeth (Ph. D.). "CHANGE IN RELIGIOUS ATTITUDES OF FRESHMAN CATHOLIC WOMEN AFTER ONE YEAR ON A SMALL RELIGIOUSLY-ORIENTED CAMPUS, A LARGE RELIGIOUSLY-ORIENTED CAMPUS, AND A LARGE SECULAR CAMPUS." University of Northern Colorado, 1972. 86 pp. Source: DAI, XXXIII, 7A (January, 1973), 3758-A-3759-A. XUM Order No. 73-282.

A study of 100 Catholic freshman women from each type of institution indicated a significant difference between campuses on the Attitude Toward God: Reality of God scale. The study's 2 major null hypotheses were accepted: that no significant change in religious attitudes would occur during the time span of the study and that there would be no significant difference between the change that occurred on the 3 campuses.

Kanjanasthiti, Euwadee (Ph. D.). "THE FEASIBILITY OF THE USE OF PROGRAMMED INSTRUCTION AS A METHOD OF TEACHING BASIC NUTRITION TO THAI STUDENTS AT COLLEGE LEVEL." Ohio State University, 1968. 159 pp. Source: DAI, XXIX, 5B (November, 1968), 1743-B. XUM Order No. 68-15,338.

A programmed instructional unit on basic nutrition tried out on 51 Ohio State University students was then translated and successfully used with 100 Thai technical college students.

Kappes, Eveline E. (Ed. D.). "AN ATTITUDE INVENTORY TO DETERMINE ATTITUDES OF COLLEGE WOMEN TOWARD PHYSICAL EDUCATION AND STUDENT SERVICES OF THE PHYSICAL EDUCATION DEPARTMENT." University of Oklahoma, 1954. Source: RESEARCH QUARTERLY (AAHPER), XXV, No. 4 (December, 1954), pp. 429-437.

From this study a valid and reliable inventory of college women's attitudes toward physical education was developed. Recommendations were made for using inventory findings as guides to planning the curriculum.

Karch, Jacqueline Quigley (Ed. D.). "CHARACTERISTICS OF WOMEN TEACHERS OF EDUCATION IN INSTITUTIONS OF HIGHER LEARNING IN THE UNITED STATES OF AMERICA." Washington University, 1956. 267 pp. Source: DAI, XVII, 4 (1957), 796-797. XUM Order No. 20,754.

The women teachers (860) were frequently reared in farm homes, regarded themselves as principally from homes of the middle to upper middle group, were within the ages of 45 to 55, were single, and attended public institutions. Their highest degrees were granted to approximately the same extent by private and state universities; they had teaching experience at either the elementary or secondary level or at both, with professional work centering mainly on the preparation of elementary teachers. In their present positions, they were characterized as being assistant professors employed on a full time rather than on a part-time basis in states away from their childhood homes. Their institutions of employment had women in more than 1/3 of their faculty positions in education.

Karlson, Shirley Mae (Ed. D.). "HEALTH CARE PROBLEMS AND COPING STRATEGIES OF EPILEPTIC ADULTS: IMPLICATIONS FOR NURSING EDUCATION." Indiana University, 1973. 272 pp. Source: DAI, XXXIII, 11A (May, 1973), 6127-A. XUM Order No. 73-10,775.

The main implication for nursing students is that they need to know the ambulatory setting in caring for epileptic adults.

Karman, Felice Joanne (Ed. D.). "WOMEN: PERSONAL AND ENVIRONMENTAL FACTORS IN ROLE IDENTIFICATION AND CAREER CHOICE." University of California, Los Angeles, 1972. 113 pp. Source: DAI, XXXIII, 4A (October, 1972), 1448-A. XUM Order No. 72-25,789.

Of 1,646 junior and senior women in U. S. colleges, 1,537 were planning to enter female-dominated careers and 109 wanted careers occupied primarily by men. The variable which most accurately differentiated the 2 groups was a propensity for using analytical thinking.

Karmel, Marylin Odom (Ph. D.). "MATERNAL ATTITUDES IN WOMEN TRAINED FOR CHILDBIRTH BY LAMAZE TECHNIQUES AND WOMEN RECEIVING NO FORMAL PRENATAL TRAINING." University of North Carolina at Greensboro, 1974. 172 pp. Source: DAI, XXXV, 4B (October, 1974), 1890-B. XUM Order No. 74-22,019.

Compared 28 women enrolled in a Lamaze Training for Childbirth class and 28 women selected from private practices of obstetricians. Found initial differences between the 2 groups in attitudes specific to childbearing and strictness concerning sex training. No difference existed in attitudes of acceptance or rejection of the child and concepts related to the family.

Karr, Donald Lee (Ph. D.). "PROBLEMS AND PERCEPTIONS OF PRACTICAL NURSING INSTRUCTORS IN RELATION TO THEIR TRADE AND INDUSTRIAL TEACHER EDUCATION PROGRAM." Ohio State University, 1969. 192 pp. Source: DAI, XXXI, 2A (August, 1970), 692-A. XUM Order No. 70-14,049.

In their first 4 years as teachers, practical nursing instructors had problems with teaching techniques, instructional materials, and classroom management. Most instructors agreed that the existing teacher education program was appropriate to their needs.

Kasmarik, Patricia Evelyn (Ed. D.). "ATTITUDE SCORE CHANGES TOWARD DEATH AND DYING IN NURSING STUDENTS." Columbia University, 1974. 94 pp. Source: DAI, XXXV, 4B (October, 1974), 1767-B. XUM Order No. 74-23,524.

Instruction in death and dying made a significant difference in attitudes. Age, experience, and prior care of the dying were positively associated with more favorable attitudes toward dying.

Kasuya, Yoshi (Ed. D.). "A COMPARATIVE STUDY OF THE SECONDARY EDUCATION OF GIRLS IN ENGLAND, GERMANY, AND THE UNITED STATES, WITH A CONSIDERATION OF THE SECONDARY EDUCATION OF GIRLS IN JAPAN." Columbia University Teachers College, 1932. 212 pp. Source: Eells, p. 8; and TCCU DIGESTS, VII (1933), pp. 1-4.

As of 1929-32, found these comparisons: (1) girls' secondary education was more commonly single sex in England and Germany and coeducational in the U. S.; (2) U. S. high schools were unitary and comprehensive while England and Germany retained dual selective-academic and mass-vocational paths; and (3) in Germany, where the teacher is the master of subjects, the educational objective was intellectual training; in England, where the gifted were more thoroughly trained, the educational objective was character formation; and in the U. S., which aimed at producing socialized citizens, culture and utility were intermingled. The best features from these and other comparisons were then related with careful modifications to fit Japan's peculiar social and cultural backgrounds.

Katrin, Susan Ellen (Ph. D.). "THE EFFECTS ON WOMEN INMATES OF FACILITATION TRAINING PROVIDED CORRECTIONAL OFFICERS." University of Georgia, 1972. 110 pp. Source: DAI, XXXIII, 8A (February, 1973), 4176-A. XUM Order No. 72-34,097.

The study reported a successful 4-month training course given to 14 female correctional officers for improving their interpersonal interactions with 3 experimental groups of women inmates.

Katzell, Mildred Engberg (Ph. D.). "EXPECTATIONS AND DROPOUTS IN SCHOOLS OF NURSING." Columbia University, 1967. 149 pp. Source: DAI, XXVIII, 4B (October, 1967), 1718-B. XUM Order No. 67-12,263.

Data from 1,439 students and from 413 dropouts indicated that students who experienced satisfactions were less likely to withdraw. Students withdrew when expected satisfactions were not realized.

Kaufman, Charles Wesley (Ed. D.). "EDUCATIONAL RETRAINING REQUIREMENTS OF THE OLDER FEMALE LABOR POOL RETURNEE." University of Arizona, 1967.

358 pp. Source: DAI, XXVIII, 4A (October, 1967), 1241-A. XUM Order No. 67-12,209.

Vocational retraining needs for women aged 35 and over were: lower social group needed complete training in local (Tucson, Ariz.) industrial occupations; already well trained higher social group needed little retraining.

Kaufman, Helen M. (Ed. D.). "THE STATUS OF WOMEN IN ADMINISTRATION IN SELECTED INSTITUTIONS OF HIGHER EDUCATION IN THE UNITED STATES." New York University, 1961. 199 pp. Source: DAI, XXII, 12, Part 1 (June, 1962), 4239-4240. XUM Order No. 62-1443.

Questionnaires to 355 college and university presidents and 156 New York University women with degrees in school administration and supervision revealed that: (1) 43.5% preferred male administrators to females; (2) only 17.2% of department heads were women; (3) women received administrative posts in such traditionally female fields as nursing and home economics; and (4) education and experience being equal, men fared better professionally than women.

Kedzuf, Mary Ann (Ed. D.). "SELF-ESTEEM, PERSONAL AND INTERPERSONAL VALUES OF NURSING STUDENTS IN DIPLOMA, ASSOCIATE DEGREE, AND BACCALAURE-ATE PROGRAMS." Northern Illinois University, 1971. 143 pp. Source: DAI, XXXII, 7B (January, 1972), 4030-B. XUM Order No. 72-4226.

Associate degree students valued stability in residence and in work requirements, were very goal-directed, and valued recognition. Diploma program students valued variety and independence and enjoyed doing things for people. Baccalaureate program students had high self concepts, valued variety and independence, and placed higher value on leading people than on doing things for others.

Keefe, Alice Elizabeth (Ph. D.). "A STUDY OF SOCIAL STATUS AS A DETERMINATE FACTOR IN THE DISTRIBUTION OF PROMOTIONS." New York University, 1958. 135 pp. Source: DAI, XIX, 1 (July, 1958), 117-118. XUM Order No. Mic 58-2128.

Nursing students with lower social class backgrounds were more likely to be favored for promotion. Social class was identified with religion and nationality of parents, education of fathers, reading and learning ability of daughter, and choice of nursing program. Scholastic ability had little relationship to promotion. Social class placement had no relationship to grades.

Keenan, Harry Charles (Ed. D.). "A STUDY TO EVALUATE ORIENTATION EMPHASIZING HUMANNESS ON FRESHMAN ASSOCIATE DEGREE NURSING STUDENTS." Boston University School of Education, 1974. 166 pp. Source: DAI, XXXIV, 9A (March, 1974), 5634-A. XUM Order No. 74-7622.

Freshman nursing students who took a seminar in human relations gained clarity about themselves, better interpersonal relations, and readiness to explore broader ranges of their vocational role and self-actualization.

Keener, Barbara Jean (Ed. D.). "AN ANALYSIS OF THE PERCEPTIONS OF THE LEADERSHIP BEHAVIOR OF MALE AND FEMALE UNIVERSITY OF FLORIDA ADMINIS-TRATORS." University of Florida, 1976. 126 pp. Source: DAI, XXXVII, 7A (January, 1977), 4023-A. XUM Order No. 77-1124.

There was little difference between male and female administrators and little justification to conclude that they behave differently. There were some differences in career orientation, development, and aspirations.

Kehle, Thomas John (Ph. D.). "EFFECT OF THE STUDENT'S PHYSICAL AT-TRACTIVENESS, SEX, RACE, INTELLIGENCE, AND SOCIOECONOMIC STATUS ON TEACH-ERS' EXPECTATIONS FOR THE STUDENT'S PERSONALITY AND ACADEMIC PERFORMANCE." University of Kentucky, 1972. 161 pp. Source: DAI, XXXIV, 3A (September, 1973), 1131-A. XUM Order No. 73-20,598.

Assessing both the psychological temperament of a fictitious 5th grade student and an essay supposedly written by this student, teach-ers expected females, blacks, and intelligent students to be signif-icantly more stable in temperament than males, whites, and less in-telligent students. Essays written by black males and white females were given a higher rating than those written by black females and white males.

Kehr, Marguerite Witmer (Ph. D.). "A COMPARATIVE STUDY OF THE CUR-RICULUM FOR MEN AND WOMEN IN THE COLLEGES AND UNIVERSITIES OF THE UNITED STATES." Cornell University, 1920. Source: Marguerite Witmer Kehr, "A Comparative Study of the Curriculum for Men and Women in the Colleges and Universities of the United States," JOURNAL OF THE ASSOCIATION OF COLLEGIATE ALUMNAE, XIV, No. 3 (December, 1920), pp. 3-26.

Recommended that women's undergraduate education: (1) prepare them for a profession such as teaching, librarianship, or business; (2) provide vocational guidance for them; and (3) offer ample home eco-nomics courses as electives.

Kehres, Marlene Kirek (Ph. D.). "COMPARATIVE ANALYSIS OF GROUP COUN-SELING WITH A MALE-FEMALE CO-COUNSELING TECHNIQUE AND A SINGLE-COUNSELOR TECHNIQUE." University of Akron, 1972. 137 pp. Source: DAI, XXXIII, 7A (January, 1973), 3294-A. XUM Order No. 72-25,698.

The male-female co-counseling technique was the most effective treat-ment program for classroom disruption, disrespect-defiance, and ex-ternal blame, while the single counselor technique was better than the control technique for classroom disturbance and disrespect-de-fiance.

Keller, Dorothy J. (Ed. D.). "MARIA MITCHELL, AN EARLY WOMAN ACA-DEMICIAN." University of Rochester, 1975. 163 pp. Source: DAI, XXXVI, 1A (July, 1975), 159-A. XUM Order No. 75-15,237.

Author related career of Maria Mitchell, Vassar College astronomy professor and observatory director (1865-1888), her views on women's education, her role in the Association for the Advancement of Women, and her efforts at getting equal pay for women academicians.

Kelley, Ann Elizabeth (Ph. D.). "CATHOLIC WOMEN IN CAMPUS MINISTRY: AN EMERGING MINISTRY FOR WOMEN IN THE CATHOLIC CHURCH." Boston University Graduate School, 1975. 285 pp. Source: DAI, XXXVI, 3A (September, 1975), 1598-A. XUM Order No. 75-18,555.

Catholic women have since the Second Vatican Council begun to assume a ministerial role on campuses. Though they cannot administer the sacraments, these women are of growing importance because of the feminist movement and pressures that women be admitted to the priesthood.

Kelley, Georgette Katherine (Ed. D.). "A COMPARISON OF MALE AND FEMALE LEVELS AND COMPONENTS OF SELF-ESTEEM." Rutgers University, 1976. 110 pp. Source: DAI, XXXVII, 6A (December, 1976), 3520-A-3521-A. XUM Order No. 76-27,329.

Male self-esteem was significantly higher than female self-esteem at the college freshman level but not in the 7th, 9th, and 11th grades. Sources of male self-esteem were intrinsic; sources of female self-esteem were extrinsic.

Kelley, Mary Bremer (Ph. D.). "THE UNCONSCIOUS REBEL: STUDIES IN FEMININE FICTION, 1820-1880." University of Iowa, 1974. 278 pp. Source: DAI, XXXVI, 1A (July, 1975), 482-A-483-A. XUM Order No. 75-13,772.

Writings of ten 19th century women novelists, though not strictly about schooling, were implicitly instructive. They taught that women who were homemakers were superior to men and were purveyors of those values necessary to a strong society.

Kelley, William Frederick (Ph. D.). "THE INSERVICE IMPROVEMENT OF COLLEGE INSTRUCTION IN CATHOLIC COLLEGES FOR WOMEN." University of Minnesota, 1949. 338 pp. Source: Dissertation, pp. 265-274.

Among 22 recommendations for improving Catholic college education for women: orientation for new lay teachers, pre-school faculty-student leadership meetings, course syllabi related to college purposes, intelligent use of inter-class visitation, and inter-institutional teacher exchanges.

Kelly, Sister Mary Owen (Ph. D.). "A SURVEY STUDY OF ART IN GENERAL EDUCATION IN LIBERAL ARTS COLLEGES FOR WOMEN IN THE UNITED STATES." University of Pittsburgh, 1969. 117 pp. Source: DAI, XXX, 6A (December, 1969), 2436-A. XUM Order No. 69-19,662.

General education art courses in 171 women's colleges tended to be aesthetic rather than strictly chronological, and relied on multi-media and multi-sensory teaching techniques.

Kelly, Paul William (Ph. D.). "PREPARING NURSING STUDENTS TO INTERACT WITH TERMINAL PATIENTS." Fuller Theological Seminary Graduate School of Psychology, 1972. 241 pp. Source: DAI, XXXIII, 8B (February, 1973), 3945-B. XUM Order No. 72-31,655.

Although the effects of training were not statistically significant, the experimental group of nursing students had favorable test scores after attending special training sessions about dealing with dying patients.

Kennedy, Larry Wells (Ph. D.). "THE FIGHTING PREACHER OF THE ARMY OF TENNESSEE: GENERAL MARK PERRIN LOWREY." Mississippi State University, 1976. 213 pp. Source: DAI, XXXVII, 12A, Part 1 (June, 1977), 7920-A. XUM Order No. 77-11,754.

Life and influence of Mark Perrin Lowrey (1828-83), Mississippi Baptist minister, Confederate general, editor, and founder in 1873 of Blue Mountain Female College.

Kenney, Irene M. (Ed. D.). "A COMPARISON OF THE STATUS OF WOMEN WITH THAT OF MEN ON FACULTIES OF EDUCATION IN SELECTED INSTITUTIONS OF HIGHER EDUCATION IN DELAWARE VALLEY." University of Pennsylvania, 1974. 257 pp. Source: DAI, XXXV, 12A, Part 1 (June, 1975), 7530-A-7531-A. XUM Order No. 75-11,926.

Notable differences were found in the status of men and women faculty members despite the fact that the women had worked a long time and were as ambitious as the men. The conclusion was that cultural attitudes hindered women's achieving equality.

Kent, Druzilla Crary (Ph. D.). "A STUDY OF THE RESULTS OF PLANNING FOR HOME ECONOMICS EDUCATION IN THE SOUTHERN STATES, AS ORGANIZED UNDER THE NATIONAL ACTS FOR VOCATIONAL EDUCATION." Columbia University Teachers College, 1936. 172 pp. Source: TCCU CONTRIBUTIONS No. 689, pp. 130-136.

Examined similarities (many) and differences (slight) in 12 southern states' home economics programs funded by federal acts during 1917-33. Study showed good effects of growing trend toward statewide and regional planning in home economics education.

Kergin, Dorothy Jean (Ph. D.). "AN EXPLORATORY STUDY OF THE PROFES-SIONALIZATION OF REGISTERED NURSES IN ONTARIO AND THE IMPLICATIONS FOR THE SUPPORT OF CHANGE IN BASIC NURSING EDUCATIONAL PROGRAMS." University of Michigan, 1968. 257 pp. Source: DAI, XXX, 1A (July, 1969), 65-A-66-A. XUM Order No. 69-12,151.

Recommended that committees be established at chapter levels of Canadian provincial nurses' associations to discuss: current issues in nursing, the need for improving nursing education, and a Canadian code of ethics for nurses.

Kesler, Suad Wakim (Ph. D.). "VALUES OF WOMEN COLLEGE STUDENTS IN THE ARAB MIDDLE EAST." Cornell University, 1965. 266 pp. Source: DAI, XXV, 12, Part 1 (June, 1965), 7408. XUM Order No. 65-5726.

Changes in values of women students at Beirut College for Women (150) and American University of Beirut (11), representing 11 countries, mainly Lebanon and neighboring Arab countries: (1) an increase in understanding, service, sociability, social status, responsibility, economic value, democratic value, leadership, independence, freedom,

liberalism, intellectual qualities, marriage, and equal rights for
women; and (2) a decrease in authoritarian value, religion, religious
exclusiveness, obedience, and conservatism.

Kessel, William George (Ed. D.). "A DETERMINATION OF CERTAIN CONTENT
DESIRABLE IN ORGANIC CHEMISTRY COURSES FOR HOME ECONOMICS STUDENTS." Indiana University, 1962. 130 pp. Source: DAI, XXIII, 10 (April, 1963),
3802. XUM Order No. 63-2602.

For a model course, a jury of college home economics professors identified desirable parts for inclusion and undesirable parts for exclu-
sion from organic chemistry textbooks written especially for home
economics students.

Ketefian, Shake (Ed. D.). "KNOWLEDGE UTILIZATION IN THE PROCESS OF
ACCEPTING SELECTED INNOVATIONS IN BACCALAUREATE EDUCATION IN NURSING."
Columbia University, 1972. 263 pp. Source: DAI, XXXIII, 6A (December,
1972), 2695-A. XUM Order No. 72-30,331.

Found that: (1) systematically obtained knowledge was the most important source in developing and evaluating an innovation in nursing
education; (2) the authority of expert persons or agencies was the
source of information such as social need; and (3) faculty involvement was very important in accepting curriculum innovations.

Keys, Elizabeth Jaffer (Ph. D.). "WOMEN'S ROLES: AN ATTITUDINAL AND
BEHAVIORAL SURVEY." University of Cincinnati, 1976. 420 pp. Source:
DAI, XXXVII, 5B (November, 1976), 2571-B-2572-B. XUM Order No. 76-25,502.

Females (274) in introductory psychology classes in a large urban
university were attempting to coordinate education, careers, marriage,
and childrearing. Those with highly educated fathers had a contemporary lifestyle and those with minimally educated fathers had a
strong career commitment and a traditional lifestyle as indicated by
a stronger religiosity.

Khosh, Mary Sivert (Ph. D.). "A STUDY OF THE RELATIONSHIP TO CAREER
OBJECTIVES OF INTEREST, VALUES AND SELECTED PERSONALITY FACTORS OF MATURE
WOMEN ENROLLED IN HIGHER EDUCATION." Kent State University, 1976. 221
pp. Source: DAI, XXXVII, 5A (November, 1976), 2670-A. XUM Order No.
76-25,367.

No significant relationships were found between women's college enrollment and such factors as marital status and children's ages.
Most women enrolled to prepare for a new career and were highly motivated. The major influence on a wife's continuing education was her
husband's attitude.

Khouri, Lorraine Mary (Ed. D.). "ARAB CHILDREN'S PLAY AS A REFLEC-
TION OF SOCIAL INTERACTION PATTERNS OF THEIR CULTURE." University of
North Carolina at Greensboro, 1976. 150 pp. Source: DAI, XXXVII, 12A,
Part 1 (June, 1977), 7614-A. XUM Order No. 77-13,402.

Boys played a slightly higher percentage of the competitive games and
the games of physical skill and mimicry. Girls, on the other hand,
chose a few more games of strategy and rhythm.

Kiang, Min-Hsien Yang (Ed. D.). "PROGRAMMED INSTRUCTION IN NUTRITION FOR BACCALAUREATE DEGREE NURSING STUDENTS." Columbia University, 1968. 224 pp. Source: DAI, XXX, 1B (July, 1969), 267-B. XUM Order No. 69-8082.

Most 5-year baccalaureate nursing students tested were favorable to a programmed nutrition course.

Kidd, Nancy Van Tries (Ed. D.). "THE EFFECT OF GROUP COUNSELING AND MINI COURSES ON WOMEN IN A COMMUNITY COLLEGE." Pennsylvania State University, 1977. 125 pp. Source: DAI, XXXVIII, 2A (August, 1977), 633-A-634-A. XUM Order No. 77-17,702.

Experimental groups, but not the control group, showed significant reduction in alienation. Significant increases in self-regard occurred for the counseling group, and in inner direction for all experimental groups. Since the control group showed differences in levels of progress, role modeling may have occurred.

Kilbourn, Donald William (Ph. D.). "A STUDY OF THE STATUS AND ROLES OF HEAD RESIDENTS IN COLLEGE AND UNIVERSITY RESIDENCE HALLS FOR WOMEN." Michigan State University, 1959. Source: Donald W. Kilbourn, "The Status and Roles of Head Residents," PERSONNEL AND GUIDANCE JOURNAL, XXXIX, No. 3 (November, 1960), pp. 203-206.

Concluded that head residents should: (1) be professionally trained; (2) receive pay and status comparable to those of academic personnel; and (3) have responsibilities appropriate to their training and status.

Kilian, Gloria LaVerne (Ph. D.). "THE RELATIONSHIP BETWEEN READABILITY OF ASSIGNED TEXTBOOKS AND READING LEVEL OF STUDENTS IN A SCHOOL OF NURSING." Kansas State University, 1976. 113 pp. Source: DAI, XXXVII, 9A (March, 1977), 5530-A-5531-A. XUM Order No. 77-5507.

Readability levels of the nursing textbooks used in the Wichita-St. Joseph (Kansas) School of Nursing were within the appropriate range for the student nurses tested.

Kim, Soon Ki (Ph. D.). "AN ASSESSMENT OF FOREIGN HOME ECONOMICS STUDENTS' SELECTED ACADEMIC AND PERSONAL CHARACTERISTICS: AN EXPLORATORY STUDY." University of Wisconsin, 1973. 164 pp. Source: DAI, XXXIV, 10B (April, 1974), 5055-B-5056-B. XUM Order No. 73-28,926.

Recommendations: (1) mandatory orientation programs in the home country and in the U. S.; (2) mandatory English proficiency; (3) special policies to motivate students to return to their home countries; and (4) special seminars on problems in home economics in developing countries.

King, Bradford Dean (Ed. D.). "LEARNING AND ORALITY: THE RELATIONSHIP BETWEEN ORAL RECEPTIVITY AND SERIAL LEARNING, VERBAL RECALL AND GRADE-POINT AVERAGE IN COLLEGE WOMEN." Boston University School of Education, 1970. 219 pp. Source: DAI, XXXI, 5B (November, 1970), 2990-B-2991-B. XUM Order No. 70-22,469.

An inverse relationship existed between women's oral receptivity and their skill at learning, requiring active effort and persistence.

King, Charlyce Ross (Ed. D.). "ATTITUDES OF COLLEGE WOMEN TOWARD STUDENT ORGANIZATIONS AT THE UNIVERSITY OF OKLAHOMA." University of Oklahoma, 1957. 202 pp. Source: DAI, XVII, 8 (August, 1957), 1693. XUM Order No. 21,886.

University of Oklahoma women students favored social over governing types of campus organizations. Major field, academic ability, and sorority or non-sorority affiliation did not affect attitudes toward campus organizations.

King, Elizabeth Camp (Ph. D.). "PERCEPTIONS OF FEMALE VOCATIONAL FACULTY MEMBERS AS SEEN BY THEMSELVES AND COLLEGE ADMINISTRATORS." Pennsylvania State University, 1974. 147 pp. Source: DAI, XXXVI, 1A (July, 1975), 145-A. XUM Order No. 75-15,793.

The most significant finding was that administrators' expectations about promoting women vocational education faculty were significantly higher than were those of the women themselves.

King, Imogene Martina (Ed. D.). "GRADUATE EDUCATION FOR THE PREPARATION OF TEACHERS OF NURSING PRACTICE AT THE UNIVERSITY OF ILLINOIS." Columbia University, 1961. 129 pp. Source: DAI, XXIII, 4 (October, 1962), 1280-1281. XUM Order No. 62-3552.

Major characteristics of the proposed curriculum: general education (25%), professional education (50%), and nursing specialization (25%), the latter chosen from among age groupings.

King, Mary Frances Gooch (Ed. D.). "A STUDY OF ADMISSION CRITERIA AND ATTRITION IN SELECTED SCHOOLS OF PRACTICAL NURSING IN VIRGINIA." Virginia Polytechnic Institute and State University, 1976. 171 pp. Source: DAI, XXXVII, 3A (September, 1976), 1512-A. XUM Order No. 76-19,886.

Admissions criteria and selection procedure of various Virginia practical nursing programs were not successful at reducing student attrition rates.

Kinsella, Cynthia Rodstrom (Ed. D.). "NEEDS OF COMMUNITY COLLEGE TEACHERS OF NURSING AND IMPLICATIONS FOR INSERVICE EDUCATION." Columbia University, 1967. 303 pp. Source: DAI, XXVIII, 3B (September, 1967), 964-B. XUM Order No. 67-9446.

The only unanimity about roles of nursing educators in community colleges was that they should instruct and advise students.

Kinsell-Rainey, Lynn Wallace (Ph. D.). "ACHIEVEMENT AND ATTRIBUTION PATTERNS AS A FUNCTION OF SEX-ROLE INTERPRETATION: A COMPARISON OF ANDROGYNOUS AND STEREOTYPED COLLEGE STUDENTS." Southern Illinois University, 1976. 83 pp. Source: DAI, XXXVII, 6A (December, 1976), 3521-A. XUM Order No. 76-28,752.

This study, which grouped male and female undergraduates as either non-sex-oriented (androgynous) or sex-oriented, concluded that androgynous females were most self reliant, self confident, and more demanding of themselves than feminine females.

Kintgen, Jean Katherine (Ph. D.). "DEVELOPING GUIDELINES FOR SEQUENCING CURRICULUM CONTENT FOR CAREER ADVANCEMENT IN NURSING." Ohio State University, 1973. 302 pp. Source: DAI, XXXIV, 2A (August, 1973), 549-A-550-A. XUM Order No. 73-18,915.

Curriculum guidelines were developed for competency progression for nurse aides, practical nurses, and registered nurses.

Kinzig, Elizabeth Steinebrey (Ph. D.). "A SURVEY OF WOMEN FACULTY MEMBERS IN THE DEPARTMENTS OF PHYSICAL EDUCATION IN COLLEGES AND UNIVERSITIES OFFERING A MAJOR PHYSICAL EDUCATION CURRICULUM FOR WOMEN." Ohio State University, 1949. 213 pp. Source: Dissertation, pp. 184-189.

Among findings: (1) most common special assignments were advising major students, directing intramurals, serving on staff committees; and (2) 46% had published books, articles, or pamphlets.

Kirkpatrick, Wynona Jeanneret (Ed. D.). "THE EMERGING ROLE OF WOMEN IN INSTITUTIONS OF HIGHER EDUCATION IN THE UNITED STATES." University of Arkansas, 1965. 214 pp. Source: DAI, XXVI, 2 (August, 1965), 797. XUM Order No. 65-8460.

Historical study from colonial times; 19th century leaders like Catharine Beecher, Emma Willard, Mary Lyon; institutions like Oberlin College; and women's educational emergence today.

Kirshstein, Rita Joy (Ph. D.). "SEX DIFFERENCES IN THE ACADEMIC WORK STRUCTURE." University of Massachusetts, 1976. 220 pp. Source: DAI, XXXVII, 9A (March, 1977), 6089-A-6090-A. XUM Order No. 77-6486.

A national sample of men and women college faculty members found that: (1) women spent less time than men in graduate teaching and research but more time in undergraduate teaching; (2) women published less; (3) women counseled more undergraduates and men counseled more graduates; and (4) women were less likely than men to evaluate their career achievement as above average.

Kissell, Patricia Darlene (Ph. D.). "THE RELATIONSHIP OF SELF-ESTEEM, PROGRAMMED MUSIC, AND TIME OF DAY TO PREFERRED CONVERSATIONAL DISTANCE AMONG FEMALE COLLEGE STUDENTS." New York University, 1974. 133 pp. Source: DAI, XXXV, 5B (November, 1974), 2280-B. XUM Order No. 74-25,001.

Among the conclusions: sequence of programmed music, time of day, and low or high self-esteem did not significantly affect preferred conversational distance among listening college female students.

Kittredge, Robert Elwin (Ph. D.). "INVESTIGATION OF DIFFERENCES IN OCCUPATIONAL PREFERENCES, STEREOTYPIC THINKING, AND PSYCHOLOGICAL NEEDS AMONG UNDERGRADUATE WOMEN STUDENTS IN SELECTED CURRICULAR AREAS." Michigan State University, 1960. 130 pp. Source: DAI, XXI, 11 (May, 1961), 3362. XUM Order No. Mic 61-1179.

Women students who were least stereotyped and least traditional in their job preferences tended to believe that a woman's place was both in the home and on the job.

Kivetz, Dolores L. (Ph. D.). "A STUDY OF SEX-ROLE ADOPTION AND ACHIEVEMENT MOTIVATION IN HIGH SCHOOL STUDENTS." University of Toledo, 1976. 286 pp. Source: DAI, XXXVII, 5A (November, 1976), 2745-A. XUM Order No. 76-24,926.

No significant sex differences were found among male and female high school students in achievement motivation or in desire to avoid success.

Kizer, Dorothy Jetty West (Ph. D.). "COGNITIVE INTERACTION AND LEARNING IN HOME ECONOMICS CLASSES." Iowa State University, 1973. 173 pp. Source: DAI, XXXIV, 7A (January, 1974), 4061-A-4062-A. XUM Order No. 74-550.

Few significant differences were found in cognitive interaction and classroom learning of 11th and 12th grade home economics classes taught by Iowa State University home economics graduates.

Klabik-Lozovsky, Nora Neli (Ed. D.). "THE EDUCATION OF RUSSIAN WOMEN: EVOLUTION OR REVOLUTION, A COMPARATIVE ANALYSIS." University of British Columbia (Canada), 1972. Source: DAI, XXXIII, 8A (February, 1973), 4141-A-4142-A. Order: National Library of Canada at Ottawa.

This 3-part study traced the education of women from the first era of Christianity to 1856, covered trends in elementary, secondary, and higher education; discussed Marxist-Leninist educational philosophy; and explained the educational system of the Soviet Union.

Klaczynska, Barbara Mary (Ph. D.). "WORKING WOMEN IN PHILADELPHIA - 1900-1930." Temple University, 1975. 301 pp. Source: DAI, XXXVI, 9A (March, 1976), 6264-A-6265-A. XUM Order No. 75-28,230.

Historical-sociological study of Philadelphia ethnic (Polish, Jewish, Blacks, Irish) and native-born working women who by the 1920s were being trained for leadership by groups like the Bryn Mawr Summer School for Working Women.

Klahn, Jacqueline Squire (Ph. D.). "CLASSROOM 'BUSINESS': A STUDY OF THE POTENTIAL FOR SEX-TYPING IN TEACHER ASSIGNED TASKS." University of Oregon, 1975. 122 pp. Source: DAI, XXXVI, 9A (March, 1976), 5803-A. XUM Order No. 76-5181.

Found no real indication of sex-typing in 40 tasks given by 23 teachers to 103 girls and 126 boys in ten 5th grade classes.

Klein, Ruth Arnold (Ed. D.). "A CRITICAL ANALYSIS OF PUBLIC SCHOOL NURSING IN NEW JERSEY." Rutgers University, 1958. 532 pp. Source: DAI, XX, 4 (October, 1959), 1328. XUM Order No. Mic 58-5726.

The majority of public school nurses had obtained only the basic nursing diploma; most were trained in hospital schools. New Jersey's certification requirements were being strengthened, but school health services were lagging behind minimal recommended standards.

Kloss, Marie Guzell (Ph. D.). "THE RELATION BETWEEN ADOLESCENT CREA-
TIVITY AND SELECTED VARIABLES: SEX, ADJUSTMENT, ART-SCIENCE PREFERENCE,
COMPLEXITY-SIMPLICITY, AND TYPE OF SCHOOL." Louisiana State University,
1972. 98 pp. Source: DAI, XXXIII, 5B (November, 1972), 2324-B. XUM
Order No. 72-28,359.

Tests administered to 99 males and 59 females revealed a significant
sex bias in favor of males. The tests showed no sex differences in
creativity. Adjustment was significantly related to female creativity. Art-science preference was uncorrelated with adjustment; however,
female science preference was associated with neuroticism.

Klotzburger, Katherine Margaret (Ph. D.). "POLITICS IN HIGHER EDUCA-
TION: THE ISSUE OF THE STATUS OF WOMEN AT THE CITY UNIVERSITY OF NEW
YORK, 1971-1973." New York University, 1976. 584 pp. Source: DAI,
XXXVII, 9A (March, 1977), 6029-A-6030-A. XUM Order No. 77-5419.

Described ways CUNY dealt with the status of women as a major social
issue, with the university environment, and with the politics sur-
rounding the status of women. Traced the development and analyzed
the operation of the Chancellor's Advisory Committee on the Status
of Women.

Knaak, Nancy Katherine (Ph. D.). "A STUDY OF THE CHARACTERISTICS OF
ACADEMICALLY SUCCESSFUL AND UNSUCCESSFUL FRESHMAN WOMEN WHO ENTERED NORTH-
WESTERN UNIVERSITY IN THE FALL OF 1954." Northwestern University, 1956.
230 pp. Source: DAI, XVII, 2 (1957), 304-305. XUM Order No. 19,002.

Honor students and probation students were similar in: high school
experience; attitudes toward the relative ease and difficulty of high
school and college courses, toward the values to be derived from a
college education, and toward Northwestern; amount of time for class
preparation; and reasons for vocational preference. Honor students
scored higher on tests of academic aptitude, English achievement, and
study habits and were more persistent in making a single vocational
choice. Probates scored higher in sociability. Honor students
scored higher in seriousness, reflectiveness, and literary interest.

Knight, Elmer Lee (Ph. D.). "A STUDY OF THE IMAGE OF MISSISSIPPI
STATE COLLEGE FOR WOMEN HELD BY SELECTED HIGH SCHOOL SENIORS IN MISSIS-
SIPPI AND SELECTED COLLEGE SENIORS ENROLLED AT MISSISSIPPI STATE COLLEGE
FOR WOMEN." University of Alabama, 1973. 209 pp. Source: DAI, XXXIV,
3A (September, 1973), 1028-A-1029-A. XUM Order No. 73-19,552.

College seniors perceived the institution positively, feeling that
it was attractive, well designed, well kept, friendly, fully accredited, with many major fields of study, and with an academic program
designed to meet women students' needs. This group's majority consensus was that the students were not being treated as adults and
that there was too much supervision. High school seniors perceived
the college positively, but lacked opinions regarding various aspects of the college. Those attending private schools had a more
definite perceptual image of the college than did those attending
public schools.

Knoebber, Sister M. Mildred (Ph. D.). "THE ADOLESCENT GIRL: AN ANALYSIS OF HER ATTITUDES, IDEALS, AND PROBLEMS FROM THE VIEWPOINT OF THE GIRL HERSELF." Saint Louis University, 1934. 293 pp. Source: DAI, II, 2 (1940), 117-118. XUM Order No. 184.

Responses of 300 girls emphasized the importance of woman's place in the family; documented the ideals, attitudes, and problems of adolescent girls in the home, school, and social environment; and pointed to adolescence as the time for developing the type of womanhood that would contribute to the wellbeing of the social whole.

Knoepfli, Heather Elizabeth (Ph. D.). "THE ORIGIN OF WOMEN'S AUTO-NOMOUS LEARNING GROUPS." University of Toronto (Canada), 1971. Source: DAI, XXXIII, 1A (July, 1972), 136-A-137-A. Order: National Library of Canada at Ottawa.

The following aspects of the group formation process were found to be significant: decisions concerning group objectives, type of group, general learning approaches, core group of members, methodology, additional members, and organization structure.

Knott, Thomas Garland (Ph. D.). "MOTIVATIONAL FACTORS IN SELECTED WOMEN CANDIDATES FOR THE MASTER OF RELIGIOUS EDUCATION DEGREE." Boston University Graduate School, 1964. 341 pp. Source: DAI, XXV, 5 (November, 1964), 3140-3141. XUM Order No. 64-11,654.

The women students (31) were motivated by Christian upbringing, church activities, and college religious experiences. Their mean scores on standardized tests were higher than the average for college women on deference, intraception, and endurance, and lower on achievement, exhibition, autonomy, succorance, heterosexuality, and aggression. Perseverance in vocation was related to formation of a strong ego ideal; higher scores on acceptance by others, witness, and order; and a low score on heterosexuality.

Knowles, Ruth Dailey (Ph. D.). "CURRICULAR GUIDELINES FOR A BAC-CALAUREATE IN NURSING PROGRAM FOR REGISTERED NURSES, BASED ON THEIR LEARN-ING NEEDS." Florida State University, 1975. 119 pp. Source: DAI, XXXVI, 4B (October, 1975), 1656-B. XUM Order No. 75-21,422.

There was agreement that programs should include: (1) nursing diagnosis, orders, intervention, and evaluation; (2) coordination and data collection with health care team; (3) self-awareness and behavior psychology; (4) electives; and (5) preparation for graduate study in nursing.

Knowling, Winifred Ann (Ph. D.). "THE RELATIONSHIP BETWEEN CHILDREN'S ATTITUDES TOWARD THE CLASSROOM AND THEIR PERCEPTIONS OF TEACHER BEHAVIOR AS INFLUENCED BY THE AGE, SEX, AND BEHAVIOR OF THE CHILDREN." University of Iowa, 1977. 143 pp. Source: DAI, XXXVIII, 4A (October, 1977), 1789-A-1790-A. XUM Order No. 77-21,144.

Girls in grades 1-6 had more positive attitudes toward the classroom environment and felt that teachers liked them more than they liked boys. There seemed to be a relationship between teacher behavior as students perceived it and students' attitudes toward the classroom environment.

Knox, Jane Eleanor (Ed. D.). "THE FORMATION OF NURSE ROLE CONCEP-
TIONS: A STUDY OF BACCALAUREATE NURSING STUDENTS." Columbia University,
1971. 169 pp. Source: DAI, XXXII, 3A (September, 1971), 1297-A. XUM
Order No. 71-24,152.

Seniors (153) had a significantly higher professional conception of
the role of the nurse and significantly lower bureaucratic conceptions than 253 neophytes. Both groups perceived the hospital practices as more bureaucratic, less professional, and less service oriented than need be. A majority identified a role model: 58% of the
neophytes' models were instructors and 30% were nurses; for the
seniors, 43% identified instructors as their role models and 49%
identified nurses. Neophytes with instructor role models reported
the highest professional conception. Both groups perceived professional role conceptions of the faculty as higher than their own.

Koba, Sister Mary Hiltrude (Ph. D.). "A LONGITUDINAL ANALYSIS OF THE
PREDICTIVE VALIDITY OF THE SRA HIGH SCHOOL PLACEMENT TEST FOR NINTH GRADE
GIRLS." Fordham University, 1974. 156 pp. Source: DAI, XXXV, 5A
(November, 1974), 2772-A-2773-A. XUM Order No. 74-25,104.

When 692 girls were tested, the best single predictor of success in
algebra was the Arithmetic Computation Score; in Latin, the Language
Arts Core; and in world history, either the SRA High School Placement
Test Reading Score or the Language Arts Score. Arithmetic scores
were the most valid criterion for predicting individual attainment
in algebra, Latin, and world history.

Kochey, Kenneth Charles (Ed. D.). "THE DEVELOPMENT OF PREDICTIVE
GRADE POINT AVERAGE MODELS FOR COMMUNITY COLLEGE DENTAL HYGIENE AND NUR-
SING PROGRAMS AND THE APPLICATION OF THESE MODELS IN A COMPUTERIZED AD-
MISSIONS SYSTEM." University of Florida, 1972. 91 pp. Source: DAI,
XXXIV, 1A (July, 1973), 92-A. XUM Order No. 73-15,511.

Success predictors for dental hygiene enrollees were high school
mathematics grades; for nursing enrollees, age and high school percentile rank. The intellectual variables of high school mathematics
grades and high school percentile rank were the best single predictors
of the first semester grades for both groups. Standardized test
scores did not relate significantly to either program.

Kohnke, Mary Florence (Ed. D.). "LITERATURE VERSUS PRACTICE IN NUR-
SING EDUCATION." Columbia University, 1972. 178 pp. Source: DAI,
XXXIII, 7A (January, 1973), 3481-A-3482-A. XUM Order No. 72-30,332.

Descriptions by nursing school administrators of knowledge, responsibility, and role of student nurses differed from the literature surveyed on knowledge, responsibility, and role of student nurses in
associate and baccalaureate programs.

Koivisto, Helmi Louise (Ph. D.). "THE ROLE OF THE HOME ECONOMICS
TEACHER IN THE EDUCATION OF SLOW-LEARNING GIRLS IN OHIO PUBLIC SECONDARY
SCHOOLS WITH IMPLICATIONS FOR TEACHER EDUCATION." Ohio State University,
1954. 288 pp. Source: DAI, XV, 6 (1955), 1057-1058. XUM Order No.
12,039.

Most (91%) of the 377 respondents taught slow learners (IQ between 50 and 90). Three-fourths stated that they were meeting the needs of these students well; ½ reported concern with 10 out of 13 problem areas; and over 3/4 reported difficulty with reading disabilities, with meeting individual differences in class, and with finding suitable techniques for teaching the slow learner.

Komanyi, Margit Hona (Ph. D.). "THE REAL AND IDEAL PARTICIPATION IN DECISION-MAKING OF IBAN WOMEN: A STUDY OF A LONGHOUSE COMMUNITY IN SARA-WAK, EAST MALAYSIA." New York University, 1973. 157 pp. Source: DAI, XXXIII, 10B (April, 1973), 4631-B. XUM Order No. 73-8177.

Encouragement of education of girls equally with boys among the Ibans of Sarawak, East Malaysia, promoted rather than destroyed traditional values.

Komorita, Nori (Ph. D.). "SELF-CONCEPT MEASURES AS RELATED TO ACHIEVEMENT IN NURSING EDUCATION." Wayne State University, 1971. 75 pp. Source: DAI, XXXII, 12A (June, 1972), 6809-A. XUM Order No. 72-14,584.

Self concept was shown to be relevant to nursing education and to the prediction of success in clinical practice.

Konstam, Varda Slomowitz (Ph. D.). "FEAR OF SUCCESS, SEX ROLE ORI-ENTATION, AND PERFORMANCE IN DIFFERING EXPERIMENTAL CONDITIONS." Fordham University, 1976. 210 pp. Source: DAI, XXXVII, 2A (August, 1976), 886-A. XUM Order No. 76-17,904.

Variables of success-non-success, feedback, sex role orientation, appropriate-inappropriate feedback were not effective in predicting differences in performance. Defensive patterns were characteristic of the high fear-of-success individual.

Kopel, Bernice Helene (Ed. D.). "HOME ECONOMISTS WORKING WITH LOW-INCOME FAMILIES AND IMPLICATIONS FOR COLLEGE FOOD AND NUTRITION CURRICU-LUM." Oklahoma State University, 1970. 147 pp. Source: DAI, XXXI, 10B (April, 1971), 6095-B-6096-B. XUM Order No. 71-11,197.

Greatest concerns reported were: having food and nutrition knowledge about low-cost foods; knowing how to teach nutrition to low income groups; understanding the people with whom they work; and planning food and nutrition programs for low income groups. The degree of concern home economists felt for low-income families was signifi-cantly affected by selected employment and educational variables.

Korben, Donald Lee (Ed. D.). "THE EFFECTS OF DISTRIBUTED PRACTICE VERSUS MASSED PRACTICE, AND BEHAVIORAL MODELING VERSUS SCRIPT MODELING, ON ASSERTIVE TRAINING WITH FEMALES." Indiana University, 1976. 195 pp. Source: DAI, XXXVII, 8A (February, 1977), 4866-A. XUM Order No. 77-3296.

The distributed practice group was effective in enhancing assertive behavior. Time format and modeling style made no significant dif-ference.

Korri, Lea Jean (Ph. D.). "INSTRUCTIONAL PROBLEMS ENCOUNTERED BY
WOMEN PHYSICAL EDUCATION TEACHERS AND THEIR RELATION TO TEACHING COMPE-
TENCY AS EXPRESSED BY PHYSICAL EDUCATION MAJORS IN MINNESOTA." University of Minnesota, 1970. 176 pp. Source: DAI, XXXI, 10A (April, 1971),
5181-A. XUM Order No. 71-8173.

Teachers reported the following problems: inadequate facilities, inadequate programs for handicapped students, inadequate provisions for
individual differences in large classes, and difficulty in motivating
students in large classes. They felt inadequately prepared to teach
handicapped children, to deal with problems relating to physical facilities, and to handle organizational and personal relationships.
Junior high teachers had more problems than senior high teachers.
Most teachers with 4 years or less experience had fewer problems than
teachers with 5 or more years of experience.

Kotcher, Elaine V. (Ph. D.). "SEX-ROLE IDENTITY AND CAREER GOALS IN
ADOLESCENT WOMEN." Hofstra University, 1975. 146 pp. Source: DAI,
XXXVI, 9A (March, 1976), 5949-A. XUM Order No. 76-4588.

Sex role identity was related to atypical occupational choice and
degree of career commitment. Young women who identified with traditionally male roles saw themselves in occupations more male-dominated
and saw their careers as central in their lives. Young women who
saw themselves in traditionally female roles expected to enter feminine occupations. A strong positive relationship existed between
perceived commitment to a career and untraditional occupational
choice. Early adolescent women chose more masculine occupations
than did young women in later adolescence. Older adolescent women
saw a career as more central to their lives than did younger ones.

Kouchok, Kawsar Hussein (Ph. D.). "EDUCATIONAL TELEVISION IN HOME
ECONOMICS IN THE UNITED STATES WITH IMPLICATIONS FOR THE UNITED ARAB
REPUBLIC." Southern Illinois University, 1970. 260 pp. Source: DAI,
XXXI, 10B (April, 1971), 6096-B. XUM Order No. 71-2385.

Most U. S. educational television stations broadcast informal home
economics related programs between July 1967 and June 1969 and included consumer information. Home economics-related programs were considered women's programs. Major factors for success were content
and the personality of the performer. Major problems were funding,
lack of a qualified performer, scheduling, and appropriateness for
specific audiences.

Kovacs, Alberta Rose (Ed. D.). "PREDICTING SUCCESS IN THREE SELECTED
COLLEGIATE SCHOOLS OF NURSING." Columbia University, 1968. 239 pp.
Source: DAI, XXXI, 1B (July, 1970), 266-B-267-B. XUM Order No. 70-12,
522.

The Scholastic Aptitude Test (SAT) was the best predictor of success
on the State Board Test Pool Examination (SBTPE). Verbal SAT proved
to be the best predictor on all SBTPE tests except psychiatric nursing.

Kozlowska, Sister Mary Viterbia (Ed. D.). "A STUDY OF THE EFFECTS
ON RACIAL ATTITUDES OF EXERCISES IN VALUES CLARIFICATION AND IDENTIFICA-
TION IN CONJUNCTION WITH THE POETRY OF A BLACK POET AND A WHITE POET."

Temple University, 1973. 258 pp. Source: DAI, XXXIV, 7A (January, 1974), 3695-A. XUM Order No. 74-1805.

Study of a white poetess and a black poetess, as well as exercises in value clarification and identification, strengthened the self concepts of 9th and 10th grade black and white girls. However, the racial attitudes of both the black and the white group remained consistent, despite changes in individual girls.

Kraditor, Aileen Sema (Ph. D.). "THE IDEAS OF THE WOMAN SUFFRAGE MOVEMENT, 1890-1920." Columbia University, 1962. 293 pp. Source: DAI, XXVIII, 11A (May, 1968), 4577-A. XUM Order No. 63-6116.

Historical study on the thinking of 26 leading suffragists about religion, the home, the new immigration, labor, the Negro, and political parties and their tactics. Suffragists were mostly middle-of-the-road in political and social outlook and demanded the right to participate in the political management of a society whose basic structure they endorsed.

Kramer, Sister Mary Albert (Ph. D.). "THE ASSOCIATE DEGREE PROGRAM AND CATHOLIC NURSING EDUCATION IN THE MIDDLE STATES AREA." Catholic University of America, 1962. 262 pp. Source: DAI, XXIII, 9 (March, 1963), 3323-3324. XUM Order No. 63-260.

Opinions of 24 Catholic leaders were that public associate degree nursing programs threatened the survival of Catholic diploma programs. Dissatisfaction with the general nursing program for registered nurses who went on for a bachelor's degree was also shown.

Kramer, Susan Saunders (Ph. D.). "AN EXPLORATORY STUDY OF THE SITUATIONAL PROBLEMS OF A SELECT GROUP OF OLDER WOMEN IN A DIPLOMA SCHOOL OF NURSING." University of Oregon, 1975. 135 pp. Source: DAI, XXXVII, 1B (July, 1976), 155-B-156-B. XUM Order No. 76-15,042.

The major problem was for women to combine their student role with responsibilities to their families. Recommendations included setting up remedial and basic skills classes; reorganizing the program to meet these students' needs; organizing special counseling groups; scheduling clinical time that would not interfere with home duties; and making financial aid more accessible.

Krause, John Ludwig (Ed. D.). "A STUDY OF TEACHER ATTITUDES TOWARD THEIR WOMEN SECONDARY SCHOOL PRINCIPALS IN NEW JERSEY." Temple University, 1964. 267 pp. Source: DAI, XXV, 2 (August, 1964), 967-968. XUM Order No. 64-9338.

Negative attitudes toward women principals did not generally exist in New Jersey's secondary schools. Stereotypes generally associated with women in leadership positions were therefore not justified by teacher attitudes toward their women principals.

Krekeler, Sister Kathleen (Ph. D.). "AN ANALYSIS OF FACTORS INHIBITING IMPLEMENTATION OF RECURRING RECOMMENDATIONS FROM NURSING EDUCATION STUDIES." University of Texas at Austin, 1974. 142 pp. Source: DAI, XXXV, 1B (July, 1974), 347-B-348-B. XUM Order No. 74-14,725.

Inhibiting factors included: lack of appreciation of education, leadership, and professionalism; disunity in nursing; tradition of dedication and self-sacrifice; apprenticeship image of nursing education; opposition of medical profession to improvements in nursing education; hospital economics; lack of support of college administration; cost of collegiate nursing; and resistance to administrative independence.

Kresojevich, Ida Zektick (Ph. D.). "MOTIVATION TO AVOID SUCCESS IN WOMEN AS RELATED TO YEAR IN SCHOOL, ACADEMIC ACHIEVEMENT AND SUCCESS CONTEXT." Michigan State University, 1972. 92 pp. Source: DAI, XXXIII, 5B (November, 1972), 2348-B-2349-B. XUM Order No. 72-29,993.

A desire to avoid success was found among each of the 80 undergraduates studied. Women with high grades were more negative toward success. Sophomores were more optimistic than seniors.

Kriger, Sara Finn (Ph. D.). "NEED ACHIEVEMENT AND PERCEIVED PARENTAL CHILDREARING ATTITUDES OF CAREER WOMEN AND HOMEMAKERS." Ohio State University, 1971. 74 pp. Source: DAI, XXXII, 12B (June, 1972), 6621-B. XUM Order No. 72-15,235.

Homemakers perceived their parents as relatively more restrictive and scored lower on an achievement test than did career women. Career women in male-dominated occupations scored higher on achievement than did those in female-dominated occupations.

Kring, Frederick Stevens (Ed. D.). "A COMPARATIVE STUDY OF SUPPLEMENTAL INCOMES OF MALE AND FEMALE TEACHERS IN THE PUBLIC SCHOOLS OF BEDFORD, CAMBRIA, AND SOMERSET COUNTIES OF PENNSYLVANIA." University of Pittsburgh, 1955. 201 pp. Source: DAI, XVI, 1 (1956), 46-47. XUM Order No. 13,872.

Both male and female teachers recognized greater economic justification for male teachers to supplement their incomes.

Krosky, Beverly J. (Ed. D.). "SEX ROLE STEREOTYPING IN HOME ECONOMICS CURRICULA IN SELECTED SENIOR HIGH SCHOOLS IN COLORADO." University of Northern Colorado, 1974. 118 pp. Source: DAI, XXXV, 9A (March, 1975), 5781-A-5782-A. XUM Order No. 75-5423.

Content analysis of textbooks and materials revealed such sex role stereotyping as passive females, females in traditional occupations, and sex-linked personality traits.

Krueger, Cynthia Sue (Ph. D.). "PROBLEMS AND PROCESSES OF PROFESSIONAL SOCIALIZATION: THE STUDENT NURSES." Washington University, 1967. 165 pp. Source: DAI, XXVIII, 10A (April, 1968), 4287-A-4288-A. XUM Order No. 68-5142.

Investigated the relationships among faculty-student conflict, student culture, professional ideology, professional character judgment, and sponsorship in the socialization of professionals.

Krueger, Elizabeth Annette (Ed. D.). "THE ADMINISTRATION OF A HYPODERMIC INJECTION: AN INSTANCE OF PROGRAMMED INSTRUCTION." Columbia

University, 1964. 647 pp. Source: DAI, XXVI, 1 (July, 1965), 322-323.
XUM Order No. 65-6169.

The program was effective in teaching most of the needed scientific
knowledge and motor skills. Learning was transferred to an actual
practice setting. The program enabled individualized learning of a
manipulative skill.

Kubat, Janice Gail Pflanz (Ph. D.). "ATTITUDES OF MEDICAL EDUCATORS
AND NURSE EDUCATORS TOWARD EXPANSION OF THE NURSE PRACTITIONER'S ROLE TO
INCLUDE PRIMARY CARE." University of Nebraska, 1970. 113 pp. Source:
DAI, XXXI, 10A (April, 1971), 5110-A. XUM Order No. 71-9570.

There were differences in attitudes toward the nurse's role: medical educators agreed that nurses should be lateral and nurse educators desired vertical expansion of the role.

Kuczynski, Hedwig June (Ph. D.). "KNOWLEDGE AND ATTITUDES TOWARD
HUMAN SEXUALITY AMONG GRADUATE STUDENTS IN THE COLLEGES OF MEDICINE AND
NURSING: IMPLICATIONS FOR CURRICULUM." Wayne State University, 1976.
147 pp. Source: DAI, XXXVII, 10A (April, 1977), 6245-A-6246. XUM Order No. 77-9418.

Since graduate nursing students were no more knowledgeable about
human sexuality than medical students or the average college graduate, the study implied the need for such education as part of medical and nursing programs.

Kuhl, Louise (Ph. D.). "A STUDY OF THE LEARNING RATE OF COLLEGE
WOMEN IN CERTAIN PHYSICAL ACTIVITIES AS RELATED TO THEIR GENERAL MOTOR
ABILITY." University of Iowa, 1941. 71 pp. Source: Dissertation,
pp. 58-60.

No significant relationship existed between general motor ability
and learning rate during an 8-week or less instructional period of
swimming, tennis, and stunts. A statistically significant relationship was found between learning rate and general motor skills in
archery.

Kumler, Katharine Walter (Ph. D.). "THE IMPLICATION OF THE CAMPUS
COOPERATIVE MOVEMENT FOR HOMEMAKING EDUCATION." Ohio State University,
1943. Source: Katharine W. Kumler, "Campus Co-Operative Living,"
JOURNAL OF HOME ECONOMICS, XXXVIII, No. 6 (June, 1946), pp. 329-332.

Suggested that the campus co-op houses provided women a satisfactory
home environment at a financial saving. The movement promoted democracy only in so far as democracy flourishes whenever people are
associated for mutual betterment without undue outside interference.

Kummer, Laura Bates (Ed. D.). "ADMISSION CHARACTERISTICS OF MASTER'S
CANDIDATES IN NURSING EDUCATION." Indiana University, 1964. 143 pp.
Source: DAI, XXV, 10 (April, 1965), 5683-5684. XUM Order No. 65-2377.

Significant differences were found between nurses and teachers in
age, undergraduate grades, time span between finishing high school
and college entrance, number of states in which candidates had

worked, years of professional experience, and marital status. Most
candidates came from educational institutions in the same geographic
region. There was a difference in the amount of representation from
other regions. The major reason for rejecting nurses was that undergraduate grades were below average. Nurses completed their bachelor's
work with higher grades. They received conditional admission if they
had not met the master's program entrance requirements. Generally,
nurses applied earlier than did the teachers.

Kuo, Ping-wen (Ph. D.). "THE CHINESE SYSTEM OF PUBLIC EDUCATION."
Columbia University Teachers College, 1914. Source: TCCU CONTRIBUTIONS
No. 64, pp. 163-171.

This history of public education in China discussed the relation of
school training to national progress and government service, elimination of classics and other major curriculum revision, teaching
methods, teacher training, and women's education.

Kuramoto, Alice Mitsuye (Ph. D.). "AN EVALUATION OF REGISTERED NURSE
STUDENTS IN A BACCALAUREATE NURSING PROGRAM: THE EFFECT OF EDUCATION ON
PERFORMANCE." University of Michigan, 1975. 114 pp. Source: DAI,
XXXVI, 10B (April, 1976), 4944-B. XUM Order No. 76-9439.

Found no significant differences between baccalaureate nursing students and registered nursing students in performance of nursing care.

Kyle, Patricia Ann (Ph. D.). "POLITICAL SEX-ROLE DISTINCTIONS: MOTI-
VATIONS, RECRUITMENT, AND DEMOCRACY OF WOMEN PARTY ELITE IN NORTH CARO-
LINA." Georgetown University, 1973. 274 pp. Source: DAI, XXXIV, 7A
(January, 1974), 4348-A. XUM Order No. 74-1438.

Women entered political party positions with less schooling, lower
income, and fewer children than did their male counterparts. Schools,
however, particularly the single-sex school, where they took politics-
related courses, were the primary agency for women's political socialization.

Labadie, Georgie Conoly Royster (Ed. D.). "VERBAL INTERACTION IN
COLLEGE NURSING CLASSES." Columbia University, 1970. 136 pp. Source:
DAI, XXXI, 7A (January, 1971), 3419-A. XUM Order No. 71-1106.

Tape recordings of 4 successive class sessions in medical and surgical nursing revealed: teachers were more active verbally in classroom discussions than students; teachers dominated the discourse;
subject matter accounted for 2/3 of the discourse; and positive and
negative reactions accounted for a small proportion of the discourse
in all classes.

La Barthe, Eileene Reid (Ed. D.). "A STUDY OF THE MOTIVATION OF
WOMEN IN ADMINISTRATIVE AND SUPERVISORY POSITIONS IN SELECTED UNIFIED
SCHOOL DISTRICTS IN SOUTHERN CALIFORNIA." University of Southern California, 1973. 142 pp. Source: DAI, XXXIV, 7A (January, 1974), 3695-A-
3696-A. XUM Order No. 73-31,364.

Status was the most powerful positive motivator: lack of status was
the number one negative motivator of women school administrators.

Recognition and achievement ranked second and third as satisfiers.
Women's liberation and interpersonal relations with peers ranked
second and third as dissatisfiers. Challenging work and leadership
opportunities caused women to enter school administration. Negligible factors were salary, security, growth, advancement, and personal
life.

Labecki, Geraldine (Ed. D.). "BACCALAUREATE PROGRAMS IN NURSING IN
THE SOUTHERN REGION, 1925-1960." George Peabody College for Teachers,
1967. 149 pp. Source: DAI, XXVIII, 5A (November, 1967), 1687-A-1688-A.
XUM Order No. 67-14,999.

Traced the development of nursing baccalaureate programs of 51 institutions and identified each school's sources of support and problems
relating to school objectives, the integration of clinical experience with content, and attrition rate.

Lafrieda, Dorothea Faith (Ph. D.). "THE RELATIONSHIP BETWEEN SPECIAL
PROGRAMS AND THE COMMUNITY ADAPTATION AND MARITAL ADJUSTMENT OF WIVES OF
FOREIGN STUDENTS." University of Miami, 1973. 252 pp. Source: DAI,
XXXIV, 5A (November, 1973), 2304-A-2305-A. XUM Order No. 73-25,914.

Wives (30) who were assigned to 3 modes of treatment (individual,
counseling, social information programs, and no treatment) generally
adapted well to new surroundings. Social life, the larger cultural
community, and community service agencies played a weak role in their
overall adaptation. Neither individual counseling nor social information programs had appreciable impact on their adaptation.

Lambertsen, Eleanor Catherine (Ed. D.). "PROFESSIONAL EDUCATION FOR
LEADERSHIP IN NURSING PRACTICE." Columbia University Teachers College,
1957. Source: Dissertation, pp. 226-231.

Nursing as an occupational title was a deterrent in clarifying the
nursing role. Principles of professional education reflecting nursing aims, curriculum, objectives, relationship between education and
experience, faculty responsibility, and philosophies of teaching and
practice were formulated. Concluded that professional education
could improve the evaluation and development of nursing education.

Lamoreaux, James Wood (Ph. D.). "RECEPTIVITY OF SPECIFIC SUBAUDIENCES
TO FAMILY PLANNING COMMUNICATIONS IN IRAN: A TYPOLOGICAL APPROACH."
Syracuse University, 1976. 226 pp. Source: DAI, XXXVII, 11A (May,
1977), 6821-A. XUM Order No. 77-9871.

Findings indicated that least modern females utilized information
more effectively than most modern females, with most modern females
using the motivation factors more than least modern females. The
division of females as least, semi, and most modern was not as effective as groupings of age, sex, and urbanization.

Lande, Sylvia (Ed. D.). "FACTORS RELATED TO PERCEPTION OF NURSES
AND NURSING AND SELECTION OR REJECTION OF NURSING AS A CAREER AMONG
SENIORS IN ROMAN CATHOLIC HIGH SCHOOLS IN NEW YORK CITY." Columbia Uni-
versity, 1964. 268 pp. Source: DAI, XXVI, 4 (October, 1965), 2143.
XUM Order No. 65-2284.

Students (934) were divided into 3 groups: (1) nursing aspirants;
(2) those who had never wanted to be nurses; and (3) those who rejected nursing after initial consideration. Aspirants preferred the
physical sciences; students in the other groups preferred languages.
Aspirants felt more assured of approval of their career choices than
did the others. For aspirants, the most frequent information sources
about nursing were people and media associated with the profession.
Most students were uninformed about the degree of independence of
nursing. Aspirants were more aware of the different levels of nursing functions.

Lane, W. Clayton (Ph. D.). "THE LOWER-CLASS GIRL IN COLLEGE: A
STUDY OF STANFORD FRESHMAN WOMEN." Stanford University, 1961. 237 pp.
Source: DAI, XXI, 11 (May, 1961), 3540. XUM Order No. Mic 61-1234.

Lower-status girls were generally different from upper-status girls
in the conditions that brought them to college, in their orientation
to family, and in ther adaptation to college life. Lower-status
girls' adjustment to college life was difficult because of such feelings as inadequacy in necessary skills and ambivalence toward their
parents.

Lang, Paula Helen (Ph. D.). "THE USE OF FEEDBACK AND BEHAVIORAL AS-
SIGNMENTS IN ASSERTIVE TRAINING GROUPS FOR WOMEN." University of Geor-
gia, 1976. 79 pp. Source: DAI, XXXVII, 7B (January, 1977), 3617-B.
XUM Order No. 76-29,541.

Although experimental groups improved more than control groups, video
feedback and extra assignments alone or in combination did not enhance treatment effects on assertive training of 32 women.

Langdon, Lois Mardelle (Ed. D.). "AN EXPLORATION OF THE VOCATIONAL
BEHAVIOR OF PROFESSIONAL NURSES WITH FACULTY ASSIGNMENTS IN PROGRAMS OF
PRACTICAL NURSING EDUCATION." University of Illinois at Urbana-Champaign,
1973. 223 pp. Source: DAI, XXXIV, 9A (March, 1974), 5662-A-5663-A.
XUM Order No. 74-5619.

Career patterns of 227 faculty in 45 practical nursing programs were
markedly different from the full-time continuing homemaker role.
Faculty had nearly continuous work patterns in supervisory nursing
positions or in-service education. Intrinsic needs ranked over job
attributes in determining satisfaction.

Lassiter, Constance Smith (Ph. D.). "THE RELATIONSHIP OF SELF-CONCEPT
AS LEARNERS TO BLACK STUDENTS COMPARED TO SELECTED VARIABLES." United
States International University, 1976. 115 pp. Source: DAI, XXXVIII,
3B (September, 1977), 1385-B. XUM Order No. 77-16,405.

Females had a more positive self-concept as learners than males in
this study of 108 black 7th, 8th, and 9th graders in Tacoma, Washington, public schools.

Lau, Estelle Pau On (Ph. D.). "ELLEN C. SABIN, PRESIDENT OF MIL-
WAUKEE-DOWNER COLLEGE, 1895-1921: PROPONENT OF HIGHER EDUCATION FOR
WOMEN." Marquette University, 1976. 142 pp. Source: DAI, XXXVII, 4A
(October, 1976), 2025-A-2026-A. XUM Order No. 76-21,752.

Social, economic, and political trends in 19th and 20th century American society and their impact on Milwaukee-Downer College. Life and career of Pres. Sabin before 1895; her educational practices and beliefs; and her roles as teacher, friend, administrator, and proponent of higher education for women.

Lawrence, Cora Jane (Ph. D.). "UNIVERSITY EDUCATION FOR NURSING IN SEATTLE 1912-1950: AN INSIDE STORY OF THE UNIVERSITY OF WASHINGTON SCHOOL." University of Washington, 1972. 287 pp. Source: DAI, XXXIII, 5A (November, 1972), 2141-A. XUM Order No. 72-28,622.

Traced the school's growth within the University as well as through outside forces such as scientific movements, changes in hospital practices, war, depression, and funding. Also emphasized the role of Elizabeth Sterling Soule, who guided the school for 30 years.

Lawrence, Roger Lee (Ph. D.). "IMPLICATIONS OF CHARACTERISTICS AND ATTITUDES OF FARM AND VILLAGE WOMEN FOR HOME ECONOMICS EXTENSION PROGRAMS." Iowa State College, 1958. 210 pp. Source: DAI, XIX, 3 (September, 1958), 477-478. XUM Order No. Mic 58-3004.

A comparison of 147 farm women with 111 village women. Village women were older; more of them worked outside the home for pay; they placed greater importance on a college education; had more problems with money management; made less use of radio as a source of homemaking information; and did not participate in as many formal organizations. The most striking difference was in their knowledge and use of the extension service. Farm women recognized the service as an information source and used it accordingly.

Laws, Ruth Mitchell (Ed. D.). "A STUDY OF THE IN-SERVICE EDUCATION NEEDS OF HOMEMAKING TEACHERS IN DELAWARE." New York University, 1956. 191 pp. Source: DAI, XVII, 4 (1957), 844-845. XUM Order No. 17,659.

Teachers (72) and 25 administrators revealed that the chief source of in-service education was summer courses at the university and services provided by the State Education Department. Most teachers indicated that family responsibility prohibited their studying for advanced degrees. Most held membership in the State Home Economics Association and attended the state professional meetings. The teachers listed improved teaching methods and better understanding of family-centered teaching as desired professional needs. The most popular activities for credit were campus workshops.

Lediger, Cecelia Reba (Ed. D.). "A FOLLOW-UP STUDY OF THE GRADUATES OF ST. OLAF COLLEGE DEPARTMENT OF NURSING, 1956-1962." Columbia University, 1966. 181 pp. Source: DAI, XXVII, 4B (October, 1966), 1202-B. XUM Order No. 66-10,302.

Of the 203 graduates surveyed, all but 3 had practiced professional nursing since graduation; 110 were in active practice and 93 planned to return; 164 were married and 111 had one or more children; 92% had been staff nurses at hospitals, while 14% had been staff nurses in public health agencies; and 49 continued formal study after completing the baccalaureate program.

Lee, Anne Marold (Ed. D.). "A STUDY OF MARRIED WOMEN STUDENTS AT INDIANA STATE TEACHERS COLLEGE, 1958-1959." Indiana University, 1960. 173 pp. Source: DAI, XXI, 4 (October, 1960), 800. XUM Order No. Mic 60-3006.

In this survey of 267 married women, 90% were vocationally oriented, generally toward teacher certification; 1/5 had husbands who were college students; 85% felt that they had inadequate funds and had the most time pressures. The need for counseling was stated most frequently by students as a way the college could serve them better.

Lee, Dong Wook (Ed. D.). "PROPOSED PROGRAMS IN THE CHRISTIAN WOMEN'S TWO-YEAR COLLEGES IN KOREA." University of Tulsa, 1974. 152 pp. Source: DAI, XXXV, 2A (August, 1974), 846-A. XUM Order No. 74-19,086.

The proposal described a general education curriculum designed to emphasize leadership development, women's education, and career education in such fields as special education, education for the aged, and pre-school teaching program.

Lee, Joan (Ph. D.). "PATTERNS OF MENTAL ABILITY IN CHINESE CHILDREN REARED IN THE UNITED STATES AND IN THE REPUBLIC OF CHINA." Columbia University, 1977. 149 pp. Source: DAI, XXXVIII, 5A (November, 1977), 2667-A. XUM Order No. 77-24,101.

Boys did better than girls in one reasoning test. Middle class and lower class girls shared one common pattern of mental ability while boys of middle and lower class shared another pattern of mental ability.

Lee, Kyung Sik (Ph. D.). "RELATIONSHIPS BETWEEN SPECIALIZATION AND ATTITUDES TOWARD POPULATION RELATED ISSUES AMONG PROFESSIONAL STUDENTS IN KOREA." University of North Carolina at Chapel Hill, 1974. 332 pp. Source: DAI, XXXVI, 1A (July, 1975), 145-A. XUM Order No. 75-15,661.

Of 1,692 students, the majority in education, nursing, and medicine favored family planning, contraceptive use, population education, and equal opportunities for the education of both sexes. The nursing and medical groups were more positive about these variables than the education group. The nursing group was the most favorable toward equality of sexes in terms of opportunities for education, employment, and careers of married women. Students in the health professions desired the 2-child family, whereas those in education desired the 3-child family.

Lee, Louise Grieshaber (Ed. D.). "FACTORS RELATED TO PROFESSIONAL ACHIEVEMENT OF WOMEN: A STUDY OF CALIFORNIA STATE UNIVERSITY AND COLLEGE WOMEN." University of Southern California, 1975. Source: DAI, XXXVI, 11A (May, 1976), 7237-A.

A survey of 250 women about their achievement revealed: opportunities for graduate study, faculty interest, support of others, high motivation, strong intellectual interest, ability to work with people, self-concepts congruent with family expectations, lack of inhibitions about the roles of women, and freedom to develop their talents.

Lee, Margaret Naomi (Ed. D.). "PREFERENCES FOR UNIVERSITY TEACHING AS THE CAREER GOAL OF BACCALAUREATE STUDENTS OF NURSING GRADUATING FROM SELECTED UNIVERSITIES IN CANADA." Columbia University, 1966. 134 pp. Source: DAI, XXVII, 9B (March, 1967), 3158-B-3159-B. XUM Order No. 67-2818.

From the 6 universities visited and 303 seniors surveyed, university teaching was first choice for respondents from basic programs and second choice for respondents from post-basic programs. Thirty-four percent from the basic programs and 65% from the post-basic programs chose teaching.

Lee, Mary Eugenia (Ed. D.). "A CURRICULUM IN NURSING SERVICE ADMIN-ISTRATION FOR THE SCHOOL OF NURSING, MEDICAL COLLEGE OF GEORGIA." Columbia University, 1969. 214 pp. Source: DAI, XXXI, 1B (July, 1970), 267-B. XUM Order No. 70-12,877.

The curriculum included: (1) general education in the behavioral sciences; (2) administrative theory and principles, and personnel administration; (3) general   studies of health systems, nursing practice and education, and the nursing profession; (4) electives or independent study in clinical nursing; (5) learning experience in the area of specialization; (6) research methods and statistics; and (7) preparation and defense of a thesis.

LeFevre, Carol Jane (Ph. D.). "THE MATURE WOMAN AS GRADUATE STUDENT." University of Chicago, 1972. Source: Carol Jane LeFevre, "The Mature Woman as Graduate Student," SCHOOL REVIEW, LXXX, No. 2 (February, 1972), pp. 281-297.

Little evidence was found that the experiences of 35 women at 3 stages of their graduate school careers (beginning, middle, and end) differed significantly from those of other graduate students. The fact that these returning women were not different kinds of students and did not face special academic problems suggested that universities had been neglecting an excellent source of good graduate students in not encouraging the intellectually gifted college-educated married women with children to apply.

Leggon, Cheryl Bernadette (Ph. D.). "THE BLACK FEMALE PROFESSIONAL: ROLE STRAINS AND STATUS INCONSISTENCIES." University of Chicago, 1975. Source: DAI, XXXVI, 7A (January, 1976), 4776-A-4777-A.

A majority of the respondents experienced more discrimination because of race than sex. For most of the younger respondents, the black liberation movement was much more important than the women's liberation movement.

Leibell, Helen Domincia (Ph. D.). "ANGLO SAXON EDUCATION OF WOMEN: FROM HILDA TO HILDEGARDE." Georgetown University, 1922. Source: Published; Same Title; New York: Lenox Hill Publishing and Distribution Co. (Burt Franklin), reprinted 1971; p. 9.

Chapters on: education in the primitive church, post-Nicene education, Christianity in Britain, prominent Anglo-Saxon women, Anglo-Saxon education and educators, the fine arts, Anglo-Saxon influence in Germany, Alcuin in Frankland, the Alfredian Renaissance, Anglo-Saxon literature, and the Dissolution.

Leigh, Mary Henson (Ph. D.). "THE EVOLUTION OF WOMEN'S PARTICIPATION IN THE SUMMER OLYMPIC GAMES, 1900-1948." Ohio State University, 1974. 490 pp. Source: DAI, XXXV, 8A (February, 1975), 5098-A-5099-A. XUM Order No. 75-3121.

Factors in the evolution were social mores and traditions in various societies, intransigence of governing bodies of organized amateur sport, the influence of feminism, the 1922 controversy in which the U. S. took a team of American women to the Women's Olympic games, and the influence of the media.

Lemen, Mildred Gene (Ph. D.). "THE RELATIONSHIP BETWEEN SELECTED VARIABLES AND ATTITUDES OF COLLEGE WOMEN TOWARD PHYSICAL EDUCATION AND CERTAIN SPORTS." State University of Iowa, 1962. 265 pp. Source: DAI, XXIII, 5 (November, 1962), 1596. XUM Order No. 62-4981.

Relationships existed between the following: (1) social background factors and attitudes toward activities and physical education; and (2) participation in recreation associations in school; (3) attitudes, ability, and leisure participation in sports. The women preferred to participate in individual sports rather than in team sports during their leisure time.

Lemmerman, Janice Lou Nausner (Ph. D.). "NURSING AND MEDICAL SCHOOL ORGANIZATIONAL INTERACTION, AND PERCEPTIONS ABOUT PHYSICIAN/NURSE ROLES AND RELATIONSHIPS." Kent State University, 1976. 241 pp. Source: DAI, XXXVII, 12B, Part 1 (June, 1977), 6054-B. XUM Order No. 77-12,430.

A vast amount of data was accumulated about the relationship between U. S. universities' medical school programs and nursing school pro-grams. Found no statistically significant differences in the roles and relationships of physicians and nurses.

Lemon, Donald K. (Ed. D.). "A STUDY OF THE ATTITUDE OF SELECTED GROUPS TOWARD THE EMPLOYMENT OF WOMEN FOR ADMINISTRATIVE POSITIONS IN PUBLIC SCHOOLS." University of Kansas, 1968. 169 pp. Source: DAI, XXIX, 6A (December, 1968), 1718-A-1719-A. XUM Order No. 68-17,415.

Comparison of attitudes of 69 school board members, 70 administrators, and 72 teachers found that: (1) women were more favorable toward working with women administrators than were men; (2) teachers were more amenable to working with women administrators than were school board members or male administrators; and (3) women school administrators had the most favorable attitude toward other women as administrators.

Lenox, Mary Frances (Ed. D.). "BLACK WOMEN: STUDENT PERCEPTIONS OF THEIR CONTRIBUTIONS." University of Massachusetts, 1975. 162 pp. Source: DAI, XXXVI, 9A (March, 1976), 5901-A. XUM Order No. 76-5356.

Students' perceptions of black women's contributions were favorable before and after experimental course about black women.

Leonard, Louise Carrell (Ed. D.). "AN INVESTIGATION BY INTERVIEW OF
THE SELF-DESCRIPTIVE FACTORS UNDERLYING THE ACHIEVEMENT PERFORMANCE OF
THE ACADEMICALLY TALENTED WOMAN." University of Kansas, 1962. 283 pp.
Source: DAI, XXIII, 8 (February, 1963), 2794-2795. XUM Order No. 63-796.

Watkins scholars (34 women) at the University of Kansas engaged in a
free expression of why they were high achievers. Found that self-
image of the high-achieving women students was affected by kind and
degree of societal acceptance.

Leserman, Jane Paushter (Ph. D.). "BOYS AND GIRLS IN WHITE: PROFES-
SIONAL ORIENTATION OF THE STUDENT PHYSICIAN." Duke University, 1976.
225 pp. Source: DAI, XXXVII, 12A, Part 1 (June, 1977), 7981-A. XUM
Order No. 77-11,832.

Women medical students were oriented more highly than men to values
considered beneficial for health care.

Leshem, Ariel (Ed. D.) and Leshem, Yonia (Ed. D.). "ATTITUDES OF
COLLEGE STUDENTS TOWARD MEN AND WOMEN WHO COMMIT SUICIDAL ACTS." Univer-
sity of Northern Colorado, 1976. 388 pp. Source: DAI, XXXVII, 11A
(May, 1977), 7042-A. XUM Order No. 77-11,070.

Results indicated that males high in authoritarianism had more negative feelings toward personal suicidal thoughts; females had a higher
frequency of personal suicidal thoughts. Occupational choice was
positively related to the level of authoritarianism.

Levine, Adeline Gordon (Ph. D.). "MARITAL AND OCCUPATIONAL PLANS OF
WOMEN IN PROFESSIONAL SCHOOLS: LAW, MEDICINE, NURSING, TEACHING." Yale
University, 1968. 139 pp. Source: DAI, XXX, 2A (August, 1969), 829-A.
XUM Order No. 69-13,353.

Women in traditionally male fields of law and medicine came from
higher social class backgrounds, had better educated mothers, and
maintained their feminine identity and sex role while in law and
medicine. Women in traditionally female fields of nursing and teaching felt that their sex role was separate from their work role and
planned to withdraw from their careers.

Levinson, Fay Van Der Kar (Ph. D.). "EARLY IDENTIFICATION OF EDUCA-
TIONALLY HIGH RISK AND HIGH POTENTIAL PUPILS: INFLUENCES OF SEX AND
SOCIO-CULTURAL STATUS ON SCREENING TECHNIQUES." University of California,
Los Angeles, 1976. 98 pp. Source: DAI, XXXVII, 11A (May, 1977), 7042-
A-7043-A. XUM Order No. 77-9350.

Analyses indicated that gender and socio-cultural status were significant influences on test scores, with girls scoring higher than boys
and Anglo subjects scoring higher than black and Spanish-speaking
subjects. A major finding was that though the tests given had similar names they measured different things.

Levitt, Morris Jacob (Ph. D.). "POLITICAL ATTITUDES OF AMERICAN WO-
MEN: A STUDY OF THE EFFECTS OF WORK AND EDUCATION ON THEIR POLITICAL
ROLE." University of Maryland, 1965. 123 pp. Source: DAI, XXVII, 6A
(December, 1966), 1880-A. XUM Order No. 66-933.

Among homemakers, working women, and men (included for comparison), working women had an active voting record and a greater sense of political efficacy and of citizen obligation than the homemakers. These characteristics tended to increase with formal education.

Levy, Betty Bollinger (Ph. D.). "TEACHERS' JUDGMENTS OF ACHIEVEMENT-RELATED AND PUPIL ROLE BEHAVIORS OF ELEMENTARY SCHOOL GIRLS AND BOYS." Columbia University, 1974. 282 pp. Source: DAI, XXXV, 10B (April, 1975), 5085-B. XUM Order No. 75-7518.

Teachers (259) valued achievement-related behaviors over pupil role behaviors and differed little in their responses to the behaviors of boys and girls.

Lewis, Audrey Eubanks (Ed. D.). "A COMPARISON OF THREE METHODS OF TEACHING BOWLING TO COLLEGE WOMEN." George Peabody College for Teachers, 1965. 117 pp. Source: DAI, XXVI, 11 (May, 1964), 6503-6504. XUM Order No. 66-4428.

No significant differences were found in achievement as a result of 3 teaching methods or in the methods' effectiveness with students of high and low motor ability.

Lewis, Clifford Gray (Ed. D.). "EXPRESSED VALUES OF COLLEGE WOMEN AT THE UNIVERSITY OF GEORGIA CONCERNING SELECTED SOCIAL FACTORS RELATED TO ACCEPTANCE AND PARTICIPATION IN PHYSICAL EDUCATION." Columbia University Teachers College, 1961. Source: TCCU DIGESTS (1961), pp. 344-345.

The smallest percentage of voluntary participation was found in the freshman class. Young women who dated regularly participated in the voluntary program more frequently than any other designated group. Women from upper class families participated more frequently in volun-tary programs than those from other social positions. Most popular activities were swimming, ballroom dancing, bowling, water skiing, and tennis. Sorority members and non-sorority members selected simi-lar activities.

Lewis, Eloise Rallings (Ed. D.). "FACULTY APPOINTMENT PRACTICES IN THE COLLEGIATE SCHOOLS OF NURSING IN THE SOUTHERN REGION WHICH OFFER NATIONALLY ACCREDITED PROGRAMS." Duke University, 1964. 280 pp. Source: DAI, XXV, 1 (July, 1964), 239. XUM Order No. 64-7757.

In 24 institutions studied, appointment practices affected faculty retention. Administrative thinking and attitudes toward working con-ditions differed from faculty thinking and attitudes. Personnel pol-icies for the school of nursing did not differ from university-wide policies. Nurse faculty members in the study were from the South and were graduates of basic professional nursing programs.

Lewis, Ida Belle (Ph. D.). "SOME PHASES OF THE EDUCATION OF CHINESE WOMEN." Columbia University, 1919. 92 pp. Source: Eells, p. 74 and Published as THE EDUCATION OF GIRLS IN CHINA, TCCU No. 104, pp. 84-89.

The boarding school girls (1,106) were highly selected. Their fathers were usually professionals and businessmen. Over ½ lived in dormi-tories. Most were between ages 10 to 18 and entered school 4 to 6 years after the legal entrance age. They studied Chinese literature, composition and writing, mathematics, English, history, geography and science, and, in mission schools, the Bible.

Lewis, Madalynne Solomon (Ph. D.). "A PHILOSOPHY OF FINNISH WOMEN'S PHYSICAL EDUCATION AS REPRESENTED IN SELECTED WRITINGS OF ELIN KALLIO, ELLI BJORKSTEN, AND HILMA JALKANEN." University of Southern California, 1970. 514 pp. Source: DAI, XXXI, 9A (March, 1971), 4525-A. XUM Order No. 71-7723.

Finnish women's physical education was developed by and for women, was aided by voluntary gymnastic associations, was stimulated by eclecticism, had high standards in professional preparation and training, used open-minded research, and had dedicated instructors. Its philosophy involved total movement, kinesthetic awareness, and control of the physical by the mental.

Lewis, Roger Owen, Jr. (Ph. D.). "CONSISTENT CAREER PREFERENCES, PERSONALITY AND WOMEN'S PERCEPTIONS OF MALE VIEWS OF FEMININITY." Ohio State University, 1974. 100 pp. Source: DAI, XXXV, 11A (May, 1975), 7062-A. XUM Order No. 75-11,386.

Those women who thought males' views of femininity were nontraditional had greater self-esteem, more intellectual ambitions, more interest in scientific careers, and more wholesome personal adjustment.

Liddicoat, James Patterson (Ed. D.). "DIFFERENCES BETWEEN UNDER- AND OVERACHIEVERS AT A SMALL LIBERAL ARTS WOMEN'S COLLEGE." Lehigh University, 1972. 134 pp. Source: DAI, XXXII, 11A (May, 1972), 6133-A-6134-A. XUM Order No. 72-15,885.

I.Q. was not the only factor affecting student achievement. No significant difference existed between the groups in reading speed, study habits, and activities; or in attitudes, personality traits, self-sufficiency, and confidence in oneself, and in all but one of the achievement motivation factors. Significant differences existed in reading comprehension, creativity, neurotic tendencies, introversion, extroversion, dominance, submission, sociability, and the achievement motivation factor of threat of failure. The typical underachiever was emotionally unstable, submissive, non-social, more creative, afraid of failure, and lower in reading comprehension. There was a significant difference in who made the decisions at home, the type of secondary school attended, the desired level of education, and grades expected for the first semester.

Life, Mary Louise (Ph. D.). "THE EFFECTS OF SUPPLEMENTARY ISOMETRIC EXERCISES WITH SWIMMING AND GOLF ON SELECTED PHYSIOLOGICAL FACTORS OF COLLEGE WOMEN." Louisiana State University, 1964. 94 pp. Source: DAI, XXV, 8 (February, 1965), 4527-4528. XUM Order No. 64-13,261.

There was no difference in the effectiveness of intermediate swimming and beginning golf in increasing fitness. Addition of the isometric program did not increase the effectiveness of the 2 courses' ability to increase fitness.

Lillis, Sister Mary Agatha (Ph. D.). "AN INVESTIGATION AND COMPARI-
SON OF THE ACADEMIC ACHIEVEMENTS OF BOYS AND GIRLS AT THE TENTH AND ELE-
VENTH GRADE LEVELS IN THREE TYPES OF SCHOOLS, SINGLE-SEX, COEDUCATIONAL,
AND CO-INSTITUTIONAL." Fordham University, 1965. 176 pp. Source: DAI,
XXVI, 8 (February, 1966), 4452-4453. XUM Order No. 65-14,154.

Between 2 groups of 10th grade boys and girls, girls scored higher
in Latin, boys were higher in history, and no difference existed in
geometry. Among 3 groups of girls, girls from single-sex schools
were higher in Latin, co-institution girls were higher in geometry,
and no difference occurred in history. Between the 2 groups of 11th
grade boys and girls, boys were higher in intermediate algebra, with
no difference in English. No significant difference was found among
scores of 10th grade girls in algebra and English.

Linder, Irene Christine (Ph. D.). "SOME FACTORS INFLUENCING WOMEN TO
CHOOSE CHURCH-RELATED VOCATIONS: A STUDY IN OCCUPATIONAL SOCIOLOGY."
State University of Iowa, 1956. 291 pp. Source: DAI, XVI, 9 (1956),
1733-1734. XUM Order No. 17,473.

Women training for church-related vocations were influenced to enter
religious work by the following: (1) little awareness of social
class (most were from the lower class); (2) unhappy relationship with
parents; (3) parents with marital and other personal problems; (4)
religious groups and experiences; and (5) a desire to serve God and
mankind.

Lindstrom, Rizpah May (Ed. D.). "STUDENT SURVIVAL IN A COLLEGIATE
BASIC NURSING PROGRAM." Stanford University, 1961. 222 pp. Source:
DAI, XXII, 10 (April, 1962), 3613-3614. XUM Order No. 62-280.

Comparison of 75 nursing students who remained and 75 who withdrew
showed: (1) no significant differences in age at admission, in admission test scores, or in dissatisfaction with academic counseling;
and (2) significant differences in number of high school courses
taken, high school grades, and grades in college science. Reasons
for withdrawing were (in order): dislike for nursing, academic
problems, changed goals, financial problems, dislike for college,
marriage, and health and environment problems.

Linsin, Jimmie (Ph. D.). "AN ANALYSIS OF THE TREATMENT OF RELIGION,
THE BLACK-AMERICAN, AND WOMEN IN THE AMERICAN HISTORY TEXTBOOKS USED BY
THE PUBLIC, PRIVATE, AND PAROCHIAL HIGH SCHOOLS OF THE CITY AND COUNTY OF
SAINT LOUIS, MISSOURI, 1972-73." Saint Louis University, 1974. 256 pp.
Source: DAI, XXXV, 5A (November, 1974), 2541-A. XUM Order No. 74-24,110.

Selected high school American history textbooks were found to be less
than ideal in the treatment of religion and the contributions of
blacks and women. Blacks and women's contributions were often ignored or understated. Some textbooks either de-emphasized religion
or had religious bias.

Lipp, Dorothy Jane (Ph. D.). "A SURVEY OF WOMEN GRADUATES OF THE
COLLEGE OF LIBERAL ARTS OF NORTHWESTERN UNIVERSITY." Northwestern University, 1952. 307 pp. Source: Dissertation, pp. 296-299.

Women graduates recommended that: (1) guidance be improved, particularly for freshmen and seniors; (2) extracurricular activities continue; (3) marriage preparation be provided in courses and extracurricular activities; (4) opportunities to acquire job skills be expanded; (5) practical aspects be emphasized in theoretical courses; (6) more survey courses; (7) instruction in the dynamics of human relationships; (8) language courses include cultural background; (9) better coordination of course sequence; and (10) refresher courses and additional credit and noncredit courses be available to women graduates.

Lipsey, Sally Irene (Ed. D.). "A PROGRAMMED COURSE IN MATHEMATICS FOR NURSING STUDENTS." Columbia University, 1965. 249 pp. Source: DAI, XXVI, 8 (February, 1966), 4693. XUM Order No. 65-14,972.

A programmed text was designed and successfully tested to enable nursing students who were weak in mathematics to learn sufficient mathematics to pass a required pharmacology course in the Bronx (NY) Community College associate degree nursing program.

Liskevych, Taras Nestor (Ph. D.). "A COMPARATIVE STUDY OF WOMEN'S VOLLEYBALL AT THE INTERNATIONAL LEVEL." Ohio State University, 1976. 153 pp. Source: DAI, XXXVII, 11A (May, 1977), 7024-A. XUM Order No. 77-10,563.

This study compared women's volleyball programs in 15 countries, especially in the Soviet Union, Japan, and the United States, and sought educational implications for the United States.

List, Davida Norma (Ph. D.). "THE ATTITUDES OF WOMEN SCHOOL TEACHERS AND PARENTS TOWARD THE TEACHER ROLE." New York University, 1961. 137 pp. Source: DAI, XXII, 12, Part 1 (June, 1962), 4427. XUM Order No. 62-1474.

Female secondary school teachers (33), aged 25-55, and 50 parents of school children were used to: (1) test whether laymen have a more positive attitude toward teachers than the teachers perceive them as having; (2) identify relationship between level of emotional security of the individual teacher and the accuracy of her perception of the laymen's attitudes toward the teacher role; and (3) examine the structure of the attitudes of the teachers and laymen toward the teacher role. The results: (1) some teachers perceived inaccurately the parents' attitudes toward the teacher role; and (2) teachers' perceptions of parents' attitudes were not related to emotional stability. Conclusion: the study revealed communications difficulties between teachers and the public.

Little, Dolores Mae (Ph. D.). "THE EFFECTS OF MODELING OF CAREER COUNSELING AND SEX OF COUNSELOR ON INTEREST IN NONTRADITIONAL OCCUPATIONS FOR WOMEN." Texas A & M University, 1973. 152 pp. Source: DAI, XXXIV, 7A (January, 1974), 3994-A. XUM Order No. 74-1026.

Female undergraduate students with undeclared majors were randomly assigned to 2 experimental groups and a control group. Group 1 saw videotapes about nontraditional occupational roles for women using 3 peer social models; counseling and reinforcement were provided by

a male counselor. Group 2 saw the same tapes but had a female counselor. The control did not see the videotapes. Findings: (1) women
who saw the tapes became more interested in nontraditional occupations; and (2) the male counselor was more effective than the female
counselor.

Little, Dorcas Elaine Turley (Ed. D.). "A SELF-INSTRUCTIONAL COURSE
IN BODY AND FIGURE CONTROL FOR COLLEGE WOMEN." East Texas State Univer-
sity, 1973. 133 pp. Source: DAI, XXXIV, 9A (March, 1974), 5691-A. XUM
Order No. 74-5770.

Conclusions: self-instructional packages can be refined and struc-
turally adapted for use in body and figure control courses; and individual instruction can be stressed in body and figure control
through the use of self-instructional learning packages.

Livingston, Inez Baisden (Ph. D.). "SOCIAL, ECONOMIC, AND POLITICAL
INFLUENCES ON THE DEVELOPMENT OF RESIDENCE HALLS FOR WOMEN IN COLLEGES
AND UNIVERSITIES IN THE UNITED STATES." Ohio State University, 1966.
208 pp. Source: DAI, XXVII, 7A (January, 1967), 2033-A. XUM Order No.
66-15,107.

The author traced the history of women's campus housing up to present-
day residence halls and examined implications for solving present and
future problems of women's housing. The major problems with residence halls today were: (1) impersonal surroundings; and (2) the
need to integrate residence hall activities with education programs.

Livingston, Omeda Frances (Ed. D.). "A STUDY OF WOMEN EXECUTIVES IN
LIFE INSURANCE COMPANIES OWNED AND OPERATED BY NEGROES WITH IMPLICATIONS
FOR BUSINESS EDUCATION." New York University, 1964. 162 pp. Source:
DAI, XXV, 10 (April, 1965), 5637. XUM Order No. 65-973.

The women studied had risen to responsible positions after starting
in clerical jobs. Their experiences as well as trends in women's
employment substantiated the writer's recommendation that the business education curriculum should prepare women, not merely for specific jobs, but for higher, more demanding positions.

Lloyd, Margaret Ann (Ph. D.). "THE EFFECTS OF ACTIVE VERSUS PASSIVE
PARTICIPATION ON EGO-INVOLVED ATTITUDES: CHANGES IN KNOWLEDGE AND ATTI-
TUDES FOLLOWING A LIFE-PLANNING WORKSHOP FOR COLLEGE WOMEN." University
of Arizona, 1973. 102 pp. Source: DAI, XXXIV, 2B (August, 1973), 858-B.
XUM Order No. 73-19,123.

The Life Planning Workshop in conjunction with assigned readings was
significantly more effective in attitudinal changes than were either
the reading alone or no treatment.

Lo, Rong-rong (Ph. D.). "MARRIAGE PATTERNS AND MODERNIZATION IN
TAIWAN." University of Minnesota, 1972. 395 pp. Source: DAI, XXXIII,
10A (April, 1973), 5840-A-5841-A. XUM Order No. 73-10,670.

Women's level of education was a major factor influencing the shift
from a traditional Chinese marriage to a modern marriage in Taiwan.

Lockhart, Barbara Day (Ed. D.). "PERSONALITY FACTORS OF UNIVERSITY WOMEN IN RELATION TO THEIR ATTITUDES TOWARD PHYSICAL EDUCATION AND PHYSICAL ACTIVITY." Brigham Young University, 1971. 116 pp. Source: DAI, XXXII, 6A (December, 1971), 3077-A. XUM Order No. 72-1759.

Data about 200 women who completed 3 tests revealed 16 personality factors that related significantly to a positive attitude toward physical activity and 4 that were significantly related to a positive attitude toward physical education. Conclusion: a relationship exists between a healthy personality and positive attitudes toward physical activity.

Lockwood, Margaret (Ed. D.). "AN EXAMINATION OF HOMEMAKING PROGRAMS IN GRADES ONE THROUGH SIX IN SELECTED PUBLIC ELEMENTARY SCHOOLS." Columbia University, 1963. 385 pp. Source: DAI, XXIV, 9 (March, 1964), 3726. XUM Order No. 64-3186.

The study's purposes were: (1) to describe homemaking programs in grades 1-6; and (2) to evaluate homemaking programs according to selected criteria. Conclusions were: (1) variations in organizing homemaking programs were necessary to fit the particular school and community; (2) departmentalized, semi-departmentalized, and consultant types of homemaking programs could be effective; and (3) the 5-point rating scale constructed for the study was an acceptable evaluation tool.

Lodge, Mary Patricia (Ed. D.). "PROPOSALS FOR THE PREPARATION OF TEACHERS OF NURSING FOR PRESERVICE BACCALAUREATE PROGRAMS." Columbia University Teachers College, 1962. Source: TCCU DIGESTS (1962), pp. 271-272.

Teachers of nursing in pre-service baccalaureate programs (268) and 75 nursing teachers in graduate education rated the following in importance: teaching, guidance and counseling, scholarship, experimentation and research, faculty relations, administration and organization relations, relation with the profession, and relations with the community.

Loehfelm, Elizabeth Eileen (Ph. D.). "RATES OF CLASSROOM BEHAVIORS BY SEX COMPARED TO TEACHER APPROVAL/DISAPPROVAL RATES." Columbia University, 1974. 133 pp. Source: DAI, XXXV, 10B (April, 1975), 5085-B-5086-B. XUM Order No. 75-9291.

Study showed that teacher approval and disapproval of classroom behavior did not differ according to the sex of the student. Pupil behavior shaped teacher behavior. Rates of approval decreased as grade level increased, but disapproval showed little variation over the grades.

Lohr, Mary Margaret (Ed. D.). "PROFESSIONAL ACTIVITIES OF PSYCHIATRIC NURSE INSTRUCTORS." Columbia University, 1962. 283 pp. Source: DAI, XXIII, 5 (November, 1962), 1666-1667. XUM Order No. 62-4906.

Professional roles and problems of psychiatric nursing instructors were identified and ways to improve their performance were suggested.

London, Arcenia Phillips (Ph. D.). "DETERMINANTS OF SELF-ACCEPTANCE OF BLACK FEMALE SCHOOL TEACHERS SELECTED FROM THE SYRACUSE PUBLIC SCHOOL SYSTEM AND FROM LITTLE ROCK, ARKANSAS, PUBLIC SCHOOL SYSTEM." Syracuse University, 1975. 164 pp. Source: DAI, XXXVI, 10A (April, 1976), 6616-A. XUM Order No. 76-7663.

Black women teachers (74) from Syracuse, NY, and 78 from Little Rock, AR, provided data about their perception of the teaching profession, their status within the community, their status in school social life, their perception of education and employment. A significant relationship was found between self-acceptance and their perceived status. The conclusion was that southern black women teachers had a higher positive level of self-acceptance.

Long, Ernest S. (Ph. D.). "DETERMINANTS OF CAREER CHOICE IN PSYCHI-ATRIC NURSING: A STUDY OF STUDENTS ENROLLED IN NON-COLLEGIATE SCHOOLS OF NURSING." Case Western Reserve University, 1958. 222 pp. Source: Dissertation.

Findings showed no significant change in group preference for psychiatric nursing after a summer course in that field. But the students became less custodial in their orientation toward mental illness, less authoritarian, and saw no relationship between interest in psychiatric nursing and mental illness among family or friends. Concluded that once a student established a preference for psychiatric nursing as a career, her preference was fairly stable and enduring.

Longstreth, Catherine Archibald (Ed. D.). "AN ANALYSIS OF THE PER-CEPTIONS OF THE LEADERSHIP BEHAVIOR OF MALE AND FEMALE SECONDARY SCHOOL PRINCIPALS IN FLORIDA." University of Miami, 1973. 266 pp. Source: DAI, XXXIV, 5A (November, 1973), 2224-A-2225-A. XUM Order No. 73-25,894.

Female (17) and 20 male secondary principals, their immediate supervisors, and a sample of their subordinates were studied. Findings included: (1) supervisors' perception of the principals' leadership behavior was not affected by the principals' sex; (2) principals of both sexes perceived their own behavior as different; (3) subordinates saw women principals as having a higher degree of representation; and (4) there was no significant sex difference in interaction between principals and subordinates. Conclusion: sex was not a significant factor in most leadership behavior. Little justification was found for the idea that women behave differently as leaders than men.

Loo, Fe Villaflores (Ph. D.). "A PLAN FOR CURRICULUM DEVELOPMENT FOR A BACCALAUREATE NURSING PROGRAM AT SILLIMAN UNIVERSITY, PHILIPPINES." University of Kansas, 1973. 131 pp. Source: DAI, XXXIV, 12A, Part 1 (June, 1974), 7520-A. XUM Order No. 74-12,593.

The curriculum, based on the local needs, included the ultimate goal of bringing about objective, systematic, and comprehensive change.

Lord, Marion Elizabeth Manns (Ph. D.). "MATURE WOMEN AND THE DEGREE OF DOCTOR OF PHILOSOPHY." University of Wisconsin, 1968. 272 pp. Source: DAI, XXIX, 12A (June, 1969), 4267-A. XUM Order No. 68-16,002.

Compared cultural, psycho-social, and educational differences between
28 women Ph. D.s, aged 40, with a control group of the same age who
had received their bachelor degrees but never intended further education. The Ph. D. women had mothers who worked more often outside the
home. They perceived the successful combining of career and family
roles as their greatest fulfillment. They were more idea-minded,
majored mostly in science and math, were less competent drivers,
married less, found undergraduate work less difficult, and received
better grades. They were less responsive to authority and more independent. The control group found ages 36-45 their most rewarding
years and averaged 3½ children. The Ph. D.'s found ages 46-55 the
most satisfying and averaged 2 children.

Love, Robert Alden (Ph. D.). "THE DEVELOPMENT, FIELD TESTING AND
EVALUATION OF THREE HIERARCHIES OF BEHAVIORALLY STATED OBJECTIVES FOR
THE CHEMISTRY CONTENT OF A COURSE OF INSTRUCTION IN PHYSICAL SCIENCE FOR
PRE-SERVICE NURSING STUDENTS." University of Maryland, 1971. 236 pp.
Source: DAI, XXXII, 6A (December, 1971), 3115-A. XUM Order No. 72-633.

After nursing chemistry textbooks and standardized tests were analyzed
and students' abilities were measured, the students tested achieved
most of the behavioral objectives formulated for the chemistry course
for nurses.

Lovett, Sarah Lee (Ed. D.). "PERSONALITY CHARACTERISTICS AND ANTECE-
DENTS OF VOCATIONAL CHOICE OF GRADUATE WOMEN STUDENTS IN SCIENCE RE-
SEARCH." University of California, Berkeley, 1968. 133 pp. Source:
DAI, XXIX, 12A (June, 1969), 4287-A-4288-A. XUM Order No. 69-10,228.

Two groups were used: (1) women science majors connected to research;
and (2) graduate women in social welfare. Findings were: the science majors were more non-person oriented; the 2 groups had different
childhood experiences and interest inventory scores; there were no
differences in their feminine role opinions; both had achievement,
endurance, autonomy, and encouragement from their parents to be independent, self-reliant children. Social workers had played with
dolls, engaged in dramatics, and played dress-up. Science women
mainly connected things, participated in artistic activity, tended
to be tomboys. Science majors had more personal distance, less
stress, more time alone, and difficulties with peer relationships.
Social workers were disciplined by appeal to feelings.

Lowrie, Kathleen H. (Ph. D.). "FACTORS WHICH RELATE TO THE EXTRA-
CURRICULAR PERFORMANCE OF COLLEGE WOMEN." University of Iowa. 128 pp.
Source: Dissertation, pp. 109-116.

This research revealed that most women participated in extracurricular activities related to their major subjects.

Lueth, Carl Anthony (Ed. D.). "SELECTED ASPECTS IN THE ATTAINMENT
AND USE OF THE DOCTOR OF MEDICINE, DOCTOR OF DENTAL SURGERY, AND BACHELOR
OF LAWS DEGREES BY WOMEN GRADUATES OF TULANE UNIVERSITY AND LOYOLA UNI-
VERSITY OF THE SOUTH." University of Mississippi, 1973. 217 pp. Source:
DAI, XXXIV, 4A (October, 1973), 1648-A-1649-A. XUM Order No. 73-23,654.

The single most facilitating factor in women's attainment and use of a degree in medicine, law, and dentistry was the influence of others, especially parents. The most impeding factor was poor counseling in high school and undergraduate school. Most of the women had decided on the career before college, had upper-middle class parents, were married to professional men, and had 2 children. Most had been employed full or part time in the 27 years after graduation (10% were not active in profession). Discrimination was highest in financially rewarding and prestigious specialties. The study showed that: (1) women's admission to professional schools should not be limited; and (2) a professional career does not detract from marriage and a family.

Lumpkin, Katherine Du Pre (Ph. D.). "SOCIAL SITUATIONS AND GIRL DELINQUENCY: A STUDY OF COMMITMENTS TO THE WISCONSIN INDUSTRIAL SCHOOL." University of Wisconsin, 1928. Source: Abstracts of Articles Supplied by Author from AMERICAN JOURNAL OF SOCIOLOGY, XXXVII, No. 2 (September, 1931), pp. 222-230; XXXVIII, No. 2 (September, 1932), pp. 232-239.

Found girl delinquents (252) had such bad socio-economic and educational situations as broken homes (66.6%), bad companions (83.4%), family poverty (95%), and modal IQ of 66-75.

Lunceford, Ronald Douglas (Ph. D.). "SELF-CONCEPT CHANGE OF BLACK COLLEGE FEMALES AS A RESULT OF A WEEKEND BLACK EXPERIENCE ENCOUNTER WORKSHOP." United States International University, 1973. 83 pp. Source: DAI, XXXIV, 4B (October, 1973), 1728-B-1729-B. XUM Order No. 73-22,678.

Compared 15 black women who attended a black female awareness weekend encounter with 15 who did not attend. Although no significant changes occurred in those who attended encounter groups, data implied that they had higher self-concepts.

Lurry, Lola Lucile (Ph. D.). "THE CONTRIBUTION OF HOME ECONOMICS TO SELECTED PROBLEM AREAS IN THE CORE CURRICULUM OF THE SECONDARY SCHOOL." Ohio State University, 1949. 385 pp. Source: Dissertation, pp. 337-338.

Conclusions were: (1) that home economics has made significant contributions to each of the problems studied; and that home economics teachers (2) should be members of the initial curriculum planning group; (3) should be core teachers of units about family living problems; and (4) could coordinate units that deal with home economics subject matter.

Lutz, Sandra Waugh (Ed. D.). "THE EDUCATIONAL AND VOCATIONAL PLANNING OF TALENTED COLLEGE-BOUND WOMEN." Texas Tech University, 1974. 192 pp. Source: DAI, XXXV, 6A (December, 1974), 3427-A. XUM Order No. 74-23,054.

Differences in the pattern and range of women's major fields and vocational choices were consistent with their talents, plans, and aspirations. This study offered implications for counseling and talent utilization.

Lyman, Kathleen Dunn (Ed. D.). "THE DEVELOPMENT OF FLEXIBILITY IN MALE AND FEMALE INTERNS IN SECONDARY ALTERNATIVE SCHOOLS." University of Massachusetts, 1975. 413 pp. Source: DAI, XXXVI, 9A (March, 1976), 6019-A. XUM Order No. 76-5358.

Women student teachers made more use than men of community resources, used greater variety of teaching strategies and materials, and were more willing to learn new subject content.

Lynch, Ann Quarterman (Ed. D.). "THE EFFECTS OF BASIC ENCOUNTER AND TASK TRAINING GROUP EXPERIENCES ON UNDERGRADUATE ADVISORS TO FRESHMAN WOMEN." University of Florida, 1968. 93 pp. Source: DAI, XXX, 1A (July, 1969), 135-A. XUM Order No. 69-10,950.

Women who wanted to be undergraduate advisors to freshman women were assigned to a basic encounter or task training or control group. The encounter group stressed becoming aware of one's own feelings. The task group focused on the role of the advisor. No significant differences were found among the groups, but all the women's self-awareness increased.

Lynn, Leslie (Ph. D.). "ACADEMIC ACHIEVEMENT AS RELATED TO SEX, ANXIETY, SELF-CONCEPT, AGGRESSION, AND DEPRESSION." Illinois Institute of Technology, 1976. 145 pp. Source: DAI, XXXVIII, 1B (July, 1977), 335-B. XUM Order No. 77-13,749.

Found some unique differences, but nothing statistically significant, between male and female college achievers and underachievers.

Lyon, Ella Rhee (Ph. D.). "CAREER INTERESTS OF MARRIED WOMEN WITH COLLEGE DEGREES." Northwestern University, 1967. 188 pp. Source: DAI, XXVIII, 6A (December, 1967), 2097-A. XUM Order No. 67-15,282.

A national survey of 400 randomly chosen married college women, ages 24-45, indicated that most women were primarily family oriented and preferred traditional female roles in occupations and education. Most chose fields in which they were already trained and which best fitted their interests and family responsibilities.

Lyons, Marjory Dyson (Ph. D.). "ANALYSIS OF HEALTH KNOWLEDGE OF COLLEGE WOMEN." State University of Iowa, 1961. 98 pp. Source: DAI, XXII, 8 (February, 1962), 275-276. XUM Order No. 61-5588.

Tests given before and after health instruction revealed that students improved significantly in health knowledge and understanding after the class, and freshman and sophomore women had significantly higher health knowledge than freshman and sophomore men. The Revised General Health Knowledge Test seemed valid in measuring achievement of health knowledge.

Lytle, Nancy Ann (Ed. D.). "DESCRIPTIONS OF NURSE ACTIVITIES CITED BY BACCALAUREATE NURSING STUDENTS BEFORE AND AFTER INSTRUCTION IN MATERNITY NURSING." Columbia University, 1968. 193 pp. Source: DAI, XXIX, 11B (May, 1969), 4238-B. XUM Order No. 69-8085.

Student nurses who received instruction in maternity care became
aware of professional skills a nurse could use to help women in labor.

McCamey, Delener Sue (Ph. D.). "THE STATUS OF BLACK AND WHITE WOMEN
IN CENTRAL ADMINISTRATIVE POSITIONS IN MICHIGAN PUBLIC SCHOOLS." University of Michigan, 1976. 128 pp. Source: DAI, XXXVII, 10A (April, 1977),
6189-A. XUM Order No. 77-7987.

Women's under-representation in administrative positions in Michigan
public schools was attributed to: (1) local school districts' lack
of interest in allowing women to become administrators; and (2) women's complacency and lack of motivation to attain such posts. Fewer
women were applying for school administrative jobs than there were
jobs available.

McCann, Marcia Clark (Ed. D.). "A GUIDANCE BASED CURRICULUM FOR A
LIFE PLANNING/CAREER DEVELOPMENT PROGRAM FOR ADULT WOMEN WITHIN AN IN-
TEGRATION MODEL." University of Massachusetts, 1977. 429 pp. Source:
DAI, XXXVIII, 4A (October, 1977), 1895-A. XUM Order No. 77-22,031.

A curriculum model was designed to show possibilities for adult
women to develop careers at various stages of their lives.

McCormack, Sister Maureen (Ph. D.). "RELIGIOUS, MORAL AND INTELLEC-
TUAL-AESTHETIC VALUES OF SELECTED CATHOLIC COLLEGE WOMEN." University of
Denver, 1968. 162 pp. Source: DAI, XXIX, 11A (May, 1969), 3887-A. XUM
Order No. 69-7012.

Used questionnaires with 1,315 Catholic college women to identify
religious, moral, and intellectual-aesthetic values; to compare values
of faculty-selected "ideal" students and other students; and to assess
the relationship between student values and certain background factors.
Found that: (1) students selected as "ideal" had better high school
grades, higher college entrance scores, higher scores on intellectual-
aesthetic values, and more frequently attended intellectual and fine
arts events; (2) academic ability, achievement indicators, background
factors, and related interests were positively correlated to students'
intellectual values; and (3) mass attendance, taking Holy Communion,
and frequent confession were positively correlated with religious
and moral values.

McCormick, Albert Grant (Ed. D.). "AN INVESTIGATION OF READING SKILLS,
GENERAL MENTAL ABILITY AND PERSONALITY VARIABLES USED IN THE SELECTION OF
PRACTICAL NURSING STUDENTS." Oklahoma State University, 1966. 76 pp.
Source: DAI, XXVII, 12A (June, 1967), 4136-A. XUM Order No. 67-7255.

Reading skills, general mental ability, and age were significantly
related to scores on standardized achievement tests administered to
entrants to 9 Oklahoma schools of practical nursing to assess their
scholastic progress. Conclusion: the 3 standardized tests were
valid for assessing applicants.

McCoy, Doris Lee (Ph. D.). "THE STUDY OF VERBAL BEHAVIOR OF MALE AND
FEMALE STUDENTS TOWARD MALE AND FEMALE TEACHERS IN THE UNDERGRADUATE COL-
LEGE." Claremont Graduate School, 1973. 144 pp. Source: DAI, XXIV,
4A (October, 1973), 1649-A. XUM Order No. 73-22,779.

Found that male teachers, as compared with female teachers, elicited more: (1) personal opinions from female students; (2) objective opinions from male students; and (3) tension-releasing responses through laughter. Female teachers elicited more information exchange and gave more orientation and clarification to all students. Both male and female students agreed that male teachers were more interested in what students said, invoked more friendly feelings from students, induced greater personal contributions from students, and used materials or illustrations more appropriate to students' life experience. Concluded that male teachers were more relevant to male and female students than were female teachers.

McCuen, Barbara Anne (Ph. D.). "PSYCHOLOGICAL ATTRIBUTES OF MALE AND FEMALE STUDENTS IN A COLLEGIATE BUSINESS SCHOOL POTENTIALLY AFFECTING THEIR RELATIVE ADVANCEMENT TO MANAGERIAL POSITIONS." Iowa State University, 1977. 286 pp. Source: DAI, XXXVIII, 2A (August, 1977), 894-A. XUM Order No. 77-16,967.

Women business administration seniors, compared to men, had lower occupational aspirations and expectations, different reasons for working, different views of their financial responsibilities after college, and shorter and less continuous career expectancies. Findings implied that if the college curriculum presented more effectively the potential rewards of the business field, women's aspirations would be raised.

McCulloch, Etta Smith (Ph. D.). "FACTORS INFLUENCING JOB SATISFACTION AND JOB SATISFACTORINESS OF NEWLY LICENSED NURSES." Florida State University, 1974. 253 pp. Source: DAI, XXXV, 5B (November, 1974), 2280-B-2281-B. XUM Order No. 74-25,456.

Two groups studied were: (1) nursing graduates new on the job, to measure their job satisfaction; and (2) their supervisors, to ascertain supervisors' satisfaction with the new nurses. Findings: (1) both supervisors and the new nurses agreed that the new nurses had too little clinical training; (2) satisfaction differed significantly among the new nurses according to type of nursing degree held, age, and hospital size; (3) associate degree (AD) nurses were more satisfied in large hospitals because orientation was more thorough; (4) little relationship existed between nurses' satisfaction with their jobs and their supervisors' satisfaction with them; and (5) supervisors were more satisfied with nurses with previous hospital experience and with AD nurses who were young.

McCullough, Elizabeth Sarah (Ed. D.). "CHANGES IN ATTITUDES OF WOMEN STUDENT TEACHERS DURING DIFFERENTIAL ELEMENTARY SCHOOL ASSIGNMENTS." University of Southern California, 1972. 146 pp. Source: DAI, XXXIII, 2A (August, 1972), 649-A. XUM Order No. 72-21,681.

To ascertain racial attitude changes, 95 women student teachers were assigned in different groups to mainly black and non-black elementary school classes. Found that the combination of grade level and racial composition of class negatively affected the attitudes of the student teachers working with middle grade blacks. Deprivation and discrimination effects may become more apparent in the middle school years, thus causing student teachers' changed attitudes. Recommended that

if attitudes are to improve, contact with black students should begin
in early rather than middle grades.

McDermott, Sister Maria Concepta (Ph. D.). "A HISTORY OF TEACHER ED-
UCATION IN A CONGREGATION OF RELIGIOUS WOMEN: 1843-1964, SISTERS OF THE
HOLY CROSS." University of Notre Dame, 1964. 365 pp. Source: DAI,
XXVI, 2 (August, 1965), 850. XUM Order No. 65-1133.

Historical account of teacher education in this single congregation
of religious women is presented within the framework of Catholic education and U. S. educational history. Begins with Saint Mary's Academy at Bertrand, MI, and encompasses events, individuals, and the
several institutions of the congregation in the U. S.

MacDonald, Gwendoline Ruth (Ed. D.). "THE EVOLUTION OF STANDARDS AND
THE DEVELOPMENT OF VOLUNTARY ACCREDITATION IN COLLEGIATE NURSING EDUCA-
TION." Columbia University, 1964. 309 pp. Source: DAI, XXVII, 12B
(June, 1967), 4456-B. XUM Order No. 67-6528.

The persistent problems hindering better accrediting procedure for
college nursing education are: obsolete traditions, poor communications within the profession, dissension and disunity about the role
of education in nursing, and shortage of qualified personnel. Recommendations were made to improve the basis for evaluating college nursing programs.

McDonald, Patricia Ann (Ph. D.). "BALTIMORE WOMEN, 1870-1900." University of Maryland, 1976. 452 pp. Source: DAI, XXXVII, 11A (May,
1977), 7272-A. XUM Order No. 77-10,285.

Public and private records indicated that Baltimore, 1870-1900, was
less prosperous than other industrial cities. Women's economic, educational, and legal status did not change. Jobs and other opportunities did not improve, but more women needed to work. Their economic
importance to the city increased but their own personal and social
conditions were poor. Educational opportunities lagged, although
breakthroughs into higher education came about for some women by 1900.

McDonnell, Sister Geraldine (Ed. D.). "CONTINUING EDUCATION NEEDS
ASSESSMENT: NURSING GRADUATES, UNIVERSITY OF SAN FRANCISCO, 1950-1975."
Brigham Young University, 1977. 154 pp. Source: DAI, XXXVIII, 2A
(August, 1977), 575-A-576-A. XUM Order No. 77-17,617.

Questionnaires from 823 baccalaureate nursing graduates, 1950-74,
indicated a need for continuing education in professional nursing
courses, refresher courses, and master's and nurse practitioner programs. Because qualified faculty were available, graduates had identified appropriate curriculum, and numbers of students were sufficient, the study concluded that a University of San Francisco continuing nursing education program was feasible.

McFatter, Bobbie Batchelor (Ed. D.). "ATTITUDES AND PERCEPTIONS OF
MEN AND WOMEN IN THE LOUISIANA COOPERATIVE EXTENSION SERVICE ABOUT THEIR
ADMINISTRATIVE MOBILITY IN THE ORGANIZATION." Louisiana State University, 1976. 132 pp. Source: DAI, XXXVII, 11A (May, 1977), 6855-A-
6856-A. XUM Order No. 77-10,383.

Women's reticence in making their aspirations known and the tradition-al bias of administrators may account for the few women administrators in Extension Service. Lack of experiential opportunity for female leadership may account for the stereotype of women as less desirable than men as managers. Women's negative self-image as potential admin-istrators was caused by their lower goals and by a lack of motivation-al models.

McFarlane, Betty Feldman (Ph. D.). "NEW DIRECTIONS: A STUDY OF ADULT WOMEN." Wright Institute, 1976. 288 pp. Source: DAI, XXXVII, 10B (April, 1977), 5364-B. XUM Order No. 77-6547.

The 8 middle-aged working class women studied had enrolled in a com-munity college. Data revealed that their early family life had been supportive and had emphasized education. As returning students, their skills in processing information were improved and their thinking be-came increasingly flexible. Conclusion: these women continued to grow cognitively.

McGavran, Margaret Ross (Ph. D.). "MARY AND MARGARET: THE TRIUMPH OF WOMEN." Cornell University, 1973. 422 pp. Source: DAI, XXXIV, 3A (September, 1973), 1248-A. XUM Order No. 73-20,167.

This psychobiography of women's rights leaders Mary Wollstonecraft (British, 1759-97) and Margaret Fuller (U. S., 1810-50) shows how their education and life experiences led them to work to make women the equal of men.

McGriff, Erline Perkins (Ed. D.). "ADMINISTRATORS OF GRADUATE PRO-GRAMS IN NURSING AS EDUCATIONAL LEADERS." Columbia University, 1967. 249 pp. Source: DAI, XXVIII, 12B (June, 1968), 5091-B-5092-B. XUM Or-der No. 68-8983.

Information from 30 administrators of graduate nursing programs re-vealed that: (1) an educational leader was seen as a scholar who shaped the entire program of study; (2) a lack of qualified faculty impeded educational leadership (but administrators' low priority to allow faculty leadership in curriculum development was inconsistent); (3) administration as such was not viewed as an area of scholarship; and (4) unless the university administration gave full support, it was unrealistic to expect nursing school administrators to achieve their goals. Concluded that nursing school administrators needed understanding and skill in nursing and experience in administration and higher education.

McIlroy, Jane Susan (P. E. D.). "AN EVALUATION OF THE PHYSICAL EDU-CATION PROGRAMS FOR WOMEN IN SELECTED INSTITUTIONS OF HIGHER LEARNING IN THREE NORTHWEST STATES." Indiana University, 1961. 363 pp. Source: DAI, XXII, 5 (November, 1961), 1492-1493. XUM Order No. 61-4067.

The study developed a score card for evaluating women's physical edu-cation programs. Conclusion: physical education programs evaluated in 22 institutions differed greatly in meeting effectively the recom-mended standards; none exceeded 81% of total program attainment; and all needed improvement in 1 or more areas.

Mack, Barbara Inhofe (Ed. D.). "CRITERIA FOR STUDYING DEMOCRATIC
PRACTICES IN THE PREPARATION OF WOMEN TEACHERS OF PHYSICAL EDUCATION."
University of California, Los Angeles, 1950. 232 pp. Source: Abstract
from Dissertation.

A checklist was developed to enable those preparing women teachers of
physical education to evaluate their own practices related to their
democratic beliefs. Found that important deterrents to implementing
democratic beliefs were: (1) widely differing interpretations of
democratic philosophy; and (2) teachers' lack of understanding and
skill about how to guide students toward becoming self-directed persons.

McKay, Charles Forrest, III (Ed. D.). "A TEST OF HOLLAND'S THEORY
OF VOCATIONAL CHOICE USING A SAMPLE OF RURAL, URBAN, AND SUBURBAN FEMALE
COMMUNITY COLLEGE STUDENTS." Virginia Polytechnic Institute, 1977. 119
pp. Source: DAI, XXXVIII, 4A (October, 1977), 2083-A-2084-A. XUM Order
No. 77-22,079.

J. L. Holland's theory that vocational choice is an expression of interest and personality was tested with 252 women students. Found
that the women's curriculum choices and "occupational daydreams"
were consistent with Holland's theory.

McKay, Rose Patricia (Ed. D.). "THE PROCESS OF THEORY DEVELOPMENT IN
NURSING." Columbia University, 1965. 162 pp. Source: DAI, XXVI, 8
(February, 1966), 4584-4585. XUM Order No. 65-10,052.

The desire to make nursing a profession has caused conflict between
nursing's service function and its scientific basis. Aware of the
conflict, this study examined the processes of theory development in
such service fields as education and social work. Those theory development processes were applied to nursing and the conclusions
reached that nursing is: (1) a set of techniques for giving services;
(2) a set of theories to explain these techniques; and (3) a set of
values which influences the services given.

McKeehan, Ethel Gibson (Ph. D.). "THE EFFECT OF TWO SCHEDULING
METHODS ON ANXIETY AND LEARNING OF DISADVANTAGED STUDENTS IN AN ASSOCIATE
DEGREE NURSING PROGRAM IN APPALACHIA." University of Tennessee, 1975.
172 pp. Source: DAI, XXXVI, 10B (April, 1976), 4945-B. XUM Order No.
76-1967.

Subjects were 37 disadvantaged students in an associate degree nursing
program in Appalachia. The purpose was to determine whether the development and implementation of an altered method of scheduling classes and clinical laboratories would decrease anxiety and facilitate
learning.

McKemie, Kate (Ed. D.). "PERCEPTION OF 'ACTUAL AND IDEAL ROLE' CON-
CEPTS OF WOMEN HEADS OF DEPARTMENTS OF PHYSICAL EDUCATION BY IMMEDIATE
SUPERIORS, DEPARTMENT HEADS, AND INSTRUCTIONAL STAFF." University of
Tennessee, 1970. 155 pp. Source: DAI, XXXII, 1A (July, 1971), 135-A.
XUM Order No. 71-17,756.

Studied actual and ideal roles of women heads of physical education departments as perceived by their (1) immediate superiors, (2) department heads, and (3) instructional staff. Found that significant relationships existed: (1) within groups as to perceived "actual role"; (2) between groups as to perceived "actual role"; (3) between groups as to perceived "ideal role"; and (4) between perceived "actual role" and perceived "ideal role" described by each group.

McKenzie, Sheila Pereira (Ed. D.). "A COMPARATIVE STUDY OF FEMININE ROLE PERCEPTIONS, SELECTED PERSONALITY CHARACTERISTICS, AND TRADITIONAL ATTITUDES OF PROFESSIONAL WOMEN AND HOUSEWIVES." University of Houston, 1971. 215 pp. Source: DAI, XXXII, 10A (April, 1972), 5615-A-5616-A. XUM Order No. 72-4117.

In some of the many complex findings, the female role was seen by 4 groups of women as: (1) traditional by elementary education majors and by conformists; and (2) modern by medical students, doctoral students, housewives, and by non-conformists.

McKevitt, Rosemary Kerr (Ed. D.). "A STUDENT-CENTERED APPROACH FOR BACCALAUREATE NURSING EDUCATION." Columbia University, 1971. 172 pp. Source: DAI, XXXII, 3B (September, 1971), 1681-B. XUM Order No. 71-24,158.

A background review included an examination of: (1) trends in nursing curriculum development; and (2) themes around which existing nursing curricula have been organized. Major recommendations were: (1) that those nursing students desiring an innovative student-centered approach would follow a largely self-designed sequence of learning experiences; and (2) that this self-designed sequence would be allowed to coexist with the traditional curriculum.

Mackey, Ann (Ed. D.). "A NATIONAL STUDY OF WOMEN'S INTRAMURAL SPORTS IN TEACHERS COLLEGES AND SCHOOLS OF EDUCATION." Boston University School of Education, 1957. 165 pp. Source: DAI, XVII, 12 (December, 1957), 2912-2913. XUM Order No. 22,121.

Collected descriptive data about women's intramural sports, using 221 checklists returned from accredited teacher training institutions in 45 states and Puerto Rico. Women's intramural programs: (1) were cooperatively supervised in over 50% of the schools by physical education departments and Women's Athletic Associations (WAA); (2) were financed in most schools by the physical education department, WAA, or student government; (3) used physical education department facilities in 98% of institutions; and (4) required a special health examination for participation in only 15% of the institutions.

McKinney, Florence Elizabeth (Ph. D.). "THE ROLE OF THE HOME MANAGEMENT RESIDENCE EXPERIENCE IN EDUCATING FOR DEMOCRACY." Ohio State University, 1949. Source: Ohio State University, ABSTRACTS OF DOCTORAL DISSERTATIONS, No. 59 (1950), pp. 179-186.

Premise of this study was that living in home management residences gave students and advisors an opportunity to practice democratic principles. Several patterns of decision making using student-advisor interaction were tried in Kansas State University home management

residences. No single best method for promoting democratic principles
was found. The need for such experimentation on other campuses was
reflected on questionnaires returned from 46 land grant institutions
by 64 home management advisors who were, for the most part, unaware
of their opportunities for promoting democratic decision making.

McKissick, Grace Chirnside (Ed. D.). "THE RELATIONSHIP AMONG THE
FACTORS OF ACADEMIC ABILITY, SELF-ACTUALIZATION, AND ACHIEVEMENT OF SEN-
IORS IN A FOUR-YEAR LIBERAL ARTS COLLEGE FOR WOMEN." University of Missouri, Columbia, 1975. 106 pp. Source: DAI, XXXVII, 4A (October, 1976),
2016-A. XUM Order No. 76-21,959.

Purposes of this study of 106 senior women were: (1) to investigate
the relationship among self-actualization factors, academic ability,
and academic achievement; and (2) to compare the effects of these
factors on liberal arts and career-oriented majors. Findings: (1)
among career majors, academic achievement varied significantly with
the woman's inner directedness, self-regard, self-actualization values, and existentialism; and (2) among liberal arts majors, academic
achievement varied significantly with spontaneity. Conclusion: best
predictors of academic achievement, in this order, were: (1) high
school grades; (2) academic ability; and (3) inner-directedness.

MacLaggan, Katherine Eva (Ed. D.). "A PLAN FOR THE EDUCATION OF NUR-
SES IN THE PROVINCE OF NEW BRUNSWICK." Columbia University, 1965. 282
pp. Source: DAI, XXVI, 8 (February, 1966), 4584. XUM Order No. 65-
10,054.

This blueprint for the future includes a transition from present ser-
vice-centered and hospital-controlled nursing education to education-
centered and a multi-purpose health service, using separate French-
speaking and English-speaking systems, and preparing 75% Nurse Grade
I and 25% Nurse Grade II, all within the ascertained needs and present
educational structure of the Province of New Brunswick, Canada.

McLane, Audrey M. (Ph. D.). "CORE COMPETENCIES OF MASTER'S PREPARED
NURSES AND IMPLICATIONS FOR PROGRAM DEVELOPMENT." Marquette University,
1975. 107 pp. Source: DAI, XXXVI, 10B (April, 1976), 4945-B-4946-B.
XUM Order No. 76-8644.

Responses about 68 desired competencies for the professional education
of master's degree nursing students indicated agreement that: (1)
nursing teachers be high-level practitioners and that nursing practitioners attain teacher competencies; (2) nurses be able to communicate
a philosophy of nursing; (3) they have interpersonal competence; (4)
they engage in clinical research; and (5) they be accountable for the
outcomes of nursing care and for humanizing the nursing care environment.

McLaughlin, Helen Garrison (Ph. D.). "THE EFFECT OF VIDEOTAPE MODEL-
ING, ORAL INFORMATION, AND WRITTEN INFORMATION, ON THE FUTURE TIME PER-
SPECTIVE AND COUNSELING-SEEKING BEHAVIOR OF WOMEN COLLEGE STUDENTS."
Ohio State University, 1973. 81 pp. Source: DAI, XXXIV, 5B (November,
1973), 2311-B-2312-B. XUM Order No. 73-26,870.

Investigated the counseling-seeking behavior of women college students and the effect of several information formats on such behavior. Wishing to influence women's future time perspectives, information about the period after children leave home was given to 3 experimental groups in 3 different formats: (1) a written paragraph; (2) videotaped discussion; and (3) live talk by older female counselor. Although the major hypotheses were not supported, the effect of videotaped modeling on the women's future time perspective was sufficiently significant to warrant further investigation.

McLeod, Marshall W. (Ed. D.). "A STUDY OF NURSING IN FLORIDA WITH IMPLICATIONS FOR NURSING EDUCATION." University of Florida, 1969. 342 pp. Source: DAI, XXXI, 3B (September, 1970), 1363-B. XUM Order No. 70-14,906.

Data from the literature, state agencies, and questionnaires were used to project Florida's nursing needs. Recommendations were made for improving and enlarging nursing practice and education. Further research was suggested.

McMahon, Gordon Green (Ed. D.). "COMPARISON OF WORK ASSIGNMENTS WITH TRAINING IN OHIO PUBLIC SCHOOLS OF PRACTICAL NURSING." Case Western Reserve University, 1963. Source: Abstract from Dissertation.

Negative findings pertaining to practical nursing education in 14 Ohio publicly supported schools included: (1) no universally accepted definition of practical nursing; (2) coordinators and clinical instructors did not agree on principles or practices of practical nurse education; (3) licensed practical nurses performed procedures they were not trained to do; (4) no conformity in curriculum and teaching materials; (5) teacher selection was inadequate; and (6) coordinators and clinical instructors were set in their ways. Suggested that graduates' work experience be analyzed as a basis for curriculum revision.

McMillan, Alta Ann (Ed. D.). "STUDENT PERSONNEL SERVICE FOR A SMALL, CHURCH-RELATED, WOMAN'S LIBERAL ARTS COLLEGE." University of Mississippi, 1967. 125 pp. Source: DAI, XXVIII, 12A (June, 1968), 4824-A-4825-A. XUM Order No. 68-2138.

Data from 74 senior women and 107 women graduates of Blue Mountain College, MS, a small women's liberal arts college: (1) identified women's problem areas; (2) established the need for a formal student personnel service; and (3) helped with a design for organizing formal student personnel services.

McMurdo, June Hackett (Ph. D.). "THE DISCOVERY OF HEALTH PROBLEMS OF COLLEGE WOMEN THROUGH THE USE OF THE DEPTH INTERVIEW." Ohio State University, 1962. 194 pp. Source: DAI, XXIII, 8 (February, 1963), 2784-2785. XUM Order No. 63-71.

Found the depth interview to be only moderately useful in uncovering health problems of 40 University of Oregon freshman women, but was not useful in uncovering problems in sex, marriage, nutrition, and physical development.

McNicholas, Ellen Theresa (Ed. D.). "THE USE OF PROGRESSIVE PATIENT CARE UNITS AS LABORATORIES FOR NURSING STUDENTS IN A PRESERVICE BACCALAUR-EATE PROGRAM." Columbia University, 1965. 225 pp. Source: DAI, XXVI, 8 (February, 1966), 4504-4505. XUM Order No. 65-14,975.

Recommendations for nursing education included: (1) a unifying phil-osophy of patient care; (2) communication for better continuity as patients move from unit to unit; (3) a dynamic nursing rehabilitative program for the chronically ill; and (4) continuing education for registered nurses.

MacPhail, Jannetta (Ph. D.). "FACTORS INFLUENCING THE CREATION OF A RESEARCH CLIMATE IN UNIVERSITY NURSING SCHOOLS." University of Michigan, 1966. 365 pp. Source: DAI, XXVIII, 1B (July, 1967), 243-B. XUM Order No. 67-8305.

Interviews with deans of 3 nursing schools and questionnaires from 150 of their nurse faculty members identified these important factors in creating a research climate in nursing schools: (1) faculty train-ing and experience in research; and (2) administrative support of faculty research. A negative concern was fear that overemphasis on research would downgrade teaching. Recommended that research be en-couraged by: (1) hiring more faculty with doctorates; (2) giving in-service training during the working day in research techniques; and (3) reducing teaching loads to allow time for research.

Madden, Sister Anselm Mary (Ph. D.). "EDITH STEIN AND THE EDUCATION OF WOMEN: AUGUSTINIAN THEMES." St. Louis University, 1962. 258 pp. Source: DAI, XXIV, 10 (April, 1964), 4077. XUM Order No. 64-3752.

Edith Stein, philosopher and teacher, was prominent in German Catholic education, 1925-1933. The 5th volume of her works and other writings were chief sources of this study. She believed: (1) that feeling should be central in women's education; (2) that feeling should be balanced by intellect and will; and (3) that the curriculum should include all areas of culture but emphasize literary-humanistic disci-plines.

Magee, Llora Belle (Ph. D.). "SUBJECT MATTER IN MONEY MANAGEMENT IN JUNIOR HIGH SCHOOL HOME ECONOMICS." Columbia University, 1937. 137 pp. Source: Published; Same Title; New York: Privately Printed, 1937; pp. 101-106.

Coverage of money management topics varied greatly in 14 home eco-nomics textbooks analyzed. Recent textbooks presented more topics on money management. Recommended a study to determine home economics pupils' minimum needs in money management. With such information, a basic core of money management textual material should be prepared.

Maher, Sister Mary Gratia (Ph. D.). "THE ORGANIZATION OF RELIGIOUS INSTRUCTION IN CATHOLIC COLLEGES FOR WOMEN." Catholic University of America, 1951. 158 pp. Source: Published; Same Title; Washington, DC: Catholic University of America Press; 1951; pp. 134-135.

This summary of religious instruction in 42 Catholic colleges for wo-men was divided into: (1) ways religious instruction was responding to contemporary Christian needs; (2) ways such instruction was hindered from responding to contemporary Christian needs; and (3) suggested ways to improve college religious instruction.

Mahoney, Sister M. Frances (Ph. D.). "AN INVESTIGATION INTO TEMPERAMENT AND TEACHER POTENTIALITY IN SELECTED GROUPS OF COLLEGE WOMEN STUDENTS." St. John's University, 1967. 179 pp. Source: DAI, XXVIII, 10B (April, 1968), 4284-B. XUM Order No. 68-3812.

Compared 2 groups of women students--a lay group and a group preparing to become nuns. Sister students scored more favorably on emotional stability, objectivity, friendliness, and personal relations. The 2 groups had many academic similarities. The study failed to clarify the relationship between a student's personality and her potentialities as a teacher.

Mahootchi, Fereshteh K. (Ph. D.). "PLANNING FOR A CURRICULUM FOR PREPARATION OF RURAL HOME ECONOMICS TEACHERS IN IRAN." Southern Illinois University, 1970. 150 pp. Source: DAI, XXXI, 10B (April, 1971), 6097-B. XUM Order No. 71-10,030.

To hasten Iran's rural development, this proposal recommended that each village (75-100 families) should have 2 elementary teachers, 1 agriculture teacher, and 1 home economics teacher, the latter to teach all girls aged 11-14. The proposed home economics curriculum was designed to improve peasants' nutrition and meet other practical needs.

Major, Alice Ruby Maria (Ed. D.). "THE TEACHER OF NURSING." Columbia University, 1967. 274 pp. Source: DAI, XXVIII, 7A (January, 1968), 2583-A. XUM Order No. 67-16,761.

Because teacher training for baccalaureate nursing faculty members failed to prepare them for many important tasks, the author recommended that master's programs be improved and more doctoral programs be developed.

Major, Dorothy Mae (Ed. D.). "CAREER PREFERENCES AND PLANNING OF HIGH-RANKING SENIOR STUDENTS IN COLLEGIATE SCHOOLS OF NURSING." Indiana University, 1960. 196 pp. Source: DAI, XXI, 9 (March, 1961), 2678-2679. XUM Order No. Mic 60-6063.

Found that 100 senior nursing students from the upper 3rd of their classes in 16 college nursing programs needed more career guidance and preferred that such guidance be based on individual counseling. Other findings: (1) students preferred clinical over theoretical parts of the curriculum; (2) many were interested in becoming teachers but needed more information about such a career; and (3) outstanding students wanted the curriculum improved to give them additional enriching experiences.

Makovic, Sister Mary Vernice (Ph. D.). "THE RELATIONSHIPS BETWEEN NUN-TEACHERS' MANIFEST PSYCHOGENIC NEEDS AND ATTITUDES TOWARD STUDENTS AND STUDENT BEHAVIOR." Case Western Reserve University, 1968. 285 pp. Source: DAI, XXX, 1A (July, 1969), 170-A-171-A. XUM Order No. 69-9355.

Those nuns who, according to standardized tests, needed nurturance,
affiliation, and succorance were more permissive and democratic toward
students. Nuns who needed deference were more authoritarian. Those
with strong autonomy, dominance, and aggression needs had permissive
attitudes. Variations in nuns' needs and attitudes were related to:
(1) teaching level; (2) type of students taught; and (3) length of
teaching experience.

Makulski, Margaret Jane Davis (Ph. D.). "CASE STUDIES OF THE ATTITUDES
OF SUPERINTENDENTS AND SCHOOL BOARD MEMBERS OF SELECTED SCHOOL DISTRICTS IN
THE STATE OF MICHIGAN TOWARD THE EMPLOYMENT OF WOMEN AS SCHOOL ADMINISTRA-
TORS." University of Michigan, 1976. 178 pp. Source: DAI, XXXVII, 10A
(April, 1977), 6186-A-6187-A. XUM Order No. 77-7979.

Causes of women's limited school administrative opportunities: (1)
lack of funds; (2) enrollment decline; (3) seniority practices; and
(4) superintendents' attitudes. More favorable attitudes toward women
as school administrators were found among women and in "urban fringe-
town" areas as compared to city and rural areas.

Mallory, Berenice (Ph. D.). "A STUDY OF THE BEARING OF REQUIRED OFF-
CAMPUS EXPERIENCE OF UNDERGRADUATE STUDENTS IN HOME ECONOMICS ON STUDENT
GROWTH AND ON CURRICULUM." Ohio State University, 1948. 284+ pp.
Source: Dissertation, pp. 278-280.

Recommended that off-campus work in home economics: (1) be planned
as an integral part of the curriculum; (2) contribute to improved
home and family life; and (3) be supervised by college personnel.
After such off-campus experience, counselors should help students to
relate their off-campus work to their future academic and vocational
plans.

Maloney, Elizabeth Mary (Ed. D.). "ANALYSIS OF MENTAL HEALTH-PSYCHI-
ATRIC NURSING CONTENT IN SELECTED MASTERS' COURSES IN THE DEPARTMENT OF
NURSING EDUCATION AT TEACHERS COLLEGE, COLUMBIA UNIVERSITY." Columbia
University, 1966. 173 pp. Source: DAI, XXVII, 11A (May, 1967), 3627-A-
3628-A. XUM Order No. 67-2821.

Surveyed 12 nursing instructors to identify the mental health-psychi-
atric nursing ideas they planned to include in courses. Among the 30
possible ideas, they did not agree on the most important, but all
planned to stress some of the ideas. Many instructors expected to
rely on the students' emotional experiences as a teaching aid.

Mamantov, Charmaine Bienvenu (Ed. D.). "AN ANALYSIS OF THE RELATION-
SHIP BETWEEN SELECTED VARIABLES AND ACADEMIC SUCCESS IN NURSING CHEMISTRY."
University of Tennessee, 1976. 103 pp. Source: DAI, XXXVII, 11A (May,
1977), 7057-A. XUM Order No. 77-10,787.

Freshmen in 3-year diploma nursing programs were put into 2 groups to
test the effect of various factors on their chemistry performance,
using the National League for Nursing Chemistry Achievement Test
(NLN-Exam). Standardized test scores on science, English, math, and
a combination of subjects; chemistry marks; and previous chemistry
experience were considered. Group I took the NLN-Exam after 1 term
of nursing chemistry; Group II took the exam after 2 terms of nursing

chemistry. Results showed no significant correlation between performance on the exam and the other two variables. Group II had a significant correlation between performance on the exam and their chemistry marks but insignificant correlations with the other test scores
and previous chemistry experience.

Manansala, Erlinda Madera (Ed. D.). "DIFFERENCES IN STYLE OF COPING
WITH STRESS AMONG MALE AND FEMALE INTERNATIONAL STUDENTS AT AN URBAN UNI-
VERSITY." Boston University School of Education, 1976. 140 pp. Source:
DAI, XXXVII, 8A (February, 1977), 4867-A. XUM Order No. 77-4071.

Female international students used counseling and other human services more often than did males for coping with adjustment problems.
Conclusion: more counselors were needed on campuses, and some knowledge of therapeutic techniques used in other countries was desirable.

Manchester, Gertrude Bradley (Ph. D.). "THE WOMAN HIGH-SCHOOL TEACHER
OF PHYSICAL EDUCATION IN OHIO: A PERSONNEL STUDY AND ANALYSIS OF PROFES-
SIONAL DUTIES AND RESPONSIBILITIES." New York University, 1935. Source:
New York University, School of Education, ABSTRACTS OF THESES (1935),
pp. 1-7.

Some conclusions: (1) women physical education teachers had broad
academic background but lacked professional teacher training; (2)
full-time teachers were better trained and more permanent than part-
time teachers; (3) salaries were inadequate for cultural and professional development; (4) teachers taught at least 2 other subjects,
and class size depended on school enrollment; and (5) their weaknesses as teachers resembled those of teachers of other subjects.

Mandrillo, Margaret Paula (Ed. D.). "A COMPARATIVE STUDY OF THE COG-
NITIVE SKILLS OF THE GRADUATING BACCALAUREATE DEGREE AND ASSOCIATE DEGREE
NURSING STUDENTS." Columbia University, 1969. 130 pp. Source: DAI,
XXX, 9B (March, 1970), 4222-B. XUM Order No. 70-4515.

Findings showed that baccalaureate students had consistently higher
averages on tests of scientific knowledge of patients' health problems than did associate degree nursing students.

Manfredi, Claire Mildred (Ed. D.). "THE DEVELOPMENT AND IMPLEMENTA-
TION OF A PRIMARY NURSING MODEL: A CASE STUDY." Columbia University
Teachers College, 1976. 196 pp. Source: DAI, XXXVII, 4B (October,
1976), 1624-B. XUM Order No. 76-21,785.

The preparation of a primary nursing model, developed with the aid
of nurses in a general hospital, included the role of affiliated
nursing students and had implications for nursing education. Concluded that nurse educators need to find ways to integrate into nursing education programs primary nursing experiences.

Manicur, Alice Roberta (Ed. D.). "PROBLEM AREAS AND ACCEPTABILITY
OF STUDENT BEHAVIOR AS INDICATED BY RESIDENCE HALL AND SORORITY WOMEN AT
INDIANA UNIVERSITY." Indiana University, 1960. 194 pp. Source: DAI,
XXI, 3 (September, 1960), 502-503. XUM Order No. Mic 60-3008.

Found no significant differences between the number of problems faced
by women living in residence halls and women living in sororities.
But the nature of their problems differed. Their opinions of punish-
able behavior were similar. Conclusion: university administrators
should not base student personnel policies on the assumption that
these 2 groups of women differ from each other.

Mann, Coramae Richey (Ph. D.). "THE JUVENILE FEMALE IN THE JUDICIAL
PROCESS." University of Illinois at Chicago Circle, 1976. 260 pp.
Source: DAI, XXXVII, 10A (April, 1977), 6782-A-6783-A. XUM Order No.
77-6838.

Parents of girl offenders were less likely to come to juvenile court
than were parents of boy offenders. Fathers of girls came more for
runaway girls than for delinquent girls. Assault and battery were
more frequently committed by girl than boy offenders. Girl offenders
spent less average time in court than boy offenders. Author concluded
than juvenile courts were harder on girl than boy offenders.

Mann, Dale Philip (Ph. D.). "AN INVESTIGATION OF THE EFFECTS OF A
TRAINING PROGRAM FOR FEMALE STUDENT NURSES IN THE RECOGNITION OF EMOTION
IN THE FACIAL REGION." Kansas State University, 1975. 127 pp. Source:
DAI, XXXVII, 2A (August, 1976), 889-A. XUM Order No. 76-17,118.

Data showed that female nursing students fully trained in recognizing
emotions (anger, disgust, sadness, fear, happiness, surprise) were
able to identify the preferred response to such emotions. Recommended including such training in nursing education programs.

Mann, Jona Jacqueline (Ph. D.). "THE RELATIONSHIP AMONG DOGMATISM,
SEXUALLY STEREOTYPIC ROLE ORIENTATION AND INTERPERSONAL RELATIONS ORIEN-
TATION OF TEACHER CANDIDATES." Iowa State University, 1976. 149 pp.
Source: DAI, XXXVII, 11A (May, 1977), 7044-A-7045-A. XUM Order No.
77-10,326.

Some findings: (1) there was no difference between feminine females
and masculine males' need for affection; (2) androgynous females had
a greater need for affection than did masculine females or androgynous
males; and (3) no relationship existed between a student's dogmatism
and that student's sexually stereotyped role orientation.

Mann, Mohindar Kaur (Ph. D.). "A STUDY OF THE ROLE OF WOMEN IN THE
COOPERATIVE EXTENSION SERVICE OF OHIO, WITH IMPLICATIONS FOR THE INVOLVE-
MENT OF RURAL WOMEN IN THE COMMUNITY DEVELOPMENT PROGRAM OF THE PUNJAB."
Ohio State University, 1962. 190 pp. Source: DAI, XXIV, 1 (July, 1963),
276. XUM Order No. 63-2531.

The history of women's role in the Ohio extension service revealed
that farm women's need for home economics education was consistently
emphasized. Recommended that women members of Punjabi village councils should help motivate rural women to support a similar extension
program in the Punjab.

Mann, Opal Hurley (Ph. D.). "DIFFERENCES BETWEEN SELECTED INDIVIDUAL
AND FAMILY CHARACTERISTICS OF HOMEMAKERS AND THEIR RECEPTION, VALUE RATING
AND DESIRE FOR HOME AND FAMILY LIVING EDUCATION." Ohio State University,

1971. 327 pp. Source: DAI, XXXII, 4A (October, 1971), 1831-A. XUM
Order No. 71-27,517.

The highest percentage of homemakers who had received educational information about home and family living: (1) lived on farms; (2) were
over 45 years old; (3) had at least a high school education; (4) were
not employed; and (5) had belonged to homemaker clubs over 5 years.
Women who had not completed high school wanted more home economics
information than they had been able to get.

Manning, Doris Elnova (Ph. D.). "VIEWPOINTS OF MALE GRADUATE STUDENTS
WITH RESPECT TO THEIR WIVES' WORKING AT DIFFERENT STAGES OF THE FAMILY
LIFE CYCLE." University of Illinois, 1967. 122 pp. Source: DAI, XXVIII,
12B, Part 1 (June, 1968), 5099-B-5100-B. XUM Order No. 68-8158.

Some findings: (1) more married men students than unmarried men were
willing for their wives to work; (2) in general men were willing for
wives to work when no children were at home; (3) more men favored
their wives' working for personal satisfaction than for a mere pay-
check; and (4) the most acceptable reason for wives' working was economic necessity.

Mantell, Michael Robert (Ph. D.). "CATASTROPHIC FANTASIES, FEAR OF
NEGATIVE EVALUATION, AND ASSERTIVENESS/NON-ASSERTIVENESS AMONG UNDERGRADU-
ATE WOMEN." University of Pennsylvania, 1976. 164 pp. Source: DAI,
XXXVII, 4B (October, 1976), 1913-B. XUM Order No. 76-22,736.

Non-assertive women were more fearful and had greater catastrophic
fantasies than did assertive women. Findings had important implications for women's assertiveness training and affective education.

Marable, June Morehead (Ph. D.). "THE ROLE OF WOMEN IN PUBLIC SCHOOL
ADMINISTRATION AS PERCEIVED BY BLACK WOMEN ADMINISTRATORS IN THE FIELD."
Miami University, 1974. 251 pp. Source: DAI, XXXVI, 1A (July, 1975),
73-A. XUM Order No. 75-14,316.

Findings: (1) administrative policies and practices which discriminated against women needed re-evaluation; (2) women, including black
women, most often held lower level administrative positions; (3)
women's assignment to administrative positions was based on traditional recruitment, selection, and placement methods; (4) blackness
was less detrimental to applicants than being female; (5) age was not
a factor; and (6) activities in civic, social, and religious groups
demonstrated leadership abilities before becoming an administrator.

Marella, Medea Marie (Ed. D.). "FACTORS INFLUENCING THE RESEARCH
ACTIVITY OF FACULTY IN GRADUATE PROGRAMS IN NURSING." Columbia Univer-
sity, 1974. 175 pp. Source: DAI, XXXIV, 11B (May, 1974), 5535-B. XUM
Order No. 74-11,803.

Nursing faculty with Ph. D. degrees and doctoral science majors ranked
research as more important, had conducted more research, and published
more than those with doctoral majors in education or nursing.

Mark, Arthur (Ed. D.). "TWO LIBERTARIAN EDUCATORS: ELIZABETH BYRNE
FERM AND ALEXIS CONSTANTINE FERM (1857-1971)." Columbia University, 1974.

372 pp. Source: DAI, XXXVI, 1A (July, 1975), 160-A. XUM Order No. 75-13,899.

Lives and careers of Elizabeth and Alexis Ferm, pioneers in the free school idea, were studied in the context of social and educational reform, anarchism, progressive education, and social reconstruction. Curricular inferences and implications of their educational ideas were given. Their theories were compared with those of other educational pioneers including John Dewey and A. S. Neill.

Markel, Marilyn Ruth (Ed. D.). "THE RELATIONSHIP OF SELECTED MEASURES OF COMPETENCE IN THE PHYSICAL EDUCATION BASIC INSTRUCTION PROGRAM FOR WOMEN AT THE UNIVERSITY OF MISSOURI-COLUMBIA." University of Missouri, Columbia, 1969. 167 pp. Source: DAI, XXX, 4A (October, 1969), 1422-A-1423-A. XUM Order No. 69-16,091.

Found that a battery of written tests helped determine whether freshman women students should be retained in physical education classes.

Marlow, Dorothy Ruth (Ed. D.). "THE ORGANIZATION AND INSTRUCTION OF MATERNAL AND CHILD HEALTH IN TEN SELECTED COMMUNITY COLLEGE NURSING PROGRAMS." Columbia University Teachers College, 1958. Source: TCCU DIGESTS (1958), pp. 390-392.

Purposes of the study were to: (1) examine selected best 10 national community college programs for preparing maternal and child health nurses; and (2) prepare an ideal program of pre-service education preparing baccalaureate maternal and child health nurses. Report covered: (1) overview; (2) general information about the nursing programs; (3) organization of maternal and child health nursing programs; (4) instructional aspects; and (5) implications for education program leading to maternal and child care baccalaureate degree.

Marple, Betty Louise N. (Ph. D.). "ADULT WOMEN STUDENTS COMPARED WITH YOUNGER STUDENTS ON SELECTED PERSONALITY VARIABLES." Boston College, 1974. 89 pp. Source: DAI, XXXV, 9A (March, 1975), 5820-A. XUM Order No. 75-5969.

Adult women students showed significantly more autonomy but were not significantly different from the younger women in social presence and thinking introversion. Younger women scored significantly higher on responsibility, socialization, and practical outlook. These and other findings established that older and younger women students differed significantly from each other.

Marple, Dorothy Jane (Ed. D.). "MOTIVATIONAL TENDENCIES OF WOMEN PARTICIPANTS IN CONTINUING EDUCATION." Columbia University, 1969. 148 pp. Source: DAI, XXX, 5A (November, 1969), 1824-A-1825-A. XUM Order No. 69-16,791.

Purposes were: (1) to study the motivations of women participants and non-participants in continuing education; and (2) to relate the participants' motivations to their satisfactions with enrollment and other continuing education factors. Women not participating in continuing education had a strong tendency toward "self-limiting adaptation." Most participants in continuing education who were motivated

to "uphold internal order" in their lives were also seeking intellectual fulfillment and were enrolled in degree programs.

Marram, Gwen Dower (Ph. D.). "VISIBILITY OF WORK AND THE EVALUATION
PROCESS: EVALUATION AND AUTHORITY FOR NURSES IN HOSPITALS AND TEACHERS
IN OPEN AND CLOSED SCHOOLS." Stanford University, 1972. 245 pp. Source:
DAI, XXXII, 12A (June, 1972), 6718-A. XUM Order No. 72-16,753.

Compared nurses and teachers in general, nurses and teachers who work
on teams with those who do not, and individual differences in perceptions within each group. Supported contention that visibility, soundness, and importance of peer evaluations are positively associated
with each other. A closer relationship was found between visibility
and soundness than between visibility and the importance of peer evaluations. Nurses believed their training was more helpful to them than
was teacher training for teachers. Nurses' also perceived that patients' evaluations were less sound than evaluations by colleagues and
less sound that students' evaluations of teachers. Nurses, more than
teachers, saw their skills as separating them from laymen. Visibility
of nurses' work to colleagues was greater than was teachers. Teachers
in teams had increased visibility which enhanced the soundness and
importance of their colleagues' evaluations of them. Team nursing did
not have the same effect on evaluations of a nurse's work by her colleagues.

Marrero Felix, Jovina (Ph. D.). "ACCEPTABILITY OF FUNCTIONS OF A BE-
GINNING NURSE SPECIALIST FROM A BACCALAUREATE PROGRAM IN NURSING IN THE
COMMONWEALTH OF PUERTO RICO." University of North Carolina, Chapel Hill,
1974. 381 pp. Source: DAI, XXXVI, 1B (July, 1975), 162-B-163-B. XUM
Order No. 75-15,670.

Studied were 351 nursing students, baccalaureate graduates, physicians,
nursing directors and supervisors, and hospital-public health agency
administrators. Found broad areas of agreement about functions of a
beginning baccalaureate nurse specialist. Acceptance of her specialized functions by the different groups indicated a changed perspective
of baccalaureate nursing tasks and a trend toward specialization.
Conclusion: this specialization has implications for the nursing
curriculum.

Marsh, J. Patricia Marsh (Ed. D.). "A STUDY OF SELECTED STATED OB-
JECTIVES OF AMERICAN HIGHER EDUCATION OF WOMEN TO 1940." Harvard University, 1959. Source: Dissertation, pp. iv-xiv.

Showed that the development of women's higher education in America
reflected women's changing economic, political, cultural, and social
demands. This history moves from finishing schools, to female semi-
naries, to colleges, and to graduate education. Included are accounts
about outstanding leaders in women's education. Included are such
changes as adding professional training in existing colleges and the
creation of new institutions to meet women's needs.

Marshall, Mary Eleanor (Ed. D.). "THE POSITION OF WOMEN IN THE ADMIN-
ISTRATION OF PHYSICAL EDUCATION UNITS IN SELECTED FOUR-YEAR, PUBLIC COL-
LEGES AND UNIVERSITIES." University of North Carolina, Greensboro, 1975.
286 pp. Source: DAI, XXXVII, 3A (September, 1976), 1453-A. XUM Order
No. 76-19,415.

Most physical education programs in 98 colleges and universities were administered on a co-educational basis with more men than women as administrators and as teachers in each rank. Women had more administrative opportunities in women's athletics.

Martin, Betty Jean Bryant (Ph. D.). "PROFESSIONAL COMMITMENT, ROLE PERCEPTION AND RATED EFFECTIVENESS OF HOME ECONOMICS COOPERATING TEACHERS." University of Missouri, Columbia, 1973. 146 pp. Source: DAI, XXXV, 4A (October, 1974), 1877-A-1878-A. XUM Order No. 74-18,593.

No significant relationship was found between cooperating teachers' effectiveness as rated by teacher educators and their own self assessment. Those cooperating teachers who had completed a graduate course in home economics curriculum construction had higher professional commitment scores than those who had not. But instruments used in this study did not prove valid as the sole guide to selection of effective home economics cooperating teachers.

Martin, Elizabeth Smith (Ph. D.). "PERCEPTION OF SELF AND EDUCATIONAL ENVIRONMENT AND THEIR RELATIONSHIP TO PERSISTENCE IN TECHNICIAN-NURSE EDUCATION PROGRAMS IN WASHINGTON." University of Washington, 1971. 180 pp. Source: DAI, XXXII, 11B (May, 1972), 6490-B-6491-B. XUM Order No. 72-15,120.

Based on the idea (from Gestalt and Phenomenology psychology) that people seek consistency between self and environment. The search for an accurate way to predict that female nursing students will persist in a personally satisfying educational environment was inconclusive.

Martin, Evelyn Bacon (Ed. D.). "A PROFILE OF WOMEN AS SECONDARY SCHOOL VICE-PRINCIPALS." Columbia University Teachers College, 1956. Source: TCCU DIGESTS (1956), pp. 412-413.

A sample of women vice principals contacted through the National Association of Secondary School Principals revealed that they: (1) were often single and advanced in age; (2) had taught many years; (3) had earned M.A. degrees and done other formal study; (4) had gained much personal satisfaction from their jobs; and (5) were not interested in rising to principalships. Recommended that talented women should be given administrative responsibilities earlier in their careers.

Martin, Georgia M. (Ed. D.). "DIFFERENCES IN EVALUATION OF COLLEGE CLIMATE BETWEEN FRESHMAN AND SENIOR WOMEN AT THE UNIVERSITY OF GEORGIA." University of Georgia, 1966. 159 pp. Source: DAI, XXVII, 12A (June, 1967), 4135-A. XUM Order No. 66-13,608.

To judge the intellectual and non-intellectual climate of the University of Georgia, the views of freshman (200) and senior (200) women were measured on a college characteristic index. Few significant differences were found between freshmen and seniors' perceptions of the university. The women concluded that: the University of Georgia had a low intellectual climate and a normal non-intellectual climate, with little opportunity for expressing artistic and aesthetic interests.

Marty, Howard Henry (Ed. D.). "THE EFFECT OF MICRO-TRAINING SESSIONS ON THE ATTITUDE AND BEHAVIOR OF FRESHMAN STUDENT NURSES TOWARD THE TERMI-NALLY ILL." University of South Dakota, 1973. 129 pp. Source: DAI, XXXIV, 5A (November, 1973), 2306-A-2307-A. XUM Order No. 73-27,533.

Findings about work with the terminally ill from 3 student nursing groups (a micro-training group who used audio-video taped instruction, a lecture discussion group, and a control group) were: (1) the micro-training group, on an immediate post-test, rated significantly higher in empathic communication with dying patients; (2) no significant differences were found among the 3 groups in their attitudes toward the dying; and (3) a 2-week delayed post-test showed that the micro-training group continued to score higher on empathic communication.

Mash, Donald Joseph (Ph. D.). "THE RELATIONSHIP OF WOMEN'S LIFE-STYLE PREFERENCE AND PERSONALITY DURING COLLEGE." Ohio State University, 1974. 145 pp. Source: DAI, XXXV, 5A (November, 1974), 2689-A. XUM Order No. 74-24,365.

Junior and senior college women at a small Ohio Catholic liberal arts college: (1) preferred less traditional life-style orientations; (2) preferred a combined family and career life style rather than either one alone; and (3) there were personality differences among those preferring family or career or dual life-styles.

Mason, Jean Jefferson (Ph. D.). "AN ANALYSIS OF LEARNING RESOURCE CENTERS IN NATIONAL LEAGUE FOR NURSING ACCREDITED BACCALAUREATE SCHOOLS OF NURSING AS A FUNCTION OF THE ACADEMIC QUALIFICATIONS OF DIRECTORS AND THE ADMINISTRATIVE, FISCAL, AND ORGANIZATIONAL STRUCTURE OF CENTERS." University of Pittsburgh, 1976. 146 pp. Source: DAI, XXXVII, 3A (September, 1976), 1359-A. XUM Order No. 76-19,921.

The quality was ascertained of 83.2% of the multi-media learning re-source centers in 161 nursing schools. The highest quality nursing school media centers were 4 to 5 years old, had the largest school populations, and spent most for media. The youngest school media centers spent the least for media and had directors who worked less than 40 hours a week. Concluded with guidelines for nursing media centers in accredited baccalaureate nursing schools.

Massie, Lois O'Neil (P. E. D.). "SELECTED PRACTICES FOR THE CONDUCT OF WOMEN'S INTERCOLLEGIATE ATHLETICS IN KENTUCKY COLLEGES." Indiana University, 1970. 270 pp. Source: DAI, XXXI, 3A (September, 1970), 1056-A. XUM Order No. 70-16,451.

Women physical educators (28) agreed that: (1) full-time women under-graduates who engage in intercollegiate athletics should meet schol-astic eligibility requirements; and (2) competition against males is undesirable. Some desirable practices included: (1) uniform stan-dards for college entrance, college employment, and grants-in-aid; and (2) games not to be played at examination times.

Masterman, Leslie John (Ph. D.). "EFFECTS OF MODELING ON SELF-REFER-ENT TALK OF MEXICAN-AMERICAN GIRLS WITH CULTURALLY SIMILAR AND DISSIMILAR COUNSELORS." Arizona State University, 1975. 127 pp. Source: DAI, XXXVI, 8A (February, 1976), 5050-A-5051-A. XUM Order No. 76-3766.

The effectiveness of a guidance counselor's first interview with 6th
grade Mexican-American girls was increased by: (1) using a videotape
to provide models; and (2) using culturally similar Mexican-Americans
as counselors.

Masterson, Albert Clark (Ph. D.). "ADVANTAGED AND DISADVANTAGED RURAL
HIGH SCHOOL GIRLS' PERCEPTIONS OF OFFICE WORK." Colorado State University,
1968. 232 pp. Source: DAI, XXX, 2A (August, 1969), 829-A-830-A. XUM
Order No. 69-5484.

Perceptions of office work held by 2 groups of rural high school girls
(498 advantaged, 477 disadvantaged girls) did not differ significantly.
Both groups of rural girls misunderstood office work. Recommended
that rural girls get a realistic introduction to office work by: (1)
having office workers as resource persons in high school business education classes; (2) requiring high school business teachers to period-
ically work in an office for refresher experience; and (3) providing
field trips to offices.

Matheny, Priscilla Herron Pugh (Ph. D.). "A STUDY OF THE ATTITUDES
OF SELECTED MALE AND FEMALE TEACHERS, ADMINISTRATORS AND BOARD OF EDUCA-
TION PRESIDENTS TOWARD WOMEN IN EDUCATIONAL ADMINISTRATIVE POSITIONS."
Northwestern University, 1973. 273 pp. Source: DAI, XXXIV, 6A (Decem-
ber, 1973), 2976-A. XUM Order No. 73-30,658.

Most female teachers: (1) saw a bias in favor of men as administrators; (2) disagreed that men's temperaments were better suited for
administration; (3) agreed that women with the same qualifications
must work harder to get an administrative job; (4) did not feel that
community attitudes and traditions make it hard for women to become
administrators; (5) believed men would and women would not prefer to
work under a man; (6) believed boards of education would hire men
over women; (7) felt women were not encouraged in college to prepare
for administration; and (8) felt that the women's movement was a plus
for getting equal pay and job opportunities for women. Almost as
many women as men aspired to administrative jobs. Most administrators
(especially women) had been sought for their first administrative job.
Women had experienced a much higher percentage of discrimination.

Matis, Edward Eugene (Ph. D.). "AN ANALYSIS OF DIFFERENCES IN INTER-
ESTS, PERSONALITY NEEDS, AND PERSONALITY STRUCTURES BETWEEN COLLEGE WOMEN
MAJORING IN SPEECH PATHOLOGY AND COLLEGE WOMEN MAJORING IN OTHER PROFES-
SIONAL AREAS." University of Alabama, 1968. 151 pp. Source: DAI, XXIX,
12A (June, 1969), 4290-A-4291-A. XUM Order No. 69-6556.

Comparison of 30 women speech pathology majors with 57 women majors
in other fields supported the hypothesis that a relationship exists
between personality needs and occupational choice. Recommended that
the same study be conducted in a number of colleges and universities
before generalizing from this one.

Matlack, Jean Yaukey (Ed. D.). "A LIFE STUDY OF A PSYCHOTHERAPIST:
MARJORIE MURRAY BURTT." University of Massachusetts, 1977. 649 pp.
Source: DAI, XXXVII, 10A (April, 1977), 6372-A-6373-A. XUM Order No.
77-8701.

Biographical account based on some 60 hours of interviews and contact with 50 former patients. Relates subject's attendance at boarding school and Bryn Mawr College, her 5 years of teaching, her medical school education, her work as pediatrician and psychotherapist.

Mattes, Linda Ann (Ed. D.). "THE STATUS OF WOMEN IN SCHOOLS OF EDU-CATION AND EDUCATIONAL ADMINISTRATION IN HIGHER EDUCATION." Auburn University, 1973. 190 pp. Source: DAI, XXXIV, 3A (September, 1973), 1099-A. XUM Order No. 73-19,651.

Findings: (1) women were more numerous than men in colleges of education than in higher education generally or in educational administration; and (2) fewer women than men were administrators or were doctoral candidates in educational administration.

Matthews, LaMoyne Mason (Ph. D.). "PORTRAIT OF A DEAN: A BIOGRAPHY OF INABEL BURNS LINDSAY, FIRST DEAN OF THE HOWARD UNIVERSITY SCHOOL OF SOCIAL WORK." University of Maryland, 1976. 262 pp. Source: DAI, XXXVII, 11A (May, 1977), 7064-A. XUM Order No. 77-10,287.

The remarkable career of black scholar Inabel Burns Lindsay was an outgrowth of: (1) a protected childhood which saved her from facing racial prejudice and gave her a positive outlook on life; (2) interaction of family, community, and the educational system which aided her quest for academic excellence, human dignity, and social justice; (3) a succession of 3 increasingly responsible positions which strengthened her leadership skills; and (4) her use of the positive aspects of her own extended family as a pattern for the Howard University School of Social Work.

Maxwell, Mary Percival (Ph. D.). "SOCIAL STRUCTURE, SOCIALIZATION AND SOCIAL CLASS IN A CANADIAN PRIVATE SCHOOL FOR GIRLS." Cornell University, 1970. 467 pp. Source: DAI, XXXI, 9A (March, 1971), 4907-A-4908-A. XUM Order No. 71-1069.

The school assured that the girls would conform to an elitist social system by its selection processes, organizational structure, and system of control.

Mayer, Evelyn Ann (Ed. D.). "STUDY OF THE ATTITUDES OF A SAMPLE OF THE INITIAL CLASS OF FIRST-YEAR WOMEN ADMITTED TO RESIDENT LIVING AT THE UNIVERSITY OF VIRGINIA." University of Virginia, 1971. 181 pp. Source: DAI, XXXII, 8A (February, 1972), 4292-A-4293-A. XUM Order No. 72-7134.

Attitudes of 50 1st-year women freshmen were examined after their 1st semester in a predominantly male institution. Some objectives were: (1) to determine reasons the women chose the University of Virginia; (2) to determine the women's ambitions and to see if they were changing; (3) to discover impressions of the university's academic offerings and effectiveness of instruction; (4) to examine reaction to the social atmosphere, university activities, and dormitory; (5) to identify their hardest adjustments; and (6) to assess whether being a minority caused the women to suffer discrimination or other disadvantages. Findings were compared with information about coeducation at Yale and Princeton, which recently admitted women. Guidelines were devised for meeting coeducation needs at the University of Virginia.

Mayer, Wilhelm Karl (Ed. D.). "VOCATIONAL INTEREST PATTERNS OF TEACH-
ING AND NON-TEACHING FEMALE COLLEGE GRADUATES." University of Florida,
1966. 97 pp. Source: DAI, XXVII, 9A (March, 1967), 2831-A. XUM Order
No. 67-3488.

To determine whether the women's form of a vocational interest test
taken during the freshman year would differentiate among 232 females
who were in 3 groups: (1) students enrolled in the college of education; (2) students in liberal arts preparing for teaching; and (3)
students not planning to teach. Conclusions were drawn after the
women graduated: (1) the test did discriminate among women who were
in teacher preparation and those who were not; (2) women graduates
from different subject fields had differing vocational interests;
(3) the test differentiated among the fields of those women who
planned to teach; and (4) foreign language and history majors were
more subject oriented than teaching oriented, while English and math
majors were both subject and teaching oriented.

Mayhew, Harry Calvin (Ed. D.). "AN ANALYSIS OF COMPREHENSIVE CONTIN-
UING EDUCATION PROGRAMS AND SERVICES FOR WOMEN AT SELECTED MIDWESTERN UNI-
VERSITIES." Ball State University, 1970. 306 pp. Source: DAI, XXXI,
4A (October, 1970), 1586-A. XUM Order No. 70-19,589.

To encourage more women to continue their education: (1) colleges,
universities, and professional schools should accommodate part-time
students; (2) opportunities should be increased for independent study,
reading, research, and credit by examination; (3) requirements for
advanced standing should be liberalized; and (4) society should provide part-time employment for women.

Mayo, Frances Moss (Ph. D.). "THE EFFECTS OF AEROBICS CONDITIONING
EXERCISES ON SELECTED PERSONALITY CHARACTERISTICS OF SEVENTH AND EIGHTH
GRADE GIRLS." North Texas State University, 1974. 136 pp. Source:
DAI, XXXV, 7A (January, 1975), 4162-A. XUM Order No. 75-890.

No significant personality differences were found between girls who,
after running 12 minutes, were rated as "low fitness" or "high fitness." Recommended that schools should help American society give
greater acceptance and encouragement to physical fitness for women.

Meacham, Esther Anne (Ph. D.). "THE RELATIVE EFFECTIVENESS OF FACE-
TO-FACE LECTURE VERSUS INSTRUCTIONAL TELEVISION IN A COLLEGE CLOTHING
COURSE." Ohio State University, 1962. 153 pp. Source: DAI, XXIV, 1
(July, 1963), 276-277. XUM Order No. 63-4684.

Concluded that a college course in clothing construction for home
economics students can be taught as effectively by instructional television as by lecture method, that any disadvantages of instructional
television can be overcome, and that its advantages outweigh its disadvantages as a learning method.

Means, Ingunn Nordeval (Ph. D.). "NORWEGIAN POLITICAL RECRUITMENT
PATTERNS AND RECRUITMENT OF WOMEN." University of Washington, 1971.
339 pp. Source: DAI, XXXII, 5A (November, 1971), 2761-A. XUM Order
No. 71-28,446.

Women elected to Norwegian public office had more education and higher occupational achievements than Norwegian women as a whole, but the educational and career attainments of these women politicians were considerably lower than were those of their male counterparts.

Mears, G. L. (Ed. D.). "EDUCATIONAL MOTIVATION OF THREE GROUPS OF MATURE WOMEN IN A METROPOLITAN AREA." University of Mississippi, 1972. 179 pp. Source: DAI, XXXIII, 5A (November, 1972), 2062-A-2063-A. XUM Order No. 72-20,237.

Subjects were 50 Memphis, TN, female high school graduates, 1952-56; 50 women college dropouts of the same period; and 50 women currently enrolled in college. The 3 groups of women did not differ significantly in intelligence. The currently enrolled women students were: (1) more active mentally and physically than the other 2 groups; (2) had fewer children under age 6 and more children over age 18; (3) had more marital disruptions; and (4) more planned careers outside the home.

Mehnert, Irene Barnes (Ed. D.). "THE EFFECTS OF AN ABBREVIATED TRAINING PARADIGM ON FEMALES LEARNING ASSERTIVE BEHAVIOR." University of South Dakota, 1974. 181 pp. Source: DAI, XXXV, 6A (December, 1974), 3430-A. XUM Order No. 74-27,260.

Author succeeded in developing and teaching verbal and non-verbal assertive behavior skills to 37 low-level assertive college women in a University of South Dakota educational psychology course.

Meixel, Carol Aneshensel (Ph. D.). "EFFECTS OF SOCIAL STRUCTURAL, SOCIAL PSYCHOLOGICAL, AND SEX ROLE FACTORS ON FEMALE AND MALE ADOLESCENTS' STATUS EXPECTATIONS." Cornell University, 1976. 230 pp. Source: DAI, XXXVII, 11A (May, 1977), 7351-A. XUM Order No. 77-11,003.

Females tended to hold somewhat liberal sex role values and stereotypes. They expected social disapproval for competitive behavior and gave preference to the wife-mother role over the work role. Males held more traditional values and stereotypes.

Melamed, Audrey Marie Ruth Van Natta (Ph. D.). "COLLEGE OF NURSING: PSYCHOLOGICAL PREDICTORS OF COUNSELING SERVICE USE." Loyola University of Chicago, 1976. 212 pp. Source: DAI, XXXVII, 5A (November, 1976), 2641-A. XUM Order No. 76-24,448.

Established that, by using standardized tests, differences between seekers and non-seekers of counseling could be identified. Education and work experience enhanced growth and maturity. Concluded that tests used could be employed in nursing schools to predict students' needs for counseling and to establish programs designed to prevent personal problems.

Melloh, Sister M. Tolentine (Ph. D.). "PLANNING FOR THE DEVELOPING OF A HOME ECONOMICS CURRICULUM FOR A JAPANESE COLLEGE." Southern Illinois University, 1963. 269 pp. Source: DAI, XXIV, 12, Part 1 (June, 1964), 5375. XUM Order No. 64-4475.

This descriptive study examined the development of home economics and higher education programs in smaller colleges in the United States and Japan.

Mellow, June (Ed. D.). "THE EVOLUTION OF NURSING THERAPY AND ITS IM-PLICATIONS FOR EDUCATION." Boston University School of Education, 1965. 184 pp. Source: DAI, XXVI, 5 (November, 1965), 2696-2697. XUM Order No. 65-9538.

The researcher intervened in therapeutic sessions as she studied the evolution of nursing therapy. The model involved the ruptured rela-tionship between a schizophrenic patient and his mother. Showed that the psychiatric nurse can be trained to provide a mother substitute and aid the patient in reliving and resolving anxieties.

Melniker, Robert C. (Ph. D.). "SELF-ACCEPTANCE AND THE MECHANISM OF IDENTIFICATION: A Q-SORT INVESTIGATION OF THE RELATIONSHIP BETWEEN LEVELS OF SELF-ACCEPTANCE, CHARACTER, PARENTAL DESCRIPTIONS AND IDENTIFI-CATION PATTERNS IN COLLEGE WOMEN." New York University, 1957. 174 pp. Source: DAI, XVII, 8 (August, 1957), 1812-1813. XUM Order No. 21,713.

College women volunteers were placed in a high self-acceptance group and a low self-acceptance group, according to an index of adjustment and values. Both groups identified with their fathers. Because both groups had an inadequately developed identification with their mothers they had an underlying dissatisfaction with self.

Melton, Alfred William (Ph. D.). "PARENTAL EXPRESSIVENESS AS PER-CEIVED BY ADOLESCENT BOYS AND GIRLS: ITS MEASUREMENT AND ASSOCIATION WITH SELECTED SOCIAL VARIABLES." Florida State University, 1971. 209 pp. Source: DAI, XXXII, 11A (May, 1972), 6569-A-6570-A. XUM Order No. 72-13,539.

Used concept of parental expressiveness as formalized by Talcott Par-sons. Adolescents (226) were tested on 148 statements, rated as low, medium and high, concerning parental expressiveness. Employed mothers employed part-time received a higher expressive rating than full-time homemakers or full-time employed mothers. Fathers whose spouse was employed part-time were also rated as higher in expressiveness by their sons. Girls rated their fathers as higher in expressiveness when their mothers were employed full-time or were full-time home-makers.

Mentzer, Rosalind Blue (Ph. D.). "A HISTORY OF THE PROGRAM OF VOCA-TIONAL HOME ECONOMICS IN THE SECONDARY SCHOOLS OF MICHIGAN 1917-18 THROUGH 1952-53." Michigan State College, 1954. 347 pp. Source: DAI, XIV, 8 (1954), 1156. XUM Order No. 8505.

After noting 5 major historical changes in Michigan secondary school vocational home economics programs, author recommended state-wide studies of pupil needs and housing and equipment needs as basis for future planning. Also recommended that histories be written of Mich-igan Home Economics Association and of part-time and adult home eco-nomics programs.

Meredith, Nancy Lynn (Ph. D.). "AN EXPLORATION OF THE ROLE OF PERSON-
HOOD AND PROFESSIONAL DEVELOPMENT IN THE PROGRAM PERFORMANCE OF EXTENSION
HOME ECONOMISTS." Iowa State University, 1972. 189 pp. Source: DAI,
XXXIII, 4B (October, 1972), 1649-B. XUM Order No. 72-26,932.

The major finding was that the extension home economist's self fulfillment was strongly related to her success in carrying out her job
as measured by: (1) her supervisor; (2) her ability to perceive
families' problems; and (3) her identified feelings toward diverse
audiences.

Merry, Pauline Estelle (Ph. D.). "A DESCRIPTIVE STUDY OF MATURE AND
YOUNGER WOMEN IN AN ASSOCIATE DEGREE NURSING PROGRAM." University of
Southern California, 1974. 88 pp. Source: DAI, XXXV, 2A (August, 1974),
823-A. XUM Order No. 74-17,366.

Mature (aged 35+) associate nursing students (27) consistently had
better grade point averages than 46 younger students, average age of
24, although there were no significant differences in their personalities and clinical performances. Author concluded that counselors
can encourage mature women to enter associate degree nursing programs
since they can expect to do as well as younger students.

Meshke, Edna Dorothy (Ph. D.). "THE EFFECTS OF UTILIZING SELECTED
COMMUNITY RESOURCES IN NINTH-GRADE AND TENTH-GRADE HOMEMAKING CLASSES."
University of Minnesota, 1942. Source: Dissertation, pp. 127-135.

Compared the effectiveness of specific teaching methods. Two experimental groups and two control groups, a 9th grade food selection
course and a 10th grade electrical equipment course, composed the
sample. Specific procedures were incorporated into the teaching
methods to distinguish between classroom instruction and store instruction. The experimental groups went to stores and used specialized instruction booklets. The findings showed a significantly higher
level of achievement for the 9th grade classes that utilized community
resources. Less of a difference existed between the 10th grade classes since all groups used the special booklet.

Messler, Eunice Claire (Ed. D.). "TRANSFORMING INFORMATION INTO NUR-
SING KNOWLEDGE: A STUDY OF MATERNITY NURSING PRACTICE." Columbia University, 1974. 61 pp. Source: DAI, XXXV, 4B (October, 1974), 1767-B-
1768-B. XUM Order No. 74-20,823.

Changes were traced in the professional literature (journals and textbooks) from 1909 to 1972 to ascertain present use of past information
on the preparation of maternity nurses. It was noted that several
topics had been repeated in the literature without apparent awareness
of their prior treatment. Author concluded with a plan for the efficient use of textual information in maternity nursing programs.

Metz, Edith Martin (Ph. D.). "DEVELOPMENT OF A STANDARDIZED TEST OF
COGNITIVE ASPECTS OF EFFICIENT BODY MOVEMENT FOR TECHNICAL AND PROFES-
SIONAL NURSING STUDENTS." University of Washington, 1964. 275 pp.
Source: DAI, XXVI, 10 (April, 1966), 5981-5982. XUM Order No. 65-5447.

Associate degree, diploma, and baccalaureate nursing degree students
who had completed basic physical science courses and a semester of
clinical practice were tested to determine the differences between
these groups' inefficiency of body movement as it related to nursing.
Significant differences were found between diploma and baccalaureate
degree students on the total test and the four educational objectives.
Comparisons of the length of time the students had been in classes
and test scores were significantly related in associate degree programs but not in diploma and baccalaureate programs.

Meyer, Gerald Dennis (Ph. D.). "SCIENCE FOR ENGLISHWOMEN: 1650-1760:
THE TELESCOPE, THE MICROSCOPE, AND THE FEMININE MIND." Columbia University, 1951. 280 pp. Source: DAI, XII, 1 (1952), 46-47. XUM Order No.
3366.

Between 1650 and 1760 interest in science grew among leisure class
women, bolstered by introduction of the telescope and microscope.
Scientific information was presented to women through popular literature. By the 1760's formal education in the natural sciences began
replacing these informal approaches to knowledge.

Meyer, Sister Mary Irene (Ph. D.). "EXPLORATIONS OF FEMININE ROLE
CONCEPTS AMONG CATHOLIC COLLEGE WOMEN AND MEN." Saint Louis University,
1966. 160 pp. Source: DAI, XXVII, 4A (October, 1966), 1111-A-1112-A.
XUM Order No. 66-9116.

Catholic college men (99) and women (142) were tested to determine
the expectations of a man's ideal woman, women in general, and self
(feminine) expectations. Men and women tested thought that the masculine viewpoint of the ideal woman was more traditional than that
of the average woman in society (women were more extreme). The
women rated themselves as more traditional than the average woman in
society, which partially confirmed the slow process of attitude
change in society.

Meyer, Peter (Ph. D.). "EFFECT OF GROUP COUNSELING UPON CERTAIN EDU-
CATIVE AND EMOTIONAL FACTORS OF FIRST YEAR STUDENTS IN AN ASSOCIATE DE-
GREE PROGRAM IN NURSING." New York University, 1963. 98 pp. Source:
DAI, XXV, 2 (August, 1964), 1009-1010. XUM Order No. 64-6561.

Demonstrated the value of group counseling in effecting change in
attitudes of first-year associate degree nursing students toward
disabled persons. Control group had no counseling sessions. Students who completed 25 counseling sessions showed a more positive
attitude toward change, but they did not differ significantly from
the control group in their academic and clinical performances. The
results suggest that more emphasis is needed on specific clinical
examples in the counseling sessions.

Miao, Greta Gustafson (Ph. D.). "THE EFFECTS OF INDIVIDUAL VARIATION
ON SOCIALIZATION IN A SCHOOL OF NURSING." Duke University, 1971. 180 pp.
Source: DAI, XXXII, 12A (June, 1972), 7097-A-7098-A. XUM Order No. 72-
16,990.

Of 4 different personality types tested, the greatest difference
occurred between the "open-wide" and "constricted-narrow" types,

with the former experiencing the most change in the first 2 years of nursing. The constricted-narrow type was more influenced by external forces in nursing commitment and the commitment level was more stable during the first 2 years. Although pattern types could be predicted from the data, the causes for these patterns could not be determined.

Michaelson, Bonnie Lee (Ph. D.). "VOCATIONAL INTERESTS, SELF-CONCEPTS, AND ATTITUDES TOWARD FEMININE ROLES AS RELATED TO THE EDUCATIONAL AND VOCATIONAL CHOICES OF COLLEGE WOMEN." Temple University, 1974. 118 pp. Source: DAI, XXXV, 6B (December, 1974), 2994-B. XUM Order No. 74-28,242.

A comparison of undergraduate women who selected either a traditionally female major or a non-traditional major revealed that: (1) traditional majors were people-oriented and interested in such occupations as raising and educating children or caring for the ill; (2) non-traditional majors had individualized interest patterns which were closely related to their major fields; and (3) fewer of the women in non-traditional majors had high self-concept scores than did the traditional women. Concluded that women's vocational choices were based on more complex factors than self-concept and vocational interest.

Mickleson, Karen Kay (Ph. D.). "THE EFFECTS OF FATHER-DAUGHTER RELATIONSHIPS ON THE DEVELOPMENT OF ACHIEVEMENT ORIENTATION AND PSYCHOLOGICAL ANDROGYNY IN FEMALES." California School of Professional Psychology, San Francisco, 1976. 139 pp. Source: DAI, XXXVII, 6B (December, 1976), 3085-B-3086-B. XUM Order No. 76-28,682.

Found that while fathers' active participation and direct encouragement aided daughters' achievement orientation, the role model of both parents was also important.

Middlebrook, Grace I. (Ed. D.). "ATTITUDES OF INSTRUCTORS OF NURSING TOWARD THEIR PREPARATION FOR TEACHING NURSING EDUCATION." Arizona State University, 1970. 136 pp. Source: DAI, XXXI, 5A (November, 1970), 2091-A-2092-A. XUM Order No. 70-21,949.

Data showed that nursing instructors with graduate education were employed more frequently and had longer tenure in their present positions than nursing instructors with basic educational background.

Mikan, Kathleen Joyce (Ph. D.). "DEVELOPMENT OF A CLASSIFICATION SCHEME OF PUPIL QUESTIONS ASKED BY NURSING STUDENTS WITHIN A SELF-INSTRUCTIONAL LEARNING ENVIRONMENT." Michigan State University, 1972. 174 pp. Source: DAI, XXXIII, 9A (March, 1973), 4803-A. XUM Order No. 73-5445.

Using nurses as monitors aided the effectiveness of multi-media self-instruction. This project categorized situations which helped students ask questions. Results showed that students asked nurse-monitors questions. Questions were more often about psycho-motor skills than about cognitive matters. Frequency of questions did not vary between stationary monitors and those who moved about the room.

Mikesell, Terrie Eileen (Ph. D.). "THE DEVELOPMENT OF OBJECTIVES FOR THE ADULT CONSUMER AND HOMEMAKING EDUCATION PROGRAM AND INSTRUMENTS TO MEASURE THE PROGRAM'S IMPACT ON PARTICIPANTS." Cornell University, 1973. 227 pp. Source: DAI, XXXIV, 10B (April, 1974), 5056-B. XUM Order No. 74-6330.

A new approach to teaching homemaking skills in disadvantaged areas is being provided by centers staffed with a home economist, teacher's aide, and child care aide. This study evaluated the learning of clients who were divided according to high exposure or low exposure to instruction. The only subjects about which high exposure clients learned significantly more were clothing and textiles.

Milburn, Corine M. (Ed. D.). "THE RELATIONSHIP BETWEEN MEN AND WOMEN SECONDARY TEACHERS' PERCEPTIONS OF IDEAL AND REAL LEADER BEHAVIOR OF THE WOMAN SECONDARY PRINCIPAL IN PUBLIC SCHOOLS." University of South Dakota, 1976. 98 pp. Source: DAI, XXXVII, 10A (April, 1977), 6392-A-6393-A. XUM Order No. 77-3449.

In schools having women principals, neither men nor women teachers were significantly biased against women administrators. Men and women teachers had different perceptions of ideal and real leader behavior: (1) women wanted leaders to show consideration; and (2) men preferred leaders to take initiative. The shortage of women secondary school principals was a problem to the researcher.

Miles, Margaret Shandor (Ph. D.). "THE EFFECTS OF A SMALL GROUP EDUCATION/COUNSELING EXPERIENCE ON THE ATTITUDES OF NURSES TOWARD DEATH AND TOWARD DYING PATIENTS." University of Missouri-Kansas City, 1976. 166 pp. Source: DAI, XXXVIII, 2A (August, 1977), 636-A. XUM Order No. 77-16,872.

There was a significant difference in attitude toward death and dying patients between those nurses who experienced a continuing education course entitled "Coping with Death and Dying in High Risk Areas of Hospitals" and those who did not.

Miller, Barbara Jeanette (Ed. D.). "EXPRESSED BELIEFS AND FEELINGS OF NINTH GRADE GIRLS TOWARD WIVES AND MOTHERS WORKING OUTSIDE THE HOME AS RELATED TO SELECTED ENVIRONMENTAL CHARACTERISTICS." University of Georgia, 1975. 132 pp. Source: DAI, XXXVI, 9A (March, 1976), 6053-A-6054-A. XUM Order No. 76-6428.

Ninth grade girls (741) generally had more positive feelings toward working wives (no children at home) than mothers. Girls whose mothers were employed full time showed that most favorable attitude toward working wives. Girls from higher socio-economic groups had the most favorable attitude towards both working wives and mothers.

Miller, Beverly White (Ph. D.). "A STUDY OF DISTRIBUTED VERSUS MASSED PRACTICE IN HUMAN ANATOMY AND PHYSIOLOGY INSTRUCTION IN A COLLEGIATE PROGRAM FOR STUDENT NURSES." University of Toledo, 1967. 53 pp. Source: DAI, XXVIII, 4A (October, 1967), 1347-A. XUM Order No. 67-12,501.

Nursing students in group A completed anatomy, microbiology, chemistry, and clinical classes in 1 semester (16 weeks). Group B took microbiology and chemistry along with sociology, psychology, and English in 2 semesters. Comparison of the 2 groups revealed that group B had significantly higher achievement scores.

Miller, Carrie Eulah (Ph. D.). "THE EFFECT OF THE HOME BROKEN BY DIVORCE UPON THE SELF CONCEPT OF SELECTED COLLEGE WOMEN." University of Denver, 1958. 142 pp. Source: Abstract from Dissertation.

Findings supported the hypothesis that students from broken homes had a less adequate self-concept than did students from complete homes. Statistically significant differences were found between the two groups' perceived sense of adequacy and their negative references to themselves.

Miller, Elizabeth Suzanne (Ph. D.). "ACHIEVEMENT MOTIVATION IN WOMEN: A DEVELOPMENTAL PERSPECTIVE." Loyola University of Chicago, 1977. 124 pp. Source: DAI, XXXVII, 12A, Part 1 (June, 1977), 7643-A-7644-A. XUM Order No. 77-13,425.

Tests taken by 124 female college graduates (66 full-time homemakers and 58 graduate students destined for the professions) indicated that the homemakers were traditional in their sex-role orientation, married, had been raised as Protestants, and never intended to hold full-time jobs. The graduate students had high mental ability, were Jewish or followed no religion, and had stopped working in order to become full-time students. Findings supported the hypothesis that certain developmental characteristics could be used to discriminate between female professionals and homemakers.

Miller, Eunice Lillian (Ph. D.). "THE VALUE OF THE DOCTORATE FOR WOMEN IN BUSINESS EDUCATION AND BUSINESS." New York University, 1957. 226 pp. Source: DAI, XVIII, 6 (June, 1958), 2030-2031. XUM Order No. 21,714.

Since most women doctoral degree holders in business education were and remained college teachers of secretarial subjects, graduate programs for them should be designed to promote their teaching abilities. The doctorate stabilized their employment, provided college promotion opportunities, and did not interfere with their personal, social, or emotional life.

Miller, Evelyn (Ph. D.). "FACTORS CONTRIBUTING TO THE ACQUISITION OF INFORMATION IN CERTAIN FIELDS: A STUDY OF CERTAIN FACTORS IN THE BACKGROUND OF ONE HUNDRED WOMEN STUDENTS MAKING EXTREME SCORES ON A TEST OF SCIENCE, FOREIGN LITERATURE, FINE ARTS, AND HISTORY AND THE SOCIAL STUDIES." Columbia University Teachers College, 1932. Source: TCCU DIGESTS, VII (1932), pp. 1-4; and Published; Same Title; New York: Privately Published; 1932.

Women (50) who obtained high scores on a comprehensive test concerning fine arts, science, foreign literature, history, and social studies were compared to 50 women with low scores on this test to determine the effect of family background and environmental factors. Results indicated that women receiving high scores were more likely to come from urban backgrounds, have foreign ancestry, have fathers employed in the professions, have working mothers, discuss cultural topics at home, and have traveled outside the U. S.

Miller, Genevieve Loretta (Ed. D.). "A STUDY OF SELECTED SOCIAL PRO-CESSES ON WOMEN'S CAREER MOTIVATION RELATED TO THE DECLINING NUMBER OF WOMEN IN THE ELEMENTARY SCHOOL PRINCIPALSHIP." Rutgers University, 1976. 102 pp. Source: DAI, XXXVII, 6A (December, 1976), 3315-A-3316-A. XUM Order No. 76-27,336.

Data revealed that: (1) the number of women administrators in ele-mentary schools declined after 1950; and (2) women principals viewed their role and goals differently than did male principals. Concluded that women's total view of their social role limits their career and life choices.

Miller, Grace Augusta (Ph. D.). "A STUDY OF THE EFFECTIVENESS OF ACADEMIC PREPARATION OF RECENT HOME ECONOMICS GRADUATES AS RELATED TO MANAGERIAL RESPONSIBILITIES IN THE FOOD SERVICE INDUSTRY." Michigan State University, 1959. 211 pp. Source: DAI, XX, 12 (June, 1960), 4647-4648. XUM Order No. Mic 60-1716.

Graduates, employers, and home economic educators identified defi-ciencies in management and technical training for food service ad-ministration and recommended more courses in personnel management, labor regulations, meat purchasing, and specialized catering.

Miller, Margaret Evelyn (Ed. D.). "PHYSICAL EDUCATION TEACHER PREP-ARATION FOR WOMEN IN SELECTED CALIFORNIA STATE UNIVERSITIES AND ENGLISH PHYSICAL EDUCATION SPECIALIST COLLEGES: A COMPARATIVE ANALYSIS." Uni-versity of Southern California, 1973. 360 pp. Source: DAI, XXXIII, 12A (June, 1973), 6716-A-6717-A. XUM Order No. 73-14,427.

Data from interviews, journal articles, curriculum catalogs, and other primary and secondary sources showed that physical education programs in California institutions were broader and allowed more opportunity for advanced study and research than the English programs. The English system included outdoor activities and more opportunities for students to teach a wider age range of school children.

Miller, Sister Mary Claudelle (Ph. D.). "AN EVALUATION OF CONCEPTS AND THEIR RELATED COMPETENCIES FOR THE STUDY OF THE FAMILY IN WOMEN'S LIBERAL ARTS COLLEGES." University of Wisconsin, 1968. 285 pp. Source: DAI, XXIX, 2B (August, 1968), 671-B-672-B. XUM Order No. 68-7115.

A Q-sort instrument was developed by the researcher, and competencies (83) relating to family development were evaluated by a panel of family specialists. Communication--listed as top priority-- values, companionship, love, and inter-personal competence were rated as most significant. A checklist of these concepts was mailed to the administrators of women's liberal arts colleges to obtain their feelings on the significance of these ideas to the present curriculum. The administrators replied that these concepts should be included in the liberal arts program and that subjects were being offered to cover these areas.

Miller, Peter John (Ph. D.). "THE EDUCATION OF THE ENGLISH LADY, 1770-1820." University of Alberta, 1969. Source: Author.

This study analyzed social and economic changes, 1770-1820; views on the nature of women; and the types of education available to middle and upper class women; i.e., women either attended boarding schools or were taught at home by a parent or governess.

Miller, Wilma K. (P. E. D.). "ACHIEVEMENT LEVELS IN TENNIS KNOWLEDGE AND SKILL FOR WOMEN PHYSICAL EDUCATION MAJOR STUDENTS." Indiana University, 1952. Source: Author.

Women physical education students (672) who had completed or were close to completing a course in methods of teaching tennis were tested to determine the effectiveness of the programs. The study showed that the method tested was reliable, valid, objective, and economically feasible.

Milligan, Jean Beattie (Ed. D.). "EXPECTATIONS OF NURSING FACULTY MEMBERS IN BACCALAUREATE PROGRAMS." Columbia University, 1972. 236 pp. Source: DAI, XXXIII, 8A (February, 1973), 4126-A-4127-A. XUM Order No. 73-2619.

Nursing faculty's roles in 14 New England baccalaureate nursing programs were viewed by administrators and by 161 faculty members. Administrators rated higher than did teachers: teaching, scholarship, and service to the university. Older and longer tenured teachers placed greater value on scholarship and on service to the university and community. Among the recommendations: development of faculty evaluation based on clear definition of expectations; and a reassessment of graduate programs so as to enhance scholarship.

Mills, Belen Collantes (Ed. D.). "RELATIONSHIP OF CAREER ATTITUDES TO STABILITY IN TEACHING AMONG FEMALE ELEMENTARY SCHOOL TEACHERS." Indiana University, 1967. 169 pp. Source: DAI, XXVIII, 6A (December, 1967), 1995-A. XUM Order No. 67-16,420.

Major causes for job stability of over 300 women elementary teachers were: (1) strong commitment to a career; (2) need to supplement husband's low income (below $8,000); and (3) having pre-school children. Insignificant factors included: (1) social origin; (2) adequacy of teacher preparation; and (3) satisfaction with homemaking.

Millsap, Margaret Israel (Ed. D.). "AN APPLICATION OF JOHN CARROLL'S MODEL FOR SCHOOL LEARNING TO A NURSING COURSE." University of Alabama, 1974. 135 pp. Source: DAI, XXXV, 11A (May, 1975), 7032-A-7033-A. XUM Order No. 75-9927.

John Carroll's model for learning stated that, given enough time, a student could master a task if the ability to understand instruction, the quality of instruction, the aptitude of the learner, and the perseverance of the student were optimal. This model was applied to teaching a group of nursing students, while a control group was taught by traditional methods. Results indicated that the experimental group achieved higher grades, although a later achievement test showed no significant difference between the 2 groups. The experimental group expressed a more favorable attitude, however, toward the learning experience.

Milner, Edward Keith (Ph. D.). "A COMPARATIVE STUDY OF LEADERSHIP
BEHAVIOR OF MALE AND FEMALE HEADS OF DEPARTMENTS OF PHYSICAL EDUCATION IN
MAJOR UNIVERSITIES AND COLLEGES." University of Iowa, 1976. 145 pp.
Source: DAI, XXXVII, 5A (November, 1976), 2722-A-2723-A. XUM Order No.
76-26,315.

Female and male physical education department administrators were
asked to describe their behaviors and the behaviors of the ideal person in their role. Faculty were given the same questionnaires and
asked to identify actual and ideal behaviors of the administrators.
Consideration of others and leadership initiative were mentioned more
in administrators' descriptions of themselves than in faculty ratings.
Faculty members rated female and male department heads differently
in 2 different situations: female faculty in integrated departments
rated female administrators as showing more initiative; male faculty
members in segregated departments rated male administrators as dis-
playing more consideration.

Minner, Sister Jeanne Francis (Ph. D.). "A CRITICAL ANALYSIS OF THE
INTRODUCTORY COLLEGE BIOLOGY PROGRAM IN CATHOLIC WOMEN'S JUNIOR COLLEGES
IN THE UNITED STATES." University of Texas, 1965. 157 pp. Source: DAI,
XXVI, 4 (October, 1965), 2080. XUM Order No. 65-10,752.

No significant differences were found between biology programs in 16
Catholic women's junior colleges and in 24 other junior colleges.
All biology programs proved inadequate when compared with national
standards. Many faculty were not trained to teach in junior colleges.
A positive relationship existed between faculty members' hours of
preparation, course organization in biology labs, and memberships in
professional organizations.

Mintz, Florence S. (Ed. D.). "DEVELOPMENT OF A MODEL FOR THE RECRUIT-
MENT OF MATURE WOMEN IN TRADITIONALLY MALE-ORIENTED OCCUPATIONAL EDUCATION
PROGRAMS." Rutgers University, 1976. 226 pp. Source: DAI, XXXVII, 6A
(December, 1976), 3581-A-3582-A. XUM Order No. 76-27,337.

Goals of this multi-media recruitment method were to: (1) present
problems mature women face on entering the labor force; (2) change
women's attitudes about careers in a male-dominated field; and (3)
provide facts about the field of mechanical technology. This method
was effective, as shown by comparing enrollments at Union County
Institute (NJ) with enrollments of mature women in similar institutions.

Mintzer, Rhoda Greenberg (Ph. D.). "VOCATIONAL MATURITY AND ITS RE-
LATIONSHIP TO INTELLIGENCE, SELF-CONCEPT, SEX ROLE IDENTIFICATION, AND
GRADE LEVEL." Fordham University, 1976. 91 pp. Source: DAI, XXXVII,
5A (November, 1976), 2643-A. XUM Order No. 76-25,782.

Data revealed a difference in vocational maturity between 160 junior
and senior high school boys and girls, with girls scoring higher at
all grade levels. Conclusions: (1) vocational maturity is a developmental process; (2) girls scored higher on self-concept but sex role
identification, intelligence, and self-concept were not strong predictors of vocational maturity.

Miraflor, Clarita Go (Ph. D.). "THE PHILIPPINE NURSE: IMPLICATIONS FOR ORIENTATION AND IN-SERVICE EDUCATION FOR FOREIGN NURSES IN THE UNITED STATES." Loyola University of Chicago, 1976. 202 pp. Source: DAI, XXXVI, 11B (May, 1976), 5515-B. XUM Order No. 76-11,719.

A large majority of immigrating Philippine nurses were middle class and under age 35 who immigrated to further their education. Their major cultural and professional problem was the language barrier. In comparison, U. S. nurses generally rated slightly higher than Philippine nurses, except that more Philippine nurses were rated excellent in job performance, interpersonal relationships, and physical fitness.

Miriani, Sister Christa (Ph. D.). "THE IMPACT OF STRUCTURED SMALL-GROUP EXPERIENCES ON THE BEHAVIORAL DEVELOPMENT AND GROUP INTERACTION OF NURSING STUDENTS." Michigan State University, 1972. 171 pp. Source: DAI, XXXIII, 9A (March, 1973), 4885-A-4886-A. XUM Order No. 73-5448.

To investigate the impact on behavior made by structured small-group meetings, an experimental group of 2nd-year nursing students met for 1 month in a security group (individuals with similar behavior characteristics) and 8 weeks in stimulation groups (individuals with complimentary characteristics). Pre and post tests revealed that only the experimental group had significantly favorable changes in practical outlook, altruism, flexibility, hedonic tone, intimacy, potency, and stratification. Findings supported the value of structured small groups for behavior change.

Mishkin, Rosalie (Ed. D.). "RELATIONSHIP BETWEEN PERSONALITY NEEDS OF MEN AND WOMEN AND OCCUPATIONAL CHOICE." Columbia University Teachers College, 1959. Source: TCCU DIGESTS (1959), pp. 478-480.

Study identified 10 personality needs: achievement, dominance, autonomy, endurance and aggression (more for males), deference, abasement, nurturance, order, and affiliation (generally female needs). The hypothesis that males and females choosing similar professions have similar needs was substantiated for the following 4 personality characteristics: achievement, autonomy, nurturance, and affiliation.

Mista, Nancy Josephine (Ph. D.). "ATTITUDES OF COLLEGE WOMEN TOWARD THEIR HIGH SCHOOL PHYSICAL EDUCATION PROGRAMS." University of Iowa, 1966. 122 pp. Source: DAI, XXVII, 2A (August, 1966), 380-A. XUM Order No. 66-7221.

Factors influencing attitude differences toward high school physical education programs of freshman women (1,126) were: earning interscholastic letters, participation in extra-curricular physical activities, living on a farm before entering college, belonging to a high school graduating class of fewer than 75 or over 140, choosing teaching as a career, self-ratings of above or below average athletic skill, and enjoyment of physical education classes.

Mitchell, Susan Barber (Ed. D.). "WOMEN AND THE DOCTORATE: A STUDY OF THE ENABLING OR IMPEDING FACTORS OPERATIVE AMONG OKLAHOMA'S WOMEN DOCTORAL RECIPIENTS IN THE ATTAINMENT AND USE OF THE DEGREE." Oklahoma State University, 1969. 155 pp. Source: DAI, XXXI, 8A (February, 1971), 4016-A. XUM Order No. 70-21,448.

A profile of women with doctorates, including motivations for pursuing the degree, satisfaction gained, and the degree's usefulness, showed that they: (1) were employed full-time at colleges and universities; (2) had published; and (3) had experienced some discrimination in the profession. Significant differences were found in: (1) sources of their motivation; (2) family responsibilities; (3) cost of getting the doctorate; and (4) importance to them of proximity to graduate school. Women with doctorates gained personal and professional satisfaction and also benefited society, but academic practices and cultural demands impeded women from obtaining doctorates.

Mitchell, Teresa Lou (Ph. D.). "AN EXPLORATORY STUDY OF SELECTED VARIABLES RELATED TO ATTRITION IN ONE SCHOOL OF NURSING." University of Missouri, Kansas City, 1970. 106 pp. Source: DAI, XXXI, 8B (February, 1971), 4798-B. XUM Order No. 71-3701.

Attrition rate (29%) of 1st-year nursing students exceeded the national norm (20.4%) but was less than the 30% freshman attrition rate at the University of Missouri, Kansas City, to which the nursing school was affiliated. Significant differences between nursing students and non-nursing students were sex and age, with nursing students being younger and mostly women. Of the 3 methods used to reduce attrition (counseling, tutoring, and motivation), motivation was most successful. Concluded that these findings could help reduce attrition among 1st year nursing students.

Miwa, Keiko (Ed. D.). "ANALYSIS OF THE EFFECT OF MAJOR AMERICAN IDEAS UPON THE ORGANIZATION OF JAPANESE HIGHER EDUCATION FROM 1946 TO 1967." Washington State University, 1969. 106 pp. Source: DAI, XXX, 3A (September, 1969), pp. 933-A-934-A.

After World War II (1946-1967), these were some of Japan's major developments in higher education: (1) simplification of the 4-year university; (2) introduction and expansion of junior colleges; (3) elimination of undue government controls; and (4) advancement of women's higher education. Financial problems curtailed further development. Women's education focused primarily on preparing women as homemakers.

Miyahira, Sara Diane (Ph. D.). "COLLEGE WOMEN'S CAREER ORIENTATIONS AS RELATED TO WORK VALUES AND BACKGROUND FACTORS." Ohio State University, 1976. 254 pp. Source: DAI, XXXVII, 8A (February, 1977), 4868-A. XUM Order No. 77-2463.

Career-oriented freshman women (196) expected to: (1) attain advanced degrees; (2) marry later; (3) have fewer children; (4) in many cases, pursue male-dominated professions; and (5) have husbands who encouraged their career ambitions. Career-oriented senior women (185): (1) had many career-oriented women friends; (2) had many intellectual interests; and (3) expected to get advanced degrees.

Mobley, Norma King (Ed. D.). "NURSE-FACULTY PERCEPTIONS OF THE SYSTEM OF NURSING EDUCATION IN RELATION TO ARTICULATION, CAREER LADDERS, AND THE OPEN CURRICULUM IN NURSING." University of Alabama, 1971. 311 pp. Source: DAI, XXXII, 9B (March, 1972), 5273-B-5274-B. XUM Order No. 72-8455.

Nursing faculty (464) from baccalaureate and associate degree programs perceived nursing education as inadequate in meeting society's
health care needs, in providing for nurses' educational and career
mobility, and in connecting segments of nursing education. The majority of nursing faculty: (1) favored efforts to improve the connections between segments of nursing education; (2) believed nursing
curricula could fit a ladder concept; and (3) favored open curriculum
plans. Views on these matters differed significantly in relation to
the academic level of the program in which nursing faculty taught and
their own academic attainment.

Moeller, Tamerra Pickford (Ph. D.). "COOPERATIVE BEHAVIORS OF FOUR-
YEAR-OLD GIRLS IN NURSERY SCHOOL SETTINGS." University of Michigan, 1974.
222 pp. Source: DAI, XXXV, 7B (January, 1975), 3648-B. XUM Order No.
75-759.

The girls' cooperative behavior in a natural setting was not affected
by the experimental tasks intended to encourage cooperative behavior;
nor were their scores on affiliation and empathy tests related to
their cooperativeness.

Moloney, Sister Mary Annetta (Ph. D.). "LEADERSHIP BEHAVIORS OF DEANS
IN UNIVERSITY SCHOOLS OF NURSING." Catholic University of America, 1967.
176 pp. Source: DAI, XXVIII, 6A (December, 1967), 2036-A. XUM Order
No. 67-15,461.

Three groups--26 deans of nursing, 26 university vice presidents, and
234 nursing faculty--had significantly different perceptions and expectations of a dean's leadership behavior. A significant relationship existed between perceived leader behavior and a person's evaluation of a dean's overall leadership.

Monaghan, Louise Kathryn (Ed. D.). "CONTINUING EDUCATION PROGRAMS
FOR WOMEN: A SPATIAL ANALYSIS OF THE PERSONALITY CHARACTERISTICS AND
NEEDS OF MATURE WOMEN PARTICIPANTS WITH IMPLICATIONS FOR PROGRAM MODELS."
Memphis State University, 1974. 98 pp. Source: DAI, XXXVI, 2A (August,
1975), 665-A. XUM Order No. 75-10,065.

A survey of mature women participants in a continuing education program found that the women considered their mothers their major source
of encouragement for education. Self-actualization and academic
achievement were more important to them than security and sense of
belonging. Findings were used to plan future courses for women.

Monahan, Oanno Richard (Ph. D.). "EDUCATING WOMEN RELIGIOUS: THE
HISTORY OF MARILLAC COLLEGE, 1955-69." Saint Louis University, 1972.
127 pp. Source: DAI, XXXIII, 6A (December, 1972), 2745-A-2746-A. XUM
Order No. 72-31,474.

Traced the 14 years after Marillac became a 4-year liberal arts college for Roman Catholic sisters. Examined its professional programs
in teacher education, social work, and nursing. Made recommendations
for improving the college program.

Montague, Anita C. (Ph. D.). "A FACTORIAL ANALYSIS OF THE BASIC IN-
TEREST PATTERNS OF TWO HUNDRED WOMEN COLLEGE STUDENTS IN VARIOUS CURRICU-

LAR GROUPS." Temple University, 1960. 119 pp. Source: DAI, XXII, 1 (July, 1961), 324. XUM Order No. Mic 60-4442.

To investigate the vocational and educational interest patterns of 200 college women in various curricula, the study obtained their responses to a 300-item inventory. One conclusion: basic interest patterns differed among women from the various divisions of colleges and for major within the same division.

Montenegro, Raquel (Ph. D.). "EDUCATIONAL IMPLICATIONS OF CULTURAL VALUES AND ATTITUDES OF MEXICAN AMERICAN WOMEN." Claremont Graduate School, 1973. 132 pp. Source: DAI, XXXIV, 7A (January, 1974), 3883-A. XUM Order No. 74-971.

Mexican American women, aged 17-24 (179 in high school; 51 in adult education programs), who provided data about their attitudes and beliefs: (1) were proud of their Mexican heritage; (2) rejected the traditional role of husband as dominant figure; (3) were strongly committed to further education; (4) were career-oriented toward female dominated fields; and (5) had no special interest in the women's movement but agreed with its goals.

Moody, Florence Elizabeth (Ed. D.). "THE DIFFERENTIAL EFFECTS OF TEACHER COMMENTS ON COLLEGE FEMALES' ACHIEVEMENT AS MEASURED BY TEST PERFORMANCE." University of Rochester, 1969. 108 pp. Source: DAI, XXX, 8A (February, 1970), 3328-A-3329-A. XUM Order No. 70-2939.

Undergraduate women (54) were labeled "self oriented" or "other" oriented on the basis of responses on a personality test and were divided into 3 groups to receive from their teachers either no comment, affiliative (other oriented) comment, or an achievement comment. Findings were: (1) no statistically significant differences were found among the 3 groups; and (2) sex-role value orientation and comment interaction were significantly related. Conclusion: while teacher comments did affect females' test performances, this effect was highly specific in terms of type of comment, level of comment, and the students' sex-role orientation.

Moore, Barbara Allen (Ph. D.). "STAFFING HOME ECONOMICS EDUCATION PROGRAMS IN THE UNITED STATES BETWEEN 1975-1981." Ohio State University, 1976. 261 pp. Source: DAI, XXXVII, 8A (February, 1977), 4917-A-4918-A. XUM Order No. 77-2464.

For this survey about staff needs, 1975-1981, a questionnaire was sent to the 376 U. S. institutions offering a B. A. degree in general or vocational home economics. Found that many existing home economics vacancies were unfilled because of too few qualified applicants and limited budgets. Between 1978 and 1981 the number of new doctorates seeking positions was expected to equal the number of home economics faculty vacancies.

Moore, Brian Edward Arthur (Ph. D.). "SOME WORKING WOMEN IN MEXICO CITY: TRADITIONALISTS AND MODERNISTS." Washington University, 1970. 238 pp. Source: DAI, XXXI, 7A (January, 1971), 3659-A. XUM Order No. 70-26,866.

Interviews with 162 Mexican women, observations of blue and white-
collar women, and questionnaire responses verified the existence of
a modernism-traditionalism conflict in some Mexican women. The degree of modernity in each woman varied. Job demands caused the women
problems with their families, in their religious beliefs, and in controlling their lives.

Moore, Dean Frazier (Ph. D.). "A COMPARISON OF SELECTED CHARACTERIS-
TICS OF LSU WOMEN GRADUATES FOR THE 1930s AND 1950s. (A STUDY OF CHANG-
ING ROLES AND ALIENATION)." Louisiana State University, 1976. 220 pp.
Source: DAI, XXXVII, 11A (May, 1977), 7330-A-7331-A. XUM Order No.
77-10,387.

Such characteristics as home location, occupation, and number of
children were compared for 276 female graduates of 1930-1940 and
241 female graduates of 1950-1960. The 2 groups had many similar
characteristics and differed only in number of children and religious
affiliation. Conclusions were that the 2 groups of females tended
to: (1) earn less than their husbands; (2) work to have money for
middle class living; and (3) hold jobs in such traditional fields as
nursing and teaching.

Moore, Eva Lanice (Ph. D.). "SATISFACTIONS AND DISSATISFACTIONS OF
COLLEGE TEACHERS OF HOME ECONOMICS." Pennsylvania State University,
1958. 165 pp. Source: DAI, XIX, 1 (July, 1958), 129-130. XUM Order
No. Mic 58-2279.

Faculty members were generally satisfied with their jobs. Comparisons revealed that: (1) older teachers were more satisfied in human
relationships than younger teachers; (2) full professors were more
satisfied than instructors with community and environmental conditions; and (3) satisfaction level increased as the level of education
and salaries rose.

Moore, Fernie Baca (Ph. D.). "THE EFFECTS OF A LARGE GROUP VERSUS A
SMALL GROUP VOCATIONAL EXPLORATION GROUP EXPERIENCE ON THE VOCATIONAL
KNOWLEDGE, ATTITUDES, AND JOB SEARCH BEHAVIORS OF HIGH SCHOOL FEMALES."
University of Colorado, 1976. 183 pp. Source: DAI, XXXVII, 5A (Novem-
ber, 1976), 2643-A-2644-A. XUM Order No. 76-23,657.

Female high school students (87) were tested before and after they
had either a 3-hour small group vocational exploration experience; a
similar experience in a class-size group; or, as part of a control
group, had no planned vocational exploration. No significant differences were found in any groups' knowledge about careers, in positive
attitudes toward career exploration, or in understanding of how to
look for a job.

Moore, Helen Boulware (Ph. D.). "RACE AND SOCIAL CLASS: SOCIO-
CULTURAL FACTORS IN THE DEVELOPMENT OF THE ACHIEVEMENT MOTIVE IN COLLEGE
WOMEN." Boston College, 1977. 148 pp. Source: DAI, XXXVIII, 2A
(August, 1977), 707-A. XUM Order No. 77-17,599.

Effects of race and socio-economic class on the motive to achieve
were investigated. Achievement motive was greater in black college
women than in white and also in women of lower socio-economic class
than middle class women. Race and social class are both factors in
the development of the achievement motive.

Moore, Linda Lee (Ed. D.). "THE RELATIONSHIP OF ACADEMIC GROUP MEM-
BERSHIP TO THE MOTIVE TO AVOID SUCCESS IN WOMEN." University of Virginia,
1971. 95 pp. Source: DAI, XXXII, 8A (February, 1972), 4355-A. XUM Order No. 72-7220.

Explored the relationship between a woman graduate student's academic
or professional field (nursing, law, arts and sciences) and her tendency to avoid success. Conclusion: presence or absence of the motive to avoid success was not related to a woman's academic field but
to the way she identified with traditional socio-cultural norms about
sex-role identification.

Moore, Marjorie Anne (Ph. D.). "A STUDY OF THE EXTENT TO WHICH SPE-
CIFIC BEHAVIORAL OBJECTIVES DIFFERENTIATE BACCALAUREATE, DIPLOMA, AND
ASSOCIATE ARTS NURSING EDUCATION PROGRAMS." University of Iowa, 1966.
174 pp. Source: DAI, XXVII, 9B (March, 1967), 3159-B. XUM Order No.
67-2655.

Qualities of leadership, judgment, and responsibility were elicited
in questionnaires to 93 associate, 236 diploma, and 226 baccalaureate
nursing faculty members. Findings: on all items, the above characteristics were considered more important for baccalaureate graduates
than for graduates of the other 2 nursing programs. Most respondents
noted differences among the programs in level of skill, preparation,
and ability to assume leadership.

Moore, Miriam Brown (Ph. D.). "AN ANALYSIS OF VALUES HELD BY TWO
GROUPS OF MARRIAGE AND FAMILY LIFE EDUCATORS AS INDICATED BY THEIR REAC-
TIONS TO A SELECTED NUMBER OF CONTROVERSIAL ISSUES." Ohio State Univer-
sity, 1961. 141 pp. Source: DAI, XXII, 7 (January, 1962), 2380-2381.
XUM Order No. 61-5109.

Family life educators (2 groups) who teach in higher education home
economics departments helped identify controversial issues in the
literature about values in marriage and family life. This study revealed inconsistencies and differences of opinion about values. In
general, however, the 2 groups agreed on 84 of the 105 statements
about controversial issues.

Moore, Nancy Voigt (Ph. D.). "COGNITIVE LEVEL, INTACTNESS OF FAMILY,
AND SEX IN RELATION TO THE CHILD'S DEVELOPMENT OF THE CONCEPT OF FAMILY."
University of Texas at Austin, 1976. 96 pp. Source: DAI, XXXVII, 8B
(February, 1977), 4117-B-4118-B. XUM Order No. 77-3960.

Girls had more sophisticated concepts of family, in this study of 84
children (aged 4-13), divided according to Piagetian cognitive levels.
Conclusion: cognitive developmental theory was relevant to studying
the family.

Moore, Sandra Elizabeth (Ed. D.). "OPPORTUNITIES FOR WOMEN IN THE
FIELD OF PUBLIC SCHOOL ADMINISTRATION IN THE NEW JERSEY COUNTIES OF CUM-
BERLAND, HUNTERDON, AND PASSAIC." Rutgers University, 1977. 116 pp.
Source: DAI, XXXVII, 12A, Part 1 (June, 1977), 7451-A-7452-A. XUM Or-
der No. 77-13,468.

Data were obtained from those certified as school administrators, principals, and/or supervisors in 3 New Jersey counties and from interviews with selected women administrators. Findings: (1) fewer women than men seek administrative posts although they have equal qualifications; (2) there is a strong prejudice against women as school administrators; and (3) only 52% of the men questioned had elementary level teaching experience (men hold 80% of U. S. elementary principalships). Recommendations: (1) since men reported hearing of vacancies by word of mouth and women did not, women need improved ways of learning about administrative openings; and (2) graduate schools should develop programs aimed specifically at women's role in educational administration.

Moore, Shirley Tuttle (Ph. D.). "A HISTORICAL STUDY OF TRENDS IN THE METHODOLOGY AND CONTENT OF ADULT EDUCATION PROGRAMS IN NUTRITION IN THE UNITED STATES." Michigan State University, 1965. 226 pp. Source: DAI, XXVII, 3B (September, 1966), 869-B. XUM Order No. 66-6152.

The history of nutrition education, 1894-1965, is an example of adult education as aided by many private and governmental bodies. In the period studied, nutrition teaching shifted from insistence that people be told what to eat to recognition of the social, psychological, and emotional factors which hinder efforts to change food habits.

Moore, Violet (Ph. D.). "HOME ECONOMICS TEACHERS SERVING AS GENERAL-ISTS AND SPECIALISTS IN SECONDARY SCHOOLS IN ILLINOIS." Southern Illinois University, 1973. 84 pp. Source: DAI, XXXIV, 9B (March, 1974), 4483-B. XUM Order No. 74-6231.

Questionnaires from 1,209 home economics teachers in junior and senior high schools of Illinois provided data about whether existing home economics positions used generalists or specialists. Findings: (1) a greater number of home economics teachers were generalists; (2) the majority of those who were specialists did not hold a master's degree; and (3) new positions likely to be available would require generalists. Conclusion: Illinois teacher education institutions should continue to prepare most home economics teachers as generalists.

Mooth, Adelma Evelyn (Ed. D.). "NEEDS OF BEGINNING COLLEGE TEACHERS OF NURSING AND ASSISTANCE THAT MIGHT BE PROVIDED BY THE ADMINISTRATOR." Columbia University Teachers College, 1962. Source: TCCU DIGESTS (1962), pp. 309-311.

To determine the nursing education administrator's role in assisting a beginning nursing teacher to be more effective, 19 administrators and 68 nursing faculty in 19 colleges and universities were interviewed. Findings: the administrator (1) is expected to acquaint beginning teachers with the institution's philosophy, policy, and legislative organization; (2) needs to be an enabler, facilitator, initiator, evaluator, and teacher; and (3) needs to understand the psychology of change and to know methods for in-service development and materials available to the teacher.

Morain, Thomas Jeffrey (Ph. D.). "THE EMERGENCE OF THE WOMEN'S MOVE-MENT, 1960-1970." University of Iowa, 1974. 272 pp. Source: DAI, XXXV, 12A, Part 1 (June, 1975), 7845-A. XUM Order No. 75-13,798.

Placed the women's movement in political and cultural context of the 1960s. Schools were among institutions discredited by the New Left, anti-Vietnam War, and civil rights movements. Women, stirred by these causes, used sex as another tool for attacking discriminatory practices in education and in society generally.

Moravek, Marjory (Ed. D.). "THE RELATIONSHIP OF SELF CONCEPT OF THE BEGINNING TEACHERS TO SELECTED ASPECTS OF THEIR VERBAL BEHAVIOR AS A BASIS FOR RECOMMENDATIONS FOR HOME ECONOMICS EDUCATION." Oklahoma State University, 1970. 142 pp. Source: DAI, XXXI, 11B (May, 1971), 6725-B-6726-B. XUM Order No. 71-11,232.

Self concepts of 15 home economics teachers were tested before and after their first year of teaching. Less positive self concepts were found for 9 teachers and more positive for 6 teachers. Their verbal behavior patterns, compared with those in other studies, were often within the average range. The study found a tendency toward a positive correlation between the teacher's self concept and the percentage of student talk.

Morelock, Judy Carol (Ph. D.). "SEX DIFFERENCES IN SUSCEPTIBILITY TO SOCIAL INFLUENCE." Pennsylvania State University, 1976. 152 pp. Source: DAI, XXXVII, 11A (May, 1977), 7361-A. XUM Order No. 77-9580.

Female and male undergraduate students were asked to express opinions on several statements, all with an attempt to influence a sex-biased answer. Males were more compliant than females when given statements on female sex-role related tasks. Females were more compliant with male sex-role related tasks. No main effect of sex influenced the answers.

Morey, Elwyn Aisne (Ph. D.). "VOCATIONAL INTERESTS AND PERSONALITY CHARACTERISTICS OF WOMEN TEACHERS." University of California, 1947. 231 pp. Source: Dissertation Abstract.

This study found measurable differences in vocational interests and personality characteristics in 680 women teachers according to their teaching level. Junior high teachers preferred academic and scientific professions; senior high teachers preferred academic occupations and intellectual amusement; and elementary teachers had a stronger interest in art and in people.

Morgan, Carolyn Stout (Ph. D.). "SUPPORT FOR THE GOALS OF THE WOMEN'S RIGHTS MOVEMENT AMONG COLLEGE STUDENTS." University of Oklahoma, 1973. 136 pp. Source: DAI, XXXIV, 9A (March, 1974), 6107-A. XUM Order No. 74-6974.

Measures of the commitment among 493 college students to 8 goals of the women's rights movement found the views of males and females highly compatible. The following women's rights goals were acceptable (in this order): public day care facilities, equal responsibility for child rearing and care; abortion on demand by women; end of sex-differentiated tracking in the educational system; equal responsibility for housekeeping; child rearing without regard to traditional sex-role stereotypes; end to the institution of marriage in its present form; and preferential treatment for women in hiring and promotions.

Morgan, Donna Davis (Ph. D.). "PERCEPTION OF ROLE CONFLICTS AND SELF CONCEPTS AMONG CAREER AND NONCAREER COLLEGE EDUCATED WOMEN." Columbia University, 1962. 84 pp. Source: DAI, XXIII, 5 (November, 1962), 1816-1817. XUM Order No. 62-4242.

This study of 120 women college graduates (60 with careers and 60 without careers) found that a woman's career position did not consistently influence self perception and role perceptions. But career women had inner conflict about role expectations. Both groups saw more differences between the ideal-woman's role and the feminine role than they saw between feminine and masculine roles.

Morgan, Janice Marie (Ph. D.). "SIMULATED TEACHING EXPERIENCES FOR SOPHOMORE HOME ECONOMICS EDUCATION STUDENTS." Iowa State University, 1973. 188 pp. Source: DAI, XXXIV, 10B (April, 1974), 5056-B-5057-B. XUM Order No. 74-9141.

Examined attitudes of sophomore home economics education majors who took an experimental course which gave them simulated teaching experiences. Result: students who took the experimental course were less anxious about student teaching. Recommendation: a simulated teaching course should be included early in the home economics teacher preparation program.

Morneau, Robert Henry, Jr. (Ph. D.). "WOMEN IN LAW ENFORCEMENT: A SOCIAL-PSYCHOLOGICAL STUDY." University of Southern California, 1975. Source: DAI, XXXVI, 11A (May, 1976), 7635-A.

Found that women law enforcement officers' positions had advanced despite their relative lack of education. They had attained equality with male colleagues and had moved ahead of males in some areas. Compared to women in more traditional jobs, female law enforcement officers were more job-oriented, more self-assured, and more satisfied.

Morrison, Linnea Setterlind (Ed. D.). "THE CONTINUING EDUCATION NEEDS OF LICENSED PRACTICAL NURSES IN MINNESOTA, 1976." Brigham Young University, 1977. 159 pp. Source: DAI, XXXVIII, 2A (August, 1977), 576-A. XUM Order No. 77-17,616.

A survey of 784 licensed practical nurses, nursing directors of 190 hospitals and 369 nursing homes revealed need for continuing education in such problem areas as: death and dying, myocardial infarction, chemical dependency, and patient education. Preference was for workshops which emphasized psycho-social aspects of these problems.

Morrison, Lonnie Leotus (P. E. D.). "A TEST OF BASIC SPORTS FOR COLLEGE WOMEN." Indiana University, 1964. 169 pp. Source: DAI, XXV, 3 (September, 1964), 1724-1725. XUM Order No. 64-6193.

Two valid, reliable, and objective batteries of test items were developed to help estimate the basic sports skills ability of college women.

Morrison, Peggy Jean (Ed. D.). "FOODS AND NUTRITION EDUCATION IN THE
HOME ECONOMICS CURRICULUM IN TWENTY-THREE SELECTED HIGH SCHOOLS." Auburn
University, 1971. 222 pp. Source: DAI, XXXII, 7A (January, 1972), 3670-
A. XUM Order No. 72-5341.

Home economics teachers (40) in 23 high schools responded to a checklist of 11 major concepts in foods and nutrition education. These
teachers reported giving above average attention to 9 of the concepts.
These and other findings were the basis of recommendations to improve
foods and nutrition education.

Morrissey, William Michael (Ed. D.). "THE STATUS AND PERCEPTIONS OF
WOMEN SCHOOL BOARD MEMBERS IN INDIANA." Indiana University, 1972. 102
pp. Source: DAI, XXXIV, 3A (September, 1973), 1037-A-1038-A. XUM Order
No. 73-6989.

A questionnaire administered to 97 Indiana women school board members
examined their perceptions about their role, function, and relationships as board members. The data showed that the older, more experienced women did not believe they were discriminated against but that
a limited amount of sex prejudice existed.

Morse, Barbara (Ph. D.). "IDENTITY STATUS IN COLLEGE WOMEN IN RELA-
TION TO PERCEIVED PARENT-CHILD RELATIONSHIPS." Ohio State University,
1973. 204 pp. Source: DAI, XXXIV, 5B (November, 1973), 2287-B-2288-B.
XUM Order No. 73-26,875.

The 67 freshman and 76 junior women as a group significantly rated
mothers higher than fathers on accepting their daughters and on certain control scales. Those women who had achieved a sense of identity
revealed less possessiveness from mothers.

Morsink, Helen Muriel (Ph. D.). "COMPARATIVE STUDY OF THE LEADER BE-
HAVIOR OF MEN AND WOMEN SECONDARY SCHOOL PRINCIPALS." University of
Michigan, 1966. 209 pp. Source: DAI, XXVII, 9A (March, 1967), 2793-A-
2794-A. XUM Order No. 67-1780.

In comparing 15 men and 15 women secondary school principals, it was
found that: (1) they did not perceive themselves significantly different in exercise of responsibility, authority, delegation of responsibility, tolerance of uncertainty, and consideration of others; (2)
men were perceived to exercise greater tolerance of freedom; (3) women
were perceived to exercise more representation, reconciliation, per-
missiveness, emphasis on production, accuracy of prediction, and other
characteristics. Concluded that in at least some characteristics one's
perceptions of a leader's behavior is related to the sex of the individual.

Moses, Elizabeth (Ph. D.). "MASTER'S STUDENTS IN NURSING EDUCATION."
University of California, Berkeley, 1966. 131 pp. Source: DAI, XXVII,
5B (November, 1966), 1525-B-1526-B. XUM Order No. 66-8346.

Personalities, values, and academic aptitudes were measured among 635
master's degree nursing students in 13 graduate U. S. programs, divided into 2 groups: college programs and those in hospital school
programs. There were many differences between the 40% generally

younger college students and the 60% generally older, more experienced, and lower socio-economic hospital school students.

Moses, Mary Louise (Ph. D.). "PREDICTORS OF SUCCESS OR FAILURE OF A SELECTED GROUP OF FRESHMAN ASSOCIATE DEGREE NURSING STUDENTS." Texas Woman's University, 1976. 174 pp. Source: DAI, XXXVII, 8B (February, 1977), 3871-B-3872-B. XUM Order No. 77-755.

Academic failure, lack of motivation, and family responsibilities were major reasons for dropping out of the associate degree nursing program. This study showed that grade point average, scholastic aptitude scores, and personality ratings of such qualities as responsibility, independence, and self criticism could be used as reliable predictors of success of freshman student nurses.

Mosley, Doris Yvonne (Ed. D.). "NURSING STUDENTS' PERCEPTIONS OF THE URBAN POOR." Columbia University, 1971. 230 pp. Source: DAI, XXXII, 3A (September, 1971), 1261-A-1262-A. XUM Order No. 71-24,160.

Questionnaire to 329 graduating associate degree students in 6 nursing programs in or near New York City revealed that: (1) most viewed the urban poor positively but a significant number were undecided or negative; (2) most, but relatively few best students, planned to work in urban areas; (3) more lower socio-economic students had cared for poor patients; and (4) more higher socio-economic students were indecisive or rejected working with urban poor.

Moss, Mattie Elizabeth (Ed. D.). "THE FEMALE UNDERGRADUATE MATHEMATICS MAJOR: ATTITUDES, EXPERIENCES AND ASPIRATIONS." Rutgers University, 1975. 204 pp. Source: DAI, XXXVI, 10A (April, 1976), 6510-A. XUM Order No. 76-8702.

Questionnaire to 182 male and female mathematics majors showed that: (1) the female math majors were satisfied with their choice of major; (2) the career choices of females did not differ significantly from those of males; and (3) both males and females expressed some dissatisfactions with their math training.

Most, Ada Franziska (Ed. D.). "A SURVEY OF PROBLEMS OF THE NEOPHYTE TEACHER IN BACCALAUREATE NURSING PROGRAMS." Columbia University, 1969. 199 pp. Source: DAI, XXX, 9B (March, 1970), 4223-B. XUM Order No. 70-4519.

Returns from some 500 new nursing teachers (under 1½ years' teaching) in 133 baccalaureate nursing programs indicated that: (1) a significant number felt themselves insufficiently prepared; (2) most reported a burdensome teaching load; (3) most did not understand their roles and responsibilities; (4) most reported negative experiences; and (5) most had difficulty in testing and evaluation.

Moulton, Robert O'Neil (Ed. D.). "ASSOCIATE DEGREE NURSING EDUCATION IN THE STATE-SUPPORTED JUNIOR COLLEGES OF ARKANSAS: A STUDY OF NEEDS." Memphis State University, 1969. 187 pp. Source: DAI, XXX, 9A (March, 1970), 3694-A-3695-A. XUM Order No. 70-1910.

Data came from catalogs of 3 state-supported junior colleges, interviews with their academic deans, the Arkansas State Board of Nursing,
University of Arkansas Nursing School, Arkansas State Manpower Commis-
sion, and the Southern Regional Education Board. Finding: academic
and plant facilities were adequate to start associate degree nursing
programs at state-supported junior colleges, but shortages of funds
and qualified faculty would hinder their establishment.

Mowder, Barbara Hogue (Ph. D.). "THE EFFECT OF SEX BIASED MATHEMATICS
ITEMS ON THE PERFORMANCE OF THIRD AND SIXTH GRADE STUDENTS." Indiana Uni-
versity, 1976. 79 pp. Source: DAI, XXXVII, 8A (February, 1977), 4997-A.
XUM Order No. 77-1921.

Sex-biased mathematics problems did not significantly affect performance of third and sixth grade boys and girls. But sixth grade girls
tended to perform better on male-biased problems. These findings
were consistent with 3 developmental theories about the development
of 8 to 12 year olds.

Mowrer, John LaDieu (Ph. D.). "ATTITUDES OF NURSING HOME ADMINISTRA-
TORS TOWARD THEIR OWN CONTINUING EDUCATION." University of Missouri,
Columbia, 1974. 154 pp. Source: DAI, XXXVI, 1B (July, 1975), 154-B.
XUM Order No. 75-16,031.

To evaluate the continuing education program for nursing home administrators, attitudes of participants in University of Missouri continuing education conferences were sought. They gave opinions about these
4 areas: professional-legal, instruction, subject matter, and administration. Participants' attitudes were more favorable than unfavorable
toward the 4 areas and toward continuing education. Those with less
education were more favorable than were those with some graduate-level
education.

Muckenhirn, Erma Florence (Ph. D.). "SECONDARY EDUCATION AND GIRLS IN
WESTERN NIGERIA." University of Michigan, 1966. 347 pp. Source: DAI,
XXVII, 12A, Part 1 (June, 1967), 4108-A. XUM Order No. 67-1781.

Despite rising enrollment trends, western Nigerian girls' secondary
education is limited by primary school dropouts, external exams, insufficient qualified teachers, low average income, early marriage,
premarital pregnancies, parental belief that girls need less education to be homemakers, and the preference for academic education over
practical vocational education. Author concluded that the gap between
male and female secondary school enrollment would not be appreciably
narrowed in the next 10 years.

Mullins, Elizabeth Ione (Ph. D.). "RADICALISM IN COLLEGE WOMEN: A
TEST OF CONTENDING THEORIES." Indiana University, 1975. 740 pp. Source:
DAI, XXXVI, 11A (May, 1976), 7687-A. XUM Order No. 76-11,373.

Data showed that the development of radical attitudes and behavior in
college women was related to: (1) the daughter's perception of her
parents' reactions to their own roles; (2) use of parents as negative
role models; (3) upbringing in a setting of sharp contrasts and inconsistencies; and (4) experience of conflict and disagreement in
family relations. The most useful explanations of radicalism were in
general agreement with the Systems Contraint Theory of behavior.

Mullis, Rebecca McNeill (Ph. D.). "A COMPARATIVE EVALUATION OF TWO
APPROACHES TO THE PHYSIOLOGICAL WELL-BEING COMPONENT OF THE CORE CURRICU-
LUM IN HOME ECONOMICS." University of Tennessee, 1976. 169 pp. Source:
DAI, XXXVII, 11B (May, 1977), 5615-B. XUM Order No. 77-10,790.

This comparison of 2 methods of teaching a home economics course revealed that: (1) total knowledge and common content scores were similar; but (2) the 2 methods produced significantly different results
as evidenced by the fact that each group acquired a different body of
knowledge.

Munley, Mary Joan (Ed. D.). "BACCALAUREATE NURSING STUDENTS AND DE-
CISION MAKING." Columbia University, 1975. 111 pp. Source: DAI, XXXVI,
1B (July, 1975), 163-B. XUM Order No. 75-13,902.

This study was based on the expectation that senior nursing students
who were relatively internally controlled would be more decisive and
self confident in facing patient care problems than would nursing students who were externally controlled. Experiments with the 2 groups
found no measurable significant differences between them.

Munson, Stuart Edwin (Ph. D.). "THE RELATIONSHIP BETWEEN PERCEIVED
CHILD-REARING PRACTICES AND DEPRESSION IN COLLEGE-AGE WOMEN." Rutgers
University, 1974. 84 pp. Source: DAI, XXXV, 10B (May, 1975), 5125-B.
XUM Order No. 75-8422.

Found that parents of depressed college women tended to be less critical and controlling than parents of the psychiatric control group,
although more so than parents of normal women.

Murdock, Betty J. (Ph. D.). "A SURVEY STUDY TO ASCERTAIN THE CURRICU-
LUM STRUCTURE UTILIZED FOR THE NON-DEGREE GRADUATE NURSE IN THE BACCALAUR-
EATE PROGRAM." University of Nebraska, Lincoln, 1973. 107 pp. Source:
DAI, XXXIV, 7A (January, 1974), 3815-A. XUM Order No. 74-648.

Found the following for 24 baccalaureate nursing faculty members responsible for curriculum decisions in programs for non-degree graduate nursing students: (1) most were oriented to nursing apprenticeship programs; (2) most were more concerned with experience than with
educational concepts; (3) most had no formal adult education experience; and (4) most made decisions based on apprenticeship backgrounds
with little or no attention to adult education concepts. Concluded
that generally held concepts about adult learners were little used in
curriculum development for the non-degree graduate nurse.

Murphy, Mother M. Benedict (Ph. D.). "PIONEER ROMAN CATHOLIC GIRLS'
ACADEMIES: THEIR GROWTH, CHARACTER, AND CONTRIBUTION TO AMERICAN EDUCA-
TION. A STUDY OF ROMAN CATHOLIC EDUCATION FOR GIRLS FROM COLONIAL TIMES
TO THE FIRST PLENARY COUNCIL OF 1852." Columbia University, 1958. 337
pp. Source: DAI, XIX, 2 (August, 1958), 267. XUM Order No. Mic 58-2541.

This historical study traced the origins of U. S. Catholic girls' education to 1727, when French Ursulines founded in Louisiana the first
and only 18th century Catholic girls' school on what was to become
U. S. soil. After independence a few Catholic girls' academies were
opened, always with an ethnic flavor but often serving a cross-section

of society (including many Protestant girls). Religion was central to the curriculum in girls' academies, which began as elementary schools and often expanded to the secondary level. By 1852 the girls' academies were a significant part of American women's education.

Murphy, Sister Mary Thomas (Ph. D.). "THE RELATIONSHIP OF PSYCHOLOGI-CAL NEEDS TO OCCUPATIONAL SATISFACTION IN RELIGIOUS WOMEN TEACHERS." Fordham University, 1965. 165 pp. Source: DAI, XXVI, 8 (February, 1966), 4455. XUM Order No. 65-14,156.

Concluded that: (1) the needs of most religious women teachers stud-ied for security, identity, and commitment were significantly related to their occupational satisfaction; and (2) length of teaching experi-ence and grade level assignment were not so important to their job satisfaction as was the fulfillment of intrinsic psychological needs.

Murray, Beatrice Louise (Ed. D.). "AN EXPLORATORY STUDY OF PERSISTENT NURSING SITUATIONS IN MOTHER AND CHILD CARE WITH IMPLICATIONS FOR PRESER-VICE EDUCATION." Columbia University Teachers College, 1962. Source: TCCU DIGESTS (1962), pp. 336-337.

Nurses and nursing students (109) were interviewed for descriptions of maternal and child care. Areas of responsibility were defined and the implications were noted for education programs for nurses of mothers and children.

Mussallem, Helen Kathleen (Ed. D.). "A PLAN FOR THE DEVELOPMENT OF NURSING EDUCATION PROGRAMS WITHIN THE GENERAL EDUCATIONAL SYSTEM OF CANA-DA." Columbia University, 1962. 236 pp. Source: DAI, XXIV, 2 (August, 1963), 705. XUM Order No. 63-5723.

This plan to meet Canada's nursing education needs and to operate within Canada's educational system encompassed the following: (1) a 4-year university baccalaureate professional nursing course and a 2-year technical nursing course (ultimately to be given in junior col-leges); (2) these nurses to be prepared in a ratio of 1 professional nurse to 3 technical nurses; (3) control of nursing education to shift from hospitals to universities; and (4) university nursing school en-rollment to be quadrupled.

Myers, Charles Nash (Ph. D.). "A PROJECTION OF DEMAND FOR DOCTORS AND NURSES IN MEXICO: 1965-1980." Princeton University, 1971. 200 pp. Source: DAI, XXXII, 3A (September, 1971), 1142-A. XUM Order No. 71-23,378.

This study projected the need for 43,000 to 49,000 new doctors and 55,000 to 63,000 new nurses in Mexico between 1965-1980. These high numbers suggest that Mexican medical and nursing education must be changed.

Naffziger, Kenneth Gordon (Ph. D.) and Claudeen Cline Naffziger (Ph. D.). "A SURVEY OF COUNSELOR-EDUCATORS' AND OTHER SELECTED PROFESSIONALS' ATTITUDES TOWARDS WOMEN'S ROLES." University of Oregon, 1971. 160 pp. Source: DAI, XXXII, 6A (December, 1971), 3035-A-3036-A. XUM Order No. 72-956.

Identified attitudes toward women held by counselors, counselor educators, and teachers according to the counselors' sex, age, education, work setting, and marital status. Findings: (1) both men and especially women counselors rejected the intra-family oriented ideal woman; (2) women counselors were more accepting of working mothers than were men counselors; (3) men counselors found career women less attractive; (4) no difference in attitudes toward women were found in the 25-34 and the 35-44 age groups; (5) counselors over age 44 felt that women should be active outside the home but also viewed the ideal woman as being a wife and mother.

Naser, Abdallah Omar (Ed. D.). "THE EDUCATIONAL PHILOSOPHY OF CERTAIN PROSPECTIVE AMERICAN AND ARAB WOMEN TEACHERS." University of Florida, 1966. 174 pp. Source: DAI, XXVII, 9A (March, 1967), 2742-A-2743-A. XUM Order No. 67-3493.

American and Arab women in their senior year of teacher education completed a 5-point scale of 103 items of agreement. Psychological principles underlying the differences in educational philosophy were calculated. Scores showed that the Arab women had greater agreement on the items but for no important psychological reasons. Significant differences between the 2 groups' educational philosophy reflected the traditional outlook of Arab women and the liberal outlook of American women as well as their diverse historical backgrounds.

Nash, John Morton (Ed. D.). "PREDICTION OF ACADEMIC ACHIEVEMENT OF WOMEN AT A PRIVATE JUNIOR COLLEGE THROUGH USE OF CERTAIN INTELLECTIVE AND FAMILY RELATIONSHIPS MEASURES." Boston University School of Education, 1970. 185 pp. Source: DAI, XXXI, 5A (November, 1970), 2113-A-2114-A. XUM Order No. 70-22,479.

To predict academic achievement of 2 groups (295 and 300) of freshman women, this study used several measures of family relationships along with such intellectual evidence as high school grade point average and American College Testing Program scores. Both groups used 3 non-academic measures, including the Gilmore Sentence Completion Test developed for this study. Other family relationship tests were used separately to distinguish the 2 groups. Conclusions: (1) prediction of academic achievement improved significantly when non-intellective measures were combined with intellective measures; (2) the intellective factor most effective in predicting academic achievement was the high school grade point index; and (3) the only effective non-intellective predictor was the Gilmore Sentence Completion Test, which had high predictive validity.

Nauright, Lynda Parks (Ed. D.). "FACULTY DEVELOPMENT PROCEDURES AND PRACTICES IN PROGRAMS OF PROFESSIONAL NURSING EDUCATION." University of Georgia, 1975. 138 pp. Source: DAI, XXXVI, 12B, Part 1 (June, 1976), 6073-B-6074-B. XUM Order No. 76-13,976.

Nursing education administrators (59) and 112 faculty members in 65 nursing programs answered questionnaires concerning their faculty development. Nursing programs were found to be active in faculty development. The most feasible and effective practices for nursing faculty development were: (1) assigning new faculty to experienced teams; (2) financing faculty attendance at professional meetings;

(3) aiding graduate study; and (4) providing faculty handbooks. The
greatest drawbacks were lack of personnel, time, and money.

Naylor, Frank McClay (Ed. D.). "A STUDY OF THE SUPPLEMENTAL INCOMES
OF WOMEN TEACHERS IN THE PUBLIC SCHOOLS OF ALLEGHENY COUNTY, PENNSYLVANIA."
University of Pittsburgh, 1956. 261 pp. Source: DAI, XVI, 6 (1956),
1093-1094. XUM Order No. 16,519.

To supplement professional income, the average woman teachers worked
31.5 days during the summer, mostly in sales and clerical positions.
Reasons for supplemental jobs, in this order, were economic necessity,
good standard of living, avocational interest, and desire for luxuries.
Most supplemental incomes were spent for current expenses. Most of
the women strongly opposed expanding the school year but said they
would give up supplemental jobs if teachers' salaries were higher.
The majority concluded that the overall effect of supplemental working
was detrimental.

Neale, Nancy Alice Kester (D. S. W.). "WOMEN'S STUDIES IN SOCIAL WORK
EDUCATION: THE IMPACT OF A SOCIAL MOVEMENT ON CURRICULUM." University
of Utah, 1977. 374 pp. Source: DAI, XXXVIII, 4A (October, 1977), 2074-
A-2075-A. XUM Order No. 77-20,949.

This historical-descriptive-exploratory study provided comprehensive
information on women's studies as a new curriculum genre in social
work education. Used a survey form and a questionnaire to gather
data. Collected course outlines and bibliographies from 86% of U. S.
accredited undergraduate and graduate social work programs. Among
the extensive findings about social work courses in women's studies
were: (1) the courses had a common core of knowledge, similar concepts, and similar organizing principles; (2) a large body of literature was available; and (3) women studies faculties had positive
teaching experiences but found attitudes of male faculty, male students, and many administrators were negative.

Nederlander, Caren Elaine Berman (Ph. D.). "A SEX EDUCATION PROGRAM
FOR FEMALES INCORPORATING GRAPHIC EXPRESSION IN THE MODIFICATION OF SEXUAL
BEHAVIOR." University of Michigan, 1976. 404 pp. Source: DAI, XXXVII,
3A (September, 1976), 1411-A. XUM Order No. 76-19,203.

Art was one of the tools used in a self-awareness program intended to
change women's behavior and to heighten their perceptions of their
thoughts, feelings, and sensations in sexual functioning. This program produced significant changes in 10 volunteers, as measured on
pretests and post-tests.

Neidig, Marilyn Boyd (Ph. D.). "WOMEN APPLICANTS FOR ADMINISTRATIVE
POSITIONS: ATTITUDES HELD BY ADMINISTRATORS AND SCHOOL BOARDS." University of Iowa, 1973. 146 pp. Source: DAI, XXXIV, 6A (December, 1973),
2982-A-2983-A. XUM Order No. 73-30,959.

Among findings from questionnaires sent to school board members and
superintendents in Iowa's 50 largest school districts: (1) no significant relationships were found between board members and superintendents with sex as a selection criterion for superintendent, assistant
superintendent, junior and senior high principals, or elementary

principals; (2) sex was less important for elementary positions than for others; (3) board members rated women as more ambitious than did the superintendents; and (4) 71% of the superintendents would hire women as assistant superintendents, 42.9% as high school principals, and 92.9% as elementary principals.

Nelle, Susan Vaylle (Ph. D.). "COGNITIVE SOCIAL LEARNING OF SEX-ROLES AND SELF-CONCEPTS IN WOMEN." University of Washington, 1975. 124 pp. Source: DAI, XXXVII, 2A (August, 1976), 889-A-890-A. XUM Order No. 76-17,577.

Workshops for 31 women dealt with sex-role stereotypes that regard males as competent but lacking warmth and regard females as incompetent but warm and expressive. One assumption was that women who observed highly competent models would raise their own competency scores but would not have a drop in warmth and expressiveness score. Although results only partially supported this hypothesis, they did suggest that masculinity and femininity are separate and independent qualities.

Nelson, Flora Bina (Ed. D.). "PHILOSOPHICAL APPROACH TO THE DEVELOPMENT OF PHYSICAL EDUCATION PROGRAMS FOR WOMEN IN INDIA." New York University, 1950. 228 pp. Source: DAI, XI, 1 (1951), 145-147. XUM Order No. 2191.

This study attempted to formulate principles for a women's physical education program in India. Indian traditions separated mind and body, subordinated women, and neglected bodily needs. Goal of this physical education program was to use biology, psychology, and sociology in order to enhance the full development of Indian women's personalities and their physical well-being.

Nelson, Helen Young (Ph. D.). "FACTORS RELATED TO THE EXTENT OF MORTALITY AMONG HOME ECONOMICS STUDENTS IN CERTAIN COLLEGES OF MINNESOTA, WISCONSIN, AND IOWA DURING 1943-50." University of Minnesota, 1952. 141 pp. Source: DAI, XII, 3 (1952), 291. XUM Order No. 3654.

Home economics dropouts (2,075) from 14 colleges cited as reasons for leaving college, first, marriage, and second, financial problems. On the basis of their complaints about the home economics curriculum, these changes were recommended: (1) offer practical courses earlier; (2) eliminate prerequisites for elementary courses; and (3) use pretests to assure that students are placed in courses that will offer them new material and new skills.

Nelson, Linnea A. (Ed. D.). "A PROPOSED CURRICULUM FOR A SELECTED SENIOR MIDDLE SCHOOL IN CHINA." University of California, Berkeley, 1946. 284 pp. Source: Eells, p. 75; and UC, Berkeley.

In developing a curriculum for the Cheng Mei School for Girls, a projected senior middle mission school in Kinhwa, China, 5 areas of need were covered: (1) physical and mental health; (2) vocational training; (3) personal-social relationships; (4) citizenship education; and (5) character training.

Nelson, Lois Florence (Ed. D.). "COMPETENCY OF NURSING GRADUATES AS
PERCEIVED BY GRADUATES AND SUPERVISORS, IN TECHNICAL, COMMUNICATIVE AND
ADMINISTRATIVE SKILLS." University of South Dakota, 1975. 131 pp.
Source: DAI, XXXVI, 9B (March, 1976), 4385-B. XUM Order No. 76-2404.

Nursing graduates (329) and 209 of their supervisors gave their opinions of nursing graduates' competencies. Findings: (1) diploma nursing graduates rated themselves higher than did baccalaureate or associate degree graduates in overall competence, technical skills, and
administrative skills; (2) baccalaureate graduates rated themselves
higher in communication skills; (3) supervisors of baccalaureate
graduates rated them higher in overall competence, technical, communication, and administrative skills than did supervisors of the other
2 types of nurses; and (4) nursing graduates and supervisors differed
in their views of their overall competence, with the least difference
being between supervisors and baccalaureate graduates and the greatest
difference between supervisors and diploma graduates.

Neri, Emperatriz B. (Ed. D.). "A STUDY OF ADMISSIONS AND RELATED
ORIENTATION PRACTICES IN SELECTED BASIC COLLEGIATE SCHOOLS OF NURSING IN
THE UNITED STATES." Indiana University, 1957. 269 pp. Source: DAI,
XVII, 11 (November, 1957), 2571-2572. XUM Order No. 22,990.

Questionnaire data and first-hand inspection of the admissions and
orientation practices of 61 U. S. collegiate nursing schools revealed:
(1) some schools accepted students with academic or other deficiencies;
(2) better schools had no barriers because of marital status, race,
and sex; (3) no orientation programs were found for students who
transferred to nursing from another department in the same university;
and (4) some schools had inadequate health admissions requirements.

Nessler, Joan (Ph. D.). "AN EXPERIMENTAL STUDY OF METHODS ADAPTED TO
TEACHING LOW-SKILLED FRESHMAN WOMEN IN PHYSICAL EDUCATION." Pennsylvania
State University, 1961. 215 pp. Source: DAI, XXII, 7 (January, 1962),
2282. XUM Order No. 61-6802.

Low-skilled freshman girls (148) were divided into 3 groups: (1) 57
in an 8-week elementary games course; (2) 57 in isolated skills practice; and (3) 34 in regular physical education classes. In a follow-
up study 80 of the girls learned to play badminton. Findings: (1)
participation in the 8-week elementary games course adapted to poorly
skilled freshman girls was more advantageous than a regular physical
education class; (2) achievement in complex skill patterns did not
necessarily result from improved isolated skills; and (3) theoretical
knowledge of a skill was not related to performance of the skill.
Concluded that low-skills persons could be brought up to average
level, but instruction could not compensate for all inadequacies.

Neuman, Robert Paul (Ph. D.). "SOCIALISM, THE FAMILY AND SEXUALITY:
THE MARXIST TRADITION AND GERMAN SOCIAL DEMOCRACY BEFORE 1914." Northwestern University, 1972. 380 pp. Source: DAI, XXXIII, 6A (December,
1972), 2865-A-2866-A. XUM Order No. 72-32,525.

In pre-1914 Germany, the Social Democratic movement disproved Marxist
claims that capitalism was destroying the family and other institutions. Women and youth groups among Social Democrats fostered exten-

sive educational and cultural programs. Such educational activities
helped integrate workers into the German mainstream and reinforced
social institutions during Germany's transition from agrarianism to
urban industrialism.

Newby, Martha Florence Redmon (Ed. D.). "CONTINUING EDUCATION FOR
NURSES IN THE MARICOPA COUNTY COMMUNITY COLLEGE DISTRICT." Arizona State
University, 1974. 82 pp. Source: DAI, XXXV, 11A (May, 1975), 7017-A.
XUM Order No. 75-10,048.

This study of continuing education courses for nurses in Maricopa
County, AZ, community colleges revealed that: (1) the program met
many nurses' needs; (2) the program could not serve those desiring a
baccalaureate degree; and (3) nurses desired short-term workshops and
seminars in the future in addition to the existing semester-long
courses.

Newkirk, Gwendolyn Anita Jones (Ed. D.). "COMMUNITY EXPERIENCES IN
HOME ECONOMICS STUDENT TEACHING PROGRAMS IN SIX TEACHER EDUCATION INSTI-
TUTIONS IN NEW YORK STATE." Cornell University, 1961. 204 pp. Source:
DAI, XXII, 12, Part I (June, 1962), 4341. XUM Order No. 62-963.

Home economics student teaching programs at 6 New York State colleges
were compared and provisions by these colleges for student teachers
to have community experiences were analyzed. Findings: (1) the 6
home economics student teaching programs were similar; and (2) community experiences for student teachers were similar: (a) becoming acquainted with the community first hand, (b) locating various community resources, and (c) planning and conducting field trips.

Ngo, Natividad Anguluan (Ph. D.). "THE RELATIONSHIP BETWEEN INTEL-
LECTIVE AND BIOGRAPHICAL VARIABLES AND STUDENT ACHIEVEMENT IN SELECTED
ADN PROGRAMS IN MICHIGAN COMMUNITY COLLEGES, AND IN THE STATE BOARD TEST
POOL EXAMINATION FOR PROFESSIONAL NURSES." University of Michigan, 1972.
253 pp. Source: DAI, XXXIII, 11A (May, 1973), 6131-A-6132-A. XUM Order
No. 73-11,216.

Achievement of 284 students in associate degree nursing programs at 6
Michigan community colleges was significantly related to high school
grade point averages; to American College Test scores; and to high
school grades in mathematics, English, biology, and chemistry. Biographical variables significantly related to high achievement were:
(1) age (students over 30 made higher grades); (2) marital status
(married students did better); and (3) father's work (fathers of more
successful students were in professional, managerial, and clerical
posts).

Nichols, Glennadee Adele (Ed. D.). "AN EXPLORATOIN OF FACTORS ASSO-
CIATED WITH CAREER DECISIONS OF NOVICE ARMY NURSES." Columbia University,
1970. 254 pp. Source: DAI, XXXI, 7B (January, 1971), 4157-B-4158-B.
XUM Order No. 70-26,794.

The value of army-sponsored further education was one of several reasons that 17% of 181 novice army nurses intended to remain in the
service (7% undecided, 76% intended to leave).

Nihlen, Ann Sigrid (Ph. D.). "THE WHITE WORKING CLASS IN SCHOOL: A STUDY OF FIRST GRADE GIRLS AND THEIR PARENTS." University of New Mexico, 1976. 200 pp. Source: DAI, XXXVII, 10A (April, 1977), 6158-A. XUM Order No. 77-6565.

Thirteen first grade girls and their working class parents were studied. Author found that the girls thought education was important but not paramount to their futures and that sociability was most important in school. Sex stereotyping, absent in early schooling, was expected to become forceful in junior high school. Author concluded that, as long as schools continue to make educated professionals out of middle class youths and blue collar workers out of working class youths, reform of sex stereotyping will be impossible.

Nikkari, John Garton (Ph. D.). "FRESHMAN-TO-SENIOR PERSONALITY CHANGES IN BASIC COLLEGIATE STUDENT NURSES AS COMPARED TO CHANGES IN FEMALES IN A LIBERAL ARTS COLLEGE IN A LARGE MIDWESTERN STATE UNIVERSITY." University of Michigan, 1969. 382 pp. Source: DAI, XXXI, 2B (August, 1970), 774-B-775-B. XUM Order No. 70-14,607.

Studied the degree and type of personality changes in nursing students between their freshman and senior years. Nursing students were divided into groups, were compared with one another, and were compared with women liberal arts majors. Very few statistically significant differences were found among the student nurse groups. Other findings: (1) student nurses had fewer personality changes than did liberal arts students; (2) student nurses were more conservative, restrictive, and practical minded than liberal arts graduates; and (3) both senior nursing students and women liberal arts students became more liberal.

Noack, Janice A. (Ph. D.). "CATHOLIC SECONDARY EDUCATION AND FERTILITY VALUES: A STUDY OF CATHOLIC GIRLS IN SELECTED SCHOOLS IN THE WASHINGTON METROPOLITAN AREA." Catholic University of America, 1969. 261 pp. Source: DAI, XXX, 9A (March, 1970), 4033-A. XUM Order No. 70-4300.

Studied fertility values of female students in 7 Catholic high schools, including 1,615 girls who had an all-Catholic education and 412 girls who had some nonsectarian education. Conclusions: (1) the effect of Catholic secondary education upon girls' average family-size preference varied with the girls' having attended a Catholic elementary school; (2) girls in the all-Catholic group who received communion at least weekly were most influenced by church teachings; and (3) both groups favored lower fertility by the end of the senior year.

Noall, Sandra Hawkes (Ed. D.). "A HISTORY OF NURSING EDUCATION IN UTAH." University of Utah, 1969. 128 pp. Source: DAI, XXX, 8B (February, 1970), 3722-B. XUM Order No. 70-3387.

Traced the history of Utah nursing education from its beginnings when midwives accompanied the first settlers to 1965 when the American Nurses Association recommended that higher education institutions provide all nursing education. Some landmarks: (1) 1894, first nursing school established; (2) 1917, nursing standards and requirements set in a nursing registration law; (3) 1920, a qualifying examination for nurses established; (4) 1942, opening of first baccalaureate nursing program; and (5) 1953, opening of first associate degree program.

Noble, Jeanne L. (Ph. D.). "THE NEGRO WOMAN LOOKS AT HER COLLEGE EDUCATION." Columbia University Teachers College, 1955. Source: TCCU DIGESTS (1955), pp. 465-467.

Black women graduates (412) who lived in 6 cities in parts of the U. S. having the largest concentration of black college graduates evaluated their college experiences. The majority of black women said the following were most important for college to give a black woman: (1) vocational education; (2) citizenship education; and (3) education for marriage and family life. Black women graduates of white colleges were less utilitarian minded and more liberal arts minded than were those black women who graduated from black colleges.

Nobles, Brenda Hudson (Ph. D.). "SEX OF THE EXPERIMENTER AND SEX OF THE SUBJECT AS VARIABLES IN VERBAL LEARNING." University of Arkansas, 1973. 91 pp. Source: DAI, XXXIV, 5B (November, 1973), 2344-B. XUM Order No. 73-27,433.

Found that males and females learned more in an experimental setting when the experimenters (male and female) were perceived as attractive rather than unattractive.

Nofsker, Julia Frank (Ph. D.). "HOME ECONOMICS OBJECTIVES AS SHOWN IN A SURVEY OF EDUCATIONAL LITERATURE." University of Wisconsin, 1932. Source: Author.

Found among selected Wisconsin high school girls that home economics teachers' personalities in smaller schools with closer contacts influenced girls more than teachers in larger schools. The girls suggested that high school home economics provide more opportunities for: (1) student initiative; (2) individual differences; (3) more advanced work; (4) field trips; (5) outside speakers; (6) broader course of study; (7) academic rather than vocational credit; and (8) explanation of goals and purposes to appeal to high school boys and girls.

Noguera, Remedios (Ed. D.). "A PROPOSAL FOR A STUDENT PERSONNEL PROGRAM FOR THE PHILIPPINE WOMEN'S UNIVERSITY." Indiana University, 1954. 242 pp. Source: DAI, XIV, 4 (1954), 618-619. XUM Order No. 7908.

Guided by the view that universities are responsible for developing the whole person, this study applied student personnel findings from the literature and from U. S. universities' programs. Filipino cultural background and resources available at Philippine Women's University (PWU) were also considered. Concluded with proposals for student personnel services to be headed by a dean of students at PWU.

Noll, Nancy Lee (Ph. D.). "OPINIONS OF POLICY-MAKING OFFICIALS IN TWO-YEAR PUBLIC EDUCATIONAL INSTITUTIONS TOWARD THE EMPLOYMENT OF WOMEN ADMINISTRATORS." Arizona State University, 1973. 154 pp. Source: DAI, XXXIV, 3A (September, 1973), 1100-A-1101-A. XUM Order No. 73-20,447.

Data on women administrators in 181 2-year public community or junior colleges indicated that: (1) none were chief executives (presidents); (2) women as presidents of governing boards were in 6 states; (3) women as presidents of faculty were in 11 states; (4) policy required previous administrative experience for male or female candidates as

top administrators; (5) males were preferred over similarly qualified
females; and (6) female candidates were judged more on emotional stability than were males.

Nolting, Earl, Jr. (Ph. D.). "A STUDY OF FEMALE VOCATIONAL INTERESTS:
PRE-COLLEGE TO POST-GRADUATION." University of Minnesota, 1967. 236 pp.
Source: DAI, XXVIII, 6A (December, 1967), 2074-A-2075-A. XUM Order No.
67-14,637.

Vocational interest test scores and subsequent careers of 316 University of Minnesota females during and after graduation revealed that:
(1) occupations were highly related to academic majors in all areas
but art; (2) the percentage of employment was greater for those with
graduate degrees than undergraduate degrees; (3) fathers' educational
level was related to daughters' educational level; and (4) those in
medicine, library science, and art had more fathers who had gone to
college.

Norod, Elizabeth Frashure (Ed. D.). "EFFECTS OF SIMULATED INSTRUCTION
IN INTERPERSONAL RELATIONSHIPS ON VERBAL BEHAVIOR OF STUDENT NURSES."
University of Rochester, 1971. 160 pp. Source: DAI, XXXII, 3A (Septem-
ber, 1971), 1400-A-1401-A. XUM Order No. 71-22,333.

Behavioral changes were examined after freshman associate degree nursing students participated in a simulated experiment about interpersonal relationships. Experimental groups used programmed material
and showed significant gains in their ability to communicate empathe-
tic understanding, level of regard, unconditionality of regard, acceptance, and genuineness. Conclusions: (1) programmed instruction
in human relations skills was effective; and (2) the Interpersonal
Interaction Inventory was a valid measure of helping behavior.

Noronha, George Eric (Ph. D.). "BACKGROUNDS IN THE EDUCATION OF IN-
DIAN GIRLS." Catholic University of America, 1939. 235 pp. Source:
Published; Same Title; Washington, DC: The Catholic University of
America, 1939; pp. vii, 219-220.

Author concluded that only as Indian education combines western democracy and the best of eastern culture will its educational system be
adequate to the needs and capacities of all children. Only in this
context will women make intelligent and forceful contributions as
citizens, homemakers, and professionals. Chapters included: status
of women, disabilities of women, and the era of Gandhi.

Norris, Betty Norman (Ed. D.). "AN ANALYSIS OF POLICIES AND PRACTICES
OF ADVANCED PLACEMENT IN SELECTED BACCALAUREATE NURSING PROGRAMS THROUGH-
OUT THE UNITED STATES." University of Virginia, 1972. 183 pp. Source:
DAI, XXXIII, 7A (January, 1973), 3164-A-3165-A. XUM Order No. 72-33,248.

Analyzed policies and practices toward advanced placement in 88 U. S.
baccalaureate nursing programs. Major findings: (1) 79 programs provided ways to recognize previous knowledge; (2) advanced placement
was given more often in liberal arts than in nursing; (3) significant
differences in advanced standing credit existed between public and
private nursing programs and between large and small nursing programs;
(4) variations were extreme in courses included in advanced placement

and in type of students included in advanced placement; (5) provisions were limited for assisting students to achieve advanced placement and for giving information about advancement placement; and (6) limited use of standardized tests to give advanced placement.

Norton, Naoma Peninger (Ed. D.). "THE HOME ECONOMIST-TEACHER AND HOMEMAKER." Columbia University Teachers College, 1956. Source: TCCU DIGESTS (1956), pp. 471-472.

Women trained as home economists who became homemakers and then turned to teaching home economics needed: (1) updating in teaching procedures and in home economics developments; (2) guidance, short reference courses, workshops, and supervisory help; (3) knowledge of psychology and guidance of teenagers; and (4) the cooperation and approval of their families in order to be effective as both teachers and homemakers.

Notter, Lucille E. (Ed. D.). "PROPOSALS FOR THE USE AND TRAINING OF PUBLIC HEALTH NURSES AIDES." Columbia University Teachers College, 1956. Source: TCCU DIGESTS (1956), pp. 474-475.

Found that despite the need for help only 23 public health nursing agencies employed nurses aides. Data indicated that professional nurses in charge of in-service education should plan on-the-job training for nurses aides in such skills as elementary home nursing care and housekeeping for the sick. A suggested instructional plan was included.

Novak, Edward Ladis (Ed. D.). "THE RELATIONSHIP BETWEEN ACADEMIC PERFORMANCE, TEST ANXIETY, RACE, SEX, SCHOLASTIC ABILITY, AND SCHOOL ORGANIZATION OF PRE-ADOLESCENT PUBLIC SCHOOL STUDENTS: A MULTI-VARIABLE APPROACH." University of Akron, 1973. 231 pp. Source: DAI, XXXIV, 1A (July, 1973), 99-A. XUM Order No. 73-16,437.

Students' sex made no significant difference in academic performance in this study of 132 4th graders and 74 non-graded counterparts from a middle class suburban community. But 99 females had a significantly higher score for test anxiety. Females also had significantly higher average scores for scholastic ability.

Novak, Sigrid Gerda Scholtz (Ph. D.). "IMAGES OF WOMANHOOD IN THE WORKS OF GERMAN FEMALE DRAMATISTS: 1892-1918." Johns Hopkins University, 1971. 281 pp. Source: DAI, XXXIV, 7A (January, 1974), 4276-A-4277-A. XUM Order No. 73-31,231.

Restricted educational and professional opportunities are among the many problems of women examined by the author in some 50 plays written by women in Germany between 1892 and 1918 and housed in the Loewenberg collection, Johns Hopkins University Library.

Nowakowski, Marie Elizabeth (Ph. D.). "THE EFFECT OF INSTRUCTION IN OCCUPATIONAL INFORMATION AND GROUP VOCATIONAL EXPLORATION ON THE VOCATIONAL ATTITUDES OF HIGH SCHOOL GIRLS." Catholic University of America, 1974. 102 pp. Source: DAI, XXXV, 2A (August, 1974), 826-A. XUM Order No. 74-16,709.

Classroom instruction in career information was given to one experimental group of girls. Discussion of vocations was conducted with another experimental group of girls. Findings: (1) neither group's scores changed significantly on measures of vocational maturity, self-concept, or vocational concept; but (2) the discussion group had a heightened awareness of both material and non-material dimensions of work value.

Nowlin, Billie Hopper (Ed. D.). "OCCUPATIONAL HOME ECONOMICS AS RELATED TO SELF CONCEPT, ACHIEVEMENT, AND HOMEMAKING." Texas Woman's University, 1974. 139 pp. Source: DAI, XXXVI, 9B (March, 1976), 4406-B. XUM Order No. 76-5063.

Comparisons of 122 occupational and 135 homemaking students in an occupational home economics high school class showed differences in educational expectations, credits in home economics, employment of mothers, reasons for taking the class, enrollment according to sex, and achievement.

Nuckols, Margaret Lynn (Ph. D.). "A COMPARATIVE ANALYSIS OF SELECTED UNITED NATIONS DOCUMENTS RELATED TO EDUCATIONAL OPPORTUNITIES FOR WOMEN DURING THE FIRST DEVELOPMENT DECADE (1960-1970)." Florida State University, 1975. 135 pp. Source: DAI, XXXVI, 6A (December, 1975), 3454-A. XUM Order No. 75-26,802.

Analysis of women's education trends in United Nations documents (1960-70) showed that: (1) educational opportunities increased because of more positive attitudes and greater social acceptance, especially in developed nations; (2) women chose an increasingly wider range of major fields of study; (3) obstacles were the same in developed and developing nations; (4) while women in developing nations had fewer baccalaureate degrees, they had more opportunities for leadership than did women with baccalaureate degrees in developed nations; (5) women everywhere received lower salaries than men; and (6) although women's activity in economic and social development increased, their participation was still limited and the level of responsibility was still comparatively low.

Nunley, Joe Edwin (Ed. D.). "A HISTORY OF THE CUMBERLAND FEMALE COLLEGE, McMINNVILLE, TENNESSEE." University of Tennessee, 1965. 153 pp. Source: DAI, XXVI, 8 (February, 1966), 4423. XUM Order No. 66-186.

Chartered as a degree-granting women's college in 1850, Cumberland Female College in 1853 offered primary, preparatory, and college courses. The 1853 college curriculum emphasized Latin, Greek, and mathematics and after 3 years' study culminated in the Mistress of Arts degree. By 1881 the curriculum had modern languages, social sciences, and sciences. Other degrees available in 1881 were English Mistress of Arts (only 1 foreign language) and Mistress of English Literature (no foreign language). By 1890 bookkeeping and dictation were taught as were such popular non-degree courses as art, music, mechanics, surveying, and speech. The school ceased to exist by century's end.

Nunn, Helen Cleola Robinson (Ph. D.). "AN EXPLORATORY STUDY OF ADULT HOMEMAKING EDUCATION IN RELATION TO TEACHER PREPARATION AND PROGRAM

PLANNING." Cornell University, 1966. 126 pp. Source: DAI, XXVII, 3A (September, 1966), 647-A. XUM Order No. 66-7843.

This study of 200 Arkansas home economics teachers who had taught adult homemaking classes showed: (1) that program planning and teacher evaluation were important aspects of teacher effectiveness; and (2) that pre-service and in-service education, especially about working with adults, would have reduced the high dropout rate in adult home-making courses.

Nuzum, Robert Edward (Ph. D.). "INFERRED PARENTAL IDENTIFICATION AND PERCEIVED PARENTAL RELATIONSHIP AS RELATED TO CAREER- AND HOMEMAKING-ORIENTATION IN ABOVE-AVERAGE ABILITY COLLEGE WOMEN." Washington State University, 1970. 114 pp. Source: DAI, XXXI, 6A (December, 1970), 2689-A-2690-A. XUM Order No. 70-24,992.

A random sample of above average freshman and sophomore women were divided according to standardized test scores into career-oriented (38) and homemaker-oriented (37) groups. Findings: (1) homemaker-oriented women had more pleasurable relationships with their fathers than did career-oriented women; and (2) both groups of women had similar relationships with their mothers. Conclusion: a positive, affective relationship with the father seems conducive to homemaker orientation in women.

Nygard, Melissa Wilcox Farley (Ph. D.). "EFFECT OF CONSCIOUSNESS-RAISING GROUPS VERSUS LECTURES ABOUT WOMEN ON THE PERSONALITIES AND CAREER INTERESTS AND HOMEMAKING INTERESTS OF FEMALE STUDENTS IN NURSING." University of Iowa, 1973. 188 pp. Source: DAI, XXXIV, 6A (December, 1973), 3151-A. XUM Order No. 73-30,963.

Compared a lecture approach and consciousness-raising approaches to changing "feminist behaviors" of 45 nursing students. On several standardized scales of behavior, no significant differences were found in relation to the different experimental approaches used. But results of an assertiveness measure suggested that those women in the consciousness-raising groups responded significantly more as-sertively to a male chauvinist than they did to a female chauvinist.

O'Brien, Sister Sheila Mary (Ed. D.). "CONGRUENCE OF GOALS AT A LIBERAL ARTS COLLEGE FOR WOMEN." Indiana University, 1975. 177 pp. Source: DAI, XXXVI, 9A (March, 1976), 5874-A. XUM Order No. 76-6337.

Findings on an institutional goals inventory administered to faculty, administrators, trustees, part-time and full-time students of the col-lege were: (1) most respondents were in agreement about the college's present purposes; (2) agreement was greater on most important goals and least important goals than on goals of medium importance; and (3) all groups agreed upon the rank order given to a new reordering of the college's priorities.

Obst, Frances Melanie (Ed. D.). "A STUDY OF SELECTED PSYCHOMETRIC CHARACTERISTICS OF HOME ECONOMICS AND NON-HOME ECONOMICS WOMEN AT THE UNIVERSITY OF CALIFORNIA, LOS ANGELES." University of California, Los Angeles, 1955. 70 pp. Source: Abstract from Dissertation.

Wanting to improve the effectiveness of advising and counseling for
home economics majors, the author compared a group of home economics
students with a group of non-home economics women students. Findings
on 4 standardized tests of interest and personality revealed that the
home economics majors differed fundamentally and significantly from
the non-majors in personality, interest, and ability. Conclusion:
(1) the home economics department should use additional tests in order to refine data about home economics majors; and (2) these data
should guide counselors in advising prospective majors and in helping
them choose areas of specialization.

O'Byrne, John Gerard (Ph. D.). "EFFECTS OF KOHLBERGIAN AND ROGERIAN
TREATMENTS ON THE MORAL DEVELOPMENT AND LOGICAL REASONING OF ADOLESCENT
GIRLS." Catholic University of America, 1976. 172 pp. Source: DAI,
XXXVI, 10B (April, 1976), 5312-B-5313-B. XUM Order No. 76-5499.

To aid moral development education, separate techniques advocated by
Roger and Kohlberg were tried on 1,250 Catholic girls aged 14-16 in
Washington, DC. Implications were applied to what school counselors
could do in advancing moral development in students.

Odita, Florence Chinyere Uwanda (Ph. D.). "DIFFERENCES IN PAY, PRO-
MOTION, JOB TITLE, AND OTHER RELATED FACTORS BETWEEN EMPLOYED MALE AND
FEMALE COLLEGE GRADUATES AS INDICATORS OF SEX DISCRIMINATION." Ohio
State University, 1972. 152 pp. Source: DAI, XXXIII, 2B (August, 1972),
945-B. XUM Order No. 72-20,997.

Major findings: (1) the difference in pay between males (they earned
more) and females was not statistically significant; (2) males were
underutilized more often than were females; (3) males received more
fellowships and scholarships than did females; and (4) no significant
difference in job behavior was observed. Conclusion: though sex
discrimination exists, it is not of the magnitude claimed in the literature.

Odom, Kathrine Pool (Ph. D.). "COMPARATIVE STUDY OF OLDER AND YOUNG-
ER WOMEN ENROLLED IN AN UNDERGRADUATE DEGREE PROGRAM AT THE OHIO STATE
UNIVERSITY." Ohio State University, 1974. 151 pp. Source: DAI, XXXV,
8A (February, 1975), 5033-A-5034-A. XUM Order No. 75-3159.

Older college women (over age 25) performed differently on vocational
interest tests than did younger college women. Intellectual stimulation as a reason for being in college was given by 40.2% of the
older women and 24.1% of the younger women; 59.8% of the older women
were there to learn an occupation or profession. Only 26.5% of the
older women chose a degree program similar to their previous choice
at age 18. The groups did not differ in their feminine-masculine
interests, in academic achievement, or in their majority wish (80%)
to combine homemaking and career.

O'Donnell, Beatrice Olson (Ph. D.). "DISCREPANCIES BETWEEN BELIEFS
OF LEADERS IN HOMEMAKING EDUCATION IN MICHIGAN AND PRACTICES IN LOCAL
HOMEMAKING PROGRAMS." Michigan State College, 1954. 412 pp. Source:
DAI, XIV, 9 (1954), 1312-1313. XUM Order No. 8507.

Data from administrators, homemaking teachers, pupils, and their parents generally supported the hypothesis that discrepancies existed between beliefs of leaders in homemaking education and actual practices in local homemaking programs. Discrepancies between beliefs and practices were greatest in: (1) home and school cooperation; and (2) use of certain teaching-learning methods.

O'Donnell, Jo Anne (Ed. D.). "A STUDY OF MAJORS AND CAREER ASPIRATIONS OF A SELECTED SAMPLE OF UNDERGRADUATE WOMEN IN THE UNIVERSITY SETTING." Washington State University, 1976. 121 pp. Source: DAI, XXXVII, 6A (December, 1976), 3454-A-3455-A. XUM Order No. 76-27,751.

While 2 groups of 20 senior women stated a preference for combining homemaking with a career, they did see child care as limiting their careers. They were finally convinced that child care responsibilities could not be combined successfully with a full-time career.

Ohlson, Virginia M. (Ph. D.). "NURSING EDUCATION AS A FORM OF ADULT SOCIALIZATION." University of Chicago, 1969. Source: Author.

Unmarried female students (450) aged 17-23 in 6 nursing schools (2 Catholic, 2 Protestant, 2 secular; 3 hospital-based and 3 collegiate) provided data about their future roles as nurses and adult women. Findings: (1) significant relationships were found between role orientation scores and the students' religious preferences, religiosity, social class, and parents' professions; (2) 16 significant differences in female role orientation scores and 21 differences in nurse role orientation scores were found between baccalaureate and diploma students and between students in religious or sectarian schools. Conclusions: (1) to assure student nurses' concern about care giving, nursing schools should orient students toward people rather than toward tasks early in the nursing course; and (2) to orient student nurses toward a career woman's role, students should have opportunities to explore professional and personal questions with married nurses who are successfully combining family and a career.

Olds, Claire Marie (Ed. D.). "SOME IMMEDIATE EFFECTS OF TWO METHODS OF PRESENTING INFORMATION ABOUT THE MULTIPLE ROLES OF WOMEN TO SELECTED COLLEGE SOPHOMORE WOMEN." University of Denver, 1966. 127 pp. Source: DAI, XXVII, 12A (June, 1967), 4102-A. XUM Order No. 67-6868.

Results were inconclusive in comparing two methods of giving information on women's multiple roles to 2 groups of 100 sophomore women. The group given the information without follow-up discussions seemed to do somewhat better on the tests.

O'Leary, Joan Grace (Ed. D.). "OPINIONS OF THE EDUCATIONAL NEEDS OF THE PRACTICING NURSE." Columbia University Teachers College, 1975. 148 pp. Source: DAI, XXXVI, 10B (April, 1976), 4946-B-4947-B. XUM Order No. 76-7783.

Compared data from practicing nurses and from in-service nurse educators about the educational needs of nurses in 15 New York state community hospitals. Even though the 2 groups disagreed on 32% of possible program topics, they agreed that further training in emer-

gency services, coronary care, and intensive care nursing was needed.
Their opinions were the same on teaching methods and location for in-
service classes but differed somewhat about the best time to hold in-
service classes. Conclusion: nurse educators and practicing nurses
must work together to build the kind of in-service program nurses
need.

O'Leary, Virginia Elizabeth (Ph. D.). "THE WORK ACCULTURATION OF 72
BLACK WOMEN INTO THE LABOR FORCE: TRAINEE ORIENTATION." Wayne State
University, 1969. 97 pp. Source: DAI, XXXII, 7A (January, 1972), 4110-
A. XUM Order No. 71-29,974.

Two purposes of on-the-job orientation sessions with newly hired
black females previously unemployed were: (1) to help the newly
hired women to accept the values (such as regularity of attendance
and interaction with supervisors) necessary to hold the job; and (2)
to build more positive self concepts. Results: the women did not
experience a positive shift of attitudes toward work; instead their
level of aspiration and expectation was raised to the extent that
many left their jobs with little evidence of regret.

Olesen, Virginia Lee (Ph. D.). "SEX ROLE DEFINITIONS AMONG COLLEGE
UNDERGRADUATES: A STUDY OF STANFORD FRESHMEN." Stanford University,
1961. 200 pp. Source: DAI, XXII, 10 (April, 1962), 3761-3762. XUM
Order No. 62-323.

Women students demanded strongly that males actively control their
immediate surroundings and show socially mature behavior. Males expected much less of females in regard to these 2 behaviors. Men made
significantly clearer distinctions between sex roles than did women.
Men and women agreed more about male roles than about female roles.
Conclusions: (1) ambiguities existed about the female sex role; and
(2) sex-role orientations of working class students agreed with those
of middle class students.

Olheiser, Sister Mary David (Ph. D.). "DEVELOPMENT OF A SISTER
TEACHER INTEREST SCALE FOR THE STRONG VOCATIONAL INTEREST BLANK FOR WO-
MEN." Boston College, 1962. Source: Author.

Using the Strong Vocational Interest Blank for Women as a model, the
author developed the Sister Teacher Interest Scale. The scale in-
vestigates whether or not women applying for admission to religious
teaching communities have interest patterns similar to those of successful Catholic sister teachers.

O'Keefe, Sister Maureen (Ed. D.). "MENTAL HEALTH EDUCATION FOR RELI-
GIOUS WOMEN." Loyola University (Chicago, IL), 1962. 203 pp. Source:
Dissertation, pp. 171-177.

Analytical study covering: (1) "An Estimate of the Current Status
of Mental Health Education for Religious Women"; (2) a detailed examination of the present status of religious (nuns) living in convents;
and (3) specific suggestions for implementing "Units of Study in
Mental Health Education for Religious Women."

O'Koren, Marie Louise (Ed. D.). "THE EFFECT OF PROGRAMMED INSTRUC-
TION IN HUMAN RELATIONS UPON THE NURSING STUDENT'S PERCEPTION OF THE
IDEAL NURSE-PATIENT RELATIONSHIP AS A FUNCTION OF OPENNESS." University
of Alabama, 1964. 142 pp. Source: DAI, XXV, 7 (January, 1965), 3916-
3917. XUM Order No. 64-12,772.

It was hypothesized but found not to be statistically significant
that programmed instruction in human relations would help 44 nursing
students' perception of their openness to an ideal nurse-patient relationship.

Okrant, Mark Jay (Ed. D.). "AN EXAMINATION OF THE SIGNIFICANCE OF
EDUCATIONAL AND REGIONAL FACTORS IN EXPLAINING WOMEN'S INTERCOLLEGIATE
ATHLETIC PROGRAM QUALITY." Oklahoma State University, 1975. 117 pp.
Source: DAI, XXXVI, 11A (May, 1976), 7643-A. XUM Order No. 76-9740.

Further research was recommended on the question pursued in this
study: to what extent, if at all, are winning college women athletic
programs affected by the academic quality of the institutions and
their locations?

Okun, Barbara Frank (Ph. D.). "A STUDY OF THE VARIABLES AFFECTING
THE OCCUPATIONAL CHOICE OF WOMEN 12-20 YEARS AFTER COLLEGE GRADUATION."
Northwestern University, 1970. 228 pp. Source: DAI, XXXI, 11A (May,
1971), 5960-A. XUM Order No. 71-1932.

Found among 55 Northwestern University women who had graduated 12 to
20 years before, no significant differences between (1) undergraduate
major and current occupation and (2) between post-college work experience and current occupation (except those who had consistently been
teachers). Their major problems were: (1) guilt over excessive time
away from families; (2) role conflict between homemaking and career;
and (3) fatigue and shortage of time.

O'Neill, Mary F. (Ph. D.). "A STUDY OF NURSING STUDENT VALUES." University of Chicago, 1972. 104 pp. Source: Dissertation.

Nursing students had: (1) significantly higher social value scores
than students in any other field; and (2) value patterns very similar
to those of faculty members.

O'Neill, Sister Mary Bernice (Ph. D.). "AN EVALUATION OF THE CURRICU-
LA OF A SELECTED GROUP OF CATHOLIC WOMEN'S COLLEGES." Saint Louis University, 1937. 591 pp. Source: Dissertation, pp. 546-551.

Identified the following trends in 9 Catholic women's colleges: (1)
increasing emphasis on the social sciences; (2) increasing numbers
of specialized professional departments; and (3) continuing use of a
general curriculum similar to that of other colleges, both Catholic
and non-Catholic.

O'Neill, Patrick Terence Hugh (Ph. D.). "SELF-ESTEEM AND BEHAVIOR
OF GIRLS WITH CONVERGENT AND DIVERGENT COGNITIVE ABILITIES IN TWO TYPES
OF SCHOOLS." Yale University, 1974. 56 pp. Source: DAI, XXXVI, 1B
(July, 1975), 451-B. XUM Order No. 75-15,367.

Girls from 3 open space and 3 conventional elementary schools were
rated on divergent and convergent thinking ability, self-esteem, and
behavior. Findings: (1) type of school was not related to the behavior of girls high in convergent thinking ability and self-esteem;
but (2) girls with high divergent thinking ability showed high self-
esteem in open space schools and low self-esteem in conventional
schools. Conclusion: since innovative programs will not help all
children equally, students' individual characteristics should be a
factor in program design.

Oppenheim, Irene Gartner (Ph. D.). "A STUDY OF THE CONSUMER ROLE OF
A SAMPLE OF YOUNG ADOLESCENT GIRLS IN GRADES SEVEN, EIGHT, AND NINE IN
IRVINGTON, NEW JERSEY." New York University, 1961. 475 pp. Source:
DAI, XXII, 2 (August, 1961), 559. XUM Order No. Mic61-2563.

This study of the purchases of 72 urban junior high school girls
grouped by social class found that social class had no significant
effect on their expenditures. The girls' spending increased with
each age level. The only family purchases influenced by the girls
were for food and soft goods. Conclusion: these data can help in
planning junior high consumer education.

Oppert, Judith Richards (Ed. D.). "THE DEVELOPMENT AND PUBLICATION
IN A PROFESSIONAL JOURNAL OF A CORRESPONDENCE COURSE ENTITLED: THE HOME
ECONOMICS TEACHER AND METRICS." University of Illinois at Urbana-Cham-
paign, 1976. 332 pp. Source: DAI, XXXVII, 10A (April, 1977), 6424-A.
XUM Order No. 77-9129.

A metrics course designed for home economics teachers was offered by
correspondence, with lessons published in a professional magazine.
The study dealt with: (1) the process of preparing the lessons; and
(2) reactions and characteristics of enrollees, dropouts, and journal
subscribers who did not enroll. Reasons course completers took the
course: (1) to serve as a resource person; (2) to advance their
salary; and (3) to renew a teaching certificate or to advance professionally.

Orbach, Noreen Rochelle Feldman (Ph. D.). "THE EVOLUTION OF A PRO-
FESSIONAL: THE CASE OF WOMEN IN DENTISTRY." University of Illinois at
Chicago Circle, 1977. 195 pp. Source: DAI, XXXVIII, 1A (July, 1977),
492-A. XUM Order No. 77-15,332.

In training and practice women dentists felt that male students,
instructors, and patients scrutinized and doubted them. Faculty did
not encourage female students to participate fully or to strive for
excellence. Female students did not have female instructors as role
models, or as empathizers, or as advisers. Concluded that women in
dentistry are not given the opportunity to fully develop a professional self-image.

Orloff, Lee Judith (Ph. D.). "SEX DIFFERENCES IN COGNITIVE DIFFEREN-
TIATION." Boston University Graduate School, 1977. 143 pp. Source:
DAI, XXXVII, 12B, Part 1 (June, 1977), 6342-B-6343-B. XUM Order No. 77-
11,143.

Investigated the hypothesis that self-image disparity and sex-role
identity are more significant factors in cognitive differentiation

than age and sex. Some findings: (1) conformity to traditional sex roles was found for girls but not for boys; (2) adjustments in early adolescence were significantly related to the development of field dependence, magnitude of self-image disparity, and conformity to traditional sex-role identity; and (3) differences between the sexes attributed to genetic factors might be caused by differences in the experiences of girls and boys.

Orr, Milton Lee (Ph. D.). "THE STATE-SUPPORTED COLLEGES FOR WOMEN." George Peabody College for Teachers, 1930. 229 pp. Source: GPCFT CONTRIBUTIONS No. 91, pp. 218-221.

Curricula of the 8 state-supported colleges for women, all in the South, reflected various emphases--liberal arts, vocational education (most often teacher training), and homemaking education. Histories of these colleges showed the South's allegiance to state support for higher education and for separate institutions for the sexes. Their vocational slant was one consequence of the South's economic stringencies.

Osborn, Barbara Louise (Ph. D.). "THE DEVELOPMENT OF AN INSTRUMENT TO DETERMINE VALUE PATTERNS OF HOMEMAKING TEACHERS." Cornell University, 1960. 225 pp. Source: DAI, XXI, 12 (June, 1961), 3679-3680. XUM Order No. Mic 61-1007.

Assuming a relationship between values patterns and teaching effectiveness, the author administered a values test to 200 homemaking teachers, 94 student teachers, and 37 business home economists. Found that: (1) the values test was reliable; and (2) responses were similar from student teachers, business home economists, and teachers.

Osborn, Ruth Helm (Ed. D.). "CHARACTERISTICS, MOTIVATION, AND PROBLEMS OF MATURE MARRIED WOMEN COLLEGE STUDENTS: A STATUS STUDY OF SELECTED STUDENTS AT THE GEORGE WASHINGTON UNIVERSITY." George Washington University, 1963. 312 pp. Source: Abstract from Dissertation.

This descriptive study of 221 married women students aged 30 or older revealed that 57% were employed full-time or part-time. Their problems were lack of time, budgeting time, mental strain, and physical tiredness. Chief reasons for seeking degrees were: (1) personal growth and self improvement; (2) enjoyment of learning; and (3) professional growth.

Osborne, Joan Skolnick (Ed. D.). "CLASS AND SEX: A SIMULATION MODEL IN WOMEN'S HISTORY." University of Massachusetts, 1977. 276 pp. Source: DAI, XXXVIII, 1A (July, 1977), 196-A-197-A. XUM Order No. 77-15,106.

Students in groups participated in a simulation model college course in women's history. The exercise challenged participating students' attitudes, biases, and interclass relationships, which the author believed paralleled the general literature describing the women's movement as based on middle class female experiences. The model brought in social and economic influences in addition to biological considerations and was used as a teaching device.

Osmond, Frederick Bramwell (Ed. D.). "ATTITUDES OF SPECIFIC GROUPS
IN SELECTED CALIFORNIA COMMUNITIES REGARDING FEMALE PARTICIPATION IN
HIGH SCHOOL INTERSCHOLASTIC PROGRAMS." University of the Pacific, 1977.
264 pp. Source: DAI, XXXVIII, 2A (August, 1977), 579-A-580-A. XUM Order No. 77-16,657.

Findings from male and female coaches, male and female students, and
parents at 5 large and 5 small California high schools: (1) all believed interscholastic athletics to be as important for girls as for
boys; (2) disagreed about allowing females to play contact sports;
(3) disagreed about equalizing reductions should funding become a
problem; and (4) all said that girls' and boys' interscholastic programs were not equal.

O'Toole, Lela (Ph. D.). "THE PURPOSES AND ORGANIZATION RELATING TO
LARGE HOME ECONOMICS UNITS IN TEN LAND-GRANT COLLEGES AND UNIVERSITIES
WITH PROPOSALS FOR EFFECTIVE ORGANIZATION." Ohio State University, 1950.
117 pp. Source: Ohio State University, ABSTRACTS OF DOCTORAL DISSERTA-
TIONS, No. 61 (1951), pp. 341-347.

This study of home economics units in 10 land-grant colleges and universities concluded with specific proposals for effective organization to: (1) further their functions; (2) promote home economics;
and (3) promote democratic values.

Ott, Timothy Joseph (Ph. D.). "ANDROGYNY, SEX ROLE STEREOTYPES, SEX
ROLE ATTITUDES AND SELF-ACTUALIZATION AMONG COLLEGE WOMEN." University
of Notre Dame, 1976. 111 pp. Source: DAI, XXXVII, 6A (December, 1976),
3527-A. XUM Order No. 76-27,292.

This study of 49 college women showed a significant correlation between: (1) their non-sex bias (androgyny) and inner direction; (2)
inner direction and sex role stereotypes; (3) non-sex bias and sex
role stereotypes; (4) non-sex bias and sex role attitudes; and (5)
sex role attitudes and sex role stereotypes.

Ozimek, Dorothy (Ed. D.). "A FOLLOW-UP STUDY OF THE GRADUATES OF
THE GENERIC BACCALAUREATE NURSING PROGRAM OF SETON HALL UNIVERSITY."
Columbia University, 1965. 198 pp. Source: DAI, XXVI, 8 (February,
1966), 4585. XUM Order No. 65-14,980.

Curriculum implications for nursing faculty drawn from a follow-up
study of 150 nurses who graduated between 1957 and 1965: (1) provide students with more critical thinking skills; (2) aid their knowing where and how to seek new knowledge; (3) teach nursing principles
based on the sciences and the humanities; and (4) encourage further
education through workshops and other short courses, especially for
inactive nurses who return to nursing.

Paduano, Mary Ann (Ed. D.). "NURSING EDUCATION IN SPAIN IN 1974."
Columbia University Teachers College, 1975. 200 pp. Source: DAI,
XXXVI, 8B (February, 1976), 3872-B. XUM Order No. 76-3269.

Study based on literature search and visits and interviews in 3 private and 3 government nursing schools in Spain found that: (1) the
curriculum was based on one approved by the education ministry in

1953; (2) curriculum implementation varied, with schools supplementing number of courses and hours of theory classes; (3) 5 of the 6 curricula failed to meet European standards; (4) progress was hindered by lack of strong professional association, insufficient communcation between nurses and education ministry, and nurses not reprsented on decision making groups; and (5) a new curriculum plan by the national nurses' association providing for university preparation of nurses was under consideration by the education ministry.

Page, Jean Vivian (Ed. D.). "WOMEN AND THE DOCTORATE AT TEACHERS COLLEGE, COLUMBIA UNIVERSITY." Columbia University Teachers College, 1959. Source: TCCU DIGESTS (1959), pp. 548-549.

Women with doctorates or working for doctorates revealed that: (1) they had received very little financial aid for their doctoral studies; and (2) average salaries of those with doctorates would not cover expenses incurred for at least 10 years. The majority felt the doctorate was valuable despite their belief that it would not assure them equal opportunities when competing with men.

Page, Mary Jean (Ed. D.). "A DESCRIPTIVE ANALYSIS OF SELECTED ATTITUDES, INTERESTS, AND PERSONALITY CHARACTERISTICS OF MATURE COLLEGE WOMEN." North Texas State University, 1971. 194 pp. Source: DAI, XXXII, 7A (January, 1972), 3699-A-3700-A. XUM Order No. 72-4101.

Undergraduate college women (184), aged 32 or older, completed a questionnaire and standardized measures of vocational interest, personal preference, and values. Most (72%) intended to become teachers and almost all were preparing for work. A significant correlation was found between husband's attitude and part-time or full-time employment. Author recommended that the university cater to the needs of mature women students.

Pagel, Irene Shirley (Ed. D.). "THE PROCESS OF CURRICULUM CHANGE IN THREE BACCALAUREATE SCHOOLS OF NURSING." Columbia University, 1971. 249 pp. Source: DAI, XXXII, 2A (August, 1971), 727-A-728-A. XUM Order No. 71-20,024.

Studied 3 baccalaureate nursing schools which had recently adopted and implemented a major curriculum change. Some findings: (1) subject matter, not students, were the focal point of the change; (2) faculties accepted full responsibility for curriculum change; and (3) covert and overt resistance to change was evident. Among recommendations: (1) an in-service program should assist faculty in implementing new curriculum; and (2) more people affected by curriculum change (students, patients, other involved groups) should be involved in planning for curriculum change.

Pagel, Lou Helen (Ed. D.). "CORRELATES OF ACHIEVEMENT CONFLICT IN COLLEGE WOMEN." University of California, Los Angeles, 1975. 171 pp. Source: DAI, XXXVI, 10A (April, 1976), 6563-A. XUM Order No. 76-9006.

Fear of success (FOS) has been suggested as barring young, intelligent women from fulfilling their potential. Gifted low FOS senior women seemed to be associated with a broader sex-role definition. Even though their FOS appeared to be associated with dissatisfaction

with self, the 202 senior women were maintaining high levels of
career aspirations.

Paley, Marlene Gershman (Ph. D.). "THE EVOLUTION OF A FEMINIST THER-
APIST." Union Graduate School, 1976. 207 pp. Source: DAI, XXXVII, 9B
(March, 1977), 4697-B. XUM Order No. 77-4333.

In this autobiographical study, the author: (1) traced her own
growth as a feminist therapist; (2) told of incidents leading to formation of a women's group whose members became more assertive after
3 months; and (3) concluded with a personal evaluation, affirming
her joy in being a woman and her desire to be an effective role model
for other women.

Paolucci, Beatrice (Ed. D.). "DECISION-MAKING IN RELATION TO MANAGE-
MENT IN CLASSES OF HOME ECONOMICS BY BEGINNING TEACHERS." Michigan State
University, 1956. 203 pp. Source: DAI, XVII, 6 (1957), 1326-1327. XUM
Order No. 20,082.

Decisions on class management made by beginning teachers in home economics: (1) were related to teachers' knowledge, skills, and information available; and (2) were based on their past experiences.
Found that the decisions varied in number but not in kinds and that
satisfactions from decisions tended to be more alike than different.

Parker, Aileen Webber (Ed. D.). "A COMPARATIVE STUDY OF SELECTED
FACTORS IN THE VOCATIONAL DEVELOPMENT OF COLLEGE WOMEN." Indiana Univer-
sity, 1961. 118 pp. Source: DAI, XXII, 4 (October, 1961), 1087-1088.
XUM Order No. 61-3220.

Undergraduate women divided into career-oriented, marriage-oriented,
and mixed groups were compared, using interviews, college records,
and standard measures of vocational interest and personal preference. Marriage-oriented girls tended to have high grades, high
socio-economic status, and interests similar to the average elementary school teacher. Interests of career-oriented girls resembled
those of the average librarian.

Parker, Richard Earl (Ph. D.). "SOCIAL HIERARCHIES IN SAME SEX
PEER GROUPS." University of Chicago, 1976. Source: DAI, XXXVII, 9B
(March, 1977), 4763-B.

Studied how the sex composition of elementary school classes affected
girls' behavior. Author's findings suggested that all-girl classes
produced more confident and assertive women than did mixed sex classes, but varied according to social ecology.

Parlato, Mary Lou (Ed. D.). "A COMPARATIVE STUDY OF THE EDUCATIONAL
AND OCCUPATIONAL ASPIRATION OF FIVE SELECTED GROUPS OF WOMEN IN ELEMEN-
TARY EDUCATION IN THE DETROIT METROPOLITAN AREA." Wayne State Univer-
sity, 1966. 292 pp. Source: DAI, XXVIII, 3A (September, 1967), 914.
XUM Order No. 67-10,500.

Among findings: (1) women college seniors and graduates wanted to
do graduate study more than did women teachers, assistant principals,
and principals; (2) under half of the 483 women studied wanted to

earn a doctorate (10% of the principals and 2% of the assistant principals had doctorates); (3) parents, husbands, and school administrators exerted major influence on respondents to seek college degrees
and career advancement; and (4) over 83% of respondents' mothers
were not college graduates. Concluded that the aspirational levels
of the women studied were low.

Parrish, Susan Elizabeth (Ph. D.). "COMPARISON OF PERSONAL VALUES
OF HOME ECONOMICS AND HUMAN ECOLOGY STUDENTS AT MICHIGAN STATE UNIVER-
SITY, 1968-1975." Michigan State University, 1975. 328 pp. Source:
DAI, XXXVI, 12A (June, 1976), 7960-A-7961-A. XUM Order No. 76-12,505.

Compared personal values of female undergraduates according to various factors, including class level, years (during 1968-75), and major subject within the home economics and human ecology departments.
Their highest values were the same, during 1968-75, including 5 long
range values (happiness, mature love, self-respect, inner harmony,
and freedom) and 5 instrumental values (honest, loving, responsible,
forgiving, and broadminded). Changes in idealism among freshmen,
transfers, and seniors suggested that by 1975 they were more realistic.

Parse, Rosemarie Rizzo (Ph. D.). "AN INSTRUCTIONAL MODEL FOR THE
TEACHING OF NURSING, INTERRELATING OBJECTIVES AND MEDIA." University
of Pittsburgh, 1969. 173 pp. Source: DAI, XXXI, 1A (July, 1970), 180-
A. XUM Order No. 70-12,704.

Using insights gained from nursing students and faculty, the author
developed an audio-visual instructional model for the professional
preparation of baccalaureate nurses. Some media were found to be
more effective than others in teaching specific nursing education
objectives and for nursing students' independent study. A main use
of the instructional model was for faculty and student nurses to ascertain and pursue professional nursing competencies and specific
nursing behavioral objectives.

Parsons, Harriet D. (Ph. D.). "OCCUPATIONAL ROLE CHOICES OF GRADU-
ATE-EDUCATED MARRIED WOMEN." University of Missouri--Columbia, 1972.
273 pp. Source: DAI, XXXIII, 9A (March, 1973), 5319-A-5320-A. XUM
Order No. 73-7070.

Factors closely related to the occupational choice of women who received a University of Missouri graduate degree, 1956-60, and were
living with husbands were: (1) number of preschool children; (2)
age of respondent; (3) number of elementary children; (4) attitude
of the husband; (5) achievement motivation; (6) level of energy;
(7) husband's education; (8) teaching as an occupation; (9) role
relationship preferences; (10) mother's education; (11) present residence; and (12) perceived adequacy of husband's income.

Parsons, Mary Ann Coward (Ph. D.). "APPLICABILITY OF CHANGE THEORY
TO CHANGE-ORIENTED AND NONCHANGE-ORIENTED DEPARTMENTS WITHIN SELECTED
COLLEGIATE NURSING PROGRAMS." University of Florida, 1976. 365 pp.
Source: DAI, XXXVII, 10B (April, 1977), 4990-B. XUM Order No. 77-
8209.

Identified 3 change-oriented departments and 3 nonchange-oriented
departments in 4 college nursing schools. The change-oriented departments had such facilitators of change as: (1) internal support
for change; (2) presence of a change agent; (3) retraining of members
for new tasks; and (4) adequate funding. Nonchange-oriented departments had such resisters to change as: (1) conformity to norms; (2)
systemic and cultural coherence; and (3) vested interest which appeared to develop because of traditional organizational structure
(strong faculty identification with a single department).

Pass, Barbara Harper (Ed. D.). "A STUDY OF ADMINISTRATIVE WOMEN IN
EDUCATION." University of Virginia, 1976. 169 pp. Source: DAI, XXXVII,
7A (January, 1977), 4038-A. XUM Order No. 76-22,859.

This study reviewed characteristics of women school administrators
as reported in doctoral research, 1957-1974. Dissertations analyzed
concluded that: (1) few women school administrators aspired to leadership positions without the support and encouragement of others;
(2) most women administrators were promoted within their own school
system and native state; and (3) their career goals were outgrowths
of their teaching careers. Author suggested that: (1) women teachers' aspirations might be raised by in-service programs; (2) female
mobility in educational administration should be analyzed; and (3)
counseling and role models might influence more women to combine
homemaking and an administrative career.

Passos, Joyce Young (Ph. D.). "A METHOD FOR ANALYZING THE PROBLEM
IDENTIFICATION BEHAVIOR OF BASIC BACCALAUREATE NURSING STUDENTS AND ITS
RELATIONSHIP TO STUDENT PREPARATION STRATEGIES, STUDENT ROLE SATISFACTION
AND FACULTY ROLE SATISFACTION." Michigan State University, 1969. 227
pp. Source: DAI, XXXI, 3A (September, 1970), 1147-A-1148-A. XUM Order
No. 70-15,102.

Study showed that both students and faculty wanted student nurses to
have more opportunities to collaborate with members of the health
team and to participate in decision making about the classroom portion of clinical courses.

Patri, Virginia Carol (Ed. D.). "WOMANPOWER AND PHYSICAL EDUCATION:
A REPORT OF A TYPE C PROJECT." Columbia University Teachers College,
1958. 275 pp. Source: Dissertation, pp. iii-vii.

An analysis of some problems affecting women's careers, especially
in physical education but also in nursing and the armed services.

Patrylow, Sarah Snyder (Ph. D.). "THE RELATION OF THE DOMINANT
VALUES OF SENIOR ASSOCIATE DEGREE NURSING STUDENTS TO THEIR ATTITUDES TO-
WARD CARING FOR THE DYING." New York University, 1970. 153 pp. Source:
DAI, XXXI, 12B (June, 1971), 7390-B-7391-B. XUM Order No. 71-13,657.

Supported the hypothesis that those nursing students with strong person-oriented values (religious and/or social) have more positive attitudes toward caring for the dying than do those with non-person-
oriented values (theoretical, economic, aesthetic, and/or political).

Patterson, Mary Gertrude (Ed. D.). "HOSPITAL NURSING SERVICE AS A MODEL FOR NURSING EDUCATION: THE EFFECT OF AN EXPERIMENTALLY STRUCTURED EXPRESSIVE ROLE IN THE REGISTERED NURSE POSITION ON PERCEPTION OF PATIENTS." University of California, Los Angeles, 1967. 164 pp. Source: DAI, XXVIII, 9A (March, 1968), 3433-A. XUM Order No. 68-3277.

The experimental treatment increased the number of contacts between individual patient and registered nurse. These 7 contacts were sequential, nonrepetitive, and relevant to patient needs. Nurses and patients in the experiment found the increased contact very satisfying. Concluded that existing nursing practices, in contrast to this experimental design, were dysfunctional to treatment of patient needs because the registered nurse was too remote from the patient.

Patterson, Patricia Louise (Ph. D.). "A DESCRIPTION AND ANALYSIS OF THE WOMEN FACULTY IN PENNSYLVANIA'S STATE-OWNED COLLEGES AND UNIVERSITIES." University of Pittsburgh, 1974. 137 pp. Source: DAI, XXXV, 8A (February, 1975), 5063-A. XUM Order No. 75-4071.

Women faculty profile: (1) most born in or near Pennsylvania; (2) had skilled, semi-skilled, or professional fathers; (3) ½ were under age 43; (4) 19% had public school-age children; (5) most had master's + degree; (6) 25% had doctorate, of which 42% felt it had not advanced them; (7) most were assistant professors, worked 9-10 months, earned $14,000-$16,999; (8) most taught (a few were also administrators, with dean as their highest position); (9) 2/3 taught nursing, physical education, humanities, social sciences, preschool and elementary education; (10) ½+ had recently served on curriculum and faculty affairs committees, few as chairpersons; (11) most wanted the intellectual challenge; (12) this plus salary and prestige were their chief rewards; (13) 87% were satisfied and would recommend their careers to other women; (14) most felt more women faculty should be hired and allowed equal access to administrative positions; and (15) those dissatisfied said their positions were less than they expected and felt that being female had disadvantaged them.

Patty, Rosemarie Selma Anderson (Ph. D.). "THE AROUSAL OF THE MOTIVE TO AVOID SUCCESS IN COLLEGE WOMEN." University of Nebraska--Lincoln, 1973. 76 pp. Source: DAI, XXXIV, 5A (November, 1973), 2768-A-2769-A. XUM Order No. 73-25,474.

Author hypothesized from the literature that some college women's ambivalence toward success was based on society's view that femininity and success (i.e., competitive achievement in a masculine world) were incompatible. Following experimental instruction and writing assignments, author found that the motive to avoid success in college women could be heightened only in those women who were already ambivalent toward success.

Paul, Catharine Manny (Ph. D.). "AMANDA LABARCA H.: EDUCATOR TO THE WOMEN OF CHILE. THE WORK AND WRITINGS OF AMANDA LABARCA H. IN THE FIELD OF EDUCATION IN CHILE; THEIR IMPORTANCE; THEIR VALUE IN THE PROGRESS OF EDUCATION IN CHILE." New York University, 1967. 210 pp. Source: DAI, XXVIII, 4A (October, 1967), 1215-A-1216-A. XUM Order No. 67-11,120.

The contributions of Amanda Labarca to women's education and Chilean education generally, documented with material from U. S. and Chilean libraries and from Labarca herself, were: (1) compiling arithmetic and reading textbooks; (2) acquainting Chileans with John Dewey's philosophy; (3) founding seasonal schools, particularly helpful to women; (4) writing the History of Education in Chile; and (5) representing Chile at the U. N.

Paul, Glendora B. (Ph. D.). "EMANCIPATION AND EDUCATION OF INDIAN WOMEN SINCE 1829." University of Pittsburgh, 1970. 220 pp. Source: DAI, XXXI, 9A (March, 1971), 4389-A. XUM Order No. 71-8006.

The equality with men of women in India in Vedic times gave way to their subjection, particularly after the Moslem conquest. Christian missions and British education lessened this discrimination by stages: 1819-54, by women missionaries; 1854-84, government grants to missions; and after 1884, with direct government aid to girls' education. The Indian National Congress (Gandhi and others) helped and the Freedom Movement depended on women's participation. Indian women's emancipation has been more political than social or economic. When education penetrates all corners of India, it will bring women economic and social emancipation, too.

Paulsen, Dorothy Louise (Ph. D.). "THE CAREER COMMITMENT OF TWELFTH GRADE GIRLS." Yale University, 1967. 183 pp. Source: DAI, XXVIII, 10A (April, 1968), 4290-A. XUM Order No. 68-5200.

Twelfth grade girls relied almost completely on the advice of people with whom they had primary relationships in making occupational plans. Conclusions: (1) peer group and mass media have little impact on occupational decisions; and (2) the family is the most important agency of socialization in developing career commitment.

Pauwels, Jacques Robert Maria (Ph. D.). "WOMEN AND UNIVERSITY STUDIES IN THE THIRD REICH, 1933-1945." York University (Canada), 1976. Source: DAI, XXXVII, 12A, Part 1 (June, 1977), 7912-A-7913-A.

In Germany in the 1920s and early 1930s the Nazis opposed women's academic aspirations. With the labor shortage and changing views of eugenics in the mid-1930s women were openly encouraged to pursue their academic ambitions (although in fact female university enrollment declined). During World War II women in unprecedented proportions enrolled in higher education, many of them indifferent or even antagonistic toward Nazi doctrines.

Payne, Effietee Martin (D. P. E.). "A CRITICAL EVALUATION OF SELECTED PHYSICAL EDUCATION FILMS FOR USE WITH GIRLS AND WOMEN." Indiana University, 1952. Source: Dissertation, pp. 423-430.

Included in this study were: (1) a catalogue of selected physical education films, annotated and evaluated, for use with women and girls; (2) a rating scale to assist in evaluating other films; and (3) a description of the process used in preparing the catalogue and rating scale.

Payne, Sister Mary Ruth (Ph. D.). "A STUDY OF VALUE CRISIS: TRADI-
TIONAL AND MODERN VALUES OF THE FEMALE STUDENTS AT THE UNIVERSITY OF SAN
ANDRES, LA PAZ, BOLIVIA." Saint Louis University, 1967. 242 pp. Source:
DAI, XXVIII, 8A (February, 1968), 3046-A-3047-A. XUM Order No. 68-1286.

Found that: (1) a severe value crisis existed among female university students who were identified as potential leaders; (2) the crisis was especially strong between their idealism and modern values;
and (3) the crisis had not been resolved while they were attending
the university.

Pearman, Eleanor Caswell (Ed. D.). "HISTORICAL STUDY OF THE EMOTION-
ALLY-SUPPORTIVE AND PATIENT-TEACHING ROLES OF THE GENERAL DUTY NURSE
FROM 1900-1970." Boston University School of Education, 1971. 284 pp.
Source: DAI, XXXII, 4B (October, 1971), 2255-B. XUM Order No. 71-
26,729.

Study traced historically nurses' emotionally supportive role in patient care and noted recent evidence to support the additional responsibility of patient-teaching role. This patient-teaching role
as a new essential to nursing care is now agreed upon by nurses, the
public, and to a lesser degree the physician.

Pearson, Kathleen May (Ph. D.). "A STRUCTURAL AND FUNCTIONAL ANALY-
SIS OF THE MULTI-CONCEPT OF INTEGRATION-SEGREGATION (MALE AND/OR FEMALE)
IN PHYSICAL EDUCATION CLASSES." University of Illinois at Urbana-Champaign, 1971. 233 pp. Source: DAI, XXXII, 10A (April, 1972), 5596-A-
5597-A. XUM Order No. 72-12,332.

Analyzed reasons for the mainly separate sex physical education programs at high school and university levels and to a lesser degree at
junior high school level.

Pearson, Millie Violet (Ph. D.). "A STUDY OF PROFESSIONAL HOME ECO-
NOMICS EDUCATION COURSES IN THE LIGHT OF THE DEMOCRATIC IDEAL." Ohio
State University, 1942. 249 pp. Source: Millie Violet Pearson, "Demo-
cratic Procedures in High-School and College Teaching," EDUCATIONAL AD-
MINISTRATION AND SUPERVISION, XXIX, No. 2 (February, 1943), pp. 87-95.

Author urged democratic procedures in teaching home economics courses so as to enhance learning and also to build cooperative citizens.

Pederson, Evelyn May (Ed. D.). "A BACCALAUREATE DEGREE PROGRAM IN
NURSING AT SAN FRANCISCO STATE COLLEGE." University of Houston, 1955.
205 pp. Source: DAI, XVI, 1 (1956), 103-104. XUM Order No. 15,414.

In line with the California Administrative Code, this program was
designed to teach general nursing by emphasizing service to patients rather than diseases. The 132 semester units of credit con-
sisted of 60 hours in nursing, 68 hours in general education, and 4
hours of electives. Degree requirements were comparable with those
of other majors. Both sexes and all social and ethnic groups were
eligible for admission.

Pegram, George Raleigh (Ph. D.). "AN INVESTIGATION OF THE SEMANTIC
SPACE AND RELATIONSHIPS AMONG THE RELATED EDUCATIONAL VARIABLES OF

ABILITY, ACHIEVEMENT, ATTITUDE, AND MEANING WITH SOPHOMORE NURSING STU-
DENTS." Ohio State University, 1971. 160 pp. Source: DAI, XXXII, 5A
(November, 1971), 2316-A-2317-A. XUM Order No. 71-27,536.

Found among Ohio State University sophomore nursing students that
their understanding of the semantic meaning of nursing and 13 other
nurse-oriented concepts was related to their academic achievement.

Pengelly, Rita Sandra Rapoza (Ph. D.). "A COMPARATIVE STUDY OF ACA-
DEMIC SELF-ESTIMATES, ACADEMIC VALUES AND ACADEMIC ASPIRATIONS OF ADOLES-
CENT MALES AND FEMALES." University of Minnesota, 1974. 131 pp. Source:
DAI, XXXV, 6A (December, 1974), 3433-A. XUM Order No. 74-26,268.

Some findings in a study of 1,577 public high school students: (1)
girls did not have more negative self-estimates than boys; (2) girls'
slightly higher academic values were statistically negligible; (3)
academic values for both boys and girls decreased at higher grade
levels; and (4) girls' educational-vocational aspirations in later
high school years were lower than those of boys. Concluded that
girls' educational aspirations declined relative to those of boys in
later adolescence.

Penn, Linda Spetner (Ph. D.). "CURRENT SEX ROLE IDENTIFICATION, SEX
ROLE STEREOTYPES, AND ROLE CONFLICT IN UNIVERSITY WOMEN." Adelphi University, 1975. 175 pp. Source: DAI, XXXVI, 1B (July, 1975), 425-B-
426-B. XUM Order No. 75-15,182.

Data from 99 female university students in the New York City area
confirmed that traditional sex role stereotypes were widespread.
All the women described men in positive terms. But their descriptions of women were divided: 3 groups of females described women in
positive terms; and 3 other groups of females described women negatively (as superficial, demanding, and overly emotional).

Penrod, Mary Jenet Elder (Ph. D.). "THE IDENTIFICATION OF PROBLEMS
OF FIRST YEAR HOME ECONOMICS TEACHERS AS PERCEIVED BY THE TEACHERS THEM-
SELVES, THE SUPERVISORS, AND THE ADMINISTRATORS." Purdue University,
1974. 182 pp. Source: DAI, XXXV, 6A (December, 1974), 3567-A. XUM
Order No. 74-26,761.

Three groups of home economics teachers, supervisors, and administrators in 3 states (IN, NC, and MO) listed among their major problems: (1) motivating students, especially uninterested and trouble-
some ones; (2) using interesting teaching methods; (3) discipline;
(4) interpersonal relations with students; and (5) finding time for
personal pursuits. The 3 groups perceived problems differently but
agreed that first-year home economics teachers' greatest problems
were in human relations.

Perez, Jose Ramon (Ph. D.). "THE RATE OF RETURN TO EDUCATIONAL IN-
VESTMENTS WITH SPECIAL REFERENCE TO PUERTO RICO." University of Michi-
gan, 1973. 166 pp. Source: DAI, XXXIV, 8A (February, 1974), 4521-A.
XUM Order No. 74-3709.

Measured the economic benefits of schooling to marginal students in
Puerto Rico by examining differences in earnings. Males' rate of

economic return for college attendance was 8%-16% and females' rate was 4%-11%. These low percentages suggested that increased school enrollments were not economically attractive. Further research was recommended.

Perez, Presentacion T. (Ph. D.). "PROBLEMS OF EMPLOYED WOMEN IN CERTAIN PROFESSIONAL GROUPS IN THE PHILIPPINES AND THEIR EDUCATIONAL IMPLICATIONS." University of Minnesota, 1954. 318 pp. Source: DAI, XV, 3 (1955), 359-360. XUM Order No. 11,113.

Of the professional and below professional Filipino women studied: (1) those in the provinces had less education than those in Manila; (2) over ½ with bachelor's degrees had received them from private co-educational and non-sectarian institutions, with the public university ranking second; and (3) criticism of their undergraduate courses included (a) little class participation, (b) no real electives, (c) too few extracurricular activities, and (d) too much theory without accompanying practice. Recommended: (1) high school vocational courses and guidance, particularly applicable to those working below the professional level; (2) in-service and summer institute for professional respondents; (3) a family life course for all women, regardless of field; and (4) the university should lead in counseling and guidance courses for prospective teachers.

Perrin, Ellen Hays (Ph. D.). "PERCEPTIONS OF WOMEN COLLEGE FACULTY MEMBERS TOWARD CAREERS IN ACADEMIC ADMINISTRATION." University of Pittsburgh, 1974. 198 pp. Source: DAI, XXXV, 12A, Part 1 (June, 1975), 7574-A-7575-A. XUM Order No. 75-13,206.

Author sought reactions from 245 randomly selected women faculty at 21 PA colleges and universities to 3 concepts: "effective administrator," "women administrators," and "myself as administrator." Their reactions to the 3 concepts were studied in relation to their age, marital status, level of education, and career aspirations. Found that: (1) respondents tended to reject the administrator role; (2) more women aged 40-59 responded positively to the "effective administrator" concept; (3) women separated from husbands scored higher on "myself as administrator"; and (4) women's career aspirations and their level of education were not significantly related to their responses to the 3 concepts.

Persinger, Staples (Ed. D.). "A STUDY OF THE SUITABILITY OF SELECTED NEW JERSEY COLLEGES TO OFFER A PHYSICAL EDUCATION MAJOR FOR WOMEN." New York University, 1964. 387 pp. Source: DAI, XXVI, 7 (January, 1966), 3745. XUM Order No. 65-6607.

After establishing need, surveying requirements, and gauging the capacities of NJ state colleges to offer the best model physical education program for women, a rating was made listing these institutions in this order: Glassboro State College, Paterson State College, Newark State College, and Jersey City State College.

Peter, Lilian Augustine (Ph. D.). "WOMEN AS EDUCATIVE GUARDIANS IN SHAKESPEARE'S COMEDIES." Indiana University, 1975. 236 pp. Source: DAI, XXXVI, 11A (May, 1976), 7443-A. XUM Order No. 76-11,439.

William Shakespeare's Portia in THE MERCHANT OF VENICE is indirectly
Bassanio's teacher; she also teaches mercy to Shylock. Rosaline in
AS YOU LIKE IT educates Orlando and Phebe. Helena in ALL'S WELL
THAT ENDS WELL is educator to Bertram and Diana. Paulina in THE
WINTER'S TALE brings Leontes to self-knowledge. These women adapt
their role-playing to the achieving of social values while furthering self-education. They teach not with arrogance but with the intent to nurture, enlarge, and restore family and personal welfare.
These Shakespeare heroines have a gift for benevolent strategems,
clever intrigue, and pleasant surprises that characterizes them, according to the author, as educative guardians.

Peters, Agnes Elaine (Sister Agnes Joseph) (Ph. D.). "CORRELATES OF
PERSISTENCE OF OCCUPATIONAL CHOICE AMONG A SELECTED GROUP OF COLLEGE WO-
MEN." Saint John's University, 1956. 221 pp. Source: Dissertation,
pp. 198-210.

Occupational choices of 782 women students in 3 NJ Catholic liberal
arts colleges indicated that: (1) their preferences were teacher,
marriage, clerical worker, researcher, journalist, and social worker; (2) 60% of students persisted in their 1st occupational choice,
almost 40% in 2nd choice, and about 32% in 3rd choice; (3) those
choosing engineering assistant and teacher persisted most; and (4)
those choosing financier and reception persisted least. Concluded
that: (1) persistence did not depend on college classification;
(2) persistence consistency was not found in any particular subject
area; (3) higher academic achievement was related to occupational
choice persistence; and (4) persistence increased when course of
study was related to occupational choice.

Peters, Sister Catherine (Ph. D.). "EMPLOYMENT OF HOME ECONOMISTS
IN TEXTILES AND CLOTHING RELATED POSITIONS NOT ASSOCIATED WITH EDUCATION-
AL INSTITUTIONS." Iowa State University, 1973. 177 pp. Source: DAI,
XXXIV, 10B (April, 1974), 5057-B-5058-B. XUM Order No. 74-9147.

Collected information from home economists in textile and clothing
related positions in business and industry to use in planning textiles and clothing curricula. The 217 home economists questioned in
36 states indicated that they expected recent graduates to: (1) perform consumer services; (2) keep up to date about new developments
in textiles and clothing; and (3) do other work, which varied widely
with the specific job and the firm's location.

Peters, David Wilbur (Ph. D.). "THE STATUS OF THE MARRIED WOMAN
TEACHER." Columbia University Teachers College, 1934. Source: TCCU
CONTRIBUTIONS No. 603, pp. 84-90.

Found no evidence to justify discrimination against married women
teachers in VA. If any relationship existed between marital status
and teaching effectiveness, such relationship was without adequate
significance to justify its use in employment policy.

Petersen, Lois E. (Ed. D.). "CAREER ASPIRATIONS OF FRESHMAN WOMEN
ENROLLED IN COMMUNITY COLLEGE OFFICE OCCUPATIONS CURRICULA." University
of North Dakota, 1976. 137 pp. Source: DAI, XXXVII, 7A (January, 1977),
4082-A-4083-A. XUM Order No. 76-30,305.

Among findings about freshman women enrolled in office occupations programs: (1) age and marital status significantly affected the women's work-related decisions; (2) their educational backgrounds and the family breadwinner's employment level were not significant variables; (3) important influences on whether a woman planned a long-term career were her liking for the job, job security, fringe benefits, husband and/or family attitude toward her working; and (4) major reasons women wanted to go to work were desire for independence and for self-fulfillment.

Peterson, Carol Jean Willts (Ph. D.). "SECONDARY SCHOOL COUNSELORS' AND NURSE EDUCATORS' PERCEPTIONS OF TRENDS IN NURSING EDUCATION AND IMAGES OF NURSING." University of Minnesota, 1969. 368 pp. Source: DAI, XXXI, 3B (September, 1970), 1363-B-1364-B. XUM Order No. 70-15,786.

Some major findings: (1) secondary school counselors scored significantly lower in awareness of recent developments in nursing education than did nurses; (2) baccalaureate and associate degree nursing faculties scored significantly higher on awareness of nursing trends than did those in practical and diploma programs; and (3) counselors' images of the nursing profession were quite favorable but somewhat traditional.

Peterson, Leona Mae (Ph. D.). "MOTIVATIONAL OUTCOMES OF A SIMULATION APPROACH IN CLINICAL NURSING INSTRUCTION." University of Chicago, 1972. Source: Author.

Found among clinical nursing students in baccalaureate programs that simulated problems and discussion should not be used when students are overworked or under excessive pressure, since they need time to respond to the problems.

Petit, Sister Rita Marie (Ed. D.). "ATTITUDINAL STUDY OF FACULTY WOMEN IN HIGHER EDUCATION IN NORTHWEST UNITED STATES." University of Montana, 1972. 172 pp. Source: DAI, XXXIII, 4A (October, 1972), 1572-A. XUM Order No. 72-25,077.

Responses from 154 deans, 41 vice presidents, and 568 faculty women from higher education institutions in 6 states agreed that: (1) men and women faculty deserved equal pay for equal work; (2) there should be an equal system of merit appointments and promotions; (3) women's lower mobility limited their employment opportunities; and (4) the potential of women in higher education had been neglected.

Petro, Carole Smith (Ph. D.). "THE RELATIONSHIP OF COUNSELOR'S SEX, SEX-ROLE STEREOTYPES, AND SEX-ROLE IDENTITY ON AFFECTIVE SENSITIVITY." State University of New York at Buffalo, 1976. 232 pp. Source: DAI, XXXVII, 8A (February, 1977), 4869-A-4870-A. XUM Order No. 77-3572.

Data from 173 practicing male and female counselors showed that the counselors: (1) held sex-role stereotypes similar to those held by the larger society; (2) perceived males as more androgynous (non-sex biased) than females; and (3) had equal capacity for sensitivity but had greater sensitivity to males than to females.

Petschauer, Peter (Ph. D.). "THE EDUCATION AND DEVELOPMENT OF AN EN-
LIGHTENED ABSOLUTIST: THE YOUTH OF CATHERINE THE GREAT, 1729-1762." New
York University, 1969. 534 pp. Source: DAI, XXXI, 7A (January, 1971),
3481-A. XUM Order No. 70-27,259.

Historical view of Catherine the Great's preparation for the Russian
throne includes: (1) her parents' cultural and intellectual influence; (2) influence of her teachers (Elizabeth Cardel and Pastor Wagner) and her friends: (3) her wide reading; and (4) her correspondence with such philosophers as Voltaire.

Pettersen, Pearl Cargill (Ed. D.). "INTERRELATIONSHIP OF KINESTHE-
SIS, FLEXIBILITY, JOINT ANGULATION AND MOTOR ABILITY IN COLLEGE WOMEN."
University of Georgia, 1970. 105 pp. Source: DAI, XXXI, 11A (May,
1971), 5829-A. XUM Order No. 71-13,107.

Found significant relationships between kinesthesis, flexibility,
joint angulation, and motor ability in 58 University of Georgia women in 3 badminton classes.

Petti, Elizabeth Rosina (Ed. D.). "A STUDY OF THE RELATIONSHIP BE-
TWEEN THE THREE LEVELS OF NURSING EDUCATION AND NURSE COMPETENCY AS RATED
BY PATIENT AND HEAD NURSE." Boston University School of Education, 1975.
195 pp. Source: DAI, XXXV, 12A, Part 1 (June, 1975), 7536-A-7537-A.
XUM Order No. 75-12,231.

Found: (1) a positive correlation between diploma nursing education
and higher competency but not between associate degree and baccalaureate degree and higher competency, which suggested possible consoli-
dation of the 3 programs into 1 collegiate nursing program for efficient preparation of the bedside nurse; and (2) the diploma nurse
who had less theory than the college graduate nurse received a higher
competency rating, suggesting a missing link between theory and
practice.

Petway, Jamesetta (Ph. D.). "BLACK WOMEN AND WHITE MANAGERS: AN
ACTION PROGRAM FOR INCREASED STRENGTH AND INFLUENCE." Case Western Reserve University, 1975. 286 pp. Source: DAI, XXXVI, 7B (January, 1976),
3680-B-3681-B. XUM Order No. 75-27,949.

One workshop was held with black secretaries to identify effective
ways for them to use their strengths and to establish support groups.
Another workshop was held with black secretaries and their white
managers to improve their relationship, increase the black women's
influence, and to establish managers as their supporters. Results:
(1) the first workshop helped all except 2 women to gain strength;
and (2) the 2nd workshop taught secretaries new ways of interacting
with their managers.

Pfeiffer, Marie Stoll (Ph. D.). "SOCIAL AND PSYCHOLOGICAL VARIABLES
ASSOCIATED WITH EARLY COLLEGE MARRIAGES." Ohio State University, 1961.
350 pp. Source: DAI, XXII, 7 (January, 1962), 2381. XUM Order No.
61-5118.

Found that: (1) fathers of most young married students studied were
clerical or white-collar employees or managers willing to support

their married children in college because they believe in social mobility; (2) group I (husband and wife were both students) had the highest marital adjustment score; (3) 2/3 of group II (husband is student, wife is not) had children, had highest pre-marital pregnancy, and had lower marital adjustment score; and (4) over 3/4 said they would still marry before finishing college but about ½ were uncertain about advising friends to marry in college. Concluded that: the particular personality needs of one's self and of one spouse was important to marital adjustment.

Pfiffner, Virginia Therese (Ph. D.). "FACTORS ASSOCIATED WITH WOMEN IN MAJOR ADMINISTRATIVE POSITIONS IN CALIFORNIA COMMUNITY COLLEGES." University of Southern California, 1972. 115 pp. Source: DAI, XXXIII, 9A (March, 1973), 4888-A. XUM Order No. 73-7260.

Data from 22 of CA's 26 top-level women community college administrators showed: (1) their motivation to become an administrator usually came from their own administrators; (2) most did not feel discriminated against because they were women; (3) most were from small families, had been married an average of 25 years, and felt that their children were more help than hindrance; and (4) all had master's degrees while 23% had doctorates. Author recommended steps for increasing the percentage of top-level women administrators in CA from the existing 4% to at least 28% (putting the number of top-level women administrators into direct proportion with the number of women faculty).

Phillips, Barbara Elyse (Ph. D.). "FEAR OF SUCCESS AND THE FEMALE DOCTORAL STUDENT: A STUDY OF THE INFLUENCE OF AGE AND MARITAL STATUS ON WOMEN'S EXPERIENCE OF GRADUATE SCHOOL." California School of Professional Psychology, San Francisco, 1977. 196 pp. Source: DAI, XXXVIII, 6B (December, 1977), 2878-B-2879-B. XUM Order No. 77-27,606.

Reasons that findings did not support the hypothesis that single women doctoral students (age 25-33) had intense fear of success because their striving was different from the female norm: (1) they had a non-traditional sex-role orientation with high priority on self-actualization; (2) their early family life had encouraged their striving; and (3) since they were redefining their role, they embraced a non-sex-biased concept of self. The single doctoral women did experience stress different from that of the married women; this stress was delineated and discussed.

Phillips, Florence Louise (Ed. D.). "A SOCIO-ECONOMIC STUDY OF COLLEGE WOMEN." Indiana University, 1958. 107 pp. Source: DAI, XIX, 8 (February, 1959), 1955. XUM Order No. Mic 59-81.

Study of 1,352 Texas Technological College undergraduate women showed: (1) a close relationship between socio-economic status and college attendance; (2) significant relationship between socio-economic status and parents' education, home town size, sorority membership, activity participation, school or division in which enrolled. employment, college residence, and class; (3) blue collar family women were under-represented; (4) a high proportion dropped out or transferred; (5) upper socio-economic women participated more in college extra-curricular activities; and (6) more white collar family women belonged to sororities.

Phillips, Lorraine Waters (D. N. Sc.). "THEORY DEVELOPMENT IN NUR-
SING: ITS PRESENT NATURE AND FUTURE EVENTS AS JUDGED BY A PANEL OF
NURSE-THEORETICIANS." Boston University School of Nursing, 1971. 250
pp. Source: DAI, XXXII, 4B (October, 1971), 2255-B-2256-B. XUM Order
No. 71-26,669.

Data from nurse-theoreticians reflected great concern that nursing
raise its status in relation to other professions. Ways to achieve
such status were to develop nursing theories and to increase communications with other disciplines.

Phillips, Madge Marie (Ph. D.). "BIOGRAPHIES OF SELECTED WOMEN LEAD-
ERS IN PHYSICAL EDUCATION IN THE UNITED STATES." State University of
Iowa, 1960. 440 pp. Source: DAI, XX, 12 (June, 1960), 4581. XUM Order
No. Mic 60-1571.

Purpose was to assemble material to help future historians interpret
women's role in the development of U. S. physical education. Information gathered from 8 selected living women physical education leaders in higher education included: family, childhood, education, professional experiences and writings, and other biographical information, together with students and colleagues' evaluations.

Phillips, Thomas P. (Ph. D.). "A SOCIOLOGICAL STUDY OF SELECTED
FACTORS ASSOCIATED WITH THE PRODUCTIVITY PATTERNS OF NURSES WITH DOCTORAL
DEGREES." Catholic University of America, 1973. 271 pp. Source: DAI,
XXXIV, 3A (September, 1973), 1377-A. XUM Order No. 73-21,638.

From 315 questionnaires the author identified only 3 factors which
affected the quantity and quality of publications nurses with doctorates wrote: (1) age at first publication; (2) length of time in
the profession; and (3) their feelings about the importance of publications. Viewed sociologically, these nurse-researchers seemed to
be more closely involved with nursing than with research, but the
group studied was not necessarily representative of nursing as an
occupational entity.

Phillips, Wilma E. (Ph. D.). "THE MOTIVE TO ACHIEVE IN WOMEN AS RE-
LATED TO PERCEPTION OF SEX ROLE IN SOCIETY." University of Maryland,
1974. 141 pp. Source: DAI, XXXV, 9A (March, 1975), 5934-A. XUM Order
No. 75-7355.

Findings about nursing graduates, aged 20-41, who were grouped according to sex-role orientation as either traditional or non-traditional: (1) expectations for career success were comparable for both
groups; (2) non-traditionals had higher aspiration level, which was
associated with expressed needs for self fulfillment and financial
independence; (3) non-traditionals had greater conflict between career and family responsibilities; (4) achievement motivation was
greater for women aged 23-41; (5) women aged 20-22 were more traditional and had a relatively lower motive to succeed; (6) the most
achievement-minded were aged 23-28; and (7) younger women had greater
need for affiliation while older women had greater need for achievement.

Phinney, Anita Louise (Ph. D.). "THE EFFECTS OF ASSERTION TRAINING
AND BIBLIOTHERAPY WITH MARRIED WOMEN." State University of New York at

Stony Brook, 1977. 267 pp. Source: DAI, XXXVIII, 6B (December, 1977), 2879-B. XUM Order No. 77-27,470.

Tested the effectiveness of: (1) assertion training plus bibliotherapy; and (2) bibliotherapy and assertion counseling. Found that both processes developed women's assertive behavior in marital situations.

Phipps, Patricia McNamar (Ph. D.). "AN EXAMINATION OF TEACHER PERCEPTIONS OF BOYS AND GIRLS WITH SCHOOL LEARNING AND BEHAVIOR PROBLEMS." University of California, Riverside, 1977. 120 pp. Source: DAI, XXXVIII, 6A (December, 1977), 3416-A-3417-A. XUM Order No. 77-27,138.

Found that: (1) teachers referred boys more often than girls for possible placement in special learning disabled programs and more often for behavior problems than for academic problems; (2) teachers referred girls for the same reasons but the referrals of girls came when they were older and further behind academically; (3) teachers perceived boys' behavior problems as being more serious than the boys' academic problems; and (4) differences in teacher perceptions of learning disabled boys and girls were not statistically significant.

Piel, Ellen Ruth (Ph. D.). "SEX AND CAREERS: RELATIONSHIPS BETWEEN SEX TYPING AND DIFFERENCES ON CAREER-RELATED VARIABLES FOR MEN AND WOMEN." University of Iowa, 1977. 198 pp. Source: DAI, XXXVIII, 7A (January, 1978), 3964-A-3965-A. XUM Order No. 77-28,503.

Most women college students' occupational choices, which fell into a social category, were markedly different from those of men and ranged from feminine-dominant to male-dominant roles.

Piemonte, Robert Victor (Ed. D.). "A HISTORY OF THE NATIONAL LEAGUE OF NURSING EDUCATION 1912-1932: GREAT AWAKENING IN NURSING EDUCATION." Columbia University Teachers College, 1976. 177 pp. Source: DAI, XXXVII, 2B (August, 1976), 701-B-702-B. XUM Order No. 76-17,291.

In its first 20 years the League: (1) strengthened nursing theory and practice; (2) improved admission standards; (3) published curriculum guides; (4) reduced hospitals' exploitation of student nurses by insisting on the 8-hour day and adding more theory to the curriculum; (5) pushed nurses' training toward the mainstream of education by encouraging college affiliation and by supporting university schools of nursing; and (6) helped set standards for nursing service by emphasizing quality in graduate nurses' performance.

Pierce, Lillian Williams (Ph. D.). "FACTORS RELATED TO NURSING STUDENTS' PERCEPTIONS OF NURSES AND NURSING." Ohio State University, 1965. 237 pp. Source: DAI, XXVI, 11 (May, 1966), 6652. XUM Order No. 65-13,270.

Nursing students' perceptions were studied in relation to various factors and were analyzed in terms of their responses on 2 scales: (1) Nurses' Own Appraisal of Nurses and Nursing; and (2) Nurses' Estimate of Public Opinion of Nurses and Nursing. Found that changes in their perceptions of nurses and nursing tended to be away from the traditional image of nursing and toward the reality of present nursing practice.

Pierson, Lloyd Robert (Ed. D.). "THE DEVELOPMENT OF ACADEMIC SUCCESS PREDICTION EQUATIONS FOR USE IN THE SELECTION AND ADVISEMENT OF STUDENT NURSES IN AN ASSOCIATE DEGREE NURSING PROGRAM." Brigham Young University, 1975. 101 pp. Source: DAI, XXXVI, 7B (January, 1976), 3311-B-3312-B. XUM Order No. 76-661.

The purpose was to develop 2 sets of prediction equations: one for screening applicants for admission to the nursing program and a second for advising student nurses. Research on the equations, which used biographical and achievement factors, revealed that college achievement had a high correlation with success.

Pieta, Barbara Ann (Ed. D.). "A COMPARISON OF ROLE CONCEPTIONS AMONG NURSING STUDENTS AND FACULTY FROM ASSOCIATE DEGREE, BACCALAUREATE DEGREE, AND DIPLOMA NURSING PROGRAMS AND HEAD NURSES." State University of New York at Albany, 1976. 198 pp. Source: DAI, XXXVII, 11B (May, 1977), 5604-B. XUM Order No. 77-10,688.

Examined the bureaucratic, professional, and service aspects of nursing as perceived by senior nurses and faculty in baccalaureate, associate, and diploma programs. Role discrepancies existed for all groups, but the greatest discrepancy was found in the service role conception. The least discrepancy was in the bureaucratic role conception. Regarding perceptions of ideal versus actual practice of nursing, similarities existed among all groups on the ideal practice; views about actual practice were more diverse.

Pillepich, Mary K. (Ed. D.). "THE ROLE OF THE ADMINISTRATOR IN THE DEVELOPMENT OF GENERAL EDUCATION IN COLLEGIATE NURSING PROGRAMS." Columbia University Teachers College, 1960. Source: TCCU DIGESTS (1960), pp. 480-482.

Examined the importance of general education in collegiate nursing programs, the relationship between professional and general education, and the administrator's responsibility to encourage general education objectives. Recommended that nursing schools: (1) use general education goals as guides in curriculum planning; (2) determine the usefulness to nursing students of general courses in natural and social sciences; and (3) encourage nursing faculties to improve their general education courses.

Piper, Patricia Ellen (Ph. D.). "SELF-CONCEPT DIFFERENCES BETWEEN WHITE MALE AND WHITE FEMALE ELEMENTARY SCHOOL STUDENTS." Duke University, 1976. 287 pp. Source: DAI, XXXVII, 7A (January, 1977), 4241-A-4242-A. XUM Order No. 77-1086.

Females were more positive toward school and/or teachers. Females saw themselves as more anxious and insecure. Among students who felt positively about themselves in all the areas of self concept measured, the differences between boys and girls were minimal. Low self-security, high social maturity, and moderate to high self-acceptance appeared among both boys and girls at the primary level, became more characteristically female during the intermediate age, and by the fifth grade was almost exclusively female.

Pipitone, Phyllis Luis (Ph. D.). "THE FUNCTION OF SELF-ESTEEM, ATTITUDES TOWARD SCHOOL, AND TEACHERS' PERCEPTIONS AMONG ABOVE-AVERAGE FIFTH-

GRADE GIRLS." Kent State University, 1974. 65 pp. Source: DAI, XXXVI, 1A (July, 1975), 221-A. XUM Order No. 75-14,224.

Standard measures of behavior and self esteem were used with 60 above-average 5th grade girls and their teachers in 8 different classes. Found that: (1) no significant difference existed between the girls' levels of self-esteem and their teachers' perceptions of this self-esteem; and (2) high self-esteem girls indicated a better attitude toward school than did low self-esteem girls.

Pittman, Jacquelyn (Ed. D.). "THE DEVELOPMENT OF GRADUATE PROGRAMS IN PSYCHIATRIC NURSING, 1932-1968, AND THE RELATIONSHIP TO CONGRESSIONAL LEGISLATION." Columbia University, 1974. 159 pp. Source: DAI, XXXV, 10B (April, 1975), 4965-B-4966-B. XUM Order No. 75-7848.

Identified such social forces affecting psychiatric nurse education as: humanitarian reforms, mental hygiene movement, progressive education, 2 world wars, and acceptance of graduate psychiatric study in general medicine. Federal acts examined included: the Bolton Act of 1942, the National Mental Health Act of 1946, the Mental Health Study Act of 1955, and the Community Mental Health Act of 1963. In line with these trends, author made 5 recommendations to improve psychiatric nursing education.

Pittman, Mildred Madelene (Ed. D.). "SELECTED VARIABLES RELATIVE TO PERSISTING AND NON-PERSISTING STUDENTS IN SIX TWO-YEAR REGISTERED NURSE PROGRAMS IN OKLAHOMA." Oklahoma State University, 1974. 81 pp. Source: DAI, XXXVI, 10B (April, 1976), 4947-B. XUM Order No. 76-9748.

Studied associate degree nursing students grouped as persisters (graduated) or non-persisters (dropouts). Significant biographical variables were age, marital status, number of children, grades, social studies and composite American College Testing scores, and previous nursing education and nursing employment. Those found likely to succeed were: (1) older married students with children; and (2) students with previous nursing education or nursing employment.

Pitts, Janet Anita (Ph. D.). "AN ANALYSIS OF PERCEIVED NURSING PROGRAM OUTCOME GOALS." University of Washington, 1974. 113 pp. Source: DAI, XXXV, 8B (February, 1975), 4004-B-4005-B. XUM Order No. 75-4037.

In the effect on clinical practice by (a) baccalaureate and (b) associate degree nursing programs: (1) nursing educators saw little difference but believed there should be a big difference in goals; (2) registered practical nurses saw some differences and believed there should be differences in goals; (3) physicians saw little difference and believed there should be little difference in goals; and (4) hospital nursing administrators saw a small difference but believed no difference should exist in goals. Pointing to these incongruities, author stated the necessity: (1) to change nursing personnel utilization; and (2) to help physicians and nursing service administrators understand the implications of the alternative programs upon nursing practice.

Plawecki, Judith Ann (Ph. D.). "FACTORS INFLUENCING THE ATTRACTION AND RETENTION OF QUALIFIED NURSING FACULTY TO INSTITUTIONS OF HIGHER

EDUCATION LOCATED WITHIN THE STATE OF IOWA." University of Iowa, 1974.
283 pp. Source: DAI, XXXV, 7A (January, 1975), 4094-A. XUM Order No.
75-1246.

Identified the following factors associated with attraction and retention of nursing faculty at Iowa higher education institutions:
(1) the work itself and the responsibilities had the greatest influence; and (2) salary, personal life, and environment were less influential.

Plummer, Toni Carolyn (Ph. D.). "FACTORS INFLUENCING THE ATTITUDES
AND INTERESTS OF COLLEGE WOMEN IN PHYSICAL EDUCATION." University of
Iowa, 1952. 47 pp. Source: Dissertation, pp. 27-29.

College women surveyed showed that their motor ability had little relation to their favorable or unfavorable view of physical education.
More important were such factors as: personal response to the group,
finance, competition of other activities and interests, physical ap-
pearance, and physical education background.

Podall, Jane M. (Ph. D.). "THE EFFECTIVENESS OF CAREER AWARENESS
WORKSHOPS WITH FIFTH GRADE GIRLS." Loyola University of Chicago, 1977.
190 pp. Source: DAI, XXXVIII, 4A (October, 1977), 1901-A-1902-A. XUM
Order No. 77-22,350.

Among 105 5th grade girls in suburban public schools, those who participated in special workshops significantly reduced their sex-role
stereotypes, as against non-participants in the workshops. The workshops did not affect self-concept. There was no relationship between
sex-role stereotype and mother's employment. Study implied that special short workshops may be better than classroom instruction in reducing girls' sex-role stereotypes.

Poe, Nancy Margaret (Ed. D.). "FUNCTIONS OF A SCHOOL NURSE." Boston
University School of Education, 1957. 281 pp. Source: DAI, XVIII, 3
(1958), 1017. XUM Order No. 24,860.

Various functions of the public school health nurse were listed,
ranked in importance and frequency by practicing public school nurses, and the results used to suggest curriculum improvement in training public school nurses.

Pohl, Margaret Louise (Ed. D.). "A STUDY OF THE TEACHING ACTIVITIES
OF THE NURSING PRACTITIONER." Columbia University, 1963. 243 pp.
Source: DAI, XXIV, 8 (February, 1964), 3297. XUM Order No. 64-1494.

Informal teaching by private duty, general duty, public health, occupational health, and office nursing practitioners was analyzed. The
typical nurse: (1) did not recognize that she was actually teaching
when she helped patients understand their health and illness; (2) did
extensive teaching and considered it an important responsibility;
and (3) did not feel adequately trained to teach. The author defined
the professional nurse's teaching function and recommended ways to
prepare professional nurses to teach patients and others.

Poland, Harold Vincent (Ph. D.). "THE RELATIONSHIP BETWEEN SELF CON-
CEPT AND SUPERVISORY AND PEER RATINGS OF SUCCESS IN NURSES' TRAINING."
Fordham University, 1961. 126 pp. Source: DAI, XXII, 4 (October, 1961),
1260. XUM Order No. Mic 61-1580.

Of 100 senior nursing students tested, findings suggested that the
successful student nurse: (1) identified more closely with her occupational role and occupational goals; and (2) had superior personality adjustment (higher self-esteem).

Poletti, Rosette Aline (Ed. D.). "NURSING EDUCATION FOR THE UNIVER-
SITY OF GENEVA." Columbia University, 1975. 248 pp. Source: DAI,
XXXVI, 3B (September, 1975), 1148-B-1149-B. XUM Order No. 75-20,220.

Relates the background of the creation of a nursing education program
at the University of Geneva, Switzerland: (1) following example of
U. S., several West European countries saw the value of university-
based nursing education; (2) Switzerland's health needs and resources were studied; and (3) theoretical and practical curriculum was
planned to meet the next 10-year needs.

Polito, Josephine Tutino (Ph. D.). "STUDENT PERCEPTIONS OF TEACHER
INFLUENCE ON CAREER CHOICES ACCORDING TO THE SEX OF THE STUDENTS." Syracuse University, 1974. 278 pp. Source: DAI, XXXVI, 10A (April,
1976), 6619-A-6620-A. XUM Order No. 76-7930.

Used taped interviews with 36 students from urban, suburban, and
rural high schools to explore how students of both sexes perceived
their teachers' influence on their career choices. Concluded that
students saw teachers as an influential force. However, male students perceived teachers' influence differently from female students.
Replies seemed to show that teachers did not consider careers to be
important to females.

Pollack, Ronald Irwin (Ph. D.). "AN EXAMINATION OF SELECTED VOCA-
TIONAL BEHAVIORS OF TWELFTH GRADE SCHOOL-AGE PREGNANT GIRLS." Wayne
State University, 1976. 263 pp. Source: DAI, XXXVII, 11A (May, 1977),
6957-A-6958-A. XUM Order No. 77-9437.

Compared matched groups of pregnant and non-pregnant high school
senior girls. Found that pregnant girls: (1) had less stable
career choices; (2) made less vocational progress after graduation;
(3) were less likely to get jobs or attend higher education after
pregnancy; and (4) along with non-pregnant girls, considered their
parents most helpful with post-high school planning and the school
counselor the next most helpful.

Pollard, Lucille Addison (Ed. D.). "WOMEN ON COLLEGE AND UNIVERSITY
FACULTIES: A HISTORICAL SURVEY AND A STUDY OF THEIR PRESENT ACADEMIC
STATUS." University of Georgia, 1965. 346 pp. Source: DAI, XXVI, 11
(May, 1966), 6452. XUM Order No. 66-2494.

In a 17-state area, by 1860, 46 private colleges and 1 state university had women faculty. Percentages of women faculty were: 1890,
26.73%; 1946, 30.99%; 1962, 21.97%. At the time of this study, women held 9% of professorships and 10% of the doctorates. Author

recommended that more women should aspire to higher education careers and should earn doctorates.

Poloma, Margaret Mary (Ph. D.). "THE MARRIED PROFESSIONAL WOMAN: AN EMPIRICAL EXAMINATION OF THREE MYTHS." Case Western Reserve University, 1970. 203 pp. Source: DAI, XXXII, 1A (July, 1971), 564-A. XUM Order No. 71-19,042.

Studied 53 couples in which the wife was an attorney, physician, or professor. Found: (1) no role conflict between wife and husband; (2) most couples said that the man should be head of the family; (3) the professional woman did not have a career in the same sense as did her male colleagues because of family demands and her husband's career; and (4) most professional women considered their traditional roles as wife and mother most important. Concluded that dual-profession families are not altering the sex roles of the traditional family.

Poole, Drusilla (Ph. D.). "A STUDY OF ROLE PERCEPTIONS OF NURSING FACULTY IN SIXTEEN STATE UNIVERSITY SCHOOLS OF NURSING IN THE SOUTHERN REGION." University of Texas at Austin, 1969. 235 pp. Source: DAI, XXX, 4B (October, 1969), 1773-B. XUM Order No. 69-15,855.

Recent growth of university-based nursing education created interest in role perceptions of nursing faculty. This study found a conflict about nursing faculty role among the 3 groups who provided data-- nursing faculty, administrators, and senior nursing students. Nursing faculty identified as their primary role the teaching of nursing as a discipline, rather than service to the university, the nursing profession, or the community. Study concluded that pre-service and in-service training of nursing faculty should prepare them for multifaceted role as collegiate faculty members.

Poole, Rachel Johnson (Ph. D.). "A COMPARATIVE STUDY OF THE EFFECTS OF ASSERTIVE TRAINING AND CAREER DECISION-MAKING COUNSELING ON SELF-CONCEPT, SELF-ACTUALIZATION AND FEELINGS OF INADEQUACY OF ADULT WOMEN COMMUNITY COLLEGE STUDENTS." University of Pittsburgh, 1977. 176 pp. Source: DAI, XXXVIII, 4A (October, 1977), 1902-A. XUM Order 77-21,225.

Found among community college women that: (1) assertive training had a significantly greater effect on self-concept than career decision-making counseling groups or a control group; (2) assertive training had no greater effect on self-actualization or feelings of inadequacy than career decision-making counseling groups or a control group; (3) more self-actualization occurred in counseling groups than in the control group; and (4) counseling groups thought that counseling helped improve their self-perceptions and their interpersonal effectiveness.

Poole, Roy Raymond (Ph. D.). "EVALUATION OF A SMALL GROUP TEACHING-LEARNING PROCEDURE DESIGN TO FACILITATE THE OCCUPATIONAL PREPARATION OF BLACK UNDERGRADUATE UNIVERSITY WOMEN." University of Oregon, 1973. 123 pp. Source: DAI, XXXIV, 3A (September, 1973), 1186-A-1187-A. XUM Order No. 73-20,223.

Found among 24 black women university undergraduates that those in a specially designed small group learning situation (as against similar students not in a small group) gathered more accurate and comprehensive occupational information suitable to black women professionals.

Pope, Rhama Dell (Ph. D.). "THE DEVELOPMENT OF FORMAL HIGHER EDUCATION FOR WOMEN IN ENGLAND, 1862-1914." University of Pennsyvlania, 1972. 615 pp. Source: DAI, XXXIII, 7A (January, 1973), 3338-A-3339-A. XUM Order No. 73-1433.

Purposes of women's higher education in 19th century England were to prepare teachers for girls' schools and provide general education. Between 1862-86, universities opened their local examinations to girls. Girls' poor scores revealed their need for higher education. Proponents' gradual tactics reduced the threat that women's higher education would disrupt society. The University of London in 1878 granted the first degrees to English women. This study included comparisons of the rise of women's higher education in England with similar movements in Germany and Russia.

Pope, Ruth Vesta (Ph. D.). "FACTORS AFFECTING THE ELIMINATION OF WOMEN STUDENTS FROM SELECTED CO-EDUCATIONAL COLLEGES OF LIBERAL ARTS." Columbia University Teachers College, 1930. 110 pp. Source: TCCU DIGESTS (September 1929-December 1930), pp. 1-4.

Purpose was to determine the reasons women students in 6 liberal arts colleges withdrew before graduation. The author followed the college careers of freshman women entering in 1925 who dropped out. The average rate of withdrawal of entering students was 48%; 88% of all withdrawals occurred by the end of the 4th semester. Major reasons for withdrawal were (in order of frequency): financial problems, academic problems, and physical and social problems. Other findings: (1) some students knew when they entered college that they would not remain long enough to graduate; and (2) 34% of those who withdrew entered other higher education institutions.

Pope, Sharon Kay (Ph. D.). "EFFECTS OF FEMALE CAREER ROLE MODELS ON OCCUPATIONAL ASPIRATIONS, ATTITUDE, AND PERSONALITIES OF HIGH SCHOOL SENIORS." University of Missouri, Columbia, 1971. 163 pp. Source: DAI, XXXII, 9A (March, 1972), 4964-A-4965-A. XUM Order No. 72-10,648.

Found that high school seniors' vocational aspirations were raised by: (1) viewing video-taped interviews with 6 career women about their jobs and women's role; and (2) viewing video-taped interviews with 5 career women and 1 man about their jobs and women's role. These 2 experiments had negligible effect on the personality characteristics of participating high school seniors.

Popper, Dorothy Karpel (Ph. D.). "THE RELATIONSHIP OF SELF-CONCEPT TO CONGRUENCE AMONG SELF, IDEAL SELF, AND OCCUPATIONAL SELF IN SIXTH GRADE PUERTO RICAN GIRLS IN AN INNER-CITY POVERTY AREA." Fordham University, 1975. 83 pp. Source: DAI, XXXVI, 3A (September, 1975), 1359-A-1360-A. XUM Order No. 75-18,922.

A major purpose was to investigate the relationships between self-concept and possible future occupation among 66 6th grade Puerto

Rican girls. Found that girls with high self-concepts were better able to foresee themselves in a future occupation than were girls of low or medium self-concept. Recommended that career development programs be started in early grades and focus on building positive self-concept in order to promote career planning as a way to productivity and self-fulfillment.

Porter, Janet B. (Ph. D.). "THE VOCATIONAL CHOICE OF FRESHMAN COLLEGE WOMEN AS INFLUENCED BY PSYCHOLOGICAL NEEDS AND PARENT-CHILD RELATIONSHIPS." University of Oklahoma, 1967. 151 pp. Source: DAI, XXVII, 11A (May, 1967), 3730-A. XUM Order No. 67-3980.

Found: (1) no statistically significant differences existed between person versus non-person occupational orientation of women from 2-parent families and father-absent families; (2) women whose relationship with their mothers involved punishment were oriented toward non-person occupations; and (3) women whose relationship with their fathers involved rewards were oriented toward person occupations.

Porter, Janice (Ph. D.). "SEX-ROLE CONCEPTS, THEIR RELATIONSHIP TO PSYCHOLOGICAL WELL-BEING AND TO FUTURE PLANS IN FEMALE COLLEGE SENIORS." University of Rochester, 1967. 151 pp. Source: DAI, XXVIII, 5A (November, 1967), 1903-A. XUM Order No. 67-13,639.

Measured various qualities of 162 college senior women and divided them into 2 groups: the self-oriented (concerned with developing their own potential and seeking fulfillment through achievement) and other-oriented (expecting fulfillment through the achievements of their children and husbands). Self-oriented women felt more strongly about pursuing graduate study. No differences were found between the 2 groups on elation-depression and ego-strength scales.

Porter, Phyllis Evelyn (Ed. D.). "STUDENT AND FACULTY PERCEPTIONS OF STUDENT PARTICIPATION IN CURRICULUM IN SELECTED BACCALAUREATE SCHOOLS OF NURSING." Columbia University, 1975. 291 pp. Source: DAI, XXXVI, 1A (July, 1975), 110-A-111-A. XUM Order No. 75-13,905.

Responses of 1,139 students and 112 faculty in 10 accredited nursing schools about student participation in curriculum review and development showed that students perceived themselves as having limited involvement in curriculum. Faculty perceived that students were more involved in curriculum matters. Students actually played a role in their own individual programs and were important in curriculum evaluation.

Poshek, Neila Ann (Ed. D.). "CONGRUENCE OF EXPECTATIONS OF BACCA-LAUREATE NURSING STUDENTS AND THE REAL WORLD OF NURSING." University of Tulsa, 1971. 115 pp. Source: DAI, XXXII, 10B (April, 1972), 5889-B. XUM Order No. 72-12,941.

Used 25 statements about: (1) nurses, (2) nursing, and (3) patients to describe "The Real World of Nursing." Measured changes in expectations of baccalaureate nursing students before and after an 8-week course in Foundations of Nursing Care. Found that although student expectations about nurses did not change after the course, their expectations concerning nursing and patients did become more realistic about "The Real World of Nursing."

Poston, Dudley Louis, Jr. (Ph. D.). "INDUSTRIALIZATION AND OCCUPA-
TIONAL DIFFERENTIATION BY SEX: UNITED STATES, 1950-1960." University
of Oregon, 1968. 225 pp. Source: DAI, XXX, 2A (August, 1969), 834-A-
835-A. XUM Order No. 69-12,631.

In 28 states examined, the author found evidence to support the hypothesis that as states become more industrialized they allocate work
roles on the basis of qualification (including educational qualifications) and ability rather than on stereotyped status, such as sex.
Between 1950-60 the greater the industrialization, the less the occupational differentiation by sex.

Potter, Nancy Dutton (Ph. D.). "MATHEMATICAL AND VERBAL ABILITY PAT-
TERNS IN WOMEN: PERSONALITY AND ENVIRONMENTAL CORRELATES." University
of Missouri, Columbia, 1974. 116 pp. Source: DAI, XXXVI, 1B (July,
1975), 426-B. XUM Order No. 75-16,037.

Goal was to establish the relationship of personality and environmental factors to high mathematical or high verbal ability. Study
of 60 college women (20 with high math ability, 20 as a control group
with a balanced math and verbal ability, and 20 with high verbal
ability) found significant differences among the ability groups in
personality, sex-role perception, and environment as shown by their
relationships with their parents. Concluded that: (1) cognitive
skills and affective skills were inter-related; (2) individuals
with a balanced ability pattern may be more emotionally healthy; and
(3) fathers play an important role in daughters' emotional and intellectual development.

Potter, Ruby Mildred (Ed. D.). "FACULTY WORK LOAD IN THE CLINICAL
FIELDS IN NURSING DEGREE PROGRAMS." University of Colorado, 1958. 194
pp. Source: DAI, XIX, 12 (June, 1959), 3279-3280. XUM Order No. Mic
59-806.

Data for this descriptive study of clinical nursing faculty workload
were gathered from 38 nursing schools in 21 states and the District
of Columbia. The average faculty member worked 46.78 hours weekly,
nearly 3/4 of which were in teaching and related activities. The
remaining time was spent in meetings, clerical, civic, administrative, and other duties. Although not assigned, 1/4 performed some
nursing service. Faculty suggested that more staff be hired and/or
more time allowed for class preparation.

Potts, Helen Jo (Ph. D.). "CHARLOTTE PERKINS GILMAN: A HUMANIST
APPROACH TO FEMINISM." North Texas State University, 1976. 431 pp.
Source: DAI, XXXVII, 12A, Part 1 (June, 1977), 7925-A. XUM Order No.
77-12,492.

Biography of Charlotte Perkins Gilman (1860-1935), author, humanist,
and editor of THE FORERUNNER. Her diagnosis of women's predicament
was that it was ideological rather than political. Her solution was
that woman through her own powers, not through political agitation,
could achieve equality. Her influence was largely ignored until
Carl N. Degler's article in the AMERICAN QUARTERLY (Spring, 1956)
called her the "leading intellectual" in early 20th century American
feminism.

Powell, Bertie Jeffress (Ph. D.). "AN ANALYSIS OF THE DOMINANT THEMES IN SELECTED LITERATURE BY AFRO-AMERICAN WOMEN WITH RECOMMENDATIONS FOR INCLUSION IN THE HIGH SCHOOL CURRICULUM." University of Pittsburgh, 1974. 268 pp. Source: DAI, XXXV, 12A, Part 1 (June, 1975), 7748-A. XUM Order No. 75-13,209.

Analyzed U. S. black women's writings since the 18th century (novels, dramas, short stories, and poetry), identified the major themes, and showed how black literature could be studied in teacher education programs and used in English classrooms to benefit both sexes and all races.

Powell, Joann (Ph. D.). "AN ANALYSIS OF FACTORS RELATING TO DECI-SIONS TO TRANSFER FROM NORTHWESTERN UNIVERSITY BY FRESHMAN WOMEN." Northwestern University, 1970. 103 pp. Source: DAI, XXXI, 7A (January, 1971), 3277-A. XUM Order No. 71-1942.

University freshman women planning to transfer, as against those planning to remain: (1) appeared to have intellectual needs not being met; (2) were less group-oriented; (3) fewer belonged to sororities; (4) dated less often; (5) came mainly from the Northeast; and (6) were mainly either Jewish or had no religious faith.

Powers, Rosemary Redditt (Ed. D.). "A SURVEY OF THE READING, MEDIA, AND OTHER SELECTED INTERESTS OF STUDENTS IN GRADES NINE THROUGH TWELVE AS RELATED TO SEX, RACE, ACADEMIC LEVEL, SOCIO-ECONOMIC STATUS, AND ACHIEVEMENT IN ENGLISH." Temple University, 1977. 323 pp. Source: DAI, XXXVIII, 4A (October, 1977), 2031-A. XUM Order No. 77-21,784.

Identified self-reported interests of 1,200 pupils from urban, suburban and rural areas; compared findings with those reported in 1961 by Paul A. Witty. Found that both sexes: (1) preferred reading fiction to essays, plays, and poetry; and (2) were influenced more than formerly in their reading choices by movies, TV, and radio. Girls, compared to boys: (1) received less parental encouragement about reading; (2) read more fiction and magazines; (3) preferred stereotypically "girl" books and periodicals; (4) watched more TV and heard more radio (time declined as girls grew older); and (5) had less parental restrictions on TV viewing.

Pratt, Gladys Awotwi (Ph. D.). "VALUES AND QUALITY OF LIFE CONCERNS OF GHANAIANS AS A BASIS FOR HOME SCIENCE CURRICULUM." Pennsylvania State University, 1977. 132 pp. Source: DAI, XXXVIII, 2A (August, 1977), 670-A. XUM Order No. 77-17,716.

Found in comparing 69 home economics and 53 non-home economics teachers in Ghana (West Africa) elementary and secondary schools and teachers colleges: (1) no significant difference in their values and quality of life concerns; and (2) that their values included family security, happiness, wisdom, inner harmony, a comfortable life; mental, physical, and emotional well-being; freedom, equality, and concern for others; human relations; development and management of resources; and family planning. Recommended adding to present Ghanaian home economics (food, nutrition, clothing and textiles, and home-making) human development and the family.

Prefontaine, Marielle (Ph. D.). "WOMEN'S ROLE ORIENTATION IN THREE TYPES OF FRENCH CANADIAN EDUCATIONAL INSTITUTIONS." Cornell University, 1969. 154 pp. Source: DAI, XXX, 3B (September, 1969), 1229-B-1230-B. XUM Order No. 69-10,462.

Quebec women students at classical colleges, normal schools, and family institutes were tested for self-concept and role orientation (family, intellectual, and professional roles). Findings: (1) classical college students were high on professional role and low on family role orientation; and (2) Montreal students were more professionally oriented and less family oriented than were students from other areas. Other conclusions: (1) data only partially supported the view that high scholastic ability women were attracted more to the professional than to the family role; (2) independence from family and exposure to outside influence were important predictors of family role orientation in normal schools and family institutes; and (3) self-concept was negatively associated with family role orientation.

Preseren, Herman John (Ph. D.). "GENERAL EDUCATION AT THE WOMAN'S COLLEGE OF THE UNIVERSITY OF NORTH CAROLINA AS REVEALED THROUGH GROUP INTERVIEWING OF THE SENIOR CLASS OF 1953." University of North Carolina, 1954. 342 pp. Source: Dissertation, pp. 239-248.

Findings among women college seniors were that: (1) they did not understand thoroughly the intent of their general education program; (2) the interrelationships among courses had not always been explained; and (3) the general education program needed constant faculty evaluation.

Preston, Wilma Vivian Humbert (Ph. D.). "COLLEGE UNDERGRADUATE PREPARATION OF KANSAS HOME ECONOMICS TEACHERS." Kansas State University, 1976. 180 pp. Source: DAI, XXXVII, 7A (January, 1977), 4178-A-4179-A. XUM Order No. 76-30,016.

Data from Kansas public school home economics teachers during 1974-75 were used to suggest certification revision, improved home economics teacher preparation programs, and improved in-service training programs.

Price, Elmina Mary (Ed. D.). "LEARNING NEEDS OF REGISTERED NURSES." Columbia University, 1965. 235 pp. Source: DAI, XXVI, 8 (February, 1966), 4585-4586. XUM Order No. 65-14,983.

Data from 1,102 nurses in 24 hospitals identified interest in and need for in-service training. Of nurses questioned, 1/2 had been licensed less than 5 years; more frequent orientation programs for less experienced nurses were recommended. Because of their interests and their influence with the less experienced, supervisors and head nurses should receive in-service education in such areas as: administrative skill, hospital equipment, new therapies, and others. Concluded that in-service education should be scheduled for selected groups of nurses, many of whom have a strong desire for self-improvement.

Price, Helen Bryan (Ed. D.). "SCHOOL APPRAISAL BY DELINQUENT GIRLS."
University of Southern California, 1975. 164 pp. Source: DAI, XXXVI,
1A (July, 1975), 111-A. XUM Order No. 75-15,568.

Findings from 54 delinquent girls: (1) their attitudes toward
school were negative; (2) most did not blame schools for their incarceration; (3) their strongest negative feelings were toward teachers' interpersonal relationships; and (4) they felt no one at school
really cared about them. Recommended that: (1) school districts
and teachers find ways to learn of students' attitudes toward school
and to show concern for students as individuals; and (2) schools
should offer more alternative courses and schedules to meet more
students' needs.

Price, Mary Alice (Ph. D.). "A STUDY OF MOTIVATIONAL AND PERCEPTUAL
FACTORS ASSOCIATED WITH LEADERSHIP BEHAVIOR OF YOUNG WOMEN IN A PRIVATE
SCHOOL." Ohio State University, 1948. 149 pp. Source: Dissertation,
pp. 100-105.

Surveyed 223 female students, aged 16-20, in a private junior college
on personality traits associated with leadership behavior. Found
that the behavior of leaders and non-leaders as perceived by others
differed in: objectivity and goal orientation, motivational techniques, and the control of emotional expression. Leaders also differed from non-leaders: (1) in their estimate of their own behavior
and leadership status within a group; and (2) in relations with their
families.

Price, Michelle Braunstein (Ph. D.). "THE TEACHERS' PART IN SEX-ROLE
REINFORCEMENT." Yeshiva University, 1976. 159 pp. Source: DAI, XXXVII,
9B (March, 1977), 4656-B. XUM Order No. 77-5011.

Study investigated whether teachers expected and attempted to promote
sex-role behavior in their students. Responses from 90 lower elementary and 78 upper elementary female teachers indicated that teachers' concepts of typical and mentally healthy behavior: (1) differed
for boys and girls; and (2) corresponded to many societal stereotypes
of masculinity and femininity. Teachers were less tolerant of behavior inappropriate to their sex in older children, especially among
boys. Conclusion: teachers' sex-role expectations seemed likely to
cause sex-typed behavior in students.

Price, Quenton L. E. (Ph. D.). "INFLUENCE OF SEX AND FAMILY LIFE
EDUCATION ON STUDENT ATTITUDE TOWARD TRADITIONAL FAMILY IDEOLOGY AND SEX
KNOWLEDGE." United States International University, 1969. 118 pp.
Source: DAI, XXXI, 11A (May, 1971), 6161-A. XUM Order No. 71-7881.

Found no statistically significant differences in sex knowledge and
family ideology between those students who had pre-college sex education and/or family life courses and those who had no such training.
But among those with training: (1) boys and girls had higher mean
test scores; and (2) the girls scored higher on traditional family
status.

Priestley, Alice E. A. (Ph. D.). "MARIA MITCHELL, AS AN EDUCATOR."
New York University, 1947. 75 pp. Source: DAI, VIII, 1 (1948), 54-56.

This biography of Maria Mitchell evaluated her contribution to women's higher education, told of her preparation to be an astronomer, her teaching and training of researchers, and the unique qualities of her leadership as Professor of Astronomy and Director of the Observatory at Vassar College.

Prince, Lillian Joan (Ed. D.). "AN ANALYSIS OF THE LEADERSHIP OF MALE VERSUS FEMALE ELEMENTARY PRINCIPALS AS PERCEIVED BY TEACHERS." Brigham Young University, 1976. 105 pp. Source: DAI, XXXVI, 12A (June, 1976), 7794-A. XUM Order No. 76-13,577.

Teachers who worked under both saw no differences in and were not affected by male and female principals' leadership behavior.

Pringle, Robert William, Jr. (Ph. D.). "ANNA LOUISE STRONG: PROPAGANDIST OF COMMUNISM." University of Virginia, 1970. 220 pp. Source: DAI, XXXI, 9A (March, 1971), 4657-A. XUM Order No. 71-6646.

Biography of Anna Louise Strong (d. 1970), American-born communist propagandist who lived in and wrote glowingly of the USSR and the People's Republic of China. Briefly relates her education at the University of Chicago (Ph. D.) and her work as school board member in Seattle, WA.

Prochazka, Robert James (Ph. D.). "PHENOMENOLOGICAL STUDY OF PRACTICAL NURSING EDUCATION." University of Missouri, Columbia, 1976. 281 pp. Source: DAI, XXXVII, 9A (March, 1977), 6091-A. XUM Order No. 77-5644.

Study of significant aspects of practical nurses' 1-year hospital training, how they functioned, how faculty evaluated and classified them, and how faculty and students reacted to each other.

Profant, Patricia McGivern (Ph. D.). "SEX DIFFERENCES AND SEX ROLE STEREOTYPES AS RELATED TO PROFESSIONAL CAREER GOALS." Ohio State University, 1968. 298 pp. Source: DAI, XXX, 1B (July, 1969), 388-B-389-B. XUM Order No. 69-11,695.

Studied differences in sex-role perceptions and sex-role stereotypes of persons with specific career goals. Compared 30 men in engineering and 30 women in home economics (relatively homogeneous fields) with 30 men and 30 women in secondary education (a field more equally divided between men and women). Their sex-role stereotypes seemed less prevalent than earlier tests showed. The tendency was for one sex to be severe in judging the other sex on masculinity and femininity. Yet they were lenient with their own sex-role expectations.

Prose, Sister M. Redempta (Ph. D.). "THE LIBERAL ARTS IDEAL IN CATHOLIC COLLEGES FOR WOMEN IN THE UNITED STATES." Catholic University of America, 1943. Source: Published: Same Title; Washington, DC: Catholic University of America Press, 1943; pp. 156-160.

Only one of 91 Catholic colleges for women met all the requirements of a model liberal arts curriculum; 9 colleges were just short of the model; and the remaining 81 colleges lacked 2 or more fields of study. Among recommendations: colleges should reassess their aims and set up curriculum to meet those aims.

Pruitt, Greta Story (Ed. D.). "WOMEN IN LEADERSHIP OF ALTERNATIVE
SCHOOLS." University of Massachusetts, 1976. 246 pp. Source: DAI,
XXXVII, 1A (July, 1976), 80-A. XUM Order No. 76-14,655.

Compared women directors of public alternative schools with male
directors and with female principals of traditional schools. Found
that women directors of alternative schools: were younger; had
fewer academic degrees; had a non-traditional career sequence; and
had high ambitions. Recommended that advanced degree programs be
created for women who are working as innovative school leaders and
that leadership roles be redefined to assure that more women will
apply for them.

Puckett, Dorothea Emma Webb (Ph. D.). "EDUCATIONAL COUNSELING
GROUPS FOR BLACK ADOLESCENT FEMALES FROM A LOW-INCOME HOUSING AREA." University of Michigan, 1976. 160 pp. Source: DAI, XXXVII, 3A (September,
1976), 1472-A. XUM Order No. 76-19,222.

Low-income black adolescent girls in a counseling group were better
able to identify their problems than were the control group (girls
of similar background). The counseling group expressed ways to
cope with their fear, anger, and depression.

Puckett, Verna B. Fraser (Ph. D.). "DECISION MAKING IN PSYCHIATRIC
NURSING WITH IMPLICATIONS FOR CURRICULUM DEVELOPMENT." University of
California, Berkeley, 1963. 291 pp. Source: DAI, XXIV, 10 (April,
1964), 4148-4149. XUM Order No. 64-2120.

An intensive analysis of the decisions made in their work with patients by 5 graduate registered psychiatric nurses was used, among
other purposes, to: (1) define a body of knowledge unique to psychiatric nursing; and (2) clarify what and how to teach student psychiatric nurses.

Qadry, Hind Tahsin (Ed. D.). "PROBLEMS OF WOMEN TEACHERS IN IRAQ."
Stanford University, 1957. 204 pp. Source: DAI, XVIII, 2 (February,
1958), 476-477. XUM Order No. 25,357.

Data from 250 women teachers at 50 Iraqi girls' primary schools provided counseling information for girls considering becoming teachers.
The schools' cultural and historical setting were described. Characteristics of teachers: (1) most of their fathers were in trade,
commerce, or civil service; (2) over 1/3 were married and 80% of
their husbands were civil servants, professionals, or military men;
(3) 75% were Muslim; and (4) ½ entered teaching after 1948. Teachers' problems with pupils included their attitudes, classroom behavior, physical conditions, and age-grade placement.

Quinn, Kathryn Irene (Ph. D.). "SELF-PERCEPTIONS OF LEADERSHIP BE-
HAVIORS AND DECISION MAKING ORIENTATIONS OF MEN AND WOMEN ELEMENTARY
SCHOOL PRINCIPALS IN CHICAGO PUBLIC SCHOOLS." University of Illinois at
Urbana-Champaign, 1976. 153 pp. Source: DAI, XXXVII, 10A (April, 1977),
6199-A-6200-A. XUM Order No. 77-9151.

Found, in comparing 85 male and 76 female elementary school principals, that: (1) there were some differences in their self-percep-

tions of their administrative behaviors; and (2) those differences were affected by marital status, teaching experience, and race.

Quint, Catherine Isabella (Ed. D.). "THE ROLE OF AMERICAN NEGRO WOMEN EDUCATORS IN THE GROWTH OF THE COMMON SCHOOL." Boston University School of Education, 1970. 267 pp. Source: DAI, XXXI, 5A (November, 1970), 2142-A. XUM Order No. 70-22,473.

Included in the contributions of black women educators to the development of U. S. education were: Sojourner Truth (1797-1883), Marie Becraft (1807-33), Charlotte Forten (1838-1914), Lucy Laney (1854-1933), Ida Wells Barnett (1862-1931), and Mary Church Terrell (1863-1954).

Quiring, Julia Dianne (Ph. D.). "THE EFFECTS OF QUESTIONING LEVEL AND FEEDBACK TIMING ON THE ACHIEVEMENT OF SOPHOMORE NURSING STUDENTS USING AN AUTO-TUTORIAL APPROACH." University of Washington, 1971. 147 pp. Source: DAI, XXXII, 8A (February, 1972), 4251-A. XUM Order No. 72-7408.

Nursing students who learned to give certain injections by using videotaped replay as part of an experimental learning package did significantly better than those who received traditional classroom instruction.

Quisenberry, Dorothy Jean (Ph. D.). "A USE OF THE SEMANTIC DIFFER-ENTIAL TO DETERMINE THE PERCEPTIONS OF STUDENTS TOWARD WOMEN HIGH SCHOOL PHYSICAL EDUCATION TEACHERS." Ohio State University, 1970. 94 pp. Source: DAI, XXXI, 7A (January, 1971), 3324-A. XUM Order No. 70-26,350.

Regarding women high school physical education teachers, college freshman women viewed them: (1) in slightly lower esteem than they did all other women high school teachers; and (2) freshman physical education majors and those who liked physical education viewed the teachers more favorably than non-majors and those who did not like physical education. Recommended further research to learn reason for the dislike and to find ways to enhance the image of women physical educators.

Quraishi, Zahida (Ph. D.). "SUGGESTIONS AND RESOURCE MATERIALS FOR THE DEVELOPMENT OF A HOME ECONOMICS CURRICULUM AT THE COLLEGE LEVEL IN PAKISTAN BASED ON THE STUDY OF HOME ECONOMICS CURRICULA OF FOUR COLLEGES IN NEW YORK STATE." Cornell University, 1953. 305 pp. Source: Eells, p. 119, and Dissertation, pp. 282-285.

Personal interviews with home economics faculties in 4 NY state colleges provided data for a suggested home economics curriculum model for Pakistan schools, some of which features would have to be slightly altered because of social and cultural differences.

Rahman, Syeda Afzalunnisa (Ph. D.). "EDUCATION OF WOMEN FOR MODERN INDIAN SOCIETY: A HISTORICAL STUDY WITH A CRITIQUE OF CONTEMPORARY EDU-CATIONAL THOUGHT." Ohio State University, 1963. 222 pp. Source: DAI, XXIV, 3 (September, 1963), 1065. XUM Order No. 63-6261.

During the Muslim period, education was free and open to all, including Hindu boys but by custom denied to girls by rich Hindu

parents. All Muslim girls attended mosque schools but only upper-
class Muslim girls received higher education. With the Muslim decline, women's education almost ended. Initially neglected under
British rule, women's education grew at mission and private schools
and became overly academic, like men's education. Gandhiji and
Tagore suggested educational reforms. With independence universal,
free, and compulsory education for boys and girls became a constitu-
tional right, although women's education still lagged. The conclusion emphasized aiding every woman to become a good homemaker, citizen, and efficient worker.

Ralson, Yvonne Louise (Ed. D.). "AN ANALYSIS OF ATTITUDES AS BAR-
RIERS TO THE SELECTION OF WOMEN AS COLLEGE PRESIDENTS IN FLORIDA." University of Mississippi, 1974. 129 pp. Source: DAI, XXXV, 11A (May,
1975), 6992-A. XUM Order No. 75-10,687.

Concluded that female administrators in Florida had pro-feminist
views and were aware of sex discrimination in academia. The Board
of Regents and Chancellor had traditional views, and their lack of
awareness of sex discrimination could be a barrier to selecting a
woman as college president.

Ramphal, Marjorie Mote (Ed. D.). "FUNDAMENTALS OF NURSING AT LOS
ANGELES STATE COLLEGE." Columiba University, 1965. 175 pp. Source:
DAI, XXVI, 1 (July, 1965), 323. XUM Order No. 65-6170.

Author developed, tried, improved, and suggested continued use of a
Fundamentals of Nursing course as a foundation for baccalaureate
nursing education programs.

Ramsay, Edith Mae (Ed. D.). "THE EXTENT OF COMMUNITY COLLEGE FACUL-
TY PARTICIPATION IN ACADEMIC GOVERNANCE AS PERCEIVED BY ASSOCIATE DEGREE
NURSING FACULTY MEMBERS AND ADMINISTRATORS." Columbia University, 1975.
298 pp. Source: DAI, XXXVI, 3B (September, 1975), 1149-B. XUM Order
No. 75-20,222.

Nursing faculty (71) and 18 administrators of 24 2-year community
college associate degree nursing programs agreed that salary, fringe
benefits, and faculty participation in governance had decided their
use of collective bargaining.

Ramseyer, Edna Geraldine (Ph. D.). "THE ROLE OF THE HOME ECONOMICS
UNIT IN OHIO COLLEGES IN EDUCATION FOR FAMILY LIVING." Ohio State Uni-
versity, 1956. 237 pp. Source: DAI, XVII, 5 (1957), 1070. XUM Order
No. 20,713.

At 16 Ohio colleges more than 90% of both the faculty and senior
men and women questioned proposed requiring or making available to
all students selected learning experiences related to education for
family living. Social science and home economics were most often
suggested as contributing to education for family living.

Rancour, Laurence Edward (Ed. D.). "AN ANALYSIS OF MASTER'S DEGREE
PROGRAMS FOR TEACHING IN ROMAN CATHOLIC WOMEN'S COLLEGES." University
of Northern Colorado, 1961. 138 pp. Source: Dissertation, pp. v-xii.

This analysis of master's degree programs in teaching offered at Roman Catholic women's colleges revealed that: (1) all were accredited by regional associations and 27.9% had approval from the National Council for the Accreditation of Teacher Education; (2) the faculty-student ratio was 8.8 to 1; (3) libraries were 70% as large as those at criterion colleges but 97.4% satisfactory by standards of the Association of College and Research Libraries; (4) 55% of decisions were made by administrative fiat, as compared to 30% in criterion colleges; and (5) 3/5 of courses were in subject matter specialties compared to 2/5 at criterion colleges.

Rand, Lorraine Mary (Ph. D.). "CHARACTERISTICS OF CAREER- AND HOME-MAKING-ORIENTED COLLEGE FRESHMAN WOMEN." University of Iowa, 1966. 211 pp. Source: DAI, XXVII, 9A (March, 1967), 2833-A. XUM Order No. 67-2667.

Data from a nationwide study of freshmen were used to compare 548 homemaking-oriented women with 300 career-oriented women. Conclusions: (1) the career-oriented derived satisfactions from their achievements in school subjects, activities, and in professional aspirations; (2) the homemaking-oriented derived satisfaction from social relationships and personal well-being; (3) the career-oriented had redefined their roles to include characteristics appropriate to both sexes; and (4) the career-oriented were not less well-adjusted than the homemaking-oriented freshman women.

Randeri, Kalindi Jaswant (Ph. D.). "THE RELEVANCE OF LIBERAL ARTS EDUCATION IN TERMS OF THE ROLE OF THE EDUCATED INDIAN WOMAN AS PERCEIVED BY STUDENTS, PARENTS, ALUMNAE AND ADMINISTRATORS." Southern Illinois University at Carbondale, 1974. 297 pp. Source: Dissertation, pp. 190-194.

Researcher summarized the expectations of the educated woman's role as primarily wife, mother, daughter-in-law, and volunteer social worker or educator, and only secondarily as wage earner. A majority of administrators thought the goals of women's education should be the same as for men's education.

Randolph, Kathryn Scott (Ed. D.). "THE MATURE WOMAN IN DOCTORAL PROGRAMS." Indiana University, 1965. 74 pp. Source: DAI, XXVI, 9 (March, 1966), 5137-5138. XUM Order No. 65-14,060.

Study revealed: (1) discriminatory practices toward mature women in doctoral programs in admission policies, financial aid, assistantships, attitudes in assessing motivation, and lack of encouragement and guidance; (2) archaic views of women were common among graduate administrators and faculties; and (3) few women persisted in doctoral programs because of these obstacles.

Ranlett, Judith Becker (Ph. D.). "SORORITY AND COMMUNITY: WOMEN'S ANSWER TO A CHANGING MASSACHUSETTS, 1865-1895." Brandeis University, 1974. 308 pp. Source: DAI, XXXV, 6A (December, 1974), 3654-A. XUM Order No. 74-28,009.

The improvement of Massachusetts women's self-image and achievement in the 30 years studied resulted in large part from the many clubs and organizations they joined which offered self-awareness, sharing, self-help, and other educational concerns. These women's clubs helped offset the disintegrating effects of urbanization, industrialization, and immigration. Physical education, professional, and other training efforts were among the reforms that came from the organizations and prepared the way for the Progressive era.

Ranzau, Marie-Louise (Ph. D.). "CORRELATES OF CREATIVITY IN NURSING EDUCATION." University of Texas at Austin, 1970. 126 pp. Source: DAI, XXXI, 11B (May, 1971), 6715-B-6716-B. XUM Order No. 71-11,596.

Found baccalaureate nursing students to be imaginative, spontaneous, clever, and self-confident in personal and social interaction.

Raskin, Betty Lou (Ph. D.). "THE RELATIVE EFFECT OF OCCUPATIONAL AND SOCIO-OCCUPATIONAL INFORMATION ON HIGH SCHOOL GIRLS' EXPRESSED OPINIONS OF WOMEN SCIENTISTS AND SCIENCE AS A CAREER." Johns Hopkins University, 1968. 71 pp. Source: DAI, XXIX, 5A (November, 1968), 1455-A. XUM Order No. 68-16,464.

Lecture 1 on career opportunities for women in science was given to 115 college-bound high school seniors. But they were more affected by Lecture 2 which added to Lecture 1 favorable information about social aspects of women in the sciences.

Rasmus, Carolyn J. (Ed. D.). "LEONA HOLBROOK: HER INFLUENCES AND CONTRIBUTIONS." Brigham Young University, 1973. 241 pp. Source: DAI, XXXIV, 5A (November, 1973), 2371-A. XUM Order No. 73-26,702.

Biographical study of Leona Holbrook, former president of the American Association for Health, Recreation and of the National Association for Physical Education of College Women, who also served as recreation director, teacher, university professor, department administrator, and community and professional leader.

Ratliff, Christina Lycan (Ph. D.). "A DISCRIMINANT ANALYSIS OF SELECTED PERSONALITY FACTORS AND ATTITUDES OF TWO GROUPS OF MATURE WOMEN: HOMEMAKER-STUDENTS AND HOMEMAKERS." New York University, 1975. 155 pp. Source: DAI, XXXVI, 12B, Part 1 (June, 1976), 6452-B. XUM Order No. 76-12,591.

Found that homemaker-students were more dominant, more internally autonomous in thinking, more radical, more self-oriented in sex-role attitudes, and less group-dependent than the homemakers. No significant differences were found in trust, suspicion, or ego strength.

Ratte, Mary Lou (Ph. D.). "THE LOTUS AND THE VIOLET: ATTITUDES TOWARD WOMANHOOD IN BENGAL, 1792-1854." University of Massachusetts, 1977. 242 pp. Source: DAI, XXXVIII, 1A (July, 1977), 415-A. XUM Order No. 77-15,112.

During the early 19th century, British concern about Bengali women reflected the British feminist movement and the thinking of 18th century philosophies. Efforts to educate women failed at first, mainly because the Bengalis resented stress on Christian morality;

the British in 1835 decided to concentrate on training a male elite. When education came for Bengali women, the conservatism in both British and Bengali societies determined that the goal of women's education would be to assure that an educated man could have an educated companion.

Ratusnik, David LeRoy (Ph. D.). "INFLUENCE OF RACE, SOCIOECONOMIC STATUS, SEX, STIMULUS PRESENTATION MODE, AND RACE OF CLINICIAN ON PRE-SCHOOLERS' PHONOLOGICAL AND GRAMMATICAL ENCODING." Northwestern University, 1974. 546 pp. Source: DAI, XXXV, 10B (May, 1975), 5186-B-5187-B. XUM Order No. 75-7974.

The language usage of Chicago pre-schoolers was tested by several instruments. Findings related to sex included the following: higher non-standard speech was demonstrated by boys; on the draw-a-man measure, girls consistently achieved higher scores than boys.

Rauner, Therese M. (Ph. D.). "A STUDY OF OCCUPATIONAL CHOICES OF COLLEGE WOMEN." Fordham University, 1959. Source: Therese M. Rauner, "Occupational Information and Occupational Choice," PERSONNEL AND GUIDANCE JOURNAL, LXI, No. 4 (December, 1962), pp. 316-317.

Women college students (186) took tests of knowledge of occupations. Mean scores indicated a lack of a realistic approach to occupation choice. Students in nursing, medical technology, and biological and industrial research tended to score higher than students in liberal arts and business. Seniors tended to achieve better scores than juniors.

Ravitz, Melvin Jerome (Ph. D.). "FACTORS ASSOCIATED WITH THE SELECTION OF NURSING OR TEACHING AS A CAREER." University of Michigan, 1955. 265 pp. Source: DAI, XV, 4 (1955), 640. XUM Order No. 11,344.

Compared 135 nursing students with 188 teaching students on occupational, personal, and cultural-demographic factors. Selecting teaching as a career was associated with an urban and business class background and being Jewish; the opposite of these cultural-demographic facts was related to selecting nursing as a career. Parents and peers of nursing students more strongly favored nursing than parents and peers of teaching students favored teaching. Implications were suggested for counselors and recruiters of women nurses and teachers.

Ray, Malcolm Douglas (Ph. D.). "CAREER COUNSELING WITH THE MATURE WOMAN." University of Oregon, 1972. 150 pp. Source: DAI, XXXIII, 1A (July, 1972), 163-A. XUM Order No. 72-20,926.

Discussed women's role in changing society and the need for counseling of mature women wanting career skills. Four case studies and their implications were presented.

Raya, Afroditi C. (Ed. D.). "PSYCHIATRIC NURSING: A CONCEPTUAL APPROACH. A TEXTBOOK FOR GREECE." Columbia University, 1975. 396 pp. Source: DAI, XXXVI, 3B (September, 1975), 1149-B-1150-B. XUM Order No. 75-20,223.

Author presented the background for psychiatric nursing education in Greece and prepared a textbook for nursing students in this specialty.   Text tried to incorporate into nursing education the values of Greek religion and culture and a philosophy of nursing care of the whole patient.

Rea, Katharine (Ph. D.). "A FOLLOW-UP STUDY OF WOMEN GRADUATES FROM THE STATE COLLEGES IN MISSISSIPPI, CLASS OF 1956." Ohio State University, 1958. 234 pp. Source: DAI, XIX, 9 (March, 1959), 2276. XUM Order No. Mic 59-418.

Follow-up study of 272 married and 237 single women graduates of Mississippi colleges, most of them teachers, compared their grade average, salary, marital status, and type of work. Black women, 26% of the total, had similar characteristics to white women graduates except in salary.

Ready, Sister Mary Claver (Ph. D.). "A SURVEY OF THE TRAINING AND FUNCTIONS OF COUNSELORS IN CATHOLIC COLLEGES FOR WOMEN IN THE UNITED STATES." Fordham University, 1958. 323 pp. Source: Author.

Survey of counselors at 108 Catholic senior colleges for women showed that: (1) counseling was largely part-time, with counselors also teaching; (2) most counselors rated their efforts as successful; and (3) since ½ counselors were trained in fields other than education or guidance, in-service training was widely used.

Redd, A. Loretta (Ph. D.). "THE INFLUENCE OF A SEX ROLE STEREOTYPE INSTRUCTION UNIT ON THE MODIFICATION OF ATTITUDES AND BEHAVIORS OF ELEMENTARY SCHOOL TEACHERS." Georgia State University School of Education, 1976. 138 pp. Source: DAI, XXXVII, 8A (February, 1977), 5002-A. XUM Order No. 77-1557.

An experimental group of 15 Atlanta (GA) elementary school teachers and a control group of 10 teachers were rated for sex stereotyped behavior. The experimental group participated in 4 instructional meetings. Found that teachers did have sex-role stereotype biases and that such biases could be significantly reduced through education.

Redick, Sharon Smith (Ph. D.). "SELECTED CHARACTERISTICS OF HOME ECONOMICS TEACHERS AND PROGRAMS FOR PHYSICALLY HANDICAPPED STUDENTS." Iowa State University, 1974. 263 pp. Source: DAI, XXXV, 8B (February, 1975), 4025-B. XUM Order No. 75-3324.

Assessed selected attitudes, characteristics, and teaching behaviors of home economics teachers and determined the characteristics of the program they provided for physically handicapped students. Examined administrator and teacher perceptions of components to be included in home economics teacher education programs for the handicapped.

Reed, Dorothy (Ph. D.). "LEISURE TIME OF GIRLS IN A 'LITTLE ITALY'; A COMPARATIVE STUDY OF THE LEISURE INTERESTS OF ADOLESCENT GIRLS OF FOREIGN PARENTAGE, LIVING IN A METROPOLITAN COMMUNITY, TO DETERMINE THE PRESENCE OR ABSENCE OF INTEREST DIFFERENCES IN RELATION TO BEHAVIOR."

Columbia University, 1932. 69 pp. Source: Published; Same Title; Portland, OR: Privately Printed, 1932; pp. 57-60.

The leisure behavior of girls of Italian parents in a U. S. ghetto
was classified in categories of satisfactory, questionable, and
delinquent. Suggestions made to overcome their deprivation included:
(1) recreation through clubs and community organizations; and (2)
vocational training.

Reed, Fay Carol (Ph. D.). "EDUCATION FOR PROFESSIONAL NURSING:
FOUNDATIONS, HISTORY, PRINCIPLES, PROBLEMS." Ohio State University,
1964. 178 pp. Source: DAI, XXV, 12, Part 1 (June, 1965), 7210. XUM
Order No. 65-3907.

Culled from the literature were these 5 basic principles of professional nursing education: (1) nursing is a profession that provides
practical service to meet human needs; (2) it encompasses knowledge
from relevant fields of learning and from original investigations;
(3) its services are intellectual and altruistic; (4) it is subject
to control of society and the nursing profession; and (5) its excellence is related to the quality of individuals that compose it.

Reed, Joy Ann (Ph. D.). "THE ROLE OF SUPPORT SYSTEMS IN THE EDUCA-
TIONAL ATTAINMENT OF MATURE WOMEN." University of Oklahoma, 1977. 138
pp. Source: DAI, XXXVIII, 4A (October, 1977), 1823-A. XUM Order No.
77-21,401.

Asked 196 women college students, aged 35-45, about the sources of
tangible and intangible support for their education and about the
relationship between those support systems and the number of semester hours completed. Found: (1) no connections between the women's
support score, number of semester hours completed, socio-economic
levels, and the educational level of parents; and (2) a marginal
relationship between the educational level of husband and the number of semester hours completed.

Reed, Suellen Brenner (Ph. D.). "THE EFFECTS OF SEX AND PRESTIGE
VARIABLES, AS TEACHER CHARACTERISTICS, ON THE ACQUISITION OF KNOWLEDGE
BY UNDERGRADUATE NURSING STUDENTS." Texas A&M University, 1976. 126 pp.
Source: DAI, XXXVII, 8A (February, 1977), 4832-A-4833-A. XUM Order No.
77-2660.

On the assumption that students will imitate teachers, this study
investigated the effect that teacher sex and prestige had on attitudes and knowledge acquired by nursing students. Found that: (1)
teacher sex and prestige had no significant effect on knowledge acquired; but (2) attitude changes related to sex and prestige of
teachers did occur (i.e., male and female students identified with
attitudes of male teachers who had medium prestige).

Rees, Jane Louise (Ph. D.). "THE USE AND MEANING OF FOOD IN FAMI-
LIES WITH DIFFERENT SOCIO-ECONOMIC BACKGROUNDS." Pennsylvania State University, 1959. 131 pp. Source: DAI, XX, 2 (August, 1959), 657. XUM Order No. Mic 59-2909.

Comparison of food patterns and socio-economic and educational status of families with elementary school children showed that: upper status families with more education were more concerned with nutrition, family food preferences, and aesthetic meal preparation and service.

Reeves, Mary Elizabeth (Ed. D.). "MEASUREMENT OF ATTITUDES OF DEANS OF WOMEN TOWARD PRINCIPLES OF GOOD COUNSELING." Boston University School of Education, 1960. 143 pp. Source: DAI, XXI, 10 (April, 1961), 2992-2993. XUM Order No. Mic 60-5636.

Found in measuring and comparing the counseling attitudes of college deans of women and college counselors that: (1) deans were more authoritarian, more persuasive, less sympathetic, and less understanding; (2) younger deans were more understanding than older deans; (3) deans who did not teach were more authoritarian; and (4) deans felt primarily responsible to their college or university while counselors felt primary responsibility to the student.

Reevy, William Robert (Ph. D.). "MARITAL PREDICTION SCORES OF COLLEGE WOMEN RELATIVE TO BEHAVIOR AND ATTITUDES." Pennsylvania State University, 1954. Source: DAI, XV, 5 (1955), 702-706.

Urban, unmarried college women (139) were tested for prediction of marital success. Those with unfavorable marriage predictions were: (1) more active sexually; (2) less communicative about sex with family members, but more ready to talk about such matters with outsiders and strangers; and (3) less conservative in sexual attitudes.

Regan, Carole Ann Bennett (Ph. D.). "ATTITUDES TOWARD PARENTS AND ACHIEVEMENT MOTIVATION OF FRESHMAN WOMEN IN A SELECTIVE URBAN UNIVERSITY IN RELATION TO MOTHERS' CAREER PATTERNS." University of Pennsylvania, 1972. 162 pp. Source: DAI, XXXIII, 12A (June, 1973), 6738-A-6739-A. XUM Order No. 73-13,458.

Influence of working mothers on their college daughters: (1) there were no significant background differences other than education between working and non-working mothers; and (2) the career-oriented pattern of the mothers was not related to their daughters' achievement motivation but was related to the daughters' attitude toward herself, marriage, father, and mother.

Regan, Patricia Ann (Ed. D.). "AN HISTORICAL STUDY OF THE NURSE'S ROLE IN SCHOOL HEALTH PROGRAMS FROM 1902 TO 1973." Boston University School of Education, 1974. 183 pp. Source: DAI, XXXV, 4B (October, 1974), 1768-B. XUM Order No. 74-20,459.

Traced the changing role of the school nurse. Recommended: (1) uniform state certification approved by concerned professional organizations; (2) released time for continuing education; and (3) state committee to coordinate congruent roles of nurse, educator, and physician in school health service.

Regina, Sister Theresa (Ph. D.). "THE WORK OF THE NUN IN EDUCATION DURING THE MIDDLE AGES." Boston College, 1938. 227 pp. Source: Dissertation.

This historical study has important chapters on nuns and education in medieval France, England, Germany, and other European countries.

Reichow, Ronald W. (Ph. D.). "AN ANALYSIS OF THE EDUCATION AND EM-PLOYER'S PERCEPTION OF ASSOCIATE, DIPLOMA, AND BACCALAUREATE NURSES IN KANSAS." Kansas State University, 1974. 129 pp. Source: DAI, XXXV, 5B (November, 1974), 2281-B-2282-B. XUM Order No. 74-25,614.

Compared and evaluated associate degree, diploma, and baccalaureate degree programs, their curricula, and students. Found no signifi-cant difference in high school grades of students in the 3 nursing programs. Surveyed major employers of nurses in Kansas about their perception of recent nursing school graduates. Found that larger hospitals ranked diploma and baccalaureate students equal overall, diploma nurses significantly better in technical nursing, and bac-calaureate nurses stronger in leadership and administrative roles. Smaller hospitals tended to favor diploma nurses in most categories. Recommended that nursing programs include more work experience.

Reid, Alice Ruth (Ph. D.). "THE CONTRIBUTION OF THE FRESHMAN YEAR OF PHYSICAL EDUCATION IN A LIBERAL ARTS COLLEGE FOR WOMEN TO CERTAIN PER-SONALITY VARIABLES." State University of Iowa, 1955. 117 pp. Source: DAI, XV, 11 (1955), 2091-2092. XUM Order No. 14,140.

Freshman women's (39) personalities were tested at the beginning and end of the freshman year at a liberal arts college for women. Women not taking physical education courses that year were compared to a group which took 3 hours per week. Students with normal personality scores improved significantly in their general motor ability.

Reilly, Dorothy Elizabeth (Ed. D.). "A COMPARATIVE ANALYSIS OF SE-LECTED NON-INTELLECTIVE CHARACTERISTICS OF COLLEGE GRADUATE AND NONCOLLEGE GRADUATE WOMEN WHO ENTERED A COLLEGIATE NURSING PROGRAM." New York Uni-versity, 1967. 262 pp. Source: DAI, XXVIII, 10B (April, 1968), 4180-B. XUM Order No. 68-4817.

Characteristics of college graduates entering a college nursing pro-gram (compared to non-college graduates): (1) most college graduates were only-children; (2) expected to be in debt after their nursing program; (3) were late deciders who scored higher on theoretical values; (4) more were married and older so that choosing nursing sug-gested it was a substitute for another career; and (5) their selec-tion of a college nursing program was prompted by their wanting to continue intellectual stimulation.

Reimal, M. William (Ed. D.). "A STUDY OF FACTORS AFFECTING ATTRITION AMONG WOMEN RE-ENTERING FORMAL EDUCATION." University of Northern Colo-rado, 1976. 130 pp. Source: DAI, XXXVII, 7A (January, 1977), 4089-A-4090-A. XUM Order No. 76-29,778.

Found in a study of 374 women who re-entered school that the proba-bility of their persisting in college could be predicted. Students most likely to drop out: (1) were under age 40; (2) had children under age 6; (3) had prior college experience; (4) had incomes over $15,000; (5) told others their troubles; and (6) did not consider child care as important as did persisting students.

Reinfeld, Miriam Carol Grossman (Ph. D.). "THE RELATION OF EARLY RECOLLECTIONS AND LOCUS OF CONTROL AMONG EARLY ADOLESCENTS." University of Georgia, 1976. 87 pp. Source: DAI, XXXVII, 7A (January, 1977), 4243-A. XUM Order No. 76-29,559.

Internally controlled middle school girls had more early recommendations at home and recollections of other family members. Externally controlled girls remembered more early happy occasions, more positive consequences of their actions, and more incidents of high self-esteem.

Reinhart, Elizabeth (Ph. D.). "A STUDY OF THE EFFECTS OF THE LEARNING CONTRACT ON COGNITIVE GAINS AND ATTITUDES OF PRACTICING REGISTERED NURSES IN SELF-DIRECTED LEARNING." Kansas State University, 1976. 140 pp. Source: DAI, XXXVII, 9A (March, 1977), 5533-A-5534-A. XUM Order No. 77-5523.

The group that used a learning contract during a self-directed study did no better in cognitive learning than the control group. But some statistically significant changes did occur: (1) in the contract group's attitude toward self-discipline and satisfaction with new skill attained; and (2) in the control group's satisfaction with independent study.

Reiter, Mary Jo (Ph. D.). "EFFECTS OF POSTURAL TRAINING ON SELF CONCEPT OF SELECTED COLLEGE WOMEN." University of Utah, 1972. 90 pp. Source: DAI, XXXIII, 7A (January, 1973), 3358-A. XUM Order No. 73-1604.

Found among college women in an experimental physical education group who were given a special posture training program that: (1) they had an increased self concept; and (2) the increased self concept may have been a result of instructor influence.

Rennebohm, Fern Helene (Ph. D.). "A STUDY OF CURRENT CONSUMER EDUCATION ISSUES, BASED UPON OPINIONS OF HOME ECONOMICS PROFESSORS, BUSINESS PROFESSORS AND OTHER PROFESSIONALS WHO ARE MEMBERS OF THE AMERICAN COUNCIL ON CONSUMER INTERESTS." University of Wisconsin, 1971. 163 pp. Source: DAI, XXXII, 6B (December, 1971), 3470-B-3471-B. XUM Order No. 71-28,362.

Forty-nine issues were ranked in level of importance by home economics professors, business professors, and other members of the American Council on Consumer Interests. Significant differences existed among the 3 groups regarding placing the responsibility for teaching consumer education in a specific high school subject area. All respondents were greatly concerned about the preparation of high school teachers of consumer education.

Repp, Eleanor Carlotta (Ed. D.). "AN EXPLORATORY STUDY OF SELECTED BEHAVIORS OF EXECUTIVE OFFICERS OF BACCALAUREATE PROGRAMS IN NURSING." Columbia University, 1970. 181 pp. Source: DAI, XXXI, 10A (April, 1971), 5094-A-5095-A. XUM Order No. 71-8965.

Author developed a classified system to describe the role of the executive officer in nursing education leadership. Presented 6 categories to provide guidance and assistance to faculty in curriculum development and identified 6 behaviors within each category. Suggested how to use the classification system in nursing education research, teaching, and administration.

Reppert, Harold Curtis (Ph. D.). "A STUDY OF THE DIFFERENTIATING VALUES OF CERTAIN PERSONALITY MEASURES APPLIED TO A STUDENT AND REGISTERED NURSE POPULATION." Pennsylvania State University, 1945. 76 pp. Source: Dissertation, pp. 58-63a.

Found, in comparing supervisors' evaluation of best and worst (a) student nurses and (b) registered nurses, that: (1) most registered nurses and the best student nurses seemed to be more serious and more content; and (2) the 2 traits, seriousness and contentment, were highly related to nursing success.

Reres, Mary Epiphania (Ed. D.). "FACTORS OF INFLUENCE ON THE DECISION TO ENTER GRADUATE STUDY IN NURSING." Columbia University, 1970. 109 pp. Source: DAI, XXXII, 7B (January, 1972), 4031-B. XUM Order No. 72-4180.

Investigated nurses' decisions to enter graduate level nursing, particularly psychiatric mental health nursing. Findings: (1) no factors which influenced the decision to enter graduate study were statistically significant; and (2) no identifiable personality traits were related to choice of specific clinical areas. Concluded that nurses specialize in areas of their greatest competence.

Rey, Lucy Davis (Ph. D.). "SEX AND THE ASPIRATION FORMATION PROCESS." University of Notre Dame, 1976. 309 pp. Source: DAI, XXXVI, 11A (May, 1976), 7675-A. XUM Order No. 76-10,520.

Found among Michigan high school students that: (1) there was no significant difference in educational or occupational aspirations of boys and girls; (2) of 51 girls, 35% indicated combining career and family roles; (3) 25% of the girls chose non-feminine stereotyped occupations; and (4) girls' occupational aspirations were influenced by socio-economic status, degree of careerist ideology, and especially mother's career experiences, whether or not she was currently employed.

Reyburn, Clella DeLyte Tallman (Ed. D.). "THE EFFICIENCY OF THE NATIONAL LEAGUE FOR NURSING, PRE-NURSING, AND GUIDANCE EXAMINATION IN DISCRIMINATING BETWEEN PERSISTENCE AND WITHDRAWAL IN SCHOOLS OF NURSING." University of Tulsa, 1963. 114 pp. Source: Dissertation, pp. iii-v.

Scores of 1,892 freshman nursing students in 50 diploma schools of nursing were used to test the validity of classification equations evolved from the National League for Nursing, Pre-nursing, and Guidance Examination in predicting which applicants would persist or withdraw during the 1st year. Although the equations were adjusted, their predictive value was improved by only 4%. Further study was recommended.

Reynolds, Hilda Faden (Ed. D.). "WORK LOAD AND DETERMINATION OF WORK LOAD OF NURSE FACULTY IN SELECTED BACCALAUREATE PROGRAMS IN NURSING." University of Southern Mississippi, 1974. 123 pp. Source: DAI, XXXV, 5B (November, 1974), 2282-B. XUM Order No. 74-25,527.

Responses from 35 nursing school faculties: (1) did not agree on who decided nursing faculty work loads (mainly an administrative-faculty shared decision or decision made by deans in private schools); and (2) over ½ of the respondents said that work loads for nursing faculty were higher than those of other faculties. Among recommendations: (1) to formulate a work load in relation to class and clinic contact hours as well as student credit hours; and (2) to increase faculty-nursing student ratio.

Rheiner, Neil Warren (Ed. D.). "THE ROLE AND STATUS OF NURSING AS PERCEIVED BY NURSES." University of Nebraska, 1970. 198 pp. Source: DAI, XXXI, 4B (October, 1970), 2081-B-2082-B. XUM Order No. 70-17,749.

Information from 558 registered nurses and student nurses revealed that: (1) their educational preparation did not prevent them from ranking nursing very high as a profession; (2) technical nurses indicated that the nurse's primary role was to perform technical tasks but professional nurses saw their primary role as meeting patients' nursing needs; and (3) the longer they were nurses, the fewer activities they saw as appropriate nursing roles.

Rhodes, Jack Wayne (Ed. D.). "DEVELOPMENT OF A CARDIOVASCULAR FITNESS TEST FOR COLLEGE WOMEN BASED ON AN INDEX OF WORK EQUIVALENCY." North Texas State University, 1970. 104 pp. Source: DAI, XXXI, 10A (April, 1971), 5185-A. XUM Order No. 71-8687.

Formulated and found valid norms for a cardiovascular fitness test for college women that was the equivalent of measured work stress.

Rhodes, Kathleen (Ph. D.). "A STUDY OF TEACHERS' CHOICES OF OBJECTIVES AND METHODS FOR TEACHING ADULTS IN HOMEMAKING." Cornell University, 1950. 190 pp. Source: Dissertation, pp. 173-175.

The author developed, tested, and found valid an instrument to identify the objectives and methods used by teachers of adults in homemaking courses. Recommended that the instrument be used before and after adult homemaking classes to help students understand and teachers evaluate course aims and results.

Rhude, Beth Esther (Ed. D.). "A DESCRIPTION OF THE VOCATIONAL AND PERSONAL DEVELOPMENT OF A FEW WOMEN B. D. CANDIDATES." Columbia University, 1967. 261 pp. Source: DAI, XXVIII, 7A (January, 1968), 2565-A-2566-A. XUM Order No. 67-16,763.

Tiedeman and O'Hara's vocational theory, when applied to 5 women Bachelor of Divinity students, had weaknesses as a research tool but was useful: (1) in clarifying the ages at which each women proceeded through each stage of her development; and (2) in comparing the women with one another and in comparing their ages and stages in vocational and personal development.

Richards, Hilda B. (Ed. D.). "AN ASSESSMENT OF FACTORS RELATED TO SUCCESS IN INNER CITY NURSING PROGRAMS." Columbia University Teachers College, 1976. 276 pp. Source: DAI, XXXVII, 3A (September, 1976), 1378-A-1379-A. XUM Order No. 76-21,034.

The following factors were related to success among 57 graduating
nursing students and 107 pre-nursing students in an inner city associate degree nursing program: age, work experience, value placed on
education, educational preparation for college or post-high school
training (especially practical nursing), family's achievement orientation and other strengths, place of attendance of elementary and/or
high school, positive self concept, cohesion of community in which
reared, and supportive persons in that community. Social class and
father's income and education were not related to success. Most pre-
nursing students selected for the program came from and attended
schools outside large cities and were from intact communities.

Richards, Ronald Warren (Ph. D.). "THE RELATIONSHIPS OF CERTAIN
STRUCTURAL CHARACTERISTICS OF HOSPITAL WARDS AND THE ROLE CONFLICT AND
JOB SATISFACTION OF NURSES." Michigan State University, 1968. 144 pp.
Source: DAI, XXIX, 10B (April, 1969), 3802-B. XUM Order No. 69-5936.

College degree nurses had a higher need for order in their work and
in the structure of their wards than hospital school trained nurses.

Richardson, Mary Sue (Ph. D.). "SELF CONCEPTS AND ROLE CONCEPTS IN
THE CAREER ORIENTATION OF COLLEGE WOMEN." Columbia University, 1972.
175 pp. Source: DAI, XXXIII, 10B (April, 1973), 5001-B-5002-B. XUM
Order No. 73-9040.

Information from 150 women college seniors revealed that: (1) career-
oriented women had a high desire to work, valued a career more than
marriage, chose less traditionally feminine occupations, had high
aspiration levels, and sought intrinsic rather than extrinsic satisfactions in work; (2) work-oriented women sought both intrinsic and
extrinsic satisfactions in work, had well-defined occupational aspirations, planned to integrate work and homemaking, and did not plan a
major career; and (3) women whose self concept closely matched their
concept of the homemaker were not career-oriented. The evidence suggested that career women experienced role conflict.

Richmond, Lee Joyce (Ph. D.). "A COMPARISON OF RETURNING WOMEN AND
REGULAR COLLEGE AGE WOMEN AT A COMMUNITY COLLEGE." University of Mary-
land, 1972. 200 pp. Source: DAI, XXXIII, 3A (September, 1972), 1028-A.
XUM Order No. 72-20,792.

Comparisons were made of 86 women returning to college and 39 college
age women. Found that high school grades were the best predictor of
academic achievement for the college age women. For many returning
women, the best predictor of academic success was verbal reasoning
ability.

Riddle, Lynne (Ed. D.). "RELATIONSHIPS BETWEEN PHYSICAL EDUCATION
ACTIVITY PREFERENCE, SOCIOECONOMIC STATUS, AND PERSONALITY NEEDS OF FRESH-
MAN AND SOPHOMORE COLLEGE WOMEN." Syracuse University, 1968. 317 pp.
Source: DAI, XXX, 3A (September, 1969), 1005-A. XUM Order No. 69-8661.

Found that, given their choice, college women select physical education activities congenial to their personalities.

Rideout, Anne Holloway (Ed. D.). "THE UPWARD MOBILITY OF WOMEN IN
HIGHER EDUCATION: A PROFILE OF WOMEN HOME ECONOMICS ADMINISTRATORS."
University of Massachusetts, 1974. 201 pp. Source: DAI, XXXV, 5A (No-
vember, 1974), 2604-A-2605-A. XUM Order No. 74-25,865.

Characteristics of leading women home economics administrators studied
in U. S. and Puerto Rican colleges and universities: 53.2% had doctorates, median age was 45, median years employed was 24, 38% had no
career interruptions, over ½ were full professors, over 1/3 earned
annually over $25,000, saw challenging work as the highest rated job
characteristic, 56.1% were or had been married with an average of 1
child, most came from small families, most of their mothers had not
worked, most saw their own positive attitudes as having aided their
careers, almost 50% had received a professional honor in the past 5
years, and saw being a woman an advantage only because they were in
home economics.

Ridgway, Eileen Mary (Ph. D.). "THE AMERICAN NURSE OVERSEAS IN PRO-
GRAMS OF EDUCATION FOR NURSING." Catholic University of America, 1963.
226 pp. Source: DAI, XXIV, 9 (March, 1964), 3698. XUM Order No. 63-
7983.

Traced the history of nursing's international involvement and described the overseas work of voluntary and official agencies. Found
that: (1) 31 agencies had 512 U. S. nurses overseas, most of them
teaching; (2) most nurses and programs were in Asia (India and Pakistan), Africa, and Latin America; (3) few American nurse educators
were involved at the decision-making level of agencies; and (4) little cooperative planning was done for recruitment, preparation, orientation, or research related to nursing education overseas.

Rie, Herbert Emmanuel (Ph. D.). "SOME FACTORS ASSOCIATED WITH AT-
TRACTION OF STUDENT NURSES TO PSYCHIATRIC NURSING." Case Western Reserve
University, 1959. Source: Published with George W. Albee; Same Title;
Cleveland, OH: Mental Health Manpower Research Office, Behavioral Sci-
ences Research Building, May 1959; pp. 103-113.

First and 3rd year nursing students in general and psychiatric hospitals were compared on what attracted or did not attract them to
psychiatric nursing education. Positive factors for attraction included: (1) age, with older 3rd year students preferring psychiatric
nursing; (2) patients' greater appreciation; and (3) the location of
the nursing school in a psychiatric hospital, instead of in a general
hospital.

Rieff, Janan Ellen (Ed. D.). "A ROLE PERCEPTION STUDY OF CHAIRMEN
OF DEPARTMENTS OF PHYSICAL EDUCATION FOR WOMEN IN INSTITUTIONS OF HIGHER
EDUCATION IN THE MIDWEST." Illinois State University, 1972. 134 pp.
Source: DAI, XXXIII, 7A (January, 1973), 3488-A. XUM Order No. 73-94.

Found general agreement among deans, chairmen, and faculty at 16
higher education institutions about perceived ideal practice and
actual practice of women physical education chairpersons. Most disagreement was about the perceived actual role. The department chairpersons had the most agreement about their ideal and actual roles.

Riegel, Bernard George (Ph. D.). "ATTITUDES TOWARD CHILDBEARING."
United States International University, 1974. 131 pp. Source: DAI,
XXXIV, 10A (April, 1974), 6773-A-6774-A. XUM Order No. 74-8916.

College women more than men considered having children a creative and
joyful experience. Catholic college women more than Protestants and
the non-religious had a more accepting attitude about childbearing.
Both sexes reflected an optimism about achieving a better self in
their offspring.

Rines, Alice R. (Ed. D.). "EVALUATION AND LEARNING THE PRACTICE OF
NURSING." Columbia University Teachers College, 1959. 130 pp. Source:
TCCU DIGESTS (1959), pp. 610-611.

Reviewing the literature plus securing course aims, teaching methods,
and evaluations from junior college nursing instructors enabled the
author to identify a pattern of student behavior in nursing education.
Author urged that this teacher evaluation of the learning process be
made part of nursing teacher education programs.

Riordan, Richard Joseph (Ph. D.). "FEMININE SEX ROLE CONCEPTS AMONG
HIGH SCHOOL COUNSELORS AND STUDENTS." Michigan State University, 1965.
172 pp. Source: DAI, XXVII, 3A (September, 1966), 680-A-681-A. XUM
Order No. 66-6163.

Measured the attitudes of male and female counselors and male and female 11th graders toward the feminine role. Found that: (1) the counselors foresaw that girls would combine marriage and careers; (2)
male students thought the feminine role was more marriage-oriented
than did female students; and (3) female students, though their
Ideal Woman was marriage-oriented, were planning to work in traditionally female jobs.

Rios Pujols, Maria de los Angeles (Ph. D.). "A STUDY OF THE USE OF
MEDIA IN THE SCHOOL OF HOME ECONOMICS AT THE UNIVERSITY OF PUERTO RICO."
University of Nebraska-Lincoln, 1974. 111 pp. Source: DAI, XXXV, 5A
(November, 1974), 2629-A. XUM Order No. 74-23,934.

Gathered data from University of Puerto Rico home economics faculty
and administrators about their media use and their competencies in
media preparation. Because many faculty were unable to use tape recording, duplicating, and projection equipment and to prepare slides,
the author recommended an in-service program to teach these and
other audio-visual skills.

Ritz, John Michael (Ed. D.). "UNIFIED ARTS: AN INTEGRATIVE APPROACH
TO CURRICULUM DESIGN FOR THE ART, HOME ECONOMICS, AND INDUSTRIAL ARTS
SUBJECT AREAS IN THE MIDDLE GRADES." West Virginia University, 1977.
226 pp. Source: DAI, XXXVIII, 4A (October, 1977), 1863-A. XUM Order
No. 77-22,726.

To replace separate classes in art, home economics, and industrial
arts, the author designed a program for middle grades combining the
3 subjects. While each subject retained its identity, relationships
among the 3 subjects were shown and understandings heightened.

Roach, Sister Marie Simone (Ph. D.). "TOWARD A VALUE ORIENTED CUR-
RICULUM WITH IMPLICATIONS FOR NURSING EDUCATION." Catholic University of
America, 1970. 159 pp. Source: DAI, XXXI, 5B (November, 1970), 2785-B-
2786-B. XUM Order No. 70-21,844.

This philosophical study considered how Christian values might be
applied in nursing education. No specific changes were proposed.
The author recommended further study.

Robbins, Harvey Abraham (Ph. D.). "A COMPARISON STUDY OF COGNITIVE
STYLES ACROSS EDUCATIONAL LEVELS, RACE, AND SEX." East Texas State Uni-
versity, 1976. 92 pp. Source: DAI, XXXVII, 5A (November, 1976), 2752-
A. XUM Order No. 76-24,539.

Found that cognitive styles differed significantly across educational
levels, between blacks and whites, and between males and females.
Racial differences were attributed to cultural variations. The validity of some differences detected was questioned.

Robbins, Rosemary Boehringer (Ph. D.). "ACHIEVEMENT PERFORMANCE AND
FANTASY AROUSAL IN COLLEGE WOMEN AS A FUNCTION OF THE MOTIVE TO AVOID
SUCCESS, PROBLEM FORMAT, AND RELATIONSHIP TO EXPERIMENTER." Temple Uni-
versity, 1973. 187 pp. Source: DAI, XXXIV, 6B (December, 1973), 2950-
B. XUM Order No. 73-30,172.

Undergraduate females were divided into 2 groups on the basis of
their measured motive to avoid success. Found that: (1) creating a
situation where the women would not face negative effects of success
did not alter their performance; and (2) using female formats in
math problems revealed no differences between the 2 groups, both of
whom performed better on female format problems. Concluded that the
relationship between women's motive to avoid success and their performance is unpredictable.

Robert, Ellen Ruth (Ph. D.). "WOMEN'S ROLES: A MARXIST-EXISTENTIAL-
IST ANALYSIS." Western Michigan University, 1973. 342 pp. Source:
DAI, XXXIV, 10A (April, 1974), 6764-A. XUM Order No. 74-8927.

Data from 110 graduates 10 years after leaving high school revealed
that: (1) women were generally less interested and knowledgeable
about public figures and more socially isolated than men; (2) working women were more knowledgeable about national affairs, felt less
powerless, voted more often, and had more friends; and (3) the wife-
mother role affected only the number of acquaintances seen during
the day. Concluded that the evidence showing the importance of women's outside employment supported the Marxian theoretical concepts
espoused by Simone de Beauvoir.

Roberts, Mary Diane (Dr. P. H.). "THE EFFECTIVENESS OF JUNIOR/COM-
MUNITY COLLEGE ALLIED HEALTH/NURSING DEPARTMENTS: A STUDY OF THE RELA-
TIONSHIP OF ORGANIZATION STRUCTURE TO PERFORMANCE." University of Texas
Health Science Center at Houston School of Public Health, 1976. 323 pp.
Source: DAI, XXXVII, 10B (April, 1977), 5002-B-5003-B. XUM Order No.
77-9278.

This study of health and nursing departments and their organizational structure found: (1) much agreement about characteristics common to effective departments; and (2) evidence that the more effective departments were in colleges with more specialized staff, formalized programs, written rules, procedures, and guidelines.

Roberts, Percival Rudolph, III (Ed. D.). "AN EXPERIMENTAL STUDY OF SELECTED EFFECTS UPON DRAWINGS PRODUCED BY COLLEGE AGE WOMEN USING POETRY AS MOTIVATION." Illinois State University, 1968. 122 pp. Source: DAI, XXIX, 9A (March, 1969), 2903-A. XUM Order No. 69-4586.

Using poetry, especially oral readings, proved effective in motivating 54 women elementary education majors to try to express their creative feelings graphically. But their drawing ratings were not significantly related to their American College Test scores.

Robey, Marguerite Carr (Ed. D.). "A METHOD FOR DESIGNING A COMPETENCY BASED EDUCATION PROGRAM TO PREPARE NURSING SERVICE ADMINISTRATORS FOR COMPLEX HEALTH CARE INSTITUTIONS." Columbia University Teachers College, 1977. 203 pp. Source: DAI, XXXVIII, 4B (October, 1977), 1652-B-1653-B. XUM Order No. 77-22,291.

By applying the theory of competency-based education, the author designed an innovative research-based doctoral program intended to prepare nursing service administrators for complex institutions. The program's goal was to teach the necessary competencies and to provide for individualized study in order to achieve them.

Robinson, Mabel Crenshaw (Ed. D.). "A SURVEY OF THE GIRLS' PHYSICAL EDUCATION PROGRAMS FOR THE SECONDARY SCHOOLS IN THE STATE OF ALABAMA." University of Alabama, 1970. 234 pp. Source: DAI, XXXI, 10A (April, 1971), 5185-A-5186-A. XUM Order No. 71-9136.

Found in a survey of girls' physical education programs in 290 Alabama high schools that: (1) co-educational activities were offered in 44% of the schools; (2) fewer than ½ of the schools had girls' intramural programs; and (3) 81% of the teachers felt their programs lacked facilities, equipment, and administrative support.

Rocereto, Irene LaVerne Rodgers (Ph. D.). "THE IMPLICATIONS OF ROOT WORK AND ROOT DOCTORS FOR THE EDUCATION OF THE PROFESSIONAL NURSE." University of Pittsburgh, 1972. 94 pp. Source: DAI, XXXIII, 12A (June, 1973), 6696-A. XUM Order No. 73-13,174.

Because patients of certain ethnic groups believe in root doctors (i.e., medicine men), this study verified information about the practice of "root medicine." Findings were used in a nursing education course about culture and health practices.

Rockwood, Catherine A. (Ph. D.). "THE PERSONAL AND FAMILY LIFE NEEDS OF COLLEGE WOMEN, WITH IMPLICATIONS FOR EDUCATION." University of Chicago, 1952. 197 pp. Source: Dissertation, p. 7.

Investigated the needs of college women to help make the objectives for the college curriculum more appropriate and effective.

Rodgers, Leland Thorpe (Ed. D.). "CHARACTERISTICS OF JUNIOR COLLEGE WOMEN HAVING PERSONAL PROBLEMS HINDERING ADJUSTMENT." University of Missouri, 1954. 467 pp. Source: DAI, XV, 1 (1955), 87-88. XUM Order No. 10,130.

Factors that influenced women's college adjustment were parent-child treatment, peer relationships, and health problems. Recommended that data about these factors be considered in admitting students to college.

Roeder, Harold Henry (Ed. D.). "A COMPARISON BETWEEN THE LEISURE READING PATTERNS OF FEMALE TEACHERS AND FEMALE NON-TEACHERS IN AN INDUSTRIAL CITY." State University of New York at Buffalo, 1968. 215 pp. Source: DAI, XXX, 4A (October, 1969), 1458-A-1459-A. XUM Order No. 69-15,193.

Found, in examining leisure reading of women teachers and non-teachers, that significant relationships existed: (1) between the number of books and magazines read by adult females and their occupation; (2) between the number of books and magazines read by non-teachers and their level of education; and (3) education was a major determinant of the number of books reported read.

Roehm, Maryanne Evans (Ed. D.). "AN ANALYSIS OF ROLE BEHAVIOR, ROLE EXPECTATIONS, ROLE CONFLICT, JOB SATISFACTION, AND COPING PATTERNS OF ASSOCIATE DEGREE, DIPLOMA, AND BACCALAUREATE DEGREE GRADUATES IN BEGINNING NURSING POSITIONS." Indiana University, 1966. 148 pp. Source: DAI, XXVII, 6B (December, 1966), 2001-B. XUM Order No. 66-12,680.

Found that significant differences existed among associate degree, diploma, and baccalaureate degree nurses on 8 items of role behavior and 7 items of role expectation. The 3 types of nurses did not differ in the amount of conflict, degree of job satisfaction, or strength of coping patterns. Concluded that after a year as a practitioner the 3 types of nurses were satisfied with nursing as a career.

Roessler, Grayce Maurine (Ph. D.). "A COMPARATIVE STUDY OF THE SIMILARITIES AND DIFFERENCES OF OPINIONS OF NURSE FACULTY IN SELECTED ASSOCIATE DEGREE AND DIPLOMA IN NURSING PROGRAMS IN THE UNITED STATES AND CANADA AS RELATED TO SPECIFIC ASPECTS OF COMMUNITY/TECHNICAL COLLEGE PROGRAMS IN NURSING." University of California, Los Angeles, 1976. 252 pp. Source: DAI, XXXVII, 6B (December, 1976), 2773-B. XUM Order No. 76-28,576.

Opinions were compared from 104 associate nursing faculty members representing 46 U. S. community colleges in 27 states and 84 faculty members from 40 Canadian colleges: (1) most U. S. programs began after 1960, Canadian programs after 1970; (2) most programs had over 90 students, Canadian faculties had 21 and more, and U. S. faculties numbered between 6 and 15; (3) U. S. faculties were more satisfied with their programs; (4) both were concerned about their lack of control over student admissions, retention, and dismissal; (5) Canadian loads were heavier; (6) the U. S. clinical teacher-student ratio was higher; (7) both were satisfied with academic freedom and professional recognition; and (8) both were dissatisfied with student evaluation.

Roffman, Marian Hentzell (Ph. D.). "WORKING-CLASS WOMEN IN MEDIEVAL FRANCE, 800-1300." University of Hawaii, 1977. Source: DAI, XXXVIII, 4A (October, 1977), 2277-A.

Wives of artisans in town and their daughters and sons learned their husband and father's craft and were involved in production and trade. Most guilds let a woman become a master only at her husband's death.

Rogers, Marion Elizabeth (Ph. D.). "AN EVALUATION OF SELECTED PHYSI-CAL EDUCATION ACTIVITIES FOR COLLEGE WOMEN: A COMPARATIVE ANALYSIS OF PHYSICAL EDUCATION ACTIVITIES TO DETERMINE THEIR EDUCATIONAL POTENTIALS." New York University, 1960. 524 pp. Source: DAI, XXII, 1 (July, 1961), 145. XUM Order No. Mic 60-3757.

Of the 55 selected women's physical education activities evaluated: 20 activities scored high in educational value and in development value; 26 scored high for contributing to adjustment; and 16 scored high in leadership value. A conclusion was that women's physical education programs should include a variety of activities to meet women's needs for development, adjustment, and leadership training.

Rogers, Nola Stark (Ed. D.). "A STUDY OF CERTAIN PERSONALITY CHAR-ACTERISTICS OF SORORITY AND NON-SORORITY WOMEN AT THE UNIVERSITY OF CAL-IFORNIA, LOS ANGELES." University of California, Los Angeles, 1952. 118 pp. Source: Dissertation, pp. 101-109.

Sorority and non-sorority freshman and senior women were compared on the basis of grade point average and standard tests of personality, temperament, ethnic distance, and political distance. Some women were also interviewed. The same general characteristics were found among freshman women (sorority and non-sorority) and senior sorority women. Statistically significant differences existed in the non-sorority senior women, whose attitudes and selected traits changed much more during college than did those of sorority seniors.

Roh, Chang Shub (Ph. D.). "A COMPARATIVE STUDY OF KOREAN AND JAPA-NESE FAMILY LIFE." Louisiana State University, 1959. 310 pp. Source: DAI, XIX, 12 (June, 1959), 3408. XUM Order No. Mic 59-1546.

Women's status in Korean and Japanese societies was changing because of industrialization, urbanization, education, and western influence. Despite similarities, these differences in family life were found: (1) the Korean family was influenced by Chinese culture; and (2) the Japanese have strong ties with groups and activities outside the family.

Rohaly, Kathleen Alice (Ph. D.). "THE RELATIONSHIPS BETWEEN MOVEMENT PARTICIPATION, MOVEMENT SATISFACTION, SELF-ACTUALIZATION, AND TRAIT ANXI-ETY IN SELECTED COLLEGE FRESHMAN WOMEN." Ohio State University, 1971. 211 pp. Source: DAI, XXXII, 7A (January, 1972), 3766-A. XUM Order No. 72-4625.

Investigated relationships among physical movement, anxiety, and self-actualization values in 143 freshman women students. Some findings: (1) there was a negative relationship between self-actu-

alization values and anxiety (i.e., women having low anxiety tended
to have greater self-actualization); (2) no significant relationship
existed between participation in physical movement and self-actualization characteristics; and (3) women who felt great satisfaction
because of physical movement also demonstrated great self-
actualization.

Romano, Nicholas C.   (Ed. D.).   "RELATIONSHIPS AMONG IDENTITY CONFU-
SION AND RESOLUTION, SELF ESTEEM, AND SEX ROLE PERCEPTIONS IN FRESHMAN
WOMEN AT RUTGERS UNIVERSITY." Rutgers University, 1975. 112 pp. Source:
DAI, XXXVI, 10A (April, 1976), 6487-A. XUM Order No. 76-8704.

Found among 140 2nd semester college freshman women that: (1) resolution of their identity crisis was associated with positive feelings
of self-esteem, but not with their sex role perception; and (2) co-
education and single-sex options are desirable in college residences.

Romine, Benjamin Houston, Jr. (Ph. D.).   "THE EFFECTS OF THE INTER-
ACTION BETWEEN A PERSONALITY CHARACTERISTIC AND AN ENVIRONMENTAL CHAR-
ACTERISTIC ON THE ACHIEVEMENT OF FEMALE COLLEGE FRESHMEN WHEN ABILITY IS
CONTROLLED." Duke University, 1969. 121 pp. Source: DAI, XXX, 12A
(June, 1970), 5301-A. XUM Order No. 70-8835.

Comparison of 250 college freshman women living in a supportive atmosphere with 344 college freshman women living in a non-supportive
atmosphere suggested that the interaction between independence from
family and the press for community on a college campus might influence student achievement.

Roraback, Catherine Mary (Ed. D.).   "THE COLLEGE-BOUND HIGH SCHOOL
SENIOR GIRLS AND NURSING AS A MAJOR FIELD OF STUDY." Columbia Universi-
ty, 1968. 163 pp. Source: DAI, XXIX, 10B (April, 1969), 3802-B-3803-B.
XUM Order No. 69-6038.

Findings about 503 high school senior girls and their possible recruitment as nursing candidates: (1) 5.2% had chosen nursing; (2)
most were unprepared or reluctant to decide about a major field; (3)
the values of those who chose nursing were work-oriented; and (4) the
values of the rest were personally oriented. Concluded that those
trying to recruit nursing candidates: (1) should be aware of the
need for realistic information about present nursing trends; and (2)
should provide curriculum patterns sufficiently flexible to permit
exploration of nurse-related activities as a possible career.

Rosato, Peter, III (Ph. D.).   "THE ROLE AND QUALIFICATIONS OF DIREC-
TORS OF ASSOCIATE DEGREE NURSING PROGRAMS IN THE SOUTHEASTERN UNITED
STATES." University of Mississippi, 1972. 187 pp. Source: DAI, XXXIII,
7A (January, 1973), 3328-A. XUM Order No. 73-1289.

The work and qualifications of directors of associate degree nursing
programs were described, using findings from 91 academic deans and
91 associate nursing directors.

Rose, Eithel Bray (Ph. D.).   "A STUDY OF FACTORS INFLUENCING SELEC-
TION AND SATISFACTIONS IN USE OF MAJOR HOUSEHOLD APPLIANCES AS INDICATED
BY THREE SELECTED GROUPS OF MARRIED WOMEN GRADUATES OF THE OHIO STATE

UNIVERSITY." Ohio State University, 1959. 185 pp. Source: DAI, XX, 9 (March, 1960), 3723. XUM Order No. Mic 60-789.

Data about appliances from 495 women were used to suggest improvements in household equipment courses for college home economics departments and for non-credit continuing education programs.

Rose, Ella Joy (Ph. D.). "THE CASE STUDY METHOD IN THE GUIDANCE OF PROSPECTIVE HOME ECONOMICS TEACHERS IN PERSONAL AND SOCIAL ADJUSTMENT." Ohio State University, 1941. 597 pp. Source: Dissertation, pp. 527-531.

Recommended using the case study method to identify likely adjustment problems among prospective home economics teachers and to guide in their solution.

Rose, Lucien Devon (Ph. D.). "PATIENT VS. TECHNIQUE: A COMPARATIVE STUDY OF PERSONALITY AND MOTIVATIONAL CORRELATES OF STUDENT NURSES." Texas Tech University, 1972. 87 pp. Source: DAI, XXXIII, 8B (February, 1973), 3960-B-3961-B. XUM Order No. 73-4070.

Found that: (1) motivation of technique-oriented nurses and patient-oriented nurses did not differ significantly; (2) technique-oriented nurses were significantly more rule bound, duty bound, and more emotionally disciplined; (3) personalities of some technique-oriented nurses were reserved while others were domineering; and (4) personalities of some patient-oriented nurses were self-confident while others were submissive. Concluded that personality tests were useful for nurse selection and job placement.

Rosen, Andrew (Ph. D.). "DIFFERENCES IN MALE-FEMALE PERFORMANCE ON THE WECHSLER ADULT INTELLIGENCE SCALE." Hofstra University, 1975. 110 pp. Source: DAI, XXXVI, 1B (July, 1975), 426-B-427-B. XUM Order No. 75-12,480.

The patterns of male and female performance on the Wechsler Adult Intelligence Scale revealed that the rates at which scores declined between ages 16 to 65 and over were equivalent for males and females.

Rosenman, Linda Sophie (Ph. D.). "MARITAL STATUS CHANGE AND LABOR FORCE READJUSTMENTS: AN ANALYSIS OF FEMALE HEADS OF FAMILIES." Washington University, 1976. 154 pp. Source: DAI, XXXVII, 12A, Part 1 (June, 1977), 7975-A-7976-A. XUM Order No. 77-12,480.

Investment in job training for women who lost their husbands by death, separation, or divorce was more likely to be made by those better educated, those in white collar or professional work, those with higher incomes, and those with day care for their children. Major barriers to their taking training were responsibility for small children and other home duties.

Rosenstein, Betty (Ed. D.). "ACTIVITY PATTERNS OF MIDDLE CLASS WOMEN IN THEIR MID-YEARS WITH IMPLICATIONS FOR ADULT EDUCATION." University of California, Los Angeles, 1967. 266 pp. Source: DAI, XXVIII, 2A (August, 1967), 462-A. XUM Order No. 67-9659.

More than other women, 337 college student wives, aged 21-72: (1)
spent more time in creative arts; and (2) cared for their family's
educational and recreational needs. Implications were noted for
adult educators.

Rosensweet, Marshall Alan (Ph. D.). "THE RELATIONSHIP OF MASCULINITY-
FEMININITY OF SELECTED ELEMENTARY SCHOOL TEACHERS AND OTHER ENVIRONMENTAL
FACTORS TO THE MASCULINITY-FEMININITY OF THEIR STUDENTS." Miami Univer-
sity, 1972. 125 pp. Source: DAI, XXXIII, 1A (July, 1972), 196-A. XUM
Order No. 72-20,290.

Found that no significant relationship existed between the masculinity-femininity of 5th graders (69 males and 59 females) and any of the
variables tested, including the masculinity-femininity of their
teachers.

Rosenthal, Evelyn Ruben (Ph. D.). "STRUCTURAL PATTERNS OF WOMEN'S
OCCUPATIONAL CHOICE." Cornell University, 1974. 122 pp. Source: DAI,
XXXV, 6A (December, 1974), 3901-A. XUM Order No. 74-26,310.

Found that occupational choice and attainment of women aged 30-44
were related to social origins, socio-economic level, education, and
experience.

Rosenthal, Jane Chenoweth (Ed. D.). "A STUDY OF THE SELF-ACTUALIZING
PROCESS OF SELECTED UNIVERSITY FRESHMAN WOMEN STUDENTS." Colorado State
College, 1967. 194 pp. Source: DAI, XXVIII, 11A (May, 1968), 4451-A.
XUM Order No. 68-453.

Author administered a Personal Orientation Inventory to college freshman home economics students to measure their self-actualization (i.e.,
how they were achieving their academic, personal, and professional
goals).

Rosenthal, Naomi Braun (Ph. D.). "CONSCIOUSNESS RAISING: INDIVIDUAL
CHANGE AND SOCIAL CHANGE IN THE AMERICAN WOMEN'S LIBERATION MOVEMENT."
State University of New York at Stony Brook, 1976. 197 pp. Source:
DAI, XXXVII, 10A (April, 1977), 6775-A. XUM Order No. 77-7780.

Described the feminist origins, growth, and transformation of women's
consciousness-raising groups. Consciousness raising helped women's
self-esteem and encouraged women to change their lives, but it did
not provide an activist base for the women's movement. Instead, consciousness raising became increasingly like group therapy.

Rossmann, Jack Eugene (Ph. D.). "AN INVESTIGATION OF MATERNAL EMPLOY-
MENT AMONG COLLEGE WOMEN--A TWENTY-FIVE YEAR FOLLOW-UP." University of
Minnesota, 1963. 202 pp. Source: DAI, XXV, 4 (October, 1964), 2658-
2659. XUM Order No. 64-7269.

Follow-up study 25 years later of 240 married women college graduates
with children at home showed that those working full-time (compared
to part-time workers and the nonemployed): (1) had a higher scholastic score in 1962; (2) were less satisfied with marriage and life
in general; (3) had more education than their husbands; and (4) had
less family income (without counting the working wife's income).

Roudebush, Alma R. (Ph. D.). "A STUDY OF THE UTILIZATION OF STUDENT JUDGMENT IN CURRICULUM REVISION IN THE HOME ECONOMICS DIVISION AT THE NEW YORK STATE COLLEGE FOR TEACHERS AT BUFFALO." Ohio State University, 1952. 470 pp. Source: Author.

Data from home economics graduates about student involvement in curriculum revision revealed that: (1) students should not take over curriculum decision making; and (2) students should be given a rationale for decisions and their views should be presented in decision-making discussions.

Rouner, Evelyn Irene (Ed. D.). "A CONTEMPORARY IMAGE OF THE HOME ECONOMICS ENROLLEES OF FORTY-SIX DOWN-STATE ILLINOIS PUBLIC HIGH SCHOOLS." University of Illinois, 1959. 175 pp. Source: DAI, XX, 9 (March, 1960), 3653-3654. XUM Order No. 60-231.

Compared home economics with non-home economics students among 1,618 high school girl graduates in terms if IQ, achievement, family background, program of studies, college entrance, and homemaking activities after graduation. The resulting profile was then related to 12 competencies reported by the American Home Economics Association in June 1959 and implications were drawn for home economics guidance, curriculum, and recruitment.

Roussell, Frances Cecile (Ph. D.). "A COMPARATIVE STUDY OF TEACHERS' ATTITUDES TOWARD MEN AND WOMEN DEPARTMENT HEADS IN LARGE-CITY SECONDARY SCHOOLS." University of North Carolina, Chapel Hill, 1972. 178 pp. Source: DAI, XXXIII, 4A (October, 1972), 1385-A. XUM Order No. 72-24, 840.

Male and female department heads differed only slightly in personal characteristics and quality of leadership. In other aspects, women department heads were, on the average, 10 years older, had 10 years' more experience in education, and had been in their present jobs 2.6 years longer. Significant differences were that: (1) departments headed by women were perceived by teachers as higher in "hindrance" (negative influence); and (2) departments headed by men were perceived as higher in "esprit" and intimacy.

Rowe, Eleanor Lasier (Ed. D.). "THE KNOWLEDGE OF AMERICAN NURSES SERVING IN ETHIOPIA, NIGERIA, AND LIBERIA CONCERNING THE ETIOLOGY AND TREATMENT OF TYPHOID, TYPHUS, AND MALARIA." Boston University School of Education, 1975. 184 pp. Source: DAI, XXXVI, 3B (September, 1975), 1151-B. XUM Order No. 75-20,965.

In-service training and other continuing educational needs were stressed by American nurses serving in the 3 African countries; they disclosed their lack of knowledge, facilities, and equipment to treat typhoid, typhus, and malaria.

Rowles, Edith Child (Ed. D.). "A BRIEF HISTORY OF SOME EARLY CANADIAN DEVELOPMENTS IN HOME ECONOMICS." Columbia University Teachers College, 1956. Source: TCCU DIGESTS (1956), pp. 556-557.

Historical development of home economics education in 6 Canadian colleges and universities out of 14 offering home economics programs.

Last chapter on: social forces that led to teaching of home economics
in Canada, and the present status of home economics in higher education in Canada.

Roy, Edgar Lucien, Jr. (Ph. D.). "THE FOUR YEAR AMERICAN CATHOLIC
COLLEGES FOR WOMEN IN 1965." Saint Louis University, 1967. 207 pp.
Source: DAI, XXVIII, 8A (February, 1968), 2961-A. XUM Order No. 68-1290.

Findings in this descriptive study of 101 Catholic 4-year colleges
for women: (1) a trend was toward greater involvement of laymen;
(2) faculty strengths were devotion to teaching and a spirit of unity;
faculty weaknesses were lack of original research and too little pressure to compete professionally; (4) tuition was the greatest single
source of income; (5) a drop occurred between 1961-65 in career-oriented majors while humanities and social science majors increased.
Prospects were for continued diversity among Catholic 4-year colleges
for women.

Roy, Manisha (Ph. D.). "IDEAL AND COMPENSATORY ROLES IN THE LIFE
CYCLE OF UPPER-CLASS BENGALI WOMEN." University of California, San Die-
go, 1972. 259 pp. Source: DAI, XXXIII, 4B (October, 1972), 1362-B.
XUM Order No. 72-25,736.

Delineated the educational influences on upper-class Bengali women
by: father and father figures, mother and mother figures, husband
and husband's younger brother, and guru (spiritual advisor). Thus,
major extended family members contributed to women's personality needs.

Roy, Sunita (Ph. D.). "FACTORS RELATED TO THE ADOPTION OF FOOD
PRACTICES BY LOW-INCOME HOMEMAKERS IN THE EXPANDED FOOD AND NUTRITION
EDUCATION PROGRAM IN OHIO." Ohio State University, 1973. 145 pp.
Source: DAI, XXXIV, 2B (August, 1973), 746-B-747-B. XUM Order No. 73-
18,948.

Found that 96 Ohio homemakers ranked high 16 out of 32 food practices
recommended by nutrition aides, and that these food practices were
related to: number of family members, number of children at home,
frequency of the nutrition aide visits, kitchen facilities, marital
status, age, education, race, income, residence, information sources,
and community.

Rozendal, Nancy Anne (Ed. D.). "THE EVALUATION OF ADMINISTRATORS OF
BACCALAUREATE NURSING PROGRAMS: A STUDY OF CURRENT PRACTICES." Boston
College, 1977. 196 pp. Source: DAI, XXXVIII, 3A (September, 1977),
1259-A. XUM Order No. 77-18,634.

Surveyed 144 nursing schools in 40 states about the type of evaluation process used to assess administrators of baccalaureate nursing
programs. Found that: (1) more than 2/3 of respondents were not
evaluated by formal plans; (2) 3/4 felt they should be evaluated by
formal plans; and (3) smaller institutions were more likely to use
formal evaluation procedures. Most administrators favored such principles of evaluation as: (1) ideal performance criteria; and (2)
measurement of actual duties performed.

Ruach, Susan Whitledge Nevius (Ed. D.). "COMMUNICATION EFFECTIVENESS AND EXTENT OF ADOPTION OF AN ORGANIZATIONAL INNOVATION IN LOCAL UNITS OF UNITED METHODIST WOMEN." Indiana University, 1975. 114 pp. Source: DAI, XXXVI, 9A (March, 1976), 5744-A-5745-A. XUM Order No. 76-6294.

This adult education study focused on the communications which took place in the merger in October 1971, of 2 Methodist women's organizations into the United Methodist Women.

Rubenstein, Frank Jay (Ph. D.). "A STUDY OF FRESHMAN NURSING STU-DENTS: ROLE CONCEPTIONS." University of Pittsburgh, 1964. 139 pp. Source: DAI, XXVI, 6 (December, 1965), 3523. XUM Order No. 65-7031.

First-year nursing students (87) entering general hospital training: (1) felt ill-prepared in their new status; (2) preferred clinical experience with patients to classroom learning; and (3) were awed by their professional responsibilities.

Rubin, Arline May (Ed. D.). "SEX ATTITUDES OF FEMALE SEX EDUCATORS." Columbia University, 1970. 149 pp. Source: DAI, XXXII, 7A (January, 1972), 4139-A. XUM Order No. 72-4183.

Information came from 303 white females and 95 males taking sex education courses in 14 colleges. Some taught or planned to teach sex education. Males had more permissive sex standards for females. Sex educators and non sex educators alike thought that adolescent girls should have more restrictive standards. Rather than give advice themselves, both would refer students with sex problems to parents, clergy, or physicians.

Rubin, Howard Stanley (Ph. D.). "THE PREVENTION OF STUDENT ATTRITION IN NURSING EDUCATION: A COMMUNITY PSYCHOLOGY APPROACH." Illinois Institute of Technology, 1971. 172 pp. Source: DAI, XXXIII, 3B (September, 1972), 1296-A. XUM Order No. 72-22,852.

Found that: (1) the American College Test was the best predictor of academic success; (2) low California Reading test scores correlated significantly with academic failure; (3) achievement test scores of students getting remediation in basic skills did not improve significantly; (4) student's adjustment was significantly related to academic success; (5) student's expressed level of satisfaction was not related to academic success; and (6) using the community psychology approach was successful in reducing the number of student dropouts.

Rubin, Stefi Gail (Ph. D.). "TRAINING FAMILY DAY CARE PROVIDERS: EVALUATION OF AN EDUCATIONAL TV SERIES VIEWED AT HOME OR IN DISCUSSION GROUPS." 364 pp. Source: DAI, XXXVIII, 3B (September, 1977), 1418-B. XUM Order No. 77-19,134.

The TV series seemed to help shape a humanistic and developmental (as opposed to custodial) child care philosophy. As an introductory education experience, viewing at best had more to do with a "consciousness-raising" process in which providers' concerns were legitimized, than with instruction aimed at knowledge or skill acquisition.

Rueckel, Patricia (Ed. D.). "THE CONTRIBUTIONS OF WOMEN IN THE PRO-
GRESSIVE MOVEMENT IN EDUCATION 1890-1919." University of Pittsburgh,
1964. 172 pp. Source: DAI, XXVI, 2 (August, 1965), 851. XUM Order No.
65-7954.

Studied women progressive educators who helped liberalize kindergar-
tens in the 1890s, women directors of private progressive experiments
in New York City and in rural areas, similarities and differences
among progressive experiments, and the experiments' contributions to
later educational practice. Included: Anna Bryan, Caroline Haven,
Bertha Newell, Jennie Merrill, Nina Vanderwalker, Patty Smith Hill,
Caroline Pratt, Lucy Sprague Mitchell, Margaret Naumberg, Harriet
Taylor, Phoebe Thorn, Cora Williams, Marietta Johnson, and Mary
Turner Harvey.

Ruslink, Doris Henrietta (Ph. D.). "MARRIED WOMEN'S RESUMPTION OF
EDUCATION IN PREPARATION FOR TEACHING: AN INVESTIGATION OF SELECTED
FACTORS THAT ENCOURAGE AND DETER MARRIED WOMEN'S ENTRY OR RE-ENTRY INTO
TWO NEW JERSEY COLLEGES." New York University, 1969. 156 pp. Source:
DAI, XXXI, 3A (September, 1970), 1123-A. XUM Order No. 70-15,978.

Found that a woman's return to school was most often deterred by
family needs which conflicted with college obligations such as class
hours and academic load, both of which can be changed by educational
policymakers.

Russell, Sarah Frances Mullins (Ph. D.). "A SURVEY OF GUIDANCE PRO-
CEDURES IN CERTAIN NATIONALLY ACCREDITED GRADUATE PROGRAMS FOR GRADUATE
NURSES." University of North Carolina, 1960. 249 pp. Source: DAI,
XXI, 7 (January, 1961), 1854. XUM Order No. Mic 60-4866.

Concerning guidance, author found in 7 accredited graduate programs
for nurses that: (1) administrators and faculty usually performed
guidance functions; (2) vocational and health guidance was given
more than emotional and personal guidance; (3) students were less
pleased with their guidance than were administrators and faculty.
Recommended that there be: (1) leadership in guidance assigned to
qualified faculty; (2) in-service programs in guidance for faculty;
(3) continuous evaluation of guidance procedure; (4) follow-up guidance for graduates in adjusting to new positions; and (5) guidance
objectives identified in each nursing school's philosophy.

Rutherford, Millicent Alexander (Ph. D.). "FEMINISM AND THE SECONDARY
SCHOOL CURRICULUM, 1890-1920." Stanford University, 1977. 211 pp.
Source: DAI, XXXVIII, 3A (September, 1977), 1205-A. XUM Order No. 77-
18,243.

Surveyed the rise of the sex-differentiated high school curriculum,
1890-1920, and found that: (1) national education journals, 1904-17,
carried articles about girls' physical, intellectual, and moral capacities but after 1917 said little about girls; (2) after 1910 few
girls were enrolled in higher mathematics and science; and (3) the
1918 Cardinal Principles of Secondary Education Report followed established practice when it called for compulsory homemaking courses
for all girls. Concluded that the post-1890 high school curriculum
became sex-biased after the women's movement made suffrage rather
than full equal rights their goal.

Ryan, Sister Margaret Loretto (Ph. D.). "GENERAL EDUCATION IN CATHO-
LIC COLLEGES FOR WOMEN." Fordham University, 1950. 213 pp. Source:
Dissertation, pp. 195-200.

Recommended that Catholic women's colleges require a general education curriculum because: (1) expanding enrollments included more
students of diverse background than when only the elite attended college; (2) the breadth of general education would help prepare women
for responsible citizenship; and (3) general education's comprehen-
siveness would integrate learning.

Sabock, Ralph Joseph (Ph. D.). "THE HISTORY OF PHYSICAL EDUCATION
AT THE OHIO STATE UNIVERSITY--MEN AND WOMEN'S DIVISIONS, 1898-1969."
Ohio State University, 1969. 483 pp. Source: DAI, XXX, 10A (April,
1970), 5464-A. XUM Order No. 70-6868.

Historic highlights affecting women's physical education at Ohio
State University: (1) 1898, physical education begun, with no sex
separation; (2) 1922, women's division separated from men's physical
education; and (3) 1968, physical education department became the
School of Physical Education, separate from the Athletic Department.

Sabri, Marie Aziz (Ed. D.). "BEIRUT COLLEGE FOR WOMEN AND TEN OF
ITS DISTINGUISHED PIONEERING ALUMNAE." Columbia University, 1965. 451
pp. Source: DAI, XXVI, 11 (May, 1966), 6454. XUM Order No. 65-10,061.

This history of Beirut College for Women, 1926-1963, viewed its effect on women's status and its influence on Arab societies, particularly on education and social work. Biographies of 10 distinguished
alumnae are presented.

Sacks, Karen Helen Brodkin (Ph. D.). "ECONOMIC BASES OF SEXUAL
EQUALITY: A COMPARATIVE STUDY OF FOUR AFRICAN SOCIETIES." University
of Michigan, 1971. 267 pp. Source: DAI, XXXII, 11B (May, 1972), 6178-
B. XUM Order No. 72-14,982.

Found that: (1) women's status in 4 African societies was directly
related to their involvement in work outside the home; and (2) women's inheritance rights were directly related to their authority
over others and their household duties.

Sacks, Michael Paul (Ph. D.). "SEX ROLES IN SOVIET RUSSIA: CONTIN-
UITY IN THE MIDST OF CHANGE. (Volumes I-II)." University of Michigan,
1974. 418 pp. Source: DAI, XXXV, 5A (November, 1974), 3143-A. XUM
Order No. 74-25,317.

Studied effects of USSR industrialization on sex roles and women's
education from the late 19th century. Found that: (1) women's educational attainment had risen rapidly; (2) schools reinforced traditional sex roles; (3) women's domestic roles severely limited their
occupational advancement; and (4) men had greater opportunities for
advanced education and job promotion. Concluded that despite industrialization and widespread female employment, women in the USSR
lacked equality and were confined by sex-role stereotypes.

Saigh, Hani Raphael (Ph. D.). "STUDENT FINANCE IN NURSING EDUCATION: A SURVEY." New York University, 1972. 188 pp. Source: DAI, XXXIII, 11A (May, 1973), 5921-A. XUM Order No. 73-11,764.

Surveyed students in 129 2-year, diploma, and baccalaureate nursing programs. Found students were from diverse backgrounds. Most were from lower income families. Single white females predominated. Non-whites and males enrolled more frequently in the 2-year nursing course than in diploma or baccalaureate programs. Recommended that student financial aid be increased and that non-whites, males, and married people be actively recruited.

Sakac, Sister John Mary (Ph. D.). "AN ASSESSMENT OF THE PLACE OF CATHOLIC FOUR-YEAR COLLEGES FOR WOMEN WITHIN THE FRAMEWORK OF HIGHER EDU-CATION IN NEW YORK STATE." Catholic University of America, 1969. 119 pp. Source: DAI, XXX, 6A (December, 1969), 2269-A. XUM Order No. 69-19,724.

Descriptive study of New York State's 18 4-year Catholic women's col-leges. Dominant trends were: (1) rising number of lay faculty be-cause of reduced numbers of sisters; (2) growing financial strain, partly because of lay salaries; and (3) increasing concern about the viability of such small institutions (only 8 of the colleges had en-rollments exceeding 750 students).

Salie, Robert Douglas (Ph. D.). "THE HARVARD ANNEX EXPERIMENT IN THE HIGHER EDUCATION OF WOMEN: SEPARATE BUT EQUAL?" Emory University, 1976. 399 pp. Source: DAI, XXXVII, 7A (January, 1977), 4174-A-4175-A. XUM Order No. 77-979.

Fifteen-year history of the Harvard Annex, later Radcliffe College, founded 1879 on British university lines as separate from but depen-dent on Harvard University for men. First suggested by Harvard Presi-dent Charles Eliot in his 1869 inaugural address. Author concluded that separate education for women was not equal to Harvard education for men.

Salley, Karen Lynn (Ph. D.). "THE DEVELOPMENT OF COMPETITIVENESS IN WOMEN." University of Arkansas, 1977. 157 pp. Source: DAI, XXXVIII, 5B (November, 1977), 2349-B. XUM Order No. 77-23,398.

Findings included: (1) non-competitive college women were more tradi-tionally sex-role oriented and less achievement-motivated; and (2) mothers of competitive women had encouraged their daughters' compet-itiveness.

Salwonchik, Marie (Ph. D.). "THE EDUCATIONAL IDEAS OF LOUISA MAY AL-COTT." Loyola University of Chicago, 1972. 150 pp. Source: DAI, XXXIII, 4A (October, 1972), 1596-A. XUM Order No. 72-25,110.

First examined educational ideas of New England Transcendentalists Ralph Waldo Emerson, Henry David Thoreau, and Amos Bronson Alcott. Then focused on girls' education in Louisa May Alcott's novels: Little Women, Little Men, and Jo's Boys.

Samarakkody, Amara (Ph. D.). "WOMAN'S STATUS AND FERTILITY RATES IN SRI LANKA." State University of New York at Buffalo, 1976. 140 pp. Source: DAI, XXXVII, 8A (February, 1977), 5219-A. XUM Order No. 77-3578.

Author found in rural Sri Lanka that, despite low female education and employment, family planning education was effective.

Sample, Dorothy Elliott (Ph. D.). "SOME FACTORS AFFECTING THE FLOW OF WOMEN ADMINISTRATORS IN PUBLIC SCHOOL EDUCATION." University of Michigan, 1976. 328 pp. Source: DAI, XXXVII, 10A (April, 1977), 6201-A. XUM Order No. 77-8028.

Among 14 findings: (1) fewer women were training for school administration; (2) fewer women applied for school administration jobs; (3) women had less interest in administration; (4) women were less interested in 12-month job; (5) black women teachers had higher aspirations for administration than white women; and (6) there was no difference between men and women administrators' attitudes toward women administrators.

Samples, Merna A. (Ed. D.). "AN EXPLORATION OF PROFESSED ATTITUDES AND VALUES OF WOMEN COLLEGE STUDENTS TOWARD FAMILY LIVING, AS INDICATED BY RESPONSES TO A LOG-FORM." New York University, 1966. 185 pp. Source: DAI, XXVII, 4B (October, 1966), 1208-B-1209-B. XUM Order No. 66-9486.

A significant relationship existed between home economics students' middle class values and the number of family life courses completed. Since many graduating home economics students were uninterested in specific home economics-related courses, the author questioned whether departments should emphasize careers in recruiting home economics majors.

Sams, Lauranne Brown (Ph. D.). "THE RELATIONSHIP BETWEEN ANXIETY, STRESS, AND THE PERFORMANCE OF NURSING STUDENTS." Indiana University, 1968. 142 pp. Source: DAI, XXIX, 5A (November, 1968), 1456-A. XUM Order No. 68-15,461.

Found that: (1) less anxious nursing students performed 2 tasks better than did more anxious students; (2) stress-causing instructions produced poorer performance; and (3) interactions were not significant between anxiety vs. stress, stress vs. complexity of the task, and anxiety vs. complexity of the task.

Sand, Janet Marilyn (Ph. D.). "IDENTIFYING PREDICTORS OF DEPRESSION IN FRESHMAN COLLEGE WOMEN." Boston University Graduate School, 1973. 127 pp. Source: DAI, XXXIII, 12B (June, 1973), 6092-B. XUM Order No. 73-14,174.

Found valid, in testing 45 college freshman women, Bibring's theory that depression results from failure to meet one's goals or to satisfy one's needs, regardless of the psycho-sexual level at which they develop.

Sanders, May Myrtle (Ed. D.). "AN APPROACH FOR SELECTING THE NURSING CONTENT OF A PRESERVICE BACCALAUREATE PROGRAM." Columbia University, 1962. 115 pp. Source: DAI, XXIII, 11 (May, 1963), 4324. XUM Order No. 63-3768.

Used recommendations from nursing faculty, health reports, and nursing literature to propose 4 courses for baccalaureate nursing students: nursing of (1) children; (2) adolescents; (3) adults; and (4) the aged.

Sanderson, Donald Ray (Ed. D.). "A COMPARISON OF SELECTED CHARACTERISTICS OF THE UNIVERSITY AS PERCEIVED BY MALE AND FEMALE ELECTED STUDENT RESIDENCE HALL LEADERS AND NON-LEADER RESIDENCE HALL STUDENTS." Oregon State University, 1970. 89 pp. Source: DAI, XXXI, 11A (May, 1971), 5801-A. XUM Order No. 71-12,669.

Similar views about the university were held by female residence hall leaders and female non-leaders. Female students in general had a more congruent view of the university environment than did residence hall male students. Sex differences influenced students' views more than did their being leaders or non-leaders. Non-leader males had the most negative view of the university environment."

Sandul, Margarethe Lorensen (Ph. D.). "CHARACTERISTICS OF THE DEAN OF THE SCHOOL OF NURSING IN INSTITUTIONS OF HIGHER EDUCATION." Arizona State University, 1976. 175 pp. Source: DAI, XXXVII, 3A (September, 1976), 1342-A. XUM Order No. 76-19,828.

Findings about 172 deans of accredited U. S. baccalaureate and master's nursing programs included: (1) 68.7% had doctorates and 89% had previous administrative experience; (2) average ages were 46-55; (3) most were female, single, and Caucasian; (4) most reported directly to a high administrator; and (5) most had held their job less than 4 years. Among experiences rated as essential for deanship were classroom teaching and course work in budget making. Most time-consuming were personnel, administration, and curriculum problems. Most satisfying was work with faculty development and student growth.

Sanford, Jutta Schroers (Ph. D.). "THE ORIGINS OF GERMAN FEMINISM: GERMAN WOMEN 1789-1870." Ohio State University, 1976. 208 pp. Source: DAI, XXXVII, 2A (August, 1976), 1161-A. XUM Order No. 76-18,038.

More important than the influences of the Enlightenment and the French Revolution on German feminism were the romantic movement and the revolution of 1848. Not until the middle 1860s did German women begin to organize, and even then they made no demands for political equality.

Sarvas, Arlene Frances (Ed. D.). "AN ANALYSIS OF THE RELATIONSHIP BETWEEN PERCEPTIONS OF VOCATIONAL FEMALE FACULTY AND ADMINISTRATORS TOWARD FEMALE FACULTY IN FOUR INSTITUTIONAL TYPES." Pennsylvania State University, 1976. 192 pp. Source: DAI, XXXVII, 5A (November, 1976), 2822-A. XUM Order No. 76-24,797.

Identified relationships between views held by 1,404 female vocational education faculty and 1,181 vocational education administrators in 4 types of schools: area vocational school, community college, comprehensive high school, and post-secondary proprietary school. Found that more significant differences existed among female faculty than among administrators (generally males).

Saunders, Carolyn Beatrice F. (Ph. D.). "VIEWS OF NURSES IN THE TEXAS NURSES ASSOCIATION, DISTRICT FOUR, CONCERNING VOLUNTARY AND MANDATORY CONTINUING EDUCATION." North Texas State University, 1977. 103 pp. Source: DAI, XXXVIII, 3A (September, 1977), 1181-A. XUM Order No. 77-19,683.

Found that 68% of the nurses favored voluntary continuing education; 21% favored a mandatory approach; and the rest had alternative opinions about continuing education. Significant correlations were noted between respondents' views and age, basic nursing education, highest degree held, and field of employment.

Saunders, Margaret Buck (Ed. D.). "A COMPARATIVE STUDY OF THE PERCEIVED BEHAVIORAL DISPOSITIONS OF FEMALE AND MALE SUPERINTENDENTS." Virginia Polytechnic Institute, 1976. 80 pp. Source: DAI, XXXVII, 5A (November, 1976), 2564-A. XUM Order No. 76-24,340.

Findings: (1) behavior of male and female superintendents was similar; (2) a relationship existed between years of service and sex (males had more experience); and (3) superintendents employed more persons of their own sex to serve on their immediate staff.

Savin-Williams, Richard Charles (Ph. D.). "DOMINANCE-SUBMISSION BEHAVIORS AND HIERARCHIES IN YOUNG ADOLESCENTS AT A SUMMER CAMP: PREDICTORS, STYLES, AND SEX DIFFERENCES." University of Chicago, 1977. Source: DAI, XXXVIII, 8B (February, 1978), 3948-B-3949-B.

Found among 20 female and 20 male adolescent (ages 11-14) summer campers who were primarily Caucasian, Protestant, upper-middle class and suburban that: (1) boys were more apt to use overt and physical behavior to express dominance over their peers; and (2) girls were more apt to use indirect and verbal behavior.

Savundranayagam, Mercia Violet Sybil Cloelia Indreni (Ph. D.). "DEVELOPMENT OF HOME ECONOMICS EDUCATION AMONG THE TAMILS OF CEYLON." Oregon State University, 1964. 166 pp. Source: DAI, XXV, 2 (August, 1964), 983. XUM Order No. 64-9226.

History of home economics education among the Tamils from early trational training through European colonization and into the post-1948 independence period. The modern curriculum blended eastern and western home management methods and prepared women for careers as well as for family living.

Saxon, Sue Virginia (Ph. D.). "TEST PROFILE CHARACTERISTICS OF SELECTED BEHAVIORAL PATTERN GROUPS OF FRESHMAN WOMEN RESIDENTS ON THE MINNESOTA COUNSELING INVENTORY." Florida State University, 1963. 65 pp. Source: DAI, XXIV, 11 (May, 1964), 4553. XUM Order No. 64-3615.

Evaluated the Minnesota Counseling Inventory as a possible predictor of women students' behavior problems. Although it identified certain characteristics of over-achieving students and of students with disciplinary troubles, the study concluded that the Minnesota Counseling Inventory should not be used as the sole predictor in screening student behavior.

Sayre, Mildred Bunce (Ed. D.). "HALF A CENTURY: AN HISTORICAL ANALYSIS OF THE NATIONAL ASSOCIATION OF DEANS OF WOMEN, 1900-1950." Columbia University Teachers College, 1950. 134 pp. Source: TCCU DIGESTS (1950), pp. 450-451.

Traced the 50-year history of the NADW, its publications, policy, and influence on women's education by state and nationally.

Scanlon, Kathryn Ida (Ph. D.). "STUDENT GOVERNMENT IN CATHOLIC COLLEGES FOR WOMEN IN THE UNITED STATES." Fordham University, 1955. 337 pp. Source: Dissertation, pp. 301-303.

Recommended formulation of a constitution for student governments in Catholic women's colleges. The advantages would be better student-faculty understanding and cooperation and less student apathy. Also recommended student leader contact with the National Student Association and the leading national Catholic student group.

Scanlon, Leone (Ph. D.). "ESSAYS ON THE EFFECT OF FEMINISM AND SOCIALISM UPON THE LITERATURE OF 1880-1914." Brandeis University, 1973. 187 pp. Source: DAI, XXXIV, 7A (January, 1974), 4218-A. XUM Order No. 73-32,405.

In assessing the effect of feminism and socialism, cited fictional women created by such writers as Olive Schreiner, Thomas Hardy, and George Bernard Shaw. The lives of such actual women as Beatrice Webb's mother, who was severely limited by her sex, and of Barbara Bodichon, a women's education pioneer, were contrasted. Concluded that feminism and socialism influenced writers to develop new literary heroes and heroines.

Schaefer, Evelyn C. (Ph. D.). "THE BEARING OF PSYCHO-SOCIAL FAMILIAL FACTORS ON THE CHOICE BETWEEN TRADITIONAL AND PIONEER FIELDS OF FEMALE SIBLINGS IN POST SECONDARY EDUCATION." Catholic University of America, 1977. 90 pp. Source: DAI, XXXVII, 12B, Part 1 (June, 1977), 6308-B-6309-B. XUM Order No. 77-11,439.

Found among 51 women students in schools of law, medicine, and dentistry ("pioneer" careers), when compared with their sisters in schools of nursing, education, and social work (traditional careers), that both pioneer and traditional women: (1) saw their parents as fostering their independence and intellectual curiosity; (2) believed that they had mastery over their own lives; and (3) exhibited little masculine envy.

Schaefer, Robert Joseph (Ph. D.). "EDUCATIONAL ACTIVITIES OF THE GARMENT UNIONS, 1890-1948: A STUDY OF WORKERS' EDUCATION IN THE INTERNATIONAL LADIES' GARMENT WORKERS' UNION AND THE AMALGAMATED CLOTHING WORKERS OF AMERICA IN NEW YORK CITY." Columbia University, 1951. 271 pp. Source: DAI, XI, 4 (1951), 945-946. XUM Order No. Mic A51-595.

Unlike most American labor unions, 2 garment workers' unions held the socialist belief that workers should be educated to bring about social change. In the 1920s a short-lived labor education movement blossomed in other unions, labor schools and colleges opened, and the American Federation of Labor established a Workers' Education Bureau. By the 1930s only the garment workers' unions continued education efforts. Influenced by the New Deal, they cut their socialist ties. They provided their members--many of whom were women--with cultural and recreational enrichment and abandoned early socialist goals.

Schaeffer, Donald Thomas (Ed. D.). "AN INVESTIGATION INTO THE DIFFERENCES BETWEEN MALE AND FEMALE ELEMENTARY TEACHERS IN THEIR PERCEPTIONS OF PROBLEMS IN PUPILS." University of Maryland, 1968. 178 pp. Source: DAI, XXIX, 12A, Part 1 (June, 1969), 4201-A. XUM Order No. 69-9328.

Found in this study of 6th grade teachers: (1) male teachers reported more problems for boys than did female teachers, and most of the boys' problems cited by male teachers were in school achievement and social relationships; (2) male and female teachers did not differ significantly in the number of problems noted for girls nor in the ranking given to problems of boys and girls; and (3) older teachers reported more problems for girls than did younger teachers. Concluded that teachers perceived boys as having more problems than girls had.

Schenk, Katherine Nixon (Ed. D.). "FACTORS ASSOCIATED WITH PLANNED CHANGE IN BACCALAUREATE NURSING PROGRAMS." University of Florida, 1969. 108 pp. Source: DAI, XXXI, 1B (July, 1970), 268-B-269-B. XUM Order No. 70-12,582.

Studied 8 baccalaureate nursing programs, 4 of which engaged in change planning and self-renewal. Found that nursing programs which had planned change: (1) were not affected by size, type of control, or location; (2) had a director of curriculum in addition to a dean; (3) had adequate financing and time for planning; (4) had high morale; and (5) allowed for shared leadership responsibility.

Schiff, Ellen (Ph. D.). "THE RELATIONSHIP OF WOMEN'S SEX-ROLE IDENTITY TO SELF-ESTEEM AND EGO DEVELOPMENT." University of Maryland, 1977. 119 pp. Source: DAI, XXXVIII, 6B (December, 1977), 2878-B. XUM Order No. 77-26,565.

Found among 100 college women: (1) no differences in self-esteem between those without sex bias and those with a masculine bias; and (2) more ego development among those without sex bias than those who were either more feminine or more masculine.

Schildhaus, Andrew Frank (Ed. D.). "STUDENT NURSE ATTITUDES TOWARD MENTAL ILLNESS FOLLOWING A PSYCHIATRIC TRAINING PROGRAM." Columbia University, 1971. 72 pp. Source: DAI, XXXII, 7A (January, 1972), 3801-A. XUM Order No. 72-4184.

No significant changes occurred in the attitudes of student nurses toward the mentally ill after an 8-week psychiatric training program.

Schirmer, Sister Mary Austin (Ph. D.). "AN EVALUATION OF TEACHER EDUCATION PROGRAMS IN A SELECTED GROUP OF CATHOLIC LIBERAL ARTS COLLEGES

FOR WOMEN." Catholic University of America, 1958. 208 pp. Source: Dissertation, pp. 174-180.

Found in teacher education programs of 66 Catholic women's colleges: (1) agreement on objectives (although only 56% had recorded teacher education objectives); (2) 47% engaged in research and experimentation; (3) offered in-service teacher education programs; and (4) 20 colleges prepared lay teachers for parochial schools.

Schlack, Marilyn Joyce (Ed. D.). "A COMPARISON OF PERSONAL CHARACTERISTICS AND LEADERSHIP STYLES OF UNIVERSITY UPPER MANAGEMENT AND MIDDLE-MANAGEMENT WOMEN STUDENT PERSONNEL ADMINISTRATORS." Western Michigan University, 1974. 164 pp. Source: DAI, XXXV, 2A (August, 1974), 852-A-853-A. XUM Order No. 74-19,076.

Found among 150 women university deans and other officers that: (1) they received higher salaries; (2) more middle-management student personnel officers pursued advanced degrees; (3) those affiliated with a feminist group were aged 20 to 40; (4) most rated themselves as middle management; and (5) those scoring higher on leadership were married, were pursuing doctoral degrees, and had mothers with professional or managerial careers.

Schloemer, Camilla Rebecca (Ph. D.). "A STUDY OF NURSE FACULTY MEMBERS: THEIR CAREER CHOICE AND RELATED FACTORS." University of Minnesota, 1967. 237 pp. Source: DAI, XXVIII, 6B (December, 1967), 2495-B-2496-B. XUM Order No. 67-14,649.

Found among 469 Wisconsin nursing teachers that they: (1) became interested in teaching nursing late, after having some nursing experiences, and by chance rather than by choice; (2) grew up in small communities, were single, and had a religious affiliation; and (3) had extended their academic preparation to the baccalaureate degree and 1/5 of them to the master's degree and beyond. Findings were then related to recruitment, retention, and programs of nursing faculties.

Schmall, Vicki Flagan (Ph. D.). "IMPACT OF A HUMAN SEXUALITY COURSE ON UNIVERSITY STUDENTS' KNOWLEDGE, ATTITUDES, AND ACCEPTABILITY OF SEXUAL BEHAVIORS." Oregon State University, 1977. 190 pp. Source: DAI, XXXVIII, 4A (October, 1977), 1753-A-1754-A. XUM Order No. 77-20,480.

Before-and-after attitudes of university students taking a sex education course showed that: (1) most became more accepting of the sexual behavior of others; and (2) women were more favorable toward virginity for both men and women.

Schmid, Andrea Bodo (Ed. D.). "AN EVALUATION OF PROFESSIONAL PREPARATION IN WOMEN'S PHYSICAL EDUCATION DEPARTMENTS IN THE STATE COLLEGE SYSTEM OF CALIFORNIA." University of California, Berkeley, 1968. 247 pp. Source: DAI, XXX, 3A (September, 1969), 1057-A. XUM Order No. 69-14,820.

Survey of the teacher education curricula in 15 California colleges graduating the 275 women high school physical education teachers studied showed that they: (1) were adequately prepared in aquatics, dance, team, and individual sports; but (2) needed more preparation in track, field, and gymnastics.

Schnaiberg, Allan (Ph. D.). "SOME DETERMINANTS AND CONSEQUENCES OF MODERNISM IN TURKEY." University of Michigan, 1968. 376 pp. Source: DAI, XXX, 1A (July, 1969), 407-A. XUM Order No. 69-12,233.

Data from 1,138 Turkish women living in Ankara and in 4 rural villages revealed that early life in a city enhanced a woman's level of modernism, mainly because of the greater availability of schooling. Concluded that providing more female education in rural areas would hasten modernism and decrease birth rate.

Schneider, Florence Hemley (Ph. D.). "THE BRYN MAWR SUMMER SCHOOL FOR WOMEN WORKERS IN INDUSTRY, A RESIDENT SCHOOL IN THE WORKERS' EDUCATION MOVEMENT." Bryn Mawr College, 1939. Source: Published as PATTERNS OF WORKERS' EDUCATION: THE STORY OF THE BRYN MAWR SUMMER SCHOOL; Washington, DC: American Council on Public Affairs, 1941; pp. 141-148.

An historical study of the Bryn Mawr Summer School, 1921-1938, a resident program for women and part of the labor education movement whose purpose was to strengthen U. S. democracy.

Schneider, Sister Mary Celeste (Ph. D.). "HOME ECONOMICS IN CATHOLIC HIGHER EDUCATION." Michigan State University, 1965. 173 pp. Source: DAI, XXVI, 8 (February, 1966), 4621-4622. XUM Order No. 65-14,269.

This historical study revealed that the first objective of home economics departments in Catholic colleges was home and family living preparation. Because most departments were small, author recommended that, where possible, regional inter-institutional cooperation be developed.

Schoel, Doris R. (Ed. D.). "THE PROGRAMMATIC CLAIMS OF VAILLOT AND KING: IMPLICATIONS FOR BACCALAUREATE NURSING EDUCATION." Temple University, 1977. 100 pp. Source: DAI, XXXVIII, 4A (October, 1977), 1864-A. XUM Order No. 77-21,787.

Explored program theories of Sister Vaillot and Imogene King and related them to nursing education curriculum. Concluded that collaboration between nurse educators and curriculum theorists will lead to program improvement.

Scholdra, Joanne Dolores (Ph. D.). "THE EFFECT OF AN EXPERIMENTAL QUESTIONING STRATEGY IN CLINICAL CONFERENCES AND EVALUATION INTERVIEWS ON THE ACHIEVEMENT OF NURSING STUDENTS." University of Washington, 1973. 115 pp. Source: DAI, XXXIII, 12A (June, 1973), 6601-A. XUM Order No. 73-13,878.

Experimental cognitive questioning of nursing students did not affect significantly their handling of patient welfare or their scores on tests on nursing care plans. Nursing students with high grade point averages performed well on cognitive achievement tests but were not more effective than other nursing students in working with patients in critical situations.

Scholz, Nelle Tumlin (Ed. D.). "ATTITUDES OF WOMEN STUDENTS TOWARD RESIDENCE HALL EXPERIENCES AT THE UNIVERSITY OF GEORGIA: A COMPARISON OF AN HONOR HALL AND CONVENTIONAL HALLS." University of Georgia, 1970. 137 pp. Source: DAI, XXXI, 11A (May, 1971), 5780-A. XUM Order No. 71-13,122.

Found among 402 women residence hall students that: (1) the program of a more liberal "honor" hall fulfilled residents' expectations during its first year of operation; (2) transfer students living there one year or less responded less positively; and (3) honor hall residents generally were more positive toward their living situations than were those living in conventional dormitories.

Schomber, Judith Hughes (Ph. D.). "JUAN LUIS VIVES AND WOMEN'S LIB-ERATION." Florida State University, 1975. 209 pp. Source: DAI, XXXVI, 8A (February, 1976), 5341-A. XUM Order No. 76-2699.

Despite his opinion that girls were emotional and fickle, Vives believed in women's potentialities, perhaps because of friendships with such able women as Queen Catherine and Sir Thomas More's daughter. Vives' proposal that women be educated provided an historical cornerstone for today's women's movement.

Schraer, Harald (Ph. D.). "SURVIVAL EDUCATION: A SURVEY OF TRENDS IN SURVIVAL EDUCATION IN CERTAIN PUBLIC SCHOOLS AND TEACHER TRAINING INSTITUTIONS AND A DETAILED STUDY OF THE ELEMENTS OF SURVIVAL EDUCATION FOUND IN THE PROGRAMS OF THE BOY SCOUTS AND GIRL SCOUTS OF AMERICA." Cornell University, 1954. 370 pp. Source: DAI, XIV, 11 (November, 1954), 1966-1967. XUM Order No. 9778.

Found among Girl Scouts and Boy Scouts of America leadership concern for and good programs about survival education (such as water safety, atomic warfare) to serve as model for public school education.

Schramm, Dwayne Gene (Ph. D.). "A STUDY OF THE OLDER WOMAN WORKER WHO HAS ATTEMPTED TO ENTER OR RE-ENTER THE WHITE COLLAR LABOR FORCE THROUGH THE ASSISTANCE OF COMMUNITY TRAINING PROGRAMS IN CLERICAL OCCU-PATIONS." University of California, Los Angeles, 1969. 165 pp. Source: DAI, XXXI, 2A (August, 1970), 694-A. XUM Order No. 70-14,326.

Older women (58) in 6 clerical training programs: (1) were high school graduates; (2) averaged 44 years of age; (3) were married; (4) had 2 to 3 children whose average age was 17; and (5) only 27.6% obtained clerical jobs during or after training; but (6) their employability was eventually aided by the training.

Schratz, Marjorie M. (Ph. D.). "A DEVELOPMENTAL INVESTIGATION OF SEX DIFFERENCES IN PERCEPTUAL DIFFERENTIATION AND MATHEMATICAL REASONING IN TWO ETHNIC GROUPS." Fordham University, 1976. 118 pp. Source: DAI, XXXVII, 2B (August, 1976), 962-B. XUM Order No. 76-17,943.

Among a small group of adolescents, white males and black females scored somewhat higher than did white females and black males on tests of mathematical reasoning and perceptual differentiation.

Schriver, Alice (Ed. D.). "A PLAN OF ORGANIZATION FOR ESTABLISHMENT OF A MAJOR FOR HEALTH PERSONNEL AT THE WOMAN'S COLLEGE, UNIVERSITY OF NORTH CAROLINA, WITH IMPLICATIONS FOR STATE UNIVERSITIES IN THE SOUTHERN REGION OF THE UNITED STATES." Columbia University Teachers College, 1952. Source: TCCU DIGESTS (1952), Part 2.

Rationale and plan for developing a health education major in a woman's college.

Schrum, Marion Margaret (Ed. D.). "THE CONCEPTS OF GENERAL EDUCATION HELD BY FIVE EMINENT NURSING EDUCATORS." Stanford University, 1958. 266 pp. Source: DAI, XIX, 4 (October, 1958), 777. XUM Order No. 58-3588.

Analyzed the educational philosophies of Isabel Hampton Robb, Mary Adelaide Nutting, Annie W. Goodrich, Isabel Stewart, and Sister Mary Olivia Gowan. They emphasized that nursing education should stress purpose rather than structure or content; favored identifying the needs of the nurse as an individual and a professional practitioner; and advocated a curriculum built around these needs.

Schubert, Florence Marguerite (Ed. D.). "THE EMERGENCE OF PREPARA-TION FOR PSYCHIATRIC NURSING IN PROFESSIONAL NURSING EDUCATION PROGRAMS IN THE UNITED STATES, 1873-1918." Columbia University, 1972. 165 pp. Source: DAI, XXXIII, 8A (February, 1973), 4143-A. XUM Order No. 73-2630.

This history of psychiatric nursing education highlighted: (1) the McLean Asylum School, 1882; (2) training schools in state mental hospitals, 1885; (3) 1st professional nurse registration act, 1903; (4) first professional psychiatric nursing curriculum, Johns Hopkins Hospital School for Nursing, 1913; (5) 1st published Standard Cur-riculum for Schools of Nursing, 1917; and (6) recommendation that accredited nursing schools require psychiatric nursing course, 1918. Among leading nurse educators mentioned: Linda Richards, Mary E. May, Sara Parsons, and others.

Schubert, Genevieve Weber (Ph. D.). "A SURVEY OF THE PROBLEMS AND NEEDS OF YOUNG HOMEMAKERS WITH IMPLICATIONS FOR HOME ECONOMICS AT THE HIGH SCHOOL LEVEL." University of Wisconsin, 1958. 192 pp. Source: DAI, XIX, 6 (December, 1958), 1362-1363. XUM Order No. Mic 58-5376.

Author recorded the problems of 104 young women homemakers as the basis for a high school home economics program.

Schuh, Sister M. John Francis (Ph. D.). "THE STATUS OF FRESHMAN ENGLISH IN SELECTED CATHOLIC WOMEN'S COLLEGES." Catholic University of America, 1953. Source: Published; Same Title; Washington, DC: Catho-lic University of America Press, 1953; pp. 143-147.

Found freshman English in Catholic women's colleges: (1) to consist chiefly of composition, reading, and writing themes emphasizing gram-mar and rhetoric; (2) to meet the needs of foreign students; (3) to yield 6 credit hours; and (4) to be satisfactory to English depart-ment administrators and teachers.

Schulte, Vivian S. Reade (Ph. D.). "RELATIONSHIPS BETWEEN THE BELIEF IN FOOD FALLACIES AND THE EDUCATION ATTAINMENT LEVELS OF UPPER-CLASS HOME-MAKERS IN NEW YORK CITY." New York University, 1962. 207 pp. Source: DAI, XXIV, 2 (August, 1963), 723. XUM Order No. 63-4919.

No substantial relationship was found between the beliefs in 291 food fallacies and the general and nutritional educational attainment levels of 302 New York City homemakers.

Schulz, Esther Ferne Dickison (Ph. D.). "DESIRABLE PERSONALITY PAT-TERNS FOR THE NURSING STUDENT: A LONGITUDINAL, COMPARATIVE STUDY." In-diana University, 1963. 102 pp. Source: DAI, XXIV, 7 (January, 1964), 2791. XUM Order No. 64-512.

Author: (1) compiled personality traits of 3 successive classes of baccalaureate nursing students; (2) found that these traits were a stereotype; and (3) concluded that the stereotype was not desirable from the viewpoint of a nursing curriculum that encouraged an indi-vidualistic approach to nursing practice.

Schultz, Jerelyn Kay Boehmke (Ph. D.). "JOB SATISFACTION, LIFE SAT-ISFACTION, AND SELF-CONCEPT OF HOME ECONOMICS COLLEGE FACULTY." Iowa State University, 1975. 176 pp. Source: DAI, XXXVI, 10A (April, 1976), 6522-A. XUM Order No. 76-9198.

Found among 238 home economics faculty in 30 colleges that: (1) they represented the upper academic ranks; (2) half were married; (3) 107 were parents; and (4) most were satisfied with their jobs, themselves, and life.

Schumacher, Elisabeth E. (Ed. D.). "THE ROLES OF THE ELEMENTARY SCHOOL TEACHER AS PERCEIVED BY FRESHMAN WOMEN STUDENTS." Pennsylvania State University, 1965. 164 pp. Source: DAI, XXVII, 3A (September, 1966), 693-A-694-A. XUM Order No. 66-8753.

Found that freshman women generally had a positive perception of ele-mentary school teachers. Statistically significant differences in perceptions of the role of elementary teachers existed between fresh-man women at the state university enrolled in teacher education, those enrolled in other programs, and those attending liberal arts colleges.

Schuyler, Constance Bradford (Ed. D.). "MOLDERS OF MODERN NURSING: FLORENCE NIGHTINGALE AND LOUISA SCHUYLER." Columbia University Teachers College, 1975. 351 pp. Source: DAI, XXXVII, 3B (September, 1976), 1179-B-1180-B. XUM Order No. 76-20,875.

In comparing the lives and nursing education philosophies of Flor-ence Nightingale's training school in London, 1860, which served as a model for Louisa Schuyler's training school in New York City, the author concluded that misunderstanding of Nightingale's philosophy contributed to American nursing schools becoming vocational schools rather than institutions of higher learning.

Schwartz, David M. (Ph. D.). "FIELD INDEPENDENCE-DEPENDENCE AND SOCIAL/SEX ROLES AMONG ELEMENTARY SCHOOL BOYS AND GIRLS." Emory University, 1976. 188 pp. Source: DAI, XXXVII, 12A, Part 1 (June, 1977), 6309-A. XUM Order No. 77-12,158.

Among 40 male and 40 female 5th and 6th graders, author found that boys defined themselves in terms of other males, sex-role preference, and dissimilarity to non-masculine interests. Girls defined themselves in relation to others of both sexes, sex-role preference, and an acceptance of female-stereotyped interests and attitudes.

Schwartz, Gerald Edward (Ph. D.). "THE GENERATION GAP: A STUDY OF INTERGENERATIONAL COMMUNICATION." Columbia University, 1977. 155 pp. Source: DAI, XXXVIII, 1B (July, 1977), 379-B. XUM Order No. 77-14,845.

Found that, in comparison with their adolescent daughters' peers, mothers were ill-prepared to communicate with their daughters about assertiveness and independence. Both mothers and adolescent daughters experienced inner tensions over their changing roles.

Scinto, Renata Galante (Ph. D.). "MEASURING ACHIEVEMENT MOTIVATION IN HIGH SCHOOL GIRLS." Hofstra University, 1977. 105 pp. Source: DAI, XXXVIII, 1B (July, 1977), 339-B-340-B. XUM Order No. 77-13,726.

High-achieving girls' motivation to achieve was not affected by the sex of figures in a test. The relationship between the girls' achievement motivation scores and their grade point average (GPA) was not greater than the relationship between IQ and GPA.

Scott, Mary Hughie (Ed. D.). "AN ANALYTIC STUDY OF CERTAIN MOTIVES AND NEEDS OF PROSPECTIVE WOMEN TEACHERS." University of Georgia, 1960. 360 pp. Source: DAI, XXI, 8 (February, 1961), 2211. XUM Order No. Mic 60-6591.

Found among 482 prospective elementary school teachers: (1) a positive relation between desirable professional characteristics and the social acceptability rank of motives prompting them to choose teaching; and that (2) those with non-professional reasons for going to college had inferior academic records and chose teaching for motives with low social acceptability ratings.

Scott, Mary Jane (Ed. D.). "IN-SERVICE EDUCATIONAL NEEDS OF A SELECTED GROUP OF HOMEMAKERS WHO ENTERED OR RE-ENTERED THE TEACHING OF HOMEMAKING." University of Tennessee, 1960. 228 pp. Source: DAI, XXI, 2 (August, 1960), 337. XUM Order No. Mic 60-2498.

Major problems of returning teachers were: (1) directing FHA activities; (2) evaluating their programs' effectiveness; and (3) finding time for home visits. Returning teachers and those who had taught continuously also had the same problems: (1) planning the adult program; (2) inadequate equipment; (3) working with pupils of differing abilities; and (4) inadequate funds and library facilities.

Scott, Nancy Ann McKay (Ed. D.). "THE EFFECTS OF RETURNING TO COLLEGE AND ASSERTIVENESS TRAINING ON SELF CONCEPT AND PERSONALITY VARIABLES OF MATURE WOMEN." University of Colorado at Boulder, 1976. 273 pp. Source: DAI, XXXVII, 8A (February, 1977), 4873-A. XUM Order No. 77-3231.

Found, among 48 mature women returning to college, significant correlations between: (1) achieved grade point averages and changes in
self-concept and personality; and (2) assistance received and changes
in self-concept and personality. Found no significant differences in
personality between those receiving and not receiving assertiveness
training.

Scruggs, Mary Marguerite (Ph. D.). "CRITERIA FOR DETERMINING EFFEC-
TIVENESS OF HOMEMAKING TEACHERS." Iowa State University, 1959. 222 pp.
Source: DAI, XX, 6 (December, 1959), 2269. XUM Order No. 59-5059.

After high school homemaking students took pre and post tests and
their teachers were observed by 2 researchers, no significant differences were found: (1) between the grade averages of 2 groups of
students; or (2) in students' attitudes toward their teachers.

Seaward, Marty Robertson (Ed. D.). "COMPARISON OF THE CAREER MATURI-
TY, SELF CONCEPT AND ACADEMIC ACHIEVEMENT OF FEMALE COOPERATIVE VOCATIONAL
OFFICE TRAINING STUDENTS, INTENSIVE BUSINESS TRAINING STUDENTS, AND REGU-
LAR BUSINESS EDUCATION STUDENTS IN SELECTED HIGH SCHOOLS IN MISSISSIPPI."
Mississippi State University, 1976. 80 pp. Source: DAI, XXXVII, 7A
(January, 1977), 4321-A-4322-A. XUM Order No. 76- 30,076.

High school girls (240) in the Cooperative Vocational Office Training
program had: (1) higher grades; and (2) higher self-concept scores.

Sechrist, Karen Richert (Ph. D.). "COMPARISON OF NURSES' RESPONSES
TO A SIMULATED PRIMARY CARE SITUATION." University of Pittsburgh, 1974.
116 pp. Source: DAI, XXXV, 8B (February, 1975), 4005-B. XUM Order No.
75-4074.

More similarity than difference was shown among 4 groups of nurses
(undergraduates, graduate, public health, and nurse practitioners)
to simulated primary care situation consisting of 4 encounters with
the same patient.

Sedlacek, Caroline Gladys (Ph. D.). "SELECTED FACTORS AFFECTING
CERTAINTY AND PERSISTENCE OF VOCATIONAL CHOICE FOR COLLEGE WOMEN." University of North Dakota, 1968. 123 pp. Source: DAI, XXIX, 11A (May,
1969), 3843-A-3844-A. XUM Order No. 69-8567.

By the end of the 2nd college year, 90% of the women studied were
preparing for traditional feminine vocations. Women who as freshmen
had been uncertain or only fairly certain of their future vocations
tended to change their choice.

Sees, Mary Carolyn (Ph. D.). "IMAGE OF NURSING: ITS RELATIONSHIP
TO CHARACTERISTICS OF STUDENTS AND FACULTY IN BACCALAUREATE NURSING PRO-
GRAMS." Syracuse University, 1974. 230 pp. Source: DAI, XXXVI, 1B
(July, 1975), 164-B. XUM Order No. 75-14,022.

Found among baccalaureate nursing students that they: (1) decided
on a nursing career during or after high school; (2) were attracted
by institutional reputation; (3) were more committed to a college
education than to the nursing major; (4) had a more advanced image
of nursing than the lay image; and (5) seniors' nursing views were

like those of the faculty. Also found that students with a professional image of nursing: (1) were more satisfied with their education than were those with an ambivalent image; and (2) wanted to pursue graduate education. Students also emphasized the necessity of
having hospital nursing experience.

Sehl, Katherine (Ed. D.). "GUIDELINES FOR PLANNING NURSING EDUCATION
PROGRAMS IN INSTITUTIONS OF HIGHER EDUCATION IN THE UNITED STATES FOR
NURSES FROM ABROAD." Columbia University Teachers College, 1959. 128
pp. Source: TCCU DIGESTS (1959), pp. 632-633.

Identified the following problem areas faced by foreign nursing students in the U. S.: (1) language; (2) cultural adjustment; (3) appropriate instructional resources and experiences; (4) appropriate
programs of study; and (5) adjustment to the educational setting.
Used this information to develop guidelines for appropriate nursing
education programs.

Sell, Dave Larry (Ph. D.). "THE EFFECTS OF PRACTICE EMPHASIS AND
FEEDBACK IN A SPEED AND ACCURACY TASK BY AGED FEMALES." University of
Southern California, 1976. Source: DAI, XXXVII, 9A (March, 1977),
5684-A-5685-A.

Found among 100 women over age 65, that those who practiced first,
learned to do a manipulative task better than those who had not
practiced.

Sell, Irene Louise (Ed. D.). "GUIDE TO MATERIALS ON DEATH AND DYING
FOR TEACHERS OF NURSING." Columbia University, 1975. 227 pp. Source:
DAI, XXXVI, 3B (September, 1975), 1151-B. XUM Order No. 75-20,226.

Author prepared an annotated multi-media teaching guide on death and
dying for nursing and health educators. The 450 entries of books,
films, tapes, and other materials covered attitudes toward dying
patients, reactions of dying patients and their families, care of the
dying child, and related topics.

Sellers, Burt A. (Ph. D.). "AN ANALYSIS OF THE RELATIONSHIP OF STU-
DENTS' SELF CONCEPTS IN SCIENCE TO THEIR MENTAL ABILITIES, SEX AND MEA-
SURES OF ACHIEVEMENT IN SCIENCE." State University of New York at Buffalo, 1975. 154 pp. Source: DAI, XXXVI, 10A (April, 1976), 6583-A-
6584-A. XUM Order No. 76-9112.

It was hypothesized and found true but not to a significant extent
that high school girls had lower self-concepts than boys in relation
to science subjects. Found that high achievers in biology who had
high ability also had the highest self-concepts in science.

Sells, Lucy Watson (Ph. D.). "SEX, ETHNIC AND FIELD DIFFERENCES IN
DOCTORAL OUTCOMES." University of California, Berkeley, 1975. 246 pp.
Source: DAI, XXXVII, 1A (July, 1976), 637-A. XUM Order No. 76-15,363.

Found: (1) low high school math scores hindered women in college
and particularly in majors with high rates of doctoral success; and
(2) a major increase of women in doctoral programs and a modest increase of minorities in college.

Semlear, Thelma Monaco (Ph. D.). "SEX DIFFERENCES IN PERFORMANCE ON LINGUISTIC CATEGORIES IN READING TESTS." State University of New York at Stony Brook, 1977. 110 pp. Source: DAI, XXXVIII, 6B (December, 1977), 2914-B-2915-B. XUM Order No. 77-26,399.

Found that boys made more errors in word analysis than girls.

Semler, Vicki Jane (Ph. D.). "A STUDY OF THIRD WORLD FAMILY PLAN-NERS' VIEWS TOWARD WOMEN'S ROLE IN SOCIETY: A COMMUNICATIONS PERSPECTIVE." Indiana University, 1977. 348 pp. Source: DAI, XXXVIII, 4A (October, 1977), 1721-A. XUM Order No. 77-22,636.

Recommended that: (1) women be promoted to decision-making positions in national and international family planning organizations; (2) training programs be started, especially for rural women, stressing job skills; (3) educational materials be prepared for young women emphasizing non-family options and activities; and (4) "consciousness raising" programs be started for family planners on women's emerging roles.

Senderak, Sister Mary George (Ed. D.). "PRIVATE COLLEGES FOR WOMEN AND JUNIOR COLLEGE GRADUATES IN NEW JERSEY." Columbia University, 1971. 150 pp. Source: DAI, XXXII, 2A (August, 1971), 756-A. XUM Order No. 71-20,028.

Most of the 215 women in 11 public and 6 private junior colleges in-dicated that they were career-oriented, were majoring in professional and vocational areas, were interested in continuing their education, and wanted to transfer to New Jersey colleges. Author concluded that women junior college graduates are potential students in New Jersey private colleges for women.

Senf, Janet Hilger (Ph. D.). "WOMEN'S EMPLOYMENT AND KINSHIP PAT-TERNS." University of Illinois at Chicago Circle, 1977. 190 pp. Source: DAI, XXXVIII, 1A (July, 1977), 504-A. XUM Order No. 77-15,333.

The single most important factor found in contacts between kin was geographical proximity. Educational differences between non-married women and their mothers had a positive influence on their contacts with kin. Educational differences between married women and their mothers had no effect on their contacts with kin.

Sense, Eleanora (Ed. D.). "A TEACHER'S GUIDE OF STUDENT NURSES' LEARNING EXPERIENCES IN DIET THERAPY CLINICAL PRACTICE RELATED TO TOTAL NURSINGCARE OF PATIENT, FOR USE IN SCHOOLS OF NURSING." New York State University, 1954. 257 pp. Source: DAI, XV, 7 (1955), 1232. XUM Order No. 12,236.

Author developed a teacher's guide for nurses learning diet therapy clinical practices. The guide was based on the literature and infor-mation from dietiticians and nurse educators, a few of whom evaluated and helped correct the manuscript.

Sepsi, Victor J., Jr. (Ph. D.). "ARCHIVAL FACTORS FOR PREDICTING RECIDIVISM OF FEMALE JUVENILE DELINQUENTS." Kent State University, 1971. 107 pp. Source: DAI, XXXII, 9A (March, 1972), 5368-A. XUM Order No. 72-9281.

Found among 210 delinquent girls in a girls' training school that their return to delinquency was significantly associated with: (1) early age at the onset of delinquency; (2) less formal education; and (3) family relationships.

Servis, Margery Ann (D. P. E.). "QUALITIES RELATED TO SUCCESS IN WOMEN'S PHYSICAL EDUCATION PROFESSIONAL PREPARATION PROGRAM." Springfield College, 1965. Source: Author.

Concluded in a study of 69 female physical education majors that the variables which most accurately predicted success were women's physical fitness, active temperament trait score, and mental ability score.

Settlemyer, Constance Ann (Ph. D.). "LEARNING AND RETENTION BY TWO AGE GROUPS OF REGISTERED NURSES IN AN INTENSIVE COURSE IN CORONARY CARE NURSING." University of Pittsburgh, 1973. 93 pp. Source: DAI, XXXV, 2A (August, 1974), 853-A-854-A. XUM Order No. 74-16,551.

Compared registered nurses under age 35 with registered nurses over age 35. Found no age-related differences in learning, in retention, or in performance by category of test item.

Sevoian, Lucile Hieser (Ph. D.). "ATTITUDES AND EXPERIENCES OF TEN- AND ELEVEN-YEAR-OLD 4-H CLUB MEMBERS ENROLLED IN CLOTHING PROJECTS IN MCLEAN COUNTY, ILLINOIS, IN 1953 WITH IMPLICATIONS FOR PROGRAM PLANNING." Cornell University, 1955. 243 pp. Source: DAI, XVI, 2 (1956), 331-332. XUM Order No. 15,428.

The 128 girls interviewed considered project work the most important phase of the 4-H Club program. The study demonstrated the value of soliciting views from even the youngest age group in 4-H Clubs.

Seward, Doris Marie (Ph. D.). "A HISTORICAL STUDY OF THE WOMEN'S RESIDENCE PROGRAM AT SYRACUSE UNIVERSITY." Syracuse University, 1953. 613 pp. Source: Abstract in Dissertation.

Traced the growth, development and trends of the women's residence programs at Syracuse University, 1870-1950.

Sexton, Larry Charles (Ed. D.). "AUDITORY AND VISUAL PERCEPTION, SEX, AND ACADEMIC APTITUDE AS PREDICTORS OF ACHIEVEMENT FOR FIRST GRADE CHILDREN." Ball State University, 1976. 141 pp. Source: DAI, XXXVII, 10A (April, 1977), 6162-A. XUM Order No. 77-7316.

Girls outperformed boys on all achievement tests. Girls' scores on language arts and, to a lesser degree, on mathematics were positively associated with visual perception and academic aptitude. Girls' visual perception had a stronger relationship to their later achievement than did either academic aptitude or auditory perception.

Shambaugh, Mary Effie (Ph. D.). "THE OBJECTIVE MEASUREMENT OF SUCCESS IN THE TEACHING OF FOLK DANCING TO UNIVERSITY WOMEN." University of California, Berkeley, 1933. 225 pp. Source: Abstract in Dissertation.

Found that: (1) a test measuring knowledge of folklore was reliable;
(2) women's attitudes toward foreign people were generally friendly;
and (3) 2 techniques of teaching folk dancing (one used a machine)
improved poor coordination.

Shanahan, John Edward, Jr. (Ed. D.). "ENERGY COMMITMENTS OF WOMEN
COUNSELORS IN SCHOOLS, COLLEGES AND AGENCIES." Ball State University,
1972. 199 pp. Source: DAI, XXXIII, 9A (March, 1973), 4850-A-4851-A.
XUM Order No. 73-6766.

Among 300 women counselors, found: (1) no differences in their energy
commitment; (2) variations in their flexibility, with secondary
school counselors being the least flexible and college counselors the
most flexible; and (3) more commitment to people and to ideas among
older women counselors than among younger counselors. Concluded that
the amount of education attained made more difference in women counselors' energy commitments than did the counselors' place of work,
sex, or self actualization.

Shannon, Amalie Roth (Ed. D.). "A DELPHI STUDY OF THE FUTURE OF
WOMEN'S COLLEGES IN THE UNITED STATES." Lehigh University, 1971. 144
pp. Source: DAI, XXXII, 5A (November, 1971), 2445-A. XUM Order No.
71-27,742.

A panel of 60 experts on women's education reached agreement on these
important issues: financial pressures, declining enrollment, dissatisfaction with sex composition of student body, and quality of
curricula. More agreement existed than was expected, but no conclu-
sive statement about the future of these women's colleges emerged.

Shannon, Mary Lucille (Ed. D.). "THE ORIGIN AND DEVELOPMENT OF PRO-
FESSIONAL LICENSURE EXAMINATIONS IN NURSING: FROM A STATE-CONSTRUCTED
EXAMINATION TO THE STATE BOARD TEST POOL EXAMINATION." Columbia Univer-
sity, 1972. 377 pp. Source: DAI, XXXIV, 9A (March, 1974), 5676-A.
XUM Order No. 74-6414.

This historical study traced the evolution of nursing licensure examinations, which began in New York in 1904 and eventually spread to
other states, whose tests were sometimes of doubtful validity. In
January 1944 the State Board Test Pool was introduced. Its licensing
test was by 1950 adopted by every state nurse licensing authority.

Shapiro, Johanna Freedman (Ph. D.). "SOCIALIZATION OF SEX ROLES IN
THE COUNSELING SETTING: DIFFERENTIAL COUNSELOR BEHAVIORAL AND ATTITU-
DINAL RESPONSES TO TYPICAL AND ATYPICAL FEMALE SEX ROLES." Stanford Uni-
versity, 1975. 276 pp. Source: DAI, XXXVI, 9A (March, 1976), 5839-A.
XUM Order No. 76-5801.

Studied counseling done by 8 male and 8 female psychology graduate
students. Found that their counseling behavior did not justify feminist claims that such male and female therapists are special oppres-
sors of women. Instead, these male and female counselors reacted
more positively toward atypical females than toward typical females.
Female counselors were, however, more reinforcing with clients and
were evaluated more positively than were male counselors by clients.

Shaw, Helen Ann McDonald Jahan (Ph. D.). "THE EFFECTS OF ROLE MODEL-ING ON THE LEVEL OF OCCUPATIONAL ASPIRATION OF NINTH GRADE GIRLS." University of Missouri, Kansas City, 1974. 126 pp. Source: DAI, XXXV, 5A (November, 1974), 2699-A-2700-A. XUM Order No. 74-23,790.

Role modeling produced significant changes in the level of girls' occupational aspiration. Girls who viewed both female role models and male reinforcers experienced greater changes in occupational aspiration than did those who viewed female models only.

Shear, Twyla Maisie (Ed. D.). "AN EVALUATION OF CORE CURRICULUM IN THE COLLEGE OF HOME ECONOMICS." Michigan State University, 1964. 225 pp. Source: DAI, XXVI, 3 (September, 1965), 1434-1435. XUM Order No. 65-6125.

Developed a useful process for curriculum evaluation and applied it to the new core curriculum in home economics at Michigan State University. Found that both faculty and students approved of the revised curriculum because of its flexibility, family focus, and balance between general and specialized courses.

Sheehan, Nancy Welburn (Ph. D.). "AN EXAMINATION OF SELECTED PER-FORMANCE FACTORS AND CORRELATES OF PIAGETIAN LOGICAL FUNCTIONING IN ELDER-LY WOMEN." University of Wisconsin, Madison, 1976. 161 pp. Source: DAI, XXXVII, 9B (March, 1977), 4656-4657. XUM Order No. 76-28,940.

Used young and old testers with 80 women, aged 62-88, to measure their Piagetian cognitive functioning. Among findings: (1) participants tested by elderly interviewers performed better; (2) visual orientation memory was consistently related to performance; and (3) neither educational level nor previous work experience was consistently related to the women's performance.

Sheehy, Sister M. Maurice (Ph. D.). "A STUDY OF A METHOD OF IMPROVING THE ATTITUDES OF INTEREST ACCURACY AND TACT IN STUDENTS OF NURSING AND THE RELATION OF THESE ATTITUDES TO SUCCESS IN NURSING." Catholic University of America, 1942. 76 pp. Source: Published; Same Title; Washington, DC: Catholic University of America, 1942; pp. 43-46.

Found that: (1) movies and discussions about attitudes improved nursing students' interest but had an insignificant effect on tact; (2) students with the highest attitude ratings were more efficient in clinical nursing practice; (3) the Revised Attitude Inventory constructed by the author gave the most satisfactory discrimination between the more and less efficient students; and (4) the more efficient students had the highest scores on the Hunt Aptitude Test for Nursing.

Sheikh, Nargis Ahmed (Ph. D.). "TEXTILE BUYING PRACTICES OF A SE-LECTED GROUP OF FEMALE PAKISTANI CONSUMERS RELATED TO SELECTED BACKGROUND FACTORS AND CLOTHING BEHAVIORS." Pennsylvania State University, 1970. 182 pp. Source: DAI, XXXII, 1B (July, 1971), 412-B-413-B. XUM Order No. 71-16,670.

Found that: (1) no consumer protection existed for textile users in Pakistan; and (2) textile buying practices of selected female Pakistani consumers were significantly related to their educational level, reading patterns, analytical habits, and experience with fabrics.

Shelton, Barbara Josephine (Ph. D.). "RESEARCH COMPONENTS IN BACCA-LAUREATE PROGRAMS OF NURSING." Saint Louis University, 1976. 66 pp. Source: DAI, XXXVII, 12B, Part 1 (June, 1977), 6055-B. XUM Order No. 77-12,134.

Findings about training in research skills given baccalaureate nursing students: (1) 141 of the 217 schools surveyed required courses in research methodology and/or statistics; (2) 38 schools not requiring such a course offered it as an elective; and (3) more university than college-based programs required a course in both research methods and statistics.

Sheppard, Jacqueline Woodards (Ed. D.). "A COMPARISON OF SELECTED FACTORS IN DESCRIBING THE MATURE PARAPROFESSIONAL WOMAN AS AN INDIGENOUS COMMUNITY RESOURCE IN AN URBAN EDUCATIONAL COMMUNITY." Temple University, 1973. 367 pp. Source: DAI, XXXIV, 4A (October, 1973), 1556-A-1557-A. XUM Order No. 73-23,360.

Author recommended that paraprofessional women serving as inner-city kindergarten aides, bus matrons, and similar helpers: (1) should be recruited because they lend stability, particularly for emotionally disturbed and culturally deprived children; (2) should be in a certified, career-ladder program; and (3) should be included in a competency-based teacher education program connected with a university where they could also get special counseling.

Sherman, V. Clayton (Ed. D.). "NURSING AND THE MANAGEMENT FUNCTION." Western Michigan University, 1975. 167 pp. Source: DAI, XXXVI, 7B (January, 1976), 3312-B. XUM Order No. 75-29,851.

Nurses (105) in supervisory roles: (1) reported inadequate preparation for their management duties; and (2) desired more training for their management tasks.

Sherwood, Elizabeth Burke (Ph. D.). "THE ANTECEDENTS OF CAREER CHOICE FOR WOMEN IN TWO PROFESSIONS." University of Maryland, 1975. 110 pp. Source: DAI, XXXVI, 10A (April, 1976), 6995-A. XUM Order No. 76-8436.

Found in comparing 20 women social workers with 20 women scientists that: (1) the social workers had a higher need for affiliation during adolescence, had more friends, went out more often, belonged to more organizations, and associated with a clique in high school; and (2) the scientists were from neighborhoods with few playmates and were less likely to have been the favored child in the family.

Shine, Elizabeth Catherine (Ed. D.). "SELECTED DEMOGRAPHIC ATTRI-BUTES AND THE FREQUENCY OF PERCEIVED ROLE STRAIN IN DEANS OF COLLEGIATE SCHOOLS OF NURSING." Boston College, 1972. 146 pp. Source: DAI, XXXIII, 10A (April, 1973), 5418-A. XUM Order No. 73-8248.

Deans (170) of college nursing schools surveyed seemed suited to their roles and had: (1) some strain from work overload; (2) some strain from a conflict between amount and quality of work; and (3) less strain over job advancement.

Shinn, Anna Hazel (Ph. D.). "SOCIAL LIVING IN CATHOLIC FOUR YEAR COLLEGES FOR WOMEN." Catholic University of America, 1959. Source: Published; Same Title; Washington, DC: Catholic University of America Press, 1959; pp. 134-142.

After profiling a wide range of social programs at Catholic women's colleges from teas and dances to card playing and student discussions, author concluded that: (1) most colleges emphasized students' personal and social adjustment; but that (2) social opportunities in some colleges were too few and too limited.

Shioda, Mary John Bosco (Ph. D.). "CULTURAL BASE FOR TEACHING RELIGION IN CATHOLIC WOMEN'S COLLEGES IN JAPAN." Saint Louis University, 1967. 248 pp. Source: DAI, XXVIII, 8A (February, 1968), 2964-A.

Religion courses were compulsory in 75% of Japan's Catholic women's colleges studied. Principal factor hindering students from understanding and accepting Catholicism was cultural difference.

Shipley, Anna Frances (Ph. D.). "ROLE PERCEPTION AND PERSONAL VALUES AS A MEANS OF PREDICTING EFFECTIVENESS FOR STUDENT TEACHING IN HOME ECONOMICS." University of Missouri, Columbia, 1975. 189 pp. Source: DAI, XXXVII, 4A (October, 1976), 2126-A-2127-A. XUM Order No. 76-21,975.

Concluded that the way students perceived the home economics teaching role and their personal values were significantly related to their effectiveness in student teaching in home economics.

Shiraishi, Reyko Ruth (Ed. D.). "EFFECTS OF A BILINGUAL/BICULTURAL CAREER GUIDANCE PROJECT ON THE OCCUPATIONAL ASPIRATIONS OF PUERTO RICAN ADOLESCENTS." Boston University School of Education, 1975. 186 pp. Source: DAI, XXXVI, 4A (October, 1975), 2171-A. XUM Order No. 75-20,932.

Role modeling, field trips, and group discussions had a positive effect on raising occupational aspirations. The girls' level of occupational aspiration was affected more than the boys' level. The project did not have a significant effect upon students' occupational choices.

Shoemaker, Gloria Maruca (Ph. D.). "RELATIONSHIPS AMONG PREDICTOR AND CRITERION MEASURES OF SENSITIVITY TO NONVERBAL COMMUNICATION." University of Pittsburgh, 1977. 179 pp. Source: DAI, XXXVIII, 4B (October, 1977), 1653-B-1654-B. XUM Order No. 77-21,238.

Studied 59 nursing faculty members to find relationships among: (1) their sensitivity to nonverbal communication; (2) self-monitoring of their expressive behavior; and (3) peer assessment of these attributes. Found that the more years in nursing, the less sensitive they were to nonverbal communication and the less they saw themselves as self-monitoring of expressive behavior.

Shootes, Queen Esther (Ph. D.). "GAINFUL EMPLOYMENT OF NEGRO HOME ECONOMICS GRADUATES WITH IMPLICATIONS FOR EDUCATION PROGRAMS." Univer-

sity of Wisconsin, 1965. 157 pp. Source: DAI, XXV, 12 (June, 1965),
7237-7238. XUM Order No. 65-6242.

Data from women home economics graduates of 5 Negro colleges in the
South indicated that: (1) their underemployment was attributed to
family ties, economic pressures to work, and geographical location
(considered least important); (2) as students they received inadequate
job information; and (3) they felt that the home economics curriculum
provided poor job preparation.

Shortridge, Lillie Mae (Ed. D.). "ATTITUDE OF FRESHMAN AND SENIOR
BACCALAUREATE NURSING STUDENTS TOWARD PROFESSIONAL NURSING BEHAVIORS."
Columbia University Teachers College, 1977. 214 pp. Source: DAI,
XXXVIII, 4B (October, 1977), 1654-B. XUM Order No. 77-22,296.

Attitude toward professional nursing behaviors held by graduating
seniors was significantly more favorable than the attitude held by
entering freshmen. In service orientation and bedside care, seniors
scored lower than the freshmen and lower than would be expected for
performance as professional nurses. Some influencing factors were
the school, current experience, work as either a nursing aide or a
practical nurse, and the family.

Shortsleeves, Judith Marie (Ph. D.). "FEMINISTS AND NONFEMINISTS:
DIFFERENCES IN THEIR SEX ROLE CONCEPTS AND THEIR ORIENTATIONS TOWARD
ACHIEVEMENT." University of Massachusetts, 1977. 193 pp. Source: DAI,
XXXVIII, 4B (October, 1977), 1959-B-1960-B. XUM Order No. 77-21,509.

Found that a woman's professional status: (1) was related to positive views toward women in general; and (2) was not related to a
more positive view of herself. A woman's commitment to feminism:
(1) was positively related to achievement; and (2) had no effect
on perceptions of self or of women in general. Concluded that a
combination of professionalism and feminism produced the most positive result in relation to achievement, self-concept, and concept of
women in general.

Showalter, Mary Emma (Ed. D.). "DEVELOPING A PLAN FOR BETTER ACCEP-
TANCE OF HOME ECONOMICS AT EASTERN MENNONITE COLLEGE." Pennsylvania
State University, 1957. 198 pp. Source: DAI, XVII, 12 (December, 1957),
2998-2999. XUM Order No. 24,039.

Recommendations from administrators, department heads, home economics
majors and graduates, and college women about ways to attract more
women to home economics courses included: (1) activities to acquaint
students, parents, and other faculties with the home economics program; (2) a home economics course as a general education requirement
for all women students; and (3) improvement of home economics program
by including professional education and strengthening child development courses.

Shridevi, Sripati (Ph. D.). "THE DEVELOPMENT OF WOMEN'S HIGHER EDU-
CATION IN INDIA." Columbia University, 1954. 407 pp. Source: DAI,
XIV, 11 (May, 1954), 1989-1990. XUM Order No. 10,184.

Indian women in prehistoric Vedic times had equal rights and opportunities. In modern times British occupation and Christian missions
evoked an energetic response from Hindu society and a drive for improved status for women. The nationalist movement under Gandhi advanced the drive. The author cited 60 women's colleges along with
many co-educational institutions as centers for women's higher education.

Shur, M. Sharon (Ph. D.). "A GROUP COUNSELING PROGRAM FOR LOW SELF-
ESTEEM PREADOLESCENT FEMALES IN THE FIFTH GRADE." University of Pitts-
burgh, 1975. 182 pp. Source: DAI, XXVI, 9A (March, 1976), 5839-A.
XUM Order No. 76-5475.

A group counseling program based on the first 4 stages of the psycho-
social developmental scheme of Erikson was effective in helping
girls learn to cope successfully with the age-relevant tasks that
confronted them.

Shurden, Kay Wilson (Ed. D.). "AN ANALYSIS OF ADOLESCENT RESPONSES
TO FEMALE CHARACTERS IN LITERATURE WIDELY READ BY STUDENTS IN SECONDARY
SCHOOLS." University of Tennessee, 1975. 101 pp. Source: DAI, XXXVI,
10A (April, 1976), 6589-A. XUM Order No. 76-1981.

An analysis of 18 books with fully drawn female characters, which
were rated by 400 secondary school students, revealed: (1) boys and
girls had similar perceptions of the characters, except in the case
of Sylvia in Up the Down Staircase, whom the boys judged as less
stereotypic; (2) the books written with a larger audience in mind
presented female characters with fewer stereotypic traits while books
with a teenage audience in mind had more stereotypic characters; (3)
the books read most widely by girls contained the characters with
the most stereotypic traits; and (4) all of the stereotyped characters
were cast in love stories.

Siegel, Hildegarde Julia (Ph. D.). "A STUDY OF PROFESSIONAL SOCIALI-
ZATION IN TWO BACCALAUREATE NURSING EDUCATION PROGRAMS." University of
Minnesota, 1967. 238 pp. Source: DAI, XXVIII, 8A (February, 1968),
3041-A-3042-A. XUM Order No. 68-1568.

Found: (1) that college students in nursing courses assimilated
faculty values about the nursing profession; and (2) that teaching
reflected faculty members' personal values about nursing and the
nursing profession.

Siegel, Idell Elaine (Ph. D.). "FEMINISM IN THE FRENCH POPULAR PLAY-
WRIGHTS: 1830-1848." University of Missouri, Columbia, 1975. 239 pp.
Source: DAI, XXXVI, 7A (January, 1976), 4684-A-4685-A. XUM Order No.
76-1044.

Pro-feminist French playwrights, 1830-48, saw a social mission in
the theater, were influenced by socialist theories and the Romantic
Movement, and thus depicted women's inferior place and subjugation.

Sikes, Joseph Neville (Ph. D.). "DIFFERENTIAL BEHAVIOR OF MALE AND
FEMALE TEACHERS WITH MALE AND FEMALE STUDENTS." University of Texas at
Austin, 1971. 64 pp. Source: DAI, XXXIII, 1A (July, 1972), 217-A.
XUM Order No. 72-19,670.

Found among 8 men and 8 women junior high school teachers that: (1) women teachers had more interactions with all students; and (2) men and women teachers' responses were the same to questions from boys and girls.

Silberstein, Ruth Leibowitz (Ed. D.). "DEVELOPMENTAL PATTERNS IN THE ACQUISITION OF SEX-ROLE IDENTIFICATION IN YOUNG CHILDREN." University of California, Los Angeles, 1977. 128 pp. Source: DAI, XXXVIII, 8B (February, 1978), 3963-B. XUM Order No. 77-30,959.

Identified a pivotal period, between ages 3 and 4, when children have a marked increase in sex-role identification. Then boys and girls interacted more with same-sex peers. Between ages 4 and 5 their interaction with opposite-sex peers decreased.

Silliman, Janet Caroline (Ph. D.). "ACADEMIC ACHIEVEMENT OF MEXICAN AMERICAN FEMALES IN A COLLEGE OF NURSING." University of Arizona, 1974. 135 pp. Source: DAI, XXXV, 6A (December, 1974), 3470-A-3471-A. XUM Order No. 74-28,295.

Found that: (1) as Mexican-American women adjusted to college life and to the College of Nursing, they became more successful in the university; and (2) there were no differences in total self-esteem scores of ethnic groups.

Silver, Evelyn Stern (Ph. D.). "INVOLVEMENT IN COLLEGE AND SELECTED STUDENT BACKGROUND CHARACTERISTICS AS PREDICTORS OF ACADEMIC PERSISTENCE FOR OLDER WOMEN UNDERGRADUATES." University of Maryland, 1977. 186 pp. Source: DAI, XXXVIII, 7A (January, 1978), 3985-A-3986-A. XUM Order No. 77-28,754.

Found that persistence in the university by undergraduate women who entered after age 21 was related to: (1) their involvement in the university's academic life, as indicated by first semester grades and class load; (2) their involvement in the university's social life, indicated by use of campus facilities and by number of campus friends; and (3) their student and family background, prior educational experiences, and commitment to educational goals.

Simcox, Charles Q. (Ph. D.). "THE EFFECT OF FACIAL ATTRACTIVENESS UPON THE EVALUATION OF FICTITIOUS BLACK AND WHITE POTENTIAL FEMALE DROPOUTS BY THE FACULTY OF SELECTED PENNSYLVANIA COMMUNITY COLLEGES: A PSYCHOLINGUISTIC INVESTIGATION." Pennsylvania State University, 1975. 162 pp. Source: DAI, XXXVI, 10A (April, 1976), 6435-A. XUM Order No. 76-6671.

Faculty members were conservative regarding the academic and occupational potential of the typical female community college student. They considered physically attractive persons with only marginal ability and motivation to be superior to the typical community college student. They believed a potential dropout would most likely succeed if she was physically attractive.

Simmons, Wilber Dean (Ed. D.). "SUPERIOR WOMEN COLLEGE STUDENTS: A STUDY OF THEIR SELF CONCEPTS AND ACADEMIC MOTIVATION." University of Illinois, 1968. 157 pp. Source: DAI, XXIX, 8A (February, 1969), 2532-A. XUM Order No. 69-1451.

Found: (1) high achieving junior and senior women at the University of Illinois from the Colleges of Agriculture, Education, and Liberal Arts and Sciences to be self-confident, independent, mature, had good rapport with faculty, and had a broad socio-cultural awareness; (2) average achievers focused mainly on social activities; (3) women in agriculture and education were socially oriented and willing to work in their fields; and (4) liberal arts women were more independent, eager for new knowledge, and had more socio-cultural awareness.

Simms, Lillian Margaret Miller (Ph. D.). "FACTORS INFLUENCING NURSES' PREFERENCE FOR AN EXTERNAL DEGREE IN A GRADUATE NURSING HEALTH SERVICES ADMINISTRATION PROGRAM." University of Michigan, 1977. 152 pp. Source: DAI, XXXVIII, 6A (December, 1977), 3218-A. XUM Order No. 77-26,360.

Among factors which influenced nurses' decisions to pursue off-campus graduate education in nursing administration were: (1) desire to fulfill personal goals and acquire new knowledge; (2) relevance of available courses to work and future career; (3) availability of faculty with expertise; (4) availability of other educational resources; and (5) proximity of classes to home and work.

Simon, Harold (Ed. D.). "THE CONSTRUCTION AND VALIDATION OF A SCALE FOR THE DETERMINATION OF ATTITUDES SYMPTOMATIC OF THE MENTAL HEALTH STATUS OF BOYS AND GIRLS IN THE JUNIOR HIGH SCHOOLS OF NEW YORK CITY." New York University, 1963. 219 pp. Source: DAI, XXIV, 3 (September, 1963), 1143-1144. XUM Order No. 63-6695.

Questionnaire constructed and administered to 624 boys and girls in 24 junior high schools helped identify students with mental health problems including quiet pupils who might not express difficulties by overt behavior.

Simons, Janet Ann (Ph. D.). "IMPRESSION FORMATION IN COUNSELING: SEX, AGE AND EDUCATION OF COUNSELORS AS COMPONENTS OF PERCEIVED COUNSELOR CREDIBILITY BY FEMALE AND MALE COLLEGE STUDENTS." Iowa State University, 1976. 134 pp. Source: DAI, XXXVII, 7B (January, 1977), 3632-B. XUM Order No. 77-1481.

Found that: (1) female counselors were rated higher than male counselors on intelligence, sincerity, religiousness, and ability to make the client comfortable on the initial interview; (2) otherwise clients preferred a counselor of the same sex; (3) male counselors were evaluated more favorably as they got older and women less favorably; and (4) there was a direct relationship between education and counselor credibility.

Simpson, Ida Harper (Ph. D.). "THE DEVELOPMENT OF PROFESSIONAL SELF-IMAGES AMONG STUDENT NURSES." University of North Carolina, Chapel Hill, 1956. 249 pp. Source: Dissertation, pp. 229-230.

The process of socializing student nurses into their professional role had 3 phases: (1) transition to task orientation; (2) attachment to significant others in the work setting; and (3) internalization of professional values. Developing a professional self-image in student nurses required that their desire to serve mankind be shifted away from a personalized concern for patient care and toward an impersonal commitment to organizational demands.

Simpson, Lawrence Alan (Ed. D.). "A STUDY OF EMPLOYING AGENTS' ATTI-TUDES TOWARD ACADEMIC WOMEN IN HIGHER EDUCATION." Pennsylvania State University, 1968. 150 pp. Source: DAI, XXIX, 12A, Part I (June, 1969), 4203-A-4204-A. XUM Order No. 69-9810.

Found that deans, department chairmen, and faculty in 6 fields of humanities and social sciences: (1) had discriminatory attitudes toward academic women when choosing between equally qualified male and female candidates; (2) selected a statistically significant num-ber of superior females in preference to less qualified males; (3) were significantly influenced by age, sex, and experience (but not degree and rank) in employment of females; and (4) those who had discriminatory employment attitudes toward academic women also had negative attitudes toward women in general.

Simpson, Wessylyne Alford (Ed. D.). "SELF CONCEPT AND CAREER CHOICE AMONG BLACK WOMEN." Oklahoma State University, 1975. 73 pp. Source: DAI, XXXVI, 11A (May, 1976), 7220-A. XUM Order No. 76-9772.

Found: (1) no significant relationship between self-concept and career choice among 50 college women, 50 college-bound high school girls, and 50 non-college-bound high school girls; (2) congruency of career choice was significantly higher among college students than among high school girls; and (3) no significant difference in career choice congruence was found between the two groups of high school girls.

Sindlinger, Walter Eugene (Ed. D.). "EXPERIMENTATION IN EDUCATION FOR NURSING AT ORANGE COUNTY COMMUNITY COLLEGE." Columbia University Teachers College, 1956. 235 pp. Source: TCCU DIGESTS (1956), pp. 614-615.

Conclusions of this descriptive study of an experimental 2-year nur-sing program: (1) competent nurses can be prepared in less than 3 years; and (2) a community college can organize, administer, and operate a nursing program that will fit into its total curriculum.

Sine, Idamae Kelii (Ph. D.). "IDENTIFICATION AND VALIDATION OF COM-PETENCIES PERCEIVED ESSENTIAL TO CERTIFIED NURSE-MIDWIFERY PREPARATION PROGRAMS." University of Utah, 1976. 127 pp. Source: DAI, XXXVII, 7A (January, 1977), 4105-A. XUM Order No. 77-768.

Identified competencies most critical to successful performance by nurse-midwives. Recommended that these competencies be used in: (1) planning a certified nurse-midwife education program; (2) pre-paring job descriptions; and (3) evaluating the effectiveness of nurse-midwives.

Singer, Sister Judith Mary (Ed. D.). "A PROGRAM FOR PREGNANT SCHOOL-AGE GIRLS IN THE EAST BATON ROUGE, LOUISIANA SCHOOL DISTRICT: A FOLLOW-UP STUDY WITH IMPLICATIONS FOR FUNCTIONAL EDUCATION." Louisiana State University, 1974. 138 pp. Source: DAI, XXXVI, 1A (July, 1975), 51-A. XUM Order No. 75-14,286.

Found among 98 school-age pregnant girls who participated in a home-bound program: (1) grades of most girls who returned to school improved; (2) most girls were black but there was no significant difference between races in the age level at which pregnancy occurred; (3) most girls came from poor homes; and (4) satisfying relationships with parents and friends were related to the girls' ages.

Singer, Michael (Ph. D.). "THE EFFECTS OF SEX AND LOCUS OF CONTROL ON HELPING BEHAVIOR IN A SIMULATED TEACHING SITUATION." University of Washington, 1974. 62 pp. Source: DAI, XXXV, 7B (January, 1975), 3566-B. XUM Order No. 74-29,500.

Found in first experiment: (1) no significant effects due to locus of control; (2) females asked for more cues than did males; and (3) internally controlled persons paired with an opposite sex confederate waited longer before asking for help. In the second experiment, on offering help, found: (1) no significant differences because of locus of control; and (2) males offered more help than did females.

Singh, Kalpa Nath (Ph. D.). "A STUDY OF THE PERSONAL AND SOCIAL BEHAVIOR OF SIXTH GRADE 4-H AND NON-4-H BOYS AND GIRLS IN TEN SELECTED WISCONSIN COMMUNITIES." University of Wisconsin, 1959. 142 pp. Source: DAI, XX, 3 (September, 1959), 822-823. XUM Order No. Mic 59-3228.

Among 70 4-H boys, 225 non-4-H boys, 78 4-H girls, and 174 non-4-H girls found: (1) significant differences in socio-economic status (with 4-H members higher), emotional stability, and certain interests; (2) 4-H boys had more social skills than did non-4-H boys; (3) no differences existed in social skills of 4-H and non-4-H girls; and (4) 4-H girls had significantly higher scores on social qualities than did non-4-H girls.

Singleton, Enrica Kinchen (Dr. P. H.). "A PROCESS OF TRAINEE ASSESSMENT FOR A FAMILY NURSE TRAINING PROGRAM." Tulane University, School of Public Health & Tropical Medicine, 1975. 410 pp. Source: DAI, XXXVI, 11B (May, 1976), 5524-B. XUM Order No. 76-10,360.

Found that, after students completed a new family health program, they: (1) had achieved at or above the 80% acceptable level of mastery of the didactic content; (2) had acquired the necessary new skills and increased their proficiency in other skills; and (3) had passed the certifying examinations prepared by 3 physicians not directly involved in the program.

Singleton, Nan Chachere (Ph. D.). "ADEQUACY OF THE DIETS OF PREGNANT TEENAGERS: EDUCATIONAL, NUTRITIONAL AND SOCIOECONOMIC FACTORS." Louisiana State University, 1974. 71 pp. Source: DAI, XXXVI, 1A (July, 1975), 210-A. XUM Order No. 75-14,287.

Found among pregnant women 18 years old or under that: (1) all had disadvantages in education, nutrition, and socio-economic background; (2) most had completed the 9th or 10th grade; and (3) most planned to continue their education.

Sink, Winifred Ray (Ed. D.). "A STUDY OF THE USE OF THE RESULTS OF THE PRE-ENTRANCE PSYCHOLOGICAL EXAMINATIONS IN THE COUNSELING OF STUDENTS

IN SELECTED SCHOOLS OF NURSING IN INDIANA." Indiana University, 1958.
114 pp. Source: DAI, XIX, 8 (February, 1959), 2067-2968. XUM Order No.
Mic 59-85.

In a study of 670 students in 20 nursing schools, found that: (1)
pre-entrance psychological exam results were not fully used; (2) using the test results as a counseling tool was helpful in students'
personal adjustment and in improving their academic achievement; and
(3) most counselors were not adequately prepared for counseling duties.

Sisley, Becky Lynn (Ed. D.). "MEASUREMENT OF ATTITUDES OF WOMEN
COACHES TOWARD THE CONDUCT OF INTERCOLLEGIATE ATHLETICS FOR WOMEN." Uni-
versity of North Carolina at Greensboro, 1973. 205 pp. Source: DAI,
XXXIV, 5A (November, 1973), 2372-A-2373-A. XUM Order No. 73-26,408.

Constructed an attitude scale which had content validity and an acceptable index of internal consistency. Found that women coaches
tested had favorable attitudes toward intercollegiate athletics for
women.

Sitton, Margaret Wilson (Ed. D.). "AN EXPLORATORY STUDY OF ATTAIN-
MENT OF BASIC CONCEPTS IN HOME MANAGEMENT BY HOME ECONOMICS EDUCATION
STUDENT TEACHERS." Texas Technological College, 1965. 210 pp. Source:
DAI, XXVI, 8 (February, 1966), 4482-4483. XUM Order No. 65-15,364.

Examined 28 student teachers and 356 high school students under
their guidance. Found that: (1) attainment of 4 basic home management concepts by student teachers could be reliably measured; (2)
the 4 concepts were interrelated and should be included in all secondary and college home management teaching; and (3) grade point average was an accurate indicator of student teacher attainment of home
management concepts.

Sitts, Marvin Ralph (Ph. D.). "A STUDY OF THE PERSONALITY DIFFEREN-
CES BETWEEN A GROUP OF WOMEN WHO HAD PARTICIPATED IN SEWING CLASSES IN AN
ADULT EDUCATION PROGRAM AND A GROUP OF THEIR FRIENDS AND NEIGHBORS WHO
HAD NOT PARTICIPATED IN ANY ADULT EDUCATION ACTIVITIES." Michigan State
University, 1960. 175 pp. Source: DAI, XXI, 5 (November, 1960), 1120.
XUM Order No. Mic 60-3426.

Found that women participants in adult education: (1) were brighter,
more aggressive, more persistent, less polished, more confident, and
possessed a less clear pattern of socially approved behavior; (2)
had enrolled in more special schools, had larger incomes, and belonged to more service and neighborhood clubs; and (3) were generally
older than non-participants.

Siu, Ping Kee (Ph. D.). "RELATIONSHIPS BETWEEN MOTIVATIONAL PATTERNS
AND ACADEMIC ACHIEVEMENT IN CHINESE AND PUERTO RICAN SECOND- AND THIRD-
GRADE STUDENTS." Fordham University, 1972. 126 pp. Source: DAI,
XXXIII, 7A (January, 1973), 3407-A. XUM Order No. 73-1519.

Found significant differences in motivational patterns and in relationships of motivational variables to achievement between Chinese
and Puerto Rican children: (1) factors of sex, grade, school experience, dominant language, and birthplace were important predictors of

achievement in one culture but did not predict it in the other; and (2) sex differences in motivational patterns were significant among Puerto Ricans but not among Chinese; i.e., Puerto Rican girls had a higher level of test anxiety than did Puerto Rican boys.

Sjoden, Barbara Virtue (Ed. D.). "CREATIVE THOUGHT PROCESSES IN DIPLOMA NURSING EDUCATION." Rutgers University, 1973. 179 pp. Source: DAI, XXXIV, 10B (April, 1974), 5176-B. XUM Order No. 74-8874.

Found in testing 91 nursing students that creative thought was not positively related: (1) to success in nursing education; (2) to length of diploma education; nor (3) to students' clinical ratings on behavioral objectives. Experimental sessions using sensory stimuli and group discussions did not increase creative thinking ability significantly.

Sklar, Kathryn Kish (Ph. D.). "HOUSEHOLD DIVINITY: A LIFE OF CATHARINE BEECHER." University of Michigan, 1969. 427 pp. Source: DAI, XXX, 9A (March, 1970), 3893-A-3894-A. XUM Order No. 70-4194.

This biographical study: (1) analyzed Beecher's career as an educator, writer on moral and religious topics, and publicist for women's education; and (2) showed how her life reflected cultural change between 1800 and 1878.

Skurski, Sister Virginia Ann (Ph. D.). "A STUDY OF THE EFFECTS OF SIMULATED INSTRUCTIONAL MEDIA ON THE BEHAVIOR OF SENIOR NURSING STUDENTS." University of Michigan, 1974. 151 pp. Source: DAI, XXXV, 7A (January, 1975), 4261-A-4262-A. XUM Order No. 75-809.

Found that the instructional media developed by the author: (1) promoted a supportive climate among senior nursing students; and (2) helped students develop healthy attitudes toward conflict.

Slaney, Fiona Jane MacKinnon (Ph. D.). "SOME CORRELATES OF ACHIEVEMENT MOTIVATION IN WOMEN IN STUDENT PERSONNEL WORK." Ohio State University, 1972. 126 pp. Source: DAI, XXXIII, 10A (April, 1973), 5523-A-5524-A. XUM Order No. 72-27,109.

In comparing graduate men and women preparing for student personnel careers and people already practicing it, found: (1) no significant differences between high and low achievement-oriented women; (2) a significant difference between graduate students and practitioners in their perception of the ideal woman, with women students viewing the ideal woman as being more active; and (3) females viewed man's ideal woman as traditionally passive but men actually viewed the ideal woman as being assertive and independent.

Slater, Shirley Tinkham (Ph. D.). "ASSESSMENT OF A CONSUMER EDUCATION IN-SERVICE PROGRAM IN RELATION TO THE TEACHING BEHAVIOR OF HOME ECONOMICS TEACHERS." Ohio State University, 1974. 177 pp. Source: DAI, XXXV, 8B (February, 1975), 4025-B-4026-B. XUM Order No. 75-3196.

The home economics teachers who went through the in-service consumer education program: (1) gained in knowledge and use of teaching materials; (2) but there was no significant change in their attitudes toward students and teaching.

Slaughter, Mary Hoke (Ph. D.). "AN ANALYSIS OF THE RELATIONSHIP BE-
TWEEN SOMATOTYPE AND PERSONALITY PROFILES OF COLLEGE WOMEN." University
of Illinois, 1968. 167 pp. Source: DAI, XXIX, 8A (February, 1969),
2554-A. XUM Order No. 69-1454.

Found among 157 university women that: (1) biological factors are
important in accounting for human behavior; (2) women were more endomorphic than men; and (3) women are more closely massed within their
endomorphic and medial groupings.

Slaughter, Peggy Sue (Ed. D.). "A COMPARISON OF THE SELF CONCEPT,
FEMININITY, AND CAREER ASPIRATIONS OF COLLEGE SENIOR WOMEN PREPARING FOR
TYPICAL AND ATYPICAL OCCUPATIONS." Mississippi State University, 1976.
73 pp. Source: DAI, XXXVII, 3A (September, 1976), 1412-A. XUM Order
No. 76-20,773.

Found no significant differences between the self concepts of women
students who planned to enter traditional female occupations and
those choosing nontraditional careers.

Slepack, Donna Grund (Ed. D.). "WOMEN IN THE GERMAN DEMOCRATIC RE-
PUBLIC: A FIELD STUDY AND COMPARATIVE ANALYSIS OF SEX BIAS IN USA AND
GDR CHILDREN'S READERS." University of Cincinnati, 1976. 232 pp.
Source: DAI, XXXVII, 5A (November, 1976), 2778-A. XUM Order No. 76-
24,502.

In the German Democratic Republic (East Germany), where 84% of women
work, found that: (1) the educational system prepared them for jobs;
and (2) sex-role stereotyping existed in elementary reading textbooks
but was less common than in USA textbooks.

Slis, Vikki Gordon (Ph. D.). "INSTRUCTIONAL SET AND OBJECTIVE SELF
AWARENESS: EFFECTS ON TASK PERFORMANCE AND CAUSAL ATTRIBUTION OF MENTAL-
LY RETARDED ADULT FEMALES." Hofstra University, 1975. 134 pp. Source:
DAI, XXXVI, 10B (April, 1976), 5362-B-5363-B. XUM Order No. 76-3978.

Concluded that mentally retarded women performed a manual task well:
(1) when given a feeling of success; and (2) when self awareness
was stimulated either by being observed or by watching themselves on
a television monitor.

Slotkin, Jacquelyn Hersh (Ph. D.). "ROLE CONFLICT AMONG SELECTED
ANGLO AND MEXICAN-AMERICAN FEMALE COLLEGE GRADUATES." University of
Arizona, 1976. 153 pp. Source: DAI, XXXVII, 3A (September, 1976),
1825-A-1826-A. XUM Order No. 76-19,731.

Found that: (1) both Anglo and Mexican-American women college graduates experienced role conflict; (2) more Mexican-American women were
employed; (3) fewer Mexican-American women perceived themselves in
the housewife-only role; and (4) Mexican-American women were more
self-oriented.

Smallwood, Kathie Beckman (Ph. D.). "THE PROBLEMS OF MATURE WOMEN
STUDENTS ENROLLED IN A SELECTED COMMUNITY COLLEGE." North Texas State
University, 1977. 213 pp. Source: DAI, XXXVIII, 3A (September, 1977),
1235-A. XUM Order No. 77-19,684.

Findings: (1) women's problems included nonacademic responsibilities, course work, future job and career, and interpersonal relations; (2) problems increased with increased course loads; (3) some problems were related to low income; (4) divorced women had the most problems; (5) younger women were more concerned with child care; and (6) older women were concerned about their ability to succeed and to pursue careers traditionally open to men.

Smith, Betty Edmiston (Ph. D.). "THE IDENTIFICATION OF PREDICTOR VARIABLES OF STATE BOARD EXAMINATION SCORES OF PRACTICAL NURSING STUDENTS IN THE STATE OF MISSISSIPPI." University of Southern Mississippi, 1976. 79 pp. Source: DAI, XXXVII, 4B (October, 1976), 1625-B-1626-B. XUM Order No. 76-23,034.

Significant predictors of practical nursing students' scores on the Mississippi State Board Examinations for practical nurses included: IQ, high school grades, GED scores, age, the National League for Nursing test scores, and junior college grades.

Smith, Cassandra Mary Ellen (Ed. D.). "SENIOR NURSING STUDENTS' PERCEPTIONS OF NURSES AND NURSING IN THE MILITARY SERVICE." Columbia University, 1971. 128 pp. Source: DAI, XXXII, 2A (August, 1971), 678-A-679-A. XUM Order No. 71-20,030.

Found that senior nursing students: (1) considered military nurses to be regimented, rigid, authoritarian, adventurous, independent, efficient, hardworking, ambitious, practical, well-educated, and neat; and (2) considered civilian nurses to be feminine, gentle, and tender.

Smith, Dorothy W. (Ed. D.). "A PLAN FOR TEACHING THE CARE OF ADULTS IN AN ASSOCIATE DEGREE PROGRAM IN NURSING." Columbia University Teachers College, 1960. 209 pp. Source: Dissertation, pp. 549-551.

Developed a teaching plan and case materials for use in training nurses to care for adults' common health problems, including mental illness.

Smith, Elizabeth Dorsey Ivey (Ed. D.). "ATTITUDES AMONG BACCALAUREATE NURSING STUDENTS IN NEW YORK CITY REGARDING WOMEN SEEKING ELECTIVE ABORTIONS." Columbia University Teachers College, 1975. 125 pp. Source: DAI, XXXVI, 8B (February, 1976), 3873-B-3874-B. XUM Order No. 76-3274.

Found that nursing students' attitudes toward women seeking elective abortion were significantly related to: (1) family size; (2) use of contraceptives; (3) death within the family; and (4) abortion status.

Smith, Harriet Oragene (Ed. D.). "A STUDY OF THE EFFECTIVENESS OF AN ALTERNATIVE PROGRAM FOR THE PREPARATION OF BEGINNING PUBLIC HEALTH NURSES." University of Southern California, 1959. 483 pp. Source: DAI, XX, 6 (December, 1959), 2233. XUM Order No. Mic 59-5026.

Evaluated an experimental course on Community Health and Nursing, given by a nursing college which lacked accreditation for preparing public health nurses. Found that: (1) the course was training students to work in public health; but (2) the evaluation methods used were not appropriate for judging all of the course's merits.

Smith, Helen Gertrude (Ph. D.). "THE EXTENT TO WHICH WOMEN STUDENTS AT A STATE COLLEGE, CLASSIFIED ACCORDING TO FIELD OF SPECIALIZATION, ARE CHARACTERIZED BY CERTAIN MEASURABLE TRAITS." New York University, 1944. 321 pp. Source: New York University, School of Education, ABSTRACTS OF THESES (October, 1944-June, 1945), pp. 49-55.

Found these characteristics among women students: (1) home economics and science majors had better adjustment to home and better health and emotional adjustment; (2) music, history, political science, business administration, and speech majors were more aggressive; and (3) speech majors had good emotional adjustment.

Smith, Hilda Lee (Ph. D.). "FEMINISM IN SEVENTEENTH-CENTURY ENGLAND." University of Chicago, 1975. Source: DAI, XXXVI, 4A (October, 1975), 2382-A-2383-A.

Found that early feminists were influenced by Descartes, Locke, and Bacon; but applied their views about women in ways that the philosophers never personally employed. Topics covered were: the roots of feminist writing; women as a distinct sociological group; descriptions of 17th century feminists, as to social class, political affiliation, personal background, marital status, occupation and personality; and a consideration of views toward women's education advanced in the early 18th century.

Smith, James Wesley (Ph. D.). "AN APPRAISAL OF THE TREATMENT OF FE-MALES IN SELECTED UNITED STATES HIGH SCHOOL HISTORY TEXTBOOKS FROM 1959 UNTIL 1976." Indiana University, 1977. 147 pp. Source: DAI, XXXVIII, 8A (February, 1978), 4723-A-4724-A. XUM Order No. 77-30,324.

Found that publishers of high school American history textbooks have been slow to improve the female image. Females: (1) had less coverage; (2) were overrepresented in stereotypical roles; (3) were less frequently authors, co-authors, or consultants for history textbooks; and (4) were less often dominant characters in pictures illustrating history textbooks.

Smith, Joan Frances (Ph. D.). "ASSESSING THE COGNITIVE STYLE OF STUDENTS IN THE NURSING CARE OF PATIENTS HAVING RETINAL DETACHMENTS." Wayne State University, 1974. 161 pp. Source: DAI, XXXV, 12A, Part 1 (June, 1975), 7625-A-7626-A. XUM Order No. 75-13,390.

An experimental group of 20 attained the clinical performance objectives in nursing care of the patients with retinal detachments to a higher degree than the control group of 20.

Smith, Joan Karen (Ph. D.). "ELLA FLAGG YOUNG: PORTRAIT OF A LEADER." Iowa State University, 1976. 331 pp. Source: DAI, XXXVII, 7A (January, 1977), 4176-A. XUM Order No. 77-1482.

Biography of a student of and colleague of John Dewey who became the first woman to be: (1) superintendent of a large city school system (Chicago); (2) president of the Illinois State Teachers' Association; and (3) president of the National Education Association.

Smith, Kathryn Muriel (Ed. D.). "DISCREPANCIES IN THE VALUE CLIMATE OF NURSING STUDENTS: A COMPARISON OF HEAD NURSES AND NURSING EDUCATORS." Stanford University, 1964. 181 pp. Source: DAI, XXV, 7 (January, 1965), 4089-4090. XUM Order No. 64-13,554.

Compared roles and values emphasized by head nurses and nursing educators in preparing nursing students for clinical practice. Found that: (1) head nurses stressed leadership, independence, conforming behavior, group orientation, friendliness, supportiveness of co-workers and patients, helpfulness, neatness, and composure; and (2) nurse educators stressed independence, team orientation, empathy with and support to patients, helpfulness, cognitive skills, and intelligence.

Smith, Lynette Elizabeth (Ph. D.). "SEX-ROLE BEHAVIOR AMONG BLACKS AND WHITES." University of Houston, 1977. 140 pp. Source: DAI, XXXVIII, 7B (January, 1978), 3417-B. XUM Order No. 77-29,684.

Found that black people: (1) had fewer sex-biased attitudes toward personality traits; and (2) had different reasons for their unwillingness to become involved with women's rights groups than did whites.

Smith, Sister M. Leonita (Ph. D.). "CATHOLIC VIEWPOINTS ABOUT THE PSYCHOLOGY, SOCIAL ROLE, AND HIGHER EDUCATION OF WOMEN." Ohio State University, 1961. 227 pp. Source: DAI, XXII, 10 (April, 1962), 3637-3638. XUM Order No. 62-815.

Presidents of U. S. Catholic colleges (69% responded) accepting women preferred that women's education: (1) reflect feminine psychology and social role; (2) develop and enrich feminine modes of thinking and acting; and (3) encourage artistic expression and the refinement of female intuitive powers.

Smith, Marie Allen (Ed. D.). "MENSTRUAL DISORDERS: INCIDENCE AND RELATIONSHIP TO ATTITUDES, MANIFEST NEEDS, AND SCHOLASTIC ACHIEVEMENT IN COLLEGE FRESHMAN WOMEN." University of Denver, 1970. 140 pp. Source: DAI, XXXI, 12A (June, 1971), 6354-A. XUM Order No. 71-2449.

Found a highly significant positive relationship between menstrual disorders and negative attitudes, tension symptoms, superstitions practiced, and feelings of depression during menstrual period. Recommended that schools use instructional and counseling programs to help remove shame of menstruation and develop pride in becoming women.

Smith, Mary-Elizabeth Reichert (Ph. D.). "PATTERNS OF INTERPERSONAL PREFERENCES IN A NURSING SCHOOL CLASS: A SOCIOMETRIC STUDY OF CHANGES IN VALUATIONAL BASES OF INFORMAL STRUCTURE IN A SCHOOL GROUP." Catholic University of America, 1952. Source: Catholic University of America, Studies in Sociology, ABSTRACT SERIES, V (1952), pp. 11-14.

Found that personal relationships among students in a nursing class during 18 months: (1) remained somewhat stable within groups; and (2) became increasingly inclusive of the class as a whole.

Smith, Norene Alys (Ph. D.). "SOCIAL AND CULTURAL FACTORS IN THE BACKGROUNDS OF WOMEN PHYSICAL EDUCATION MAJORS." University of Iowa,

1967. 216 pp. Source: DAI, XXVIII, 2A (August, 1967), 472-A. XUM Order No. 67-9105.

Found in comparing women physical education (PE) majors with women arts and science majors that: (1) PE majors came from large cities and from either very large or very small high schools; (2) parents of both groups were similarly educated; (3) fathers of PE majors read more sports magazines and engaged in more recreational activities; (4) PE majors were motivated by a desire to be a leader; and (5) arts and science majors had higher American College Testing scores.

Smith, Robert Ernest, Jr. (Ph. D.). "SELF CONCEPT IN FEMALE DELIN-QUENTS." Ohio State University, 1972. 142 pp. Source: DAI, XXXIII, 8A (February, 1973), 4103-A-4104-A. XUM Order No. 73-2130.

Found that self-concepts of delinquent and non-delinquent girls differed significantly. Delinquents had: (1) a lower self-concept on adaptability and conformity; and (2) a higher self-concept on inquiring intellect and confident self-expression.

Smith, Sharon Jean (Ph. D.). "DIMENSIONS OF WOMEN'S LOCUS OF CONTROL BELIEFS IN RELATION TO ACADEMIC ACHIEVEMENT AND EXPECTATION, VOCATIONAL ASPIRATION, AND ATTITUDES TOWARD THE WOMEN'S MOVEMENT." University of California, Berkeley, 1977. 172 pp. Source: DAI, XXXVIII, 8A (February, 1978), 4701-A-4702-A. XUM Order No. 77-31,543.

Undergraduate women (410) who favored the women's movement tended to believe that: (1) they controlled their personal lives internally; (2) control of the social system was external; and (3) socialization rather than feminine nature was responsible for differences in men's and women's interest.

Smith, Stanley Marion (P. E. D.). "PRE-STUDENT-TEACHING EXPERIENCES IN PHYSICAL EDUCATION BY MEN AND WOMEN MAJORS IN SELECTED INDIANA COL-LEGES AND UNIVERSITIES." Indiana University, 1969. 181 pp. Source: DAI, XXX, 8A (February, 1970), 3309-A. XUM Order No. 70-1703.

Found that neither women nor men's physical education programs nor small to medium-large institutions provided sufficient pre-student teaching experiences in classroom participation and observation. Recommended several steps toward providing more such experiences.

Smith, Virginia Whitmore (Ph. D.). "IDENTIFICATION AND ANALYSIS OF FACTORS THAT CONTRIBUTE TO RETENTION AND ATTRITION OF NEW FACULTY IN BACCALAUREATE NURSING PROGRAMS." George Peabody College for Teachers, 1973. 173 pp. Source: DAI, XXXIV, 7A (January, 1974), 3794-A-3795-A. XUM Order No. 73-32,649.

Data from 390 faculty in 44 baccalaureate nursing programs revealed that: (1) those nursing faculty staying in their jobs believed they had a high potential for job satisfaction; (2) relationships among job satisfaction, remaining, and leaving a job were more significant for respondents grouped by their preferences rather than by their job plans; (3) faculty members with more teaching experiences were more satisfied with intrinsic factors; and (4) reasons faculty were leaving included family problems, job-related reasons, and the desire to attend graduate school.

Smoyak, Shirley Anne (Ph. D.). "A PANEL STUDY COMPARING SELF-REPORTS OF BACCALAUREATE AND DIPLOMA NURSES BEFORE GRADUATION AND AFTER THEIR FIRST WORK EXPERIENCES IN HOSPITALS." Rutgers University, 1970. 212 pp. Source: DAI, XXXI, 11A (May, 1971), 6182-A-6183-A. XUM Order No. 71-12,274.

The comparison of 2 groups--195 students in 7 baccalaureate programs and 167 students in 6 diploma programs--revealed that the 2 groups were more alike than different, both before graduation and after working 6 months in a hospital. Factors compared were family and socio-economic backgrounds, career choice and planning, clinical learning experiences, viewpoints about the baccalaureate degree, and nursing activities and experiences.

Sneed, Ruth (Ed. D.). "HOME VISITING AS A TEACHING TECHNIQUE IN HOME ECONOMICS." Columbia University Teachers College, 1956. Source: TCCU DIGESTS (1956), pp. 626-627.

Home economics teachers (13) and their pupils followed suggestions from 46 home economics teachers in 46 states on preparing for and conducting home visits. Found that: (1) home economics teachers' satisfaction with their work increased because of home visits; and (2) mothers of home economics pupils understood school home economics programs better after a visit from the home economics teacher.

Snow, Barbara M. (Ed. D.). "AN ANALYSIS OF THE RELATIONSHIP OF CERTAIN FACTORS TO THE SOCIAL ACCEPTANCE STATUS OF COLLEGE FRESHMAN WOMEN." Pennsylvania State University, 1957. 93 pp. Source: DAI, XVIII, 1 (January, 1958), 142-143. XUM Order No. 25,102.

In a study of 20 variables among 168 freshman women, found that body symmetry (appropriate body weight), morale, social adjustment, and emotional stability were significantly related to social adjustment.

Snyder, Peggy Pope (Ph. D.). "PERSONALITY, ACHIEVEMENT VARIABLES AND DOGMATISM LEVEL DIFFERENCE BETWEEN ANDROGYNOUS AND TRADITIONAL FEMININE CAREER PROFESSIONAL WOMEN." Catholic University of America, 1977. 90 pp. Source: DAI, XXXVIII, 4A (October, 1977), 1906-A-1907-A. XUM Order No. 77-21,341.

Concluded that: (1) no significant personality differences existed between the no sex-bias women and the feminine career women; and (2) women's perceptions of male attitudes had a highly significant influence on women's career choices.

Snypes, Doris Virginia (Ed. D.). "EDUCATIONAL PRACTICES RELATED TO CRITICAL THINKING IN SELECTED BACCALAUREATE PROGRAMS IN NURSING." University of Alabama, 1965. 155 pp. Source: DAI, XXVI, 10 (April, 1966), 5982. XUM Order No. 66-2921.

Questionnaires from 46 faculty members in 5 baccalaureate nursing programs disclosed that: (1) in only 2 of the 5 schools did objectives relate to critical thinking; (2) inconsistencies existed within

departments and schools as to which aspects of critical thinking
should be developed; and (3) most respondents did not list critical
thinking as a course objective.

Sobol, Evelyn G. (Ph. D.). "THE RELATION BETWEEN SELF-ACTUALIZATION
AND THE BACCALAUREATE NURSING STUDENT'S RESPONSE TO STRESS AS EVIDENCED
BY LEVEL OF STATE-TRAIT ANXIETY." New York University, 1977. 164 pp.
Source: DAI, XXXVIII, 4B (October, 1977), 1654-B-1655-B. XUM Order No.
77-20,759.

Found among 144 female senior students in 4 baccalaureate nursing
programs that anxiety and self-actualization were negatively correlated. Recommended that nursing programs take steps to reduce anxiety among students and faculty and to increase levels of self-actualization.

Solloway, Jerry G. (Ph. D.). "A CLINICAL ASSESSMENT OF A COMMUNITY
COLLEGE AFFILIATED GUIDANCE CENTER FOR WOMEN." Michigan State University,
1970. 192 pp. Source: DAI, XXXI, 5A (November, 1970), 2081-A-2082-A.
XUM Order No. 70-20,533.

Found among women clients of the New York Guidance Center for Women
that: (1) more women were satisfied with the Center than the staff
judged were helped by the counseling; (2) counseling was seen by many
women as supporting decisions already made; and (3) the women liked
the counseling regardless of their age, education, employment, and
marital status.

Solomon, Adrian (Ph. D.). "IDENTIFICATION, DIFFERENTIATION, AND EX-
TENSION OF SELF: A STUDY OF PERCEPTIONS OF SELF, MOTHER, AND DAUGHTER
IN A SAMPLE OF COLLEGE WOMEN." Cornell University, 1955. 76 pp. Source:
DAI, XV, 6 (1955), 1121. XUM Order No. 11,920.

Concluded, from 89 college women's perceptions of themselves, their
daughters, and their mothers, that the women: (1) wanted their
daughters to be like themselves; and (2) had cultivated both similarities and differences with their own mothers.

Solomons, Helen Harris (Ph. D.). "SEX-ROLE-MEDIATED ACHIEVEMENT BE-
HAVIOURS AND INTERPERSONAL DYNAMICS OF FIFTH-GRADE COEDUCATIONAL PHYSICAL
EDUCATION CLASSES." Bryn Mawr College, 1976. 292 pp. Source: DAI,
XXXVII, 10B (April, 1977), 5445-B. XUM Order No. 77-6538.

Found that individual 5th grade girls who performed as well as (or
even better than) boys were not perceived as being as highly skilled
as boys. Concluded that the differing perceptions of girls' performance reflected society's role expectations for girls.

Sorensen, Gladys Elaine (Ed. D.). "IDENTIFICATION OF SCIENTIFIC
KNOWLEDGE BASIC TO A SPECIMEN OF NURSING CARE." Columbia University,
1965. 201 pp. Source: DAI, XXVI, 2 (August, 1965), 992. XUM Order
No. 65-8863.

This study: (1) developed a method for identifying concepts, principles, and facts basic to nursing care by taking one patient case
study and recording potential problems and nursing actions; and (2)
analyzed the literature to identify facts and principles basic to
nursing care.

South, John Craig (Ph. D.). "AN ITEM FACTOR ANALYSIS OF SOME VALUE DIMENSIONS AND THEIR RELATION TO A MEASURE OF SUCCESS IN STUDENT NURSE TRAINING." Ohio State University, 1959. 67 pp. Source: DAI, XX, 9 (March, 1960), 3821-3822. XUM Order No. Mic 60-797.

The study failed to establish a strong relationship between nursing students rated by their peers as "best" and "poorest" and such values selected by nursing students as acceptance and compliance; calm assurance vs. frightened bewilderment; concern for self; independence vs. dependence.

Sovie, Margaret Doe (Ph. D.). "THE RELATIONSHIP OF LEARNING ORIENTATION, NURSING ACTIVITY AND CONTINUING EDUCATION." Syracuse University, 1972. 238 pp. Source: DAI, XXXIII, 9A (March, 1973), 4781-A. XUM Order No. 73-7774.

Found in comparing nurses who took continuing education programs with nursing colleagues who were potential continuing education enrollees that: (1) all nurses had some continuing learning activities; (2) nurse participants in continuing education programs allowed time for a wide variety of learning experiences; and (3) past participation in such programs was as important as formal education level in predicting total educational activity.

Spafford, Ivol O. (Ph. D.). "THE CONTRIBUTION OF HOME ECONOMICS TO GENERAL EDUCATION." Ohio State University, 1935. 340+ pp. Source: Dissertation, p. v.

Appraised home economics in selected programs at elementary and secondary level and discussed curriculum planning and evaluation.

Spann, Annabelle E. (Ph. D.). "A FOLLOW-UP STUDY OF ALABAMA AGRICULTURAL AND MECHANICAL COLLEGE HOME ECONOMICS GRADUATES WITH IMPLICATIONS FOR CURRICULUM IMPROVEMENT." University of Wisconsin, 1958. 162 pp. Source: DAI, XVIII, 6 (June, 1958), 2125-2126. XUM Order No. Mic 58-1931.

Found that: (1) most of the 64 responding home economics alumnae were teaching but only 25% of those teaching were in home economics; (2) only 18% of respondents were in their preferred occupation; and (3) most alumnae recommended improvement in: guidance, student-staff relations, physical facilities, and follow-up services. Author recommended improving the home economics curriculum, offering in-service programs for teachers, and improving recruitment practices.

Spaulding, Barbara George (Ph. D.). "FACTORS RELATED TO THE CHOICE OF HOME ECONOMICS AS A COLLEGE MAJOR BY WOMEN." Purdue University, 1972. 83 pp. Source: DAI, XXXIII, 9A (March, 1973), 4855-A-4856-A. XUM Order No. 73-6114.

Found that girls who decided to major in home economics were influenced more than other college girls by: (1) college social life; (2) friends' career plans; (3) parents and teachers' wishes; and (4) farm magazines. Home economics majors and non-majors differed little in intelligence and socio-economic status.

Spears, Betty Mary (Ph. D.). "PHILOSOPHICAL BASES FOR PHYSICAL EDU-
CATION EXPERIENCES CONSISTENT WITH THE GOALS OF GENERAL EDUCATION FOR
COLLEGE WOMEN." New York University, 1956. 301 pp. Source: DAI, XVI,
11 (1956), 2088. XUM Order No. 17,675.

Established principles to assure that non-professional undergraduate
women's physical education courses will enhance women's general education.

Spellman, Dorothy Marie (Ph. D.). "AN INVESTIGATION OF THE AVAIL-
ABILITY OF WOMEN AND OTHER MINORITY GROUP MEMBERS TO BE HIRED FOR TEACH-
ING AND ADMINISTRATIVE POSITIONS IN HIGHER EDUCATIONAL INSTITUTIONS IN
MISSOURI." Saint Louis University, 1973. 146 pp. Source: DAI, XXXIV,
9A (March, 1974), 5668-A. XUM Order No. 74-4573.

Found among Missouri blacks and women Ph. D. graduates in 1971 and
1972 that: (1) they were a decided minority; (2) very few black
women were Ph. D. graduates; and (3) blacks in general were poorly
represented. Gave 7 recommendations to improve the position of women
and blacks in higher education.

Spelman, Mary Marguerite (Ed. D.). "INDEPENDENT STUDY IN MASTER'S
PROGRAMS IN NURSING." University of Florida, 1970. 208 pp. Source:
DAI, XXXI, 11A (May, 1971), 5804-A. XUM Order No. 71-13,461.

Found among 256 nursing faculty in Master's programs in 38 institutions that: (1) independent study, other than for the thesis, was
slight; (2) there was a need to disseminate information on independent study and to increase the use of independent study.

Spence, Betty A. (Ph. D.). "SEX OF TEACHERS AS A FACTOR IN THEIR
PERCEPTION OF SELECTED LEADERSHIP CHARACTERISTICS OF MALE AND FEMALE ELE-
MENTARY SCHOOL PRINCIPALS." Purdue University, 1971. 131 pp. Source:
DAI, XXXII, 6A (December, 1971), 2985-A. XUM Order No. 72-1957.

Found among 192 teachers from 9 elementary schools with female principals and among 149 teachers from 7 elementary schools with male
principals that: (1) male and female principals were perceived differently; (2) male principals were scored higher on Tolerance of Uncertainty; (3) female principals were scored higher on Production
Emphasis; (4) female teachers scored male principals higher on Reconciliation, Tolerance of Uncertainty, Tolerance of Freedom, Consideration, Predictive Accuracy, and Integration; and (5) female
teachers scored female principals higher on Representation and Production Emphasis.

Spencer, Louise Walcutt (Ed. D.). "ELEVEN YEARS OF CHANGE IN THE
ROLE OF DEAN OF WOMEN IN COLLEGES, UNIVERSITIES, AND TEACHERS COLLEGES."
Columbia University Teachers College, 1952. 447 pp. Source: TCCU DI-
GESTS (1952), Part 2, pp. 795-796.

Found among 628 Deans of Women representing 71% of U. S. colleges
and universities that, compared with similar studies in 1926 and
1936, there was: (1) a decrease in average length of service; (2)
improvement in academic qualifications; (3) decline in real income;
and (4) closer coordination of services to students.

Sperry, Irwin V. (Ed. D.). "A STUDY OF A SECONDARY SCHOOL PROGRAM IN PREPARATION FOR MARRIAGE AND FAMILY LIVING WITH IMPLICATIONS FOR THE PREPARATION OF SECONDARY SCHOOL TEACHERS IN THE AREA OF HOME AND FAMILY LIFE." Wayne State University, 1949. 293 pp. Source: Dissertation, pp. 229-231.

Among recommendations for preparing secondary school teachers of family life courses were: (1) problems studied should be viewed positively; (2) first-hand experience in child development, possibly in a nursery school, should be included; and (3) skills in smooth human relationships should be enhanced.

Spicer, Mildred Gertrude (Ph. D.). "MAJOR EQUIPMENT, WORK SPACE, AND STORAGE SPACE FOUND IN 160 FARM AND VILLAGE HOMES IN NEW YORK STATE, AND IMPLICATIONS FOR HOMEMAKING EDUCATION AT THE SECONDARY LEVEL." Cornell University, 1941. 203 pp. Source: Dissertation, pp. 191-193.

Concluded that teachers could help students discover a family's resources for improving the conditions of household work.

Spitze, Hazel Taylor (Ed. D.). "THE RELATION BETWEEN SELECTED WOMEN'S KNOWLEDGE AND USE OF CONSUMER CREDIT: A BASIS FOR ADULT EDUCATION PROGRAM PLANNING." University of Tennessee, 1961. 138 pp. Source: DAI, XXII, 6 (December, 1961), 1972. XUM Order No. 61-4673.

Found among 100 urban women attending home economics classes that those with greater knowledge about consumer credit paid lower rates for credit.

Squires, Frances Helen (Ph. D.). "AN ANALYSIS OF SEX DIFFERENCES AND COGNITIVE STYLES ON SCIENCE PROBLEM SOLVING SITUATIONS." Ohio State University, 1977. 139 pp. Source: DAI, XXXVIII, 5A (November, 1977), 2688-A-2689-A. XUM Order No. 77-24,708.

Among 13-year-olds, found that girls' verbal (reading) abilities were superior to those of boys in solving science problems.

Stack, Sister Jeanne Mary (Ph. D.). "A COST STUDY OF OHIO HOSPITALS THAT CLOSED THEIR DIPLOMA SCHOOL OF NURSING BETWEEN 1968 AND 1972." Bowling Green State University, 1976. 217 pp. Source: DAI, XXXVII, 8A (February, 1977), 4760-A. XUM Order No. 77-2703.

Found that: (1) closing its diploma school did not result in a hospital's financial advantage; (2) a hospital continued to support nursing education after closing its diploma school; and (3) there may be increased costs of recruiting, orienting, and providing in-service education to college-trained nurses.

Staelin, Charlotte Dennete (Ph. D.). "THE INFLUENCE OF MISSIONS ON WOMEN'S EDUCATION IN INDIA: THE AMERICAN MARATHI MISSION IN AHMADNAGAR, 1830-1930." University of Michigan, 1977. 349 pp. Source: DAI, XXXVIII, 3A (September, 1977), 1582-A. XUM Order No. 77-18,125.

Concluded that although Christian missions started women's education in India, continuing educating women for the professions depended on an indigenous cultural heritage.

Staley, Kathleen Holmes (Ph. D.). "FAMILY, EDUCATION, AND PERSONALITY INFLUENCES ON FEMALE PRE-MEDICAL ATTRITION: A LONGITUDINAL STUDY." University of Iowa, 1976. 219 pp. Source: DAI, XXXVII, 5A (November, 1976), 2755-A. XUM Order No. 76-26,336.

Found, among reasons that women who were interested in medical careers never apply to medical schools: (1) there was no significant difference in proportion of pre-medical males and females planning to apply to medical schools; (2) female applicants had a higher grade point average than female non-applicants; and (3) females were influenced not to apply because of grades, pre-medical classes, change of interests, difficulty of medical education, and influences from college counselors and professors, parents, relatives, fiances, and friends.

Stanaland, Peggy (P. E. D.). "A STUDY OF SELECTED CULTURAL/SOCIAL CHANGES AND THEIR INFLUENCE ON PHYSICAL EDUCATION SERVICE PROGRAMS FOR WOMEN IN HIGHER EDUCATION WITH IMPLICATIONS FOR CHANGES IN WOMEN'S PROGRAMS." Indiana University, 1968. 268 pp. Source: DAI, XXIX, 2A (August, 1968), 472-A-473-A. XUM Order No. 68-11,000.

Concluded that: (1) static and dynamic values have not been a part of planning physical education programs for college women; (2) writers recommending activities were unaware of the changing status of women; and (3) an increasingly automated society should be (but has not been) the cause for re-evaluating activities.

Stanek, Richard James (Ph. D.). "AN INVESTIGATION OF THE INFLUENCE OF AGE, SEX, AND EDUCATION ON RESPONSES TO A SEMI-CONTROLLED ASSOCIATION TEST." Loyola University, 1956. 103 pp. Source: Dissertation, pp. 89-92.

Findings on Loyola Language Study administered to 400 males and 400 females included: (1) group characteristics of age, sex, and education significantly affected communality of response; (2) females attained higher scores and more communality of response; (3) the more educated respondents gave more common responses; and (4) the older the subject the less able to attain communality of response.

Stang, Genevieve Elaine (Ph. D.). "THE EFFECT OF A MICRO-TEACHING EXPERIENCE ON MODIFYING THE ATTITUDES TOWARD TEACHING SCIENCE HELD BY PROSPECTIVE WOMEN ELEMENTARY SCHOOL TEACHERS." University of Minnesota, 1967. 227 pp. Source: DAI, XXVIII, 12A (June, 1968), 4940-A-4941-A. XUM Order No. 68-7387.

There was no evidence of modified attitudes toward teaching science among 59 prospective women elementary school teachers after experiencing a micro-teaching unit.

Stanton, Marjorie L. (Ed. D.). "ADMINISTRATIVE BEHAVIOR OF ADMINISTRATORS OF BACCALAUREATE NURSING PROGRAMS." Columbia University Teachers College, 1975. 182 pp. Source: DAI, XXXVI, 8B (February, 1976), 3874-B. XUM Order No. 76-3277.

Baccalaureate nursing program administrators gave first priority to their policy making concerns and least priority to their research behavior concerns.

Staples, Ethel Janes (Ph. D.). "THE INFLUENCE OF THE SEX OF THE
THERAPIST AND OF THE CO-THERAPIST TECHNIQUE IN GROUP PSYCHOTHERAPY WITH
GIRLS: AN INVESTIGATION OF THE EFFECTIVENESS OF GROUP PSYCHOTHERAPY WITH
EIGHTH GRADE, BEHAVIOR-PROBLEM GIRLS, COMPARING RESULTS ACHIEVED BY A
MALE THERAPIST, BY A FEMALE THERAPIST, AND BY THE TWO THERAPISTS IN COM-
BINATION." New York University, 1958. 303 pp. Source: DAI, XIX, 8
(February, 1959), 2154. XUM Order No. Mic 58-5886.

Eighth grade girls (24) with behavior problems were assigned for 20
weeks to 1 of 4 groups: with a female therapist, a male therapist,
both a male and female therapist, or a control group. A tentative
conclusion was that the co-therapist technique may be injurious to
girls of that age and that they react differently to therapists of
different sexes.

Stark, Saidee Ethel (Ph. D.). "DEVELOPMENT OF CRITERIA FOR THE EDU-
CATIONAL EVALUATION OF ADVERTISING MATERIAL USED BY HOME ECONOMICS TEACH-
ERS." Columbia University Teachers College, 1930. 184 pp. Source:
TCCU DIGESTS, VI (1929-1931), pp. 1-3; Published as THE DEVELOPMENT OF
CRITERIA FOR THE EDUCATIONAL EVALUATION OF ADVERTISING MATERIAL USED BY
HOME ECONOMICS WORKERS; NY: Association of National Advertisers, 1930.

Data from 260 home economics teachers, 47 state superintendents of
education, and advertising experts indicated that: (1) no commercial
company should have access to a home economics class unless it can
make an educational contribution; and (2) commercial company material
should be prepared under the supervision of an education expert.

Stavely, Martha Rowena (Ed. D.). "A HISTORY OF STANFORD'S PROGRAM
IN EDUCATION FOR WOMEN DURING THE LAST FIFTY YEARS." Stanford University,
1944. 429 pp. Source: Author.

Analyzed changes in women students at Stanford during 50 years (for
34 years the number of women was limited). Findings included: (1)
a decrease in age at entering; (2) a decrease in time elapsed between
entry and graduation; (3) a shift in major from humanities to social
sciences; (4) improved health; and (5) a more active part in extracurricular activities.

Stead, Floyd Lorenzo (Ed. D.). "AN APPLICATION OF THE DELPHI METHOD
OF FORECASTING TO NURSING EDUCATION PLANNING IN WEST VIRGINIA." West
Virginia University, 1975. Source: DAI, XXXVI, 7A (January, 1976),
3312-B-3313-B.

Survey of administrators of West Virginia nursing education programs
showed: (1) increased cooperation by central decision makers; (2)
stronger demand for intense preparation and prerequisite educational
requirements; and (3) accelerated attention to the image and visibility of the professional nurse.

Stedman, Rose Edith (Ph. D.). "THE RELATIONSHIP OF MASCULINITY-FEM-
ININITY TO PERCEPTION OF SELF, CHOSEN OCCUPATION, AND COLLEGE TEACHING
AMONG UNIVERSITY HONOR STUDENTS." University of Minnesota, 1963. 178
pp. Source: DAI, XXIV, 3 (September, 1963), 1078-1079. XUM Order No.
63-6084.

Study of 113 honor sophomore women compared with 102 honor sophomore
men concluded that: (1) the self Masculinity-Femininity (MF) score
was reflected in their vocational preferences; and (2) although in-
triguing relationships occurred, MF was probably not a major factor
in the vocational perception of academically able women.

Steel, Catherine Mary (Ph. D.). "THE EFFECTS OF GROUP ASSERTIVE
SKILL TRAINING ON THE DEVELOPMENT, MAINTENANCE, AND GENERALIZATION OF
ASSERTIVE SKILLS IN UNASSERTIVE FEMALE UNDERGRADUATES." University of
Missouri--Columbia, 1976. 287 pp. Source: DAI, XXXVII, 9A (March,
1977), 5615-A. XUM Order No. 77-5660.

Assertive skill training was given for 4 weeks to 3 groups of women;
a control group did not receive training. The experimental groups
became significantly more assertive on the College Self-Expression
Scale and on the Overt Assertion Test Rating Scale developed by the
experimenter. This gain in assertiveness was accompanied by shift
toward a more internal locus of control.

Steele, Shirley May (Ph. D.). "INVESTIGATION OF SIMULATION TECHNIQUES
WITH TEACHERS IN THE AREA OF CHILD HEALTH NURSING." Ohio State Univer-
sity, 1973. 239 pp. Source: DAI, XXXIV, 2A (August, 1973), 672-A-673-
A. XUM Order No. 73-18955.

Found that using simulation in conjunction with clinical laboratory
facility training was effective in training nurses to care for
children.

Steffen, John David (Ph. D.). "THE EFFECTS OF TWO BEHAVIORAL MODELS
OF GROUP COUNSELING ON THE ACADEMIC PERFORMANCE OF SELECTED COLLEGE WO-
MEN." University of Minnesota, 1968. 265 pp. Source: DAI, XXIX, 10A
(April, 1969), 3426-A-3427-A. XUM Order No. 69-6857.

Found no statistically significant differences between 2 groups of
women students who received different types of academic counseling.

Stein, Alida Anisman (Ed. D.). "IMAGES OF CONTEMPORARY AMERICAN WO-
MEN AS REFLECTED BY PROGRAMS AND ACTIVITIES OF AUXILIARIES OF PROFESSIONAL
ASSOCIATIONS." University of Northern Colorado, 1974. 108 pp. Source:
DAI, XXXV, 9A (March, 1975), 6253-A-6254-A. XUM Order No. 75-5444.

Concluded that women members of volunteer organizations were nurturers
and that their extra-home activities were extensions of their mother-
ing role.

Stein, Peter Joseph (Ph. D.). "THE IMPACT OF SELECTIVITY, THE COLLEGE
EXPERIENCE AND THE SOCIAL-HISTORICAL CONTEXT ON THE ATTITUDES OF COLLEGE
WOMEN." Princeton University, 1969. 284 pp. Source: DAI, XXX, 11A
(May, 1970), 5087-A. XUM Order No. 70-8392.

Found among 14,000 1st and 4th year women at 45 colleges: (1) Jewish women changed more regarding the female role; (2) Protestant women changed most in religious autonomy; (3) Roman Catholic women
moved toward greater secularism and autonomy; and (4) a strong association existed between a daughter's values and her mother's educational achievement.

Steinberg, Carol Lee (Ph. D.). "SEX-ROLE ORIENTATION AND FEAR OF FAILURE MOTIVATION IN COLLEGE WOMEN." State University of New York at Albany, 1976. 121 pp. Source: DAI, XXXVII, 3B (September, 1976), 1417-B-1418-B. XUM Order No. 76-19,677.

Found that the fear of failure theory developed by Birney, Burdick, and Teevan was not an accurate predictor. Recommended that future research aimed at developing a theory about women's fear of failure should define "achievement" in terms appropriate to all women (regardless of their traditional versus non-traditional sex-role orientation).

Stenzel, Anne Katherine (Ph. D.). "A STUDY OF GIRL SCOUT LEADERSHIP TRAINING: NON-PROFESSIONAL LEADERS OF ADULTS AS CONTINUOUS LEARNERS." University of California, Berkeley, 1963. 275 pp. Source: DAI, XXIV, 9 (March, 1964), 3618-3619. XUM Order No. 64-2139.

Study of 75 women scout leaders found that "learning oriented" approach to group leadership was the critical prerequisite for a superior volunteer leader of adults.

Stephens, Shelby Mitcham (Ed. D.). "AN EVALUATION OF COLLEGE HOME ECONOMICS CURRICULUMS IN SELECTED COLLEGES IN THE SOUTHERN REGION OF THE UNITED STATES." Cornell University, 1957. 244 pp. Source: DAI, XVIII, 3 (1958), 1036. XUM Order No. Mic 58-865.

Administrators and graduates of 16 home economics programs indicated that: (1) general education programs were not meeting students' needs; and (2) some weaknesses in the programs were rigidity and irrelevant courses.

Stericker, Anne Bradford (Ph. D.). "FEAR-OF-SUCCESS IN MALE AND FEMALE COLLEGE STUDENTS: SEX-ROLE IDENTIFICATION AND SELF-ESTEEM AS FACTORS." Loyola University of Chicago, 1976. 116 pp. Source: DAI, XXXVI, 11B (May, 1976), 5819-B-5820-B. XUM Order No. 76-11,724.

Study of 124 female and 107 male students found that self-esteem and sex-role identification were not significantly related to fear-of-success, but were related to several sub-categories.

Sterling, Virginia Dix (Ph. D.). "AN INTEGRATED PROGRAM IN AUDIO-VISUAL EDUCATION FOR PROFESSIONAL UNDERGRADUATE WOMEN IN PHYSICAL EDUCATION." State University of Iowa, 1952. 175 pp. Source: DAI, XII, 5 (1952), 716. XUM Order No. 4108.

Survey found sufficient audio-visual materials available but little used by staff and students in Women's Physical Education Department, State University of Iowa. Recommended A-V instruction units to aid training programs.

Stevenson, Florence Byrd (Ph. D.). "WOMEN ADMINISTRATORS IN BIG TEN UNIVERSITIES." Michigan State University, 1973. 222 pp. Source: DAI, XXXIV, 9A (March, 1974), 5553-A-5554-A. XUM Order No. 74-6141.

Found in a survey of all full-time women administrators in the Big Ten universities that they felt their advancement had been hindered

by discrimination, non-assertiveness, interrupted careers, and lack
of sponsorship and support.

Stewart, Frieda Imogene (Ed. D.). "THE INCREASING COLLEGE-AGE POPU-
LATION OF WOMEN IN OHIO AND ITS IMPLICATIONS FOR NURSING EDUCATION IN
OHIO." Columbia University Teachers College, 1959. 75 pp. Source:
TCCU DIGESTS (1959), pp. 676-678.

Identified the need to expand Ohio's pre-service nursing education
and designed an expansion plan.

Stewart, Hester R. (Ph. D.). "DEVELOPMENT AND EVALUATION OF INDIVID-
UALIZED COMPETENCY-BASED MODULES WHICH CAN BE INCORPORATED INTO SUPER-
VISION COURSES IN HOME ECONOMICS EDUCATION." Southern Illinois Universi-
ty, 1974. 154 pp. Source: DAI, XXXV, 12A, Part 1 (June, 1975), 7778-A.
XUM Order No. 75-13,283.

Competencies identified by 100 home economics teachers and student
teachers were used as the basis for modules which were then judged
for effectiveness.

Stiehl, Ruth Rasco (Ph. D.). "CHARACTERISTICS OF ROLE-MODELS AND A
DESCRIPTION OF THEIR INFLUENCE ON PROFESSIONAL SOCIALIZATION AS PERCEIVED
BY STUDENTS IN TWO ELEMENTARY EDUCATION AND NURSING PROGRAMS." University of South Florida, 1977. 262 pp. Source: DAI, XXXVIII, 2A (August,
1977), 740-A-741-A. XUM Order No. 77-16,909.

Role models who seemed to influence elementary education majors and
student nurses in 2 urban universities in their professional development were caring, concerned, knowledgeable, intelligent, and creative.

Stier, Sister Jane (Ph. D.). "THE ROLE OF WOMEN RELIGIOUS ACTIVE IN
EDUCATION AND OTHER APOSTOLATES DURING THE RENAISSANCE: AN HISTORICAL
STUDY." Catholic University of America, 1966. 201 pp. Source: DAI,
XXVII, 9A (March, 1967), 3116-A. XUM Order No. 67-1273.

Studied Renaissance origins of rules, customs, and attitudes still
governing Roman Catholic women religious orders and concluded that
they were inconsistent with today's theology and sociology.

Stiffler, Elizabeth J. (Ed. D.). "DEGREE OF ACHIEVEMENT OF AFFECTIVE
OBJECTIVES RELATED TO PROBABLE SUCCESS IN TEACHING HOME ECONOMICS."
Pennsylvania State University, 1974. 92 pp. Source: DAI, XXXV, 12A,
Part 1 (June, 1975), 7778-A-7779-A. XUM Order No. 75-10,804.

Study of 203 Pennsylvania State University home economics graduates:
(1) found them significantly more self-actualizing as seniors than
as sophomores; and (2) found the level of self-actualization and degree of openmindedness to be related to cognitive indicators of success in teaching.

Stindt, Jewell Elizabeth (Ph. D.). "SEX BIASES AND GENDER-ROLE STER-
EOTYPES IN POST-SECONDARY TEXTBOOKS." University of Michigan, 1976.
164 pp. Source: DAI, XXXVII, 10A (April, 1977), 6230-A-6231-A. XUM
Order No. 77-8046.

Content analysis of 377 textbooks used in a 16,000-student community college (60% female) showed that: (1) women were underrepresented as authors, co-authors, and contributors; (2) there were many gender role stereotypes; and (3) there was much other evidence of sex bias. Recommendations followed to eliminate sex bias.

Stodt, Martha McGinty (Ed. D.). "AUTONOMY AND COMPLEXITY IN WOMEN TEACHERS IN LEADERSHIP POSITIONS." Columbia University, 1972. 166 pp. Source: DAI, XXXIII, 1A (July, 1972), 199-A. XUM Order No. 72-19,528.

Comparison of autobiographies of 58 women classroom teachers, half of whom became school administrators, indicated that the administrators: (1) had a greater sense of control over their own lives; and (2) were motivated to seek more decision-making responsibility.

Strain, Sibyl Marjoria (Ph. D.). "AN EXPLORATORY INVESTIGATION OF WOMEN'S STUDIES IN SELECTED INSTITUTIONS OF HIGHER EDUCATION WITH EMPHASIS UPON THE HISTORICAL BACKGROUND OF THE STATUS OF WOMEN AND THE SPECIAL NEEDS OF WOMEN IN HIGHER EDUCATION." University of Southern California, 1977. Source: DAI, XXXVII, 11A (May, 1977), 6986-A-6987-A.

Reviewed the history of male-female relations since primitive times. Surveyed women's studies in California colleges and universities and analyzed experts' views on strengthening these studies.

Strathairn, Pamela Lei (Ed. D.). "ELECTIVE AND REQUIRED ASPECTS OF WOMEN'S PHYSICAL EDUCATION AT STANFORD UNIVERSITY." Stanford University, 1962. 138 pp. Source: DAI, XXIII, 6 (December, 1962), 2001. XUM Order No. 62-5448.

Found that the primarily elective program of women's physical education was within Stanford University's general education program.

Straub, Kathleen Mary (Ed. D.). "A STUDY OF CHANGES IN JOB SATISFACTION OF NURSE PRACTITIONERS FOLLOWING AN INSERVICE EDUCATION PROGRAM." Columbia University, 1964. 141 pp. Source: DAI, XXV, 9 (March, 1965), 5087-5088. XUM Order No. 65-4749.

Concluded from an experimental program with 35 nurse practitioners that their job satisfaction increased as a result of a cooperatively developed in-service education program.

Strauch, A. Barry (Ph. D.). "AN INVESTIGATION INTO THE SEX X RACE X ABILITY INTERACTION." Pennsylvania State University, 1975. 118 pp. Source: DAI, XXXVII, 2A (August, 1976), 898-A. XUM Order No. 76-17,228.

Findings did not support the hypothesis that black women outperform black men while white sexes are more similar. Study suggested that black women had a history of greater achievement motivation than black men.

Strauss, Elaine R. (Ed. D.). "ANALYSIS OF CHANGE IN FEMALE SELF-ESTEEM AS A RESULT OF PARTICIPATION IN THE CRYSTAL AND BOLLES METHOD OF CAREER/LIFE PLANNING." Northeastern University, 1977. 157 pp. Source: DAI, XXXVIII, 6A (December, 1977), 3300-A. XUM Order No. 77-24,429.

A teaching unit was judged effective, although statistically not significant, in elevating women's self-esteem in relation to job satisfaction in business and industry.

Strickler, John Wesley (Ed. D.). "AN ANALYSIS OF SELECTED INTERVIEW VARIABLES AS PREDICTORS OF TEACHING EFFECTIVENESS AMONG FEMALE ELEMENTARY TEACHER CANDIDATES." Ball State University, 1966. 177 pp. Source: DAI, XXVIII, 3A (September, 1967), 991-A-992-A. XUM Order No. 66-13,752.

Female students (111) during their 4 years of teacher education at Ball State University were rated each year on 10 characteristics of a model teacher. Study found that either the subjects changed from year to year or that there was little agreement on the characteristics that were rated. Concluded that teaching was so complex that a total assessment would be better than an atomistic assessment.

Strinden, Gertrude Marcelle (Ph. D.). "CONSUMER CONCERNS OF LOW-IN-COME FAMILIES AS PERCEIVED BY LOW-INCOME HOMEMAKERS AND BY HOME ECONOMICS TEACHERS: AN EXPLORATORY STUDY." University of Minnesota, 1975. 269 pp. Source: DAI, XXXVII, 1A (July, 1976), 159-A-160-A. XUM Order No. 76-14,968.

Compared selected consumer practices as perceived by 32 pre-service and in-service home economics teachers and 44 randomly selected low-income homemakers; found significant differences. Findings had important implications for training teachers to be effective in consumer education programs intended for low-income persons.

Strobel, Marian Elizabeth (Ph. D.). "IDEOLOGY AND WOMEN'S HIGHER EDUCATION, 1945-1960." Duke University, 1976. 291 pp. Source: DAI, XXXVI, 10A (April, 1976), 6903-A. XUM Order No. 76-9148.

Traced the post World War II debate among women's colleges about liberal arts versus vocational curriculum. Found: (1) little connection between this debate and actual late 1940s curricular changes; and (2) confusion among 1950s women students about their goals. Concluded that greatly increased numbers of women college graduates coincided with the heightened social consciousness of the 1960s to produce awareness of the limitations of traditional female roles and traditional education.

Strohmann, Rose Carol (Dr. P. H.). "A CORE CURRICULUM AS A BASE FOR CAREER MOBILITY IN NURSING PRACTICE." University of Texas Health Science Center at Houston School of Public Health, 1975. 196 pp. Source: DAI, XXXVII, 8B (February, 1977), 3872-B-3873-B. XUM Order No. 77-2978.

Author developed a 2-year junior college nursing education program for San Jacinto College using core curriculum and a concept of upward career progression: students progressed from nurse's aide, end of first semester; to state licensed vocational nurse, end of first year; and state registered nurse, end of second year. Author explored how this technique can be used for baccalaureate and graduate nursing education.

Stromborg, Marilyn Frank (Ed. D.). "THE RELATIONSHIP BETWEEN IMAGE OF NURSING AND SEX ROLE IDENTITY FOR SENIORS IN DIPLOMA, ASSOCIATE DE-

GREE, AND BACCALAUREATE NURSING PROGRAMS." Northern Illinois University, 1974. 261 pp. Source: DAI, XXXV, 4B (October, 1974), 1768-B-1769-B. XUM Order No. 74-23,163.

Study of 430 graduating student nurses indicated that their image of nursing was positively affected by their age, parental occupation, and type of nursing program in which enrolled.

Strong, Charles Richard (Ph. D.). "A STUDY OF ATTITUDES TOWARD THE SELECTION OF WOMEN FACULTY IN COLLEGIATE SCHOOLS OF BUSINESS IN THE SOUTHEASTERN U. S. A." University of Alabama, 1972. 164 pp. Source: DAI, XXXIII, 6A (December, 1972), 2573-A-2574-A. XUM Order No. 72-33,136.

In judging resumes of men and women for collegiate business department positions, chairmen and deans showed: (1) marked preference for men over women when applicants were equally qualified; (2) marked preference for women who were obviously better qualified; and (3) that those who consistently rejected women believed women professors were unacceptable in the business community.

Strong, Willa Allegra (Ed. D.). "THE ORIGIN, DEVELOPMENT, AND CUR-RENT STATUS OF THE OKLAHOMA FEDERATION OF COLORED WOMEN'S CLUBS." University of Oklahoma, 1957. 248 pp. Source: DAI, XVII, 12 (December, 1957), 2910. XUM Order No. Mic 57-4642.

Found that the Oklahoma Federation of Colored Women's Clubs contributed to: (1) educational development of community life; (2) development of community leaders; (3) "moral integration" of the community; and (4) adjustment to social change. Criticized the Federation for lacking continuity in administrative programs, long-range planning, and year-round consultative services for local clubs.

Stroops, Sylvia Lynn (Ed. D.). "PERSONALITY TYPES AND VOCATIONAL IN-TERESTS OF WOMEN STUDENTS MAJORING IN TWO DIFFERENT AREAS OF TEACHER ED-UCATION." University of Alabama, 1971. 80 pp. Source: DAI, XXXII, 9A (March, 1972), 5027-A-5028-A. XUM Order No. 72-8472.

At 3 universities compared personality types and vocational interests of undergraduate women majoring in health and physical education with an equal number majoring in home economics education. Found that: (1) both groups were extroverts, "sensors," and perceivers; (2) health and physical education majors were "feelers"; (3) home economics education majors were "thinkers"; and (4) vocational interests within both groups were varied.

Stucke, Doris Geneva (Ed. D.). "FACULTY DEVELOPMENT PRACTICES IN BACCALAUREATE NURSING EDUCATION." Columbia University, 1967. 301 pp. Source: DAI, XXVIII, 10B (April, 1968), 4181-B. XUM Order No. 68-5546.

Baccalaureate nursing administrators (128): (1) agreed on the need for better orientation of new faculty; and (2) believed that their faculty needed self-development to function on a more mature professional level.

Stutler, Douglas Lee (Ph. D.). "THE INTERRELATIONSHIP BETWEEN ACA-DEMIC ACHIEVEMENT OF COLLEGE FRESHMAN WOMEN AND MEASURES OF ANXIETY AND

ABILITY." Oregon State University, 1973. 81 pp. Source: DAI, XXXIV,
5A (November, 1973), 2400-A. XUM Order No. 73-25,381.

Found that the academic achievement of 1,080 college freshman women
at the University of Northern Colorado appeared to be randomly related
to anxiety measures.

Styles, Margretta Madden (Ed. D.). "ARTICULATION BETWEEN FLORIDA PUB-
LIC JUNIOR COLLEGES AND BACCALAUREATE DEGREE NURSING PROGRAMS IN STATE
UNIVERSITIES." University of Florida, 1968. 201 pp. Source: DAI, XXX,
4B (October, 1969), 1773-B-1774-B. XUM Order No. 69-17,047.

Shows need for better cooperative planning to facilitate transfer of
Florida nursing students from junior college to university baccalaureate degree nursing programs.

Sullivan, John Cavanaugh (Ph. D.). "A STUDY OF THE SOCIAL ATTITUDES
AND INFORMATION ON PUBLIC PROBLEMS OF WOMEN TEACHERS IN SECONDARY SCHOOLS."
Columbia University Teachers College, 1940. 140 pp. Source: TCCU CON-
TRIBUTIONS No. 791, pp. 114-120.

Found among 1,479 white women high school teachers and 244 Catholic
teaching sisters that women teachers were more conservative and less
informed.

Sullivan, Kathleen Anne (Ph. D.). "CHANGES IN GIRLS' PERCEPTIONS OF
THE APPROPRIATENESS OF OCCUPATIONS FOR FEMALES THROUGH FILMS WHICH COUNTER
SEX-STEREOTYPING." Fordham University, 1975. 125 pp. Source: DAI,
XXXVI, 8A (February, 1976), 5164-A. XUM Order No. 76-4160.

Before and after viewing experimental films encouraging women to enter
male-dominated occupations, 60 black, white, and Hispanic 9th grade
girls were asked to specify their career choices. Found that the experimental program developed positive attitudes toward the appropriateness of such occcupations for women.

Sulochana, Aaron (Ed. D.). "A GUIDE TO THE TEACHING OF DIAGNOSTIC AND
THERAPEUTIC NURSING MEASURES." Columbia University, 1964. 155 pp.
Source: DAI, XXV, 9(March, 1965), 5219-5220. XUM Order No. 65-4750.

After reviewing the literature, author found that the preparation of
teachers of nursing must be based upon the disciplines of physics and
chemistry. Author then prepared a guide for teachers of nursing
fundamentals for baccalaureate programs in India.

Sulzer, Wilmot E. (Ph. D.). "AN INVESTIGATION OF THE RELATIONSHIP
BETWEEN CONFORMITY AND MENTAL HEALTH IN WOMEN SECONDARY SCHOOL TEACHERS."
New York University, 1964. 94 pp. Source: DAI, XXV, 10 (April, 1965),
5755-5756. XUM Order No. 65-988.

Found, among 31 women secondary school teachers, no significant relationship between conformity and mental health.

Summerlin, Edith Buton (Ph. D.). "A STUDY OF THE CRITERIA AND PROCE-
DURES UTILIZED FOR INITIAL FULL-TIME FACULTY APPOINTMENT IN SELECTED BAC-
CALAUREATE PROGRAMS IN NURSING." American University, 1976. 123 pp.

Source: DAI, XXXVIII, 1A (July, 1977), 130-A. XUM Order No. 77-14,618.

Administrators of 32 baccalaureate nursing programs indicated that:
(1) appointment policy for nursing teachers was the same as in other
university departments; (2) having the doctoral degree was not used
as a criterion for appointment to academic ranks; and (3) faculty
shortage compelled administrators initially to appoint new faculty in
a classification other than traditional academic rank.

Summerville, Barbara Ellen (Ph. D.). "CAREER ORIENTATION OF WASHING-
TON COMMUNITY COLLEGE WOMEN." Washington State University, 1970. 96 pp.
Source: DAI, XXXI, 3A (September, 1970), 1043-A. XUM Order No. 70-16,823.

Found in an inventory of 615 randomly selected freshman women in
Washington state community colleges that their orientation toward a
career or homemaking could be identified. Dominance, aggression, and
achievement were consistently associated with career orientation;
nurturance, heterosexuality, affiliation, and succorance were related
to homemaking.

Sumner, Mary R. (Ed. D.). "WOMEN IN THE BUSINESS AND OFFICE OCCUPA-
TIONS AS DEPICTED IN THE AMERICAN NOVEL: 1890-1950." Rutgers University,
1977. 227 pp. Source: DAI, XXXVIII, 7A (January, 1978), 3890-A. XUM
Order No. 77-27,964.

Found that most fictional secretaries had limited career goals, even-
tually married and quit working. Recent fiction depicted women who
refused to quit work as accepting divorce in consequence of their
career commitments. Recommended that popular fiction be used in education programs to develop students' awareness of women's occupational
roles.

Sundarrao, Kasturi (Ed. D.). "STUDY OF THE PATIENT CARE ACTIVITIES
PERFORMED BY STAFF NURSES IN SELECTED HOSPITALS IN INDIA." Columbia University Teachers College, 1977. 164 pp. Source: DAI, XXXVIII, 7B (January, 1978), 3130-B. XUM Order No. 77-27,898.

The performance of hospital nurses in Tamil Nadu State, India, was
studied as a basis for curriculum evaluation for nursing education
programs.

Svinth, Marian Kelley (Ph. D.). "AN EXPLORATORY STUDY OF THE EFFECTS
OF AN ASSERTION TRAINING PROGRAM ON THE ASSERTION LEVEL, WORK MOTIVATION,
AND CAREER INFORMATION-SEEKING BEHAVIOR OF UNDERGRADUATE COLLEGE WOMEN."
University of Oregon, 1976. 124 pp. Source: DAI, XXXVII, 9A (March,
1977), 5615-A-5616-A. XUM Order No. 77-4763.

Found among 27 undergraduate college women that those so exposed did
develop a higher assertive behavior and work motivation.

Swalec, John Joseph, Jr. (Ph. D.). "ACHIEVEMENT OF PRACTICAL NURSING
GRADUATES AT ILLINOIS PUBLIC COMMUNITY COLLEGES." Illinois State Univer-
sity, 1975. 119 pp. Source: DAI, XXXVI, 11A (May, 1976), 7381-A. XUM
Order No. 76-9903.

Found a high correlation between practical nursing graduates' achievement on State Board examinations and 2 of the 28 variables considered:
(1) faculty experience; and (2) student's age.

Swan, Florence B. (Ph. D.). "RELATION OF HOME ECONOMICS PROFESSORS'
PHILOSOPHIC POSITIONS TO THEIR CURRICULUM BELIEFS." Pennsylvania State
University, 1975. 117 pp. Source: DAI, XXXVI, 11A (May, 1976), 7251-A-
7252-A. XUM Order No. 76-10,798.

College and university home economics professors (175) taking a
Philosophy of Education test showed that: (1) while most took the
progressive position; (2) the differences among them were related to
specific teaching areas in home economics, age, and experience.

Sweeney, Eleanor McDonald (Ph. D.). "AGE, SEX, AND STIMULUS DIFFI-
CULTY IN THE DISCRIMINATION LEARNING OF CHILDREN USING THE FILM MEDIA."
Fordham University, 1975. 99 pp. Source: DAI, XXXVI, 8A (February,
1976), 5164-A-5165-A. XUM Order No. 76-4195.

Responses of 90 children, ages 6-11½, to information on film showed
that age, sex, and stimulus difficulty are variables to be considered
in producing films for children.

Swope, Mary Ruth (Ed. D.). "HIGH SCHOOL GUIDANCE COUNSELORS' PERCEP-
TIONS OF SELECTED CAREERS FOR WOMEN COLLEGE GRADUATES." Columbia Univer-
sity, 1963. 269 pp. Source: DAI, XXV, 1 (July, 1964), 208. XUM Order
No. 64-7208.

Investigated perceptions and knowledge among 302 high school counselors concerning the careers of nurse, elementary teacher, home economists, secretary, and scientist. Found that counselors perceived:
(1) the role of women to include both homemaking and a career; (2)
some careers as inappropriate for women; (3) themselves as incapable
of advising equally well about some careers; and (4) women's employment opportunities as undergoing basic changes.

Swort, Arlowayne (Ed. D.). "THE ANA: THE FORMATIVE YEARS, 1875-1922."
Columbia University, 1974. 458 pp. Source: DAI, XXXVI, 1B (July, 1975),
165-B. XUM Order No. 75-15,764.

History of the socio-economic forces that gave rise to the American
Nursing Association and its influence on state nurses' associations,
licensure of nurses, and the professionalization of nursing.

Symms, Dorothy Eugenia (Ed. D.). "A SURVEY OF HOUSING FOR WOMEN STU-
DENTS AND IMPLICATIONS FOR EDUCATIONAL DEVELOPMENT THROUGH HOUSING EXPERI-
ENCES." University of Colorado, 1957. 303 pp. Source: DAI, XVIII, 5
(May, 1958), 1745. XUM Order No. Mic 58-1244.

Responses from 238 members of the National Association of Deans of
Women and of the Intercollegiate Association of Women Students indicated need for: (1) more resident housing staff; and (2) their academic training and faculty status.

Tait, Helen Steele (Ph. D.). "THE EFFECT OF ASSERTION TRAINING ON
SELECTED PERSONALITY DIMENSIONS OF WOMEN." University of Missouri, Kansas

City, 1976. 141 pp. Source: DAI, XXXVIII, 2A (August, 1977), 642-A.
XUM Order No. 77-16,876.

Found among 60 women, over half of them college educated, that assertion training can be a valuable tool for increasing both assertive
skills and self-acceptance.

Taitt, Adelaide Lenora (Ed. D.). "COUNSELING AND RECIDIVISM: A
STUDY OF WOMEN PARTICIPANTS IN THE TEACHERS COLLEGE, COLUMBIA UNIVERSITY
RIKERS ISLAND CORRECTIONAL INSTITUTION FOR WOMEN PROJECT." Columbia Uni-
versity, 1974. 118 pp. Source: DAI, XXXV, 6A (December, 1974), 3438-A.
XUM Order No. 74-26,622.

Supportive counseling had positive effects on 10 adolescent girls in
a New York City correctional public school institution when the counselors assisted the girls after their incarceration in meeting: (1)
food, clothing, shelter, and other survival needs; (2) in meeting
their feelings of self worth, guilt, fear, and personal problems;
and (3) in discussing their education or job training.

Taj, Kokab (Ph. D.). "A COMPARATIVE STUDY OF THE ATTITUDES OF MARRIED
WOMEN AND COLLEGE STUDENTS TOWARD FAMILY PLANNING IN A SELECTED COMMUNITY
OF HYDERABAD, WEST PAKISTAN." Southern Illinois University, 1969. 117
pp. Source: DAI, XXX, 10B (April, 1970), 4682-B. XUM Order No. 70-7320.

Researcher found similar attitudes favoring family planning among 300
married Pakistani women and 200 Pakistani college women.

Talbot, Dorothy McComb (Ph. D.). "PROFESSIONALIZATION AMONG STUDENT
NURSES IN PERU: A SOCIOLOGICAL ANALYSIS." Tulane University, 1970. 339
pp. Source: DAI, XXXI, 9A (March, 1971), 4911-A. XUM Order No. 71-8085.

Responses from 522 nurses at 2 nursing schools and 8 three-year hospital schools showed that secular hospital schools had the largest
percentage of students with high professionalism scores, followed by
universities, and then by the non-secular hospital schools. Professionalism also increased according to progress in school (class year)
and having mothers in a professional occupation.

Talburtt, Margaret Anne (Ph. D.). "PROMOTING CREATIVE RISK-TAKING IN
WOMEN." University of Michigan, 1976. 213 pp. Source: DAI, XXXVII, 3A
(September, 1976), 1434-A-1435-A. XUM Order No. 76-19,255.

Researcher found in an experiment with 25 university women majoring
in education that creative risk-taking could be taught and was a
necessary experience if women were to realize their potential (risk-
taking: i.e., discriminating among options in 1 or more critical
decision situations).

Taloumis, Thalia (Ph. D.). "THE RELATIONSHIP OF AREA CONSERVATION
TO AREA MEASUREMENT AS AFFECTED BY SEQUENCE OF PRESENTATION OF PIAGETIAN
AREA TASKS TO BOYS AND GIRLS IN GRADES ONE THROUGH THREE." New York University, 1973. 220 pp. Source: DAI, XXXIV, 2B (August, 1973), 775-B-
776-B. XUM Order No. 73-19,450.

Grades 1-3 children at the higher grade level scored higher on 2 Piaget area measurement tasks than did children at the lower grade level.
Boys did not score higher than girls.

Tangri, Sandra Florence Schwartz (Ph. D.). "ROLE-INNOVATION IN OCCU-
PATIONAL CHOICE AMONG COLLEGE WOMEN." University of Michigan, 1969. 266
pp. Source: DAI, XXX, 9A (March, 1970), 4021-A. XUM Order No. 70-4207.

One-third of female graduating seniors were found to be Role-Innovators (those who chose male-dominated occupations); 1/3 were Traditionals; and the remaining 1/3 fell in between. Role-Innovators had
greater commitment to vocation, better educated mothers, greater autonomy, and greater concern about self-identity.

Tanner, Christine A. Waers (Ph. D.). "THE EFFECT OF HYPOTHESIS GENER-
ATION AS AN INSTRUCTIONAL METHOD ON THE DIAGNOSTIC PROCESSES OF SENIOR
BACCALAUREATE NURSING STUDENTS." University of Colorado at Boulder, 1977.
464 pp. Source: DAI, XXXVIII, 7A (January, 1978), 4062-A-4063-A. XUM
Order No. 77-29,983.

Found that the experimental techniques used in teaching the basic
principles of coronary nursing care, though promising, needed further
investigation. The experimental method used: (1) a cue-based order
of presentation, with cues related to plausible nursing diagnosis;
and (2) practice in generating and testing multiple hypotheses.

Tanner, Linda Rose (Ph. D.). "THE EFFECTS OF VARIATION IN WORD FAMI-
LIARITY, STORY CONTENT, AND INSTRUCTIONAL EFFORT ON BOYS' AND GIRLS' COM-
PREHENSION OF LITERAL AND INFERENTIAL QUESTIONS." University of Minneso-
ta, 1976. 119 pp. Source: DAI, XXXVII, 12A, Part 1 (June, 1977), 7520-
A-7521-A. XUM Order No. 77-12,864.

Of 120 6th grade students reading various kinds of writings, girls
excelled in narrative literature, boys in technical exposition.

Tashjian, Helen Elizabeth (Ed. D.). "AN EVALUATION OF A CAREER LADDER
MODEL FOR NURSING EDUCATION." Boston University School of Education,
1971. 476 pp. Source: DAI, XXXII, 4B (October, 1971), 2256-B. XUM
Order No. 71-26,745.

Author's sequential nursing program from associate to baccalaureate
degrees was endorsed by 50% of a jury of experts; most curriculum
items received over 80% jury acceptance.

Tate, Mildred Christine Jackson (Ph. D.). "AN ANALYSIS OF THE RELA-
TIONSHIP BETWEEN SELECTED PERSONAL SOCIO-ECONOMIC CHARACTERISTICS OF A
RANDOM SAMPLE OF ADULT WOMEN AND THEIR REASONS FOR ENROLLING IN AN URBAN
COMMUNITY COLLEGE." Michigan State University, 1971. 135 pp. Source:
DAI, XXXII, 12A (June, 1972), 6735-A-6736-A. XUM Order No. 72-16,523.

Women students (259) said that their major reasons for attending an
urban community college were to earn a degree, gain knowledge, and
enter a profession. Less important were personal reasons, social
usefulness, and higher income. Least important was filling leisure
time.

Tatman, Clarice (Ph. D.). "A SURVEY OF THE SPEAKING ACTIVITIES OF GRADUATES OF A LIBERAL ARTS COLLEGE FOR WOMEN." State University of Iowa, 1958. 123 pp. Source: DAI, XIX, 7 (January, 1959), 1869-1870. XUM Order No. Mic 58-5867.

Regarding public speaking activities of 932 Mount Holyoke women graduates, researcher found that 7% had no speaking activities in 1957, 89% reported some speaking activities, and 4% only told stories to children. Majors in languages, history, and psychology were more likely to become public speakers than were majors in mathematics or physical sciences.

Taylor, Annie Alford (Ph. D.). "THE CURRENT STATUS OF BLACK WOMEN IN AMERICAN HIGHER EDUCATION ADMINISTRATION." Arizona State University, 1977. 156 pp. Source: DAI, XXXVIII, 3A (September, 1977), 1261-A-1262-A. XUM Order No. 77-17,884.

Survey showed few black women were top administrators in colleges and universities. Those few were mainly directors of special services or programs, or assistants to directors or deans. The typical black woman college administrator was aged 20-30, married, had a master's degree, and had previously either taught or been an administrator.

Taylor, Green Yarbrough (Ed. D.). "A STUDY OF CERTAIN CHARACTERISTICS OF SENIOR WOMEN STUDENTS PREPARING TO TEACH IN THREE AREAS OF EDUCATION." University of Alabama, 1956. Source: Author.

Researcher found: (1) elementary and secondary school majors more interested in aesthetic and social service pursuits than in outdoor, scientific, or clerical activities; (2) special field majors (art, music, etc.) were most interested in mechanical, artistic, and persuasive activities; and (3) secondary school majors were more interested in literary activities than were special field majors.

Taylor, Mary Emily (Ed. D.). "EMPLOYED WOMEN IN RECENT PERIODICAL SHORT FICTION: THE FICTIONALIZED PORTRAIT OF EMPLOYED WOMEN PROJECTED AGAINST A BACKGROUND OF FACTUAL DATA." Indiana University, 1955. 196 pp. Source: DAI, XV, 11 (1955), 2066-2067. XUM Order No. 14,589.

Working women were distortedly portrayed in magazine fiction during 1952-53 as: (1) having higher level positions and more glamorous jobs; and (2) being younger, better educated, better groomed, and more sophisticated than in actual life. Single women were favored.

Taylor, Suzanne Saunders (Ph. D.). "THE ATTITUDES OF SUPERINTENDENTS AND BOARD OF EDUCATION MEMBERS IN CONNECTICUT TOWARD THE EMPLOYMENT AND EFFECTIVENESS OF WOMEN AS PUBLIC SCHOOL ADMINISTRATORS." University of Connecticut, 1971. 198 pp. Source: DAI, XXXII, 1A (July, 1971), 145-A. XUM Order No. 71-18,452.

Information from 84 Connecticut school superintendents and 321 school board members showed that attitudes toward women as administrators were: (1) favorable when respondents were female school board members; and (2) judged neutral to favorable by males. Males who had worked for females were more favorable than those who had not. Concluded that administrative career opportunities for women were limited.

Temple, Kathe D. L. (Ed. D.). "RELATIONSHIP OF SELF-CONCEPT AND AD-
JUSTMENT TO STUDENT NURSES FROM THREE NURSING PROGRAMS." University of
Northern Colorado, 1971. 115 pp. Source: DAI, XXXII, 7B (January, 1972),
4031-B. XUM Order No. 72-3308.

Found healthier self-concept and better adjustment in 2nd year students in a nursing-concepts baccalaureate school as against 2nd year
students in a hospital diploma school or a typical baccalaureate
school.

Temple, Wathena E. (Ed. D.). "A STUDY OF THE BASIC COURSE IN THE DI-
VISION OF HOME ECONOMICS OKLAHOMA AGRICULTURAL AND MECHANICAL COLLEGE."
Oklahoma State University, 1951. 220 pp. Source: Dissertation, pp. 167-
171.

Traced the development of the basic home economics course, identified
changes, evaluated strengths and weaknesses, suggested remedies, and
defined the problems encountered by the home economics teaching staff.

Templin, Lucinda de Leftwich (Ph. D.). "SOME DEFECTS AND MERITS IN
THE EDUCATION OF WOMEN IN MISSOURI: AN ANALYSIS OF PAST AND PRESENT EDU-
CATIONAL METHODS AND A PROPOSAL FOR THE FUTURE." University of Missouri,
Columbia, 1926. 256 pp. Source: Published; Same Title; Privately
Printed, 1926; pp. 6-12.

Cultural and social history of women's education in Missouri and especially of women in junior colleges. Case studies of particular
types of higher education serving women: Stephens College, Linden-
wood College, The Principia, Washington University, Northeast Missouri
State College, and the University of Missouri.

Tenzer, Amy (Ed. D.). "PARENTAL INFLUENCES ON THE OCCUPATIONAL CHOICE
OF CAREER WOMEN IN MALE-DOMINATED AND TRADITIONAL OCCUPATIONS." Columbia
University Teachers College, 1977. 132 pp. Source: DAI, XXXVIII, 4A
(October, 1977), 2014-A. XUM Order No. 77-22,308.

Results suggest that parental influence on female vocational development may be more closely related to the type of parental role models
with which a girl identifies rather than the sex of the models. The
influence of the mother is probably greater than previously believed.

Tessler, Sharlene Estella (Ph. D.). "PROFILES OF SELECTED WOMEN COL-
LEGE PRESIDENTS REFLECTING THE EMERGING ROLE OF WOMEN IN HIGHER EDUCATION."
Boston College, 1976. 146 pp. Source: DAI, XXXVII, 2A (August, 1976),
840-A. XUM Order No. 76-18,927.

A typical woman college president was the youngest or oldest in a
middle class American, English, or American-Irish family where there
were fewer than 4 siblings; graduated from a private women's college
with a B. A. degree in a social science; later obtained a master's
and Ph. D. degrees; a former teacher with 20 years' experience; appointed president of an eastern college between ages 40-49; returned
to teaching in an academic department after serving as president for
6 years or less; possessed leadership qualities of responsibility,
realism, efficiency, and energy.

Tetreault, Alice Ida (Ed. D.). "AN ANALYSIS OF SELECTED FACTORS AS-
SOCIATED WITH PROFESSIONAL ATTITUDE OF NURSING STUDENTS IN A BACCALAUREATE
PROGRAM." North Carolina State University at Raleigh, 1974.   104 pp.
Source: DAI, XXXVI, 1A (July, 1975), 154-A. XUM Order No. 75-15,168.

Of 157 nursing students tested, those with the highest regard for the
nursing profession were: (1) between ages 24-26; (2) who saw nursing
as highly positive and highly active; (3) who had the most formal and
informal nursing experiences; and (4) who perceived their nursing
teachers as taking strong positions on their beliefs.

Thames, Anna-Marie (Ph. D.). "WOMEN'S STUDIES IN THREE INSTITUTIONS
OF HIGHER EDUCATION IN CALIFORNIA." University of California, Los Ange-
les, 1975.   219 pp. Source: DAI, XXXVI, 6A (December, 1975), 3461-A.
XUM Order No. 75-27,009.

Women's studies at 3 California institutions of higher education succeeded when there was strong support from the administration, faculty,
and students. At California State College in Long Beach faculty pressure and large enrollments led to a minor in women's studies. UCLA
faculty and administrator support led to a bachelor's degree in women's studies. In the community colleges, only 1 of 8 campuses made
an effort to advance women's studies.

Thavilab, Vichien (Ed. D.). "AN ANALYSIS OF ANDRAGOGICAL THEORY AS
APPLIED TO IN-SERVICE EDUCATION FOR FACULTY MEMBERS OF A SCHOOL OF NURSING
IN THAILAND." Boston University School of Education, 1972.   173 pp.
Source: DAI, XXXIII, 4A (October, 1972), 1407-A. XUM Order No. 72-25,
472.

Using diagnostic needs expressed by its graduates, author developed
an in-service nursing education program for a Thailand school of
nursing.

Thetford, Mary Louise (Ed. D.). "VOCATIONAL ROLES FOR WOMEN IN JUNIOR
FICTION." Rutgers University, 1974.   121 pp. Source: DAI, XXXV, 6A
(December, 1974), 3311-A. XUM Order No. 74-27,348.

Career fiction (5 books) in junior high school libraries more often
portrayed women as working in service occupation, such as teaching.
Unlike men, these women listened more than they spoke, suggesting
passivity. Praise for women occupational competency was less than
for men. Researcher recommended career fiction that portrayed options and life styles open equally to women and men.

Thistle, Linda (Ph. D.). "THE EFFECTS OF CONSCIOUSNESS-RAISING VS.
ENCOUNTER AND SAME VS. MIXED SEX GROUPS ON SEX ROLE ATTITUDES AND SELF-
PERCEPTIONS OF GRADUATE STUDENTS IN A COUNSELOR/PSYCHOTHERAPIST TRAINING
PROGRAM." University of Southern California, 1975. Source: DAI, XXXVI,
11A (May, 1976), 7222-A-7223-A.

Consciousness-raising technique seemed an excellent way to change
sex-role attitudes, for men to become effective non-biased counselors,
and for women counselors to develop self-esteem.

Thom, Eleanor Wai-chun (Ed. D.). "A PLAN FOR THE ORGANIZATION AND AD-MINISTRATION OF A PROPOSED PRIVATE SECONDARY SCHOOL FOR GIRLS IN CANTON, CHINA." Columbia University Teachers College, 1946. 217 pp. Source: Eells, p. 76; and Dissertation.

After giving background of women's education in China, the study out-lined the organization and physical facilities for a proposed private secondary school for girls; discussed school's objectives and philos-ophy; and described group living, curriculum, teaching materials, teaching staff, guidance, administration, public relations, and com-munity service.

Thomas, Alice Elizabeth (Ed. D.). "AN ANALYSIS OF HOME ECONOMICS IN-SERVICE INSTRUCTION-IMPROVEMENT ACTIVITIES IN CALIFORNIA UNIVERSITIES AND COLLEGES." University of California, Los Angeles, 1976. 267 pp. Source: DAI, XXXVII, 3A (September, 1976), 1347-A-1348-A. XUM Order No. 76-20,215.

Found that successful in-service programs for college home economics staff depended on organization, leadership, and exchange of ideas. Formally structured activities were more likely to succeed. However, frequency of participation was not necessarily a sign of teaching suc-cess.

Thomas, Ann Grace (Ed. D.). "ASSERTION TRAINING FOR PROFESSIONAL WOMEN: A CASE STUDY." University of Massachusetts, 1976. 263 pp. Source: DAI, XXXVII, 9B (March, 1977), 4658-B. XUM Order No. 77-6407.

Found that professional women functioned more reactively than proac-tively; were relationship oriented; valued their own and others' self worth; were frequently fearful of failing or hurting others; and were highly motivated to change. Positive reactions or modeling from others aided their assertiveness. Their assertiveness was blocked mostly by males using manipulative or passive-aggressive behavior.

Thomas, Ellis Amilda (Ph. D.). "CHANGES IN SELECTED TRAITS OF FRESH-MAN MAJOR STUDENTS AFTER PARTICIPATION IN A SELF-DEVELOPMENT PROGRAM IN THE COLLEGE OF HEALTH, PHYSICAL EDUCATION, AND RECREATION AT THE TEXAS WOMAN'S UNIVERSITY IN DENTON, TEXAS." Texas Woman's University, 1970. Source: Author.

Of the 46 freshman women studied, those in a self-development pro-gram were better informed in literature, drama, and sports, and pos-sessed better reading comprehension than those not participating in the program.

Thomas, Gail Elaine (Ph. D.). "RACE AND SEX EFFECTS IN THE PROCESS OF EDUCATIONAL ACHIEVEMENT." University of North Carolina at Chapel Hill, 1975. 214 pp. Source: DAI, XXXVII, 3A (September, 1976), 1826-A. XUM Order No. 76-20,077.

Variation in the educational achievement of black and white high school senior females was more by race than by sex; being female produced slightly depressed achievement.

Thomas, Ruble Joan Thompson (Ed. D.). "BACKGROUND AND PERSONALITY CHARATERISTICS OF CREATIVE COLLEGE WOMEN." Mississippi State University, 1977. 312 pp. Source: DAI, XXXVIII, 7A (January, 1978), 4063-A. XUM Order No. 77-28,566.

Compared traits and background of 214 college women from 49 states who gave outstanding creative performances in art, basketball, dance, gymnastics, and music. Found that musicians, artists, and dancers were significantly more creative than basketball players and gymnasts.

Thomas, Sandra Carol (Ph. D.). "THE WOMEN OF CHILE AND EDUCATION FOR A CONTEMPORARY SOCIETY: A STUDY OF CHILEAN WOMEN, THEIR HISTORY AND PRESENT STATUS AND THE NEW DEMANDS OF A SOCIETY IN TRANSITION." Saint Louis University, 1973. 378 pp. Source: DAI, XXXV, 5A (November, 1974), 2799-A. XUM Order No. 74-24,150.

Reviewed legislation, education (particularly higher education), feminist activities, and class-related problems of Chilean women.

Thompson, Ann Elizabeth (Ed. D.). "IDENTIFICATION AND EVALUATION OF CONCEPTS FOR COMPETENCIES OF HOME ECONOMIST IN EXTENSION AS A PROGRAM ORGANIZER." Oklahoma State University, 1967. 147 pp. Source: DAI, XXVIII, 12B (June, 1968), 5101-B-5102-B. XUM Order No. 68-8509.

Identified 4 concepts for in-service education that would add competencies to extension home economists: (1) continuing education; (2) promoting relationships within the extension program and among other programs; (3) exploring the place of evaluation in program development; and (4) relating the program development process to the professional leadership role.

Thompson, Eleanor W. (Ph. D.). "A STUDY IN IDEAS ON EDUCATION IN MAGAZINES FOR LADIES AND OTHER PERIODICALS." Columbia University Teachers College, 1946. Source: TCCU DIGESTS, XX (1945-1947), pp. 245-248.

Education content noted in women's magazines for 1830-60 included: philosophies of education; curriculum for the instruction of women; growth of public education; training of children; education for the physically, mentally, and socially handicapped; and medical education.

Thompson, Florence M. (Ph. D.). "PROVISIONS FOR STUDENT ACTIVITY PROGRAMS IN COLLEGE RESIDENCE HALLS FOR WOMEN." University of Chicago, 1946. 165 pp. Source: Dissertation, pp. 108-119.

Found among students and head residents of women's college residence halls that: (1) activities varied from hall to hall; (2) there was little relationship between effectiveness of activities and their availability; (3) students felt they had more responsibility to initiate activities than the head resident did; and (4) student-head resident participation was by house meetings, house councils, committee meetings, and student initiation. Group life was a positive factor in good mental hygiene.

Thompson, James Newton (Ed. D.). "STABILITY AND CHANGE IN MEASURED ATTITUDES AND VOCATIONAL INTERESTS OF WOMEN IN A TEACHER EDUCATION PRO-

GRAM." University of Missouri, Columbia, 1967. 115 pp. Source: DAI, XXVIII, 10A (April, 1968), 4035-A. XUM Order No. 68-3662.

Vocational interests of women preparing to be teachers were found to be constant when tested over a period of 20-44 months during their 4-year teacher education programs.

Thompson, Susanne (Ph. D.). "A COMPARATIVE STUDY OF WOMEN STUDENTS IN HOME ECONOMICS, ARTS AND SCIENCES, AND EDUCATION WITH RESPECT TO CERTAIN SOCIAL AND PERSONALITY CHARACTERISTICS." Cornell University, 1940. 199+ pp. Source: Dissertation, pp. 186-199.

Found in studying the social background and personalities of 300 Louisiana State University women students that: (1) those in home economics and those in education had a rural, middle class, and religious background; (2) the status was low for home economics, intermediate for education, and high for arts and sciences; and (3) there were few differences in social background when the Louisiana women home economics majors were compared with University of Kentucky women home economics majors, except that the Kentucky women were more extroverted.

Thornburg, Mary Lou (Ph. D.). "MEASUREMENT OF PROFESSIONAL ATTITUDE HELD BY WOMEN PHYSICAL EDUCATION MAJOR STUDENTS IN SELECTED INSTITUTIONS." University of Iowa, 1967. 106 pp. Source: DAI, XXVIII, 7A (January, 1968), 2544-A-2545-A. XUM Order No. 67-16,849.

Author made, tested, and found valid a scale to measure the professional attitude held by college women physical education majors.

Thornton, Vivian J. (Ph. D.). "THE EFFECT OF EXTERNAL CONSTRAINTS ON THE LEADERSHIP STYLE OF SUCCESSFUL ADMINISTRATORS IN TWO TYPES OF NURSING PROGRAMS." Wayne State University, 1977. 98 pp. Source: DAI, XXXVIII, 5A (November, 1977), 2605-A. XUM Order No. 77-24,027.

Successful administrator of associate degree nursing programs tended to be relationship-oriented while successful administrators of baccalaureate degree nursing programs tended to be task-oriented.

Thorpe, Jo Anne Lee (Ph. D.). "A STUDY OF INTELLIGENCE AND SKILL IN RELATION TO THE SUCCESS ACHIEVED BY COLLEGE WOMEN ENGAGED IN BADMINTON AND TENNIS SINGLES COMPETITION." Texas Woman's University, 1964. 155 pp. Source: Dissertation, pp. 118-120.

College women of higher intelligence were no more successful than those of lower intelligence when matched in physical sport.

Thrash, Patricia Ann (Ph. D.). "WOMEN STUDENT LEADERS AT NORTHWESTERN UNIVERSITY: THEIR CHARACTERISTICS, SELF-CONCEPTS, AND ATTITUDES TOWARD THE UNIVERSITY." Northwestern University, 1959. 180 pp. Source: DAI, XX, 9 (March, 1960), 3638. XUM Order No. Mic 60-457.

Found the following characteristics of 60 university women student leaders: (1) superior intelligence (high academic averages), emotional stability, friendliness, and thoughtfulness; significant interest in literary areas, service, and artistic areas; little interest

in clerical, mechanical, and scientific areas; realistic self-awareness and self-acceptance; and love for others, faith in God, and a
sense of commitment. Subjects described the university climate as
both conforming and creative, both social and intellectual in emphasis.

Thrower, Lynda (Ed. D.). "A STUDY OF THE EFFECT OF A DOCTORAL PROGRAM
UPON WOMEN AS PERCEIVED BY GRADUATES AND CANDIDATES IN SECONDARY EDUCATION
AT THE UNIVERSITY OF ALABAMA." University of Alabama, 1976. 150 pp.
Source: DAI, XXXVII, 12A, Part 1 (June, 1977), 7671-A-7672-A. XUM Order
No. 77-12,246.

Women (23) doctoral graduates and candidates in secondary education
at the University of Alabama during 1970-75 agreed that special considerations should not be made for women doctoral students but that
women should be afforded equal economic and professional opportunities.

Thumm, Helen M. (Ed. D.). "THE ORGANIZATION AND ACADEMIC FUNCTIONS
OF THE FACULTY IN EDUCATIONAL UNITS IN NURSING IN SELECTED INSTITUTIONS
OF HIGHER EDUCATION." Indiana University, 1961. 231 pp. Source: DAI,
XXII, 3 (September, 1961), 794-795. XUM Order No. 61-3229.

Found that faculty organization varied among 7 nursing schools studied. Concluded that: (1) patterns of faculty organization were
adopted from other colleges within the same institution; (2) time-
consuming committee and departmental meetings produced little action
or policy making; (3) administrators believed faculties were content
with existing organization; and (4) field instructional faculty had
little influence on curriculum planning.

Tilley, William Ritchie (Ed. D.). "A SURVEY OF PRACTICAL NURSING AND
PRACTICAL NURSE EDUCATION IN FLORIDA." Florida State University, 1956.
228 pp. Source: DAI, XVI, 8 (1956), 1390-1391. XUM Order No. 17,032.

Survey of Florida's Licenced Practical Nurses (LPN) showed that:
71% graduates of a program and 45% non-graduates were doing institutional work; 9% graduates and 31% non-graduates were on private duty;
15% graduates and 22% non-graduates were inactive; 3 out of 4 graduates were working in general hospitals of over 100 beds and usually
where they were trained. Described educational program and future
supply of LPNs at 12 public education centers.

Timbers, Gary Dean (Ph. D.). "ACHIEVEMENT PLACE FOR GIRLS: TOKEN
REINFORCEMENT, SOCIAL REINFORCEMENT AND INSTRUCTIONAL PROCEDURES IN A
FAMILY-STYLE TREATMENT SETTING FOR 'PRE-DELINQUENT' GIRLS." University
of Kansas, 1974. 39 pp. Source: DAI, XXXV, 9B (March, 1975), 4636-B.
XUM Order No. 75-6261.

Praise and other token reinforcements helped girls aged 10 to 16 in
a pre-delinquent center learn such social skills as greeting teaching
"parents" and dressing appropriately.

Tinsley, Joyce Robertson (Ph. D.). "THE DIFFERENTIAL EFFECTS OF AN
AUDIO PROGRAM LEARNING TAPE AND OPEN GROUP DISCUSSION ON WOMEN'S ATTI-
TUDES TOWARD WOMEN AND WORK." University of Missouri, Kansas City, 1973.
137 pp. Source: DAI, XXXIV, 7A (January, 1974), 3894-A. XUM Order No.
74-1752.

Found no significant statistical differences between the attitudes of experimental and control groups of unemployed women toward women and the world of work.

Tipple, Marjorie Elaine (Ph. D.). "SEXUAL DISCRIMINATION: ATTITUDES TOWARD THE HIREABILITY OF WOMEN FOR PROFESSIONAL ADMINISTRATIVE POSITIONS IN PUBLIC EDUCATION." University of Michigan, 1972. 157 pp. Source: DAI, XXXIII, 11A (May, 1973), 6037-A-6038-A. XUM Order No. 73-11,277.

Found that: (1) discrimination against hiring women as administrators existed among school board members and superintendents; (2) no significant differences existed in attitudes toward hiring women administrators in urban, suburban, and rural school districts; and (3) hopeful signs included women's demand for equal opportunity and their increasing drive for success.

Tjosvold, Mary Margaret (Ph. D.). "AN ANALYSIS OF SELECTED FACTORS IN PERSONNEL MANAGEMENT DECISIONS WHICH SUPERINTENDENTS PERCEIVE AS AFFECTING THE EMPLOYMENT AND PROMOTION OF WOMEN IN PUBLIC SCHOOL ADMINISTRATION IN MINNESOTA." University of Minnesota, 1975. 182 pp. Source: DAI, XXXVII, 1A (July, 1976), 89-A. XUM Order No. 76-14,972.

Study deals with various factors affecting Minnesota school district superintendents in their recommending and/or promoting women to school administrative positions.

Tobiason, Roif Van Cott (Ed. D.). "THE RELATIVE EFFECTIVENESS OF INDIVIDUAL AND GROUP DESENSITIZATION IN REDUCING STUDENT NURSES' ANXIETY." Arizona State University, 1971. 109 pp. Source: DAI, XXXII, 7A (January, 1972), 3707-A. XUM Order No. 72-3011.

Compared the effects of individual versus group systematic desensitization with 2 randomly selected groups (16 each) of female nursing students. Found no statistically significant differences between the 2 approaches.

Tobin, Frances Mae (Ed. D.). "A SUGGESTED DRUG ABUSE EDUCATION PROGRAM FOR FRESHMAN WOMEN STUDENTS ATTENDING AN URBAN COLLEGE." Columbia University, 1972. 171 pp. Source: DAI, XXXII, 12A (June, 1972), 6751-A. XUM Order No. 72-17,227.

Used responses from 625 first-year college women plus appropriate textbooks and curriculum guides to develop a drug abuse education program. Concluded that: (1) drug use was probably exaggerated; (2) since students did not live on that urban campus, parents bore chief responsibility to curb drug abuse; and (3) drug abuse education should continue.

Tobin, Rosemary Barton (Ph. D.). "VINCENT OF BEAUVAIS' DE ERUDITIONE FILIORUM NOBILIUM: THE EDUCATION OF WOMEN." Boston College, 1972. 211 pp. Source: DAI, XXXIII, 2A (August, 1972), 601-A. XUM Order No. 72-22,889.

A textual examination of the classical work on women's education by Vincent of Beauvais, 13th century Dominican encyclopedist and educator, in its Medieval setting.

Tolbert, Rodney Nuckels (Ed. D.). "COMPARISON OF THE TEACHING PER-
FORMANCE OF MEN AND WOMEN IN ELEMENTARY SCHOOLS." Pennsylvania State Uni-
versity, 1966. 113 pp. Source: DAI, XXVII, 12A (June, 1967), 4095-A.
XUM Order No. 67-5978.

A comparison of male and female elementary teachers, using classroom
observation and a teaching evaluation scale, revealed no significant
differences in 16 areas of performance and effectiveness.

Tomaselli, Mary Vivian (Ed. D.). "A COMPARATIVE ANALYSIS OF SELECTED
CHARACTERISTICS OF BACCALAUREATE NURSING STUDENTS WHO ELECT INDEPENDENT
STUDY AND THOSE WHO REMAIN IN TRADITIONAL LECTURE CLASSES." Columbia
University, 1975. 104 pp. Source: DAI, XXXVI, 1B (July, 1975), 165-B-
166-B. XUM Order No. 75-13,912.

Locus of control was internal for baccalaureate nursing students
taking independent study, while those taking traditional courses
showed an external locus of control.

Tomjack, Lynn John (Ed. D.). "THE EFFECTS OF POST-SECONDARY EDUCATION
ON INITIAL OFFICE EMPLOYMENT FOR SELECTED FEMALE EMPLOYEES IN SELECTED
MIDWEST STATES FOR 1973, 1974 AND 1975." University of Northern Colorado,
1976. 254 pp. Source: DAI, XXXVII, 11A (May, 1977), 6914-A-6915-A.
XUM Order No. 77-11,086.

Data from 46 business organizations in a 9-state area about female
employees with various educational backgrounds indicated that the extent of post-secondary education had a direct and lasting effect on
salaries and the initial job titles received by new office employees.

Tonkinson, Myrna Ewart (Ph. D.). "CHANGING CONSCIOUSNESS: THE IMPACT
OF THE WOMEN'S LIBERATION MOVEMENT ON NON-ACTIVIST WOMEN IN A UNIVERSITY
COMMUNITY." University of Oregon, 1976. 209 pp. Source: DAI, XXXVII,
6A (December, 1976), 3744-A. XUM Order No. 76-27,687.

Author found cautious support for feminism among University of Oregon
married faculty women and graduate women, with professional women more
favorable than housewives in supporting feminism, abortion, day care,
and the equal rights amendment.

Topalis, Mary (Ed. D.). "THE ADMINISTRATOR'S RESPONSIBILITIES AND
FUNCTIONS AS PERCEIVED BY ADMINISTRATORS OF BACCALAUREATE NURSING PRO-
GRAMS." Columbia University, 1968. 197 pp. Source: DAI, XXIX, 12A
(June, 1969), 4259-A-4260-A. XUM Order No. 69-9920.

Found that: (1) many baccalaureate nursing programs are influenced
by traditional needs of nursing rather than the orientation and
structure of higher education; and (2) despite various titles of administrators, their functions differed more in degree than in kind.

Toporoff, Ralph (Ph. D.). "GENERATING ROLE TYPES CONCERNING THE OC-
CUPATIONAL PARTICIPATION OF WOMEN IN THE TWENTIETH CENTURY." Washington
State University, 1972. 264 pp. Source: DAI, XXXII, 12A (June, 1972),
7107-A. XUM Order No. 72-18,494.

Using U. S. census data, author presented socio-psychological history of women in the work force, 1900-60, covering educational influences, minorities, immigrants, and class structure.

Torres, Gertrude Julia (Ed. D.). "ADMINISTRATORS AND FACULTY OF BAC-CALAUREATE NURSING PROGRAMS PERCEPTION OF THE EVOLVING FUNCTIONS OF THE PROFESSIONAL NURSE." Columbia University, 1973. 199 pp. Source: DAI, XXXIV, 7A (January, 1974), 3800-A-3801-A. XUM Order No. 73-13,296.

Concluded that societal changes, external and internal pressures for change, and the setting in which the professional nurse functions have influenced administrators and faculty perception of the profes- sional nurse's evolving functions. Found no significant relation- ship between these evolving functions and such variables as age, edu- cation, or teaching experience.

Torres, Josefina Torres (Ed. D.). "A PROPOSAL FOR ASSOCIATE DEGREE PRE-SERVICE NURSING EDUCATION IN PUERTO RICO." Columbia University, 1965. 263 pp. Source: DAI, XXVI, 2 (August, 1965), 992-993. XUM Order No. 65-8865.

From a survey of needs, author developed a pre-service associate degree nursing education plan for the main learning centers in Puer- to Rico.

Torres - Matrullo, Christine (Ph. D.). "ACCULTURATION AND PSYCHO- PATHOLOGY AMONG PUERTO RICAN WOMEN IN MAINLAND UNITED STATES." Rutgers University, 1974. 98 pp. Source: DAI, XXXV, 6B (December, 1974), 3041-B. XUM Order No. 74-27,664.

Examined psychological stress of acculturation of 72 Puerto Rican women aged 18-55 in adjusting to living in North American society. Education was found to be significantly related to their attitude change.

Torrez, Daniel Saiz (Ph. D.). "THE EFFECT OF A VOCATIONAL EXPLORA- TION GROUP ON VOCATIONAL KNOWLEDGE, ATTITUDES, AND JOB SEARCH BEHAVIORS OF MALE VERSUS FEMALE HIGH SCHOOL STUDENTS." University of Colorado at Boulder, 1976. 136 pp. Source: DAI, XXXVII, 8A (February, 1977), 5083-A. XUM Order No. 77-3244.

Found that use of Vocational Exploration Group was not effective with 114 high school juniors and seniors in career exploration and job search behavior. Girls scored lower than boys on the Vocational Exploration questions.

Toth, Kolman Frank (Ed. D.). "SEPARATION FROM THE TEACHING PROFES- SION ON THE PART OF MASTER'S DEGREE GRADUATES FROM THE UNIVERSITY OF PITTSBURGH." University of Pittsburgh, 1961. 224 pp. Source: DAI, XXII, 3 (September, 1961), 795. XUM Order No. 61-3293.

Compared reasons that men and women left teaching. Noted that many women's teaching careers were only temporarily interrupted by mar- riage and childbearing.

Tracy, Janet Florence (Ed. D.). "THE USE OF SELECTED LEARNING PACK- AGES IN HOME ECONOMICS." University of Illinois at Urbana-Champaign,

1975. 176 pp. Source: DAI, XXXVI, 9A (March, 1976), 5889-A-5890-A.
XUM Order No. 76-6991.

Found among 425 home economics students and 10 home economics teachers
who used learning packaged material in home planning and interior design courses that: (1) teachers needed help to use the packaged
learning material; and (2) students also found shifting from group to
individual learning difficult.

Trail, Billie M. (Ph. D.). "COMPARISON OF ATTITUDES TOWARD WOMEN AND
MEASURES OF INTERESTS BETWEEN FEMINIST, TRADITIONAL FEMALE AND MALE UNI-
VERSITY STUDENTS." Texas A & M University, 1975. 204 pp. Source: DAI,
XXXVI, 8B (February, 1976), 4236-B. XUM Order No. 76-3678.

Of 171 university students, those identified as feminists were more
liberal in their attitudes, values, and interests. Women had more
interests than men.

Trail, Ira Davis (Dr. P. H.). "THE RELATIONSHIPS OF ROLE CONFLICT
AND ALIENATION TO TYPES OF EDUCATIONAL PREPARATION FOR NURSING." Univer-
sity of California, Los Angeles, 1971. 216 pp. Source: DAI, XXXII, 7B
(January, 1972), 4042-B-4043-B. XUM Order No. 72-2925.

Found that: (1) the bachelor degree nurse had more role conflict
than the diploma nurse but less than the associate degree nurse; (2)
the bachelor degree nurse was more alienated; and (3) the nurse working in coronary care and in intensive care units was less alienated
in her interactions but more alienated toward authority.

Trammell, Chloe Keith (Ed. D.). "THE DEVELOPMENT OF PERFORMANCE CRI-
TERIA TO ASSIST IN THE EVALUATION OF CLINICAL PERFORMANCE IN A BEGINNING
MEDICAL-SURGICAL NURSING COURSE." University of Alabama, 1974. 127 pp.
Source: DAI, XXXVI, 2A (August, 1975), 691-A. XUM Order No. 75-18,313.

Experts' rankings of 132 desirable nursing behaviors were used in an
instrument developed to evaluate students' clinical performance in a
beginning medical-surgical course.

Treacy, Sister Mary Denis (Ph. D.). "THE EFFECT OF INTEREST-CENTERED
'TAKE-HOME TESTS' ON LEARNING IN ELEMENTARY ALGEBRA." New York Univer-
sity, 1959. 229 pp. Source: DAI, XX, 11 (May, 1960), 4404. XUM Order
No. Mic. 60-1099.

Contrary to previous studies, an interest-centered "take-home" test
had no appreciable effect on high school girls' efficiency in algebra.

Treas, Judith Jennings (Ph. D.). "OCCUPATIONAL ATTAINMENT PROCESSES
OF MATURE AMERICAN WOMEN." University of California, Los Angeles, 1976.
288 pp. Source: DAI, XXXVII, 1A (July, 1976), 624-A-625-A. XUM Order
No. 76-15,963.

Among findings for mature women workers aged 30-44: (1) education
is more important for white women's first job than for white men's
first job; and (2) black women get poorer jobs than comparably educated white women.

Triplett, M. Evelyn (Ed. D.). "A SURVEY OF THE PROFESSIONAL QUALIFI-
CATIONS, RESPONSIBILITIES, INADEQUACIES, AND NEEDS OF WOMEN PHYSICAL EDU-
CATION TEACHERS IN KANSAS SECONDARY SCHOOLS WITH IMPLICATIONS FOR TEACHER
EDUCATION." University of Oklahoma, 1958. 318 pp. Source: DAI, XIX,
5 (November, 1958), 1022-1023. XUM Order No. Mic 58-3880.

Found that the 289 women high school physical education teachers:
(1) were dissatisfied with their student teaching experiences; (2)
felt inadequate to work with ill and/or disabled students; (3) were
not generally members of state and national physical education organizations; and (4) desired in-service education.

Trogdon, Jean Webb (Ed. D.). "A STUDY OF INFORMATION SOURCES UTILIZED
BY HOME ECONOMICS EDUCATORS." North Carolina State University, Raleigh,
1974. 140 pp. Source: DAI, XXXVI, 1A (July, 1975), 93-A. XUM Order
No. 75-15,162.

North Carolina home economics educators (725) preferred receiving information and instruction from their own agencies through workshops
and institutes, and by graduate study in nearby centers in the late
afternoon during the spring semester.

Troy, Donald Joseph (Ph. D.). "RESPONSIBILITY FOR CONTEMPORARY MAR-
RAIGE EDUCATION: HOME, SCHOOL AND CHURCH." Boston University, 1971.
298 pp. Source: DAI, XXXII, 4A (October, 1971), 1934-A-1935-A. XUM
Order No. 71-26,494.

Concluded that the nuclear family needs the secondary school's help
in preparing young people for marriage by means of compulsory marriage education courses.

Tryon, Bette Jean Whitelock (Ph. D.). "BELIEFS ABOUT MALE AND FEMALE
COMPETENCE BY KINDERGARTENERS AND SECOND GRADERS." Syracuse University,
1976. 52 pp. Source: DAI, XXXVIII, 5A (November, 1977), 2547-A-2548-A.
XUM Order No. 77-24,579.

Author found significant differences between kindergarteners and 2nd
graders in regard to their beliefs about the competence of males and
females, supporting earlier studies showing that sex-role stereotyping begins early and increases with age.

Tseng, Anthony Tsai-pen (Ph. D.). "THE BIOGRAPHICAL INVENTORY: A
CROSS-CULTURAL STUDY." University of Utah, 1974. 169 pp. Source: DAI,
XXXV, 4B (October, 1974), 1960-B-1961-B. XUM Order No. 74-21,359.

Taiwanese university students (2/3 female) were administered a translation of Alpha Biographical Inventory to develop Chinese keys for
predicting academic performance and major field selection of Chinese
college students.

Tucker, Beverly Stoup (Ph. D.). "THE DEVELOPMENT OF DIRECTIONALITY
OF SELF-CONCEPT OF LOW SOCIOECONOMIC YOUNG CHILDREN AS IT RELATES TO
GRADE, SEX AND RACE." Florida State University, 1977. 97 pp. Source:
DAI, XXXVIII, 4A (October, 1977), 2016-A-2017-A. XUM Order No. 77-22,164.

Among findings for low socio-economic boys and girls in kindergarten through 3rd grade: (1) no significant difference in their self-concepts; and (2) the sex of the child did not make a difference in the directionality of self concept.

Tucker, David Leo (Ph. D.). "PATTERNS OF INTELLECTUAL FUNCTIONING AS RELATED TO SEX DIFFERENCES IN BEGINNING READING." University of Illinois at Urbana-Champaign, 1974. 179 pp. Source: DAI, XXXV, 11A (May, 1975), 7040-A-7041-A. XUM Order No. 75-11,679.

Compared most successful and least successful boy and girl readers, kindergarten to grade 3. Results were then related to the language arts curriculum.

Tures, Robert Stephen (Ed. D.). "THE ANALYSIS OF SEX DIFFERENCES IN INTELLIGENCE, ACHIEVEMENT, BEHAVIOR, AND PERSONALITY OF THE SAME STUDENT SAMPLE AT THE THIRD AND TENTH GRADE LEVELS: A LONGITUDINAL STUDY." West Virginia University, 1971. 115 pp. Source: Dissertation, 107-110.

Found among 45 Iowa elementary school children that girls' higher achievement over boys disappeared by grade 10, thus disproving the supposition that feminism in elementary schools helps girls and hinders boys.

Turnbull, Marianne Madonna Malone (H. S. D.). "THE EFFECTS OF AN ELIMINATION OF SELF-DEFEATING BEHAVIOR WORKSHOP ON SELF-SELECTED DEFEATING BEHAVIORS OF UNDERGRADUATE WOMEN." Indiana University, 1976. 233 pp. Source: DAI, XXXVIII, 1A (July, 1977), 121-A. XUM Order No. 77-14,369.

Results of a workshop designed to eliminate women's self-defeating behavior: (1) experimental groups had positive changes in mental health, reduced self-defeating characteristics, and the follow-up had positive effects; and (2) the control group had minimal behavior change and progressed at a much slower rate.

Turner, Edna May (Ph. D.). "EDUCATION OF WOMEN FOR ENGINEERING IN THE UNITED STATES, 1885-1952." New York University, 1954. 218 pp. Source: DAI, XV, 4 (1954), 529-530. XUM Order No. 10,651.

Historical account of women's engineering education in various types of engineering schools: land grant, state, municipal, private, denominational, and others. Concluded that the proportion of 3 women per 1,000 engineering graduates over the last 6 decades can only be changed by the recognition that women have engineering abilities equal to men.

Turner, Margery Jean (Ed. D.). "AN EVALUATION OF THE PHYSICAL EDUCATION PROGRAM FOR ITS EDUCATIVE POTENTIAL FOR DEMOCRATIC LEADERSHIP DEVELOPMENT IN COLLEGE WOMEN." New York University, 1957. 162 pp. Source: DAI, XVIII, 6 (June, 1958), 2056-2057. XUM Order No. Mic 58-604.

Concluded that, for developing women's democratic leadership: (1) clubs and organizations are highly effective; (2) large group activities offer the most potential while individual activities offer the least; and (3) goal-centered activities have more potential than do non-goal-centered activities.

Turner, Mary Ann (Ph. D.). "SENIOR GIRLS' ATTITUDES TOWARD HIGH SCHOOL PHYSICAL EDUCATION AND THEIR RELATIONSHIP TO PROGRAM QUALITY AND OTHER FACTORS." Ohio State University, 1965. 230 pp. Source: DAI, XXVI, 7 (January, 1966), 3747. XUM Order No. 65-13,285.

Found: (1) little relationship between the quality of 3 high school women's physical education programs and the attitudes of students toward those programs; (2) no relationship in 2 of the 3 schools between physical fitness and students' attitudes toward physical education; and (3) the higher the parents' level of education and employment, the lower their daughter's attitude toward physical education.

Tuska, Shirley Anne (Ph. D.). "SELF-CONCEPTION AND IDENTIFICATION AMONG WOMEN PLANNING AND NOT PLANNING TO TEACH." University of Chicago, 1963. 153 pp. Source: Dissertation.

Prospective women teachers were compared with women who had no desire to teach as to their personal view of self, parental relationships, and teachers and teaching.

Tuttle, Helen Irene (Ed. D.). "ACTUAL AND IDEAL PERCEPTIONS OF THE ROLE OF THE DEAN OF WOMEN BY STUDENTS, ADMINISTRATORS, FACULTY, AND STAFF AT UPPER IOWA COLLEGE." University of Mississippi, 1968. 199 pp. Source: DAI, XXIX, 4A (October, 1968), 1113-A-1114-A. XUM Order No. 68-14,354.

Found that perceptions of the dean of women's actual and ideal roles varied among students, faculty, staff, and administrators. Discipline was perceived to be the dean of women's foremost actual academic role by freshman women, upperclass men, and men staff members. But freshman men, faculty men, and faculty women believed the dean of women's main role was to establish an academic climate.

Tyrrell, Linn Ann Acton (Ph. D.). "SEX ROLE ATTITUDES OF YOUNG AND RETURNING FEMALE COMMUNITY COLLEGE STUDENTS." University of Michigan, 1976. 225 pp. Source: DAI, XXXVII, 6A (December, 1976), 3368-A-3369-A. XUM Order No. 76-27,607.

Study compared the sex-role attitudes of 2 groups from 230 community college women, a younger group aged 17-22 and an older group over age 35 who previously had worked.

Tyson, Margaret Gould (Ed. D.). "PREPARATION OF TEACHERS OF NURSING FOR VIRGINIA." Columbia University, 1963. 136 pp. Source: DAI, XXIV, 8 (February, 1964), 3298. XUM Order No. 64-1506.

Because of the shortage of both faculty and students, author recommended that: (1) the University of Virginia not develop a master's degree program for preparing teachers of nursing; (2) continuing education for teachers of nursing be developed; (3) enrollments in baccalaureate programs be increased; and (4) holders of bachelor's degrees be encouraged to prepare for teaching nursing.

Ullian, Dorothy Zelnicker (Ed. D.). "THE DEVELOPMENT OF CONCEPTIONS OF MASCULINITY AND FEMININITY." Harvard University, 1976. 182 pp. Source: DAI, XXXVII, 7B (January, 1977), 3590-B. XUM Order No. 76-30,213.

Interviews with 70 males and females, aged 6-18, led to the conclusion that there are significant changes with age in the mode of interpreting and organizing the biological, social and psychological differences between males and females.

Ulton, Sister M. Paulette (Ph. D.). "A STUDY OF PARENT-CHILD RELATIONSHIPS; THE EMPHASIS ON HOME DISCIPLINE AS IT AFFECTS THE CONDUCT AND PERSONALITY OF A GROUP OF PRE-ADOLESCENT GIRLS." Catholic University of America, 1936. Source: Published; Same Title; Washington, DC: Catholic University of America, 1936; pp. 164-178.

Studied the effect of home discipline on girls aged 7-8 and concluded that their personality traits were influenced by parental personality traits.

Unteregger-Mattenberger, Judith (Ph. D.). "THE ROOTS OF A SOCIAL MOVEMENT--AN EXPLORATORY STUDY OF WOMEN'S SELF-CONCEPTIONS AND CHANGING SEX ROLES IN SWITZERLAND." University of Minnesota, 1975. 422 pp. Source: DAI, XXXVI, 7A (January, 1976), 4782-A. XUM Order No. 76-437.

Author explored the problems of highly educated Swiss women who pursued both a career and marital and parental obligations. Found that the women shifted role priorities to being a mother; their role obligations tended to be ambivalent and contradictory.

Urell, Catherine (Ph. D.). "THE CONTENTMENT OF WOMEN TEACHERS IN ELEMENTARY SCHOOLS." New York University, 1935. 461 pp. Source: New York University, School of Education, ABSTRACTS OF THESES (1935), pp. 1-7.

Found among 500 women elementary school teachers that their contentment as teachers was related to: (1) adjustment to social status as teachers; (2) rapport with professional colleagues; (3) absence of fatigue; (4) a high value placed in intrinsic elements in teaching; (5) absence of conflict with pupils' interests; (6) age (older teachers were more content); and (7) job stability (frequent changes indicated discontent).

Utz, Vernon Ray (Ed. D.). "THE RELATION OF CERTAIN PERSONALITY, VALUE AND INTEREST FACTORS TO A CHOICE OF ELEMENTARY OR SECONDARY TEACHING LEVELS AMONG WOMEN AT THE UNIVERSITY OF OREGON." University of Oregon, 1970. 211 pp. Source: DAI, XXXI, 10A (April, 1971), 5140-A-5141-A. XUM Order No. 71-10,790.

Concluded that personality, value, and interest factors distinguished between university women preparing to be teachers and those who were not. Psychological differences were also found between those preparing to teach at the elementary school level and the secondary school level.

Vail, John Paul (Ed. D.). "THE EFFECTS OF ENCOUNTERTAPES FOR PERSONAL GROWTH ON CERTAIN SPECIFIC ASPECTS OF THE INTELLECTUAL, BEHAVIORAL, AND SELF-CONCEPT DEVELOPMENT OF CULTURALLY DISADVANTAGED NEGRO GIRLS."

University of Georgia, 1970. 154 pp. Source: DAI, XXXI, 10A (April, 1971), 5141-A. XUM Order No. 71-3794.

Author used "encountertapes" to counsel leaderless groups of 34 black culturally deprived girls, but found no different effect as a result of the experimental treatment.

Vaillot, Sister Madeleine Clemence (Ph. D.). "TOWARD EDUCATION FOR COMMITMENT: AN INVESTIGATION OF STUDENT NURSES' PROFESSIONAL WORLD." Boston College, 1960. 442 pp. Source: Dissertation, pp. 405-408.

Author explored student nurses' professional beliefs by applying French existentialist philosopher Gabriel Marcel's thought as to how individuals achieve personal commitment.

Valley, John Allen (Ph. D.). "THE INFLUENCE OF RACE AND SEX UPON A COUNSELING INTERVIEW DESIGNED TO INCREASE NEED FOR ACHIEVEMENT IN UPWARD BOUND STUDENTS." Ohio State University, 1975. 240 pp. Source: DAI, XXXVI, 11B (May, 1976), 5774-B-5775-B. XUM Order No. 76-10,062.

Found that female counselors had no more effect than male counselors nor did black female counselors have more effect than white female counselors on raising the achievement level of black and white high school boys and girls.

Van Arsdale, Mary E. (Ed. D.). "A COLLEGE UNIT IN HOME AND FAMILY LIFE: A STUDY IN MOTHER-CHILD RELATIONSHIPS." University of California, Los Angeles, 1949. 325 pp. Source: Abstract from Dissertation.

Autobiographies of students in a Marriage and Family Life course were used to identify their attitudes about mother-child relationship and family cooperation.

Van De Grift, Margaret Kim (Ph. D.). "NUTRITIONAL EDUCATION: AN APPRAISAL OF TEACHING TECHNIQUES PLANNED FOR BEHAVIOR CHANGE." Texas Woman's University, 1972. 182 pp. Source: Dissertation, pp. 133-147.

Surveyed nutrition teaching techniques of 160 secondary school home economics teachers in 15 states during 1971-72. Found and analyzed 24 teaching techniques in terms of those which stressed behavior change in proper food selection.

Van Heerden, Leonora Engela (Ph. D.). "JOB SATISFACTION AND PERSONALITY OF THE HOSPITAL DIETITIAN." Cornell University, 1971. 163 pp. Source: DAI, XXXII, 9B (March, 1972), 5269-B-5270-B. XUM Order No. 72-9955.

Information from 391 full-time hospital dietitians showed that their: (1) personalities differed significantly depending on whether they specialized as administrators, administrative assistants, therapeutic dietitians, clinical research dietitians, or teaching dietitians; (2) personalities affected specific aspects of their jobs; and (3) job satisfaction depended on their personality traits, age, salary, and hospital service.

Van Hook, Barry Lee (Ed. D.). "THE CONTRIBUTIONS OF GLADYS BAHR TO CONSUMER AND ECONOMIC EDUCATION AT THE SECONDARY SCHOOL LEVEL." Northern Illinois University, 1973. 154 pp. Source: DAI, XXXIV, 8A (February, 1974), 4816-A-4817-A. XUM Order No. 74-2808.

Through documentary research and a survey of opinion of national leaders, author described the influence of educator Gladys Bahr in preparing teachers of consumer education and economics education for the secondary school level.

Van Meir, Edward James, Jr. (Ed. D.). "LEADERSHIP BEHAVIOR OF MALE AND FEMALE ELEMENTARY PRINCIPALS." Northern Illinois University, 1971. 249 pp. Source: DAI, XXXII, 7A (January, 1972), 3643-A. XUM Order No. 71-29,823.

To test the rationale most often given that men are better adminis-trators than women, 175 teachers (160 women, 15 men) were asked to rate 25 elementary school principals (10 women, 15 men). Women ele-mentary school principals were rated higher than men in: (1) com-posite leadership; (2) reducing conflicts and disorders; (3) being persuasive; and (4) showing foresight.

Van Peborgh, Mary Jean (Ed. D.). "A RE-ENTRY PARADIGM FOR EDUCATION-ALLY DISADVANTAGED WOMEN AT A COMMUNITY COLLEGE." University of Southern California, 1975. 158 pp. Source: DAI, XXXV, 9A (March, 1975), 5764-A. XUM Order No. 75-6451.

Concluded that educationally and economically disadvantaged women could successfully re-enter education in a community college if those in charge: (1) secured institutional commitment; (2) appointed an advisory committee to help recruit them; (3) identified faculty with talents to work with them; (4) and established appropriate cour-ses, goals, and objectives. Author believed that the essentials were to build self-confidence, improve communication skills, secure sup-port services, offer individual instruction, and integrate learning experiences.

Vanahian, Paul (Ed. D.). "PROPOSAL FOR IMPROVING THE FIELD WORK PRO-GRAM OF THE HOME AND FAMILY LIFE DEPARTMENT AT TEACHERS COLLEGE." Colum-bia University Teachers College, 1957. 105 pp. Source: Dissertation, pp. 82-91.

Information from participating students and staff was used to im-prove the field work experience required in Columbia University Teachers College Home and Family Life program.

Vance, Mary Jane H. (Ed. D.). "A CHRONOLOGICAL HISTORY OF THE DE-VELOPMENT OF THE OBJECTIVES FOR TEACHING HOME ECONOMICS IN THE HIGH SCHOOLS OF THE UNITED STATES DURING THE 1918-1972 PERIOD." East Texas State University, 1976. 404 pp. Source: DAI, XXXVII, 11A (May, 1977), 6997-A. XUM Order No. 77-9637.

Looking for objectives in teaching home economics as recorded in professional journals, 1918-72, author found this order of concerns: (1) development of attitudes, interests, and appreciation for home economics among students; (2) development of skills; and (3) ac-

quisition of knowledge. Also found that: (1) writers concerned
with higher education wrote more perceptive home economics teaching
objectives; and (2) home economics education grew during periods of
large federal funding: 1917-36 and 1963-68.

Vanuxem, Mary (Ph. D.). "EDUCATION OF FEEBLE-MINDED WOMEN." Columbia University Teachers College, 1925. Source: TCCU CONTRIBUTIONS No.
174, pp. 65-67.

Author discussed educational implications for: (1) mentally defective
girls and women who must remain institutionalized; and (2) for those
capable of living in a normal community.

Varshney, Sarojini (Ph. D.). "SURVEY OF ATTITUDES OF SELECTED WOMEN
TOWARDS EDUCATION BEYOND HIGH SCHOOL." University of Utah, 1965. 166
pp. Source: DAI, XXVI, 8 (February, 1966), 4408. XUM Order No. 65-
14,525.

Found among 691 women in post-secondary education that their choice
of major often did not fit their plans because they were not fully
aware of the relationship between their plans and their choice of
major.

Vaughan, Peter Bernard (Ph. D.). "A DEVELOPMENTAL STUDY OF RACE-
ESTEEM AND SELF-ESTEEM OF BLACK BOYS AND GIRLS IN THIRD AND SEVENTH
GRADES." University of Michigan, 1977. 186 pp. Source: DAI, XXXVIII,
6A (December, 1977), 3735-A. XUM Order No. 77-26,374.

Found among 75 black girls and boys in 3rd and 7th grades that: (1)
self-esteem and race-esteem were related, but more for girls than
boys; and (2) self-esteem but not race-esteem was related to the
parents' instilling pride in black heritage, again more for girls
than boys.

Venson, Gloria Mathis (Ph. D.). "THE EFFECTS OF TIME RELATED MODERN
EDUCATIONAL DANCE PROGRAMS ON THE SELF-CONCEPT OF FOURTH, FIFTH, AND
SIXTH GRADE GIRLS IN A SOUTHERN URBAN CITY." Southern Illinois University at Carbondale, 1977. 96 pp. Source: DAI, XXXVIII, 5A (November,
1977), 2569-A-2570-A. XUM Order No. 77-24,043.

Found among 144 elementary school girls that, regardless of grade
differences, modern dance education contributed to their self-concept.

Verro, Olga (Ph. D.). "SELECTED CHARACTERISTICS, VOCATIONAL INTER-
ESTS, AND REASONS FOR THE ENROLLMENT OF THE SECONDARY STUDENTS IN TRADI-
TIONAL AND OCCUPATIONAL HOME ECONOMICS PROGRAMS." University of Connec-
ticut, 1976. 563 pp. Source: DAI, XXXVIII, 1A (July, 1977), 135-A.
XUM Order No. 77-14,513.

Students in traditional and occupational home economics differed in
their: (1) demographic and educational characteristics; (2) hobbies,
interests, and activities; (3) interests in education and training
in high school; and (4) vocational interests and occupational choice.

Vice, Jackie Ann (Ph. D.). "CAREER DEVELOPMENT OF WOMEN IN ENGINEER-ING: FACTORS INFLUENCING A NON-TRADITIONAL CAREER." Ohio State University, 1977. 190 pp. Source: DAI, XXXVIII, 8B (February, 1978), 3861-B. XUM Order No. 77-32,000.

Women in engineering (200), compared to 193 non-engineering college women: (1) were more nearly neutral about sex roles; (2) had stronger desires to work, except when their children were under age 5; (3) had stronger interests in science, math, and mechanics; (4) valued their job opportunities, salaries, and fringe benefits; (5) were more intellectually self-confident, less emotional, more career-oriented, and less altruistic; (6) wanted to marry later and have fewer children; and (7) were more involved in college activities and leadership positions.

Vincent, John Dale (Ed. D.). "THE REPORTED DIFFERENCE IN SELF-CON-CEPT OF JUNIOR HIGH SCHOOL PUPILS WITH REGARD TO PERMANENCE AND MOBILITY OF FAMILIES." University of Northern Colorado, 1977. 109 pp. Source: DAI, XXXVIII, 4A (October, 1977), 1869-A. XUM Order No. 77-22,394.

Found among 240 junior high school students that girls from mobile families had higher self-concepts than did girls from more settled families.

Voss, Paul Ronald (Ph. D.). "SOCIAL DETERMINANTS OF AGE AT FIRST MARRIAGE IN THE UNITED STATES." University of Michigan, 1975. 358 pp. Source: DAI, XXXVI, 10A (April, 1976), 6995-A. XUM Order No. 76-9536.

High school students interviewed before graduation and 7 years later when married showed that: (1) marriage and education are more competing activities for women than men; and (2) early marriage aids men's more than women's further education.

Wagenschein, Miriam (Ed. D.). "INSTITUTIONAL HOUSING, SELECTIVE CLIENTELES, AND SOCIAL CLASS OF WOMEN STUDENTS." Stanford University, 1963. 313 pp. Source: DAI, XXIV, 1 (July, 1963), 151-152. XUM Order No. 63-4579.

Women students at a small college and at a large university differed little in their background, intelligence, and social status. Expectation of success and its actual achievement varied little, regardless of a student's social class.

Waggener, Frances Pauline (Ph. D.). "DEVELOPING AND TESTING A CUR-RICULUM GUIDE FOR TEACHING METHODS OF HOME ECONOMICS WITH EMPHASIS ON REACHING THE DISADVANTAGED LEARNER." Southern Illinois University, 1974. 364 pp. Source: DAI, XXXV, 12B, Part 1 (June, 1975), 5974-B. XUM Order No. 75-13,257.

Found that a curriculum guide to train home economics teachers for work with the disadvantaged made no significant difference in their sensitivity to people. Concluded that home economics teacher educators need to emphasize: (1) individualized instruction; (2) teacher-pupil evaluation; and (3) the importance of examining students' records.

Waggoner, Bernice E. (Ph. D.). "A COMPARISON OF THE PROFILES OF
TEMPERAMENT TRAITS OF WOMEN UNDERGRADUATE STUDENTS AND FULL-TIME TEACHERS
IN PHYSICAL EDUCATION DEPARTMENTS IN SELECTED COLLEGES AND UNIVERSITIES
IN THE UNITED STATES, WITH IMPLICATIONS FOR THE GUIDANCE OF YOUNG WOMEN
SEEKING CAREERS IN THIS FIELD." Texas Woman's University, 1966. 220 pp.
Source: Dissertation, pp. 149-187.

Found that women in physical education had above average intelligence,
were below average in sociability, and had a high degree of emotional
stability.

Wagner, Anna Elizabeth (Ph. D.). "COMPETENCE OF THE LICENSED PRAC-
TICAL NURSE IN A SKILLED NURSING FACILITY IN WESTERN PENNSYLVANIA."
University of Pittsburgh, 1977. 123 pp. Source: DAI, XXXVIII, 4B
(October, 1977), 1655-B. XUM Order No. 77-21,239.

Recommended that educators of practical nurses learn by task analysis
the competencies required of their graduates and provide the necessary training, including in-service training.

Wahaib, Abdul Amir (Ph. D.). "EDUCATION AND STATUS OF WOMEN IN THE
MIDDLE EAST WITH SPECIAL REFERENCE TO EGYPT, TUNISIA AND IRAQ." Southern
Illinois University, 1970. 99 pp. Source: DAI, XXXI, 8A (February,
1971), 3915-A. XUM Order No. 71-2414.

A historical study to show Arab women's progress toward emancipation
and equal participation in 20th century societies of Egypt, Tunisia,
and Iraq.

Waicis, Linda (Ph. D.). "RELATIVE EMPHASIS ON CONSUMER EDUCATION
CONCEPTS IN PART F FUNDED AND NONFUNDED HOME ECONOMICS PROGRAMS IN PENN-
SYLVANIA HIGH SCHOOLS." Pennsylvania State University, 1976. 124 pp.
Source: DAI, XXXVII, 11A (May, 1977), 6997-A-6998-A. XUM Order No.
77-9610.

Found that home economics courses emphasized consumer education in
Pennsylvania public high school homemaking programs. There were no
apparent differences in federally funded and non-funded programs,
both of which were information-centered and process-centered, a
combination educators considered most desirable.

Wakefield, Samuel (Ed. D.). "A STUDY OF TEACHER ATTITUDES TOWARD
FEMALE PRINCIPALS IN ALEXANDRIA, VIRGINIA." George Washington Univer-
sity, 1972. 142 pp. Source: DAI, XXXIII, 9A (March, 1973), 4770-A.
XUM Order No. 73-5816.

Found that women principals were more acceptable than men principals
to elementary teachers in Alexandria, VA.

Walawender, Marge Lisowski (Ph. D.). "THE BEHAVIOR AND ROLE EXPEC-
TATIONS OF FOREIGN AND AMERICAN GRADUATE WOMEN." Cornell University,
1964. 255 pp. Source: DAI, XXVI, 2 (August, 1965), 841-842. XUM Order No. 64-8743.

Comparison of 57 foreign and 57 American women graduate students
showed that their major field had a stronger influence on their
cultural adjustment than did the geographic area from which they
came.

Waldrop, Mary Ford (Ph. D.). "MINOR PHYSICAL ANOMALIES AND INHIBITED BEHAVIOR IN ELEMENTARY SCHOOL GIRLS." University of Maryland, 1974. 77 pp. Source: DAI, XXXV, 10B (April, 1975), 4956-B. XUM Order No. 75-7372.

Previous research showed that 40% of boys considered hyperactive had minor physical anomalies. In contrast, this study found that elementary school girls whom their teachers judged to be under active (were inhibited, fearful, inattentive, and socially ill at ease) had significantly more minor physical anomalies than other girls.

Walker, Arda Susan (Ph. D.). "THE LIFE AND STATUS OF A GENERATION OF FRENCH WOMEN, 1150-1200." University of North Carolina, 1958. 459 pp. Source: DAI, XIX, 8 (February, 1959), 2071. XUM Order No. Mic 58-5974.

Concluded that women gained marked freedom in 12th century France for several reasons, among them the general democratization of society. The Medieval church helped women's status but not so much as is sometimes claimed and not because of the cult of the Virgin Mary.

Walker, Jean (Ph. D.). "FACTORS CONTRIBUTING TO THE DELINQUENCY OF DEFECTIVE GIRLS." University of California, Berkeley, 1922. Source: Dissertation, preface and pp. 115-122.

Found that schools were: (1) not providing sufficient practical training for handicapped girls; nor (2) diagnosing their problems soon enough.

Walker, Kathryn Elizabeth (Ph. D.). "HOMEMAKING WORK UNITS FOR NEW YORK STATE HOUSEHOLDS." Cornell University, 1955. 244 pp. Source: DAI, XVI, 1 (1956), 113. XUM Order No. 15,437.

By finding the average time required to do specific homemaking tasks, this study provided objective information to help women decide about working outside the home and doing community service.

Walker, Lorraine Olszewski (Ed. D.). "NURSING AS A DISCIPLINE." Indiana University, 1971. 176 pp. Source: DAI, XXXII, 6B (December, 1971), 3459-B. XUM Order No. 72-1528.

Contrasts nursing education as a practical and theoretical discipline; provides a rationale for a more theoretical basis for nursing education.

Wallace, David William (Ph. D.). "THE EFFECTS OF A SYSTEMATIC TRAINING PROGRAM IN RESPONDING SKILLS ON DENTAL HYGIENE STUDENTS AT TEXAS WOMAN'S UNIVERSITY." North Texas State University, 1977. 122 pp. Source: DAI, XXXVIII, 3A (September, 1977), 1237-A. XUM Order No. 77-19,691.

Concluded that the systematic training program in communication skills was an effective strategy for improving dental hygiene student-patient rapport.

Wallace, John A. (Ed. D.). "THE ORGANIZATION, OPERATION AND EVALUA-
TION OF A EUROPEAN FIELD TRIP IN INTERNATIONAL ECONOMICS FOR TWENTY-THREE
WOMEN COLLEGE STUDENTS." University of Pennsylvania, 1949. 364 pp.
Source: Dissertation, pp. 284, 296-297.

Case study of 23 women college students of international economics
and what they learned about international economics on a European
field trip.

Wallace, Margaret Ann Jaeger (Ed. D.). "THE RELATIONSHIP BETWEEN BE-
HAVIORAL TRAITS, SELF CONCEPT, AND PERFORMANCE OF PEDIATRIC NURSING STU-
DENTS." Duke University, 1964. 179 pp. Source: DAI, XXV, 8 (February,
1965), 4555-4556. XUM Order No. 65-2803.

Concluded that student readiness for pediatric nursing experience:
(1) cannot be predicted by the relationship between their self-concept and performance; but (2) can be predicted by examining the relationships between certain behavioral traits and performance and between previous nursing performance and pediatric nursing performance.

Wallace, Sharon (Ph. D.). "IDENTIFICATION OF QUALITY OF LIFE INDICA-
TORS FOR USE IN FAMILY PLANNING PROGRAMS IN DEVELOPING COUNTRIES." Pennsylvania State University, 1974. 141 pp. Source: DAI, XXXV, 11B (May,
1975), 5518-B-5519-B. XUM Order No. 75-9855.

Statements about the "Quality of Life" were ranked "of most concern"
and "of least concern" by 76 mainly women home economists from 18
developing countries and 25 mainly women Thailand teachers.

Waller, Ruth Ellen Pariser (Ph. D.). "LIFE-STYLE AND SELF-APPRAISAL
IN MIDDLE-AGED, MARRIED, EDUCATED WOMEN." University of Wisconsin, 1974.
115 pp. Source: DAI, XXXV, 7A (January, 1975), 4173-A-4174-A. XUM Order No. 74-19,944.

Examined the extent to which homemaking and child rearing offered
satisfaction to 97 college-educated women in 4 career lifestyles:
(1) the typical "housewife" felt isolated and discouraged; (2) the
"housewife-volunteer" was pleased with herself, her marriage, and
her life in general; (3) the woman who interrupted her career for
child rearing was happy but had reservations about whether she was
doing what she liked; and (4) the "continuous career" woman was confident about her competence but less satisfied with her marriage and
life.

Wallisch, William Joseph, Jr. (Ed. D.). "THE ADMISSION AND INTEGRA-
TION OF WOMEN INTO THE UNITED STATES AIR FORCE ACADEMY." University of
Southern California, 1977. Source: DAI, XXXVIII, 8A (February, 1978),
4619-A.

Explained background conditions enabling smooth entrance, uneventful
integration, and low attrition of women cadets in the Air Force Academy because of positive academy atmosphere and extensive staff
planning.

Walshok, Mary Lindenstein (Ph. D.). "THE SOCIAL CORRELATES AND SEXU-
AL CONSEQUENCES OF VARIATIONS IN GENDER ROLE ORIENTATION: A NATIONAL

STUDY OF COLLEGE STUDENTS." Indiana University, 1969. 281 pp. Source:
DAI, XXX, 11A (May, 1970), 5088-A-5089-A. XUM Order No. 70-7515.

Found that women committed to unconventional roles often had high
socio-economic status, professional parents, secular values, urban
upbringing, close relationships with their fathers, and residential
mobility.

Walt, Dorothy Elizabeth (Ph. D.). "THE MOTIVATION FOR WOMEN TO WORK
IN HIGH-LEVEL PROFESSIONAL POSITIONS." American University, 1962. 197
pp. Source: DAI, XXIII, 5 (November, 1962), 1817-1818. XUM Order No.
62-4217.

Compared favorable and unfavorable job occurrences for women in high-
level professional positions. Concluded that jobs met women's needs
for self-actualization, self-realization, and for identification with
a group.

Walter, Gladys W. (Ed. D.). "EDUCATION OF GIRLS IN INDIA UNDER THE
METHODIST CHURCH." Columbia University Teachers College, 1949. 191 pp.
Source: Dissertation.

An historical study of elementary, secondary, higher, and vocational
education for girls under the aegis of the Methodist Church. This
missionary body helped prod the British Government in 1854 to begin
support of popular education in India.

Walters, James Coates (Ph. D.). "ATTITUDES CONCERNING THE GUIDANCE
OF CHILDREN: A STUDY OF THE DIFFERENTIAL EFFECTS OF AN INTRODUCTORY
COURSE IN CHILD DEVELOPMENT ON THE ATTITUDES OF COLLEGE WOMEN." Florida
State University, 1954. 104 pp. Source: DAI, XIV, 11 (1954), 2054.
XUM Order No. 9681.

Attitudes concerning guidance of children changed in the control
group of women students but a greater change occurred in the experimental group of women students who took a 3-hour child development
course supplemented by laboratory observation of children.

Walthall, Nancy (Ph. D.). "A STUDY OF THE EFFECTIVENESS OF THE RESI-
DENT COUNSELOR IN THE ADJUSTMENT OF A SELECTED GROUP OF FRESHMAN WOMEN."
Northwestern University, 1957. 267 pp. Source: DAI, XVII, 12 (Decem-
ber, 1957), 2944. XUM Order No. 23,555.

Evaluated the effectiveness of dormitory resident counselors in
helping freshman women resolve problems. Found that effective counseling depended primarily on human relationships. Recommended that
resident counselors be screened carefully for personality and basic
attitudes.

Waltz, Carolyn Feher (Ph. D.). "AN EXPLORATION OF THE RELATIONSHIP
BETWEEN THE NURSING PRACTICE PREFERENCES OF NURSING FACULTY, NURSING
STUDENTS' PERCEPTIONS OF FACULTY CHARACTERISTICS, AND NURSING STUDENTS'
PREFERENCES FOR NURSING PRACTICE." University of Delaware, 1976. 289
pp. Source: DAI, XXXVII, 5A (November, 1976), 2680-A-2681-A. XUM Order
No. 76-24,234.

Found in a study of 170 nursing students and 14 faculty members before, during, and after clinical training that clinical faculty members influenced students' preferences for specific nursing practices.

Wang, Amerfil Manongdo (Ed. D.). "EDUCATIONAL ATTITUDES OF NURSING INSTRUCTORS AND THEIR PERCEPTION OF LEADER BEHAVIOR IN BACCALAUREATE NURSING STUDENTS." Columbia University, 1975. 156 pp. Source: DAI, XXXVI, 1B (July, 1975), 166-B. XUM Order No. 75-13,914.

Faculty for beginning baccalaureate nursing students related leadership to logical decision-making and critical thinking, while faculty for senior baccalaureate nursing students related leadership to self-criticism and social sensitivity.

Ward, Mary Jane Morrow (Ph. D.). "A STUDY OF FAMILY NURSE PRACTITIONERS: PERCEIVED COMPETENCIES AND SOME OF THEIR IMPLICATIONS FOR NURSING EDUCATION." University of Colorado, 1975. 317 pp. Source: DAI, XXXVI, 8B (February, 1976), 3875-B. XUM Order No. 76-3964.

Identified the most frequent health problems which family-nurse practitioners must treat to help nursing educators develop appropriate training for future family nurse practitioners.

Warden, Jessie A. (Ph. D.). "SOME FACTORS AFFECTING THE SATISFACTION AND DISSATISFACTION WITH CLOTHING OF WOMEN STUDENTS IN THE COLLEGE OF EDUCATION AND THE COLLEGE OF LIBERAL ARTS." Pennsylvania State University, 1955. Source: Dissertation, pp. 134-142.

The 80 women students questioned said that clothes could help one to feel more competent.

Warnecke, Richard B. (Ph. D.). "DROPOUTS FROM COLLEGIATE NURSING: A TYPOLOGICAL STUDY OF ROLE CONFLICT." Duke University, 1966. 157 pp. Source: DAI, XXVII, 11A (May, 1967), 3954-A. XUM Order No. 67-6116.

Measured student's conflict over the ascribed versus achieved status of women and questioned the validity of marriage versus career conflict.

Warner, Beverly Alice (Ph. D.). "THE RELATIONSHIP BETWEEN REPORTED SELF AND BODY IMAGE SATISFACTION AND ATTITUDES TOWARD AGING OF SENIOR NURSING STUDENTS ENROLLED IN HOSPITAL SCHOOLS OF NURSING." New York University, 1969. 79 pp. Source: DAI, XXXI, 3B (September, 1970), 1365-B. XUM Order No. 70-15,988.

Confirmed the hypothesis that the greater the nursing student's body and self-image satisfaction, the more positive would be her attitudes toward aging.

Warning, Margaret Cynthia (Ph. D.). "THE IMPLICATIONS OF SOCIAL CLASS FOR CLOTHING BEHAVIOR: THE ACQUISITION AND USE OF APPAREL FOR GIRLS SEVEN, EIGHT, AND NINE YEARS OF AGE IN THREE SOCIAL CLASSES IN DES MOINES, IOWA." Michigan State University, 1956. 182 pp. Source: DAI, XVII, 6 (1957), 1409-1410. XUM Order No. 20,089.

Found that the clothing worn by girls ages 7-9 varied according to the social class of their families.

Warren, Carrie Lee (Ed. D.). "AN INVESTIGATION OF THE GROUP APPROACH TO WEIGHT REDUCTION AND IMPROVEMENT OF PHYSICAL FITNESS IN COLLEGE WOMEN." University of Texas, 1966. 119 pp. Source: DAI, XXVII, 9A (March, 1967), 2861-A. XUM Order No. 67-3243.

Found among college women that those interested in weight loss and physical fitness accomplished these goals more effectively as participants in a physical education discussion group.

Warren, Phyllis Ann (Ph. D.). "VOCATIONAL INTERESTS AND THE OCCUPA- TIONAL ADJUSTMENT OF COLLEGE WOMEN." University of California, Berkeley, 1958. 109 pp. Source: Dissertation, pp. 90-96.

Found, using Strong Vocational Interest Blank, that: (1) college women whose work coincided with their interests had greater job sat- isfaction; and (2) housewives who did outside work were more satis- fied with their marriages than were full-time homemakers.

Warwick, Eunice Blowers (Ph. D.). "ATTITUDES TOWARD WOMEN IN ADMIN- ISTRATIVE POSITIONS AS RELATED TO CURRICULAR IMPLEMENTATION AND CHANGE." University of Wisconsin, 1967. 303 pp. Source: DAI, XXVIII, 4A (Octo- ber, 1967), 1256-A-1257-A. XUM Order No. 67-9024.

Studied attitudes of teachers and administrators toward women admin- istrators and the relationship of these attitudes to curricular im- plementation and change. Found no evidence that men and women pro- fessionals disliked working with women administrators. Most teachers said that women were not encouraged to enter school administration and agreed that if competing with a woman of equal training and exper- ience a man would be selected. These factors contributed to women's low professional goals.

Washington, Ethel O. (Ed. D.). "NEEDED CHANGES IN HOME ECONOMICS CURRICULUM CONSISTENT WITH THE 'REPORT OF SUPERINTENDENT'S COMMITTEE ON ACHIEVEMENT.'" Wayne State University, 1976. 222 pp. Source: DAI, XXXVII, 11A (May, 1977), 6998-A-6999-A. XUM Order No. 77-9466.

Information from 75 Detroit school district junior high school home economics teachers indicated the changes needed in curriculum, bud- get, class size, and instruction to meet the aims set by the "Report of Superintendent's Committee on Achievement."

Waters, Sister Catherine Cecelia (Ph. D.). "SEX-ROLE ATTITUDES AND THE MANIFEST NEEDS, VOCATIONAL MATURITY, AND CAREER ORIENTATION OF COL- LEGE WOMEN." Fordham University, 1976. 127 pp. Source: DAI, XXXVII, 5A (November, 1976), 2654-A. XUM Order No. 76-25,802.

Major recommendation was for counselors and educators to help col- lege women explore their life-style options.

Waters, Elinor Bloch (Ed. D.). "EXERCISING NEW OPTIONS: ADULT WOMEN COMPARED WITH MEN AND YOUNGER WOMEN AT A COMMUNITY COLLEGE." Wayne State University, 1973. 87 pp. Source: DAI, XXXIV, 7A (January, 1974), 3896-A-3897-A. XUM Order No. 73-31,790.

Compared reasons for attending college, feelings about their college
experience, and plans for the future of 3 groups: (1) adult women
students; (2) young women students; and (3) men students. Found
that: (1) older students were more enthusiastic about the impact of
college on their lives; and (2) there were no sex differences regarding job and educational goals.

Waters, Kathleen Graham (Ph. D.). "A PROFILE OF BLACK FEMALE OFFICE
PERSONNEL IN SOUTHWESTERN ATHLETIC CONFERENCE UNIVERSITIES." Kansas
State University, 1976. 144 pp. Source: DAI, XXXVII, 7A (January,
1977), 4108-A. XUM Order No. 76-30,029.

The average black woman office worker in 7 mainly black universities
was young, well educated, had a need for achievement, and chose to
work rather than had to work. Professional growth was the most important factor in her feeling about her employment status.

Waters, Virginia (Ph. D.). "TEACHER DIFFERENTIAL APPROVAL AND DIS-
APPROVAL OF BOYS AND GIRLS IN THE CLASSROOM." Columbia University, 1973.
148 pp. Source: DAI, XXXIV, 6B (December, 1973), 2916-B. XUM Order No.
73-28,262.

Found no significant difference in rate of approval given to boys
and girls. But the significant difference found between rate of
disapproval and combined rates of approval and disapproval favored
boys at each grade level.

Watson, Georgia Brown (Ph. D.). "A STUDY OF THE CURRICULA IN SE-
LECTED COLLEGES FOR WOMEN." George Peabody College for Teachers, 1949.
108 pp. Source: Dissertation, pp. 95-102.

Learned from 15 private women's liberal arts colleges and their alumnae that education courses were the only vocational training common
to all 15 colleges. Most students planned to be teachers or homemakers (9 colleges offered home economics). Many alumnae said the
colleges needed to provide vocational guidance.

Watson, Helen Belle (Ph. D.). "THE COMPARATIVE RELATIONSHIP OF HIGH
SCHOOL PHYSICAL EDUCATION PROGRAMS IN TENNESSEE TO THE DEVELOPMENT OF
STRENGTH AND MOTOR ABILITY OF COLLEGE WOMEN." University of Michigan,
1955. 203 pp. Source: DAI, XV, 9 (1955), 1547-1548. XUM Order No.
12,664.

Found that: (1) women's physical education programs contributed to
motor ability but did not significantly affect strength development;
and (2) women who had good high school physical education programs
participated in more high school recreational activities.

Watson, Joellen Beck (Ph. D.). "THE CHARACTERISTICS OF CLINICAL
AGENCIES FOR CLINICAL EXPERIENCES IN BACCALAUREATE NURSING EDUCATION:
A STUDY OF FACULTY PERCEPTIONS." Boston College, 1976. 152 pp. Source:
DAI, XXXVII, 10B (April, 1977), 4991-B. XUM Order No. 77-8682.

Author found that nursing faculty perceptions of the best clinical
experiences to prepare basic nursing students were not congruent
with experiences which clinical agencies actually offered.

Watson, John W. (Ed. D.). "EFFECTS OF A THERAPEUTIC ENVIRONMENT ON THE SELF CONCEPT OF DELINQUENT GIRLS." Brigham Young University, 1976. 143 pp. Source: DAI, XXXVII, 9A (March, 1977), 5721-A. XUM Order No. 77-4860.

Found that the counseling program at Kern Youth Facility, Bakersfield, CA, did improve the self-concepts of 80 delinquent girl inmates.

Waugh, Lillian Jane (Ph. D.). "THE IMAGES OF WOMAN IN FRANCE ON THE EVE OF THE LOI CAMILLE SEE, 1877-1880." University of Massachusetts, 1977. 274 pp. Source: DAI, XXXVIII, 1A (July, 1977), 416-A. XUM Order No. 77-15,136.

The Loi Camille See of 1880, a law designed to prevent women from entering the professions, reflected contemporary prejudice against women. But French feminists exploited favorable stereotypes of women, such as being natural teachers, in order to broaden their employment opportunities.

Way, Joyce Washnok (Ed. D.). "A COMPARISON OF BACKGROUND PROFILES, CAREER EXPECTATIONS AND CAREER ASPIRATIONS OF MEN AND WOMEN PUBLIC SCHOOL ADMINISTRATORS." Western Michigan University, 1976. 154 pp. Source: DAI, XXXVII, 6A (December, 1976), 3333-A-3334-A. XUM Order No. 76-28, 431.

Compared to men, Michigan women school administrators were older, had more teaching experience, held their previous jobs longer, had less administrative experience, moved into their administrative posts by internal promotion, were in larger school districts, had more bachelor's and doctoral degrees, had experienced more sex discrimination in their careers, and aspired more to become state and federal school program administrators.

Weber, Shirley Mae (Ph. D.). "THE DEVELOPMENT AND EVALUATION OF EIGHT UNITS OF PROGRAMMED INSTRUCTION DESIGNED TO TEACH BASIC NUTRITION." Cornell University, 1965. 346 pp. Source: DAI, XXVI, 10 (April, 1966), 6014. XUM Order No. 66-4682.

Programmed instruction used by 119 junior high school home economics students led to deeper understanding of nutrition.

Weeks, Ruth T. (Ph. D.). "THE RELATIONSHIP OF GRADE, SEX, SOCIO-ECONOMIC STATUS, SCHOLASTIC APTITUDE, AND SCHOOL ACHIEVEMENT TO FORMAL OPERATIONS ATTAINMENT IN A GROUP OF JUNIOR HIGH SCHOOL STUDENTS." Kent State University, 1973. 125 pp. Source: DAI, XXXIV, 5A (November, 1973), 2405-A. XUM Order No. 73-27,261.

Studied the development of formal operations abilities (as defined by Piaget) among junior high school students and related this development to differences in grade, sex, socio-economic status, scholastic aptitude, and school achievement. Concluded that more research was needed, particularly on sex differences.

Wegner, Kenneth Walter (Ed. D.). "AN ANALYSIS OF INTEREST PATTERNS AND PSYCHOLOGICAL NEED STRUCTURES RELATED TO L-I-D RESPONSE PATTERNS ON THE STRONG VOCATIONAL INTEREST BLANK FOR WOMEN." University of Kansas,

1961. 207 pp. Source: DAI, XXII, 11 (May, 1962), 3931-3932. XUM Order No. 62-1877.

Analyzed several vocational interest tests given to 399 entering college women at the University of Kansas.

Weick, Lucinda Kathryn (Ed. D.). "AN ANALYSIS OF THE INFLUENCE OF EXPERIENCE IN PHYSICAL ACTIVITIES ON CERTAIN PSYCHOLOGICAL-SOCIAL AND PHYSICAL NEEDS OF UNIVERSITY FRESHMAN AND SOPHOMORE MEN AND WOMEN." University of Missouri-Columbia, 1971. 201 pp. Source: DAI, XXXII, 6A (December, 1971), 3080-A-3081-A. XUM Order No. 71-30,716.

Concluded that women's physical education activity programs provided appropriate situations for participation in, and working with, groups; open expression of opinion; and acceptance of responsibilities.

Weigley, Emma Seifrit (Ph. D.). "SARAH TYSON RORER (1849-1937), A BIOGRAPHICAL STUDY. AN INVESTIGATION INTO THE LIFE, CAREER, AND TEACHINGS OF AN EARLY CONTRIBUTOR TO THE DEVELOPMENT OF HOME ECONOMICS." New York University, 1971. 523 pp. Source: DAI, XXXII, 5B (November, 1971), 2834-B. XUM Order No. 71-28,567.

Mrs. Rorer, called the first American dietitian, was an active adult educator who operated the Philadelphia Cooking School (1883-1903), wrote for the Ladies' Home Journal (1897-1911), and published over 50 cookbooks. She foresaw women's changing life styles as female employment and urbanization increased.

Wein, Roberta (Ph. D.). "EDUCATED WOMEN AND THE LIMITS OF DOMESTICITY, 1830-1918." New York University, 1974. 180 pp. Source: DAI, XXXV, 8A (February, 1975), 5073-A-5074-A. XUM Order No. 75-4277.

Examined relationships between domestic values and educated women's responses to these values during the 19th and early 20th centuries. Studied careers of Elizabeth Peabody, Wellesley President Alice Palmer, and Bryn Mawr President Martha Carey Thomas. By the 20th century, the tendency was to professionalize domesticity (with careers in domestic science, etc.), but college women also made intellectuality subservient to domesticity.

Weiner, Leona (Ed. D.). "BACCALAUREATE DEGREE PROGRAM IN NURSING: A NEW CURRICULUM APPROACH." Columbia University, 1968. 146 pp. Source: DAI, XXIX, 7B (January, 1969), 2505-B-2506-B. XUM Order No. 69-681.

Author provided a model for baccalaureate nursing curriculum development based on nursing goals, professional commitment, technical skills, and communication with patients.

Weiner, Lucy Gay (Ph. D.). "SEX DIFFERENCES IN ACHIEVEMENT: AN ATTRIBUTION APPROACH." State University of New York at Albany, 1977. 131 pp. Source: DAI, XXXVIII, 7A (January, 1978), 4065-A-4066-A. XUM Order No. 77-29,176.

Author tested hypothesis that men, unlike women, attributed success to internal causes and failure to external causes so that men, un-

like women, had heightened self-reinforcement for success and less
self-punishment for failure.

Weinroth, Elissa Dosik (Ph. D.). "MOTIVATION, JOB SATISFACTION, AND
CAREER ASPIRATIONS OF MARRIED WOMEN TEACHERS AT DIFFERENT CAREER STAGES."
American University, 1977. 154 pp. Source: DAI, XXXVIII, 6A (December,
1977), 3206-A. XUM Order No. 77-27,446.

Found among married women elementary school teachers in an affluent
suburban school system that their motivational needs, job satisfactions, and career aspirations were affected by age, teaching experience, and age of their children at home. Recommended rewarding
teachers for superior accomplishments and recruiting women of all
ages to administrative and supervisory posts.

Weir, Velna Jan Townsend (Ed. D.). "LEADERSHIP AMONG ADMINISTRATIVE
WOMEN IN PUBLIC EDUCATION IN NEBRASKA." University of Nebraska Teachers
College, 1961. 279 pp. Source: DAI, XXII, 9 (March, 1962), 3080-3081.
XUM Order No. 62-142.

Found that women administrators had similar leadership characteristics
to men administrators, that 40% of women administrators were firstborn children, that 67.5% held master's degrees, and 3.7% held doctorates.

Weiss, Elma Steck (Ed. D.). "THE VALUE AND USE OF INSTRUCTIONAL
TELEVISION IN TEACHING WOMEN BEGINNING GOLFERS." Arizona State Univer-
sity, 1971. 78 pp. Source: DAI, XXXII, 4A (October, 1971), 1907-A.
XUM Order No.71-24,915.

Conclusion was that the television camera as tested was not sufficiently helpful to justify its use in college women's beginning golf
classes.

Weiss, George David (Ed. D.). "THE EDUCATION OF WOMEN ELEMENTARY
TEACHERS IN RELATION TO THEIR ROLE IN SOCIETY." Pennsylvania State University, 1962. 189 pp. Source: DAI, XXIII, 3 (September, 1962), 944-
945. XUM Order No. 62-4106.

Found about education and life patterns of women teachers that: (1)
only 8.6% seemed concerned about women's disadvantages when competing with men; (2) employed women had little interest in professional
advancement; (3) their preparation was adequate for personal and professional needs; and (4) their preparation for work in community affairs was only moderately adequate.

Weiss, Karen Lea (Ph. D.). "EFFECTS OF DIFFERENTIAL MEDIA TREATMENTS
ON NEWLY ADMITTED MATURE WOMEN STUDENTS." University of Maryland, 1977.
150 pp. Source: DAI, XXXVIII, 6A (December, 1977), 3303-A. XUM Order
No. 77-26,574.

Found that 2 different media approaches using information letters
and other materials had little positive effect on improving the adjustment and academic success of newly admitted older (over age 25)
women college students; their age rather than the information media
made for their success.

Weissman, Esther Irene (Ed. D.). "THE RELATIONSHIP BETWEEN THE MARITAL STATUS, FEMININE IDENTITY CONFLICT, AND SELF-ACTUALIZATION OF WOMEN DOC- TORAL STUDENTS." Boston University School of Education, 1974. 124 pp. Source: DAI, XXXV, 6A (December, 1974), 3441-A. XUM Order No. 74-26, 449.

Found that: (1) single women had a significantly higher level of feminine identity conflict than married women; (2) educational status, employment investment, and relationship involvement did not differen- tiate between high and low feminine identity conflict groups; and (3) feminine sex roles needed more flexibility.

Welch, Cathryne Ann (Ed. D.). "SATISFYING AND STRESSFUL EXPERIENCES IN THE PRACTICE OF NURSING." Columbia University, 1975. 188 pp. Source: DAI, XXXVI, 3B (September, 1975), 1151-B-1152-B. XUM Order No. 75-20, 237.

Found that satisfying and stressful experiences did not vary with type of nursing education received by 276 registered professional women nurses in 11 New York City general hospitals.

Weller, Robert Hubert (Ph. D.). "FEMALE WORK EXPERIENCE AND FERTIL- ITY IN SAN JUAN, PUERTO RICO: A STUDY OF SELECTED LOWER AND MIDDLE IN- COME NEIGHBORHOODS." Cornell University, 1967. 184 pp. Source: DAI, XXXVI, 4A (October, 1975), 2445-A-2446-A. XUM Order No. 75-22,995.

Education was one factor used in examining the relationship between employment and fertility among 559 women in Puerto Rico. Concluded that education and socio-economic type of neighborhood are associa- ted more with fertility than was labor force status.

Welliver, Thomas Joseph (Ed. D.). "RISK-TAKING JUDGMENTS AND OTHER RELATED VARIABLES OF COLLEGE WOMEN WHO ARE HIGHLY DECIDED OR HIGHLY UN- DECIDED ABOUT THEIR CAREER GOALS." State University of New York at Al- bany, 1973. 121 pp. Source: DAI, XXXIV, 10A (April, 1974), 6397-A. XUM Order No. 74-9296.

Found that freshman women who had definitely decided their educational and vocational goals were significantly more confident of their de- cision-making judgments and had less need for social acceptance com- pared to freshman women who had not made those decisions.

Wellman, Mabel Thacher (Ph. D.). "A STUDY OF HOME ECONOMICS EDUCATION IN INDIANA HIGH SCHOOLS." University of Chicago, 1925. 163 pp. Source: Dissertation, pp. 121-123.

Courses in vocational home making departments in Indiana high schools had more uniform organization than did courses in general home eco- nomics departments.

Wells, Margaret Cairncross (Ed. D.). "HISTORY AND EVALUATION OF THE GRADUATE COURSE FOR WOMEN IN STUDENT PERSONNEL ADMINISTRATION AT SYRACUSE UNIVERSITY." Syracuse University, 1950. 468 pp. Source: Dissertation, pp. 391-409A.

Surveyed 132 women graduates of the student personnel administration course. Found that: (1) women employed in non-education jobs considered the program less useful; and (2) women in education jobs were generally satisfied with the program.

Wentworth, Virginia Rance (Ph. D.). "AN INVESTIGATION OF SEX-ROLE STEREOTYPE IN STUDENT COUNSELORS' DESCRIPTIONS OF THE HEALTHY ADULT MAN AND THE HEALTHY ADULT WOMAN AND THEIR RESPONSES TO HYPOTHETICAL MALE AND FEMALE CLIENTS." Indiana University, 1977. 196 pp. Source: DAI, XXXVIII, 5A (November, 1977), 2570-A. XUM Order No. 77-22,711.

Found among 120 student counselors that female counselors tended to stereotype people less often than did the male counselors.

West, Eula Lee (Ph. D.). "THE ROLE OF WOMEN IN THE AMERICAN SOCIETY WITH IMPLICATIONS FOR THE PROFESSIONAL PREPARATION OF WOMEN FOR TEACHING PHYSICAL EDUCATION IN COLLEGE." New York University, 1961. 220 pp. Source: DAI, XXII, 12, Part 1 (June, 1962), 4262. XUM Order No. 62-1435.

From a literature search of the role of women in American society and the goals of general education for college women, author drew implications for objectives to serve physical education teachers of college women.

West, Sidney Duncan, Jr. (Ed. D.). "ATTITUDES OF HIGH SCHOOL TEACHERS, PRINCIPALS, GUIDANCE COUNSELORS, LIBRARIANS, AND TEACHER EDUCATORS TOWARD THE SOCIAL, EDUCATIONAL, AND ECONOMIC ROLES OF WOMEN." University of Florida, 1975. 288 pp. Source: DAI, XXXVII, 7A (January, 1977), 4301-A-4302-A. XUM Order No. 77-138.

Found that women from 17 of 20 different status groups (principals, counselors, teachers with different majors) had more favorable attitudes toward women's rights than their male counterparts. Whites, individuals with doctorates, and residents of larger counties had more favorable responses. Those at all other income levels had significantly higher responses than those earning $10,000-$15,000.

Westcot, Lynn Washburn Bertholf (Ed. D.). "PERSONALITY CHARACTERISTICS OF BACCALAUREATE NURSING STUDENTS." Illinois State University, 1977. 140 pp. Source: DAI, XXXVIII, 4B (October, 1977), 1655-B-1656-B. XUM Order No. 77-20,943.

Found that senior baccalaureate nursing students were more professional than freshman students and that the nursing education program did professionalize the students.

Westrum, Helen J. (Ed. D.). "SELF CONCEPTS OF GAINFULLY EMPLOYED WOMEN IN TWO COLLEGES IN WASHINGTON STATE." Oregon State University, 1975. 97 pp. Source: DAI, XXXV, 7A (January, 1975), 4117-A. XUM Order No. 74-29,740.

Self-concept analysis of 583 women employed in 2 colleges produced these conclusions: (1) married women had the highest self-concept scores, followed by divorced women, and finally by single women; and (2) the longer a woman had held her job, the higher was her self-concept score.

Westwick, Carmen Rose (Ph. D.). "THE RELATIONSHIP OF CONGRUITY OF PERCEPTIONS AND ORGANIZATIONAL CLIMATE IN SELECTED COLLEGIATE SCHOOLS OF NURSING IN THE UNITED STATES." University of Denver, 1972. 191 pp. Source: DAI, XXXIII, 7A (January, 1973), 3334-A. XUM Order No. 72-33, 076.

Study of 13 baccalaureate and master degree nursing schools showed that the openness of their administrative organization was affected by size of school, size of parent institution, and academic calendar system.

Wheeler, George (Ph. D.). "MASCULINE RESPONSES TO SCHOOLING: A COMPARISON OF THIRD GRADERS OF DIFFERING ETHNIC BACKGROUNDS AND SEX ON READING TEST SCORES AND A MODIFIED SEMANTIC DIFFERENTIAL." University of New Mexico, 1972. 160 pp. Source: DAI, XXXIII, 7A (January, 1973), 3273-A. XUM Order No. 73-1535.

Tested reading achievement among 48 Anglo-American males, 48 Anglo-American females, 48 Mexican-American males, and 48 Mexican-American females. Anglo-American girls had highest vocabulary, comprehension, and total reading scores. Concluded that sex differences were probably greater than ethnic differences.

Whiddon, Nancy Sue (Ed. D.). "A MODEL FOR UNDERGRADUATE PROFESSIONAL PREPARATION PROGRAMS FOR WOMEN ATHLETIC COACHES IN SOUTHEASTERN SENIOR COLLEGES AND UNIVERSITIES." Florida Atlantic University, 1977. 161 pp. Source: DAI, XXXVIII, 7A (January, 1978), 4029-A-4030-A. XUM Order No. 77-27,776.

Found in a survey of 47 undergraduate schools of physical education that almost all offered programs or courses for prospective women coaches but some did not comply with Title IX. Author designed a model program for women coaches that would meet Title IX requirements and upgrade women's intercollegiate athletic coaching.

Whitaker, Sue Hicks (Ph. D.). "CRITERION-REFERENCE EVALUATION INSTRUMENTS DEVELOPED TO MEASURE SELECTED COMPETENCIES OF PREPROFESSIONAL STUDENTS IN HOME ECONOMICS TEACHER EDUCATION PROGRAMS." University of Wisconsin, Madison, 1976. 382 pp. Source: DAI, XXXVII, 10A (April, 1977), 6315-A. XUM Order No. 76-29,948.

The researcher developed and tested the validity of a Packet of Evaluation Instruments for use in competency-based home economics teacher education programs.

White, Barbara Anne (Ph. D.). "GROWING UP FEMALE: ADOLESCENT GIRL-HOOD IN AMERICAN LITERATURE." University of Wisconsin, Madison, 1974. 342 pp. Source: DAI, XXXV, 9A (March, 1975), 6167-A. XUM Order No. 74-28,834.

Studying recent fiction, the author analyzed patterns of female adolescent experience as depicted by women authors. Found that adolescent females were most often depicted as trapped, with few having positive alternatives as ways of escape.

White, Bette C. (Ph. D.). "THE PERCEPTIONS OF CAMPUS RESOURCE PER-
SONNEL HELD BY UNDERGRADUATE WOMEN AT THREE PRIVATE COLLEGES." Michigan
State University, 1970. 118 pp. Source: DAI, XXXII, 1A (July, 1971),
150-A. XUM Order No. 71-18,327.

Women undergraduates who were questioned about the role of deans of
women at small, church-related college campuses considered deans of
women competent in handling rules and regulations and acting as arbi-
trators but unimportant as counselors.

White, Bonnie Yvonne (Ed. D.). "SUPERORDINATE AND SUBORDINATE PER-
CEPTIONS OF MANAGERIAL STYLES OF SELECTED MALE AND FEMALE COLLEGE ADMINIS-
TRATORS." Brigham Young University, 1976. 127 pp. Source: DAI, XXXVII,
2A (August, 1976), 841-A. XUM Order No. 76-18,355.

Found no differences in the managerial style self-perceptions of male
and female college administrators.

White, Dorothy Bailey (Ed. D.). "A DESCRIPTIVE STUDY OF THE STATUS
OF WOMEN ADMINISTRATORS IN TEXAS PUBLIC SCHOOLS, 1968-1973." University
of Houston, 1975. 170 pp. Source: DAI, XXXVI, 9A (March, 1976), 5735-
A. XUM Order No. 76-6064.

Texas was below the national average in its number of women school
administrators. The only exception was supervisors, 59% of whom were
women. A major obstacle was women's lack of professional preparation;
few women met academic requirements for certification in administration.

White, Dorothy Thompson (Ed. D.). "EDUCATIONAL PREPARATION OF TEACH-
ERS OF NURSING FOR THE COMMUNITY COLLEGE." Columbia University Teachers
College, 1961. Source: TCCU DIGESTS (1961), pp. 613-614.

Information from 35 community college nursing administrators and
nursing instructors was used to identify a model community college
nursing education program.

White, Elizabeth Herrick (Ph. D.). "WOMEN'S STATUS IN AN ISLAMIC
SOCIETY: THE PROBLEM OF PURDAH." University of Denver, 1975. 269 pp.
Source: DAI, XXXVI, 11A (May, 1976), 7625-A. XUM Order No. 76-8185.

Twenty-one Muslim nations were ranked according to the number of
traditional laws affecting women's status which they continue to en-
force. Correlation of this rank with female literacy rates and
school enrollment indicated a strong linear relationship between the
enforcement of traditional restrictions and low female educational
achievement. The most educated women were the most emancipated;
education was most widespread among wealthy urban women.

White, Isabella Waddell (Ph. D.). "THE USE OF CERTAIN TESTS IN THE
PREDICTION OF ACADEMIC SUCCESS AS APPLIED TO STUDENTS OF HOME ECONOMICS."
Pennsylvania State University, 1942. 92 pp. Source: Dissertation, pp.
80-84.

Home economics women students and men engineering students were compared on results of the standard mental ability test and a vocational

interest test. The tests were then evaluated in terms of their predicting academic success of home economics students.

White, Kinnard Paul (Ph. D.). "PROFESSIONAL CAREER INVOLVEMENT AMONG
FEMALE ELEMENTARY SCHOOL TEACHERS." Indiana University, 1964. 72 pp.
Source: DAI, XXV, 5 (November, 1964), 2865-2866. XUM Order No. 64-12,
103.

Author tested the validity of scales designed to identify which women
elementary school teachers were most and least professionally involved
in their teaching careers.

White, Opal Hinsey (D. N. Sc.). "A STUDY OF SELF-AWARENESS IN GRADU-
ATE STUDENTS IN PSYCHIATRIC NURSING." Boston University School of Nur-
sing, 1969. 170 pp. Source: DAI, XXX, 9B (March, 1970), 4223-B-4224-B.
XUM Order No. 70-3748.

Found that psychiatric nursing students had to be involved emotionally in relationships with patients and with their teacher before
they began to develop their own self-awareness.

White, Patricia Elizabeth Clifton (Ed. D.). "A STUDY OF THE STATUS
OF WOMEN COUNSELORS IN THE VIRGINIA COMMUNITY COLLEGE SYSTEM." College
of William and Mary in Virginia, 1976. 151 pp. Source: DAI, XXXVII,
6A (December, 1976), 3434-A. XUM Order No. 76-28,443.

Found in Virginia community colleges that the status of women counselors, in relation to men counselors, was: (1) similar in rank and
salary; and (2) not as good in travel funds to professional meetings
and in tuition aid.

White, Sarah Elizabeth (Ed. D.). "PERCEPTIONS OF HIGHER EDUCATION OF
A SELECTED GROUP OF ACADEMICALLY SUCCESSFUL COLLEGE WOMEN." University
of Denver, 1961. 216 pp. Source: DAI, XXII, 10 (April, 1962), 3476-
3477. XUM Order No. 62-1218.

Women who continued in college gave such reasons for continuing as
desire to gain a degree, prepare for a career, develop intellectual
capacities, and meet college men (though none said that finding a
husband was a major goal). These women felt strongly about the importance of a college education for women. Women college dropouts
saw uncertain long-range value in higher education.

Whitesel, Lita Sue (Ph. D.). "CAREER COMMITMENT OF WOMEN ART STU-
DENTS." University of California, Berkeley, 1974. 177 pp. Source:
DAI, XXXV, 8A (February, 1975), 5243-A. XUM Order No. 75-3673.

Assessed the career commitment of 64 women graduate art students.
Found that: (1) students' parents were supportive of their art
careers; (2) the majority of the students' mothers worked outside
the home; and (3) lack of encouragement caused other women students
to drop out of art before reaching graduate school.

Whitmore, Faith Dorcas (Ed. D.). "STUDENT PERSONNEL AND GUIDANCE
SERVICES IN SCHOOLS OF NURSING." University of Colorado, 1958. 434 pp.
Source: DAI, XIX, 10 (April, 1959), 2582. XUM Order No. Mic 59-817.

Responses from nurse educators and a survey of the literature showed these student guidance needs: (1) more guidance staff and their in-service training; (2) budgeting and program planning; and (3) specialized and placement services. Six recommendations were given to help meet these student guidance needs.

Whitney, Mary Ellen (Ed. D.). "THE WOMAN STUDENT PERSONNEL ADMINIS-TRATOR: AN ANTHROPOLOGICAL APPROACH TO THE STUDY OF ONE INDIVIDUAL IN A SOCIAL SYSTEM." Columbia University, 1967. 314 pp. Source: DAI, XXVIII, 7A (January, 1968), 2509-A-2510-A. XUM Order No. 67-16,768.

Concluded that deans of women needed to reinterpret their functions, considering their own characteristics and capabilities and the needs and wants of college students.

Wieczorek, Rita Reis (Ed. D.). "ATTITUDES OF BACCALAUREATE NURSING STUDENTS TOWARD DYING CHILDREN." Columbia University, 1975. 118 pp. Source: DAI, XXXVI, 6B (December, 1975), 2726-B. XUM Order No. 75-27, 073.

Attitudes of nursing students toward dying children were not changed by a special instructional unit related to the topic, but the small group discussions with classmates in the special instructional unit helped them share their feelings about dying children.

Wight, Jean Audrey Johnson (Ed. D.). "GUIDELINES FOR DEVELOPING UNIVERSITY HOME ECONOMICS INTERNATIONAL PROGRAMS, WITH EMPHASIS ON UNDER-GRADUATE CURRICULUM DEVELOPMENT DIRECTED TOWARD SERVICE IN OTHER COUN-TRIES, PARTICULARLY LATIN AMERICA." Oklahoma State University, 1970. 234 pp. Source: DAI, XXXI, 11B (May, 1971), 6727-B. XUM Order No. 71-11,301.

Visits to 4 land-grant universities and a literature review on Latin American family problems led author to prepare undergraduate home economics intercultural and international curriculum guidelines on family resources, nutrition, health, and housing.

Wightwick, Mary Irene (Ph. D.). "VOCATIONAL INTEREST PATTERNS, A DEVELOPMENTAL STUDY OF A GROUP OF COLLEGE WOMEN." Columbia University Teachers College, 1945. 231 pp. Source: TCCU CONTRIBUTIONS No. 900, pp. 209-221.

Studied 115 college women's vocational interests over an 8-year period. Found that: (1) 64% of them retained the same vocational choices throughout 4 years of college; (2) after 8 years, 44% held jobs consistent with their pre-college vocational choices; and (3) 73% held jobs consistent with their post-college choices. Concluded that vocational counseling could be improved if standardized tests were refined.

Wilber, Cornelia Faith (Ph. D.). "AN INVESTIGATION OF THE RELATION-SHIP AMONG SEX-ROLE IDENTIFICATION, PSYCHOLOGICAL ADJUSTMENT, AND OTHER SELECTED VARIABLES FOR STUDENTS AND WORKERS." Southern Illinois University at Carbondale, 1977. 138 pp. Source: DAI, XXXVIII, 5A (November, 1977), 2571-A. XUM Order No. 77-24,045.

Studied relationship between individuals (55 males and 70 females) categorized as psychologically androgynous or sex-typed and as psychologically adjusted. Among conclusions: (1) sex-role stereotyping did not affect psychological adjustment; (2) androgynous persons were not better adjusted, and sex-typed individuals were not less well adjusted; (3) group membership determined psychological adjustment; and (4) neither group membership, education, age, nor sex predicted one's sex-role orientation.

Wilcoxon, Linda Ann (Ph. D.). "THERAPEUTIC EFFECTS OF SELF-INSTRUCTIONAL TRAINING FOR NONASSERTIVE WOMEN." Pennsylvania State University, 1976. 220 pp. Source: DAI, XXXVII, 11B (May, 1977), 5886-B. XUM Order No. 77-9611.

An assertive training program was found to be effective among 35 nonassertive college women, with some acceptable discrepancies.

Wiley, Sister Mary Louise (Ed. D.). "A STUDY OF THE ADMINISTRATIVE ORGANIZATION OF BACCALAUREATE NURSING EDUCATION IN SISTER FORMATION OF THE RELIGIOUS SISTERS OF MERCY." Columbia University, 1967. 266 pp. Source: DAI, XXVIII, 9A (March, 1968), 3448-A. XUM Order No. 68-2448.

Analyzed the administrations and program content of baccalaureate nursing education programs in the 9 colleges where nursing sisters of the Religious Sisters of Mercy are professionally prepared.

Wilhelm, Cynthia L. (Ph. D.). "A STUDY OF THE EFFECTS OF SYSTEMATIC HUMAN RELATIONS TRAINING ON NURSING STUDENTS." Indiana State University, 1976. 129 pp. Source: DAI, XXXVII, 4A (October, 1976), 2001-A-2002-A. XUM Order No. 76-23,360.

Senior women nursing students exposed to a 16-hour training program improved their skills in human relations, empathy, assertion, and self-exploration.

Wilkens, Diane (Ph. D.). "IDENTIFICATION THROUGH REGRESSION ANALYSIS OF SOME VARIABLES THAT CHARACTERIZE PREGNANT HIGH SCHOOL GIRLS." Southern Illinois University, 1974. 148 pp. Source: DAI, XXXV, 7B (January, 1975), 3404-B. XUM Order No. 75-147.

The author identified information about sex and contraception which should be presented in high schools as part of a pregnancy prevention program.

Wilkins, John Grover (Ph. D.). "CHARACTERISTICS OF MID-CAREER WOMEN ENROLLED IN PROGRAMS AT THE UNIVERSITY OF PITTSBURGH THROUGH THE OFFICE OF CONTINUING EDUCATION FOR WOMEN FROM 1964 TO 1968." University of Pittsburgh, 1968. 160 pp. Source: DAI, XXXI, 3A (September, 1970), 1002-A-1003-A. XUM Order No. 70-13,790.

Women in an adult education program who had a vocational orientation maintained higher grade point averages.

Wilkinson, Fred James (Ph. D.). "A PROGRAM OF DEVELOPMENT FOR THE DEMONSTRATION SCHOOL OF THE WOMEN'S TEACHER TRAINING COLLEGE IN RAMALLAH, JORDAN." Harvard University, 1962. Source: Author.

Explored the contribution made to teacher education by the demonstration school of a women's teacher training college in Jordan.

Wilkinson, Janet Simpson (Ed. D.). "AN INVESTIGATION OF THE NOTE-TAKING SKILLS OF SELECTED FEMALE COLLEGE STUDENTS." University of Virginia, 1969. 121 pp. Source: DAI, XXXI, 1A (July, 1970), 88-A-89-A. XUM Order No. 70-8075.

College sophomore women who used shorthand notetaking received higher scores than those who did not use shorthand, indicating the advantage college-bound high school students would have in taking high school shorthand as an aid to academic success in college.

Williams, Claudia Cowan (Ph. D.). "FEMININE ROLE AS PERCEIVED BY WOMEN TEACHER TRAINEES." Arizona State University, 1972. 77 pp. Source: DAI, XXXIII, 3A (September, 1972), 980-A. XUM Order No. 72-23,182.

Found that a woman teacher trainee's perception of feminine role influenced her decision about teaching at the elementary or the secondary school level. The women teacher trainees studied showed no conflict over feminine role.

Williams, Eugene, Sr. (Ed. D.). "JOB SATISFACTION AND SELF-CONCEPT AS PERCEIVED BY BLACK FEMALE PARAPROFESSIONAL TRAINEES." University of Miami, 1972. 125 pp. Source: DAI, XXXIII, 10A (April, 1973), 5458-A. XUM Order No. 72-31,920.

Found among 87 black women trainees as Head Start and Follow Through teaching aides that: (1) age, marital status, and race of supervisor were not important factors in trainees' job satisfaction; and that (2) trainees with higher self-concepts were slightly more satisfied with their jobs than were trainees with lower self-concepts.

Williams, Josephine Justice (Ph. D.). "THE PROFESSIONAL STATUS OF WOMEN PHYSICIANS." University of Chicago, 1949. 227 pp. Source: Dissertation, pp. 107-112.

Author proved with documentation the hypothesis that a medical woman's status is lower than that of a medical man.

Williams, Julia Anne McCoy (Ed. D.). "SEX ROLE CONFLICT AND ACADEMIC ACHIEVEMENT: A STUDY OF SUPERIOR WOMEN STUDENTS." University of Illinois at Urbana-Champaign, 1970. 200 pp. Source: DAI, XXXI, 12A (June, 1971), 6419-A-6420-A. XUM Order No. 71-14,995.

Found that intrapersonal conflict hurt 200 academically able women's academic achievement more than did interpersonal conflict. Most high-achieving women were in traditional fields and were not as likely to have changed fields.

Williams, Mary Louise (Ed. D.). "EFFECTS OF CLINICAL SETTING ON SELECTED FACTORS RELATED TO ANXIETY AND TO ACHIEVEMENT IN PSYCHIATRIC NURSING EDUCATION." University of Southern California, 1976. Source: DAI, XXXVII, 3A (September, 1976), 1436-A.

Examined the effect that a 6-week clinical practicum had on the
anxiety and achievement levels of 2nd year associate degree nursing
students. Found that: (1) reduced anxiety could not be attributed
to the practicum; and (2) students' academic achievement was well
above the average.

Williams, Mary Margaret (Ph. D.). "THE COLLEGE AND UNIVERSITY EDUCA-
TION OF REGISTERED NURSES: WHENCE AND WHITHER?" Stanford University,
1963. 273 pp. Source: DAI, XXIV, 3 (September, 1963), 1145. XUM Order
No. 63-6454.

After historically surveying nursing education programs, author found
the greatest improvement in the baccalaureate programs. Problems
which still confronted graduate education in nursing included: "inadequate faculty qualifications, absence of an identified body of
graduate nursing control, and underdevelopment of the investigational
function."

Williams, Patricia Jean (Ed. D.). "CAREER ASPIRATIONS OF SELECTED
WOMEN TEACHERS AS RELATED TO THEIR PERCEPTIONS OF THE CHANCES OF SUCCESS
IN BECOMING A SCHOOL ADMINISTRATOR." University of Northern Colorado,
1977. 131 pp. Source: DAI, XXXVIII, 8A (February, 1978), 4507-A. XUM
Order No. 77-30,880.

Information from 72 women teachers showed that 30% were interested in
becoming school administrators and that 75% saw a good chance that
women could obtain school administrative posts. Study inferred that:
(1) women's aspirations were products of their own self-image; (2)
women in their 20s were more insecure in their sex-role identification;
(3) women in their 30s could better realize their own potential; and
(4) women over age 40 were more traditionally oriented.

Williamson, Maude (Ph. D.). "THE EVOLUTION OF HOMEMAKING EDUCATION,
1819-1919." Stanford University, 1942. 329 pp. Source: Dissertation.

Surveyed the history of homemaking education in the context of women's
education, 1819-1919.

Willis, Bernice Holley (Ed. D.). "RELATIONSHIP BETWEEN SELF-CONCEPT
AND RACE AMONG FOURTH, FIFTH AND SIXTH GRADE STUDENTS." Duke University,
1976. 165 pp. Source: DAI, XXXVIII, 3A (September, 1977), 1279-A. XUM
Order No. 77-18,786.

Found among 2,304 4th, 5th, and 6th grade students who completed self-
observation scales that girls' responses about their relationships
with teachers were more positive than were boys' responses.

Willis, Gwendolyn Hankerson (Ph. D.). "THE EFFECT OF OCCUPATIONAL
STEREOTYPES AND SELF-PERCEPTIONS OF COLLEGE WOMEN, TRADITIONALISTS AND
NON-TRADITIONALISTS, ON OCCUPATIONAL CHOICE." Georgia State University,
School of Education, 1977. 117 pp. Source: DAI, XXXVIII, 7A (January,
1978), 3818-A. XUM Order No. 77-29,338.

Found among 160 undergraduate women in an urban university that: (1)
their occupational stereotypes and self-perceptions had significant
effect on occupational choice; (2) women who chose "male occupations"

saw themselves with "male qualities" such as aggression, achievement orientation, dominance, self-control, and independence; and (3) women who chose "female occupations" saw themselves with such qualities as nurturance, affiliation, succorance, and abasement.

Willis, Jo Ann (Ph. D.). "TRAINED PEER COUNSELOR EFFECT ON THE PERSONAL GROWTH OF FRESHMAN STUDENTS AT A PRIVATE, LIBERAL ARTS COLLEGE." Oregon State University, 1977. 124 pp. Source: DAI, XXXVII, 7A (January, 1977), 4153-A. XUM Order No. 77-339.

Freshman college students rated trained men peer dormitory counselors as more scholarly, reflective, and critical in their thinking; trained women peer dormitory counselors were rated as better adjusted emotionally and more caring of others. Under the counselors, freshman women achieved more than did freshman men.

Willman, Marilyn Dawn (Ph. D.). "ATTITUDES AND PROBLEMS OF STUDENT NURSES." University of Texas, 1961. 146 pp. Source: DAI, XXII, 6 (December, 1961), 1953-1954. XUM Order No. 61-4727.

Among nursing students found that: (1) juniors had most difficulty with personal and social adjustment and with clinical practice; (2) seniors were concerned with the future; and (3) freshmen were concerned with such maturation problems as courtship, sex, marriage, home, family, and adjustment to the nursing school.

Wilson, Beverly Dawn (Ph. D.). "SELF-PERCEPTION AND PEER PERCEPTION OF A GROUP OF COLLEGE WOMEN PHYSICAL EDUCATORS." Ohio State University, 1970. 107 pp. Source: DAI, XXXI, 7A (January, 1971), 3326-A. XUM Order No. 70-26,389.

Investigated selected perceptions of college women physical educators. Found that: (1) college male physical educators viewed the women physical educators less favorably than they viewed themselves; and (2) negative stereotyping was a problem within the physical education profession.

Wilson, Glenys (D. N. S.). "AN EVALUATIVE STUDY OF A CORE COURSE FOR HEALTH OCCUPATIONS." University of California, San Francisco, 1974. 99 pp. Source: DAI, XXXIV, 11B (May, 1974), 5536-B. XUM Order No. 74-11, 201.

A multi-sensory, self-paced course minimized differences and promoted active, individualized learning by registered nurses and medical assistants.

Wilson, Grace H. (Ph. D.). "THE RELIGIOUS AND EDUCATIONAL PHILOSOPHY OF THE YOUNG WOMEN'S CHRISTIAN ASSOCIATION." Columbia University Teachers College, 1933. 156 pp. Source: TCCU CONTRIBUTIONS No. 554, pp. 136-137.

The YWCA's chief educational role was to provide character training.

Wilson, Isabella Chilton (Ph. D.). "DETERMINING OBJECTIVES FOR HOMEMAKING INSTRUCTION." Columbia University Teachers College, 1935. 99 pp. Source: Published with subtitle: A Method of Ascertaining Relative

Worths of Certain Homemaking Abilities for the Instruction of White Students in the Junior High Schools of the Bituminous Coal Fields of Southern West Virginia; New York: Privately Printed, 1935; pp. 93-95.

For this study, a jury: (1) ranked various homemaking skills as to their value in a junior high school homemaking course designed for white children in southern West Virginia; and (2) assessed the increase in competency likely to result from teaching such homemaking skills.

Wilson, Jennifer Ann Dahlby (Ed. D.). "THE AGRICULTURAL EXTENSION MODEL'S APPLICABILITY TO CONTINUING EDUCATION IN NURSING." Columbia University Teachers College, 1976. 184 pp. Source: DAI, XXXVII, 8A (February, 1977), 4884-A. XUM Order No. 77-4198.

Researcher examined extension agriculture education as a possible model and recommended that: (1) continuing nursing education be similarly organized through University Extension; and (2) the same type of local, state, and national pattern be followed, headed by a Federal Division for Continuing Nursing Education.

Wilson, Margaret Scoon (Ph. D.). "CONFORMITY AND NONCONFORMITY OF COLLEGE GIRLS TO THE STANDARD OF THEIR PARENTS." University of Pennsylvania, 1952. 215 pp. Source: Margaret S. Wilson, "Do College Girls Conform to the Standards of Their Parents?" MARRIAGE AND FAMILY LIVING, XV, No. 3 (August, 1953), pp. 207-208.

The college girls studied generally conformed to their parents' standards.

Wilson, Marian L. (Ed. D.). "RELATIONSHIPS AMONG SELECTED VARIABLES AND THE INVOLVEMENT OF HOME ECONOMICS TEACHERS IN PROFESSIONAL GROWTH ACTIVITIES." University of Massachusetts, 1973. 154 pp. Source: DAI, XXXIV, 10B (April, 1974), 5058-B-5059-B. XUM Order No. 74-8648.

Found among 140 high school home economics teachers that those who participated in professional growth activities had higher professional commitment.

Wilson, Pauline Park (Ph. D.). "COLLEGE WOMEN WHO EXPRESS FUTILITY: A STUDY BASED ON FIFTY SELECTED LIFE HISTORIES OF WOMEN COLLEGE GRADUATES." Columbia University Teachers College, 1950. 166 pp. Source: TCCU CONTRIBUTIONS No. 956, pp. 127-135.

Conclusions: (1) parental training is largely responsible for shaping a child's pattern of life; and (2) if this pattern is too narrow and rigid, a sense of futility results.

Winder, Thelma Vivian (Ed. D.). "FINANCIAL EXPERIENCES OF FAMILIES: FAMILY FINANCIAL EXPERIENCES OF SELECTED GRADUATES OF MORGAN STATE COLLEGE AND THE IMPLICATIONS OF THESE EXPERIENCES FOR TEACHING FAMILY FINANCE." New York University, 1957. 310 pp. Source: DAI, XVIII, 3 (March, 1958), 1036-1037. XUM Order No. Mic 58-501.

Information about the family finances of 40 college graduates was used to improve the content of a college family finance course.

Wingenfield, Sister M. Grace Regina (Ph. D.). "PRACTICES IN THE ORI-
ENTATION OF FRESHMEN IN CATHOLIC COLLEGES FOR WOMEN IN THE UNITED STATES."
Fordham University, 1954. 207 pp. Source: Dissertation, pp. 167-168,
191-194.

Found that the Catholic women's colleges studied needed psychologists,
full-time counselors, and a systematic testing program to improve
women students' orientation.

Wingett, Terry Jean Hamilton (Ph. D.). "CAREER ATTITUDE MATURITY AND
SELF CONCEPT OF EIGHTH GRADE GIRLS AFTER A CAREER EDUCATION EXPERIENCE."
University of Wyoming, 1974. 170 pp. Source: DAI, XXXV, 7A (January,
1975), 4175-A. XUM Order No. 75-243.

A career education program for 8th grade girls had little effect on
mature career attitude but did improve self-concept.

Winkler, Mary Carlyle (Ed. D.). "THE LIFE STYLES OF WOMEN WITH EARNED
INDIANA UNIVERSITY DOCTORATES." Indiana University, 1968. 144 pp.
Source: DAI, XXIX, 6A (December, 1968), 1694-A. XUM Order No. 68-17,297.

Among 128 women with doctorates studied, 96% were working in education, 60% were married (69% of the married had children), and a
third reported facing obstacles because of being women.

Winsor, Helen Bruce (Ed. D.). "A SYSTEMS APPROACH TO THE DEVELOPMENT
AND EVALUATION OF MASTER'S DEGREE PROGRAMS IN HOME ECONOMICS EDUCATION."
Oklahoma State University, 1974. 219 pp. Source: DAI, XXXVI, 11A (May,
1976), 7252-A. XUM Order No. 76-9801.

Used responses from home economics educators in 42 states to evaluate
the 1971 Guidelines for Graduate Programs in Home Economics, the
first such national standards set in home economics. Found that:
(1) not all guidelines were equally important; (2) guidelines essential to a sound master's program were identifiable; and (3) flexibility was desirable in applying the guidelines.

Wirtz, Peter George (Ed. D.). "AN ANALYSIS OF ATTITUDE CHANGE AMONG
FRESHMAN WOMEN AT THE UNIVERSITY OF NEBRASKA AS A RESULT OF AN EXPERI-
MENTAL SORORITY PLEDGE EDUCATION PROGRAM." University of Nebraska, 1970.
120 pp. Source: DAI, XXXI, 8A (February, 1971), 3912-A. XUM Order No.
71-3665.

All freshman sorority women studied became more socially mature,
more religiously liberal, better able to express impulses, more auto-
nomous, more like seniors in their thinking, and more esthetic in
their interests.

Wisch, Patricia Bogin (Ed. D.). "A PROFILE OF MATURE RETURNING WOMEN
AT TEMPLE UNIVERSITY IN SEPTEMBER, 1974, AND THE EFFECTS OF A SPECIAL
SEMINAR ON THEIR LEVELS OF ANXIETY AND POTENTIAL FOR SELF-ACTUALIZATION
DURING THEIR FIRST SEMESTER." Temple University, 1976. 352 pp. Source:
DAI, XXXVII, 1A (July, 1976), 209-A-210-A. XUM Order No. 76-15,872.

Concluded that a special seminar designed for mature women during
their first semester decreased anxiety levels and increased their
potential for self-actualization.

Wiser, James Eldred (Ph. D.). "CHEMISTRY USAGE BY BOOKS AND TEACHERS IN HOME ECONOMICS COURSES." George Peabody College for Teachers, 1949. 195 pp. Source: Published; Same Title; Nashville, TN: George Peabody College for Teachers, 1949; pp. 24-29, 174-190.

Analyzed 40 books used by home economics teachers and found 972 chemical terms and explanations used in relation to foods and nutrition, clothing and textiles, and home care. Study focused on essential chemistry course needs of home economics students.

Wisniewski, Lawrence John (Ph. D.). "CHOOSING A MAN'S JOB: THE EFFECT OF SOCIALIZATION ON FEMALE OCCUPATIONAL ENTRY." McMaster University (Canada), 1977. Source: DAI, XXXVIII, 7A (January, 1978), 4397-A-4398-A.

Author compared women in such traditional jobs as elementary school teacher and nursing assistant with women in such nontraditional jobs as pharmacist and policewoman. Found that: (1) socialization experiences provided occupational orientation leading to job goals; and (2) professional women more than non-professional women valued education and did well in school.

Wissman, Sally Wile (Ed. D.). "A COMPARATIVE STUDY OF PLACEMENT AGENCIES FOR WOMEN OFFICE WORKERS, WITH SPECIAL REFERENCE TO SCHOOL PLACEMENT AND GUIDANCE PROGRAMS." Harvard University, 1939. Source: Author.

Studied the public school's role in preparing and placing women graduates in jobs in Boston and other urban areas.

Withycombe-Brocato, Carol Jean (Ph. D.). "THE MATURE GRADUATE WOMAN STUDENT: WHO IS SHE?" United States International University, 1969. 384 pp. Source: DAI, XXXI, 5B (November, 1970), 2973-B-2974-B. XUM Order No. 70-20,716.

Found that the typical mature woman graduate student: (1) was about 40 years of age, married, with 2 or 3 children; (2) had parents with more than a high school education who were self-employed, professional, or businessmen and women; and (3) was married to a college-educated professional.

Witkin, Mildred Hope (Ph. D.). "THE RELATIONSHIP BETWEEN PERSONALITY FACTORS AND ATTITUDES TOWARD WOMEN'S ROLES AND THE CAREER ASPIRATIONS OF FEMALE COLLEGE STUDENTS." New York University, 1973. 179 pp. Source: DAI, XXXIV, 4A (October, 1973), 1664-A-1665-A. XUM Order No. 73-19,456.

Found a moderately high correlation between career aspirations and attitudes toward women's roles; a moderately low correlation between career aspirations and autonomy, intellectual disposition, and response bias; and very low correlation between career aspirations, femininity, and grade point average.

Wittmann, Margaret Elaine (Ed. D.). "NURSING EDUCATION IN THE FEDERAL REPUBLIC OF GERMANY." Columbia University, 1970. 257 pp. Source: DAI, XXXII, 6B (December, 1971), 3459-B-3460-B. XUM Order No. 72-1266.

Surveyed 19th and 20th century pre-nursing preparation, nursing education curriculum, and professional nursing duties in 20 West German nursing schools. Recommendations were given for improving West German nursing education along with implications for improving U. S. nursing education programs.

Woerner, Janet Beth (Ed. D.). "A COMPARISON OF MEN AND WOMEN TEACHERS IN COMPREHENSIVE HIGH SCHOOLS AND MEN AND WOMEN TEACHERS IN VOCATIONAL SCHOOLS ON TEN FACTORS RELATING TO WOMEN'S WORK ROLE." Rutgers University, 1976. 120 pp. Source: DAI, XXXVII, 12A, Part 1 (June, 1977), 7658-A. XUM Order No. 77-13,298.

Significant differences were noted between 196 men and women teachers in vocational high schools on such factors as: partner, economic mobility, and challenge. Recommended that stereotyped sex roles be dispelled in the professional preparation of both men and women high school teachers.

Wolf, Margret S. (Ed. D.). "NURSES' VIEWS OF AN IDEAL PSYCHIATRIC WARD." Columbia University Teachers College, 1975. 125 pp. Source: DAI, XXXVI, 9B (March, 1976), 4386-B. XUM Order No. 76-5498.

The more education psychiatric nurses had, the more they preferred a structured work situation, clarity of rules and order, and limited patient autonomy. Nurses educated outside the U. S. preferred more staff-patient interaction than did nurses educated in the U. S.

Wolf, Robin Vair (Ph. D.). "THE VALUE CHANGE THEORY OF FEMALE EDUCATIONAL PARTICIPATION AND PROFESSIONAL EMPLOYMENT: A CRITIQUE IN THE LIGHT OF THE EVIDENCE." University of California, Berkeley, 1977. 312 pp. Source: DAI, XXXVIII, 8A (February, 1978), 5071-A. XUM Order No. 77-31,592.

Critique of Betty Friedan's value change theory in her Feminine Mystique. Author believed that college-educated women have continually led all other women in the work force because: (1) they had fewer children and were thus better able to enter professional work in middle life ("work choice"); and (2) their husbands supported their working because it raised family standard of living ("income utilization").

Wolfe, Delight (Ed. D.). "THE CONCEPT OF AUTHORITY AND ITS IMPLICATIONS FOR NURSING EDUCATION." Boston University School of Education, 1973. 312 pp. Source: DAI, XXXIV, 4A (October, 1973), 1564-A-1565-A. XUM Order No. 73-23,631.

Author redefined authority as individual and group relationships to achieve human welfare and applied this definition toward eliminating sex bias in nursing education.

Wolfson, Karen Thelma Peyser (Ph. D.). "CAREER DEVELOPMENT OF COLLEGE WOMEN." University of Minnesota, 1972. 148 pp. Source: DAI, XXXIII, 1A (July, 1972), 169-A. XUM Order No. 72-20,160.

Variables related to education and marriage were the most powerful predictors of college women's vocational patterns. Career commitment correlated closely with amount of education.

Wolkon, Kenneth A. (Ph. D.). "PREDICTION OF PIONEER VOCATIONAL CHOICE IN COLLEGE WOMEN." Boston College, 1970. 133 pp. Source: DAI, XXXI, 5A (November, 1970), 2121-A-2122-A. XUM Order No. 70-22,800.

Found that working women were either "pioneers" (i.e., employed in fields dominated by at least 75% men) or "traditional" (i.e., employed in fields commonly dominated by women). Among findings: (1) "pioneers" demanded that rewards be intrinsic; (2) more Jewish than Catholic women were "pioneers"; and (3) "pioneers" tended to be second born ("traditionals," first born).

Wolters, Patrice Ruth (Ph. D.). "PRESCHOOL CHILDREN'S IMITATION OF SHARING BEHAVIOR AS A FUNCTION OF AGE OF MODEL, SEX OF MODEL, AND SEX OF SUBJECT." University of Oregon, 1976. 138 pp. Source: DAI, XXXVII, 6A (December, 1976), 3390-A-3391-A. XUM Order No. 76-27,695.

Preschool girls and boys (56 of each) tended to imitate older models more than they imitated same-age models in one instance of sharing, but not in another instance of sharing.

Womack, Jan George (Ph. D.). "A STUDY OF MOTIVATOR AND HYGIENE FACTORS OF ADULT WOMEN STUDENTS IN NURSING PROGRAMS AT AREA VOCATIONAL-TECHNICAL SCHOOLS." University of Oklahoma, 1976. 83 pp. Source: DAI, XXXVII, 12A, Part 1 (June, 1977), 7477-A. XUM Order No. 77-12,764.

Found that achievement, recognition, and work itself were satisfying to women practical nursing students and helped motivate them to succeed.

Wong, John C. (Ed. D.). "THE EFFECT OF INSTRUCTION IN HEALTH OCCUPATIONS AND OF VOCATIONAL INTEREST APPRAISAL ON THE PREFERENCE OF HEALTH OCCUPATIONS AMONG FEMALE COLLEGE FRESHMEN AND SOPHOMORES." University of Missouri, Columbia, 1971. 185 pp. Source: DAI, XXXIII, 1A (July, 1972), 233-A-234-A. XUM Order No. 72-10,567.

The preferences for health occupations in an experimental group of women were significantly different after a 3-month health occupation exploration program; the control group was almost unchanged.

Wood, Ada May (Ed. D.). "EMPLOYMENT OPPORTUNITIES FOR WOMEN IN CALIFORNIA." Stanford University, 1952. 174 pp. Source: Dissertation, pp. 165-167.

Found that: (1) job discrimination was widespread against women; and (2) employment patterns of white and black women and women of other races were very dissimilar. Recommended improving job counseling procedures.

Wood, George Kipling (Ph. D.). "ACADEMIC ACHIEVEMENT AND ATHLETIC PARTICIPATION AMONG COLLEGE WOMEN." University of Maryland, 1975. 141 pp. Source: DAI, XXXVI, 10A (April, 1976), 6538-A. XUM Order No. 76-8458.

Found that the academic achievement of women athletes and non-athletes did not differ. The academic achievement of athletes was not predicted to the same positive degree as for non-athletes.

Wood, Paul Leslie (Ed. D.). "THE RELATIONSHIP OF THE COLLEGE CHARAC-
TERISTICS INDEX TO ACHIEVEMENT AND CERTAIN OTHER VARIABLES FOR FRESHMAN
WOMEN IN THE COLLEGE OF EDUCATION AT THE UNIVERSITY OF GEORGIA." University of Georgia, 1963. 185 pp. Source: DAI, XXIV, 11 (May, 1964),
4558. XUM Order No. 64-4459.

Study measured the relationship between entering freshman women's
perceptions of the college environment and their academic ability,
home, family, and religion.

Wood, Shirley Jean (Ph. D.). "RECIPROCAL ROLE EXPECTATIONS OF WOMEN
PHYSICAL EDUCATION TEACHERS AND CHAIRMEN." University of Illinois at Urbana-Champaign, 1971. 176 pp. Source: DAI, XXXII, 8A (February, 1972),
4407-A. XUM Order No. 72-7114.

College women physical education teachers were satisfied with their
department chairperson's leadership to the degree that they saw their
own expectations and that of their administrators as similar.

Woods, Mary Jane (Ph. D.). "VARIATIONS IN FACULTY ROLE ORIENTATION
RELATED TO SEX, MARITAL STATUS AND FACULTY RANK." University of Texas at
Austin, 1975. 313 pp. Source: DAI, XXXVI, 10A (April, 1976), 6573-A-
6574-A. XUM Order No. 76-8128.

Studied faculty according to sex, marital status, and faculty rank.
Found: (1) single women valued altruism, intellectual stimulation,
and achievement more than single men did; and (2) no significant
differences between faculty men and women in male-female attributes.

Wooten, Mattie Lloyd (Ph. D.). "THE STATUS OF WOMEN IN TEXAS." University of Texas at Austin, 1941. 431 pp. Source: Dissertation, p. ix.

The chapter, "Women and Education," discussed women students, women
faculty, and women administrators in Texas public schools and in
higher education.

Worden, Vincent James (Ed. D.). "THE INFLUENCE OF A PARENT EDUCATION
PROGRAM ON EDUCATIONAL ACHIEVEMENT AND ASPIRATION AMONG PORTUGUESE IMMI-
GRANT YOUTH." Clark University, 1975. 109 pp. Source: DAI, XXXVI, 8A
(February, 1976), 5169-A. XUM Order No. 76-2570.

Evaluated the influence of a parent education program on the educational achievement and aspiration of Portuguese immigrant youth with
an 80%-90% drop out rate. Found that children from small families,
especially girls, tended to remain in school longer.

Work, Gerald George (Ph. D.). "CORRELATES OF ACADEMIC ACHIEVEMENT
FOR FEMALE SOPHOMORE ELEMENTARY EDUCATION MAJORS." Ohio University,
1967. 110 pp. Source: DAI, XXVIII, 8A (February, 1968), 2926-A-2927-A.
XUM Order No. 68-1963.

Found that the academic achievement of female sophomore elementary
education majors resulted, in part, from their desire either to conform or to assert their independence.

Wozniak, Dolores Ann (Ed. D.). "A DESCRIPTIVE STUDY OF THE CLINICAL LABORATORY EXPERIENCE IN ASSOCIATE DEGREE NURSING PROGRAMS." Columbia University, 1971. 171 pp. Source: DAI, XXXII, 3A (September, 1971), 1406-A-1407-A. XUM Order No. 71-24,171.

Concluded that teachers in associate degree nursing programs used the principles of learning readiness, relatedness, motivation, success, and failure better than they used principles of purposefulness, individualization, and discovery.

Wright, Jeanette Tornow (Ed. D.). "A STUDY OF STUDENT PERSONNEL SERVICES IN JUNIOR COLLEGES FOR WOMEN IN NEW ENGLAND." Boston University School of Education, 1967. 392 pp. Source: DAI, XXIX, 12A, Part I (June, 1969), 4210-A-4211-A. XUM Order No. 69-7838.

Student personnel services in women's junior colleges varied considerably. Schools with programs in addition to liberal arts had significantly more services. Major deficiencies were sex education and personal counseling.

Wright, Lorraine Mae (Ph. D.). "NURSING STUDENTS' ACQUISITION OF THERAPEUTIC COUNSELOR CHARACTERISTICS." Brigham Young University, 1975. 121 pp. Source: DAI, XXXVI, 11B (May, 1976), 5516-B. XUM Order No. 76-686.

Associate degree nursing students scored higher than did baccalaureate nursing students on therapeutic counselor characteristics.

Wu, Wu-tien (Ph. D.). "CLASSROOM CLIMATES IN CHINESE AND AMERICAN ELEMENTARY SCHOOLS: A CROSS-CULTURAL STUDY." University of Kentucky, 1975. 204 pp. Source: DAI, XXXVI, 10A (April, 1976), 6575-A. XUM Order No. 76-7741.

Found that classroom climate affected academic performance more directly than did intelligence test scores. Within both Chinese and American groups, boys and girls differed but both sexes were influenced by classroom climate.

Wuhl, Gloria Bleier (Ph. D.). "SEX DIFFERENCES IN TEACHERS' GENDER EXPECTATIONS ABOUT READING AND THEIR RELATIONSHIP TO TEACHER-STUDENT INTERACTION AND FIRST GRADE READING ACHIEVEMENT." University of Pennsylvania, 1976. 117 pp. Source: DAI, XXXVII, 11A (May, 1977), 7053-A. XUM Order No. 77-10,237.

This study focused on teacher-pupil interaction during 1st grade reading instruction as related to pupil gender. Found that pupil reading achievement related directly to teacher expectations and indirectly to classroom behavior.

Wuterich, Joan Gale (Ph. D.). "JUAN LUIS VIVES' THE INSTRUCTION OF THE CHRISTIAN WOMAN: A CRITICAL EVALUATION AND TRANSLATION." Boston College, 1969. 373 pp. Source: DAI, XXX, 9A (March, 1970), 3752-A. XUM Order No. 70-3381.

A translation and critical evaluation of Vives' The Instruction of Christian Women, considered the first modern comprehensive statement of principles of female education.

Wybourn, Marjory Ada (Ed. D.). "PROPOSALS FOR IMPROVING THE CLOTHING AND TEXTILE EDUCATIONAL EXPERIENCES OF HOME ECONOMICS STUDENTS FROM OTHER LANDS." Columbia University Teachers College, 1958. Source: TCCU DI-GESTS (1958), pp. 701-702.

Young women (214) from 50 countries suggested ways to make clothing and textile programs in U. S. colleges and universities more functional. They suggested: (1) more flexible programs; and (2) more effective communication between students and teachers.

Yaczola, Sophia (Ed. D.). "PROFESSIONAL LABORATORY EXPERIENCES FOR TEACHERS OF NURSING IN ASSOCIATE DEGREE NURSING PROGRAMS." Columbia University, 1964. 190 pp. Source: DAI, XXVI, 1 (July, 1965), 217-218. XUM Order No. 65-4769.

Study elicited suggestions to improve the laboratory experiences of those preparing to become teachers of nurses in associate degree nursing programs.

Yanico, Barbara Jean (Ph. D.). "SEX BIAS IN CAREER INFORMATION: EF-FECTS OF LANGUAGE ON ATTITUDES." Ohio State University, 1977. 183 pp. Source: DAI, XXXVIII, 5B (November, 1977), 2441-B-2442-B. XUM Order No. 77-24,728.

Found among 45 men and 45 women college students that, even after reading material aimed at reducing sex bias in occupations, they still rated 20 occupations somewhat along sex-biased lines.

Yager, Barbara (Ed. D.). "SOME CHARACTERISTICS OF WOMEN WHO HAVE CHOSEN COLLEGE TEACHING IN PHYSICAL EDUCATION." University of Southern California, 1964. 112 pp. Source: DAI, XXIV, 12 (June, 1964), 5182. XUM Order No. 64-7154.

Found that 422 women entering college physical education teaching: (1) included over 75% from the middle class; (2) had undergraduate physical education major; (3) had taught either elementary or secondary school; (4) were not married and were under age 30; (5) had wanted to work with college students; and (6) had earned a master's degree.

Yehia, May Ahdab (Ph. D.). "ATTITUDES TOWARDS WOMEN'S WORK COMMIT-MENT: CHANGES FROM 1964 TO 1975." Wayne State University, 1976. 238 pp. Source: DAI, XXXVII, 5A (November, 1976), 3215-A. XUM Order No. 76-26,195.

Women students in 1964 had a medium to high work commitment pattern while in 1974 more women wanted to have a full range of careers.

Yerxa, Elizabeth June (Ed. D.). "THE EFFECTS OF A DYADIC, SELF-AD-MINISTERED INSTRUCTIONAL PROGRAM IN CHANGING THE ATTITUDES OF FEMALE COL-LEGE STUDENTS TOWARD PHYSICALLY DISABLED PERSONS." Boston University School of Education, 1971. 226 pp. Source: DAI, XXXII, 4A (October, 1971), 1931-A-1932-A. XUM Order No. 71-26,749.

Tested and validated a self-instruction program that changed the attitudes of women college students toward the physically disabled.

Yingling, Doris Beaumont (Ed. D.). "A DESCRIPTIVE STUDY OF THE DEVEL-
OPMENTAL PROCESS INVOLVED IN ENCOURAGING COOPERATIVE EDUCATIONAL PLANNING
USING THREE HOSPITAL SCHOOLS OF NURSING IN BALTIMORE, MARYLAND." Univer-
sity of Maryland, 1956. 158 pp. Source: DAI, XVI, 12 (1956), 2431-2432.
XUM Order No. 17,826.

Described the group meetings, discussions, and agreements worked out
when 3 nearby hospital schools of nursing began to cooperate in their
nursing education programs.

You, In Jong (Ph. D.). "THE IMPACT OF THE AMERICAN PROTESTANT MIS-
SIONS ON KOREAN EDUCATION FROM 1885 TO 1932." University of North Carolina
at Chapel Hill, 1967. 324 pp. Source: DAI, XXVIII, 8A (February, 1968),
2999-A. XUM Order No. 68-2254.

Protestant missions, 1885-1932, which pioneered in women's education
(including higher education), laid the foundations for Korea's modern
educational system.

Young, Alberta (Ph. D.). "FURTHERING GOOD HUMAN RELATIONSHIPS; RE-
SOURCE MATERIALS ON HUMAN RELATIONSHIPS DESIGNED FOR USE IN A TEACHER ED-
UCATION PROGRAM FOR HIGH SCHOOL TEACHERS OF HOME ECONOMICS." Ohio State
University, 1945. 552 pp. Source: Dissertation, pp. 522-539.

Resource materials were developed for use with prospective home economics teachers to help improve human relations in the classroom.
These resource materials showed how everyday situations were handled
and should enable to students to learn democratic relations with
stress on: (1) helping others see the goals; (2) earning others'
respect; (3) securing cooperation; (4) controlling conflict situations; and (5) improving techniques for persuasion.

Young, Barbara Jean Hicks (Ed. D.). "A STUDY OF MOTHERS ON PUBLIC
ASSISTANCE IN A COMMUNITY COLLEGE." Indiana University, 1974. 126 pp.
Source: DAI, XXXV, 9A (March, 1975), 5881-A-5882-A. XUM Order No. 75-
5585.

Studied welfare mothers enrolled in Jefferson College, KY, sponsored
by the Work Incentive Program of the Department of Public Assistance.
Found among those responding that: (1) over half finished 1 year;
(2) 60% had a 2 point average; (3) 60% had improvements in self-
image, confidence, and determination to pursue goals; (4) half had
increased interest in social and political issues and their children's education; and (5) 30% hoped for a better economic situation.
Reasons some could not continue in college were financial, academic,
and/or personal.

Young, Elizabeth Barber (Ph. D.). "THE CURRICULUM OF THE WOMAN'S
COLLEGE OF THE SOUTHERN STATES." Columbia University Teachers College,
1930. 218 pp. Source: TCCU DIGESTS, VI (1929-1931), pp. 1-4.

Studied private women's colleges in 6 Southern states. Found more
uniformity than diversity in organization and in the number and types
of subjects required for entrance and graduation.

Young, Leila Rosen (Ph. D.). "CAREER COMMITMENT, SEX ROLES, AND COL-LEGE EDUCATION." State University of New York at Stony Brook, 1976. 158 pp. Source: DAI, XXXVII, 3A (September, 1976), 1815-A-1816-A. XUM Order No. 76-19,697.

Among 1,400 senior men and women at the University of Michigan, found that women: (1) had lower occupational goals; (2) felt that a career and family conflicted; and (3) thought vocational education and a full liberal arts education were incompatible.

Young, Lucie Stirm (Ph. D.). "A FRAME OF REFERENCE FOR NURSING EDUCA-TION." University of Pittsburgh, 1965. 251 pp. Source: DAI, XXVII, 4B (October, 1966), 1202-B. XUM Order No. 66-8187.

Examined 435 publications to study concepts of nursing held by nurses, hospital administrators, and the public. Findings substantiated nur-ses' multi-dimensional roles, including giving leadership and working as part of a health team.

Young, Robert Arch (Ed. D.). "RESULTS OF VALUES CLARIFICATION TRAIN-ING ON THE SELF-CONCEPT OF BLACK FEMALE UPPERCLASS RESIDENCE HALL STU-DENTS AT MISSISSIPPI STATE UNIVERSITY." Mississippi State University, 1977. 47 pp. Source: DAI, XXXVIII, 7A (January, 1978), 3967-A. XUM Order No. 77-28,575.

Self-concepts were unchanged after black women upperclassmen used leading values clarification sourcebooks and engaged in training sessions about values.

Young, Wanda Ena (Ph. D.). "FAMILY STUDIES PROGRAM DEVELOPMENT AT THE COLLEGE LEVEL: A DELPHI STUDY." Michigan State University, 1977. 223 pp. Source: DAI, XXXVIII, 3A (September, 1977), 1266-A. XUM Order No. 77-18,568.

Agreed that the family studies program should give an understanding of human development, communication, and integrative processes to help individuals and families improve the management of food, shelter, textiles, and human relationships.

Young, William H., III (Ed. D.). "STUDENT DECISIONS AS A FACTOR IN MASTER'S DEGREE PROGRAMS IN NURSING." Pennsylvania State University, 1976. 163 pp. Source: DAI, XXXVII, 11A (May, 1977), 6990-A-6991-A. XUM Order No. 77-9778.

Found that the primary reasons nurses enroll in post-baccalaureate educational programs are to satisfy their desire for autonomy, cre-ativity, responsibility, persuasiveness, and achievement.

Youngen, Lois Joy (Ph. D.). "ATTITUDES TOWARD PHYSICAL ACTIVITY AS A FUNCTION OF THE APPROVAL MOTIVE IN FIRST-YEAR COLLEGE WOMEN." Ohio State University, 1971. 170 pp. Source: DAI, XXXII, 11A (May, 1972), 6176-A-6177-A. XUM Order No. 72-15,332.

There was conflicting evidence regarding whether or not 196 college freshman women engaged in physical activities because of their need for social approval.

Youngner, Alva Haynes (Ed. D.). "THE PROFESSIONAL COMMITMENT OF GEORGIA HOME ECONOMICS TEACHERS, AND ITS RELATIONSHIP WITH SELECTED ACTIV- ITIES."   University of Georgia, 1977. 137 pp. Source: DAI, XXXVIII, 7A (January, 1978), 3990-A-3991-A. XUM Order No. 77-29,820.

Found a high professional commitment among Georgia home economics teachers, which could be predicted by professional journals read regu- larly and professional organization offices held.

Youssef, Nadia Haggag (Ph. D.). "SOCIAL STRUCTURE AND FEMALE LABOR FORCE PARTICIPATION IN DEVELOPING COUNTRIES: A COMPARISON OF LATIN AMER- ICAN AND MIDDLE EASTERN COUNTRIES." University of California, Berkeley, 1970. 299 pp. Source: DAI, XXXI, 7A (January, 1971), 3670-A. XUM Or- der No. 71-871.

Analyzed the difference in non-agricultural employment of women in Latin America (Roman Catholic Chile and Mexico) and the Middle East (Muslim Egypt, Morocco, and Pakistan). Found that: (1) the Middle East had low women's employment and Latin America had high women's employment; (2) different employment rates resulted from differences in women's reactions to work opportunities rather than the labor market demands; (3) both areas have traditional social orders that discourage women from working; but (4) in Latin America the clergy's authority and male control have collapsed as ethnic and class differ- ences have widened.

Yu, Miriam (Ph. D.). "AN EXPLORATORY STUDY OF WOMEN IN TRADITIONALLY MALE PROFESSIONS AND TRADITIONALLY FEMALE PROFESSIONS AND THE ROLE OF CREATIVITY IN THEIR CAREER CHOICES." University of Michigan, 1972. 220 pp. Source: DAI, XXXIV, 1A (July, 1973), 181-A. XUM Order No. 73-16, 357.

Among 211 Michigan professional women found that: (1) women in trad- itionally male positions were more outgoing, less intelligent, more venturesome, more practical, and more natural; (2) women in tradi- tionally female roles were more rigid and imaginative; (3) creative professional women in traditionally male professions were less sophis- ticated, less reserved, but more venturesome than the creative women in traditionally female professions; (4) all creative professional women were reserved, intelligent, assertive, sensitive, imaginative, adventurous, experimenting, self-assured, and self-sufficient; and (5) creative women married later and had more marital conflict.

Yurchuck, Elizabeth Ruth (Ed. D.). "PLANNING NURSING CARE: COMPE- TENCE AND ATTITUDES OF SENIOR STUDENTS IN SELECTED BACCALAUREATE NURSING PROGRAMS." Columbia University Teachers College, 1976. 172 pp. Source: DAI, XXXVI, 12B (June, 1976), 6076-B. XUM Order No. 76-13,502.

Most senior baccalaureate nursing students studied favored planning nursing care, but demonstrated questionable competence in actual planning.

Zaky-el-Deen, Magda (Ed. D.). "THE EFFECT OF TWO MODES OF PRESENTA- TION OF CAREER INFORMATION AND OTHER SELECTED VARIABLES UPON THE ATTITUDES TOWARD PROFESSIONAL EDUCATION IN NURSING AMONG NINTH GRADE STUDENTS IN CATHOLIC HIGH SCHOOLS." New York University, 1972. 120 pp. Source: DAI, XXXIII, 12A (June, 1973), 6812-A-6813-A. XUM Order No. 73-8209.

Studied attitudes of 9th grade girls toward professional nursing education. Found that: (1) neither a film on nursing education nor a lecture based on the film affected their attitudes toward nursing education; (2) intelligence was not directly related to attitudes toward nursing education; and (3) attitudes toward nursing education were not related to the girls' socio-economic status. Concluded that better interpretation of nursing was needed to improve nursing recruitment.

Zardus, Joan Lois (Ph. D.). "THE EFFECT OF A RELAXATION TRAINING PROGRAM ON THE DEVELOPMENT OF BADMINTON IN COLLEGE WOMEN." Boston University, 1972. Source: Abstract from Dissertation.

Found no differences in badminton skills in a group of college women who used an experimental relaxation training program.

Zasowska, Sister Mary Aloiseanne (Ed. D.). "A DESCRIPTIVE SURVEY OF SIGNIFICANT FACTORS IN THE CLINICAL LABORATORY EXPERIENCE IN BACCALAUREATE EDUCATION FOR NURSING." Columbia University, 1967. 258 pp. Source: DAI, XXVIII, 4B (October, 1967), 1591-B-1592-B. XUM Order No. 67-12,714.

Study made recommendations on the better use of the clinical laboratory experience, based on responses from 214 teachers in 81 U. S. baccalaureate nursing programs.

Zeaman, Jean Burgdorf (Ph. D.). "SOME OF THE PERSONALITY ATTRIBUTES RELATED TO ACHIEVEMENT IN COLLEGE: A COMPARISON OF MEN AND WOMEN STUDENTS." Michigan State University, 1956. 99 pp. Source: DAI, XVIII, 1 (January, 1958), 290-291. XUM Order No. 21,399.

Comparisons of achieving men students with low achieving men students and achieving women students with low achieving women students revealed that: (1) low achieving men had more tension, anxiety, depression, and insecurity than men achievers; (2) no such differences existed between women; and (3) anxiety affected men's school performance but did not affect women's performance. One conclusion was that society's greater demands and expectations for men account for low achieving men's problems and conflicts in school.

Zebas, Carole Jean (P. E. D.). "REWARD AND VISUAL FEEDBACK RELATIVE TO THE PERFORMANCE AND MECHANICAL EFFICIENCY OF HIGH SCHOOL GIRLS IN THE STANDING BROAD JUMP." Indiana University, 1974. 122 pp. Source: DAI, XXXV, 7A (January, 1975), 4237-A-4238-A. XUM Order No. 75-1544.

Neither videotaped feedback nor monetary reward affected high school girls' performance in the standing broad jump.

Zehr, Sherrill Ann (Ph. D.). "THE NURSING DEANSHIP: A FUNCTIONAL ROLE ANALYSIS WITH IMPLICATIONS FOR DECANAL ROLE PREPARATION." University of Minnesota, 1975. 217 pp. Source: DAI, XXXVII, 1B (July, 1976), 156-B-157-B. XUM Order No. 76-15,009.

A profile of deans of 117 accredited baccalaureate nursing programs showed that: (1) most were over age 50; (2) most had held their present positions for 5 years or less; (3) most had been teachers of nursing; (4) a third had clinical nursing experience; (5) over 2/3 had doctorates; (6) 42% had received their highest degree within the last 10 years; (7) few had been nursing majors at the doctoral level; and (8) deans in larger, graduate nursing schools gave less time to student affairs and more time to administration and to public relations. Concluded that the deanship was a middle management position with diversified functions.

Ziegler, Rosilene (Ph. D.). "SEX DIFFERENCES IN CAUSAL ATTRIBUTION FOR ACHIEVEMENT." University of North Carolina at Chapel Hill, 1976. 132 pp. Source: DAI, XXXVIII, 2B (August, 1977), 924-B. XUM Order No. 77-17,501.

Found that women graduate students in female fields feared success and lacked self-confidence. Women in male fields, unlike men in those fields, had a stronger belief in the recurrence of successes and attributed their academic failures to lack of effort.

Ziegler, Shirley Melat (Ph. D.). "ANDROGYNY IN NURSING: NURSE ROLE EXPECTATION, SATISFACTION, ACADEMIC ACHIEVEMENT, AND SELF-ACTUALIZATION IN MALE AND FEMALE STUDENTS." University of Texas at Austin, 1977. 155 pp. Source: DAI, XXXVIII, 5B (November, 1977), 2124-B. XUM Order No. 77-23,056.

Data from 121 junior and senior male and female nursing students on sex-role orientation, nurse-role orientation, and academic achievement revealed that: (1) juniors described the typical nurse as non-sex biased and seniors were unconcerned about sex bias in nurses; (2) females had higher grade point average; and (3) junior males had higher grade point average than senior males but senior males had higher grades than junior females. The conclusion was that sex-role orientation of nurses was not significant.

Zimders, Signy Ruth (Ph. D.). "EMPLOYMENT PATTERNS OF WOMEN AND ETHNIC PERSONS IN SCHOOL ADMINISTRATIVE POSITIONS IN FORTY-NINE DISTRICTS IN THE SEVEN COUNTY MINNEAPOLIS-ST. PAUL METROPOLITAN AREA." University of Minnesota, 1976. 196 pp. Source: DAI, XXXVII, 12A, Part 1 (June, 1977), 7471-A. XUM Order No. 77-12,882.

Found in the Minneapolis-St. Paul (MN) area during 1969-74 that: (1) women principals and superintendents numbered fewer than 3%; (2) the number of women secondary school teachers dropped slightly; and (3) ethnic personnel remained below 2%.

Zimmer, Sister M. Kathryn (Ph. D.). "ROLE OF AMERICAN BENEDICTINE INSTITUTIONS OF HIGHER EDUCATION FOR WOMEN." Catholic University of America, 1962. 170 pp. Source: DAI, XXIII, 9 (March, 1963), 3264-3265. XUM Order No. 63-304.

Survey of 14 Benedictine higher education institutions for women showed the following values which have primacy in 20th century education: importance of worship, high regard for intellectual and manual labor, importance of the family, moderation, and respect for authority.

Zimmerman, Jeanne Noll (Ed. D.). "THE STATUS OF WOMEN IN EDUCATIONAL ADMINISTRATIVE POSITIONS WITHIN THE CENTRAL OFFICES OF PUBLIC SCHOOLS."

Temple University, 1971. 242 pp. Source: DAI, XXXII, 4A (October, 1971), 1826-A. XUM Order No. 71-26,538.

Found from studying 167 Pennsylvania women public school administrators that: (1) over half held positions that did not exist 5 years previously; (2) 65% had not held other leadership positions; (3) 80% had taught an average of 14.8 years; (4) over 74% had jobs concerned with instruction; (5) 60% were offered their jobs without applying for them; and (6) 60% had no aspirations beyond their present job.

Zimmerman, Patricia Ann (Ph. D.). "THE EFFECT OF SELECTED VISUAL AIDS ON THE LEARNING OF BADMINTON SKILLS BY COLLEGE WOMEN." University of Iowa, 1970. 166 pp. Source: DAI, XXXI, 9A (March, 1971), 4534-A-4535-A. XUM Order No. 71-5852.

It was found that the extra use of videotape instruction with an experimental group of women physical education majors did not enable them to learn badminton skills significantly better than a control group receiving normal instruction.

Zimmerman, Ruth Larson (Ph. D.). "AUTOBIOGRAPHICAL STUDIES OF FRESHMAN COLLEGE WOMEN FOR APPRAISAL OF PERSONAL AND SOCIAL ADJUSTMENT." University of Wisconsin, 1949. 491 pp. Source: Dissertation, pp. 467-468.

Studied 240 freshman women's autobiographical essays to identify their ideals, moral values, and motivation. Found that the essays revealed such details as social adjustment, family relationships, and influential persons outside the family. Recommended that guidance personnel have access to the essays to assist them in counseling.

Zissis, Cecelia (Ph. D.). "THE RELATIONSHIP OF SELECTED VARIABLES TO THE CAREER-MARRIAGE PLANS OF UNIVERSITY FRESHMAN WOMEN." University of Michigan, 1962. 273 pp. Source: DAI, XXIII, 1 (July, 1962), 128-129. XUM Order No. 62-2812.

Marriage and career plans of 550 women college freshmen showed that: (1) the career group had masculine traits, more working mothers, and career plans that required education beyond the baccalaureate degree; and (2) the marriage group had feminine personality traits, more educated fathers, and career plans easily entered with a high school education and minimal college training.

Zuckerman, Diana M. (Ph. D.). "SELF-CONCEPT, FAMILY BACKGROUND, AND PERSONAL TRAITS WHICH PREDICT THE LIFE GOALS AND SEX-ROLE ATTITUDES OF TECHNICAL COLLEGE AND UNIVERSITY WOMEN." Ohio State University, 1977. 115 pp. Source: DAI, XXXVIII, 8B (February, 1978), 3923-B-3924-B. XUM Order No. 77-32,016.

At two 2-year technical colleges and 4 universities, examined educational and career goals, career commitment, and sex-role attitudes of 541 women students (3 groups: 455 whites, ages 18-25; 40 blacks, ages 18-25; 46 whites over age 26). Found that: (1) these women were more nontraditional (than a general sample) as to career goals, career commitment, and attitudes toward women; (2) the 3 groups responded similarly on major variables; (3) black women had signifi-

cantly lower scores than white women on attitudes toward women; (4)
older white women expected greater career commitment than did younger
white women; (5) unconventionality and nonreligiousness predicted
nontraditional goals and/or attitudes; and (6) mother's education
predicted higher education goals.

Zumbrun, Arleen Farris (Ed. D.). "COMPARISON OF ATTITUDES OF SUPER-
INTENDENTS AND BOARD OF EDUCATION PRESIDENTS IN INDIANA CONCERNING THE
EFFECTIVENESS OF WOMEN AS PUBLIC SCHOOL ADMINISTRATORS." Ball State Uni-
versity, 1976. 127 pp. Source: DAI, XXXVII, 10A (April, 1977), 6214-A.
XUM Order No. 77-7620.

Found that attitudes toward women school administrators differed significantly: (1) between superintendents and school board presidents;
and (2) between superintendents and male school board presidents compared with female school board presidents. Concluded that: (1)
these different attitudes toward women school administrators might
cause serious conflict; (2) the most favorable circumstances for a
woman administrator were a large district, an earned doctorate, and
relative youth with fewer than 10 years' administrative experience;
and (3) affirmative action alone did not improve women administrators'
employment opportunities.

Zungolo, Eileen Elizabeth Hendrick (Ed. D.). "A SYSTEMS ANALYSIS OF
CLINICAL LABORATORY EXPERIENCES IN BACCALAUREATE NURSING EDUCATION."
Columbia University, 1972. 288 pp. Source: DAI, XXXII, 12A (June,
1972), 6697-A-6698-A. XUM Order No. 72-17,230.

Concluded that student nurses' laboratory experiences, generally
thought highly important to their training, failed to integrate nursing theory with nursing practice.

Zwanger, Lea D. (Ed. D.). "PREPARATION OF GRADUATE NURSES IN ISRAEL,
1918-1965." Columbia University, 1968. 444 pp. Source: DAI, XXXI, 2B
(August, 1970), 776-B. XUM Order No. 70-13,785.

Traced the development of Israeli nursing education during 1918-65
(largely instituted by U. S.-prepared nurses), the assimilation and
re-education of foreign-trained nurses, and the education of African
nurses in Israel. Concluded that graduate nurse education must be
a part of Israel's higher education system and should reflect the
country's particular conditions.

Zweifach, Marilyn S. (Ph. D.). "EFFECTS OF A CROSS-AGE TUTORING
THERAPY PROGRAM FOR DISADVANTAGED ADOLESCENT GIRLS." Boston University,
1974. 142 pp. Source: DAI, XXXIV, 9B (March, 1974), 4682-B. XUM Order No. 74-7617.

Author attempted with mixed success to increase the self-esteem and
maturity of 30 disadvantaged girls aged 12-16 by combining personal
tutoring and participation in discussion groups.

Zylawy, Roman Ihor (Ph. D.). "ASPECTS OF WOMEN'S IDEOLOGY AND THE
RISE OF THE FEMININE ETHICS FROM THE XVIIth TO THE XVIIIth CENTURY AS
REFLECTED IN THE WORKS OF MARIVAUX AND PREVOST." University of Colorado,
1973. 173 pp. Source: DAI, XXXIV, 7A (January, 1974), 4297-A-4298-A.

XUM Order No. 73-32,611.

The rise of women, including their education, in 17th and 18th century France is described largely through the writings of Pierre Cariet de Marivaux (1688-1763) and Antoine Francois Prevost D'Exiles (1697-1763).

■ NOTE ■

Due to an indexing error, the user must add 2 to each of the page numbers given below. For example, an entry cited as being on page 100 will actually be found on page 102. This error will be corrected in any subsequent edition.

SUBJECT INDEX

Abortion, 228, 337, 367

Academic freedom, 142

Accountability, 73

Accreditation, 282-283

Accreditation of nursing schools, 62-63, 116-117, 192, 207, 267, 337-338

Achievement, academic, 7, 8, 9, 16, 17, 18, 23, 24, 26, 27, 28, 29, 33-
     34, 41, 42, 43, 45, 47, 48, 52, 58, 61, 62, 63, 67, 68, 69, 71, 74,
     75, 77, 78, 79-80, 82, 83-84, 86, 87, 90, 92, 97, 98, 101, 105, 108-
     109, 111, 114, 116, 117, 118, 123, 124, 127, 128, 129, 131, 134, 138-
     139, 139-140, 141, 141-142, 143, 146, 149, 151, 155, 156, 161-162,
     163, 164, 165, 166, 167, 170, 172-173, 176, 179, 180, 181, 182, 189,
     193, 196, 200-201, 213, 215, 216-217, 217-218, 219, 221, 223, 224, 225,
     231, 235, 239, 243, 244, 246, 253-254, 260, 261, 266, 268, 269, 273,
     274, 275, 276, 283-284, 286, 287, 288, 289, 290, 293, 296, 299, 300,
     302, 303, 305, 307, 311-312, 313, 315, 319-320, 321, 323, 328, 330-331,
     332, 333-334, 335, 337, 339, 340, 341, 342, 347-348, 349, 350, 351,
     353-354, 355-356, 362, 365, 371, 374, 377, 383, 385, 386-387, 392,
     394, 395-396, 400, 402, 403, 406, 407, 409, 410
     See also Success, prediction of

Administration, educational, 8, 13, 20, 21, 23, 26, 34, 36, 39, 43, 46,
     47, 55, 56, 59, 77, 80, 84, 86, 87, 94, 96, 97, 100, 102-103, 112,
     113, 116, 120, 121, 123-124, 124-125, 126, 128, 130, 131, 137, 139,
     140, 143, 144, 147, 150, 155, 156, 161, 164, 169-170, 172-173, 174-
     175, 178, 180, 186, 190, 192-193, 194-195, 200, 201-202, 203, 205-206,
     208, 209, 218, 220, 222, 223, 226-227, 230, 236-237, 241-242, 252,
     254-255, 256, 260, 261, 263, 265, 279, 280-281, 282-283, 284, 286,
     288, 289, 290-291, 294, 296-297, 300, 303, 307, 309, 310-311, 312-313,
     314, 317, 332, 338, 339, 344, 347, 349-350, 351, 359, 360, 362, 364,
     365, 366, 372, 375, 377, 383, 385, 386, 387, 391, 393, 396, 406, 409-
     410, 410-411, 412
     See also Deans of women
               Nursing education administration
               Physical education administration
               President, higher education
               Principals
               Student personnel services
               Superintendents

Administration, physical education
     See Physical education administration

Eugene, OR, 373

Europe, 46-47, 271, 288-289, 350
See also specific countries

Evaluation
See Testing and evaluation

Evanston, IL, 276

Evelyn College for Women, Princeton, NJ, 124

Examinations, 273
See also Testing and evaluation

Existentialism, 296, 374
See also Philosophy of women's education

Extension education, 363, 398
See also Adult education

Extracurricular activities, 50, 126, 147, 187, 221, 265, 347, 363, 377, 399

Eye care, 338

Faculty women
See Higher education women faculty
Job discrimination
Marriage and careers
Sex bias

Family, influence of, 22-23, 33, 35, 39, 43, 44, 46, 48, 49, 50, 63, 66, 68, 69, 71, 72, 74, 75, 77-78, 80, 83, 89, 95, 101, 109, 111, 114, 115, 120, 125, 126-127, 130-131, 134, 135, 137, 139-140, 141, 142, 146, 147, 149, 150, 155, 159, 165, 169, 170, 174, 176, 181, 182, 187, 188, 189, 193, 202, 209, 212, 215, 217-218, 221-222, 226, 230, 231, 232, 233, 235, 238-239, 240, 247, 254-255, 258, 262-263, 265, 266, 269, 271, 272, 274, 275, 276, 277, 278, 283, 285, 287-288, 289, 290, 292-293, 294, 298, 299, 300, 302, 303, 304, 306, 308, 312, 318, 322-323, 327-328, 330, 332-333, 336-337, 339-340, 340-341, 343, 345, 352-353, 360, 366, 368, 370, 372, 373, 374, 376, 377, 380-381, 382, 387, 392, 397, 398, 400, 401, 403, 410, 411-412
See also Fathers, influence of
Mothers, influence of

Family life education, 2, 18, 58, 226, 241, 261, 278, 282, 297, 309, 311, 315, 325, 345, 370, 374, 375, 393, 398, 407
See also Home economics education

Family planning, 135, 173, 176, 240, 309, 322, 357
See also Birth control
Birth rate

Family resources education
See Home economics education

Home management
   See Home economics

Homemakers
   See Housewives and homemakers

Hospital nursing schools, 63, 230-231, 234, 247, 257, 277, 279, 289, 293,
   294, 305, 345, 355, 357, 360, 365, 382, 388, 406
   See also Nursing education, diploma programs

Housewives and homemakers, 66, 69, 70, 81, 85-86, 90-91, 95, 96, 109,
   110, 115, 118, 128-129, 136, 157, 170, 174, 175, 179-180, 195, 202-
   203, 210, 211, 217, 222, 228, 234, 242, 243, 244, 245, 281-282, 283,
   284, 293, 300-301, 303, 304, 307, 309, 317, 318, 319, 336, 352, 355,
   356, 367, 379, 383, 384, 386

Houston, TX, 139

Howard University, Washington, DC, 209

Humanities
   See General education

Hunterdon County, NJ, 226-227

Hyderabad, Pakistan, 357

Iban women, Sarawak, East Malaysia, 167

Illinois, 41, 45, 66, 99, 118-119, 134, 161, 164, 182-183, 227, 276, 279,
   280-281, 285, 303, 323, 330-331, 338, 355-356, 360, 364-365

Illinois State Teachers Association, 338

Income
   See Salaries and income

Independent study
   See Teaching methods

India, 3-4, 12, 18, 31, 53, 69, 88, 91, 122, 202, 237, 242, 258, 281-282,
   283, 284-285, 294, 304, 328-329, 345, 354, 355, 381
   See also Hindu women, India
               Indians (from India)

Indiana, 112, 143, 148, 176, 201-202, 230, 260, 333-334, 340, 352, 388,
   399, 412

Indiana State Teachers College, 176

Indiana University, Bloomington, IN, 201-202, 399

Indians (from India), 115

Individualized instruction
   See Teaching methods

Physical education for women, philosophy of, 5
    See also Philosophy of women's education

Physicians, women, 82, 110, 150, 179, 208-209, 272, 395
    See also Medical education

Piagetian theory (Jean Piaget, 1896-), 226, 325, 357-358, 385

Pittsburgh, PA, 368, 394

Planning, educational, 5, 224, 227, 231-232, 234, 253, 271, 313, 347, 406,
    408
    See also Administration, educational
            Nursing education,   administration

Plays, dramatic, 243
    See also Literature

Poetry, 168-169, 276, 297
    See also Literature

Politics, women in, 10-11, 25, 41, 64, 67, 82, 90, 93, 99, 130-131, 135,
    164, 169, 172, 179-180, 203-204, 210-211, 227-228, 232, 238, 258
    See also Law and law enforcement, women in

Popes
    See Roman Catholic education

Population control
    See Birth control
        Birth rate
        Family planning

Portland State College, OR, 77

Portugal, 46-47

Portuguese-Americans, 403

Poughkeepsie, NY, 279

Poverty, 304
    See also Developing countries
            Disadvantaged students

Pratt, Caroline, 306

Pregnancy
    See Motherhood

Preschool, 12, 23, 29, 73, 103, 104, 108, 122, 144, 152, 223, 285, 305,
    306, 330, 402
    See also Child care
            Day care

Tahrir College of University of Baghdad, Iraq, 8

Taiwan
  See China, Republic of (Taiwan)

Tamil Nadu State, India, 355

Tamils, 311

Taylor, Harriet, 306

Teacher aides, 84, 216, 395

Teacher education, 5, 6, 8, 9, 14, 15, 17, 18, 21, 25, 26, 27, 32, 35,
  36, 38, 40, 41, 55, 56, 58, 59, 61, 62, 63, 67, 68, 72, 75, 76-77,
  80, 82, 86, 87, 88, 90, 92, 95, 96, 99, 103, 104, 105, 106, 107, 108-
  109, 112-113, 117, 118, 119, 121-122, 123, 125, 126-127, 134, 136,
  140, 142, 143, 146, 149, 151, 154, 157, 158, 161, 166-167, 171, 172,
  176, 189, 191-192, 194, 195, 199, 201, 202, 205, 206, 210, 218, 219,
  223. 227, 229, 235, 239, 244-245, 250, 251, 253, 276, 277, 282-283,
  286, 290, 295, 301, 306, 312, 313-314, 314-315, 316, 318, 319, 321,
  322, 323, 326, 327, 334, 335, 340, 342, 343, 344, 345, 346, 347, 348,
  350, 352, 353, 357, 359, 363-364, 365, 370, 373, 375, 382, 384, 387,
  389, 390, 394-395, 401, 403, 406
  See also Higher education

Teacher-student relations, 64, 96, 97, 104, 134, 147-148, 151, 154, 164,
  170, 190-191, 199-200, 260, 271, 274, 278, 279, 282-283, 302, 303,
  310, 312, 327, 329-330, 335, 346, 373, 377, 381-382, 384, 392, 396,
  404, 405

Teachers College, Columbia University
  See Columbia University Teachers College

Teaching as a career, 5, 9, 13, 17, 27, 28, 56, 70, 77, 80, 83, 87, 92,
  93, 95, 98, 103, 106, 110, 116, 125, 133, 134, 137, 138-139, 144, 148,
  149-150, 151, 153, 156, 163, 166-167, 168, 169, 171, 175, 179, 180,
  183, 185, 186, 190-191, 195, 199-200, 201, 205, 206, 221-222, 228,
  234, 236, 248, 255, 256, 257, 260, 262, 279, 285, 304, 315, 320, 351,
  354, 356, 360, 361, 367, 368, 370, 372, 373, 383, 385, 387, 389, 392,
  396, 398, 400, 401, 403, 405, 408, 410-411
  See also Higher education women faculty

Teaching methods, 2, 31, 41, 45, 49, 52, 54, 55, 56, 61, 62, 63-64, 66,
  67-68, 68, 70, 78, 82, 85, 86, 89, 90, 91-92, 95, 96, 103, 106, 108,
  109, 109-110, 112, 114-115, 118, 122, 123, 130, 136, 137, 141, 143,
  145, 146, 147, 150, 152, 154, 157, 159, 160-161, 165, 168, 170-171,
  172, 173, 174, 180, 184, 189-190, 196-197, 198, 207, 210, 211, 213,
  215, 216-217, 219, 221, 225, 228, 229, 232, 234, 236, 238, 241, 242,
  245, 246-247, 249-250, 251, 255, 260, 261-262, 263, 270, 272-273, 281,
  284, 286, 290, 292, 295, 301, 305, 309, 320, 321, 323-324, 325, 327,
  329-330, 333, 335, 336, 337-338, 341, 344, 345, 346, 348, 349, 351-
  352, 358, 365-366, 367, 368-369, 373-374, 375, 377, 381, 383, 385,
  387, 393, 394, 398, 404, 405, 406, 407, 408-409, 411, 412

Technology education, 67, 132, 220
  See also Engineering education

ABOUT THE COMPILER-EDITORS

Franklin Parker is Benedum Professor of Education at West Virginia University in Morgantown. His previous books include *African Development and Education in Southern Rhodesia, Battle of the Books,* and *George Peabody.* Betty June Parker is a graduate student at West Virginia University.